WITHOUT NATURE?

Without Nature?

A NEW CONDITION FOR THEOLOGY

Edited by

DAVID ALBERTSON AND CABELL KING

FORDHAM UNIVERSITY PRESS

New York 2010

Fordham University Press has no responsibility for the
persistence or accuracy of URLs for external or third-party
Internet websites referred to in this publication and does not
guarantee that any content on such websites is, or will
remain, accurate or appropriate.

Library of Congress Cataloging-in-Publication Data

Without nature? : a new condition for theology / edited by
David Albertson and Cabell King.—1st ed.
p.   cm.
Proceedings of a conference held in 2005 at the University
of Chicago.
Includes bibliographical references (p.   ) and index.
ISBN 978–0-8232–3069–3 (cloth : alk. paper)
ISBN 978–0-8232–3070–9 (pbk. : alk. paper)
1. Nature—Religious aspects—Christianity.
2. Ecotheology.   I. Albertson, David.   II. King, Cabell.
BT695.5.W58   2009
231.7—dc22
2009016298

Printed in the United States of America
12 11 10   5 4 3 2 1
First edition

CONTENTS

v

ACKNOWLEDGMENTS

We would like to thank William Schweiker, who inspired the University of Chicago Divinity School's 2005 conference "Without Nature? A New Condition for Theology" with his 2004 graduate seminar, "The Post-Human and the Death of Nature." It was Schweiker's idea that ecological collapse and genetic manipulation may be united and may indicate a broader cultural shift, and we thank him for letting us run with it. We are also both students of Kathryn Tanner and have adopted her interdisciplinary ethic as a matter of course. Together Tanner and Schweiker have advised us over the three years of the project's duration, and we thank them for their wise counsel, patience, and unreserved support. We owe a special thanks to Richard Rosengarten, dean of the University of Chicago Divinity School, and Wendy Doniger, director of the Martin Marty Center, who together green-lighted the project well before we knew how to pay for it. We received invaluable administrative support from Sandra Peppers and from Judy Lawrence.

The greatest reward for coordinating the project was the opportunity to bring together thinkers we admire and to watch their conversation about our questions unfold. We thank all of our contributors for indulging an ambitious interdisciplinary agenda. Each of the contributors visited Chicago twice, first for a closed-door working group, and then a year later for the public conference. We appreciate their humility and generosity. Particular thanks to Peter Raven, Stuart Newman, Edward Soja, and Michael Fischer, who stepped into the unfamiliar walls of a divinity school and entertained a curious theological dialogue regarding their matters of expertise.

These meetings were greatly enriched by the participation of many colleagues at the University of Chicago, to whom we owe a debt of thanks: Michael Hogue, John Schroedel, Rob Saler, Andrea White, Ted Steck, Sir Peter Crane, Mary Mahowald, Virginia Parks, Karin Knorr-Cetina, and especially J. Ronald Engel.

Finally, we are eager to recognize the indispensable and generous financial support of the University of Chicago Divinity School and the Martin Marty Center, the John Templeton Foundation, the Franke Institute for the Humanities at the University of Chicago, and the Center for Ecozoic Studies.

WITHOUT NATURE?

Without Nature?

David Albertson

One must have the strength—and from time to time make use of
it—to shatter and to unravel a past, in order to be able to live. . . . Yet
if we condemn our mistakes and consider ourselves freed of them, still
the fact remains that we are descended from them. In the best case,
we come into conflict with our inherited Nature, indeed to the point
of a struggle for a new, austere discipline against things long
accustomed and even innate. We cultivate a new domestication, we
implant a new instinct, a second Nature, so that the first dries up. As
if it were an attempt to give oneself a new past *a posteriori*, out of
which one would prefer to have sprung, in contradiction to that from
which one did. Always a dangerous attempt, because it is difficult to
find limits in denying the past, and because second Natures are often
weaker than the first. . . . But now and then the victory is won, and
for those who struggle on there is even . . . a remarkable consolation:
namely, to know that the first Nature at some time was a second
Nature, and that each victorious second Nature will become a first.[1]

FRIEDRICH NIETZSCHE, *On the Uses and Disadvantages*
of History for Life (1874)

In 1989, the naturalist Bill McKibben observed the "end of nature," the
dissolution of the widely held perception that nature stands substantively
independent of human action.[2] One used to consider nature to be the
permanent, static backdrop to the drama of human affairs: weather patterns, topographical contours, animal populations, genetic composition.
Increasingly we now reckon with the malleability of these "natural" phenomena, which previously formed a limiting network bounding human
agency from without. Whereas nature may have once denoted the edge
of human intervention, it is decreasingly distinct from other products of
industry.

Take mountains, for instance. Geographical formations would appear
an indubitable instance of pure nature: the ultimately solid, the intransi-
gently and wholly wild, the ground beneath our feet. Yet in the last century, coal-mining engineers developed "mountaintop removal mining."
The technique, a common practice in the western United States, explodes

I

all land above the seam and then digs out the coal with giant mechanical shovels. A routine mountaintop removal uses so much explosive—fifteen times that used in the Oklahoma City bombing—that foreign governments have mistaken them for secret nuclear weapons tests.[3] When the accessible coal seams are exhausted, the original soil can be replaced, but it is often deposited elsewhere to create a wholly new topographical feature. The mountaintop is simply relocated. Reshaping the natural landscape on this scale has more than aesthetic consequences and can significantly change patterns of erosion and water runoff, multiplying rainfalls into small floods.[4] Soil harvested while removing mountaintops contains toxic heavy metals such as lead, arsenic, and selenium, often carried by runoff into local aquifers. One can easily marvel (or cringe) at the modern capacity to reshape nature according to our needs. Moving mountains, once the measure of faith, is now an everyday practice.

But such power over nature and the decline of its pristine state are not distinctively modern. Three thousand years ago, the Incan population of present-day Peru and Bolivia began irrigating the Lake Titicaca basin. The landscape was hostile to farming: a desert in dry summer months, frosted over through the winter, a veritable swamp in the spring. Population growth among the Incas compelled the invention of an expansive network of canals and raised fields that channeled mountain runoff but also altered the local ecology. Archaeologist Clark L. Erickson documents the radical effects of Incan raised-field technology: redirection of rivers, changes in erosion patterns, and significant microclimate shifts. He calls the result "a totally human-created landscape" spanning more than 120,000 hectares (roughly half the size of Rhode Island).[5] It was only recently that we discovered that these impressive plateaus were not works of nature but rather, as anthropologist Michael Moseley notes, "the largest man-made structures ever constructed."[6] Whether raising up new plateaus or removing the tops of mountains, human technologies have created the "natural" givens of geography for centuries.

Shifts in biological nature can seem more dramatic. In 2003, it was documented that in one area of the North Pacific there are now six pounds of plastic waste for every one pound of zooplankton. The largest patch of garbage flotsam is approximately the size of Texas.[7] Such changes in the natural environment are soon reflected, of course, in human nature. In May 2006, physicians from the University of Massachusetts presented new evidence of the danger of "endocrine disruption" in children from environmental contaminants—namely, unregulated estrogen and testosterone additives found in some cosmetics and shampoos. The results of endocrine disruption include the onset of puberty in preschool-age children, breast enlargement in young boys, dramatically early menstruation in young girls; comparable results have been documented in alligators in Florida in the 1980s and fish in England in the 1990s.[8]

Are we now "without nature" in a way we were not before? As many environmental thinkers now recognize, recent transformations of "nature" as environment and "nature" as human nature are parallel and to some degree linked. While the spheres of human and nonhuman "nature" are often addressed distinctly in bioethical and ecological ethics, in this volume we consider them in tandem. Is it possible that ecological collapse and genetic manipulation are symptomatic of conceptually broader and more globally operative cultural shifts—a changing understanding and valuation of "nature" itself? By joining these questions together, we seek to stimulate second-order and cross-disciplinary reflection on how alterations of "nature" impact theological categories.

This situation raises a series of challenging questions. In asking about nature's destabilization, we are also asking about the sustainability and ecology of Western Christian religious discourse itself, given its historic reliance upon concepts of "nature" and "human nature." Western Christian theological traditions have invested heavily in some version of "nature" to express the meaning of grace. Yet in the last century, both Protestant and Catholic theologians have challenged the viability of a "pure" concept of nature, and in the human sciences, concepts of nature are viewed with suspicion. Would the loss of such an ecological or biological constant place new conditions on Christian theology in the present? Would the end of nature render grace less comprehensible? Without its customary notions of nature, how would Christian theological ethics begin to address the "end of nature" in bioethics and environmental ethics? What does the Christian notion of the "supernatural," or the idea of transforming human nature (through grace), have to do with the technological quest to transcend human limits?

The ambiguity of this volume's title reflects its two guiding questions. First, we contemplate the situation theology would face in the present, given the hypothesis of the loss of nature. Would the decline of nature lead to a diagnosis of ill health for Christian theology, a "new condition"? Second, we consider different ways forward for theology. Would the end of nature entail new limitations placed on Christian theological ethics, a new boundary "condition" that cannot be escaped? Thus we do not assume the end of nature as a fact nor address it independently as something to be demonstrated. The logical form of our question is conditional: If nature were no longer to be what it was, what consequences would follow for Christian reflection—especially its reflection upon environmental and biological phenomena?

In some ways the question of nature's disappearance or dissolution looks not that new after all. In the *Laws*, Plato already expresses anxiety about fashionable new philosophers misleading the young by suggesting that the gods exist not by nature (*physis*) but by craft (*technē*), that is, by cultural and legal convention (*nomos*), such that justice, he says, varies as a function of geography. The wise man rather "ought to support *nomos* and also *technē*, but acknowledge that both alike exist precisely by nature, . . . so far as either is the creation of the mind in accordance with right reason." Plato's desire to conserve the regularity of nature in order to ward off cultural relativism sounds familiar to twenty-first-century ears. Without nature, the young would think that "what justice is, is dictated by the victory of the violent" and that "living according to nature" really means "living in dominion over others."[9]

Aristotle distinguishes nature (*physis*) both from custom (*hexis*) and from craft (*technē*). And even in his milieu he has to confront the deflationary account of Empedocles, who suggests in the context of organic elements (in tones reminiscent of those whom Stuart Newman calls "biological postmodernists") that "of nothing that exists is there nature, but only the mixture and separation of component parts; nature is only a name we give to these."[10] On the contrary, says Aristotle, nature is the immanent principle and source of the self-movement that animates living things (*archē kinēseos*).[11] Following Aristotle, it is Boethius, at the turn of the sixth century, who is the first Latin author to contrast something done "naturally" versus "artificially" (*naturaliter, artificialiter*).[12] He does so in order to explain, a few sentences later, the incoherence of some of his contemporaries' theological positions.

Cicero is the first to use "another nature" (*quasi altera natura*).[13] But the first clear contrast of first nature and second nature arrives within a theological judgment of Augustine. For Augustine, the powerful human drive to sin has the force of a natural principle: "Our habitual evil . . . is also by the learned customarily called 'second Nature.'"[14] Hence Augustine distinguishes the "first nature of humankind," created perfect by God, and human nature after the Fall, "so to speak a second nature" (*quasi secunda natura*), a nature that the advent of grace then restores.[15] Grace is the divine answer to the fatal doubling of human nature.

Making sense of (and even worrying about) "nature" stands among the oldest questions in European traditions of anthropological, scientific, and theological reflection. But our wager is that something has shifted under our feet in the way we relate to nature—as if a mountain has been picked up and moved. If something fundamental has shifted, if the possibilities of how we ask the old question of nature have been redefined, then ours appears to be a unique time for thinking about nature. But then how do we move forward into what Friedrich Nietzsche calls the "dangerous attempt" of releasing oneself from a past, the past of nature? Nietzsche's words, cited above, represent a warning to those who might revisit the meaning of nature for ethics and theology today: nature's past, its present avatars, its questionable future. For contemplating a new condition "without nature" means to deny, to unravel, or to negate a past once taken as secure. Nietzsche's play with the idea of "second nature" is especially trenchant. We can oppose nature's past and the older, more stable concepts long familiar. With the advantage of hindsight, we search for pasts of nature that might have been. We carry these meager gleanings with us as we try to take steps forward—without nature but with something new. But can any second nature give back what has been lost? Nietzsche warns of two dangers that threaten the attempt to break with nature's past. One could end up denying the past without limit, finally severing ineluctable and even productive historical influences—as if to burn one's map out of frustration with being lost. Or one could concoct an arbitrary, imaginary second nature, an artificial substitute perhaps weaker than the original.

There are a few obvious ways of moving forward into a future Christian theological ethics under the condition of being "without nature." One could propose an improved concept of nature. One could suggest a solution to nature's troubles out of the resources of Christian theology itself. One could introduce a methodological distinction that enables theology to ignore new developments in the environment and biotechnology. These alternatives are familiar and attractive, but each effectively circumnavigates the very problems raised by nature's new inaccessibility. The contributions in this volume attempt instead to linger with these difficulties and thus to resist the impulse to propose a theological answer prematurely. A few principles guide this strategy.

First, in addressing what it means to think theologically "without nature," there is a constant danger of attempting a resolution of the condition merely at the level of the concept. One might attempt to measure the weak points of past concepts of nature, analyze their problems, and then fabricate a new concept, one that has been expressly designed and produced for our new condition. Along these lines, one might try to find a more dynamic, flexible, reciprocal notion of nature, or one that is holistic, relational, organic, or one that takes into account the wisdom of many different traditions, hoping that an amalgam of different substrates forms a stronger composite. But down this path, as Nietzsche warns, the denial of the past soon knows no limits, and we may quickly sever any real connection between historical "first" natures and the improved "second" nature that we have thus synthesized. Will this synthetic nature-concept be any stronger? What is the utility of fabricating a better ideal concept, when the real effects have already outstripped us? On closer study, this desire to reconceptualize may turn out to be only an intellectual reflex, a delaying tactic, that can obstruct a critical contemplation of the actual past from whence the problems arose. So the contributors in this volume attempt a broader response to the question of nature beyond simply fabricating a new concept of nature.

A second principle guiding this volume is that theology itself, particularly Western Christian theology, cannot simply exempt itself from the situation of being "without nature." It too stands under this condition. "Nature" can be defined as the context for human life (ecology and geography) or as the identity of human life (genetics and anthropology). But nature has another important meaning. In a history not unrelated to the fates of these first two senses of nature, Western Christian theology has relied heavily upon nature to express the meaning of "grace." Augustine's innovation of a distinct doctrine of *gratia* as special divine intervention was formulated in opposition to the perceived capacities of a corrupted ("second") human nature. Boethius captures the distinction with typical clarity: we should receive death as a punishment for sin *per meritum naturae*, but God confers salvation *per donum gratiae*.[16] Grace, divine action, the subject matter of theological reflection, becomes intelligible by contrast with "nature": grace as gift and gratuity (as opposed to normal dues), as excess (as opposed to adequation), as God's surprising action (as opposed to regular human capacities).

Different Christian traditions relate the pair with different emphases. Catholic traditions tend to interpret grace as a superaddition to nature—nature being anchored in grace, having its natural end in the creature's movement toward God, but also needing the supplement of further grace to reach that end. Reform traditions tend to view nature as that which is overcome in grace, since God's presence arrives in perfectly sovereign freedom from the givens of nature. God does not add grace to nature, because nature is precisely what is being overcome in grace. Eastern Christian traditions tend to imagine grace as the fullness, the illumination from within, of nature's true identity.

Despite these differences, we can say that most Christian theologies require some initial term to identify the distinction of grace and that this term, "nature," is traditionally imagined in connection both with the physically created world and with human identity and capacities. If we were to be without nature in these latter two senses, would grace become less intelligible? Would theology and theological ethics have trouble articulating themselves? If nature is passing, what would that mean for the theological understanding of creation (the "natural world")? For the intelligibility of grace as a gift, as something more than what is already given? For the ability to explicate a theological anthropology? For any theologically informed ethics?

Through the first half of the twentieth century, many Protestant and Catholic theologians agreed that more dynamic understandings of grace were required. In his several historical studies, Henri de Lubac stresses the graced, gifted character of nature within Augustinian traditions and thus the relative autonomy of grace from nature. Nature is already a gift of grace; therefore it is a mistake to overemphasize the self-sufficiency of nature "before grace." There is nothing before grace, nothing before divine action, hence there is no "pure nature."[17]

Louis Dupré contextualizes de Lubac's point within a longer historical narrative. Dupré describes the divorce of theology from the sciences that took place in the late Middle Ages and early modernity once a new notion of nature gave license to the sciences to seek their own fortune autonomously. Once a theological notion of "pure nature" changed from being a working hypothesis to something real in its own right, theology entered into a fundamentally different relationship with the sciences:

> Once the order of grace had become marginal to nature, however much it might claim to remain its ultimate goal, its potential for intrinsically affecting culture vanished. Theology lost thereby much of its original role. Instead of shaping the very substance of culture, as it had done in the past, it became reduced to a science among others with a method and an object exclusively its own. Because of its remoteness other sciences could freely ignore it and, where it continued to retain a modicum of (mostly political) authority, went out of their way to avoid any contact with it. Incapable of remedying a condition inherent in the modern concept of culture yet still controlling the consciences of the majority of its members, theology had little choice but to move forward on its self-made path.[18]

In the twentieth century, the question of nature and grace was not so much resolved as suspended until further notice. Hans Urs von Balthasar explains what was at stake in a 1953 article on the theological concept of nature.[19] "Behind apparently subtle differences far removed from real life," he writes, "there stand decisions which strike at the nervecord, the very lifeblood, of theology." In his survey of Karl Barth, Karl Rahner, Henri de Lubac, and other contemporaries, he suggests that if the requisite conceptual differentiations become ever more finely nuanced, and if "solutions to early phases can no longer simply count as finally valid for the present-day state of the problem," then this only demonstrates the importance of the problem.

Even in its theological use, the course of the twentieth century in Western Christian theology left nature weaker. The historical uniqueness of our moment, then, is the relative simultaneity of three trends: nature is destabilized not only through environmental degradation and genetic technologies but also within the very Christian theologies that intend to address these two challenges. How, then, does one relate Christian theological ethics today to the question of nature?

There are a few customary ways of approaching nature from the province of theology. One can outline a natural theology, extrapolating statements about God on the basis of putative knowledge of nature. One can construct a theology of nature, or ecotheology, taking nature as creation and as a fragile environment for stewardship, preservation, and justice. One can identify ethical questions raised in the domains of nature: bioethics and environmental ethics. It goes without saying that these are valuable contributions. But we can also postpone the moment of theological engagement with nature in order to interrogate what kind of posture and premises it entails. Ecotheology, theologies of creation, and natural theologies all attempt to levy a theological perspective (that is, a particular understanding of grace) to a field: ecology, creation, or nature. But the very ground on which one establishes a stable understanding of grace has been shaken.[20]

There is a fallacy that we might call the "therapeutic model" of theology's self-comportment. According to the therapeutic model, theologians hear the dilemmas of the sciences and then answer their perceived deficiency by providing the necessary understanding of God, world, or self that allows the nontheological sphere to overcome its dilemma. But to operate in this way only reifies a particular construal of the nature and grace at the disciplinary level—supplementing natural and social sciences with theologomena that purportedly complete their (so to speak, "natural") findings by adducing (so to speak, "supernatural") doctrines that fulfill their otherwise incomplete intentions or ends. This method, however, not only underestimates the complexity of any robust theological engagement with other disciplines (an engagement that is inexorable); given our concerns, it only begs the question.

This therapeutic model of theologizing interprets ethical dilemmas as conceptual problems that can be solved by supplying an appropriate theological judgment. Yet this assumes that theology stands apart as an unaffected whole, isolated from the crisis it purports to resolve. But theology is never so isolated in fact. The withdrawal of nature is not a local condition affecting only biotechnology and ecology. Intratheological judgments regarding nature and grace, despite the evident variance of terms, are indissociable from the concrete state of "nature"—nature on the ground, so to speak. If one chooses to abstract the theological treatment of nature and grace from the meaning of nature for the sciences, that denial of engagement itself reflects a theological judgment about nature. Hence there is an irreducible connection between what "nature" means for the articulation of grace and what it means (if anything) as an ecological, biological, geographical, or anthropological given.

If we cannot address the condition of being "without nature" either by inventing a new nature-concept, or by withdrawing Christian theology from every liaison with nature altogether, what alternative is left? Historical memory and theological principle alike point one toward a renewed engagement with the contemporary natural and social sciences. Our wager in this volume is that a dialogue with the sciences—in their plurality, in their cultural embeddedness, and in their own struggles to think what "nature" means today—holds the first step for Christian theology's own resolution of the problem of nature.

It was precisely the revival of discourse about "nature" in the Latin West around 1100 that accelerated the emergence of differentiated disciplines of knowledge and their separation from ecclesiastical theology. The main thread by which we receive the problem of nature in dialogue with the human and natural sciences—the translation of Aristotle from Arabic sources and their troubled integration into the curriculum of the thirteenth-century University of Paris—begins in fact in the twelfth century.[21] The twelfth century was the age of the "discovery of nature," in the words of medieval historian Marie-Dominique Chenu, and the construction of a new kind of knowledge, *scientia naturalis*.[22] Among circles of scholars at Chartres and Paris, progressive theologians and natural philosophers generated an ideal of autonomous *natura* that whetted the appetite for the wave of Aristotelian translations in the thirteenth century.

Older Christian thought viewed nature as a "book" written by God, a kind of second volume after the book of Scripture, which can be interpreted through reading other books.[23] But in the twelfth century, influenced by methods of Islamic natural science, something changed in Western Europe:

> In place of this symbolic understanding of nature, there emerged an original interest in the structure, constitution, and laws proper to physical reality. Reason begins increasingly to seek to acquire knowledge of these things through scientific methods. . . . The increasing knowledge of the natural world thus parallels the effort to found a *scientia naturalis*. . . . "Discovered nature" thus becomes the subject of a *scientia naturalis*. At the same time, nature is nothing but that which *scientia naturalis* discovers.[24]

Thierry of Chartres, for example, ventures a new reading of Genesis "according to natural science" (*secundum phisicam*).[25] His philosophical writings theorize nature as a realm of relative autonomy that God ruled but preserved intact, such that human minds could know the physical world of nature without divine illumination or intervention. William of Conches writes that "nature is a certain power immanent in things that produces like from like"[26] and that "nature, fleeing imperfection, struggles by a formative power to bring to completion each particular thing in its own kind."[27] Bernard Silvester and Alain de Lille pen new myths personifying *Natura* as a lesser deity carrying out God's plans.[28]

The new autonomy of nature—and soon natural science—from theology did not occur without controversy. Thierry of Chartres was accused of being a sorcerer; William of Conches was threatened with censure. In Adelard of Bath's *Quaestiones naturales*, one of the first works of natural science in the Latin Middle Ages,[29] Adelard's nephew challenges his argument. The nephew protests that "your whole line of reasoning is weakened, and the execution of all things should rather be referred to God." Adelard replies:

> I am not slighting God's role. For whatever exists is from him and through him. Nevertheless, that dependence on God is not to be taken in blanket fashion, without distinction. One should attend to this distinction, as far as human knowledge can go; but in the case where human knowledge completely fails, the matter should be referred to God. Thus, since we do not yet grow pale with lack of knowledge, let us return to reason.[30]

Later theologians interested in the new natural sciences were fond of citing the judgment of Albertus Magnus, teacher of Thomas Aquinas: "It is not our concern to deal with God's miracles when we are discussing natural things in natural terms [*de naturalibus naturaliter*]."[31]

The initial twelfth-century interest in *natura* motivated the efforts of translation to introduce Arabic and Greek sources, including Aristotle, in the thirteenth century. The newly received natural philosophy of Aristotle dramatically expanded the sphere of legitimately natural knowledge. The new space of nature made room for scientific disciplines to emerge and diverge, liberated from their theological monitors in the arts faculty. The famous condemnations of radical Aristotelians in the Parisian arts faculty in 1270 and 1277 are evidence of this struggle for discursive autonomy under way in thirteenth-century schools. Carlos Steel notes that

> the confrontation and tension between theology and philosophy ultimately led to a situation in which the natural philosophers could do their research in great intellectual freedom. This eventually favorable attitude in Latin Christian Europe toward natural philosophy and the pursuit of scientific knowledge is of great historical importance as a condition for the modern scientific revolution.[32]

Once scholars at Oxford and Paris began applying mathematical analysis to physics in the fourteenth century, the foundations of the natural sciences as we know them today had been laid.

The lesson of this historical context is clear: the development of a concept of "nature" independent of its theological use was intimately wrapped up with the emergence of multiple scientific disciplines. Therefore, to question the status of "nature" for contemporary theology and ethics is also to meditate upon the present conditions of interdisciplinary collaboration. We do not need only to ask where we stand with regard to the history of the theological use of "nature," but at the same time to ask how theology's present relationship to other scientific disciplines is conditioned by that history. "Nature" is not only the common ground upon which the sciences gather, but their autonomous territory freed from the dominion of theology. If that ground is no longer stable, if the perimeter of that territory has become less secure, then a new détente between theology and science becomes possible. The interdisciplinarity of this volume, therefore, is not elective, arbitrary, or merely fashionable. Rather, the project is therefore essentially collaborative: it interrogates the viability of "nature" as a point of intersection for dialogue across disciplines, whether it is "human nature" studied by the human and social sciences or the "natural" environment studied by the physical sciences.

For this reason we have chosen to address the question of nature across four disciplines. "Ecology and Nature" addresses nature as context in terms of the natural sciences, and "Geography and Nature" addresses nature as context in terms of the social sciences. Likewise, "Genetics and

Nature" addresses nature as identity in terms of the natural sciences, while "Anthropology and Nature" addresses nature as identity in terms of the social sciences. By addressing both senses of nature in both disciplinary fields, we have brought theologians into dialogue with each of the four areas; we have also reserved a distinct fifth area for cross-disciplinary reflections by theologians and ethicists under the title "Theology without Nature?" These five areas in the five parts of this volume, then, arise out of three senses of nature at play: nature as context, nature as identity, and nature in its more elusive theological use. Each of the fields of inquiry brings its own questions to the table concerning the possibility of a new "natural" condition.

"Ecology and Nature" begins by considering our relation to the natural environment in a time when what might be designated as "natural" remains unclear. It may not make sense, for example, to discuss the preservation or conservation of unspoiled nature if the entire globe is now impacted by pollution and changing weather patterns. Even those areas most unequivocally named "wilderness" are marked out precisely by the limits of human activity, and being thus demarcated are in some measure tamed. Is there still a "natural" world beyond the limits of human construction? What is the consequence of an increasingly malleable environment—either for its destruction or for its beneficent manipulation? What happens when we lose the external other that stands against human artifice? What constraints for theories of nature are imposed by the escalation of environmental abuse? With or without "nature," what responsibility do moral agents retain for their material environment?

"Genetics and Nature" regards the fixedness or stability of the essence of things, specifically concerning human identity. Biotechnological advances enable us now to redefine the genetic structure of organic material and alter the previously unalterable. We can now intervene in our own biological futures and introduce a radical discontinuity with our own biological pasts. Additionally, the chemicals introduced into the environment by industry, agriculture, and medicine are having dramatic effects on both plant and human life. What happens to our sense of the "nature" of things when responsibility for their biological identity is subject to human activity? The questions here are somewhat analogous to those in the first area, as they relate specifically to the definition of the human and our responsibility thereto. To what extent do novel biotechnologies pose equally novel questions about the link between human finitude and transcendence?

"Geography and Nature" concerns the social dimension of our lived experience in nature taken as context for human life. How do human communities construct and maintain—spatially, ritually, ethically, discursively—the regions of habitations in which they dwell? What are the everyday beliefs and practices that inform the construction of the common social environment we take as a given? What factors construct place and space, and which ones destructure them? The question can also be put theologically in terms of the doctrine of creation: How do we place ourselves in creation in social relationships? Is creation malleable and subject to human expression? Is it a fixed arena imposing limits? What do we learn of God from the space of creation? What do we learn from the dimensions of the natural world about the bodily dimensions of being human?

"Anthropology and Nature" attends again to the human, construed not in terms of biological malleability but in terms of the social construction of human identity. What constitutes a human being? If human identities arise out of traditions of self-formation, what happens when traditions fragment and hybridize in global networks of cultural exchange? What is the status of the generic term "human identity" in this situation? How will complex technological structures alter human identity in the twenty-first century? Would a renewed "humanism" promote or diminish universal human flourishing? What happens to anthropology without a definitely delimited *anthropos*? What theoretical resources, if any, are available to reconstruct a stable notion of human nature? What would be its utility, if any? And what would now be the conditions for meaningful consensus on the question?

Part V, "Theology without Nature?", covers the area that is the most difficult to define, as it invites us to consider each of the other areas in concert. Here we hope to pose the methodological questions raised at the junctures of the more content-driven areas. Are we able to consider all four areas together in the construction of a theologically informed sense of self and world? What happens to grace after the end of nature? In what sense can one speak, at least from within the Christian tradition, of passing beyond nature? Which elements of religious or philosophical traditions can inform the present moment by their diverse readings of human perfectibility, identity, finitude, and transcendence?

That the papers in this volume are the products of an actual dialogue among representatives of these five areas is demonstrated by their remarkable cohesion. In the first stage of dialogue, natural and social scientists presented state-of-the-art reports from their field on the meaning of "nature" or nature's decline in the present. The theologians and ethicists discussed these papers with the scientists in seminars and developed their own conceptual trajectories in reaction to them. As a result, the topics chosen respond thematically (and often explicitly) to the conceptual concerns of the field-leading scientists. We invite readers to engage all five areas of reflection upon "nature" alongside our contributors with the boldness appropriate to what Nietzsche calls a "dangerous attempt."

The World in Order

Lorraine Daston

Nature without Us

In a 1986 poem the Polish poet Wislawa Szymborska imagines not just
the indifference of nature (as Turgenev and Hardy had already imagined
it in the nineteenth century) but still more its utter meaninglessness:

> The lake's floor exists floorlessly,
> And its shore exists shorelessly.
> Its water feels itself neither wet nor dry
> and its waves to themselves are neither singular nor plural.
> They splash deaf to their own noise
> on pebbles neither large nor small.

> And all this beneath a sky by nature skyless
> in which the sun sets without setting at all
> and hides without hiding behind an unminding cloud.
> The wind ruffles it, its only reason being
> that it blows. . . .

> Time has passed like a courier with urgent news.
>   But that's just our simile.
>   The character is invented, his haste is make-believe,
>   His news inhuman.[1]

This is a nature that is adamantly inhuman (the last, emphatic word of the poem), refusing us not just mercy but even sense, even the simplest ontology of nouns: "a sky by nature skyless." This is an unsparing vision not so much of us "without nature" as of nature without us.

Considering the themes of this volume, this vision of nature without us might come as something of a relief, despite the poet's bleak intentions. Environmentalists dream of a pristine nature untouched by human hands, of reclaiming the wilderness lost to urban sprawl and toxic waste dumps. Ethicists are haunted by nightmares of genetic engineering: species boundaries dissolved and human nature changed beyond recognition. Together the environmentalists and the ethicists, along with many other thoughtful observers, might well wonder: Wouldn't nature be better off without us, or at least, with a great deal less of us? Whereas previous ages conceived of nature as a parent, "Mother Nature," sometimes benevolent, sometimes violent, the current generation is perhaps the first to regard nature as a child in need of protection from our abuses.

And yet we are hardly the first human generation to modify nature, and to modify it profoundly. Indeed, it might be argued that whatever it means to be human is bound up with the manipulation and transformation of nature. Modes of human life now regarded as particularly close to nature, such as farming and fishing, are simply the oldest of these human modifications of nature and differ in degree but not in kind from the modifications introduced by urbanization. A farm is in principle as artificial as a city. The same might be said, *mutatis mutandis*, for the continuity from the artificial selection practiced over millennia in the domestication of plants and animals to the genetic modification of organisms. Long before the advent of automobiles and highways, human beings had radically altered the landscape through agriculture and deforestation; long before the appearance of genetically modified strains of rice and corn, farmers and gardeners had bred new varieties of tulips and pears, pigeons and horses that differed strikingly from their wild ancestors.

Human nature is itself a kind of garden, not a wilderness. As Aristotle observes in the *Nicomachean Ethics*, it is quintessentially human to convert first nature into second nature, to instill habits in children that will either enhance their natural gifts or counter their natural infirmities.[2] Uncultivated human nature, nature without culture, ceases to be human at all. Advances in science and technology have certainly expanded the scope and accelerated the pace of the human modification of nature and perhaps thereby converted quantitative into qualitative change. But the general pattern is all too familiar—and it is human, all too human.

Still more eerily familiar, at least to the historian of *longue durée* Western attitudes toward nature, are the emotional responses to the most recent human modifications of environments and genomes. Reactions are, of course, individually and culturally variable, but fear and horror feature prominently and widely. The fear in question is not just the prudential fear that environmental degradation could have catastrophic consequences for the lives and property of millions of people, as in the case of the melting of the polar ice caps due to global warming. It is also fear tinged with guilt, a fear of nature punishing human hubris, a version of *nemesis divina*. The two kinds of fear, prudential and guilty, are often intertwined. For example, when in recent years the number and severity of storms in Germany dramatically increased, the media pointed an accusing finger at deforestation—both as physical cause *and* as provocation for what more than one newspaper called "nature's revenge."[3] A delicate environmental balance had been disturbed (the physical cause), and the disruption of that balance transgressed a norm (the moral cause).

If fear is the emotion evoked by human destruction of the environment, horror is the characteristic response to manipulation of the natures of organic species, most especially human nature. The emblematic case is the human monster that seems to straddle species boundaries.[4] It is the tampering with specific natures, not necessarily the outlandishness or ugliness of the hybrid, that triggers horror, as it did for the many medieval and early modern European writers who condemned the practice of grafting fruit trees as monstrous meddling with nature, however pleasing the product.[5] We no longer recoil at nectarines and carnations (those "streaked gillyvors" reviled as "nature's bastards" in Shakespeare's play *The Winter's Tale*), but new reproductive technologies often evoke the same shudder today.[6] As in the case of guilty fear over environmental damage, the element of human hubris is key to these reactions. We do not regard nature's clones (otherwise known as identical twins) as abominations nor admonish parents for the good fortune of having a healthy, handsome baby. Yet laboratory clones and designer babies are intuitively assigned to a different and dangerous category, that of the "unnatural." If the supernatural inspires awe and the preternatural prompts wonder, it is horror that signals the unnatural.[7]

In the spirit of Szymborska's poem, we might dismiss all these responses as a foolish mixture of superstition and sentiment, the legacy of centuries of futile attempts to make nature mean anything at all in human terms. It is true that the long Western history of extracting norms from nature—nature as the will of God, nature as the art of God, nature as

God's minister and judge—have been largely discredited by scientists, phi-losophers, and theologians alike. Yet the category of the unnatural remains morally electrified. Even if no one seriously suggests that natural history be taken as a primer for human ethics in the manner of the medieval besti-ary (consider, for example, the mating behavior of the praying mantis or the child-care arrangements of the cuckoo), the charge "unnatural mother" has not lost its sting. If the issue of homosexual marriage can ignite a ferocious debate that eclipses far graver political issues facing the nation, it is in large part because the emotions stirred are so powerful. Since Augustine, homosexuality has been the paradigmatic example of a crime *contra naturam* in Christian theology,[8] and in many quarters, crimes against nature still provoke the distinctive response of horror. Horror is not simply an intensification of fear or even terror. Nor is it simply a magnification of disapproval, indignation raised to the nth power, as it were. Horror registers a highly specific transgression: human violations of the perceived order of nature, including human nature.

I would like to reopen the question of norms from nature. My argu-ment is both historical and philosophical. Historically, I try here to show how various conceptions of natural order not only have sustained specific norms, both moral and aesthetic, but have moreover served as the model for what a norm, *any* norm, can be. Philosophically, I argue that the ap-peals to nature, though often and (in my opinion) rightly criticized, none-theless do capture something profound about values *in general*, regardless of their specific content. This argument hinges on the connection between normativity and order. I conclude that we cannot do without nature, even if we divest nature of all divine authority whatsoever. The human impulse to make nature meaningful, the object of Szymborska's icy skepticism, is not a psychological failing; it is an epistemological and ethical necessity.

Norms from Nature: Nature as Justice and Nature as the Will of God

The attempts of Western intellectuals to extract norms from nature stretch back to Greek and Roman antiquity and are ongoing (e.g., in cur-rent versions of evolutionary ethics). Over the millennia, the authority of nature has been enlisted in many causes: to justify and to condemn slavery, to praise breast-feeding and to blame masturbation, to elevate the aes-thetic of the sublime over the beautiful and to undergird human rights. Nature has sometimes signed up on the side of reformers and revolution-aries (as in the Enlightenment) and at other times on that of conservatives and reactionaries (for much of the nineteenth and twentieth centuries). It would take many volumes (yet to be written) to do justice to this long and motley history of invoking nature to buttress human values of the Good, the True, and the Beautiful.[9] Here I describe only two episodes, which I have chosen because of their broad and durable influence and also because the argument of one is philosophical and the other, theological. Although nature's normative authority has often been grounded in divine dictates, particularly in the Latin Christian tradition, not all appeals to nature's way are religious. The two examples I sketch are "Nature as Justice" (drawing primarily on the arguments of Plato and Aristotle) and "Nature as the Will of God" (relying on Augustine and Thomas Aquinas).

NATURE AS JUSTICE

Like any truly interesting and important word, "nature" is a mille-feuille of layered meanings. In order to understand how nature yielded a norm of justice in political philosophy, we must recall that the first, most venerable conception of nature is literally specific: that which makes something the kind (or species) of thing it is, its ontological identity card, if you will. This is the primary meaning not only of the English word "nature" and its cognates in many other modern European languages, but also of its Latin root *natura*, as well as of the ancient Greek word *physis*. In the order derived from specific natures, perfection consists in becoming the best of one's kind, not in changing kind: the rose does not aspire to become a squirrel, nor the squirrel an eagle, nor the eagle a human being. Although the species may be arranged in a hierarchy ascending from the lowliest rock to the gods, it is at once futile and wrong to climb the ladder: there is no social mobility in the Great Chain of Being. It is the idea of fixed natural kinds rather than the considerably later notion of natural laws that informs the ancient and still potent vision of nature as justice.

Closely related to the ideal of justice based on specific natures is that of functional specialization and organic integration. The most familiar example is the human body: among the heart, lungs, kidneys, and other organs, each has its specialized function; all are integrated in the individual organism when it is alive and healthy. The word "organ" derives from the Greek *organon*, or "tool," the most artificial of artifacts, and Aristotle used the term indifferently to refer to man-made instruments (including mental instruments like logic) and to the functional parts of living beings. Organic nature and art exemplify the same kind of order. The same standards of workmanship, of fitting tool to task, apply equally to human and natural productions; as Aristotle writes in the *Physics*, if nature made boats, it would be by the same methods as the shipwright.[10] Moreover, the highest standards require that each tool be fitted to only one purpose, and in this respect Aristotle at least judges nature's handiwork superior: "for nature makes nothing as the cutlers make the Delphic knife, on the cheap, but one thing for one purpose; so that each tool will be turned out in the finest perfection, if it serves not many uses but one."[11]

This ideal of an organic order based on extreme specialization echoes Plato's utopian polis, founded on the principle that each citizen plies only the trade or function for which he is fitted by nature (*kata physin*). Injustice is defined as the violation of specialization, either when citizens "interchange their tools and their honors or when the same man undertakes all these functions at once."[12] Although this organic order may follow nature, as in the case of Plato's *Republic*, it is hardly immutable. On the contrary, it is quite fragile, vulnerable to social subversions of all kinds. So pliable is nature on this view that the Guardians (the ruling class in Plato's utopia) must be forbidden from indulging in acting, lest playing a part out of character warp the qualities that suit them for their job: "Or have you not observed that imitations, if continued from youth far into life, settle down into habits and (second) nature in the body, the speech, and the thought?"[13] Just as a knife's edge may be dulled by using it as a screwdriver, so the Guardians may be denatured by imitating the habitus of a different class.

I use Plato's *Republic* to illustrate an organic order because it is among the most detailed and influential examples, not because it is unique. The history of political theory abounds with other cases, many of them intertwined with analogies drawn from natural history (e.g., the division of labor in the beehive) or human anatomy and physiology (e.g., the mapping of the three estates of feudal society onto the parts of the body). All are based on an ontology of specific natures, combined with the principle of optimal specialization and division of labor. These natures do not carry necessity; on the contrary, they can all too easily be corrupted by usage. And although these orders are usually hierarchical, they do not aim at any single vision of the noble or the good. Because they are essentially interdependent, each part must be good of its kind in order for the whole to flourish. The medieval body politic would disintegrate if it had two hearts and no arms and legs (representing the aristocracy and the commoners, respectively); the artisans in Plato's *Republic* may be less noble than the Guardians, but they are no less necessary. Each component is ideally what it is and only what it is; because the fit of tool to task and part to whole is optimal, change can only mean decay.

Such orders do not derive so much their legitimacy as their plausibility from natural analogies: Do such natures exist as are needed to fill the functions? Can they be joined neatly together with other, equally vital natures to form a viable whole? Will that whole be stable? When, for example, Plato argues that the seemingly contradictory traits of gentleness and ferocity can be united in the Guardians, he cites the well-trained watchdog as proof that such combinations are possible, not "contrary to nature [*para physin*]." Similarly, when fifteenth-century French theorists of the state tried to stave off civil war, they argued that just as a body with more than one head would be an unviable monster, a state with multiple contending monarchs would be disastrous for all.[14] The force of these analogies was as much illustrative as justificatory.

But it is surely not accidental that the illustrations are so often drawn from the realm of organic nature, at least before the mid-seventeenth century. Aristotle provides a clue as to why nature's handiwork might be preferred to that of human artisans as the most arresting illustration of functional parts integrated into a whole. Even though nature and art work by the same methods, natural products are distinguished from artificial ones in two crucial respects, according to Aristotle. First, natural objects contain the principle of motion within themselves, where motion means not simply locomotion but also any kind of change—especially change conceived as development toward a well-defined final state, the telos of the thing in question. Put another way, the ontological identity of natural products is indelible; artificial products may be classified, but only nature can create genuine natural kinds. Second, the proof that these ontological identities are indeed inherent rather than imposed is that in nature, like reproduces like. Beds, ships, houses, boxes, and any number of other artifacts may be made from the wood of trees, but trees remain trees. And whereas beds will never bring forth baby beds, the trees from which the beds are made generate other trees.[15] Only nature is capable of impressing genuine specific natures onto formless matter, and only genuine specific natures will perpetuate their own kind more or less faithfully.

This is why analogies to organic nature proved so magnetic for political and social theorists concerned to establish human orders of comparable coherence and stability. The ontology of natural kinds, which Aristotle articulated but surely did not invent from whole cloth, is also the point of intersection between the temporal and organic orders common to the natural and social realms. Because only natural kinds can be expected to breed true, they are the models and guarantors of the future. Hence the otherwise puzzling medieval allegorical depictions of Dame Nature as obsessively concerned with any hindrance to the orderly perpetuation of her species:[16] she is the manufacturer and preserver of natural kinds, not simply a synonym for some overarching order of natural laws. Organic orders are in themselves static, at least as compared to human timescales; Plato lays out the organization of his Republic for the most part without any reference to historical processes. Since the division of labor within the polis is posited as optimal, any change must be for the worse. Yet all things mortal must die; the rhythm of generations is ineluctable. It is significant that one of the few passages in the *Republic* that deals with change does so in terms of the reproduction of natural kinds. In the founding myth or "noble lie" that explains how the Republic has come to divide its members into three classes, fashioned of gold, silver, and bronze respectively, Plato relies on the principle that like reproduces like to insure the perpetuation of organic order across generations: golden parents (the Guardians) will usually produce golden offspring; silver parents (the Auxiliaries), silver children; and bronze parents (the Workers), bronze progeny.[17]

It need hardly be pointed out that moral orders based upon specific natures are mostly (though not unexceptionably) conservative, hostile to social mobility in any direction and to liberal principles of equality and individual autonomy.[18] Yet they are not conservative in quite the same fashion that post-Enlightenment political and social theories allegedly grounded in nature have been. The moral order of specific natures enjoyed neither the universality nor the inevitability of an order derived from a metaphysics of natural law. There is no escape from the dictates of nature in the doctrines of social Darwinism or, for that matter, in a novel by Turgenev or Zola: natural law is inexorable and relentless. But there is considerable slippage in the order of natural kinds: Plato admits that sometimes silver parents will bear a golden or brazen child; Aristotle concedes that some slaves have the souls of free men and that some women are superior by nature to the husbands to whom they are subordinated. These cases are "contrary to nature [*para physin*]," but whether they are unnatural in the sense of monsters or marvels is left open, and nearly two millennia of literature framed within these categories supply abundant examples for both negative and positive interpretations of individuals who deviate from their natural kind.

Such a moral order of specific natures need be neither theological (nature as God's minister and proxy) nor anthropomorphic (nature personified), although the Christianized versions imagined by the theologians of late antiquity and the Middle Ages have made these versions most familiar to us. Aristotle's nature does not deliberate; Plato's ideal of justice as optimal specialization is not propped up by the gods. Insofar as specific natures wield moral authority, they do so as exemplars of order per se, before it became mandatory to distinguish whether the order in question was natural or human. Good consists in each thing striving to be the best of its kind, not the best of all; evil, in aspiring to the prerogatives of another kind—the rose that wants (absurdly and subversively) to become a squirrel.[19] This order lays no claim to universality, much less to uniformity; on the contrary, diversity of types and functions is the cornerstone of its distinctive form of regularity.

NATURE AS THE WILL OF GOD

In contrast, nature conceived as the will of God by Christian theologians makes universality its hallmark. The *locus classicus* for this tradition is the passage in Augustine's *Confessions* in which he condemns sodomy as a crime *contra naturam* and therefore against God, "the author of nature." Although Augustine agrees, true to Roman tradition, that ordinarily local custom ought to be respected by native and foreigner alike ("when in Rome . . ."), where custom violates divine edict, as incorporated in nature, nature trumps:

> For even that society which is betwixt God and us, is then violated, when the same nature of which he is the author, is polluted . . . when God commands anything to be done, either against the customs or constitutions of any people whatsoever, though the like were never done heretofore, yet it is to be done now. . . . For as amongst those powers appointed in human society, the greater authority is set over the lesser, to command obedience; so is God set over all.[20]

An appeal to nature was not a novelty in Roman law, but to grant nature supreme authority as God's proxy represented a radical break with republican and early imperial jurisprudence. Roman law recognized a category of "natural law," which governed human relationships insofar as these derived from a state of nature, common to humans and animals alike (particularly with respect to procreation and care of offspring)—a kind of lowest common denominator. Unlike civil law, which extended only to a particular political unit, the jurisdiction of natural law was all of humanity for all time. But this universality by no means granted natural law greater authority than the more restricted civil law; quite the contrary. It was axiomatic among Roman jurists that slavery, for example, contradicted natural law, which dictated that all human beings are free and equal, but it was equally axiomatic that slavery was licit under civil law and that civil law superseded natural law. Conversely, crimes that would later in Christian ethics be branded as *contra naturam*, such as parricide and incest, were rather condemned as *nefas*, sacrilegious. In early Roman law, nature did not serve as a basis for moral norms, and, *a fortiori*, not as the most fundamental basis for such norms.[21]

The first appearance of the category of crimes *contra naturam* in Roman law dates to the *Novellae* of Justinian in the sixth century CE in relation to homosexuality (echoing Augustine), and only through a slow process of diffusion and amalgamation with Judeo-Christian elements did the moral category of the unnatural take root, applied above all to perceived threats to the family, whether from parricide, incest, or nonprocreative sexuality.[22] Christian commentators identified the natural order with God's creation and thus with divine sovereignty; hence to defy nature was to defy God, and by the tenth century CE the older Roman category of *nefandum* had converged with the newer category of crimes *contra naturam* in the arch-transgression of heresy.[23] By this convoluted trajectory, nature (here understood as universal nature, the entirety of creation, but with special emphasis on reproduction) was equated with divine authority, and subversions of natural order, with crimes against God. In this spirit Thomas Aquinas, writing in the thirteenth century, excoriated bestiality as not just wrong but unnatural because in violation of the species boundaries established by "the author of nature," that is, God. It is therefore a far more serious sin than mere fornication.[24] Such damaging associations made crimes *contra naturam* the most abominable of all crimes, *nefas* in the root sense of ineffable, unspeakable.

Note the specificity of crimes against nature: even the most heinous murder does not qualify—unless it is one family member doing in another, particularly a parent killing a child or vice versa. The horror characteristically evoked by "unnatural acts" in the Latin Christian tradition is correspondingly specific and has a partial—but only partial—analogue in Greek and Roman literary responses to sacrilege. There is scant evidence that ancient authors found sodomy or homosexuality repugnant (although these practices were sometimes scorned or satirized as lowly).[25] But acts of parricide—for example, Medea's murder of her sons in the plays by Euripides and Seneca—did call forth horror because they were interpreted as a descent into brutishness. After Jason discovers how the children died, he curses Medea as a "she-lion, not a woman, with a nature more savage

than Scylla the Tuscan monster."[26] Nowhere in Euripides's *Medea* nor in
Seneca's Latin reworking of the play (first century CE) is the act of infanti-
cide described as "unnatural," although a mother's murder of her own
children was later to become the very archetype of an unnatural act. In
both plays, abuse is heaped upon Medea for her atrocious deed, but it
is condemned as "unholy," "horrific," and "savage" in Euripides, and as
"abominable," impious, and a "horror" in Seneca—but not as "against
nature."

This is all the more striking because other passages in both plays invoke
the wrath of nature against other human misdeeds: in Euripides, the
chorus of Corinthian women expects rivers to run backward from their
sources because men like Jason now break their oaths sworn by the gods;
in Seneca, the audacious Argonauts are punished for "the sea's outraged
laws."[27] Although deviations from the natural order are cause for morally
tinged alarm in both cases (akin to the guilty fear provoked by the recent
storms in Germany, mentioned earlier), the unnatural is a sign of or response to grave moral transgressions, not a synonym for them, as it would
come to be in Latin Christianity.

The Very Idea of an Order

These two examples of norms derived from nature contrast a positive ideal
of justice with a negative specter of horrific malfeasance; a philosophical
argument from analogy with a theological argument from divine sovereignty; natural order understood as the harmony of specific natures with
natural order as the edicts of God the creator. In neither case is one likely
to find the norms compelling; on the contrary, many will find them to
be particularly repellent examples of the naturalistic fallacy, of trying to
transmute the "is" of nature into the "ought" of ethics. After all, Aristotle
used the same argument about organic specialization in nature to legitimate the human institution of slavery; the religious marginalization and
even persecution of homosexuals as guilty of unnatural acts is alas still too
topical to need belaboring.[28] Aren't these sobering examples of why we
should stop seeking norms in nature? The skeptic might press the point:
at best, nature's authority is borrowed (whether overtly from God or co-
vertly from social convention) and therefore redundant; at worst, it is a
dangerous weapon in the arsenal of the most repressive and regressive
elements of society. Skeptics may very well second John Stuart Mill's view
that invocations of nature are "the most copious sources of false taste, false

philosophy, false morality, and even bad law."[29] Or as journalist Jessica Mitford expressed the same sentiment rather more pithily: "Nature, nature, how I hate yer."[30]

How can these unedifying histories support the philosophical claim that nature is and should be a source of values? My argument will depend on a distinction between the content of specific norms and a more general claim to what philosopher Christine Korsgaard has called "normativity": roughly, the justification that gives any and all norms their force.[31] It is a notorious fact that specific norms vary dramatically across cultures and over time. This also holds for norms that appeal to nature, which run the gamut from apartheid-style racism to Sierra Club environmentalism. But *normativity* is a far more uniform and durable phenomenon; there is no known human culture, past or present, without norms, however wildly diverse these may be. Moreover, even the most cosmopolitan observers, well versed in the mutability of norms across time or space, find it difficult to brush aside the norms of the society in which they were raised. The most vehement relativist cannot help but honor some norms, flimsy conventions though these may be. There is honor among thieves.

"Normativity" sounds like a word badly translated from the German, one of those bloated abstractions that make the mind go blank and the stomach growl. But the meaning of normativity is quite simple: it is the quality of telling us what *should* be, as opposed to describing how things actually are. There are many houses in the mansion of "should," including the "shoulds" of how we should act, how we should know, and what we should admire—otherwise known as the Good, the True, and the Beautiful. What all these "shoulds" have in common is a certain wistful, counterfactual mood, a kind of subjunctive yearning: "If only things were the way they should be!" Since David Hume, most modern philosophy has insisted on the counterfactual dimension of norms in morals, epistemology, and aesthetics: a chasm yawns between what should be and what is. We have all been trained to insist upon the distinction between "is" and "ought," between descriptions of what in fact is the case and prescriptions of what should be the case. To blur this distinction is to commit the naturalistic fallacy, a peculiarly modern kind of category mistake identified by those eager to put the natural and the human asunder.

This modern intellectual reflex is closely related, both historically and conceptually, to another cornerstone of post-seventeenth-century science and philosophy: the anthropomorphism taboo. This is the prohibition, articulated forcefully by leading figures of the scientific revolution such as René Descartes and Robert Boyle, against applying human categories to nature. Boyle was particularly scathing about the maxims of Scholastic physics, such as "Nature does nothing in vain" or "Nature abhors a vacuum." It is undeniable that this policy of treating nature as nothing but brute, passive matter has been wildly successful in subsequent physics and also in some parts of biology, but it should be remembered that the price for this ban on anthropo*morphism* was an overweening anthropo*centrism*: the universe is divided into two asymmetric parts, humans and everything else. And it is humans who, along with God, have been granted a monopoly on all thought and activity, *res cogitans*, in Descartes' terms. Without this ban on anthropomorphism in the name of anthropocentrism, Boyle feared that humans might be tempted to worship nature as a goddess, which would be not only idolatry but also an obstacle to the technological exploitation of nature: "the veneration wherewith men are imbued for what they call nature has been a discouraging impediment to the empire of man over the inferior creatures of God."[32]

It is possible to imagine a scientific stance that eschews both anthropomorphism *and* anthropocentrism (Darwin would be a worthy representative of this program), but it is Boyle's metaphysics that has remained philosophically dominant.[33] The prohibition of anthropomorphism in the service of anthropocentrism supplied the metaphysics that divided the natural and the human into two immiscible realms and widened the gap between them. By the time Immanuel Kant was writing about the realms of natural necessity and human freedom in the late eighteenth century, he could take the absolute distinction between them for granted. And in terms of philosophical categories, we still largely inhabit the house Kant built—that is, we are still asking his questions, even if we are no longer giving his answers.

I do not wish to call into question the distinction between the natural and the human, but I do intend to query the gap between them. There is at very least an arresting analogy between the two realms, which Kant himself eloquently expressed: "Two things never fail to fill me with awe, the starry heavens above and the moral law within."[34] What awed Kant was the regularity exhibited by both the astronomical laws that governed the movements of the heavenly bodies as well as the moral laws that governed human conscience. The word "law" is used here in two different senses, but the justification for metaphorically (and anthropomorphically) extending the notion of human laws to laws of nature was precisely the stern regularity exhibited by both. The emotion of awe is as specific as horror. It is characteristically evoked by the "cosmic" in both root senses

of that word, that is, all-encompassing order and exquisitely designed or-
nament. The recognition of an order is key to all kinds of norms. The
vaster, the grander, and the firmer the order, the stronger is its claim to
that peculiar compound of wonder, fear, and respect known as awe. As
Kant acknowledged, awe (*Ehrfurcht*) is a rare response, but both natural
and moral orders command it.

There is a temporal as well as a spatial dimension to this analogy between natural and moral orders. Kant's image of the "starry heavens
above" conjures up a panorama of the dazzling night sky ablaze with stars.
But the laws Kant probably had in mind were those of celestial mechanics,
which describe the inexorable regularity of the motions of the stars and
planets, stretching backward and forward through all time. Like Kant, the
Victorian novelist George Eliot drew moral solace from the "great conception of the universal regular sequence, without partiality and without
caprice."[35] Although the very determinism of such a universal, regular sequence precluded genuine moral agency in the voluntarist ethical systems
to which both Kant and Eliot subscribed, its relentless uniformity could
serve at least as a figure for a universal moral order purged of the arbitrary.

One need not, however, wait for Newtonian celestial mechanics to find
moral inspiration in the temporal regularities of nature. The seasons run
their course; the sun circles the ecliptic; oaths and compacts are honored.[36]
When the chorus in Euripides' *Medea* expects rivers to run backward now
that men break their oaths, or Heraclitus says the Fates will harry the sun
should it deviate from its course just as they punish perjurers, one and the
same sort of order is being described, although modern metaphysics compels us to read these utterances as metaphorical. There need be no causal
relationship posited between natural and social predictability (which
would presuppose that the two realms have been clearly distinguished);
both simply exemplify what it means to *be* an order. The most salient of
these commonalities is predictability, the guarantee that the sun will continue to rise and set and that promises will be kept. Any order worthy of
the name, whether social or natural, demands a temporal dimension that
extends into the future. It is the order that links the past and the present
to the future, the continuity that is the precondition for rationality and
morality alike.

This is why social customs are honored, even if it is common knowledge that they are conventions, variable over history and cultures. The
ancient Greek historian Herodotus, a cosmopolitan traveler and percep-
tive ethnographer, was fully aware that different peoples—the Greeks, the
Persians, the Egyptians—worshiped different gods, observed different

customs, and embraced different values. But this knowledge did not weaken his belief in the sanctity of custom. He tells a story of an extreme clash of customs:

> When Darius was king, he summoned the Greeks who were with him and asked them what price would persuade them to eat their fathers' dead bodies. They answered that there was no price for which they would do it. Then he summoned those Indians who are called Callatiae, who eat their parents, and asked them (the Greeks being present and understanding by interpretation what was said) what would make them willing to burn their fathers at death. The Indians cried aloud, that he should not speak of so horrid an act. So firmly rooted are these beliefs; and it is, I think, rightly said in Pindar's poem that custom is king of all.[37]

"Custom is king": this later became the motto of those who wish to assert the multiplicity and relativity of social norms and moral standards against those who seek absolutes in both domains.

Yet there is scant evidence that either the poet Pindar, who coined the phrase, or Herodotus, who invoked it, meant to endorse relativism and indict custom as morally flimsy; quite the contrary. Rather, Herodotus aimed to emphasize the necessity of custom, regardless of its specific content, to create and sustain a social order. Those who defy local customs, even if they come as conquerors wielding absolute power (as in the case of Darius's ill-fated son Cambyses, whose downfall supplies the context for this anecdote), do so at their peril. Nature without order is chaos; society without order is anarchy. In states of chaos or anarchy, the past is no guide to present and future; there are no regularities, be they human promises or natural cycles, to support justice or knowledge.

I do not wish to burden the analogy between natural and human orders with more weight than it can bear. It is an analogy, not an identity. Nor do I have any stake in arguing a chicken-and-egg issue about whether it was the natural order that inspired conceptions about human order or vice versa; the arrows of influence probably always point in both directions. The question does not even make sense unless the natural and human orders are cleanly distinguished. But even when they are, the analogy continues to vibrate sympathetically in the space between them. Neither can do without the other. Even Descartes and Boyle reached for the metaphor of human law to describe the most inexorable natural regularities, despite their antipathy toward anthropomorphism; even Kant could not resist the link awe forged between the realms of necessity and freedom, despite his strict separation of the two realms. We have already seen how Aristotle and Plato, Augustine and Aquinas gestured toward natural order as the model for the just society and the virtuous family. My point here is not to defend the specifics of any of these analogies. Rather, I wish to draw our attention to the prevalence, even inevitability, of such analogies and the reasons for them. Whatever it means to be a norm, a way things should be, depends on the concept of an order, regardless of the content of particular norms—or the kind of order, human or natural.

We are now in a position to understand the inveterate habit, so perplexing and irritating to modern philosophers, of conflating prescription and description. The way things are is in principle no guide to how things should be. Yet people notoriously respond to anomalies not only with surprise but also with indignation. The word "normal" perfectly captures this confusion: it simultaneously means what does happen most of the time and what is supposed to happen. Someone who deviates from normality in the first sense of being unusual is likely to be branded "abnormal" in the second, disapproving sense. Even natural anomalies—for example, particularly destructive earthquakes or hurricanes—can sometimes elicit an outraged reaction: this is not how things are supposed to be; no reasonable and prudent person could have been prepared for this event. These easy slides from description to prescription drive philosophers to distraction, and they are indeed difficult to defend in their specifics. It is unjust to classify all human variability as deviance; it is futile to rage like King Lear against the wind—or against Hurricane Katrina. But there is a kernel of philosophical sense in this psychological nonsense. Order per se defines the normative, even if we can reasonably argue about the desirability of this or that specific order. The way in which most people come to understand what an order is in the abstract is on hand from the concrete examples, both natural and social, that pattern their daily experience. It is provincial to mistake one's own familiar order for order tout court, but the intuition that order in general is intrinsically normative hits a deep truth.

Conclusion: Chaos Is Unnatural

I began with Szymborska's poem about nature without humans. Are we now in a position to reclaim meaning from nature, to render its news human? My answer is a cautious and qualified yes. First the qualifications: the prospects of specific norms inspired by nature are not much improved—or rather, I see no reason to privilege them above norms of more purely human derivation. One reason is that nature exemplifies so many different kinds of orders: the order of the stars and planets is not that of the weather; the order of specific natures is not that of universal natural laws; the order of local ecologies, with their distinctive and symbiotic flora and fauna, is not that of cosmological uniformities of gravitation. Nature is every bit as fertile in variety as culture is; the hope that norms extracted from nature converge more convincingly than those freely invented by art is illusory. In other words, the strategy of naturalization to combat relativism is doomed. To glorify certain human values as "natural," whether in the liberal cause of human rights or the conservative one of social Darwinism, does not lend them one iota more of certainty, universality, or permanence. Opponents can always retort, "Which nature?" and counter with examples of another order, equally natural, to support the opposite position.

Yet the very variety of natural orders suggests why we cannot do without nature. Nature is a repository of all imaginable orders. This is why the word "nature" is so embarrassingly rich in definitions. There are specific natures (the nature of maple trees, the nature of salamanders, the nature of salt crystals); there are local natures (the tropics and the tundra, the lush valleys and the bald mountain peaks); there are universal natures (fire burns everywhere, zero degrees Kelvin is absolute zero even in the remotest galaxy). It is, so to speak, in the very nature of the word "nature" to mean many things. Therefore, whatever specific norms are drawn from one sense of nature are more than likely to be in competition with, if not contradiction to, other specific norms drawn from nature. It was just this proliferation of norms from nature that led critics like Mill to throw up their hands in exasperation; nature will never speak with one voice, so why listen?

But the polyphony of nature is precisely the point: it is difficult—perhaps impossible—to imagine an order that is not manifestly, flamboyantly on display in nature. Nature is that delightful paradox, a disorderly *Wunderkammer* of all possible orders. Renaissance *Wunderkammern* dramatized the fecundity and plenitude of nature in their floor-to-ceiling displays, juxtaposing flies in amber and stuffed crocodiles, two-headed cats and striped tulips, magnets and petrified wood in order to overwhelm the spectator with the glorious miscellany of it all. Although the *Wunderkammer* systematically favored the rare and the singular over the commonplace and the ordinary, even everyday nature overflows with variety; the surprises of ethnography (fancy thinking that!) pale beside those of natural history (fancy *being* that!). All human dreams of order, revolutionary or reactionary, local or global, are ultimately figured, made vivid and alluring, in nature's *Wunderkammer* of possible orders. Nature's teeming bounty, however, diverges from that of the *Wunderkammer* in one crucial respect: even at its most intricate and improbable, nature exhibits some kind of order. The *Wunderkammer* aimed to astonish by defying all expectations; nature is the source of all expectations. And without well-founded expectations, the world of causes and promises falls apart.

Order is not always a smiling word. It sometimes has a stern, steely ring to it, the snap of manacles and the clang of the prison door slamming shut. Polities that make "law and order" their motto are notoriously prone to cruelty and repression. But these dictatorial regimes take the name of order in vain. It is the essence of tyrannies and totalitarian governments to destroy the expectations of their unfortunate citizens. Everyone is kept in a state of fear by the unpredictable exercise of power at the whim of the ruler. Terror is wrought of violence combined with randomness, a very different shade of fear from that provoked by equally dangerous but more calculable risks. The very arbitrariness of dictators is their most loathed and effective weapon: no one knows when or why the Gestapo or the KGB or the Stasi will strike next. Kafka's inscrutable bureaucracies operate with the same deliberate caprice, by rules so complicated and opaque that they negate all regularity. One can never know whether tomorrow will be like today. These are examples not of order but rather of institutionalized anarchy.

Of all nightmares that bedevil the collective human imagination, that of chaos is the most terrifying. Human history is stained with orders that have been bloody, tyrannical, and ruthless, orders that suffocate like an iron vise. And many philosophers, poets, and scientists have judged the order of nature to be heartless, inexorable in its workings and indifferent to human joys and sorrows. Order itself can become a nightmare. But the horrors of excessive order shrink beside those of no order at all. Endless civil war is a greater calamity than the most oppressive dictatorship; a universe formless and lawless is the ground zero of all cosmogonies, be it divinity or natural law that is called upon to create a cosmos worthy of the name. A land in which no promise is kept, in which the sun may or may not rise on the morrow, in which the past is no guide to the future, is a no-man's-land. Nothing human, indeed nothing living, can long survive in an environment wholly at the mercy of chance.

It is chaos, the destruction of all order, that is the true unnatural. The unnatural consists not in violations of the will of God (however construed) but in the pathology of will known as the arbitrary: dictates and edicts based on nothing more than caprice, willing for the sake of willing alone. It is true that nature also sometimes seems capable of caprice—those freakish concatenations of causes that produce the odd monster or maelstrom or aurora borealis. But nature's caprices are not only by definition rare; they are impersonal. Nature does not will; nature cannot be arbitrary in the root sense of the word. People who have suffered under tyrannies report that one of the most dehumanizing aspects of such regimes is the element of humiliation implicit in being at the mercy of another's caprice—even if the outcome is only confusion rather than violence. The extreme case of being completely subject to the will of another person is slavery, but all arbitrary decisions exercised by authorities injure human dignity. If the authority is personal, insult is added to injury. We become the victims of another's disdain as well as power; we have been denied the bare recognition owed to all fellow humans qua humans. Nature's power to injure is immense—witness the destruction of earthquakes, volcanoes, and tsunamis. But nature can never insult.

Reread in this light, Szymborska's poem now consoles. Nature is inhuman (Szymborska might have added: and also undivine)—so much the better. Nature is not a person nor the minister of a personal god or gods. Nature just is. But for just this reason, we humans cannot do without nature, even if nature (like Eliza Doolittle in *My Fair Lady*) can do jolly well without us—"without your calling it the tide comes in." Our needs go beyond the technologies of food, clothing, and shelter, the air we breathe, and the water we drink. Nature also supplies the raw materials for meaning, even if nature by itself is meaningless. We humans need to use nature to make meaning, because nature is the fount of all order—or rather, orders. It is the prime example and therefore irresistible metaphor of the world in order—or rather, of many possible worlds in many possible orders. And without some concept of order to knit time together, to link memories of the past to hopes for the future, we cannot mean anything to one another.

PART ONE

Ecology and Nature

Perhaps in its most intuitive sense, "nature" means the natural environment, the ecosphere that provides a stage and backdrop for the drama of human culture. Although culture has always influenced how nature is understood and accessed, human beings in the present historical moment are altering nature to an unprecedented degree. As we continue to impact the natural environment surrounding us, how ought we to understand the stability of ecological "nature"? Can the extrahuman biosphere be transformed beyond recognition? Does it make sense to speak of being "without nature"?

Or, as Peter Raven suggests, is the contrary the truth: nature would sooner be without us than we without nature? For Raven, it is our relationship to nature, not nature itself, which is being altered. But this emerging new relationship is unsustainable, since it jeopardizes our unavoidable dependence upon the natural environment. Viewed from the perspective of the ecosphere itself, the human transformation of nature has amplified dramatically in the last few centuries. The rapid acceleration of unsustainable environmental pressures has not only led to gross disparities among human groups but has also precipitated waves of extinction. In the past, human culture helped to shape the experience of nature. But the economic expansion of the modern era is now limiting nature's own expanse, killing off its species, human and otherwise. Raven sees the greatest (and most dangerous) eclipse of nature in the aggregate loss of biodiversity. All human culture depends vitally upon the resources donated by the natural environment, and when such biodiversity becomes progressively extinguished, human life will inevitably soon follow. Nature, then, must be actively sustained not only for its own sake but because we are intimately part of it. Being "without nature," for Raven, would be tantamount to the extinction of the human species itself.

William French seconds Raven's judgment that we are not "without nature," but he points out that many modern philosophers, theologians, and ethicists have proceeded as if we already were. The dualism and an-thropocentrism of modern philosophy places subjectivity in the fore-ground in religious reflection, whether in terms of the person of Jesus or the personhood of human beings. Even the natural-law tradition of Catho-lic theology, notes French, has been attenuated as recent interpretations seek to harmonize it with Kant. Yet such "thinking without nature" can generate theoretical blind spots. When nature is seen as separate from and passively enduring human action, mistaken estimates inevitably arise in the arenas of technological impact, efficient economic distribution, and international security.

Like Raven, French affirms that just as one cannot live without a sus-tainable relationship to nature, so, too, ethical reflection attempting to abstract itself from its natural environment is equally doomed, whether in a theological or economic vein. But while French reviews the historical decline of thinking in terms of nature, Cabell King looks toward the fu-ture, proposing a possible theoretical surrogate. One way to remember the forgotten centrality of nature is to view the natural environment as space, a space produced through liturgical action. Moreover, if nature has always been coproduced by culture, then a deeper imbrication of second nature with first nature need not occasion hand-wringing. Nature is more than its wildness. Rather, the spatial production of nature grants a perspective by which to see how culture (and particularly religion) helps to establish and therefore sustain our relationship to nature. According to King, the Christian liturgy provides one resource for strengthening the bonds to nature by reestablishing the structures of natural space that can help order social life.

How is ecological nature in jeopardy, and what perspectives can illumi-nate its survival? Can we sustain the human enterprise without untamed, unadulterated wilderness? How has the present relation to the ecological world been determined by past attitudes, and what capacities for theologi-cal and ethical reflection do they enable (or prevent) today?

Our Common Responsibility to Nature

Peter H. Raven

From the standpoint of our future survival, to assert that we have entered or are entering a new world without nature is both patently absurd and extremely dangerous. We evolved our distinctive characteristics in the context of a planet that is, as far as we know, unique precisely because of its biological systems, which in turn moderate and control the operation of the physical systems with which they interact. We depend on these systems for the air we breathe, the food we consume, the protection of the topsoil on which we grow our crops, most of our medicines, and every aspect of our lives. Because of the nature of our bodies, it is clear that we shall always depend on the operation of these biological systems and can never become independent from them. What has changed, however, is our relationship with nature. As Lorraine Daston puts it so elegantly in her contribution to this volume, we have come to see Mother Nature as our child, and the necessity for us to care for nature has become ever more obvious and has grown in intensity with the passage of time.

What does the outstanding environmental author Bill McKibben mean, then, when he speaks of the "end of nature"?[1] He means that the demands of an explosively growing human population, together with our greedy and often wasteful consumption of all that the Earth provides have essentially put an end to our historical vision of nature as a paradise, a Garden of Eden that existed somewhere else or somewhere in our collective memory of the past as a kind of a perfect place where the destructive and manipulative actions of humanity were not evident. With numbers that seem very small to us today, however, our ancestors were damaging the lands where they lived with their cultivation of crops and particularly their herds of goats, sheep, and cattle—to such a degree that the authors of the Bible and the prophets had already begun to enjoin them to care for and not to destroy Creation. A clear understanding that we were responsible for the fate of the Earth had begun to grow. How did this situation develop, and where has it led?

I shall in this paper explore the growing intensity of our impacts on the natural systems that support us, emphasizing especially the critical importance of biological extinction in limiting both the Earth's productive capacity and our ability to innovate in the development of a sustainable planet in the future. Our destruction of nature is now proceeding at a staggering and unprecedented scale, but despite our ignorance we remain fully dependent on nature, and its end would clearly precipitate ours as well.

The Long View

To grasp the gravity of our present relation to nature, it is helpful to gain some chronological perspective.[2] Human beings have been in existence for perhaps 2 million years of the 4.6-billion-year history of our planet, our distinctive features having evolved among the great apes that inhabited the plains and forests of Africa at that time. Life originated much earlier, at least 3.8 billion years ago, and the origin of complex, multicellular organisms was perhaps 800 million years in the past. Major groups of organisms emerged onto the land starting about 450 million years ago and ultimately became exceedingly diverse there, with complex ecological relationships developing among them.

For most of our 2-million-year history, we have had a relatively minor effect on the sustainability of our planet. As recently as 10,500 years ago, when crop agriculture was developed for the first time in the Fertile Crescent of the eastern Mediterranean, there were no more than 3 million to 4 million people on Earth—a number smaller than the population of Chicago. Those several million people constituted the entire human population of the world—of Eurasia, Africa, Australia, and the Americas combined. Although our ancestors had by that time domesticated dogs, learned to use fire, weapons, and other tools, fashioned small sculptures and impressive rock paintings, and exhibited by the nature of some of their burials their belief in an afterlife, they cannot truly be said to have developed civilization in the sense in which we understand it today.

Starting, then, about 10,500 years, or only about 420 human generations, ago, our numbers began to grow as the cultivation of crops made food supplies much more dependable than they had been earlier. The small, scattered villages of the eastern Mediterranean grew into towns, and groups of people began to war with one another over supplies of food or to gain possession of the land on which food could be grown. The eventual establishment of the ancient Israelites in the lands bordering the eastern Mediterranean ultimately involved the conquest of the people that they encountered there and further battles for the fertile lands on which larger and richer settlements were eventually established. Agriculture developed independently in several other regions during the same period, always following a strikingly similar course.

Within these growing settlements, specialized professionals, such as weapons makers, farmers, religious and civic leaders, poets, storytellers, and artists began to appear. The path was set for the invention of written language about 3,500 BCE, starting with the cuneiform writing of ancient Sumeria, which then spread to other areas and eventually developed into the kinds of alphabets that we use today. Other forms of writing, notably the hieroglyphic script of the Nile Valley, developed at more or less the same time but did not spread to other regions. By the time Abraham and his wife migrated from Sumeria to live among the Canaanites, thought to be around 2,800 BCE, written language had been established for centuries.

Not surprisingly, early views of human history in this region extend back to around the time writing was developed, 5,000 or 5,500 years ago, this period marking the start of the reckoning of years in the Hebrew calendar. The world population continued to grow, so that by the time of Christ, there were several hundred million of us, approximately equal to the population of North America or Europe at present. These numbers reached perhaps half a billion people by the early years of the Renaissance in southern Europe. As new lands were colonized by Europeans and brought into more intensive cultivation, visions of Paradise were still possible. From the perspective of European colonialists, what they saw as unspoiled lands in North and South America, Africa, and Australia seemed to promise a boundless harvest that would be available to them forever.

Although sporadic references to the exhaustion of land, especially land that was cultivated or grazed heavily, were made in classical times, a sense of global limits began to arise about five centuries ago in Renaissance Europe, when exploration throughout the world was soon followed by waves of colonization in the New World, Asia, Australia, and Africa. The rapid extension of often unsustainable forms of land use rapidly changed the face of the continents.[3]

Such optimistic views began to turn to doubt as some noticed signs of environmental stress. Yet even in the 1790s, when the Reverend Thomas Malthus declared that people would be unlikely to be able to grow enough food to meet the needs of their rapidly growing population, there were only about 850 million of us, well under the population of either China or India at present. Malthus's dire predictions were never fully realized, however, because of the intensive application of newly harnessed forms of energy to agriculture, which allowed new lands to be plowed, cultivated, fertilized with new synthetic compounds, and ultimately protected from pests by manufactured pesticides. These gains in agricultural productivity were ultimately bolstered through improvements in crop breeding that allowed harvests to be increased greatly.

The human population continued growing, reaching 1 billion people for the first time in the Napoleonic times of the early nineteenth century and, more than a century later, 2 billion around 1930, ultimately reaching 2.5 billion people in 1950. From that point until now, a period of only fifty-five years, the human population has grown to 6.5 billion, nearly tripling in size over this relatively short period. Along with rapid growth, material expectations have risen continuously, as have the levels of consumption for those able to fulfill them. The spread of technology since the Industrial Revolution has led to the consumption of a rapidly growing proportion of all natural productivity, increasing pollution to a previously unimaginable degree and changing the character of our lands, our waters, and the whole Earth.

Specifically, the last fifty years have seen the loss of an estimated 20 percent of our topsoil to erosion—an asset of critical importance that is only slowly replaced on a timescale measured in centuries. Some 18 percent of our agricultural lands have become unavailable for food production because of salinization related to irrigation practices or overfertilization, desertification, or urban sprawl. We have cut down around a third of the forests that were present in 1950 without replacing them. We have increased the amount of atmospheric carbon dioxide, the major greenhouse gas that drives global warming, by about a sixth, with consequences that are easily demonstrable and now widely understood. We have depleted the stratospheric ozone layer by 6 percent to 8 percent, thus increasing the incidence of malignant skin cancer in temperate latitudes by about a fifth; the so-called "ozone hole" measured over Antarctica in the southern summer of 2006 and 2007 was the largest ever observed.

To summarize our impact on the biosphere in another way, it is estimated that we are currently using, diverting, or wasting on a continuing basis nearly half of the total terrestrial output that results from the process of photosynthesis and consuming about 55 percent of the renewable supplies of fresh water.[4] Overall this condition can only be described as unsustainable; we are using the world's resources much more rapidly than they can be renewed and leaving for our children and grandchildren a planet that will be much less diverse, rich, healthy, and resilient than the one in which we live now.[5] Another way of looking at our rate of consumption now has been developed by the Global Footprint Network.[6] Using carefully considered and presented statistics, this institute has calculated that at the present levels of population and consumption and with current technologies, we are using about 120 percent of the world's productivity, up from an estimated 70 percent in 1970. Even if there were no improvements in the conditions of human existence and no further growth in our numbers, the present level of consumption obviously cannot be sustained indefinitely. In financial terms, it amounts to spending not only the interest from an investment but also the capital.

The negative effects of our unsustainable levels of resource consumption are felt particularly by the world's poor. Considering that 2 to 3 billion people will be added to the world population before it could possibly be stabilized around the middle of the current century, the possibilities for improving the lot of the poor and grossly deprived people of the world seem truly bleak. At present, half of the world's 6.5 billion people live on less than $2 per day and a quarter on less than $1. Half of the world's people are malnourished in some way, and at least one in eight is literally starving—receiving so few calories that their brains cannot be formed properly when they are children and their bodies are literally wasting away as adults. A quarter of the world's people do not have access to dependable supplies of clean water; a single flush of a toilet in an industrialized country uses more water than an individual among the hundreds of millions of the world's poorest people would see in a day. In the poorest parts of the world, the lives of women and children are particularly awful. They spend most of their time gathering supplies of water and firewood and cooking in smoky huts in which the air is filled with carcinogenic particles, and they have no practical chance to gain an education or to contribute to the advance of their families, their nations, or the world as a whole.[7]

The 18 percent of the world's people who live in industrialized countries control more than 80 percent of the world's resources and produce an equivalent amount of pollution, leaving the remaining 20 percent of the world's resources for more than 80 percent of the world's people. Hence in the United States, with 4.5 percent of the world's population, we base our economy and our standard of living on our consumption of about a quarter of the world's resources and produce a corresponding fraction of global pollution. People collectively are already using considerably more than the world can produce sustainably, so that virtually all of the resources on which we depend are declining. If everyone reached the standards of consumption characteristic of industrialized countries at present, we would go much further beyond the sustainable capacity of the planet, provided that we kept using present technologies, and that would be true without any population growth. A stable population, a reasonable level of consumption, and the development of many new technologies, especially in the field of energy, would be necessary before sustainability could be achieved worldwide, particularly to address the grossly inequitable and unjust consumption of resources.

Certainly, much could be accomplished through increased assistance from the rich to the poor. Though a clear moral and practical imperative, redistribution of resources is not well accepted as a strategy for sustainability by the world's wealthy nations—nor by the affluent citizens of developing countries, for that matter. A great deal of effort clearly needs to be expended on developing better technologies and finding appropriate levels of consumption that do not squander the available resources. For example, in the United States we use twice as much energy per capita as the people of any other nation. Is our standard of living twice that of Sweden, Germany, or France? What benefit are we actually gaining by wasting so much energy, and are there not ample reasons for considering ways to conserve it more effectively?

Extinction: The End of Life

This long view of human population growth and the present inequities in resource consumption help to explain the alarming levels of species extinction at present. As a consequence of the human pressures on the environment just chronicled, much of our endowment of biodiversity is under siege.[8] While we will never be "without nature," we are presently witnessing a massive reduction in the diversity of nature's life. "Nature" will look very different by the close of the present century.

It is difficult to estimate the magnitude of this loss to the planet's richness, partly because of our limited knowledge of biodiversity generally. It appears that there are at least 12 million species of eukaryotic organisms (organisms other than bacteria and viruses), of which we have named and catalogued only about 1.8 million. We confine our attention to eukaryotic organisms because it has become evident that there are millions of different kinds of bacteria, and we have at present no way of estimating their numbers. Among the eukaryotes are the animals, plants, fungi, and microorganisms other than bacteria. We have discovered, classified, and named perhaps one sixth of them, so our degree of ignorance is profound; even of those to which we have given names, we have a reasonable amount of information about only a few, perhaps fifty thousand to a hundred thousand species. In the tropics, where more than half of the world's eukaryotic organisms live, we have classified only about six hundred thousand species, a number that certainly represents well under a tenth of the kinds of organisms that actually occur there. Thus the destruction of tropical forests and other habitats in the warmer parts of the Earth results in the destruction of a largely unknown set of organisms, the great majority of them never seen by a scientist and most likely to disappear from the face of the Earth forever without ever having been recognized.

Even though most organisms have not yet been catalogued, we can use data from the few groups that are relatively well known, like the vertebrates, vascular plants, butterflies, and a few others, to estimate the rate of extinction of the whole group. To trace the history of species in the fossil record, we select groups of animals that have hard parts, like mollusks or vertebrates, and therefore have a relatively complete representation through geological time. Doing so, we can estimate an average life for species of 2 million to 4 million years, so that about one species per million per year goes extinct—perhaps ten species a year if the total number of eukaryotic species is approximately 10 million. Six major pulses of extinction have occurred in the past, the most recent at the end of the Cretaceous period about 65 million years ago, and so the rate of extinction during the past 65 million years puts into relief the recent acceleration of extinctions.

If we consider the rate of extinction during the past four or five centuries, we can estimate that hundreds of species per year have been lost and that the rate has now climbed to thousands of species per year. Particularly striking has been the extinction of about a thousand species of birds on the islands in the Pacific, amounting to approximately a tenth of the world's bird species, over the past thousand years as the Polynesians colonized the area. Some of the birds were hunted, but land clearing for growing crops was apparently the chief reason that so many of them disappeared in such a short period of time.

At the present time, it can be estimated that thousands of species of eukaryotic organisms are becoming extinct each year. Habitat destruction is the major cause of this loss. As mentioned above, we have lost about a third of the world's forests since 1950 and are cutting into the rest rapidly. It is estimated that the tropical moist forests of the world, which may contain half of the total biodiversity on this planet, will have been reduced to about 5 percent of their original area by the middle of this century. At present, we are growing crops on about 11 percent of the world's land surface and grazing domestic animals on another 20 percent (180 million people with 3.3 billion sheep, goats, and cattle), although these pastures are becoming virtually unsustainable. A third of the world's land surface, therefore, is severely and directly affected by agriculture, and much of the rest is being altered as a result of other human activities. For example, as the world's population becomes more concentrated in large cities, urban sprawl coupled with the relentless drive to supply those cities with commodities available in the countryside is reducing habitat extent and diversity everywhere.

As a result of this rapid, catastrophic loss of habitat nearly everywhere, we can estimate that perhaps two thirds of all species of eukaryotes on Earth may be lost by the end of the present century. This staggering loss, amounting to at least 6 million species, would be comparable in scale to that estimated to have occurred at the end of the Cretaceous period 65 million years ago, when the dinosaurs disappeared altogether and the character of terrestrial life was changed permanently. It took 10 million years for life to recover, resume the evolutionary processes of the past, and build the complex ecosystems that are characteristic of the modern world.

There are several reasons, however, for thinking that the scale of extinction in this century may be even greater. One reason is that the rapid spread of invasive species throughout the world is driving many species to the brink of extinction; it is estimated that about a third of the threatened or endangered plant species in the continental United States are menaced mainly by invasive alien species. In Hawaii, almost all species that are in danger of extinction have reached that status because of invasive alien plants or animals. As people and goods move between the continents and islands in increasing numbers, the spread of such species can only be accelerated, with highly destructive consequences.

Selective harvesting of particular kinds of plants, animals, and fungi poses yet another threat to their continued survival. Thus the hunting of "bush meat," wild vertebrates killed for human consumption, is spreading like an epidemic worldwide. In addition, almost all of the world's major fisheries are overexploited, and the prospects of their continued productivity are dim if present practices continue. In this connection, the exhaustion of traditional sources of protein in the bordering oceans by European and Asian fishing boats is driving the people of West and Central Africa to intensify their harvest of native forest animals. At the same time, the increased use of plant products as medicinal supplements in Japan, Europe, and the United States is causing the plants used for these purposes to be harvested unsustainably throughout the developing countries of the world, where they are the primary sources of medicine for the people.

Another truly serious problem affecting the future of biodiversity is that of global warming. Global warming is now widely understood to be a serious threat to many human functions, but its most permanent damage may be in the massive loss of biodiversity that it will cause, changing and eliminating habitats throughout the world. The organisms that we are losing include those that could be used to rebuild sustainable ecological communities—ecosystems—in the face of climate change. Limited areas that have been set aside for the preservation of particular sets of species may be vulnerable to the changes associated with a warmer climate, since their original habitats may change drastically and thus become unsuitable for the organisms that originally occurred there. These changes are obviously taking place in a landscape in which the habitats have been fragmented, invaded by alien species, and otherwise disturbed—all factors that greatly increase the impact of global warming.

The projected global increases in temperature are unprecedented within at least the past ten thousand years. General estimates indicate a rise in average annual temperatures in temperate regions of 0.4 to 2 degrees Celsius by 2030, relative to 1990, and 1 to 6 degrees Celsius by 2070. With as little as a 1 degree Celsius rise in temperature, the bioclimates of some species will disappear entirely while the ranges of others may be greatly reduced or fragmented.[9] It is becoming widely recognized that mountainous regions should be given priority as conservation areas because of the possibility of migration upward as the climate changes; however, many of the most critical areas for biodiversity are essentially flat, and such opportunities are thus absent. One study has estimated that 15 percent to 37 percent of the species in the areas analyzed could be on the way to extinction by 2050, depending on the magnitude of the climate change that occurs by that time.[10] If these projections are valid worldwide, that would suggest the possible loss of 1.5 to about 4 million species, the great majority of them unknown, within the next fifty years or so, and this on the basis of climate change alone. The only solution to global climate change is a reduction in the emission of greenhouse gasses, but the United States and a few other countries are so resistant to this conservative step that it will probably be attained only very slowly.

In addition to the extinction of individual species, the progressive limitation of ecosystem services becomes a serious problem as natural communities are devastated by human actions. Watershed protection can be disrupted, the fertility of fragile soils destroyed, wetlands rich in biodiversity damaged, and climatic patterns disrupted. Crop pollination may be curtailed to the point that productivity declines, and the often surprisingly balanced assemblages of insects, birds, and other animals that provide a kind of natural integrated pest management in agricultural situations may be distorted and lose their ability to function well. Overall, the loss in ecosystem services associated with the loss of biodiversity may be the most serious problem we shall be facing as a result of global warming. The species lost will never be regained once they are lost, and future generations will face an irreversible loss of values that they might otherwise have had in the direct provision of goods and services, aesthetic and cultural values, and the ability to react to further global change in ways we do not understand yet.

In a narrower sense, the loss of the direct values of biodiversity is also a source of great concern. More than 90 percent of our food comes directly or indirectly from just over one hundred species of plants, and especially from just three members of the grass family: maize, wheat, and rice. More than three hundred thousand species of plants have been described and named, and well over five thousand of them have been used as sources of food at some time. We have no idea how many of the remaining species are unrecognized sources of food that might be useful in particular places in the future, when we shall have to grow a great deal more food than we do currently and obtain as much as we can locally to avoid insupportable costs for energy.

In addition, about two thirds of the people in the world depend directly on plants as their source of medicine, and there are doubtless many more plant sources that could be used if we understood their properties better. Even for those of us who routinely purchase our medicines in a drug store, about a quarter of all our prescriptions supply us with medicines that either came from plants originally or still come from them. For example, aspirin (salicylic acid) is synthesized but has properties similar to those of a molecule originally obtained from willow (*Salix*) bark. On the other hand, all steroids are made from a base molecule that is obtained from cultivated species of the genus *Solanum*, the same genus as potatoes and tomatoes. Taxol is mostly harvested directly from yews (*Taxus*), either wild or cultivated. Over five thousand kinds of antibiotics have come onto the market since the end of World War II and, with very few exceptions, they are derived from bacteria or fungi. The list of ways in which we can use individual kinds of organisms to improve our lives is practically endless: sources of paper and other commodities; biomass as a source of energy; building materials derived from plants at present, the sources of which can be improved through scientific breeding and other methods.

The quest for sustainability will ultimately be greatly assisted by modern discoveries in molecular biology, which have revealed in great depth the ways that organisms develop their characteristics, grow, and function. Watson and Crick's postulate of the double helical model for DNA was published just over fifty years ago, in 1953, and the mechanisms for the production of proteins were not well understood for nearly another decade. Subsequently, Boyer and Cohen in 1973 first successfully transferred a gene from one unrelated kind of organism to another. During the 1980s, molecules produced as a result of the genetic modification of DNA came into widespread use in medicine; genetically modified crops were tested and spread rapidly to occupy about an eighth of the world's croplands by the early 2000s. Soon organisms genetically modified by the techniques of modern biology will be ubiquitous, making possible, along with the application of many other techniques, substantial advances in the Earth's sustainability. Even now, we have produced complete or partial base sequences for the genomes of a number of different kinds of organisms, both prokaryotic and eukaryotic. As a result of these advances, we are rapidly increasing our ability to interpret patterns of variation in different organisms on the basis of evolution in gene families. The discoveries being made in this way promise to lead to new levels of understanding of how the genes associated with particular traits vary among organisms and how they function in different ways in different species, a set of observations that has the potential to shed great light on the properties of the genes and their function.

At any rate, the genes that might be useful in promoting sustainability, whether by improving existing organisms or by discovering new uses of them, are disappearing rapidly with the organisms themselves. The loss of more than two thirds of total terrestrial biological diversity over the course of the century that we have just entered must be judged a tragedy in the making. By ignoring this loss, we are destroying the very elements that we might use to build a better future for ourselves and our children—a moral crime for which it will be impossible to forgive us in the future. Surely no religion can condone such wasteful and ignorant destruction of creation.

Our Perceptions of Nature

In the writings of Aldo Leopold, a great conservationist and philosopher, we find some of the most stirring essays on this topic, such as his "Sand County Almanac." This book immediately became a landmark of the movement toward what we would now call sustainability and is surely one of America's finest gifts to the world conservation movement. Leopold's "land ethic" speaks of a complex world dominated by human beings, who thus have either the power of good, nurturing care of their land or the ability to degrade and destroy it. In his words, it "changes the role of *Homo sapiens* from conqueror of the land-community to plain member and citizen of it."[11]

Gradually the concern for the environment that has developed throughout the industrialized world has assumed a broader focus on the deteriorating condition of the whole world, which is increasingly seen as directly related to poverty. The first United Nations conference on the environment, held in Stockholm in 1972, began to bring these problems home to all people. In the same year, the Club of Rome published *The Limits to Growth*, which is based for the first time on the use of comprehensive mathematical models of the planet's environment.[12] The book's authors calculate that if the trends in world population growth at that time continued, the limits to growth on the planet would be reached within a hundred years. At the same time, they point out that the underlying conditions could be changed to produce sustainability for the indefinite future if we have the collective will to take the necessary steps to bring this condition about.

"Sustainability" is a concept that gained prominence with the publication of a report authored by the World Commission on Environment and Development in 1987, *Our Common Future*, on the global environment in a human context. The report calls for sustainable development, "development which meets the needs of the present without compromising the ability of future generations to meet their own needs." To some extent, its conclusions were built into the declarations of the Rio de Janeiro Earth

Summit held five years later (in 1992), but in practice there has been relatively little subsequent progress toward attaining global sustainability.[13]

Our collective inability, or perhaps unwillingness, to deal with conditions in the poorer parts of the world, on the one hand, and excessive consumption in more affluent parts of the world and among the rich people who live in developing countries, on the other, pose serious moral problems; in addition, they constitute obstacles to the development of global sustainability. While the majority of us ignore what conditions are like in most of the world, levels of consumption are rising globally, with China (1.3 billion people) and India (1.1 billion people) leading the way. By the middle of the twenty-first century, over 2 billion people will be added to the present population of 6.5 billion; half of these will attain high levels of affluence, adding over 1 billion "new consumers" to the world population.[14] They will severely strain the productive capacity of our planet as their levels of affluence grow. Inasmuch as they are likely to be using those technologies now available, increasing strains on the productive capacity of the Earth can be anticipated.

Our Response: Possible Strategies

Although we are completely dependent on nature for all conditions of our lives, we continue to act as if that were not the case. The assertion that nature has ended or is ending and that we have in some sense become independent of it amounts to nothing less than a collectively authored suicide note for humanity. For at least a half century, it has been evident that we cannot expect a healthy, peaceful, and productive future if we continue to live off Earth's capital rather than the interest from that capital, which is natural productivity. We shall certainly reach sustainability at some point in the future, since it is patently impossible to consume indefinitely more than our planet is able to produce. Consequently, our guiding question should be transformed. Instead of asking: How far can we go in consuming our natural resources unsustainably? we ought to ask: What kind of world do we want? The more topsoil, agricultural land, and forests we consume, the more we pollute the air we breathe and the water we drink, and the more genetic and biological diversity we allow to slip through our fingers, the less interesting, resilient, and healthy the resulting world will be and the more catastrophic crashes of major ecological and economic systems are likely to take place.[15]

Global security depends ultimately on environmental sustainability rather than on devoting a huge proportion of the world's economic output to military expenditure.[16] Food security, health, social justice—all are dependent on rising above our parochial and perhaps ingrained views of how to live and learning together how to manage our planetary home for our common benefit. Empowering women throughout the world, seeking means to raise their status and alleviating their poverty (microcredit has proved an effective strategy in this important effort), is among the most important means for achieving sustainable development. Science and technology need to be fully applied in our striving toward global sustainability, but they alone will clearly not be enough.[17]

As I suggest in a review of the historical development of the concept of "sustainability," it now seems that regulation of economic policy, with allowances for supporting the actions of the private sector, will have more impact on the environment than direct legislative initiatives.[18] The true value of the materials that we use should become the basis of the sustainable commerce of the future, and the irrational taxes that so often drive unsustainable activities by misstating the value of their materials should be abandoned. Indeed, Norman Myers and Jennifer Kent have estimated that perverse subsidies leading to the destruction of natural resources worldwide amount to some $1.5 trillion annually, a sum larger than the economy of any nation except for the five largest.[19] Hence recognizing the undesirable nature of these subsidies and eliminating them is a step of fundamental importance as we build toward a sustainable world.

Many activities undertaken by corporations over the past two decades suggest that they are recognizing global sustainability as an important element in their own achievement of success. Certainly green architecture and green engineering are flourishing in many parts of the world, involving such considerations as energy conservation and life-cycle analysis for the materials used in construction, a system that evaluates their impact on the environment from the time they are mined and manufactured through the end of their use. Green consumerism and a heightened interest in global warming, for example, are leading individuals and corporations as well as governments to modify their traditional activities.

Four hundred generations ago, most human beings were still living in highly dispersed small groups engaged in hunting animals and harvesting products, including food, from wild plants. For more than 99 percent of the estimated 2 million years that humans have existed on Earth, the conditions for success differed greatly from the ones that are operative today. Survival strategies before the development of agriculture and in early urban development differed greatly from those that would seem to be optimal in the modern world. Selfishness, the concentration of resources, competition to maintain the status of the small band—whether genetically hardwired or deeply imbedded in our social consciousness—are traits that we recognize all too readily among our fellow human beings and the social groups that we have built. Clearly we have not yet developed formulas adequate to govern the peaceful coexistence and cooperation of nations, each with millions of inhabitants and varying amounts of goods and technologies, in such a way that a sustainable world will be the result. Indeed, excessive greed and the kind of strong competition that doubtless served our ancestors well seem clearly to characterize many of our actions now and lead to the kinds of social inequality that are so difficult to deal with.

Civilization has changed so rapidly that we still possess outlooks valid some four hundred generations ago. As the elements of what we consider civilization developed, we gained many values that we cherish but perhaps not the wisdom to protect them in the face of our seemingly endless greed. New standards of thinking and living are needed for an increasingly overcrowded world in which haves and have-nots are struggling to gain their own futures as modern states battle, as rich-poor divides are deepened, and as we seek a humanistic form of globalization that must avoid subsidies further benefiting the rich if we are ever to develop a just and stable world. In fact, these subsidies amount to what Willy Brandt termed "a blood transfusion from the sick to the healthy,"[20] and what we presumably need to seek is exactly the opposite.

By pursuing strategies of the sort just reviewed, it might actually be possible to improve the potential condition of the world and to counteract humanity's tendency to behave as if we were still highly dispersed hunter-gatherers rather than members of a rapidly growing human race comprising 6.5 billion people, some very rich but many living in abject poverty. How might we build the political will to accomplish this? In view of the failure of the United States and other leading industrialized countries to address responsibly the agenda proposed at the Earth Summit in Rio de Janeiro in 1992, we cannot legitimately view the future with a sense of optimism. Nonetheless, there are many choices available to us that, if the correct course is taken, hold promise for a better future.[21] To name one significant example, a global plan for the preservation of species, properly funded, would result in the greatest gift that we could possibly give to our descendants.

For the world at large, frameworks such as that developed by The Natural Step, an influential Swedish organization, will provide convenient blueprints to help guide us along the path of sustainability. At the same time, Kai Lee's principle that sustainability can perhaps best be viewed as an ideal, like justice, should be kept carefully in mind as we travel in that direction.[22] In this connection, the kinds of grassroots activities that contribute to sustainability on a local basis have become a powerful force throughout the world, even when they simply serve to reemphasize traditional ways. Whether establishing local clinics and sustainable industries in the Biligiri Rangan Hills of south India or people-based ecotourism centers in native lands in Kenya, rebuilding a broken landscape at the Bookmark Biosphere Reserve in South Australia, learning how to ranch sustainably on the vast grasslands of the Malpai Borderlands of New Mexico and Arizona, or simply rooting out alien plants on Albany Hill in the San Francisco Bay area, the people who are pursuing sustainability in direct and personal ways will hugely affect the shape of the world in the future. Outstanding books such as those by Yvonne Baskin and Gretchen Daily, explaining in detail how nature works and how we benefit from it in untold ways, play an important role in stimulating our desire to achieve sustainability.[23]

The basic conditions of change must certainly come from within us. Collectively, we cannot continue indefinitely to consume more than the world is capable of producing, regardless of how abhorrent we may find the concept of "limits to growth." In particular, a small minority of Earth's residents cannot continue to consume such a large majority of Earth's potentially sustainable productivity. By doing so, they will ultimately destabilize their own future as well as the futures of all other people. Population control, consumption control, and the use of appropriate technology must all be brought into play if our common objective is to achieve a sustainable world in the new millennium.[24] As Paul Hawken puts it so well, we need completely new ways of thinking about our place on Earth and the ways in which we relate to the functioning of natural systems if we are to find a better way to live in harmony with nature.[25] Nothing less than a new industrial revolution and a new agriculture are required to make possible the sustainable world of the future.[26] The task is incredibly challenging but it is nonetheless one that we must undertake if we responsibly understand the realities of our situation and if we are concerned for the enduring good of those who come after us. It is also a fundamentally spiritual task. As William Cronon puts it, "If wildness can stop being (just) out there and start being (also) in here, if it can start being as human as it is natural, then perhaps we can get on with the unending task of struggling to live rightly in the world—not just in the garden, not just in the wilderness, but in the home that encompasses them both."[27] In that sense, we should not talk of the end of nature but of the reestablishment of a strong connection that binds us to nature and enables us to find our home in it.

In the most appropriate words of Gandhi as we chart our course for the future: "The world provides enough to satisfy every man's need, but not every man's greed." These words illustrate why E. O. Wilson concludes that humanity would be able to overcome its drive to environmental domination and self-propagation with reason—why, in short, we are not necessarily suicidal in our approach to the world.[28] Although we may not focus on its importance, we implicitly continue to recognize our connection with nature. In the spirit of Gandhi, one of the greatest leaders of our times, let us take his thoughts to heart and find the new inspiration that we so badly need at this incredibly challenging time. Global arguments may have little impact on the behaviors of individuals unless those individuals perceive the crisis as unbearably severe, something that impinges on people's lives in dramatic and frightening ways. By then it will be too late. Our ethics and our values must change, and they must change because we come to understand that by changing we will be happier people, guaranteeing a decent future for our children on a healthier planet in more vibrant democracy in better neighborhoods and communities.

Many of the world's life-support systems are deteriorating rapidly and visibly, and it is already clear that in the future our planet will be less diverse, less resilient, and less interesting than it is now. In the face of these trends, the most important truth is that the actual shape of that future world will depend on what we do now within our institutions from out of the spiritual dimensions of our own dedication. Nonetheless, there is much that we can do about the situation and much that we can preserve for the future. The time to act will never be more favorable than it is today.

With Radical Amazement: Ecology and the Recovery of Creation

William French

Surely humanity in the twentieth and twenty-first centuries has entered into a fundamentally new condition: our increased numbers and immensely expanded powers are enabling us to reshape the planet—its ecosystems and climate patterns, even ourselves as a species. The scale and tempo of planetwide ecological transformation and disruption are as remarkable as the burgeoning bioengineering capabilities that now allow the blending of genetic materials across species lines. Both developments appear to undermine the traditional understanding of nature's stability and permanence, a vast given order standing firm against the vicissitudes, fragility, and brevity of individual human lives.

The expansion of human powers has crossed important thresholds in the twentieth century, and in the twenty-first we will begin to reap what we have sown. E. O. Wilson rightly suggests that humanity has become a "geophysical force," and Peter Raven, like many other biologists and ecologists today, offers in this collection an eloquent account of the range and scope of our impact upon the Earth community.[1] The Book of Ecclesiastes speaks of the fragility of human life, with its allotted seasons and times for birth and for death, but it likewise comforts with the words: "a generation goes, and a generation comes, but the Earth remains forever" (Eccles. 1:4). Today it is apparent that the human condition on Earth has changed markedly, for we now face the prospect that vast expanses of Earth and a widening number of its long-established species will most decisively not remain forever.[2] Unlike Ecclesiastes's generation, ours faces the reality of broad destruction, loss, endangerment, and extinction.

Several years ago Bill McKibben argued that humanity now faces the "end of nature," in the sense of a truly wild or untouched nature.[3] McKibben's insight is surely correct, for humanity's heavy touch now reaches to all earthly ecosystems. But his point is clearly not that human life or animal life can actually live now without nature at all. He was not suggesting that ecosystems will cease to capture solar energy through photosynthesis or pull that energy up through complex food chains, nor that the atmospheric or hydrological systems would fail to sustain life on our planet. Indeed, by claiming that we face a radical new development, McKibben emphasizes humanity's utter dependency on the environing order of nature as well as our moral responsibilities for restraining ecologically unsustainable production and consumption.

In what follows I argue that the two momentous developments focused on in this volume—the emergence of broad ecological degradation and new biogenetic engineering capabilities—while certainly posing new threats, challenges, and ranges of moral responsibility, do not confront us with a condition of being "without nature." In fact, the emergence of the ecological sciences in the last century has helped open peoples' eyes across the globe to humanity's inextricable dependency upon the well-being of Earth's ecosystems and stable climate patterns. Five hundred years ago human numbers were small, our technological, industrial, and agricultural powers relatively weak, and the natural order of the planet seemed vast and relatively stable compared to the vulnerability and brief life span of individual humans. Down through the millennium, the natural order seemed solid and incapable of being fundamentally altered or damaged. The order of nature seemed to be a given, something whose existence and ongoing presence could be comfortably assumed, a solid stage upon which human lives danced in our brief course. It is understandable, given this view of the apparent sturdiness of nature, how in Western Europe and elsewhere, religious and ethical views came to concentrate attention on human life, human value, and human vulnerability.[4]

It is not that the expanding threats of ecological degradation and climate change confront us with a situation such that we stand "without nature" in some "new condition for theology," as this volume's title suggests. Rather, I suggest that for dominant streams of modern philosophy and Protestant theology, thinking "without nature" has been the norm.

Catholic theology and ethics, because of their continuing affirmation of the doctrine of creation and the natural-law tradition of moral reasoning, sustained a focus on "nature" a bit longer. But beginning in the nineteenth century and rising ever more strongly in the twentieth, one can see powerful shifts in Catholic theology and ethics away from holding "nature" as a core theological or ethical category.

Rather than viewing theological reflection "without nature" as a recently emerging condition, I argue that it is in fact a deeply entrenched problem for dominant streams of Protestant and Catholic thinking across the history of the modern period. Where once both Catholic and Protestant thinkers understood humanity as within the environing order of God's creation, the rise of modern science in Western Europe, pushed by the powerful new mechanistic vision of Galileo Galilei, Francis Bacon, and Isaac Newton, offered a fundamentally new understanding of the natural world as a vast machine. While many people accepted that the new mechanistic scientific account could adequately account for the workings of the nonhuman natural order, many balked at attempts to extend the authority of mechanistic causality to explain the complexity of human reasoning and action. The rising authority of the new science mobilized a resistance to attempts to subsume the human into the order of nature understood in this mechanistic account. Thus the new science spurred many philosophers and religious leaders to insist that though the heavens and nature may function like a vast machine, the human sphere is a realm apart. Thus the ascendancy of the new mechanistic account of nature gave impetus to protecting the distinctive status of human rationality, intentionality, subjectivity, and "dignity" by the adoption of a strict metaphysical dualism between the human realm and the nonhuman natural world. The price for philosophically protecting the human from being subsumed into mechanism was an insistence on the radical separation of the human from nature.

Indeed, one can trace historically the expanding attempts to apply the potent metaphor and model of "machine" and watch the metaphysical dualism erupt sharply in reaction. Newton and Bacon and other "fathers of modern science" employed the model of machine to account for nature in general; later, René Descartes and his followers extended the mechanistic model to account for the anatomy and motion of animals. But when Julien Offray de La Mettrie published *Man the Machine*, riots broke out, and his book was burned for its heresy in suggesting that human will and action can be explained in terms of categories that are appropriate for explaining the functioning of animal and plant life and matter in motion.[5]

Modern Protestant and Catholic theologies easily accommodated themselves to Newton's mechanistic account of nature as a field of objects for human use. Once this account became authoritative, Western religious thought tended to retreat from directly engaging the sphere of nature, since dominant streams of thought had already affirmed a sharp distinction between, as Immanuel Kant came to put it, the "sphere of persons" and the "sphere of things."[6]

To early modern religious thought, the power of the Newtonian world-picture suggested a sharp metaphysical dualism between the realm of natural causality and the sphere of human action, history, and freedom. Once the authority of this world-picture was accepted, philosophy and theology tended to pull away from making central reference in their core categories to "nature" and instead came to concentrate attention on the sphere of persons: subjectivity, rationality, and historical agency. As this dualism became increasingly entrenched, mainstream Western philosophy and theology functionally came to operate, in this sense, "without nature."[7] But it was not then nor does it remain today the case that their understanding was an account truly "without nature." Rather, these movements reflected a view of the world sustained by the acceptance of the ruling mechanistic account of nature authorized by emerging modern science in Western Europe.

One of the main reasons the emerging ecological narrative has such a powerful intellectual and emotional shock value is that it cuts directly at the commonplace affirmation of the vastness of the natural world and our comfortable sense of its dependable solidity and stability.[8] Protestant and Catholic acceptance of the emergent dualist metaphysical scheme that arose in response to the new Newtonian mechanistic world-picture was facilitated by their common view that the order of nature, so vast and seemingly stable, was a given fixture of reality and thus deserving of little direct theological or ethical attention. A huge new taxonomy of terms—endangerment, extinction, degradation—has arisen in recent decades, helping to focus attention on the increase of human numbers and our power to produce, consume, and destroy.

What appears frighteningly clear and real today is the dynamism of humanity's juggernaut of growth.[9] By contrast, it is the nonhuman world that increasingly appears fragile and vulnerable. But we must understand nature's vulnerability rightly. The ecological sciences remind us forcefully that given humanity's dependency on the well-being of natural ecosystems, nature, even in its very vulnerability, can most potently clobber human communities and nations as it reacts to human incursion into planetary ecosystems and human impacts on the global climate system.

The Legacy of Metaphysical Dualism and Anthropocentrism

Kant and other dominant voices in modern European philosophy responded to Newtonian mechanism by reifying a metaphysical dualism between the realm of persons and that of the nonhuman world. With science viewed increasingly as the authoritative discipline for understanding the nonhuman physical world, many philosophers and theologians increasingly understood their distinct field of study to require a "turn to the subject." This movement supported an ethical concentration on the value of persons.

Dualism led to dual standards for evaluating the rightness of human action. Actions that impinge on the life or interests of other humans are to be evaluated under the standards of ethics. Human actions that impact on the nonhuman natural world are by contrast commonly held to be evaluated by standards of productive and consumptive efficiency, the practical concerns for the maximization of mastery, control, and use. In this way modern ethical anthropocentrism, by restricting intrinsic moral value only to the sphere of rational human persons, sustains a powerful justification for technical and industrial rationality to become the sole arbiter of human action upon the nonhuman natural world. Even though modern science has moved far beyond the Newtonian model via multiple revolutions, among them the rise of Darwinian and Einsteinian science, at the level of popular culture the legacy of the Newtonian world-picture is still sustained by the assumptions built into and displayed by many of the dominant productive and consumptive practices of contemporary industrialized societies.

The productive efficiency delivered by the modern division of labor is indeed impressive, but it comes at a significant cultural, cognitive, and ecological cost. Where a century ago the majority of the people of France or the United States farmed the soil, picked the crops, caught the fish, and raised the farm animals, in short, were directly engaged with food production, today most people work in other sectors of the economy. Actual engagement in food production is restricted to small percentages of the population. As Albert Borgman reminds us, this movement of people away from being food producers to simply food shoppers thins out our population's direct experience with and appreciation for the way we depend on soil, rains, fertilizer, pollinators, aquifers, and complex ecosystems as well as their plant, animal, and fish species.[10]

As agriculture in many developed nations has been transformed into "agribusiness" by the introduction of industrial factory-farming techniques, we see dominant food production, transport, and retailing practices that buy high productivity through high fossil-fuel and irrigation inputs, monocrop or monospecies specialization, and the transport of processed food stuffs, often for great distances. Urban and suburban populations who purchase food at the receiving end of this productive system engage with the food chain through the mediation of a remarkable high-tech, high-fossil-fuel-input, and high-efficiency system of corporate practices. But what is lost in the convenience of this form of food shopping is any sustained encounter by the consumer with the land or lakes and seas, any sustained appreciation for how weather impacts corn production or how magnificent tuna are before they are killed and squeezed into cans or little pouches. What is lost is any sustained encounter and respect for the plants, animals, fish, and the ecosystems that sustain them and upon which we depend.[11]

Though science for the professionals has undergone many theoretical revolutions since Newton, the general public's dominant understanding of nature is shaped by day-to-day productive and consumptive practices that support a functional acceptance of a Newtonian world-picture. We tend to understand the nonhuman order as a field of objects, things, in motion. It is a field from which we humans are said to be fundamentally distinct. Yet it is a field to which the ecological sciences now remind us that we are inextricably linked and upon which we are totally dependent.

Modern Western philosophy and Christian theology have come to be deeply shaped by this dualized world-picture and its human-centered ethical understanding. This notion that the human is fundamentally apart from the world is a broad and deep stream in much of modern ethical and religious thinking and it is heightened in much of postmodern thinking.[12] In what follows I examine two cases of philosophers who display some of the breadth and power of both dualism and anthropocentrism. In a later section I examine how this dualism and anthropocentrism have had a broad impact on twentieth-century Protestant and Catholic theology and ethics.

William James, the Harvard psychologist and philosopher, in his 1910 essay "The Moral Equivalent of War," calls for the eradication of war because of the rise of horrific new weapons, but he wants to sustain what he calls the "manly virtues" of courage and self-sacrifice for the communal good that he sees as positive outcomes of humanity's warring past. To secure peace between nations, he proposes drafting young people into a shared crusade against a common foe, namely nature. He envisions an international conscription of young people to join "the army enlisted against Nature." Their pride and confidence would be enhanced in what James celebrates as the "immemorial human warfare against Nature."[13] He envisions the draining of swamps, tilling of fields, building of roads, cutting of canals, and chopping down of forests. James's language displays optimism that humanity's engagement with nature can be always contained within the control of our agenda of manipulation, mastery, and use. It exudes confidence that in such a war with nature, humanity will benefit, because nature, while potent, is fundamentally a passive and stable realm that cannot strike back in reaction to human incursion.

We certainly know today, in ways James could not, that nature as a complex ecological system does not stand passively in the face of the frenzy of human historical activity in the twentieth and twenty-first centuries. Nature, we now know, is a dynamic field of forces and systems of energy that react in complex and potentially disruptive and destructive ways to many human practices of expanded use and extraction. Where James envisioned a war against nature with no human casualties and many social and international benefits, the ecological sciences, by resensitizing us to the fact of human communities' and nations' dependency on the well-being of the dynamic planetary ecosystems, remind us that in such a war there will be significant human and nonhuman casualties. The ecological sciences underscore how any stance of war against nature is folly, for human communities depend fundamentally upon nature's well-being for our own.[14]

More recently, John Rawls, another Harvard philosopher, illustrates another example of the ongoing potency of ethical anthropocentrism. He does not call, like James, for war against nature. Rather he just forgets about nature in his lengthy discussion of justice until page 512, where he devotes two paragraphs to a reflection on how to begin to think about justice owed to the nonhuman world.[15] His view of justice is widely influential but it also serves as a potent historical illustration of the dominant tendency in modern ethical and social philosophy to view the human as categorically separate from nature.

Rawls works out of a social-contract model to articulate the obligations of justice. In his two paragraphs devoted to the possibility of human obligations of justice owed to the nonhuman world, he argues that humans have no strict obligations to creatures that lack a sense of justice. Still, he concludes, we have a general moral obligation not to be "cruel." This, he understands, should prohibit the eradication of any whole species, which would be a "great evil." While he holds we have "duties of compassion" and "humanity" owed to animals, these issues lie, he holds, outside his theory of justice. But he rightly concludes:

> [A] correct conception of our relations to animals and to nature would seem to depend upon a theory of the natural order and our place in it. One of the tasks of metaphysics is to work out a view of the world which is suited for this purpose. . . . How far justice as fairness will have to be revised to fit into this larger theory it is impossible to say.[16]

Rawls's project illustrates his sustained confidence that the concerns of justice apply only to human agents, yet in his telling afterthought he reflects on the fact that humans live in a world that we share with myriad life-forms—both plant and animal. By his recognition of the need for a "larger theory" or ethical framework, he admirably acknowledges the limits of his approach to thinking about justice, but he sadly spends almost no energy even sketching out how this expanded attention to "the natural order and our place in it" might require a similar corresponding expansion of our sense of the obligations of justice.[17] After having come so far with the social contract's anthropocentric understanding of justice and other principles of ethics, Rawls sees the need to ground an ecologically expanded vision of justice within an ecologically broadened account of human life. He sees that the notion that humanity is fundamentally apart from the rest of nature is inadequate and must give way to an understanding of "our place in" nature. Rawls is right to put his finger on the need to engage the traditional tasks of metaphysics for thinking about the natural world and our place in it.

My view is that dominant productive and consumptive practices in contemporary societies that together energize the global economy sustain at the general cultural level dominant metaphysical assumptions about a "thingified" and "objectified" nonhuman natural world that were first articulated in the emergence of early modern Newtonian science. Though science at the professional level has undergone significant revolutions, at the general cultural level and increasingly across the world the language of the global economy and global trade sustains a metaphysical dualism that sets the human apart from the world of resources that we harvest, extract, manipulate, transport, and consume. This metaphysics of the global economy is both a metaphysics that carries on the legacy of dualism from the Newtonian worldview and one that lulls us into complacency as humanity's disruption of the planet surges forward. Ecologists such as

Raven are right to condemn sharply this dualistic metaphysics as dangerously deluded and to argue that the contemporary ecological sciences must
serve as the ground of any adequate metaphysics for our age.

Twentieth-Century Christian Theology's Turn away from Creation

Modern metaphysical dualism, with its account of the human as separate
from nature, and the anthropocentric ethical concentration this reinforced
came to shape the mainstreams of both Protestant and Catholic theology.
The neoorthodox, existentialist, and eschatologically centered theologies
that dominated Protestant thinking stressed Christology, not the doctrine
of creation, and the sphere of history, not of nature, as the primary field
of God's action and disclosure. Likewise these theological streams tended
to promulgate subject-centered theological anthropologies that understand the human as historical, rational agents, and subjects, sharply distinct
from the rest of the created order.[18] It should not be surprising that the
thought forms of an age surging with the scientific, technological, industrial, and economic advances of the industrial-revolutionary period in
Western Europe should have a bias toward focusing the spotlight on historical dynamism and allowing nature, located backstage, to be cast into
the shadows. While Hegel had complex views on the interaction between
history and nature, many were influenced by his understanding of history
as the arena of freedom and subjectivity and of nature as the converse, the
arena of blind necessity, mechanism, a field of mere objects. "History" and
"nature" in both philosophy and theology became contrasting categories
loaded with the heavy baggage of multiple associations.

   In the *Church Dogmatics*, for example, Karl Barth holds Christology as
the true foundation of theological and anthropological knowledge. He
states, "the nature of the man Jesus alone is the key to the problem of
human nature."[19] In his and other theological writings of the period, we
find a potent Christological concentration that tends to be tied in with a
theological anthropology that places a high emphasis on the freedom and
subjectivity of humans and our distinctive difference from and superiority
over the rest of nature. As Joseph Sittler, a prominent American Lutheran
theologian, put it in 1972, the view of a "fundamentally 'dis-graced' natural world" leads theologians to concentrate on the drama of God's mighty
acts in history, but to constrict God's operational sphere of activity and
will to the sphere of history, not God's providential sustaining action in
the sphere of nature.[20] As Gustaf Wingren put it a year later, much of

contemporary Christian theology is engaged in a strong "flight from creation."[21]

One can see a similar movement in twentieth-century Catholic circles, inspired by Karl Rahner, Bernard Lonergan, Bernard Häring, and many others, of "turning to the subject" and to history.[22] Neither of these turns necessarily needed to be developed using the natural order as a conceptual foil for understanding human subjectivity, human "dignity," and the dynamism of historical action, but with great frequency the category of "nature" was and in many quarters continues to be so employed.[23] Liberation theologians strongly shared this general concentration on God's action in history and the goal of human freedom from poverty and oppression. Indeed, Gustavo Gutiérrez speaks for many Catholic thinkers across the last half of the twentieth century when he boldly announces: "Other religions think in terms of cosmos and nature: Christianity rooted in Biblical sources, thinks in terms of history."[24]

By so separating the human from the rest of nature, the metaphysical dualism engendered by the Newtonian world-picture and sustained by much of Enlightenment and modern anthropocentric ethics led to the dualizing of a set of categories that came to function as philosophical foils one to another. Across broad streams of modern philosophy and Christian theology one can see a privileging of the category of "history" as the dynamic home and constructive product of humanity and a diminishing of the category of "nature." History enjoys linear progress, while nature has mere cyclical repetition.

During this same period, while the Vatican promulgated several encyclicals addressing what in Catholic circles is dubbed the "social question," namely the intertwined injustices of poverty, oppression, and economic and political inequality, scant attention was paid to emerging environmental issues. Not until very recently have there been any magisterial documents to help call Catholics' attention to how the analysis of social-justice concerns must now be situated within a grander frame of the "ecologic crisis."[25]

Indeed, the long pontificate of John Paul II tended to enshrine a personalist-centered view stressing human subjectivity, dignity, agency, and history. This pope's views were strongly shaped by his 1950s doctoral dissertation's emphasis on the phenomenological movement's understanding of the human. His concentration of attention is well captured in the title of one of his major books, *The Acting Person*.[26] Pope John Paul II's strong embrace of the Newtonian world-picture is vividly displayed in his encyclical *Laborem exercens* (1981), where he describes "human work" as an activity of "subjects" who "dominate" and "transform" the natural sphere of objects and thus "humanize" it and bring it "dignity" through this transformative process. He cites Genesis 1:26–28 to reiterate the legitimacy of humanity's "dominion" and even "domination" of the natural order through our work. Work, he holds, makes us "co-creators" with God as we exert our sovereignty over the natural order.[27]

In the last fifty years the controversies triggered in the Catholic community over continued papal condemnations of birth control and gay relations have led many moderate and liberal Catholic thinkers to pull away from the Church's heritage of natural-law reasoning. This heritage remains of one of Catholicism's most distinctive ethical traditions and has ancient roots extending back to the Stoics. Thomas Aquinas in the thirteenth century developed this tradition with a powerful and comprehensive systematic treatment, and it has subsequently been further invigorated by generations of Catholic thinkers. The Stoics argued that humanity lived within the natural ordering of the cosmos and that together this great whole constituted one grand city, a "cosmopolis." From this, the natural-law heritage emphasized the fundamental unity of humankind despite our obvious broad cultural, ethnic, and religious differences and likewise affirmed that all people share common capacities for right reason to guide general moral judgments about paths for or against human flourishing. The Stoics held that right reason allows people of all cultures to discern the same fundamental moral obligations and truths. The natural-law heritage as developed by Aquinas and many twentieth-century Catholic thinkers includes a general affirmation of both this common humanitywide moral objectivity but also humanity's general participation within the broader community of the natural world, whose ordering is sustained by God's governance through laws both divine and natural.[28]

Indeed, across the last fifty years a strong shift in Catholic moral reasoning has been precipitated in part by the Second Vatican Council's call for Catholics to base their ethical reflection more deeply in engagements with scriptural themes and sources. In addition, these decades saw mounting theological concentration on the human subject and a moral emphasis on the human person and human relations. Figures noted above—Bernard Häring and Pope John Paul II—and others such as Emmanuel Mounier and Charles Curran contributed greatly to invigorating in broad streams of modern and contemporary Catholic ethics a personalist emphasis that moved away from more traditional metaphysical or creation-based models of ethical reflection.[29]

While this new personalist emphasis is eloquent in prizing human subjects and their relations with one another, it typically pays scant attention to humans' relationship with the order of nonhuman nature, which continues to be construed, following the ongoing strength of the Newtonian world-picture, as a field of physical objects or mere nonrational life-forms.

The concentration on "the person" is likewise evident in the efforts of Catholic philosophers Germain Grisez and John Finnis to articulate a "revised natural law theory."[30] Many scholars have noted that this project sustains a new basis for a universalist ethic but owes more of a debt to Kantian insights and perspectives than to themes found in the writings of Thomas Aquinas.[31] In Grisez's and Finnis's approach, even natural-law thinking is pulled into an accommodation with the Newtonian dualism shaping Kant's thought and in this fashion is pulled far away from what I would call the creation-centered frame found in a number of Aquinas's treatises.[32] As Lloyd Weinreb puts it, the Grisez-Finnis attempt to recover the natural-law tradition does so by developing a "natural law without nature."[33] As Richard Gula rightly notes, natural-law reasoning in the last few decades has developed primarily along two lines. The first, the currently dominant school, continues the natural-law tradition's stress on a universal ethic but locates the origins of this ethic in humanity's common participation in the "order of reason." The second, now a minority view, likewise affirms a universal ethic but locates the grounding of that ethic in the "order of nature."[34] The combined powers of modern personalism and the "turn to the subject" of the transcendental Thomists—Rahner and Lonergan—have pushed the emphasis on the "order of reason."

There is surely some irony present when thinkers now try to appropriate the mantle of the "natural-law" tradition even as they concentrate intense focus on human subjectivity, historical agency, and freedom and pay little attention to how the human is conditioned and sustained by an environing natural order. This raises our attention to the myriad ways different dominant disciplines and intellectual traditions today manage to reflect, analyze, and evaluate "without nature."

Technological, Economic, and Strategic Thinking without Nature

Thinking without nature in the last century has become widespread in part because of increasing specialization within the division of intellectual disciplines and academic fields of expertise. As general philosophical treatments of wealth, property, and justice give way to works in political economy, and these in turn separate out into further specialties of modern economics, political science, military science, strategic theory, and international relations, the dynamic of specialization by concentrating attention intensely on one particular sphere tends to pull attention away from other important spheres of reality.

In core streams of mainstream modern economic theory, for example, the reality of our dependency on natural systems is marginalized even as the future is "discounted." Similarly, we can see how in the rise of strategic theory the focus of attention turns to nation-states, threats to their national security, and steps by which they can preserve such security. Not surprisingly given the history of America's recent wars, our leaders and general populace have tended to concentrate on threats posed by other hostile nations' military potential and increasingly those posed by terrorism. Only very recently are world leaders beginning to understand that our emerging ecological problems, like global climate change, pose genuine national and global security threats.

TECHNOLOGICAL AND PRODUCTIVE RATIONALITY

There have certainly been major scientific revolutions since Newton's, notably those marked by Darwin, Einstein, and the rise of ecology, biogenetic engineering, and many more, and these have clearly had an immense impact on scientific theory, experimental practice, and concrete innovation. But at the general societal and cultural level, Newton's view of nature as a vast field of objects and things is carried forward historically with great vigor by many of the dominant life practices in developed, industrial, high-consumption societies.

As Martin Heidegger reminds us, technology generates and structures a way of seeing the nonhuman natural order as a "standing reserve" of resources awaiting human appropriation and use. Technology "sets upon" nature, and the rise of the global economy increases the tempo of this "setting upon."[35] Indeed, it is not an exaggeration to hold that the world's major institutions—governments, corporations, and even universities—are caught up in a broadly shared set of values that stress growth and view the nonhuman natural world as the requisite field of resources.[36]

As David Loy provocatively holds, the global economy today functions in reality as the most successful world religion, for it is an aggressively proselytizing worldview that seeks conversion across all societies and inculcates pervasive ritualized practices of shopping and consumption promoting and sustaining the dominance of a potent set of consumerist values that lure us by their attachment to potent visions of personal fulfillment and construals of the "good life." The powerful ideology of the global market enshrines belief in a transcendent deity, named by Adam Smith as the "invisible hand," in whose providential care egoistic behavior is "transubstantiated" into efforts that promote the common good. Worship of this deity is promoted via dominant journals, consumerist practices, mall development, and massive annual spending on advertising aimed at promoting a belief in the "good life" and a particular form of "salvation" via the consumption and ownership of myriad goods.[37]

ECONOMIC RATIONALITY

Clearly it is not just dominant streams of Christian theology that have tended for too long to think "without nature." Indeed, in the division of intellectual labor that marks the proliferation of diverse disciplines in universities and in corporate, governmental, professional, and lobbying communities today, we see this bracketing off of "nature" across a wide range of disciplinary perspectives and governmental, professional, and institutional conversations. Dominant schools of economics so concentrate attention on capital and labor that nature typically gets treated as such a vast sphere of renewable resources that we are admonished to celebrate rising gross domestic product (GDP) rates and rates of productivity and consumption and taught to fret little about resource shortages or ecological degradation.[38] The well-being of our great-grandchildren's generation is said by economists to be appropriately "discounted" due to its futurity. So our decisions are dominated by short-term interests, not long-term sustainability concerns. As Al Gore rightly notes: "The future whispers while the present shouts."[39]

The market mechanism typically locates present or future ecological degradation or damage borne from a consumptive or productive practice as lying outside the pricing decision; hence it is dubbed an "externality." The term is telling. An externality is a cost or a benefit that lies outside the range of costs or benefits deserving of consideration in the establishment of the price of a resource, commodity, or service. Because externalized costs are not monetized into the price paid for a commodity or service, the purchaser has no incentive to attend to a range of real world impacts—damages and costs—that flow from production and consumption. They remain out of sight and thus out of mind.

To take one example, when we purchase a gallon of gas, we pay a price that fails to include the long-range social and ecological costs of that gallon's contribution to carbon dioxide emissions and future global warming potentials. As Lester Brown and many ecological economists have noted over the years, because our current market mechanism fails to incorporate significant social and ecological costs that flow from certain productive and consumptive patterns and practices, we, as a collectivity of consumers and a general society of citizens, make important consumptive and lifestyle choices daily in a context where planetary-significant information is systematically hidden from our range of conscious attention. To the extent that past, present, and future ecological costs of a given productive or consumptive practice are not monetized into the actual market price, whole societies are making calculations on a daily and hourly basis about rational action and behavior that are functionally deeply flawed because the market, as reflected in the price, is thinking "without nature." When we think thus, our entire range of economic rationality becomes biased because of the limits of information that are being conveyed by our pricing structure.[40]

STRATEGIC RATIONALITY AND NATIONAL SECURITY

Another important example of thinking "without nature" is found in the emergence of strategic theory. This discipline developed in the twentieth century in response to perceived threats to American national security. Strategic theory's origins, forged under the pressures of World War II and the Cold War, not surprisingly push it to concentrate attention on nation-states, their military capabilities, and the threat level these may pose. The fixation on threats posed by potentially hostile nations' conventional or nuclear military strength was dramatically broadened in the wake of the dust and death of the September 11 attacks to include a vigilant scanning of the horizon for terrorist threats posed by non-nation-state actors.

Environmentalists have been trying for the last three decades to overcome the political marginalization of ecological concerns by suggesting that such concerns need to be appreciated in their full gravity as national and indeed global security threats. Against those who glibly dismiss environmental trends and problems as of interest only to "tree huggers," environmentalists employ critical analogies drawn from strategic theory to underscore the profound seriousness of some of the looming threats posed by species extinction, ecosystem degradation, and climate change.[41] However, it is still the case that the governmental attention of almost all nations remains far more concentrated on near- to mid-term threats posed by potentially hostile nation-state actors and terrorists and on national desires for economic expansion and a rising GDP index than on the need to take even modest steps to address long-term ecological trends and impacts.

How might ecological concerns rise to the level of constituting genuine national and global security threats? If we mean by national security the ability of our government to help insure the health and well-being of our citizenry, then clearly the emerging ecological pressures pose threats of such impact and scale that they deserve to be treated as national security priorities. Vast U.S. expenditures seemed warranted in the general public mind to protect us from Soviet arsenals during the Cold War. Back then, the world was locked into a bipolar superpower conflict. The Soviet Union and the United States were dubbed "superpowers" because our nuclear arsenals gave us awesome military powers far beyond the "Great Powers" of Europe in the nineteenth century. With the collapse of the Soviet Union and the end of the Cold War, everyone acknowledges that the United States remains the world's sole military superpower. On the economic front things are different, and many scholars and journalists note that there are a number of economic superpowers—the United States, the European Economic Community, Japan, and recently China and India.

But if we shift to an ecological lens, then we might see that the world is still racked by the threat of a bipolar superpower competition, namely, the emerging clash of the expanding global economy against the limits and balances of the global biosphere. While these are not nation-states, they are nevertheless two vastly dynamic systems of power and energy. And the way they engage is fully as important as the way the United States and the Soviet Union engaged.

The global biosphere deserves to be recognized as a real superpower because in the positive sense its energies and primary producers—plants and plankton—are the fundamental resource and energy sources for all of the nation's economies. In this sense the global ecosystem is the ultimate economic superpower. Similarly, in a negative sense one must name the global ecosystem a superpower because its dynamic energies react most potently to human impact on it. Where William James viewed nature as relatively passive in the face of humanity's war on nature, today we know that nature possesses a vast "retaliatory capacity" against human abuse. Nature does not strike back from a command center but by natural systems' reactions. Still its reactions can be vast and destructive to human communities, undermining the security of cities, nations, and whole regions. In these ways one can see that nation-states and their understanding of their security need to be informed by planetary ecological concerns.

The recent history of the United States is a powerful illustration of the dynamic asymmetry of threat perception. Huge military budgets have become normalized because a potent, enduring national consensus holds that such spending is prudent in light of known hostile nations, nuclear arsenals, "rogue nations," and now terrorist threats.[42] However, the same citizenry that willingly accepts year after year huge expenditures of tax dollars to support far and away the world's greatest military arsenal regularly balks at any suggestion that we need to divert far more modest portions of the national treasure to help mitigate looming global warming threats or other dangers rising from trends of ecological degradation.[43]

If we reflect on the last fifteen years of the administrations of Presidents William Clinton and George W. Bush, we will see an unnerving trail of inaction in the face of rising global warming threats. President Clinton in his first year tried to make good on a campaign promise by imposing a broad-ranging BTU tax on fossil fuels to function as a disincentive for their use and as an inducement to jump-start the development of more fuel-efficient technologies. His plan called for roughly a 25-cent tax increase on a gallon of gas. But tax increases in the United States have been rendered politically disadvantageous, and Clinton was forced to abandon his proposed energy plan. Congress passed a far more modest gas tax of 4.3 cents per gallon. Though Clinton tried to begin addressing the challenge of global climate change, in part due to the strong encouragement of his vice-president, Al Gore, he failed to move Congress or America on this issue.

While President Clinton supported the United Nation's Kyoto Protocol and its attempt to marshal an international effort to address global climate change concerns, President Bush's tenure has been marked by a stepping away from the Kyoto Protocol process and a rejection of any measures to address climate change concerns. In the early years of his administration he argued that we should not respond to climate change threats because we lack sufficient scientific certitude about the reality and potentials of global warming to warrant incurring any economic expense to address what may turn out to be a nonissue. In his last year in office, President Bush publicly accepted that global climate change does in fact constitute a real concern, but this did not lead him to push for any tangible legislative steps to begin to address this issue. Happily our nation's new leader, President Obama, appears committed to moving the United States toward policies for ecological sustainability and for reducing our country's emission of carbon dioxide through the promotion of solar and wind power and through other policy steps.

America's irresponsibility in energy usage is not just an American concern but has truly global implications as it helps so strongly to push climate change potentials. The population of the United States makes up roughly 4 percent of the world's population but contributes roughly 25 percent of the world's oil consumption and roughly 25 percent of the world's atmospheric carbon dioxide emission. As we look across the Clinton and Bush administrations, we see an expanse of years, precious years that could have been used to begin addressing global ecological challenges. As Al Gore reminds us, these years are like the precious years lost, in Winston Churchill's view, while England failed to respond to the rising threat of Hitler's advancing buildup of the Luftwaffe. In one of his finest speeches to Parliament, Churchill invoked a biblical passage from Joel 2:25 to excoriate the negligence of Stanley Baldwin's government in the face of the imminent and rising German threat. As Churchill thundered, these years, these lost opportunities, are the "years the locust hath eaten." He warned rightly that the price would be a "terrible reckoning"[44]—just as today we see climate change, habitat destruction, species extinction, and aquifer depletion. Business as usual is no longer acceptable given the scale of the threats rising before us.

Divergent Frames and Distinctive Spotlights in Modern and Postmodern Thought

Developments in the nineteenth and twentieth centuries gave rise to two equally powerful and equally true narratives about our relationship to the natural world. First, the rise of the modern social sciences increased our appreciation for the dynamic social and cultural origins of our accounts of reality—our views of humanity and the world. Second, the rise of the ecological sciences increased our appreciation for the ecological foundations that empower and sustain both human and nonhuman communities and their complex histories. The first account—the social sciences— speaks of the importance of human culture, society, historical agency, language, songs and stories, myths, historical paradigms, the human "construction of reality,"[45] while the second—the ecological sciences—speaks of solar energy, ecosystems, primary producers and food chains, human dependency, water and oxygen cycles, energy inputs, the need for sustainability, and evolutionary heritages—in short, the natural "construction of the human species" and the ecological sustenance of human communities, economies, and histories. The rise of the social sciences has tended overall to support the view that nature is a passive sphere and a view of the human as distinct from and separate from nature. The rise of the ecological sciences has tended to support the view of humanity in all of our activities as a part of nature, shaped by the planet's evolutionary past, sustained by the planet's current ecosystems, and limited by the planet's natural constraints.

Both accounts are framed in powerful narratives and both are, in many respects, true. Each account is couched in a different lexicon, a different vocabulary and discourse of central terms and categories that are presented as particularly important. Each shines its spotlight on a different sphere of human relationality. Both accounts, I submit, are needed to provide a coherent account of reality, the human condition, and God's ways in the world. If we must be attentive to the social construction of reality, then we must balance this with an equally robust emphasis on the ecological foundations of human experience. The first school pulls toward a notion of reality as humanly constructed.[46] The second pulls toward a notion of reality as a given whose terrain is ordered by forces beyond the human and whose character is discerned by humans, not so much constructed by humans.[47] The turn to the subject, stressing the social construction of nature, must be met by an equally strong turn to the natural world, stressing the embodied natural foundations of human existence, personal experience, and human society.[48]

In the last thirty years, these two frames of the social sciences and the ecological sciences have together raised strongly divergent critiques of the set of value assumptions grounding much modern thinking. In this sense both have affirmed a need to move beyond the assumptions of the "modern" and embrace the "postmodern."

The initial employment of the term "postmodern" arose among architects and artists but quickly spread to philosophical circles and literature faculties and then moved widely across the humanities and social sciences. This intellectual movement, the one that continues to attract much attention and conversation in university circles, is highly human-centered and stresses cultural differences and the "construction" of reality. It affirms an antifoundationalist or antiuniversalist epistemology that stresses how all truth claims are thoroughly perspectival; likewise, it affirms a deep sensitivity to the plurality of valid truth claims rooted in the plurality of disciplines and the world's diverse cultural and religious histories and traditions. This dominant stream of postmodern thinking centers its attention on the categories of culture, history, and texts and rightly foregrounds the radical differences between and among the diverse human cultures, histories, and textual traditions.[49]

At the same time as the ascendancy of postmodern views across various sectors of the intellectual world, we can also see the rising of a divergent stress on the shared ecological grounding of all human cultures that is profiled in postmodern ecological thinking. Whereas dominant streams of postmodern thinking place sharp emphasis on the differences between human cultures, "ecological postmodernism," by locating human cultures within a commonly shared planetary frame, highlights shared specieswide and planetwide ecological histories, needs, vulnerabilities, and threats.[50]

In short, while the dominant stream of postmodernism has tended to center its understanding of the human condition in history—in the diversity of humanity's historical agency in culture-building—an emerging stream of ecologically-informed postmodernist thinking stresses how human history is sustained within a planetary order of ecosystems and climate patterns that have a complex and evolving history of their own. Both currents of postmodern thinking attend to the dynamism of human history and agency, but they relate this focus to different frames of reference.

Where postmodernism continues and in some ways even heightens the anthropocentrism of dominant modernist streams of Western philosophy and theology, "ecological postmodernism" decenters this anthropocentric concentration by acknowledging the intrinsic value of a wide diversity of life-forms and also stressing how humanity has evolved from and been sustained by the creative dynamics of the remarkable planetary ecosystem. If we might, within limits, accept the truth of the social construction of reality, ecological postmoderns will remind us, too, of the ecological grounding of human experience, history, and creativity. Where the dominant school of postmodern thinkers emphasizes human agency, ecologically-informed postmoderns wish to emphasize the primary agency of the planetary ecosystem that over the millennia has given birth to all life-forms, including our own.

By locating human agency and history within an ecological frame, ecological postmodernism holds an appreciation for many of the thought forms sustained in the nature-centered frame of thinking found in the wide array of premodern views and practices of the world's diverse cultural and religious traditions. Premodern peoples tended to have a greater appreciation of humanity's dependency on the living powers of the planet because the then-dominant practices of agriculture, hunting, and village-based production and consumption kept people in close day-to-day contact with the natural world, providing direct reminders of their dependency on local food chains and natural resources.

The modern period, with its heightened technologies, industrialization, division of labor, and now industrialization of agriculture, forestry, and fishing, greatly lessens the number of people who directly engage nature in a sustained fashion. These developments have attenuated general society's attentiveness to the natural order and our dependency on it. Twentieth-century urbanization in the United States coincided with widespread shifts from labor to service occupations. These demographic shifts were precipitated and reinforced by the rise of new technologies and dominant practices that have occluded our relationship to the natural order.

Decreased awareness and declining direct engagement do not alter the reality of dependence, and people today require nature as much as ever. But for broad ranges of our general urban and suburban populations our daily experience of nature has changed dramatically in the modern period. It is easy to valorize rural life and occupations and to disparage contemporary urban and suburban modes of life, so it is important to be humble about the historical record of actual changes. That being said, one must rightly engage the fact that there has been a quiet revolution in recent generations. The changes are brought into relief in my own life when I consider the lives of my grandmother and grandfather on their farm, Bellevue, in Gaithersburg, Maryland, in the 1920s and thirties. In the twenties and thirties they raised Holstein cows and grew corn to feed them. My grandfather raised much of the food eaten on the farm. My grandparents could see the stars vividly at night because suburbia, with its bright lights around every parking lot, had not yet washed over the region. When my grandparents needed lumber, they harvested one of the trees in their woods. Though I grew up in a home in the woods of that farm, my present life obscures my reliance on the Earth's resources and distances me from its beauty and powerful rhythms. When I need lumber, I go to Home Depot.

Albert Borgman rightly suggests that one of the main attributes of modern technology is convenience. In the nineteenth century, heat in the home on a winter morning required lighting up the wood-burning stove, and that meant that in the late summer and early fall, intentional focus was paid to the issue of gathering and chopping logs. One was keenly aware of how heat in the home was achieved because one had a sustained practice that focused powerful reminders about one's dependence on one's local environment. The end need generated a disciplined practice that promoted and sustained a sharp awareness of one's links to nature. Technological advances across the century in home heating, first with coal, then oil, gas, and electricity, eliminated the old practices and also the level of awareness that they sustained. For Borgman, a key element of modern technology is how it liberates us from ongoing monitoring and worry.

Now we can purchase a furnace, set the thermostat, program the temperature cycle, and then happily forget about it. A key attractive feature of modern technology is its self-regulating capacity. But Borgman notes that this attractive feature comes at some cost. The thermostat is a great convenience because once we set it, we can forget about it and turn our attention elsewhere. But for Borgman this is precisely the problem. In forgetting we discount the whole chain of connections that actually bring heat into our homes. We forget about our dependency on gas, coal, oil, or wood and thus trivialize over time our dependency upon the planet's natural systems that sustain us.[51]

Happily, the rise of ecological awareness is allowing people the opportunity to recover a recognition of our utter dependency on the environing natural biosphere. While many postmodernists bristle in angry reaction to notions of some normatively weighty "natural law"—hearing them as arrogant assertions of a totalizing metanarrative—for most ecological postmodernists, language of nature's laws seems appropriate, serious, and deeply relevant.[52]

Ecological Threat and the Recovery of Awe

As Peter Raven's essay in this collection well illustrates, the ecological sciences give us today a remarkable and humbling account of the complexity of life sustained on Planet Earth and of the vast tragedy playing out in our own time as the rise of human numbers and human industrial, technological, and agricultural powers overwhelm the sustainability of many ecosystems, aquifers, coral reefs, and fishing grounds, threaten to push the "Sixth Great Extinction" event in Earth's history, and give rise to the potent disruptions of global climate change.

Raven's story, with all of its pathos and worry of impending loss, was not a story that was known last century. My grandfather Buck Diamond, on his dairy farm in Maryland in the 1930s, for example, had little knowledge or concern about the sort of planetary challenges we face today. Many of these challenges had not yet even arisen. His dominant concentration was appropriately localized to his family, his cows and fields on Bellevue Farm, and the doings of Gaithersburg, the nearby town. He was aware of the broader events of the world, but the speed of the media and the availability of easy international travel had not yet matured. Our concerns today, of necessity, must be broader than his.

But this new, remarkably moving and tragic story offers us a great gift: its capacity for jolting our eyes open. I believe that the Catholic priest Thomas Berry and other religious thinkers have it right in believing that the ecological sciences are giving today's generations a remarkable gift of a grand new narrative of beginnings and of our situation and place in the world and in its vast history.[53] Scientists appropriately articulate this story with no resort to God-talk. However, it would seem that here is a story that no religious believers—Christian, Buddhist, Muslim, Jewish, Hindu, Sikh, indigenous, or others—can ignore. If you love Jesus, then extend love to all of creation. If you are Jewish and believe in *tikkun olam* (the repairing of the world), then try to stop global warming or deforestation. If you are Buddhist, then push the requirement of loving-kindness toward all sentient life into concrete actions aimed at protecting species and their habitats from development and destruction. If you are Vaisnava Hindu, then emulate how Vishnu saved the Earth, the goddess Bhu Devi, and try to sustain the earthly community.

This evolutionary, ecological account, I would argue, is a powerful resource for reflecting on God's (or the gods') ways of creating and sustaining the world and its plant, animal, and human communities and for reflecting on humanity's newly expanded range of felt loyalties and moral responsibilities of planetary care.

In this way the traditional Christian affirmations of the doctrines of creation and providence—and the beliefs of all other great world religious traditions—can be reappropriated and invigorated in an ecological key. Indeed, Berry and others rightly suggest that both Christian believers and believers in other religious traditions must not dismiss the world of scientific studies as distant from theology, religious stance, or faith. If God or others' gods are affirmed as creators and loving sustainers, then it is imperative that religious people across the globe engage how scientists are currently understanding the concrete ways that life is daily, monthly, and across the centuries actually sustained on this planet. Any adequate concept of God or the gods today needs to engage with how life on Earth was materially created and how it continues materially to be sustained.

Berry appeals to the great Christian theological tradition spoken of by Augustine and others again and again down through the centuries as the "Two Books of Revelation."[54] This tradition holds that God as Creator and Sustainer is revealed certainly in Scripture but also in the natural order of God's creation. This physical realm is also honored as a sacred book, disclosing something of God's intentions for the world and God's ways of sustaining it. From this perspective, it would seem that from the stance of faith there can be no truly secular disciplines. For theists, all disciplines exhibit something about how God creates and sustains both human and nonhuman life-forms in the world we inhabit and know.[55]

Berry is right when he says that faith communities are being offered the great gift of a "new creation story." The ecological sciences underscore how any stance like the Genesis account is a gripping and grand story of origins. Like Genesis, the new scientifically based story of origins makes powerful and truthful claims about the human condition, our greatness and our failings, and about humanity's relations to nature. However, unlike Genesis, this new scientific story is empirically grounded and transculturally developed. It thus functions as a truly universal story because it offers a scientific account of life on Earth, a frame that includes all of the histories of the world's peoples.[56] This ecologically informed worldpicture provides the roughly 2 billion Christians living today with an important new hermeneutical lens for reading the Hebrew Bible, the New Testament, and the theological classics of the churches down through the centuries. Muslims, too, are equally being given a new lens through which to read the Koran and the classics of their heritage, and Jews, of course, now enjoy an invigorated creation-centered reading of the Hebrew Bible and the Talmud, even as Hindus, Buddhists, Jains, and indigenous peoples across the world are given this gift of a new way of reading and appropriating the materials of their traditions with eyes opened to new concerns, new senses of the expanse of the sacred, and new appreciation for the radical giftedness of being alive on Earth.

But if Berry is eloquent on the significance of ecology's "new creation story," Raven's narrative reminds us powerfully that this story is conjoined with a striking and deeply tragic "story of the Fall" rooted in humanity's overreach and willingness to let present desires for high consumption—or, for politicians, reelection—trump the claims and needs of the planet's future. Like the great opening narratives of the Hebrew Bible, the new ecological story is one of deeply creative blessing and a complex picture of human greatness and compassion coupled with a stark assessment of destructive human negligence, blindness, and hard-heartedness.

Reinhold Niebuhr remains eloquent on the disclosive force of the paired stories of the "Myth of Creation" and the "Myth of the Fall" found in the opening of the Hebrew Bible. The first provides an assurance of the goodness of God and of God's created order. The second functions powerfully to remind us of the morally corrupting capacities of human sinfulness. This reminder teaches us of the need for humility, self-critique, and strategies for effective policy change that engage the power relations and the less-than-perfect drives that pervade and motivate human society.[57]

If the emergence of the ecological sciences offers us, as Berry suggests, a remarkable new creation story, Raven's narration of humanity's evolutionary history on the planet underscores that the doctrine of the Fall needs to be reinterpreted similarly in light of new ecological understandings. The new world-picture being offered today by the ecological sciences coheres in most interesting and moving ways with some of the dominant themes of the Hebrew Bible.[58] Emerging ecological perspectives offer the stimulation of a potent new lens by which we can examine both old and long-familiar texts and a wide array of dominant societal practices.

The emergence of the ecological world-picture offers a radically new way of interpreting a very old paradigm for understanding the human condition, historical progress, and the ways of God in the world. It stands in stark contrast to the main currents of much modern philosophy and Christian theology and ethics. Its stress on humanity's relationship to the rest of nature pulls it into close convergence with many of the sensitivities of premodern Western and non-Western thinking that similarly framed the human not as separate from nature in some distinct sphere of history but as a part of the general order of creation. Thus this new paradigm is simultaneously both deeply radical in its divergence from dominant streams of modernist thought and deeply conservative and traditionalist in affirming the need to conserve and protect the planetary order of nature in solidarity with all those premodern peoples who similarly understood the key frame for understanding human existence as a nature- and creation-centered frame.

By disrupting the accommodation made by dominant schools of Western philosophical and religious thinking in the modern period with the Newtonian world-picture, the emergence of ecological understanding offers a potent opportunity for Western philosophy and theology to reengage the thought forms of premodern Western thinking even as it offers important new openings for conversation with the worldviews of non-Western religious traditions and communities. The rise of ecological understanding compels in the Christian community a strong recovery of the doctrine of creation.

Where the accommodation with Newtonian dualistic metaphysics has allowed too many to accept the natural order as a vast and stable "given," the emergence of ecological understanding invites eyes to open to the marvelous complexity, beauty, force, and living dynamism of Earth. In my view it is the rise of ecological understanding that is allowing many of us to think "with nature" for the first time. Where once it seemed we could afford to take the natural order and the climate system for granted, now, punished by rising anxiety over new awareness of emerging ecological threats, we are training our attention and vision in new ways. And as Iris Murdoch reminds us, our ability to act morally and responsibly is based on the quality of our attention and vision. As she puts it: "[O]ur ability to act well . . . depends partly, perhaps largely, upon the quality of our habitual objects of attention."[59] Happily, the rise of ecology is concentrating our attention in new directions.

And this is why the ecological world-picture is such a radically new and yet interestingly traditional paradigm for thinking, living, and believing. As the great Jewish thinker Abraham Heschel says, "taking things for granted" is a fundamental failing. As he puts it, "Indifference to the sublime wonder of living is the root of sin," but "[t]he way to faith leads through acts of wonder and radical amazement. . . . Wonder or radical amazement is the chief characteristic of the religious [person's] attitude toward history and nature."[60] Ecological understanding is a powerful new vehicle for prompting a newfound wonder and amazement about the ordinary world all around us and in us. If one looks out upon the world—on the vastness of the Amazon or the intimacy of a wondrous maple tree on a local street—and if one looks rightly, then does not one see a dynamic of life that is filled with sacred power and majesty and is deserving of our care?

In the World: Henri Lefebvre and the Liturgical Production of Natural Space

Cabell King

Ecologically we are in a time of crisis of a sort that demands the attention of religious thinkers. Still, a robust theology must not be reactionary. Further, it is rare that theology can be the source of conclusive policy recommendations. In his *Travail of Nature*, H. Paul Santmire intelligently argues that "Christian thought is both promising and not promising for those who are seeking to find solid traditional foundations for a new theology of nature. Which historical tendencies within the tradition are promising and which are not, moreover, is by no means self-evident."[1] The Christian tradition is not univocal, and the particulars of contemporary problems are not explicitly addressed by our historical sources. Theology, nevertheless, may provide valuable commentary on policy and on the broad cultural features that precipitate crisis and motivate response. Indeed, Christian theology is always ethical theology, inasmuch as it is concerned with perception and activity and not just the relation of ideas.

Whatever theology contributes, then, to our understanding of the human-nature relationship, its task is not to *solve* crisis. To maintain otherwise is to situate theology in a relationship of dependence on history where theological claims are secondary to historical circumstance. It is also to trivialize those disciplines specifically dedicated to the particular practical concerns at issue. Paradoxically, theology that asserts definitive solution surrenders its prophetic voice, conditioned, as it were, by the problem it proposes to answer. The alternative to reactionary theology is sustainable theology, which, in conversation with other disciplines and attentive to the particular concerns of the day, represents the justice and charity of the gospel. Crisis informs a sustainable theology without defining it or its agenda. What sort of relation might humans have had with nature that would have averted crisis before it was named? What sort of relation might we continue to have if and when the crisis is resolved? The principles that direct our actions and experiences of the world ought to be ones that survive any particular threat. Yet theology ought not to be blind to specific ills and injustices, which reveal the shortcomings of our understanding and practice. The prophetic authority to criticize an historical state of affairs requires also criticism of theological exercise itself.

Strikingly, ecological science consistently asserts its own prophetic voice. The concluding chapter of Rachel Carson's *Silent Spring* depicts a crossroads. We have been traveling one road, a smooth and easy road that terminates in disaster; there is another, more difficult road that "offers our last, our only chance to reach a destination that assures the preservation of the earth."[2] Gus Speth, dean of Yale University's School of Forestry and Environmental Studies and cofounder of the National Resources Defense Council, titled his 2004 assessment of the global environmental situation *Red Sky at Morning.* Red skies in the morning betoken foul weather, and Speth's title is a warning. Jesus knew the significance of a rosy dawn, and in Matthew 16 he uses it to school the Pharisees and Sadducees. Asked to provide a heavenly sign, Jesus replies, "When it is evening, you say, 'It will be fair weather, for the sky is red.' And in the morning, 'It will be stormy today, for the sky is red and threatening.' You know how to interpret the appearance of the sky, but you cannot interpret the signs of the times" (Matt. 16:2–3). Significantly, Jesus responds to his interrogators' request for a heavenly sign by directing their attention to a natural sign. There is perhaps here a hierarchy of signs with heaven at the top, nature at the bottom, and the signs of the times in between. But Jesus is not dismissive of the natural sign, for "whoever is faithful in a very little is faithful also in much" (Luke 16:10). In his concise response, Jesus brings the natural, the social, and the divine into conversation. Nature, the heavens, and the times communicate analogously.

Indeed, in our time, environmental scientists insist that the natural is precisely the sign of the times. The sky is red and threatening. The scientific observation is nearly inseparable from ethical imperative. "This is really not a political issue, it is a moral issue," Al Gore repeatedly warned the world in 2006 while marketing his film, *An Inconvenient Truth*. While Christian theology must hear the voice of ecological science, it must be careful not to confuse it with its own distinct, prophetic voice. While Christian theology is fundamentally ethical, it is not *merely* ethical, and Christian action does not ideally proceed from fear.

Underlying and contributing to documented ecological abuse as well as contested therapeutic responses is a subtle idolatry. With twentieth-century philosopher Henri Lefebvre I caution against reifying nature, assigning reality to an ideal-typical notion of wildness. When we imagine ecological nature as untouched, pure, or raw, all human contact with it occasions crisis. Human presence is then seen as poison—and growing populations and increased consumption make the poison exponentially more potent. We ought not to abandon this ideal type, which Lefebvre (and others in this volume) sometimes calls "first nature," but we ought also to acknowledge that even in its recognition, first nature is domesticated "second nature." Too often the language of second nature buries first nature, trivializing human dependence on very real ecological systems and boasting of human industry. For these reasons, I instead prefer the language of "natural space" to the nominal form, "nature," as the former designates complex, interdependent, socially produced spaces characterized by creative fecundity. To reorient the discussion in terms of natural space is fundamentally hopeful, not fearing human encroachment into the wild but boldly seeking to live well in relation to the world.

Wild Nature

Bill McKibben's *The End of Nature*, a book that informed the conversations leading to the present volume, provocatively identifies nature with the absence of humanity. Nature, for McKibben, designates a world untouched. It is even the horizon against which we recognize human activity. As the reach of human activity extends, nature withdraws and disappears, and, curiously, human activity becomes less significant. The journalist remembers walking in the woods and hearing the distant sound of a chain saw. That sound becomes a metaphor for the human challenge to the independence of nature:

> Now that we have changed the most basic forces around us, the noise of [the] chain saw will always be in the woods. We have changed the atmosphere, and that will change the weather. The temperature and rainfall are no longer to be entirely the work of some separate, uncivilizable force, but

instead in part a product of our habits, our economies, our ways of life. Even in the most remote wilderness, where the strictest laws forbid the felling of a single tree, the sound of [the] saw will be clear, and a walk in the woods will be changed—tainted—by its whine. The world outdoors will mean much the same as the world indoors, the hill the same thing as the house.[3]

McKibben paints a vivid picture, one that alarms but does not surprise those of us who love the outdoors. Often the natural world feels distant. Stars in the night sky are obscured by the lights of the city. Artificial lighting divorces our daily rhythms from the natural light cycle, as global trade—particularly in food—and heating and cooling technologies conspire to minimize the distinctiveness of the seasons. Transportation technology collapses distance, and architecture, rather than topography, dominates our everyday landscape. For McKibben, climatic impacts are particularly remarkable at least in part because they extend human impacts beyond spaces of human habitation. The shadow of human industry looms large over the remaining wilderness—such as it is—and threatens the possibility of any authentic experience of nature.

McKibben's anxiety is common among American naturalists who routinely observe the domestication of natural spaces and animal populations. Ellen Meloy documents a year spent observing desert bighorn sheep in Colorado in her text, *Eating Stone*. Her writing is descriptive and poetic, winsome for its wilderness aesthetic. In the final chapter, she laments:

The end of the wild world, the emptiness, will come—indeed, has arrived. . . . It is a reduction of diverse nature into a simplified biota that is entirely managed and dependent. It is a loss of autonomous beings, the self-willed fauna that gave us metaphor, that shaped human minds capable of identity with all existence.[4]

Like McKibben, Meloy prizes the otherness of nature. They agree that when nature is enveloped by human activity, the communicative power of nature is diminished. Made dependent, nature loses meaning.

These authors portray a dire scene with great affect. Like the proverbial butterfly that flaps its wings and changes the weather on the other side of the world, humans, by our daily practices and patterns of consumption, effect consequences across the globe, including increasing deforestation rates, biodiversity loss, pollution levels, changing temperatures, and decreasing availability of clean water. These, in turn, affect economies, public health, and myriad other social concerns. Each of these, naturally, demands attention, but the claim made by McKibben and Meloy entails more even than the broad ecologically and socially abusive consequences of human action. Their primary concern is semiotic: when nature ceases to be autonomous, it no longer imparts meaning nor does it provide the texture necessary for human meaning-making. Nature becomes "tainted" when hill and house are indistinguishable.

Two claims motivate this thesis. First, natural forces are distinct from human forces. Nature is something distant, a place we retreat to. Though it is not strictly a site from which humanity is absent, it is divided from everyday life. Second, humans have altered the "most basic forces of nature," which, according to the first claim, makes them less natural. Consequently, the previously natural world becomes, in terms of meaning, identical to the built environment.

Regarding the second claim, it is not self-evident what it would mean for human activity truly to alter the forces of nature. Natural forces operate without intent and lack the pretext of productive activity. There is a present quality to the natural that presumes no consciousness of past or future. To be clear, human activity cannot subvert the forces of nature; that would be like the pieces on a chessboard rewriting the rules of the game. In his contribution to this volume, Peter Raven aggressively rejects for precisely this reason the suggestion that humanity occupies now—or ever will—a world without nature.[5] Though there is reason to be concerned about the world's ecological future, the future of nature itself is not at stake, since it denotes the biological systems upon which all human existence depends and within which it operates. A world without nature would be a world without order, singular or plural, without the laws that enable us now constructively to debate the consequences of human action and the fate of our own planet.[6]

Nature, as Raven implies, is the condition of comprehensibility. In the same way, the rules of chess enable a skilled player to plot several moves in advance, to anticipate the decisions of her adversary. Without its ordering rules, the game would no longer be chess. A world without nature is indistinguishable from the *tohu wabohu* of Genesis 1:2, the precreative void. The absence of nature is formlessness, and without nature, the world not only would be inhospitable but would simply cease to be. A world without nature is no world at all. The sometimes apocalyptic language of contemporary environmentalism might summon images of barrenness and death, but they are images consistent with nature, as frightening as they may be. The conditions of human existence are changing, but nature persists. It is precisely this continuing participation in nature that Raven insists we acknowledge.

Regarding the first claim, we do ourselves a disservice to misconstrue nature as something wholly other, outside the human, always pressing against the human and defining its limits. This division of nature from the everyday is analogous to the way some are inclined to divide the religious from the secular. Though the quality of wildness is conceptually useful, severing nature from human activity is destructive. This severance is among the greatest threats to our ecology. The strict separation of sacred and profane, natural and unnatural, deprives the profane and unnatural of any lasting significance and marginalizes the sacred and natural to the point of inaccessibility. If nature excludes all that is human, meaning truly is at stake. In this division, nature assumes the significance of eternity, and meaning abides only where the human is absent. This division betrays the complexity and richness of life, where, as the Christian Gospel promises, one might find a life abundantly meaningful (John 10:10). If there is a distinction between nature and unnature, we must recognize it within human community; if it bears meaning, nature must encompass and include us.

While I insist that nature survives amidst human activity, I am concerned not to trivialize what might be termed *human sprawl*—our encroachment into undeveloped spaces. I do not discount the significance of wildness and I concede that naturalness denotes an untamed quality. But if we are careless in identifying nature, we undermine our own interests. Nature becomes a fiction, and our responsibility for it becomes oppressive. In a challenge to his own language, McKibben does not maintain that nature is incompatible with all human habits, economies, and ways of life. His walk into the wilderness begins at the back door of his rural home. He calls the forest "a world apart from man" when he has walked only a hundred yards. He is able to disregard the proximity of his home, the trail on which he walks, the property lines he has crossed or not crossed, the boundaries of his woods, but the dim consciousness of the indirect consequences of excessive carbon emissions extinguishes the idea of nature. His attention to one sort of interference and inattention to the other circumstances of his experience are somewhat comical but not nonsensical. It is not the presence of all mediating structures to which McKibben objects, only those that somehow disable the authentic experience of it, that diminish its capacity to confront the individual with otherness. Implicitly, McKibben affirms that there are ways of impacting and inhabiting the world that are more or less natural than others.

I propose, therefore, that nature is always with us as the condition of existence. Its enduring laws are a prerequisite to our making sense of our

selves and our world. McKibben is correct to identify nature with meaning, as it is the condition of meaning. But meaning does not inhere in
nature alone, waiting to be discovered. Meaning emerges among the social
relationships founded on its back and in relation to it. We are neither with
nor without nature, in this time or any other, as a matter of existence.
Rather, we *live* with or without nature as a matter of social practice.

Social Nature

In the second scriptural account of creation, the first person is formed
"from the dust of the ground" (Gen. 2:7) Throughout the Old Testament,
apar, the word translated as "dust," refers to earth. In Genesis 3:19, for
example, God tells Adam that he will return to the ground (*'adamah*), for
he is dust (*apar*) and to dust he will return. Though some elements of the
account set this figure apart from rest of the new creation—most especially
God's direct and tactile involvement in his formation and the giving of
life—his identity, his nature, is pointedly shared with the world. It is an
organic picture of a man intimately bound to his origin. Additionally, the
name of the first man, *'adam*, is probably not etymologically related to
'adamah, but the author unites the two by their similar sounds. The playful
pun equates human and earth, and captures vividly the confusion of our
word, "nature," which we use richly to denote the outside world and interior essence. The stuff of earth courses through human veins.

The Hebrew word *'adam* used in the creation story does not necessarily
designate a particular male figure but corresponds to something like our
notion of humankind. Arguably, the man formed from the earth is a universal figure, an everyman. The suggestion is that each person, even now,
is formed of the earth. As a graduate of Dartmouth College, I am re-
minded of my college alma mater, which expresses a similar relation to the
land. The first verse concludes:

> Though 'round the girdled earth they roam,
> Her spell on [Dartmouth's children] remains;
> They have the still North in their hearts,
> The hill-winds in their veins,
> And the granite of New Hampshire
> In their muscles and their brains.

In these proud lines, identity and context collapse into each other as the
richness of place, including ecological nature, becomes a part of a socially

constructed identity, aptly articulated in terms of physical likeness. Juxtaposing the scriptural account and the college song invites the conclusion not just that the identification of the person and the world proceeds from a moment of creation, a temporally discrete origin, but that the person is continually recreated in reference to his or her environments, particularly those that somehow inscribe meaning.

The kinship of human and ecology is not a diminution of human uniqueness, as some commentators have feared, but recognition that nature provides the texture of life. The first Genesis creation account (1:26–28) emphasizes the hierarchical priority of humans, asserting their likeness to God and establishing their dominion. Human primacy, as depicted here, need not discount the strong ties between human and nonhuman creation. These verses, too, depict a community of living things. Dominion may denote responsibility, but not necessarily opposition. From the beginning, man and woman come to themselves in their relation to the fish of the sea, the birds of the air, the cattle, the wild animals, and every creeping thing. Verse 29 introduces them also to the flora of the garden. The first couple depends on ecological nature for sustenance and for companionship.

The assignation of dominion anticipates Genesis 2:19, where *'adam*, himself formed of dust, turns to name each of the animals, who, like him, are formed "out of the ground." The language of this verse emphasizes, again, the man's terrestrial heritage and his likeness to the animals, but it also depicts his authority and his unique capacity for production. Naming, of course, is a privilege of those with power; to name is to delimit the terms of discourse. Michael Scanlon writes that naming is "the primordial human *praxis* of 'the image and likeness' of God who created the world through the divine Word. . . . We are like God because we can speak."[7] It is certainly not unreasonable to observe some parallel between the tactile project of God's forming the first man and the conceptual project of *'adam*'s naming the animals. Like nature in the material of their being, like God in their words, humans occupy an intermediate space bound to nature and invariably transforming it. Naming demonstrates human authority, but the animals are the occasion for human speech. They constitute, in this scene, the first natural resource.

If the man is composed of the world, the world, too, represents the man. As in the act of naming, human activity imprints nature, such that every instance of nature known and named by humans is a second nature. The concluding lines to the second verse of Dartmouth's alma mater announce:

The still North remembers them,
The hill-winds know their name,
And the granite of New Hampshire
Keeps the record of their fame.

The solid, unmoving stone is embossed with the legacies of those it has birthed. The person mediates in a process of production wherein nature is both the raw material and the finished product. But the two natures, origin and product, are not identical precisely because the latter has a name. Produced nature is nature *for us*.

Lefebvre explores the relationship of sociality and naturalness in his essay, "Nature and Nature Conquered." There he anticipates two heuristic divisions we have made in this collection: (1) the nature outside us and the nature within us;[8] and (2) nature as resource and nature as social product.[9] These aspects of nature are never discrete, and Lefebvre's discussion sometimes confusingly traffics between them.[10] Though conceptually distinguishable, these aspects tellingly share the same name. In a single word, notions of context, identity, resource, and product are bound in a confused dialectical unity. Their division, compelled for philosophical clarity, does violence to nature. Nature is both the stage on which we stand and we who are standing; it is the script we read and the world created by our words. Though our specific interest in this portion of the volume's larger project concerns ecological nature, real and physical threats to the world's health, we can perhaps begin to see how questions of science and sociality and of ecology and anthropology are nestled within one another. They are anticipated already in the Genesis texts and recollected in the title of Lefebvre's essay. Humans occupy the position of conquerors with dominion over the very source of their energy and strength. It is the plurality of coincident natures that makes nature so enlivening. It is, when we see it, without pretense. This is why McKibben and Meloy are correct to identify nature with meaning, though I have here challenged them for not crediting the complex sociality of nature as the source of that meaning.[11] Lefebvre writes, "With all its imprecision, and because of that imprecision, the notion of nature designates cosmic reality without implying ontology or cosmology."[12]

For Lefebvre, the dialectical quality of nature precludes its apprehension as simple object. Nature asserts itself and demands focused attention. Lefebvre insists that nature is known via praxis, which allows for confusion, tension, and contradiction. Praxis splits the polarizing dichotomy between romanticism, which imagines human participation in natural givenness, and scientism, which coldly taxonomizes nature from a secure and distant vantage. These alternatives are trite and reductionistic, but nature, Lefebvre insists, "has not been exhausted."[13] If we can quell our totalizing tendencies, nature may still surprise us. Praxis includes abstraction, as it includes language and discourse, but cuts through abstraction in practical action. Lefebvre uses praxis to designate the adversarial complementarity of abstraction and practicality united in persons.

Lefebvre illustrates the dialectic of nature in a discussion of language. An individual's internal discourse, he explains, is "a ground bass to our conscious life." That is, language is the condition of consciousness. As discourse, consciousness depends on—is even constituted by—language, a conventional system of signs. These signs come to the individual from outside the self. The signs—and often the objects they signify—are products of human industry, the labor of conscious individuals. The structure of consciousness, therefore, proceeds from a socially produced "semantic field." Inasmuch as nature participates in human consciousness, it is transformed by the linguistic categories of social and inner discourse.

One might counter that nature is preconscious. It exists as a thing in and for itself before it is domesticated by consciousness. This is not inaccurate, nor is it an insignificant observation in a time when human activity almost surely impacts natures of which we have no awareness, possibly with deleterious consequences for humans. Still, the *only* thing we could say of a preconscious, external nature is that it might exist. Nature speculatively identified in this way bears no meaning for us and, inasmuch as it is outside consciousness, is not the least bit interesting. It is a nature of which we are *entirely* unaware so we cannot make any ethical decisions about it. Arguably, it has no value, as value is a relational quality. Nevertheless, according to Lefebvre we should nurture some recognition of the priority of nature: "One could even define nature as the 'foundation,' or the 'foundation' as nature, or perhaps nature as the pre-objective or the pre-subjective, or as detotalized totality (or perhaps vice versa)."[14]

Insisting on the social construction of nature is not a way to escape real environmental problems. Hopefully it focuses our attention and acknowledges the *truth* of nature in its complex, dialectical reality. Redirecting our attention to the dynamic human-world relation emphasizes the quality of our relating to the landscape over the landscape itself. It invites us to realize significant connections between our selves and our ecology and radically to reenvision nature within and around human life rather than at its edges. Ecological crisis comes into relief not as a crisis for nature itself but as a crisis at the meeting place of humans and nature:

> Today nature is drawing away from us, to say the very least. It is becoming impossible to escape the notion that nature is being murdered by "anti-nature"—by abstraction, by signs and images, by discourse, as also by labour and its products. Along with God, nature is dying. Humanity is killing both of them—and perhaps committing suicide into the bargain.[15]

Lefebvre provocatively personifies nature in the language of withdrawal and death. That this is unusual language proves the point: modern nature is often inert, silent, *merely* material. At best it is the context for human life; more often it is relegated to the periphery. The problem is abstraction, which Lefebvre explains is the reification of a sign. "Abstract space," he says, "functions 'objectally,' as a set of things/signs and their formal relationships. . . . Formal and quantitative, it erases distinctions, as much those which derive from nature and (historical) time as those which originate in the body (age, sex, ethnicity)."[16] Abstraction results when signifiers are divided from their signs, when human activity becomes *mere* work. Nature as object is empty. To reach for it is to grasp at nothing, so it withdraws.

This crisis of abstraction is vividly demonstrated by our inability to account for the value of nature. The value of natural resources, for example, is commonly calculated only after resources have been extracted; their value is determined in the exchange market. Imagine an independent fisherman in the Philippines who harvests his catch by tossing a stick of dynamite into a coral reef.[17] He collects the dazed and injured fish, as well as much broken coral, and sells them at market prices. Both the fisherman and his government document fiscal gains according to the sale price of the harvest, though surely the value of the lost coral habitat, a breeding ground for marine life and a tourist attraction, exceeds the fisherman's profit. In routine accounting, nature as nature is assessed no value and gains value only when transformed into commodity. There is something perverse about a system of accounting that registers destruction as gains and will no doubt register others when human industry labors to rectify the consequent problem. Some economists have tried to determine values for "ecosystem services," natural systems that provide necessary goods, like the coral reef.[18] Their staggering figures, exceeding the Gross World Product several times over, emphasize human dependence on natural processes, but even they reduce nature to imprecise economic value. Both are inadequate accountings of the world, reducing it in one way or another to exchange value.

Returning to Lefebvre's observation, the withdrawal of nature—its reduction to symbol—coincides with a devaluation of human life and of religious myth. The abstraction of signs echoes through the semantic field of

human consciousness, robbing meaning from all corners of life. To cite
Lefebvre proves remarkably apposite in the present volume, where we are
suggesting that contemporary crises of environment and identity are
bound together. The human, God, and Nature itself are together mur-
dered when the idea of the thing veils the thing itself. Lefebvre's warning
about the danger of abstraction is a call to authentic, personal living, to
perceive others, including God and nature, for their distinctiveness.

Nature as Fetish

Distinctiveness ought not to be confused with independence. Natural resource expert R. Bruce Hull reports that presently:

> [Forty] to 60 percent of the biosphere is directly manipulated to satisfy
> human needs. . . . Humans use over half the accessible fresh water on Earth
> and have transformed nearly half of the land surface through agriculture,
> forestry, and urbanization. Approximately one-fourth of bird species
> present at the dawn of humanity are now extinct, and favored species such
> as corn, wheat, rice, cattle, bees, and tulips have been domesticated, trans-
> ported, planted, and nurtured so that they grow and live just about every-
> where on Earth. . . . [Invasive species] outcompete native species and have
> started a biological revolution that will transform American ecological sys-
> tems in perpetuity.[19]

There can be no question of the absolutely radical, often ruthless overrun-
ning of nature by human activities of growth, development, production,
and settlement. Further, much human activity is incalculably destructive.
But the danger is not that nature may be enveloped by the human.[20] The
danger is precisely the opposite: the contention that nature was ever not
human. The affirmation of nature's independence denies nature its social
reality and creates of it a fiction. Guardians of nature are thus situated to
protect unreality. They assume a defensive and fearful stance because any
activity that appears to encroach on the natural threatens its perceived
integrity. Consequently, they are separated further from life-giving nature, the condition of meaningful human activity.

Refusal to acknowledge nature as a social product results in fetishism.
The myth of independent nature pushes this reified idea to the boundaries
of human life. As humans reach across the globe, these boundaries now
require that nature be quite small. We have already cited several figures
who concede that nature may no longer exist. If it does, it is confined

to designated wild spaces, governmentally preserved parks, forests, and wildernesses. Those who insist that nature is space or process absent human intervention describe nature as untamed or uncivilized. But this truly amounts to nature as vacation destination, nature as theme park; nature becomes a fantasy.

Denying the dialectical unity of self and nature results in a form of alienation. It is a form of secularism, inasmuch as the realm of meaning and order is relegated to specific spaces away from everyday life and becomes an obstacle to living abundantly and responsibly *in* nature. Thus withdrawn, nature is comparatively irrelevant. Well-intentioned "enviros" dutifully struggle to reduce their ecological footprints, but the world on whose behalf they labor is one they will never see.

It is no wonder that a green lifestyle can seem a paralyzing burden. Drive a smaller car, drive it less often, take the bus. Install a low-flow showerhead, replace your incandescent lightbulbs with energy-saving fluorescent bulbs, and replace your washer and dryer with more energy-efficient appliances. Better yet, hang your clothes outside to dry. Lower your thermostat in the winter and resist using your air conditioner in the summer. Reduce your consumption, reuse paper bags and plastic containers, recycle your waste. Compost in the backyard, turn lights off when not using them, water your lawn less frequently, and plant a tree or buy carbon offsets every time you take a plane flight. Eat less and consider becoming a vegetarian. Campaign for sustainable practices, policies, and industries with your vote and with your money. Cataloguing these practical steps is not to trivialize them but to acknowledge that they can be overwhelming. They are particularly overwhelming when we are removed from nature and deprived of its meaning.

For what do we labor and compromise if the very idea of nature precludes our interaction with it? The dogmatic assertion of nature's independence, as it makes nature an idol or a fetish, alienates us from the nonhuman world. Divorcing nature from common human experience, it is the assertion of dominion in its most offensive form. And those practical steps intended to rescue nature—when nature is conceived to be so discrete—exaggerate the distance between nature and humanity, disabling the dialectical richness of Lefebvre's praxis. Jean-Joseph Goux writes:

> Fetishism is always the valorization or the overvalorization of a *thing*, as opposed to a relationship involving people. . . . To justify the transposition of the term *fetish* into . . . disparate fields, we must seek their common core of reification, of alienating insistence on the thing. Fetishism is a means of

linking the imaginary to the object, thus of clinging to the real, of investing it, without resorting to relations among people, that is, to the symbolic relation, which implies control by an alterity, that is, a form of transcendence. According to Hegel, the fetishist does not recognize God's law.[21]

The error of fetishism is objectification, the myth of discreteness. Fetishism values the idea made thing over the exciting, dynamic interplay of person and place. Goux explains that fetishism links the imaginary and the object. In the case of nature, the fetishist identifies the illusion of human noninterference with real objects like forests, rivers, deserts, and mountains. These objects are real and invaluable, as are the systems they represent, but the idea is empty. Nature ought to be *subjectified*, recognized in the complex interrelationality of social existence.

Natural Space

If nature assumes shape and meaning in social consciousness, we cannot dismiss that some spaces are clearly more natural than others. We register degrees of naturalness that include the Arctic National Wildlife Refuge, Lake Powell above the Glen Canyon Dam, a Midwestern farm, and a struggling weed in a neglected window box in Brooklyn. Each of these spaces has been produced, though more or less cultivated and engineered. A city park is an example simultaneously of nature and of industry with its carefully selected vegetation, well-articulated walking paths, definite boundaries, and social and economic functions. Greater London is so thickly forested, believe it or not, that in 2002 the U.K. Forestry Commission officially recognized the city as a forest and appointed the city's first Forestry Conservator. Nearly 20 percent of the greater metropolitan area is covered densely enough in trees to be considered woods.[22] Even in very practical terms, nature and humans cohabit. It is, indeed, one of the greatest advantages of discovering the social character of nature that we can begin to discover it in our neighborhoods and homes, even in elements of the built environment.

I object to reified nature but do not dismiss the experience of nature's wildness. To apprehend nature is to encounter an unnamable other—not an independent other, because the encounter brings human and nature into the semantic field of consciousness; unnamable because it is the encounter, not the thing-in-itself, that manifests naturalness. The encounter is distinctive, is called natural, because it reveals creative possibility. It is

life-giving—even when it is threatening—because it provides the material
that gives texture to thought and life. Of a world without humans we can
say nothing, but some experiences reveal the *possibility* of human absence
and disclose the double determination of the self as both given and produced. What is significant is not real human absence but the impression
of absence, because it compels the realization of the confused dialecticism
of individual and social identity. Nature, Lefebvre proposes, is:

> the place and the instant where the absence of man is revealed, and which
> gives anyone who comes into contact with it the fascinating impression of
> presence as absence: abyss and possible action. In this inaccessible place, at
> the heart of this absence, something comes back to us which is not in
> memory: our origins, the origins "we" came from at a time when effectively
> "we" were not *there* because we had not yet begun to be. *There* the finite
> and the limitless interact, the chasm and what emerges from it. . . . The
> place from which man is absent is also the place where man begins, taking
> shape and moving ahead of himself.[23]

Our starting point is not the thing-in-itself but the utter incomprehensi-
bility of the thing we cannot think. Raven asserts that nature is the condition of human life. The orders of nature are prerequisite to the sense-
making activity of human consciousness. In the encounter with natural
spaces we are invited to consider the abyss on the other side of our consciousness. It is an "inaccessible place," as Lefebvre writes, but in some
times and spaces we can take a glimpse. We can stand on the edge of the
world and peer into our origin. So nature, if it must be a noun, is the
inaccessible condition and origin of life. Natural spaces, then, are those
actual spaces, practically and socially determined, that give life.

Nature, as I understand it, is not prescriptive, though I am intrigued to
consider, with Lorraine Daston, the possible normativity of order. Nature
is communicative, providing us with the words by which we name it. The
richness of our language, the textures of our thoughts, and the integrity of
our other relationships depend on the skill with which we preserve the
naturalness of space. Human excellence and well-being do not compete
with ecological health, though particular situations may certainly require
difficult choices. Remember that the most unspoiled nature available to us
in Christian mythology is a garden that the first universal man was assigned to "till and keep" (Gen. 2:15). The most paradisiacal image of
nature in Christendom is a civilized one. So we bear a responsibility—
though it ought to be more desire than chore—to heed the first divine
command, which enjoins us to fruitfulness, to the cultivation of rich, deep,
textured, abundant life.

Christianity already has a tradition of intentionally producing space wherein, collectively and individually, worshippers partake in the mysterious and inaccessible. Christian liturgy is a means by practical exercise to participate in antinomic truths. Liturgical theology is a promising resource in exploring how Christians specifically might produce natural spaces. Inherent in social space are dynamics of power whereby some features of space are prioritized and some are obscured. Done right, liturgy reveals more than it obscures, cutting through abstraction to find a disclosive symbolic discourse. Likewise, an ecological liturgy will construct environments and establish patterns of behavior that reveal destructive structures, systems, and ideas, privilege the powerless, and nourish the community.

In a small text called *World as Sacrament*, Alexander Schmemann provocatively invites the world into Christian liturgy. He rejects the utilitarian role of religion, whereby its purpose is to answer problems posed from outside the church. The church, for example, lacks insight regarding what percentage of our energy ought to come from wind farms. The church's end is Truth and life in Truth. Liturgy, as the actualization of the church in the world, ought not to be identified with particular cultic acts, explicitly religious, explicitly ecological, or otherwise. Quite simply, it is the response of humans in community to the meeting of divine and human elements. Within the church there is already a consciousness of the dialectical quality of human existence. Christians are in the world but not of it, as they are also born of dust and possess dominion. Among Christian dichotomies, Schmemann notes that in the Eucharist material food is given by God as communion with God: "It is divine love made food, made life for man."[24]

Schmemann's understanding of the world is explained in terms of creation, fall, and redemption. Creation, simultaneously material and spiritual, is affirmed from its outset. The Fall occasions abstraction, specifically the division of the sacred and profane. The fallen world embraces the secular assertion of autonomous things and fails to notice that God is still all in all:[25]

> When we see the world as an end in itself, everything becomes itself a value and consequently loses all value, because only in God is found the meaning (value) of everything, and the world is meaningful only when it is the "sacrament" of God's presence. Things treated merely as things in themselves destroy themselves because only in God have they any life. The world of nature, cut off from the source of life, is a dying world.[26]

In Christ, who is the paradigm of dialectical existence, the one in whom divine origin and human productivity are most clearly modeled, the church is restored. Alienation is overcome.

Michel de Certeau wonderfully complements Schmemann's model with an anthropological model consistent with Lefebvre's. On the first page of *Practice of Everyday Life* de Certeau rejects radical individualism and writes, "Analysis shows that a relation (always social) determines its terms, and not the reverse, and that each individual is a locus in which an incoherent (and often contradictory) plurality of such relational determinations interact."[27] What a remarkable picture of our position in the world! Each of us is a locus of a plurality of relational determinations. De Certeau has in mind cultures, economies, political orders, and interpersonal relations, but there is also room here for Lefebvre's double determination, the interplay of nature and history. To de Certeau the individual is a node of social interaction. There is no individual apart from the networks she occupies. As I understand him, Lefebvre agrees but makes room in the interplay of social relations for the voice of nature. That is, included in the plurality of relational determinations are biology and physiology, both forming and being formed.

Schmemann also understands the human as node of transactions. The human receives the world and, in the act of naming, offers it to God.[28] That is, conscious life—characterized by receiving and naming—is worship:

> Honesty to the gospel, to the whole tradition Christian tradition, to the experience of every saint and every word of Christian liturgy *demands* [affirmation of God]: to live in the world seeing *everything* in it as a revelation of God, a sign of His presence, the joy of His coming, the call to communion with Him, the hope of fulfillment in Him. . . . In [Christ] the world has become again a *liturgy*, a *communion*, an *ascension*.[29]

This liturgical picture is fundamentally hopeful. Acutely conscious of the state of the world and all of its empirically determined ills, concerned always to slice through abstraction for the sake of truth, liturgy contains the promise of salvation for the individual and all creation.

Lefebvre, Schmemann, and de Certeau are constructive interlocutors not only for their rich understandings of social dialectics and human identity but also for their attention to everydayness, to ethics as praxis. The apocalyptic prophecies of environmental science arouse urgency. Discrete expressions of ecological concern, though laudable, are divorced from liturgical celebration. They find their source in an abstract notion of nature rather than in meaning-giving *mysterion*. They are liable, therefore, to overwhelm a well-intentioned individual. I am inclined to think that liturgy, alternatively, enables an attitude toward nature that is more worshipful than instrumental. Liturgy decenters the individual, emphasizing participation in a larger community and relationships with the world and the divine while admitting what seems to me obvious: that we can make sense of a world only inasmuch as it is *for us*.

PART TWO

Genetics and Nature

With this section, our discussion shifts from the outside world to the natures of things in themselves. In what respect does it make sense to speak of the natural integrity of things, especially of living beings? Without discounting the distinctions of individuals or the malleability of species over time, we are concerned here to interrogate the notion of biological natures or constitutive essences and to ask how these natures are impacted by human activity, most dramatically in cases of genetic manipulation. The contributors to this section primarily discuss biological nature and genetics, but by their proximity to the previous section on ecological natures, we propose that shifts in our understanding and treatment of the ecological world are inextricably related to the biological identity of life itself. This is why ecological ethics and bioethics are close cousins.

Acknowledging that gene-centered biologists increasingly eschew the idea of naturality for its imprecision, cell biologist Stuart Newman argues that the conceptual distinction of natural and artifactual remains firmly rooted in biological science. It is the mechanisms of development, rather than genetic change itself, which are decisive. The obfuscation of the nature-artifact distinction, Newman argues, relies on a reductive "biological postmodernism," an outdated gene determinism that often serves commercial or political interests more than it represents scientific fact. Newman analyzes the rhetorical maneuvers and often dubious scientific claims behind debates over genetically modified (GM) crops and human applications of biotechnology, such as cloning and stem cells. He sees the revival of creationism as symptomatic of the same problem: the inability of evolutionary biology, to date, to provide a full account of some critical mechanisms of the biological phenotype. This unanswered question, justly exposed by some fundamentalist Christians, is the same lacuna exploited by postmodern biologists in order to assert that no form of life exists naturally and that biotechnological innovations ought to face no special scrutiny. In response, Newman explains new developments in systems biology that attempt to explain morphological continuities (or "natures") through biophysical mechanisms in the evolution of cells.

Newman is ultimately more wary of genetic experimentation than is Ronald Cole-Turner, who withholds definitive prescription in his investigation of the shifting boundary between artificial and natural life. He directs attention to the fecund and young field of "synthetic biology," which is distinct from genetic engineering and concerns artificial synthesis of natural processes and structures, perhaps to accomplish new ends or to operate in new contexts. The project of synthetic biology is to create life against nature; the naturally occurring forms of nucleotide codes in DNA, for example, are deliberately contradicted in order to improve the rationality of the sequence or to substitute synthesized nucleotides in their stead. Nature provides a negative example for new forms of life whose raison d'être is that they live precisely nonnaturally. Of course, technology alone does not answer the questions it provokes about how and under what conditions it should be adopted, and Cole-Turner refrains here from asserting a theological "answer" to the myriad issues raised. He recommends, however, that these technologies invite theological consideration of the human capacity to create. On the one hand there may be theological warrants for caution, but on the other, Cole-Turner is excited by the promises and possibilities of new technologies and the multivocal theological reflection that must necessarily follow the consequent developments in "life" and "culture."

Gerald McKenny's contribution picks up the question of nature as normative from Lorraine Daston's introductory essay. Drawing on the writings of Michael Sandel, Leon Kass, and Francis Fukuyama, members of President George W. Bush's Council on Bioethics, McKenny proposes three ways that nature is given normative status in contemporary discussions of bioengineering. Sandel asserts the normativity of nature's independence from human activity; Kass identifies in nature an exemplary moral order, not always independent but mandating complementary activity; and Fukuyama insists on the normative inviolability of natural boundaries, the integrity of natural kinds. In practice, the three positions are not often discrete, even for McKenny's paradigmatic figures, and at times he identifies elements of each position in Newman's chapter. And like Newman, McKenny acknowledges that the tide among scientists is to reject the definiteness of nature and the clarity of its prescriptions. Ultimately critical of each of the positions, McKenny argues that we are in some way without nature, which cannot bear the weight of any of these positions, and he recommends that a more compelling ethics will defend the "goods" of nature, rather than nature itself.

Renatured Biology: Getting Past Postmodernism in the Life Sciences

Stuart A. Newman

> We must consider the possibility that at some point in the future,
> different groups of human beings may follow divergent paths of
> development through the use of genetic technology. If this occurs,
> there will be different groups of beings, each with its own "nature,"
> related to one another only through a common ancestor (the human
> race). . . . For all we know . . . they might not treat each other as
> moral equals.
>
> ALLEN BUCHANAN ET AL. (2000), *From Chance to Choice: Genetics and Justice*

Charles Darwin was a "naturalist," as were the other post-Enlightenment founders of modern biology: Carl Linnaeus, Georges-Louis Leclerc, Comte de Buffon, Gregor Mendel, Matthias Schleiden, and Theodor Schwann, to name only a few. The term was still a job description less than a century ago, when the collected works and a brief biography of William Bateson, the British scientist who introduced Mendel's ideas to the English-speaking world and coined the term "genetics," were published under the title *William Bateson, Naturalist*.[1] These days, however, there are few notions more derided by contemporary gene-centered biology and its commercial offshoots than "nature" and "the natural." The term is sometimes handled by bioethicists and policy analysts, but then only with rubber gloves. In a recent policy forum in the journal *Science* a group of twenty-two bioethicists, philosophers, and biologists addressed the question of the morality of introducing human brain tissue into the

Some material in the "Genetically Modified Crops" section appeared in a different form in Stuart A. Newman, "Genetically Modified Crops and the Attack on Nature," *Capitalism Nature Socialism* 20.2 (2009): 22–31. Some material in the "The Evolution Wars" section appeared in a different form in Stuart A. Newman, "Evolution: the Public's Problem and the Scientists'," *Capitalism Nature Socialism* 19 (2008): 98–106.

heads of nonhuman primates, first dispensing with distractions: "We unanimously rejected ethical objections grounded on unnaturalness or crossing species boundaries. Whether it is possible to draw a meaningful distinction between the natural and the unnatural is a matter of dispute."[2]

It is safe to assume that the biologists among the report's authors were not the ones who first formulated this position—an irate literature records the judgment of mainstream science on the purported social construction of empirical distinctions.[3] Nonetheless, echoing an assertion in a 1999 report by the British Nuffield Council on Bioethics that "[t]he 'natural/unnatural' distinction is one of which few practicing scientists can make much sense," the *Science* article's half-dozen basic and clinical scientist authors did in fact sign onto a statement that the distinction between the natural and the artifactual is irrelevant in considering the ethical implications of animals cobbled together from more than one species.[4]

Nature, in the sense of a world neither made nor influenced by human activity, is fundamental to any conception of science. In particular, there was a world before there were humans, and while much of it has been transformed, much has not: the structure of atoms, the Earth's topography, the anatomical plans and physiology of most organisms, the distinctness of biological species. Questions as to what extent (if at all) technologically untransformed nature represents a positive value and in which domains the natural and the artifactual become inextricable, are all, of course, "matters of dispute." That there is a conceptual difference between the natural and the human-made is not.[5] Indeed, Keekok Lee, in her remarkable book *The Natural and the Artefactual*, distinguishes seven different senses of "nature," several of which she argues are loci of values jeopardized by certain technological activities.[6]

As evidenced by the comments quoted above from the Nuffield Council Report and the *Science* article, however, since the 1980s, along with the emergence of genetic methodologies capable of transforming the material character of biological systems, radically skeptical assertions of the meaninglessness of the distinction between the natural and artifactual have been made by an increasingly vocal group of bioethicists and science writers.[7] Though representing itself as the carrier and defender of a liberating and opportunity-laden technological culture, this movement, which I refer to as "biological postmodernism," is instead, I argue, traducing the most incisive findings of contemporary biological science while enabling commercial forces to fashion a world where there is in fact little distinction between organisms and artifacts.

As we see below, technologies such as the introduction of new genes into developing organisms ("transgenesis"), generation of organisms from preexisting genetic prototypes ("cloning"), and production of organisms of multiple parental or species lineages by mixture of embryonic cells at early developmental stages ("chimerism"), can sometimes give rise to viable plants and animals, and these may have particular scientific, medical, or commercial uses. In each of these cases, however, the techniques employed are different from the intricate and often gradual processes involved in the coevolution and "complexification" of organisms, their subsystems, and the mechanisms by which they develop. The resulting products are therefore artifactual. Just as important, a theory of biological change that could illuminate the relationship of alterations at the cellular or subcellular levels, induced by either natural or artificial means, to changes effected at the level of the whole organism is, as we also see below, available only in rough form. This is despite strong claims that have been made for the triumph of Darwinism and gene-based explanatory models.

Science has been distorted and society in general deceived by corporate executives denying the deadly effects of smoking and pollution, governmental officials denying the causes of global warming, and religious fundamentalists denying evolution. The styles of these abuses differ, however. Corporate leadership and the U.S. government claim to respect the methods and outcomes of science. Dismissal of uncomfortable facts therefore requires the interested parties to suppress evidence, fire whistle-blowers, and fund obliging investigators. The religious perspective is less fearful of and therefore less deferential to science. Whereas scientifically trained religionists wishing to complement mainstream scientific accounts with extraempirical tenets (e.g., advocates of "intelligent design") may seek to identify implausible or unpersuasive aspects of standard narratives, the more fundamentalist of such thinkers are less reticent about resorting to a supernatural counternarrative that permits them to dismiss scientific findings out of hand.

Biological postmodernists, while sharing the "proscience" modernizing creed of the corporations that typically sponsor their work, also have characteristics in common with religious fundamentalists. Participants in this trend have brought together certain waning biological theories and concepts in the form of an ideology concerning how living systems operate, develop, and have evolved. Like the fundamentalists, therefore, they promulgate a narrative concerning the nature of life that conflicts in significant ways with contemporary scientific thought. Ironically, this reductive, essentially nihilistic set of views is increasingly taken as the hallmark of an informed secularism by libertarians and many liberals.

Biological postmodernism is exemplified in writings on genetically engineered foods by some agricultural scientists and policy analysts.[8] It arises in discussions of human embryo research and prospects of human cloning and genetic modification.[9] Perhaps most surprising is its role in the arguments by which scientists and science advocates have defended the reality of biological evolution against recent creationist assaults. More specifically, biological postmodernism, in adhering to an increasingly questioned exclusively neo-Darwinian paradigm for evolutionary change, represents acceptance of a notion of biological species without boundaries supported by a pseudomaterialistic genetic essentialism.

The particular examples I have chosen and the order in which I present them constitute a progression. Specifically, the postmodernist maneuvers around the first area, GM crops, represent the most transparently commercially influenced and intellectually shallow of these efforts. Those pertaining to the second area, research in human embryology, are a bit more nuanced. While in some cases no less disingenuous on the part of scientists and bioethicists who advance them, postmodern stratagems in developmental biology reflect, as well, unresolved conceptual questions in the field itself. Finally, the postmodernism of creationism's opponents in the evolution wars represents a poor defense necessitated by an evolutionary theory that, while well established, is underdeveloped in its comprehension of notions of origination and innovation of phenotypic characters.[10] Though the least "interested" and commercially driven of the implementations of biological postmodernism discussed here, those relating to evolution may be most indicative of problems with conceptualizations of the biological world as it exists independently of human activity.

To avoid misunderstanding, I must emphasize that my goal here is not to condemn biotechnology in general nor to privilege some version of nature over culture or civilization, charges that some recent commentators have lodged against virtually anyone with reservations about these techniques.[11] Rather, I propose to demonstrate the extent to which the contemporary discourse around biology has been permeated and distorted by an irrational "religion of technology" and what has been characterized by the philosopher Mary Midgley as the "dreams, dramas, myths or fantasies out of which faiths are constructed to fill the vacuum which is left when more familiar ones are abandoned."[12]

In order to understand the peculiar synergy of the cultural and scientific notions represented by biological postmodernism, it is helpful to recount briefly the trajectory of recent intellectual history that has led to its easy acceptance by many secular and more than a few liberal religious thinkers.

Biology during the Transition from the Modern to the Postmodern

The revolutions (scientific, political, industrial) that occurred in social organization and scientific thought in European-centered societies beginning four centuries ago shook the foundations of belief systems inherited from earlier periods. The recognition that supposed eternal verities—oppressive rulers with divine claims and one's station in society prominent among them—were products of human action, albeit obscured by overlays of history and ideology, produced in many an optimism concerning human agency and the possibility of changing things for the better.

Scientifically, the new fields of chemistry and physics propounded laws of transformation of matter from one form to another that contradicted older notions of permanence and also put new powers into human hands. Geology and biology in the nineteenth century also discerned laws of transformation—for example, of mountains and species—that while not under full human control, were nonetheless no longer at the whim of a supernatural creator. The industrialization associated with these political and scientific upheavals had its dark, satanic side, but its ravage of ecosystems, creation of new means of warfare and mass killing, and destruction of traditional societies could be considered and portrayed as side effects of overall "progress," at least until the twentieth century.

The modern era, beginning with the Enlightenment (or even earlier, according to some historians), gave rise in the late nineteenth and early twentieth centuries to the self-conscious literary, aesthetic, and philosophical movement known as modernism. Particularly relevant to the postmodernist style of thought that later emerged as both an extension and a rejection of it was modernism's questioning of realistic modes of representation. This tendency, represented by the work of writers and artists such as James Joyce, Virginia Woolf, T. S. Eliot, Pablo Picasso, and Piet Mondrian, has been described as a reaction to the disparities between the ideals and the reality of progress. According to the cultural critic Terry Eagleton:

> All the beliefs that had served nineteenth-century middle-class society so splendidly—liberalism, democracy, individualism, scientific inquiry, historical progress, the sovereignty of reason—were now in crisis. There was a dramatic speed-up in technology, along with widespread political instability. It was becoming hard to believe that there was any innate order in

the world. Instead, what order we discovered in the world was one we had put there ourselves.[13]

Science during this period of social uncertainty was undergoing turmoil of its own. The field of modern physics, particularly, had the misfortune of producing two theories—special relativity (1905) and quantum mechanics (1925)—that were theoretically elegant, experimentally sound, but completely at odds with common sense. Additionally, some of its best minds were enlisted to produce the atom bomb, the most powerful destructive device the world had ever seen, which, despite some misgivings and protestations by involved scientists, was used on two population centers, leaving hundreds of thousands dead and many more maimed and sickened.[14]

Biology, in contrast, appeared to be a paragon of conceptual and moral rectitude.[15] The rise of the gene provided a seemingly simple and straightforward explanation for the mysteries of physiology, development, and evolution. Ready and lucid metaphors for gene function were proffered in the form of the blueprint or computer program, the latter, like the discovery of the double-helical structure of DNA, a mid-twentieth-century product. Far from engendering weapons of mass destruction such as nuclear bombs, biology produced the Green Revolution.[16] The fascist and communist enemies of the Western democracies even embodied particular distortions and rejections of the gene's preeminence—racial purity and Lysenkoism—the suppression of which became part of the good fight against the associated political ideologies.[17]

Still, science and technology, though clearly improving the lives of many in the Western world (but only some in economically weaker venues), was failing to address the deeper disquiet of the modern era.[18] The so-called Cold War, seemingly perpetually on the verge of breaking out into a nuclear holocaust, violent wars of decolonization in Asia, Africa, and South America, and poverty and social conflict resulting from the legacy of slavery, racism, and constitutional plutocracy in the United States led to a sometimes corrosive questioning by intellectuals of the bases and tenets of the bourgeois social order. Philosophers of the Frankfurt School, such as Walter Benjamin, Theodor Adorno, and Herbert Marcuse, beginning in the 1930s, and allied thinkers such as Simone de Beauvoir and Michel Foucault fostered a turn towards cultural criticism in the academy while influencing the rise of militant international student movements of the sixties and early seventies. The effect of the academic work was to focus the skepticism of the earlier modernist critique of literature and art onto civilization itself, changing the intellectual landscape for both its advocates and opponents in an irreversible fashion.[19] An offshoot of this enterprise was "science studies" or "social studies of science," a field of scholarship that could cast an unsparing light on the production and use of scientific knowledge itself.[20]

Literary and aesthetic modernism and the cultural criticism that grew from it (like the Freudian theory with which they were sometimes allied) were concerned with the necessarily incomplete and provisional nature of knowledge of the self and the external world. The logic of cultural criticism, taken beyond its original purview, also spawned postmodernism, a theoretical stance in which the very notion of objective reality was called into question.[21] According to the postmodernist philosopher of science Bruno Latour, modernism, in its querying of the nature-culture boundary, conceded too much autonomy to each side, the two being inextricably entangled in his view.[22] Postmodernism was lambasted by some on the political right, who, lumping it with feminism and cultural theory, portrayed it as a leftist attack on the notion of scientific authority. But postmodernist positions on the nature of science and social reality also encountered resistance—and ridicule—from scientists and cultural critics on the left who were otherwise receptive to the aims of the earlier cultural critique.[23]

Confined to disagreements on the truth-value of scientific concepts and the extent to which any field of inquiry can legitimately appropriate and manipulate the terms of another, these matters are of mainly academic concern. But as postmodernist thought in the eighties and nineties drifted away from its politically radical roots, it met up with a set of societal changes that would make its epistemological relativism more congenial to the entrepreneurial program than it ever was to any socialist insurgency. In Terry Eagleton's words:

> [W]hat nobody could have predicted was that Western civilization was just on the brink of going non-realist itself. Reality itself had now embraced the non-realist, as capitalist society became increasingly dependent in its everyday operation on myth and fantasy, fictional wealth, exoticism and hyperbole, rhetoric, virtual reality and sheer appearance. . . . The radical modernists had tried to dismantle the distinction between art and life. Now, it seems that life had done it for them. . . . A radical assault on fixed hierarchies of value merged effortlessly with that revolutionary levelling of all values known as the marketplace.[24]

Among the things affected by these changes were the manner in which science was conducted and how natural distinctions and nature itself were conceived, valued, and even ascribed reality. The 1980s saw the simultaneous rise of the aggressively procorporation Reagan administration, which weakened legal restrictions on commerce, of gene analysis and splicing technologies, of patents on living organisms, and of new modes of technology transfer between the publicly funded academic and private commercial sectors. This complex of changes created a need by its potential beneficiaries for a cultural narrative that would justify manipulation and commodification of living systems. During the same period, the increased coherence and visibility in the United States of religion-based opposition to embryo research and the teaching of evolution created the appearance of a reactionary monolith against which the promoters of the new biotechnology could define themselves ideologically as "liberal" and "libertarian."

Postmodernism as a theoretical manifestation of late-capitalist social change and its cultural artifacts—the reconfiguration of family structure, social roles, and gender identities, the melding of "high" and "low" art, Transformer toys and video games, virtual reality and "reality TV"—was ready at hand to provide intellectual cover and a level of comfort (no more "shock of the new") for the new biotechnology. The intersection of market-oriented biomedical research with the now-fashionable ablation of natural distinctions also gave a new lease on life to obsolete early- and mid-twentieth-century notions in the biological sciences. These concepts—genetic reductionism, the fluidity of species boundaries, and evolution as a process of random search with no inherent directionality—had been coming under increased scientific criticism and by the 1980s were in the midst of being replaced by "systems biology"–based ideas.[25] Their lingering, however, proved particularly favorable to a corporate imperative that, echoing the manifesto of the philosopher Francis Bacon in his prescient seventeenth-century utopian fantasy, *The New Atlantis*, sought to employ biotechnology in the "effecting of all things possible."[26]

The postmodernist turn, for example, by devaluing nature and natural distinctions, has supported arguments, more influential in the United States than in Europe, that genetic engineering of crops is no different in principle from either traditional plant breeding or, for that matter, the natural evolutionary process. Coordinately with these efforts, evolution, for its part, has been mischaracterized by biological postmodernists, taking their cue from neo-Darwinian evolutionary theorists, as a product of random search that readily crosses and blurs species boundaries, potentially transforming all biological forms into all others.

Because, as noted above, the material definitions of the embryonic-developmental and evolutionary processes have each been flash points in the assault on both women's reproductive autonomy and the teaching of evolution, there has been a tendency among liberal and libertarian defenders of science in the United States to endorse reflexively all research with embryonic stem cells and to dismiss any suggestion that evolution is anything other than random and opportunistic. More broadly, technophilic bioethicists and other liberal and libertarian commentators have refrained from engaging a traditionalist critique that, despite some scientific shortcomings, reflects a deep (and, some secularists would also argue, healthy) suspicion of the transformation of life, particularly human life, into items subject to selection and material perfection. Finally, postmodernism-influenced opponents of creationism and "intelligent design" have weakened their advocacy of a scientific approach by ignoring the growing acknowledgment within naturalistic evolutionary biology itself of the inadequacy of Darwinian mechanisms alone to account for biological complexity.[27]

Allegations of the pernicious influence of postmodernism have become a familiar refrain from writers defending such purported biological realities as human nature and biological race.[28] This strain of academic anti-postmodernism, which takes as its target "political correctness" and other aspects of what it sees as feminism and cultural theory gone awry, has been criticized elsewhere.[29] In the political realm, strangely, postmodernism has been targeted by individuals who show little evidence of having accepted modernity.[30] My critique of the biological postmodernism of corporate-friendly deniers of natural boundaries avoids these contentious arenas by dealing mainly with questions of genetics, embryonic development, and evolution, where scientific consensus on the basic data, if not their interpretation, is often available.

Two additional points need to be made before presenting my main arguments. First, the scientists, commentators, and corporate spokespeople whose views I criticize here have not, in any case that I am aware of, overtly advocated or expressed sympathy with postmodernist thought. Indeed, most would almost certainly be scandalized to find themselves associated with a philosophical movement that is often characterized as an attack on scientific objectivity and even the notion of truth. It is indeed ironic that the rise of biotechnology as a means of production, against the background of an entrenched genetic determinism in developmental biology and evolutionary theory, has brought so many of the "players" in the new life sciences into such close affinity with the postmodernist bête noire. Second, biological postmodernism has been promulgated using ideas about living systems that, however questionable, are still widely accepted and have only recently begun to generate concerted opposition from within science. Although I believe it to be a dubious ideology, I do not thereby mean to suggest that all its exponents in the agricultural and medical fields hold these views in a cynical fashion.

Biological Postmodernism: Three Domains

In the following sections I elaborate on the three examples, mentioned above, of widely followed issues in which either active promotion or tacit acceptance of a postmodern concept of living systems has led to denial of biological facts by scientists and others who present themselves as defenders of science against antiscience New Ageism or religious fundamentalism: (1) attempts by biotechnology companies and some agricultural scientists to undermine public resistance to GM food crops; (2) controversies around human applications of biotechnology involving cloning, stem cells, and chimeras; and (3) the battle over teaching creationism and "intelligent design" in U.S. public schools.

GENETICALLY MODIFIED CROPS

Since the first proposals were made to introduce exogenous genes into food and fiber plants, there have been questions raised about the capacity of the methods to create superweeds or adversely affect the health (i.e., by toxicity or allergenicity) of those who consume them.[31] By 2005, however, when more than 90 percent of the annual soybean crop and 50 percent of the corn crop in the United States had come to be genetically engineered—a transformation in agricultural production that took less than a decade—efforts at regulation that had made sense in a precautionary framework could now be portrayed as irrational.[32] Indeed, as some advocates would have it, resistance to GM food now implies that one wishes to avoid eating, to undermine the U.S. economy, and, for leaders of countries with undernourished populations, to deprive their citizens of food aid.[33]

Up to now, virtually all genetic modification of food and fiber crops has been directed towards enhancing the economic aspects of crop production (i.e., resistance to herbicides and insect damage, increasing shelf life) rather than improving nutrition or flavor.[34] There have thus been enormous financial incentives associated with introducing genetic engineering methods into agriculture with little concomitant benefit to the consumer other than, in certain cases, pricing. But the grip that agribusiness corporate directors have come to exert on food and other crop production since GM products were first introduced in 1996, in the form of patents that prohibit replanting of saved seed as well as pressures on farmers via their insurance companies not to seek alternatives, suggests that any efficiencies in production arising from genetic engineering will in the long term not even be reflected in lower prices.

With the hazards of GM crops not allayed and the benefits to the general public not compelling, the means by which several important traditionally bred food crops came to be replaced by GM counterparts in the United States with little opposition, compared with Western Europe, is of great interest.[35] While the institutional and anthropological aspects of conflicts around GM foods have been written about incisively, additional insight can be gained by considering the role in this process of biological postmodernism.[36]

The relationship between an organism's genotype—the full complement of its genes—and its phenotype—its form and array of functional attributes over the range of environments in which it is viable—is one of the great unsolved problems in biology. It is studied by developmental biologists, physiologists, ecologists, and behaviorists, among other scientists, and there is little consensus across or even within these fields as to what the rules and regularities of the genotype-phenotype relation are. The simplistic notion of "one gene, one trait" suggested by some classic Mendelian studies was rejected as a general principle early on by plant and animal geneticists.[37] But equally misleading concepts such as the "genetic program" or the "genetic blueprint," collectively referred to as genetic reductionism or determinism, held on despite their inability to provide explanatory links between genotypes and anything but the most basic molecular aspects of phenotypes.[38]

In conventional agronomy, breeders select phenotypic variants associated with spontaneous mutations of genes that have coevolved with all the other genes of the particular plant over tens or hundreds of millions of years. Methods of chemical- or radiation-induced DNA mutagenesis used earlier in the twentieth century, prior to the GM era, can change the sequence, or rearrange the position in the chromosomes, of the coevolved genes. These "classic" mutagenesis methods and some newer genetic engineering techniques that simply inactivate existing genes, while they may have unpredictable effects on the organism's morphological phenotype (shape, form, arrangement of parts; see the following sections), do not add molecular functionalities uncharacteristic of the species. In contrast, "transgenesis," the most commonly used GM technique, involves introducing genes from distant species into a plant or animal's genome— bacterially derived herbicide or pest-resistance factors in soybeans and corn or fish-derived antifreeze proteins in tomatoes, for example. But throwing an entirely new component into a plant's biological mix can potentially change the levels of the hundreds to thousands of potentially toxic molecules every plant is capable of manufacturing. Moreover, different transgenic insertions of the same gene into the same plant can result in vastly different phenotypes due to variations in the position of insertion in the chromosomes. In addition, GM transgenesis can inadvertently induce extensive scrambling of the genome.[39]

It is significant in this regard that "lateral gene transfer"—that is, natural transgenesis—into plants or animals from evolutionary distant sources such as bacteria has been extremely rare in the history of life.[40] In cases where it has been documented to have occurred, it has had major consequences to the plant's phenotype.[41]

Scientific advocates of GM crops take comfort in the observation that "phenotypes and metabolic pathways tend to be buffered from the effects of mutations."[42] However, such buffering mechanisms, whereby a plant or animal can develop into a form characteristic of its species despite alteration or even complete inactivation of many genes, are products of integration of the genome through coevolution of genes and natural selection for developmental stability.[43] They would only fortuitously and inexactly pertain to transgenic organisms. The assertion that the outcomes of transgenesis are more predictable than traditional breeding or mutagenesis because the manipulations are more precise at the DNA level simply ignores the findings of cell physiology and evolutionary biology.[44]

Introduction of products based on novel technologies have traditionally been advertised as "new and improved" or even "revolutionary"; in particular, their differences from existing counterparts have been emphasized and portrayed as beneficial. With regard to GM food, it became clear early on that this strategy of differentiation would not work; people were too suspicious of significant changes in what they eat for them to respond positively to such claims. It became necessary instead to reassure the public that nothing in the nature of their food crops would change despite the new methods (sold to potential investors, paradoxically, as unprecedented in their power) used to produce them. By conflating GM transgenesis with conventional mutagenesis, traditional selective breeding, and evolution itself and portraying it as nothing new, several stratagems of biological postmodernism were brought to bear on selling GM foods to the public and, more important, to corporate and governmental leaders. In the United States these were mainly directed to undermining distinctions between the natural and artifactual. Insofar as such maneuvers were successful, agribusiness was aided by academic and think-tank intellectuals and regulatory agencies, which, regardless of the political party in power, seemed only too eager to go along with them.

Genetically Modified Crops as Substantially Equivalent to Traditionally Bred Crops Before GM crops were placed on the market in the United States and Europe, a series of reports were published by national and international deliberative bodies that had considered potential hazards of GM crops. Among the earliest and most influential of these reports was the document *Field Testing Genetically Modified Organisms: Framework for Decisions*, published in 1989 by the National Research Council (NRC), an arm of the U.S. National Academy of Sciences. Despite earlier discussions at the National Academy itself and throughout the international scientific community that acknowledged some of the complexities and pitfalls of transgenic manipulations mentioned above, the NRC report stated quite simply that "no conceptual distinctions exist between genetic modification of plants and microorganisms by classical methods or by molecular techniques that modify DNA and transfer genes."[45] Since "classical" methods included spontaneous mutagenesis, that is, the source of the genetic variation in coevolved genes in cultivated populations of plants, the assertion was a stretch. The further statement that "the same physical and biological laws govern the response of organisms modified by modern molecular and cellular methods and those produced by classical methods" finally spun the report into the realm of the postmodern; as noted above, the "biological laws" governing the genotype-phenotype relationship (the only biological laws relevant in this case) are all but unknown with regard to organisms with changes in existing coevolved sets of genes and are nonexistent for organisms containing genes imported from other species.

The main conclusion of the NRC's report was that "the *product* of genetic modification and selection constitutes the primary basis for decisions on the environmental introduction of a plant or microorganism and not the *process* by which the product was obtained."[46] Four years later, when the international Organization for Economic Cooperation and Development (OECD) met to produce the report *Safety Evaluation of Foods Derived by Modern Biotechnology*, the U.S. position, based on the NRC's dismissal of any special issues arising from genetic modification of crops, held sway, crystallizing into the OECD's doctrine of "substantial equivalence" of

GM and traditionally bred plants.[47] While initially serving as a basis for international consensus on the global marketing of GM foods, the "substantial equivalence" doctrine came under increasing attack in the United Kingdom and other European Union countries over the next decade as new data from field and laboratory tests exposed it as unscientific and ill defined. In the United States, however, it remained the operative principle governing the regulation of transgenic GM crops.[48] But at this late date there are still no adequate testing methods in place to screen for phenotypes harmful to the environment or human and animal health potentially generated by transgenic GM techniques.[49] While this is also true for conventionally bred crops, as noted above, the phenotypic novelties that may arise from transgenesis are likely to be different from those latent in the population or inducible by alteration of existing coevolved genes.

Genetically Modified Foods as Organic Foods   The U.S. Congress, in a farm bill enacted in 1990, directed the U.S. Department of Agriculture (USDA) to establish criteria for certification of foods as "organic." Though not a scientific term, "organic" on a label was meant to assure people that food crops have been produced by a management system that "promotes and enhances biodiversity, biological cycles and soil biological activity . . . based on minimal use of off-farm inputs and on management practices that restore, maintain and enhance ecological harmony."[50] Imprecise as this may be, it is fairly obvious what kinds of processes and products consumers of organic food favor: as distant as feasible from the high-tech, chemical-intensive monoculture characteristic of the large-scale, absentee-owned, contract-farmed, agricultural enterprises.

Apart from questions of whether organic farming embodies all the health and environmental advantages claimed by its supporters, there is the issue of people's right to know what they are eating. The debate over the definition of organic food is thus an example of what the science and technology analyst Sheila Jasanoff refers to as "boundary work" by which the demarcation between the natural and the unnatural is negotiated in any society.[51]

With the doctrine of substantial equivalence in hand, corporate leaders in the agricultural biotechnology sector and their academic allies took up the cause of negotiating the natural/unnatural boundary and had the Clinton administration's Secretary of Agriculture Dan Glickman issue proposed USDA standards making GM food (as well as food irradiated to increase shelf life or grown with the aid of toxic sewage sludge) eligible for labeling as organic. A massive public protest in the form of several hundred thousand letters prevented the USDA from implementing this proposal in 2000.

Traditionally Bred Foods as Genetically Modified Foods With substantial equivalence in disrepute everywhere but in the United States and the U.S. campaign to get GM foods labeled as organic a failure, deregulating the technology entirely, so as to end all public awareness and scrutiny of it, moved to the top of the industry's agenda.[52] The final arrow in the biological postmodernists' quiver was therefore released: the denial of any distinctiveness whatsoever to genetic engineering technology.

In 2003 a commentary on new research on the origins of maize was published in the journal *Science*.[53] The article itself was an unexceptionable summary of what is known about the cultivation of maize over the past four thousand years, placed in the context of retrospective knowledge of the genes involved. Only the last sentence, which concluded that "the rapid adoption of superior GM crops today . . . is far from a new phenomenon," referred to present-day technology, but the piece in effect denied that GM foods represent novel agricultural products by the maneuver of defining all cultivated crops, extending back to the New Stone Age, as genetically engineered. The author, an academic scientist and a member of the board of directors of Sigma-Aldrich, a company that markets pharmaceutical products extracted from transgenic corn, was not explicit about her intention of shifting the discourse concerning genetic engineering of crops by obfuscating its differences from traditional breeding practices until confronted by other scientists in *Science*'s letters column. And indeed, the magazine's editors colluded in helping her slip this "reframing" of the field past readers and into the scientific literature when they permitted her to give the article its provocative title, "Agriculture: Prehistoric GM Corn," and allowed her to leave her corporate affiliation off the author's note.

Some of the comments received by *Science* in response to the article are instructive. One correspondent stated, "N.V. Fedoroff's Perspective 'Prehistoric GM corn' . . . seems calculated to obscure important issues in the debate over the safety of genetically modified organisms (GMOs)," while another asserted, "It is not a question of whether genetic engineering is good, bad, or irrelevant, but clarity of understanding requires that a distinction be recognized." In her reply Fedoroff stated, "[I]t is time to eliminate the altogether artificial boundary between what humans did before molecular techniques were developed and what they do now to improve their crop plants," and then went on to conflate spontaneous mutations, radiation-induced mutations, and transgenesis.[54] As noted above, the last of these, the characteristic method for producing GM crops, is entirely different from the first two.

HUMAN DEVELOPMENTAL BIOLOGY

The controversy around abortion, though heated and divisive, is an old one. The dispute has focused on whether a developing human before a given age or stage of development has a "right to life" or is indeed due any individual regard, but there has never been any question on either side of the issue that what is eliminated by an abortion is an embryo or fetus. Starting in 1978, however, with the first human birth (in the United Kingdom) resulting from in vitro fertilization (IVF), the embryo became objectified in a new way. Even though the original goal of IVF was reproduction, the embryo's independence from a woman's body made it easier to discard if it failed to meet certain standards or to improve, to buy and sell, and to transform into something with other uses. In just a few years after the first IVF birth, the British Committee of Inquiry into Human Fertilisation and Embryology published the Warnock Report on human fertilization, which proposed that the developing human prior to day 14 of development be redefined as a "pre-embryo."[55] This designation, which is not used in the scientific or popular literature for the developmental stages of any other organism (a fertilized frog egg, for example, is called simply an embryo), established a biological entity that while no longer a human embryo (which some people found inappropriate as an experimental system), could nonetheless be studied to gain knowledge of human development.

It should be recognized that objections to modifying or otherwise experimenting on human embryos is not the same thing as seeking to limit women's reproductive autonomy by curtailing the right to obtain an abortion. Opponents of human embryo research argue that adapting the methods by which mouse embryos have been cloned and genetically modified to human embryos (even if only to produce stem cells) will clearly enable the production of full-term cloned and GM humans. There are no laws in the United States or most other countries to prevent this, nor is there currently a consensus to move in that direction. For every scientist working in this field who disavows the goal of generating full-term cloned humans, there are several bioethicists providing arguments against such misgivings.[56] But one can simultaneously hold a pro–reproductive choice position and still have concerns about the ways in which scientific advances in experimental embryo manipulations enable the production of altered humans. Put another way, accepting that a woman has a right to terminate her pregnancy does not thereby create a right for others to do what they wish with the embryo or fetus.

Defining an unmanipulated human embryo as something other than an embryo in order to circumvent taboos on its objectification clearly resembles the postmodernist maneuvers discussed above in relation to GM food crops. It is significant, however, that on the conceptual level it has exactly the opposite goal: to enforce rather than erase distinctions between the artifactual and the natural. Of course, such reversals present no problem for biological postmodernists, for whom such distinctions are arbitrary and subject to redefinition as required. Thus, in the case of GM crops, since no one seeks to restrict scientists' experimentation on plants but only the release into the environment, marketing, or public ignorance of the products of this research, it is in the interest of agribusiness owners to obscure the difference between GM and traditional crops. In contrast, since there are objections, for various reasons, to experimentation on human embryos, it is in the interest of those who wish to do so to reinforce any distinction between embryos destined to develop into persons and those used in the laboratory. Louis Guenin, for example, calls any in vitro–produced human embryo donated to medicine (even beyond the fourteen-day "pre-embryo" cutoff stipulated by the Warnock Report) an "epidos-embryo"—an embryo for the common good—for which a moral imperative pertains to its utilization.[57]

Under these circumstances and in view of the evolving technology, two important questions present themselves: (1) At what point do manipulations such as cloning and genetic manipulation actually transform an embryo into an artifact, fortifying, if only after the fact, arguments for excluding it from moral consideration for purposes of experimentation or organ harvesting? (2) As increased success with manipulations leads toward the production of full-term clones and GM humans, by what rationalizations will entities whose artifactual nature was asserted in the course of process (1) come to be selectively portrayed as "substantially equivalent" to humans?[58]

The various ways in which human biological entities have been reframed and redefined to accommodate new reproductive technologies and research strategies can be appreciated in the examples that follow.

Clones as Persons and/or Artifacts The report in 1997 of the cloning of a mammal, Dolly the sheep, elicited a burst of enthusiasm from technophilic business executives and politicians hoping to see full-term human clones in their lifetime.[59] Some religious thinkers were quick to give their endorsement to this enterprise. According to Ted Peters, a fellow at the Center for Theology and the Natural Sciences and a professor at Pacific Lutheran Seminary, "Surely, [a cloned human] would be just as much a child of God and loved by God. They would have their individuality, they would have their dignity, and certainly they would have their own souls."[60]

The "certainly" is a little troublesome. No commentators in this vein, secular or religious, addressed the patently artificial character of the cloning process, which involves combining nonviable fragments of two seriously damaged cells, an egg that has had its nucleus extracted and the isolated nucleus of a somatic (differentiated tissue) cell. (Even IVF, opposed by some on the basis of unnaturalness, still employs the material entities that have evolved as part of the human species to produce a human being—an egg and a sperm.) One may ask what ensures the humanity of the resulting assemblage. The ensuing organism may look human (or in Dolly's case, like a sheep), but so, presumably, would one constructed of chemically synthesized egg-cytoplasmic components and nuclei containing synthetic human DNA. Would such manufactured organisms also have souls (assuming these exist) just by virtue of the fact that they looked like people? The DNA of humans and the DNA of chimpanzees have extensive identity along most of their sequences;[61] the synthetic DNA in our hypothetical example could easily be made intermediate between the two species.

For religious believers for whom the notion of a living soul (particularly a human soul) is a regulative concept, the very prospect of creating such mixtures would seem to provide motivation for supporting barriers to certain forms of biological manipulation. As we have seen, however, genetic essentialism and the technological imperative are often sufficient to overcome any qualms along these lines.

The question of how much human DNA is needed to qualify an organism for a soul was not at issue for the biologists Richard Lewontin and the late Stephen Jay Gould, both of whom are known for their opposition to overemphasizing genes as determinants of key human characteristics. Yet when the cloning of a mammal was first announced, each stated that a full-term cloned human would not represent anything unprecedented biologically, since identical twins, a normal part of human communities, are also individuals having the same DNA.[62] Apart from the social novelty of producing people asexually from existing prototypes (which one would imagine to be a compelling distinction for these Marxist-oriented scientists), the conflation of clones with twins seems oddly nonmaterialistic. For one thing, the DNA of differentiated cells is chemically altered compared to that of the fertilized egg.[63] And while the reversal of these alterations when a clonal embryo starts its (usually unsuccessful) developmental trajectory occurs by mobilization of available biochemical processes, these processes, not having been under evolutionary selection to perform this particular function, can only do it in a fortuitous and approximate fashion.

Significantly, both religious commentators such as Peters and secular ones such as Lewontin and Gould seek to erase the differences between clones and "naturals" by taking DNA sequence alone, rather than the species-specific developmental process, as the defining characteristic of the human. It is ironic that genetic essentialism provides their common meeting ground.

Blurring the distinction between humans constructed from portions of damaged cells and humans produced by fertilization will ease the way for acceptance of this form of "reproductive choice" once certain technological glitches are overcome.[64] Scientists who wish to pursue this work in the short term, however, must contend with the significant portion of the public that objects to experimentation on human embryos and whose representatives control the purse strings for research funding. Some of these scientists—such as Rudolf Jaenisch of the Massachusetts Institute of Technology, whose own work in this area has led him to state, "Out of all the animals ever cloned, I'm not sure whether any normal clone has yet been produced"—have emphasized the aberrant nature of clonal embryos and their permanent unsuitability, in the human case, for being brought to full term.[65] Jaenisch has gone so far as to suggest that since "[a] cloned embryo has an exceedingly low potential to ever develop into a normal baby because of the overwhelming problems associated with reproductive cloning. . . . [w]hether the cells that result from this process are a new embryo or simply rejuvenated skin cells is as much a question of philosophy as of science."[66]

Things were now ripe for the biological postmodernists to rush in. In December of 2002 Stanford University announced the establishment of a new Institute for Cancer/Stem Cell Biology and Medicine under the direction of Dr. Irving Weissman. Some of the institute's proposed work with human embryonic stem cells (ES cells) would involve producing customized early-stage embryos in which a cell nucleus from an individual with a genetic condition under investigation (or perhaps later a patient who is a candidate for grafting of ES cell–derived tissues) would be transferred to an egg whose own nucleus had been removed. That is, clonal embryos would be produced—though Stanford was at pains to emphasize that this was not the case. Stanford's official spokesperson was quoted in news reports at the time as stating, "We're not cloning embryos, and we're not going to clone embryos." Of course they were planning to clone embryos, just not bring them to full term. This could have been made clear in a scientifically accurate fashion. Instead, Weissman himself asserted that his planned research was "not even close" to cloning.[67]

At around the same time, the International Society for Stem Cell Research (ISSCR) was established, a self-described "independent, nonprofit organization formed . . . to foster the exchange of information on stem cell research."[68] This organization, in which Irving Weissman serves as an officer, began working to ensure that what developed from an enucleated egg into which a somatic cell nucleus had been inserted was no longer referred to as an "embryo." This term was to be reserved (according to the society's online glossary) exclusively for the product of fertilization of an egg by a sperm. Thus the ISSCR put itself in the position of holding that the entity that gave rise to Dolly the sheep (a "somatic cell nuclear transfer [SCNT] product," in the society's terminology) was not an embryo. The logical conclusion is that Dolly herself was not an actual sheep and that any individuals that might in the future be generated from human SCNT products would not be exactly human.

Contrary to the religious philosophers who asserted that full-term clones would be endowed with souls by a loving God and the Marxists who claimed they were ordinary people no different from twins, one of the major liberal groups that arose in support of ES cell research, the Genetics Policy Institute, characterized efforts to produce full-term clones as a "crime against humanity."[69] Its objections, however, which relate primarily to the safety of the procedure, could potentially be allayed by successes with animal cloning.

The choice of terminology in regard to cloning technology, like that concerning GM crops, has large financial implications. During a 2004 ballot initiative campaign to direct the state of California to provide more than $3 billion in funding for stem cell research, a group of individuals including Stanford Nobel laureate Paul Berg unsuccessfully sued a coalition of the initiative's opponents to prevent them from referring to SCNT products as "cloned embryos." One of their arguments was that since the prospective recipients of the funds had no intention of implanting the SCNT products in a woman's uterus, the products were thereby not embryos. The attribution of inherent material properties to an object by virtue of the intentions of its possessor is, strictly speaking, magical thinking.

However, biological postmodernism provides an equally apt way of conceptualizing this maneuver.

Chimeras as . . . What? As seen above, despite the manipulations necessary to produce genetically engineered crops and clonal embryos, the resulting organisms retain enough of the identity of their originating species to leave at least a rhetorical opening to anyone who would define them as natural. In fact, the extraordinary resistance of species character to being altered by genetic manipulation (see next section) conflicts with the expectations of neo-Darwinism, the standard model of evolutionary change (see next section). It represents a constraint on what biotechnology can accomplish, but it is a surmountable constraint if the technologist is inclined to take things further.

Chimeras are animals in which species identity may be blurred beyond recognition. The term can be used for any organism that contains grafted tissues originating in another species. But whereas an organism that has undergone its full course of development will not be changed in any essential fashion by such grafts, if performed during embryogenesis the effect can be more profound. An extreme version of animal chimerism can be brought about by mixing cells from early developmental stages of different species of animal to create a composite embryo. If brought to full term, the resulting body contains organs and tissues that are a mosaic of cells of the originating species. This is the technique that was first used successfully in the 1980s to produce "geeps," animals that had an appearance and biological character part way between goats and sheep.[70]

Unlike hybrid animals such as the mule (the outcome of the mating of a donkey and a horse), chimeras produced by embryo-cell mixing are not infertile but they also do not reproduce their own kind. Female geeps produce both goat and sheep eggs; males geeps produce a mixture of goat and sheep sperm. The mating of two geeps may produce a goat, a sheep, or a goat-sheep hybrid (which is not viable) but not another geep. Embryo chimeras are therefore true biological artifacts—organisms of indeterminate species identity whose progeny are nonetheless typical members of recognizable species.

Though unquestionably artifactual, embryo chimeras did not mobilize postmodernist reframing exercises until humans were put into the mix. In 1998, the report that a U.S. patent had been applied for on "chimeric embryos and animals containing human cells" elicited the unusual public pronouncement from an official of the U.S. Patent and Trademark Office that nothing so offensive to public morality would be permitted to be patented.[71] The patent application was a preemptive ploy to bring the technical possibility of making human-animal chimeras to the public's attention, and at the time it was announced, some scientists portrayed it as a slander on their profession.[72] Philip Leder, the biologist who, a decade earlier, had obtained the first patent on a transgenic animal, the OncoMouse, stated on the National Public Radio program *All Things Considered*, "The creation of chimeras is an outlandish undertaking. No one is trying to do it at present, certainly not involving human beings."[73] But a few years later a group of Rockefeller University scientists announced that they intended to produce human-mouse embryo chimeras as an aid to studying the potential of human embryonic stem cells to develop into various tissue types, and in June 2006 they reported their success in constructing embryo chimeras containing human and mouse cells.[74]

Production of chimeras in which human neural stem cells are introduced into the brains of embryonic monkeys or mice are also under way. One of the investigators performing these studies is Irving Weissman of Stanford University, mentioned above. Weissman has stated that he would like to construct a mouse that has a brain composed entirely of human cells. When questioned in a Public Broadcasting Service report whether "scientists like yourself working in this field [are] treading through a legal and ethical minefield when you do this kind of research," Weissman replied, "Absolutely. It's a good thing we're treading on ethical grounds. It means we're getting close to important issues."[75] The implication of this seems to be that the transgressiveness of the proposed manipulations is desirable in itself, a doctrine best known as a tenet of postmodernist art.

The malleability of species identity and its limits are perennial elements in discussions of the future of the human species.[76] Emergence of human subspecies that may eventually have little to do with or have an antagonistic relation to one another is anticipated by both advocates and critics of human applications of gene manipulation analogous to those used in GM crops.[77] Whether or not a breach of species boundaries or change in species nature can be accomplished by these methods, it is unquestionable that they can be achieved by chimerism.

Chimerism therefore provides a reference point *in extremis* for evaluating the report on human-nonhuman neural grafting described at the beginning of this paper, a report that "unanimously rejected ethical objections grounded on unnaturalness or crossing species boundaries."[78] What lies down this increasingly mainstream biological postmodernist road can be judged from a catalogue essay by Christoph Cox for the 2005 art exhibit "Becoming Animal" at the Massachusetts Museum of Contemporary Art. Cox discusses the writings of the philosophers Gilles Deleuze and Félix Guattari for whom, he claims:

> there are no essential differences within nature, no absolute differences between minerals, vegetables, animals, and humans. Rather, matter is a vast continuum, a field of virtual forces, intensities, thresholds and powers that, under particular conditions, is actualized in the things and bodies we know. But these things and bodies are not fixed, stable, or given once and for all. They themselves are bundles of forces and capabilities that are constantly undergoing changes prompted by encounters with other entities into which they enter into relationships.[79]

Neo-Darwinian evolutionary theory makes the strong assertion that even in the natural course of things, species have vague boundaries and are always on their way to becoming something else (see next section).[80] However, an increasing number of evolutionary biologists and philosophers of biology have suggested instead that species are "natural kinds." This is not because they have preordained essences but because they exhibit causal homeostatic mechanisms that enforce their type-specificity.[81] If species barriers are real, then, not ephemeral or chimerical, it becomes reasonable to consider their preservation, like the preservation of wilderness areas, wetlands, languages, and species themselves, as a positive value. I return to this in the concluding section. In the penultimate one I describe how biological postmodernism relates to current ferment in evolutionary theory and how this is playing out in the conflicts in the United States around the teaching of evolution.

THE EVOLUTION WARS

The fact that organic evolution occurred and continues to occur is as solid as any conclusion science has yet produced. To take issue with this, considering the interconnected biological, chemical, geological, and physical facts that enter into our knowledge of evolution, is to take issue with much of modern science. Significantly, though, many people of the developed world, particularly in the United States, continue to reject a naturalistic account of the origination of complex biological systems and the genesis of species.

Skepticism about evolution appears to be based more on received views influenced by religious belief than on the persuasive force of contemporary antievolutionary counternarratives. Nonetheless, there exist several schools of thought that represent themselves as scientific and seek to capitalize on inadequacies or flaws in various versions of the account of mainstream biology.[82] While "Young Earth creationism" adheres closely to biblical accounts of the genesis of the world and its creatures, holding that life was established on Earth around six thousand years ago, the more recently established "intelligent design" movement generally accepts the age of the Earth as determined by science and even allows a role for evolution in molding many biological features (the overall structure of the bodies and appendages of insects, humans, and other many-celled organisms, for example) but asserts that other features, such the flagella, the microscopic beating whips on the surface of cells, are "irreducibly complex" and can only have been generated by a "designer" located outside the frame of naturalistic thought.[83]

The mainstream secular characterization of this debate is that it represents a clear choice between rationalism and irrationalism. However, few contemporary religionists, even the most fundamentalist, question mechanistic and other naturalistic accounts of observable phenomena. This is clearly a departure from traditional cultures in which animistic explanations of things like fire and the weather were standard. Nor do most religious believers in the developed world reject out of hand medicines and surgical procedures based on the conception of the living human organism as a material object that obeys the laws of physics and chemistry. And whatever they may think about how a cell's flagella originated, the idea that its motion occurs by standard physicochemical processes is uncontroversial to the large majority of religionists.

Why, then, do so many people reject an evolutionary account of the origination of complex biological systems? First, it must be recognized that in contemplating the origins of the world as we know it, most members of advanced technological societies, including a fair number of scientists, are comfortable bringing supernatural causation into the picture at some point, usually in the distant past.[84] So it is not simply a matter of who believes in science and who believes in divine intervention (most people seeming to believe in an amalgam of the two) but whether the scientific narrative on offer is persuasive enough to force people to reevaluate and possibly abandon their received worldview.

Second, for most people, experienced life is more important than what occurred three billion or even six thousand years ago. People's experience of organismal types—wild and domestic animals and plants—focuses and indeed depends on the constancy of the species' identities, not the possibility that they are on their way to changing into something else.[85] Excluding perhaps existentialist philosophers and constitutional cynics, the feeling that life is fundamentally meaningless is usually a source of unhappiness. It should therefore not be expected that biological postmodernist jibes, such as the essay in the *Guardian* on the evolution wars by the environmental writer George Monbiot titled "A Life with No Purpose," would be effective in recruiting the general citizenry to an evolutionary perspective. The gist of this article is contained in the following passages:

> [A]s soon as you consider the implications [of Darwin's theory], you must cease to believe that either Life or life are affected by purpose. . . . Darwinian evolution tells us that we are incipient compost: assemblages of complex molecules that—for no greater purpose than to secure sources of energy against competing claims—have developed the ability to speculate. After a few score years, the molecules disaggregate and return whence they came. Period.[86]

Such ultimate questions are, of course, irrelevant to the criteria that most people use in judging whether their lives are meaningful. Moreover, Darwinism itself, which concerns populations of organisms, not molecules, has nothing to do with these issues except in an ideological sense (see below). The failure to persuade of such thumbs-in-the-eye as Monbiot's or similar ones by the arch-Darwinist Richard Dawkins[87] is therefore not surprising, and this is not just a matter of the obduracy of fundamentalists.

In making the case for a scientific alternative to traditional accounts of natural phenomena with people who do not have a big incentive to relinquish what their parents and churches have told them, it is helpful at least to have a good theory.[88] Does Darwin's theory of evolution by natural selection meet this standard?

The Problem of Evolutionary Innovation   Incremental changes in an existing structure—the alterations in beak shape of the finches that so impressed Charles Darwin during his voyage to the Galapagos Islands, for instance—can indeed be attributed to natural selection.[89] Even most creationists do not deny this. But when it comes to the *innovation* of entirely new structures ("morphological novelties") such as bodies or body axes organized as segments (seen in earthworms, insects, and vertebrates such as humans but not in jellyfish or octopuses), or the uniquely structured hands and feet of tetrapods (four-limbed animals, a subset of vertebrates), Darwin's mechanism comes up short. This is a reality that is increasingly acknowledged by biologists, particularly those working in the field of evolutionary developmental biology, or "EvoDevo."[90]

Contrary to the expectations of the standard Darwinian model, the fossil record is deficient in transitional forms between major innovations.[91] And although our current knowledge of the cellular and genetic mechanisms of the development of animal forms is relatively sophisticated, there are few plausible scenarios involving gradual changes in developmental processes that would take an organism from one adult form (e.g., an unsegmented worm) to one embodying an innovation (a segmented worm).

While evolutionary innovation is therefore a conspicuous problem for Darwinian gradualism, more satisfactory scientific accounts of this process have emerged from recent work in developmental biology. Significantly, these alternatives do not conform to the notion that form and structure in the living world result from a purely opportunistic process of culling among random variants, with the only criterion for evolutionary persistence being "whatever works." The belief that a scientific-materialist worldview implies this second possibility was termed "Darwinian fundamentalism" by the late Stephen Jay Gould.[92] Biological postmodernism draws sustenance from Darwinian fundamentalism because of its allied supposition that living systems are arbitrary assemblages of gene-determined traits, with no preferred (i.e., "natural") forms or routes of change.

The example of segmentation in vertebrates illustrates the scientifically more incisive view of innovation that is currently emerging from evolutionary developmental biology. Living tissues are physical materials, albeit highly complex ones. The recognition that materials can undergo abrupt changes in organization due to their inherent physical properties is quite familiar from everyday experience: a violin string can vibrate or not, depending on minor differences in the tension under which it is held, and water can form waves or vortices depending on the directionality of minor agitations. In analogous fashion, certain networks of interacting genes and their protein and RNA products in embryonic tissues can act as "biochemical clocks," which means that the levels of several of the proteins produced by the tissue fluctuate periodically with time. Scientists have shown that segmentation in the vertebrate body is based on such molecular clocks. Successive waves of the involved molecules sweep across the length of the embryo from one end to the other, affecting tissue cohesion in a periodic fashion, thereby producing a spatial periodicity (i.e., segments) in the tissue.[93] Since whether or not a given molecular-genetic network behaves as an oscillator depends on small variations in the constituent genes and their products, segmentation, as a morphological novelty, can have emerged multiple times, in a relatively sudden fashion, from unsegmented ancestors of modern segmented animals.[94]

Segmentation is just one case of how the origination of phenotypic novelties can be understood by taking account of the physical nature of developing systems. Others are the formation in aggregates of cells of layers, interior spaces, tubes, and branched structures, in particular, all the constructional features that enter into animal bodies and their organs.[95] In general, if living tissues are physical materials, their forms and behaviors must be subject to forces and determinants apart from their genes; indeed, they must exhibit condition-dependent variability, a phenomenon that has been termed "phenotypic plasticity." Another way of expressing this is that an organism's properties, particularly at early stages in its evolution, are not uniquely determined by its genes.

The EvoDevo view of organismal innovation thus implies that disparate phenotypes inherent to an organism's constitution at a given stage of its evolution can be alternatively triggered by minor genetic changes or even environmental changes.[96] In evolutionary terms, natural selection, acting in an incremental fashion on these alternative developmental pathways, can reinforce their realization and make them independent of the original triggers. The remarkable stability or "robustness" of the phenotype, particularly in animal species, against environmental change and even much genetic alteration is thought to be the result of this progressive evolutionary reinforcement of developmental trajectories, termed "canalization."[97] In addition, if the "self-organization" of living tissues (of which the molecular clock phenomenon mentioned above is just one example) was efficacious in originating and innovating forms during early evolution, then the rapid burst of morphological evolution of animals that occurred more than half a billion years ago (the "Cambrian explosion") becomes much more understandable.[98]

The real possibility that the evolutionary origination and complexification of organismal features has been the result of a plasticity-based "phenotype first, genetic programs later" scenario, rather than the gradualist, gene-driven processes of neo-Darwinism, makes the whole enterprise of improving phenotypes of plants and animals by genetic tinkering (see previous sections) scientifically naïve. Natural selection has indeed led to the phenotypes of modern-day organisms being resistant to perturbation. But as complexity theory has shown us, while evolved systems are typically highly robust to perturbations encountered (and fortified against) during the evolutionary process by which they were generated, they are often exquisitely vulnerable to unforeseen disturbances.[99]

Hegemony of the Darwinian-Mendelian Synthesis Phenotypic plasticity, a relatively common property of developing organisms that was appreciated by many nineteenth-century biologists and provided the basis for Jean-Baptiste Lamarck's (generally mischaracterized and not entirely incorrect) pre-Darwinian evolutionary concepts, is only now reentering biology after becoming an all-but-taboo subject in evolutionary theory during the twentieth century.[100] Darwin's theory, which holds that the competition between individuals marginally different from one another with respect to the small inherited morphological, physiological, or behavioral variations encountered in any natural population has been sufficient to generate the entire array of biologically distinct types seen on the face of planet, avoided cases in which the same organism could take on different forms under different conditions.

Indeed, the main conceptual effect of Darwin's theory of evolution by natural selection was to marginalize the concept of organismal plasticity and, once the theory's scientific hegemony was established, to consign all the real phenomena that fit this description to a theoretical limbo. Furthermore, by making the claim (in the first chapter of *The Origin of Species*) that the small effects that can be brought about by domestication are of precisely the same kind as those that have driven large-scale ("macro") evolution, that is, that the natural (natural selection) could be understood by means of the artificial (artificial selection), Darwin himself laid the foundation for the elision of the natural and artifactual that we have seen pervading modern, technology-oriented biology.[101]

The other major scientific reason for the marginalization of the concept of organismal plasticity was the successes in applying the Mendelian paradigm early in the twentieth century. The nineteenth-century monk Gregor Mendel, in performing his remarkable experiments on various plants, carefully picked traits to study whose different versions were uniquely tied to alternative states of specific genes. Much genetic research in the first half of the twentieth century, using a similar strategy, also identified strict gene-trait correlations (particularly with regard to simple biochemical pathways) in other organisms. This led to a deep-seated conviction on the part of most biologists that the Mendelian mode of inheritance was essentially applicable to all traits in all organisms at all stages of their evolutionary histories. But even Mendel himself, who cautiously described his most famous findings as "the law valid for peas," did not suggest this, and it is demonstrably not the case.[102]

The Mendelian paradigm deals with factors, or genes, that are associated with biological characters. As such, it focuses on the *logic* of intergenerational transmission of traits (the alternative forms of characters) rather than the *mechanisms* of character generation. When joined with Darwinism in the form of the "neo-Darwinian synthesis," it gave rise to a theory of evolution concerned with little other than the distribution and fate of genes at the populational level. The supposed ability of changes in gene frequencies to account for all significant features of living organisms is considered by the philosopher Daniel Dennett to be one of the most powerful ideas ever produced by science.[103]

Other strains of early-twentieth-century biological science, represented by such figures as the British theorist of the physical basis of form generation D'Arcy W. Thompson, the Soviet evolutionary developmental biologist B. Zavadovsky, the African-American reproductive biologist E. E. Just, the Soviet geneticist I. I. Schmalhausen, the British developmental geneticist C. H. Waddington, and the German-born U.S. developmental physiologist Richard Goldschmidt, were, in contrast, not exclusively genocentric. These scientists sought to bridge the gap between inheritance and form by bringing physical, physiological, and environmental determinants of organismal form into a more comprehensive "systems" approach to scientific understanding of developmental and evolutionary processes and phenomena and the connections among them.[104] During the emergence of gene-centered biology in the mid-century, the quantitative techniques and computational methods for management of complexity that are required for the pursuit of systems biology were yet to be invented. Consequently, the successes of the Mendelian approach in its relevant domains undermined any motivation in the scientific mainstream to consider an expanded framework.

Cold War politics also played an important part in the nearly total suppression of the systems approach in mid- to late-twentieth-century biology in the United States and Western Europe. The adoption by the Soviet Union of the anti-Mendelian policy of Lysenkoism in agriculture and then in research biology and the purging of geneticists from the scientific institutes presented the capitalist powers with a vivid example of the corruption of science by a command economy.[105] The Soviet scientific managers had initially appealed to a theory of evolution that incorporated phenotypic plasticity, an approach that had a legitimate warrant in sophisticated postrevolutionary philosophy of science. And although the failures of Lysenkoist agricultural policy were hardly worse than those of the Mendelism-based agricultural policies earlier on, Soviet biology was severely damaged by Lysenkoism.[106]

While the propagandistic uses made of the Soviet Union's descent into Lysenkoism thus had considerable force and effectiveness, the resulting distortion of Western biology by the consequent digging in of Mendelian exclusivity, with dismissal and even derision by mainstream scientists of alternative systems views, is rarely noted. So entrenched was this way of thinking that despite the fact that the concrete accounts of developmental processes beginning to emerge during the last decades of the twentieth century (such as the segmentation example described above) employed genetic methodologies and mechanisms in conjunction with conditionally acting physical mechanisms (e.g., cell-cell adhesion, molecular diffusion, biochemical oscillation), the entire enterprise has nonetheless been portrayed, inaccurately, as the triumph of the Mendelian paradigm.[107]

Evolutionary Postmodernism Lysenkoism represented an ideological distortion of evolutionary biology that may be thought of as characteristic of top-down socialism: environmental determinism gone wild, living systems with no inherent nature other than a capacity to be molded to the aims of social managers. Although this view, like the political system that engendered it, has vanished, the genetic-determinist ideology that it both reacted to and provoked, in its parceling of life into separable, swappable, and most importantly, patentable modules, comports well with the worldview of advanced capitalism.

Working in the classic naturalist mode of Darwin himself, who was concerned with the inheritance of traits rather than genes, a number of scientific and popular writers have presented elegant and persuasive (to those inclined to be persuaded) accounts of the role of natural selection in the molding of particular characteristics and propensities in the plant and animal worlds.[108] As with Darwin's original theory, they make no attempt to deal with the aspects of life that need to be explained in order to recruit to an evolutionary narrative people who would just as soon hold onto their religious beliefs concerning where life came from, why it is organized the way it is, and how novel forms originate.

Biological postmodernism, however, drawing on a late-twentieth- to early-twenty-first-century gene-centered evolutionary ideology (what the philosopher Mary Midgley has called "evolution as a religion" and the historian and philosopher of science Michael Ruse, "evolutionism"), purports to answer all these questions.[109] But it does so with a wave of the hand: a theory (neo-Darwinism) in which the forces generating biological variation and the natural constraints on those variations are barely relevant. According to a prominent neo-Darwinian theorist, "our understanding of the molecular basis of development—however fascinating and important in revealing the hidden history of what has happened in evolution—sheds little light on what variation is potentially available for the use of selection."[110] The neo-Darwinian literature evinces little bad conscience about this state of affairs.

With their genetic-determinist blinders on, standard evolutionary accounts do not draw on the novelty-generating phenomena of large-scale phenotypic conversion of a population by external factors (seen even in present-day organisms like plants and social microbes) and evolutionary change occurring in preferred directions due to the material properties of developmental systems.[111] What is offered instead is an accounting of the distribution of gene variants in populations over time and space, plus the assertion that such gene changes fully explain phenotypic changes (because what else is there?). But this is inadequate. Evolutionary theory conceived in this fashion will be unable to answer several questions—for example, which features of an organism are changing over the course of evolution, and which of these changes amount to minor variations in phenotype or else to morphological novelties, new species, or even new phyla.

Genetic-determinist ideology, moreover, has had cultural ramifications that extend well beyond its belatedly loosening grip on scientific research. Given neo-Darwinism's doctrine that genes determine all biological properties and that all evolutionary changes are thus reducible to genetic changes, it is not surprising that, once genetic engineering became feasible in the 1980s, genes also came to be seen as the medium by which biological characteristics could be transferred from one type of organism to another. The evolutionary biologist E. O. Wilson, for instance, quotes approvingly the following statement from a talk by the entomologist Thomas Eisner:

> A biological species, nowadays, must be regarded as more than a unique conglomerate of genes. As a consequence of recent advances in genetic engineering, it must be viewed also as a depository of genes that are potentially transferable. A species is not merely a hard-bound volume of the library of nature. It is also a loose-leaf book, whose individual pages, the genes, might be available for selective transfer and modification of other species.[112]

More recently, a news report in the journal *Nature*, focusing on a newly identified gene whose unknown function is, according to one of the scientists involved, a matter of "wild speculation," is titled "Homing in on the Genes for Humanity" simply because the gene has changed rapidly over the course of human evolution.[113]

This view of life ignores everything about the context-dependence of gene function within organisms, including the fact that the role of an identical gene in two different kinds of organisms or in a given type of organism at two different stages of its evolutionary history can vary dramatically. The scientific literature is replete with examples of genetically engineered bacteria, plants, mice, and farm animals having properties different from predicted ones.

The creationists, for their part, have smaller fish to fry: the presence and operation of nanoscale molecular machines within the cell present genuine challenges to neo-Darwinian incrementalist scenarios. Even Francis Crick, the codiscoverer of the structure of DNA, was not convinced that conditions on the prebiotic Earth were compatible with the chemical evolution of the genetic material.[114] In the quarter century since Crick first expressed these doubts, increased knowledge of the complexity of the nanomolecular systems within the cell has only made the question of origination and innovation at this level more puzzling.

But rather than intelligent design's facile positing of a nanoengineer God, what is called for are new scientific principles of self-organization on the small scale. There are earlier precedents for new theories emerging to organize and explain anomalous findings. The structure of individual atoms, for example, as manifested in their interactions with light upon being heated, was completely enigmatic until Erwin Schrödinger and Werner Heisenberg independently developed the unprecedented and counterintuitive laws of quantum mechanics in 1925. The best physicists of the early twentieth century acknowledged that the old ideas were not adequate to these phenomena. Present-day neo-Darwinists provide a poor contrast insofar as they persist in the hand-waving consignment of all problematic aspects of the origination of complex subcellular entities to the putative universal solvent of random variation and natural selection.

As with the pressure to foist genetically engineered foods on the public and the drive to overcome reservations about the production of modified human embryos and quasi-humans, the advocacy of the standard concept of evolution is too often characterized by a disdainful attitudinizing toward received beliefs and value systems that, give or take where to draw exact lines of demarcation, are actually shared by most people on both sides of these issues. All three efforts are bound together by biological postmodernism, an antitheory of biological change that attributes agency to genes rather than to the complex systems that contain them and, making little or no attempt to provide accounts of why organisms have the properties they do, denies the existence of "the natural" as a regulative category. The scientific mainstream, which should rightly be prevailing in the evolution debate (since the living world is manifestly a product of evolution), is so committed to neo-Darwinism's "context of no context" that they are barely holding on in their attempts to prevent supernatural accounts of the history of life from being placed on par with naturalistic ones in the educational system.[115]

Conclusion

We are misled about the character of the world we live in if we believe that the changes we can induce in organisms with our recently invented biological technologies are the same as the formative processes that brought about organisms in the first place or caused them to diversify over the long course of evolution. We are similarly deceived if we imagine that knowledge of the genetic constitution of organisms is all that is needed to make and remake them without doing harm. As we see above, however, these false notions of life, its nature, and its history are definitely in the air, and they have increasingly been dominating the discourse on agricultural and biomedical policy in the United States. A recent commentary by the physicist Freeman Dyson in *Technology Review* encapsulates every aspect of biological postmodernism:

> The epoch of species competition came to an end about 10 thousand years ago when a single species, *Homo sapiens*, began to dominate and reorganize the biosphere. Since that time, cultural evolution has replaced biological evolution as the driving force of change. . . . And now, in the last 30 years, *Homo sapiens* has revived the ancient pre-Darwinian practice of horizontal gene transfer, moving genes easily from microbes to plants and animals, blurring the boundaries between species. We are moving rapidly into the post-Darwinian era, when species will no longer exist, and the evolution of life will again be communal. . . . In the post-Darwinian era, biotechnology will be domesticated. There will be do-it-yourself kits for gardeners, who will use gene transfer to breed new varieties of roses and orchids. Also, biotech games for children, played with real eggs and seeds rather than with images on a screen. Genetic engineering, once it gets into the hands of the general public, will give us an explosion of biodiversity. Designing genomes will be a new art form, as creative as painting or sculpture. Few of the new creations will be masterpieces, but all will bring joy to their creators and diversity to our fauna and flora.[116]

Possibly his avowed Christian faith has convinced Dyson that the deity would not let us mess things up too badly. A century of experience with increasingly powerful technologies, however, suggests that such belief is ill placed.

Beyond Freeman Dyson's dangerously naïve but sweet-tempered invocation of a genetic utopia lies biological postmodernism's "hammers of the witches." Like the so-named fifteenth-century handbook for prosecuting evil-doers, *Malleus maleficarum*, this recent genre seeks to stigmatize critics of its defended doctrine (genetic engineering, in this case) by accusations of nature worship.[117] Although writers in this mode tend themselves to assume a worshipful stance toward "science" (actually a set of sometimes conflicting practices rather than a uniform entity) primarily, many claim, for its supposed capacity to criticize itself, they seem to be particularly disinclined to confront scientific-based criticisms of their preferred technologies. Of course, warnings about nuclear waste and weapon proliferation, chemical pollution, environmental degradation, loss of animal habitats and species, and global warming (all products or outcomes of the best science and technologies of their times) were first raised by people knowledgeable in these fields. But instead of inviting scrutiny of genetic technologies, modern-day hammerers such as Princeton University's Lee Silver and Henry I. Miller, a former U.S. Food and Drug Administration official and a current fellow of Stanford University's corporate-funded Hoover Institution, prefer caricature and contempt. Miller, for example, refers to scientist-critics of the genetic engineering of crops, for example, as "professional agitators."[118] It is this arrogant and defensive attitude of its promoters more than its scientific misconceptions that highlights the ideological nature of the postmodern take on biology.

Finally, as welcome as genuine scientific examination of the latest commercial fixes might be, judgments concerning the wisdom of proceeding with one or another transformative technology raise issues well beyond those discussed in the present paper. Among the most important are the irrationalities of the capitalist system as a whole in its relation to the natural world.[119] But even confining ourselves to the scientific questions discussed here, it is clear that many of the debates around the potentially positive and negative consequences of genetic and other biotechnologies involve concepts of nature and the natural that extend beyond any one discipline. With respect to the biological world, knowledge of how organisms are organized, how they develop, and how their organization and development have evolved is the necessary base for understanding the nature of living things. Only with such understanding can we reasonably discuss what might be desirable to keep or to change. Unfortunately, classic neo-Darwinism, with its excessive theoretical reliance on the agency of genes, is not a reliable guide to the nature of life. Only as a multileveled, integrative theory of biological organization and change becomes more established in the public arena will it become possible to overcome the paradoxical dualism of our time, in which different groups on the one hand exaggerate and on the other reject the efficacy of biological science, while transformation of living nature proceeds apace.[120]

Synthetic Biology: Theological Questions about Biological Engineering

Ronald Cole-Turner

The disappearance of nature as a normative framework for human thought and action is nowhere more tangibly felt than in the context of contemporary biological engineering. Biological engineering, or "synthetic biology," as it is often called to distinguish it from genetic engineering, functions precisely on the boundary between natural and artificial, living and nonliving, organic and synthetic. On the one hand, like any technology, synthetic biology must work in and with nature. It operates entirely within the sphere of living nature: biological systems from metabolic pathways to ecosystems. But the whole point of synthetic biology is to synthesize nature, to replace it with an engineered surrogate. When we take up the field of synthetic biology, nature may still be the matrix and the premise but it is hardly the norm or the telos of our actions.

The first section of this paper attempts to define and locate the field of synthetic biology within the context of recent work in the biological sciences. The second section describes a broader cultural and social context in which synthetic biology is being developed, first by reviewing some of the ethics discussion that has already arisen about this new field and then by turning to theological considerations about its religious and philosophical implications.

What Is Synthetic Biology?

The goal of synthetic biology, simply put, is "to extend or modify the behavior of organisms and engineer them to perform new tasks."[1] Another researcher in the field describes the goal this way: "to expand our understanding of biomolecular networks and enhance our ability to engineer novel cellular behavior."[2] Most simply stated, the goal is "to understand and program cell function."[3] Or in more journalistic terms:

> This nascent field has three major goals: One, learn about life by building it, rather than by tearing it apart. Two, make genetic engineering worthy of its name—a discipline that continuously improves by standardizing its previous creations and recombining them to make new and more sophisticated systems. And three, stretch the boundaries of life and of machines until the two overlap to yield truly programmable organisms.[4]

In other words, "the vision is undeniably grand: think of it as Life, version 2.0."[5] The aim of synthetic biology is to reduce organisms to their simplest organic components, add newly created organic components to the mix, and reassemble the parts into novel organisms.

Though the goal of synthetic biology is somewhat straightforward, it is a field still searching for a definition, primarily because the field is divided into two distinct and competing approaches. According to a recent summary by leading researchers in the field, "Synthetic biologists come in two broad classes. One uses unnatural molecules to reproduce emergent behaviours from natural biology, with the goal of creating artificial life. The other seeks interchangeable parts from natural biology to assemble into systems that function unnaturally."[6] For researchers in the first class or group (which includes the authors of the preceding sentences), the primary challenge of synthetic biology is to synthesize novel biological components. For those in the second group, the challenge is to catalogue natural biological components or parts and use these parts to create entirely new functions within organisms or whole new organisms. The rivalry between the two camps is not so great as to prevent collaboration or vigorous competition, nor is it likely to prevent convergence between the two approaches in the future. It is, however, so significant that it results in two rather distinct definitions of the field, each with its own history. According to researchers in the first group, synthetic biology "attempts to recreate in unnatural chemical systems the emergent properties of living systems."[7] No one knows, for example, what might happen if the selection pressures of Darwinian evolution were brought to bear upon synthetic DNA. For group 1 synthetic biologists, the field is *synthetic* because biological parts such as DNA are synthesized or engineered by humans and their machines.

Those scientists who focus on synthetic biology as the synthesis of new biological components claim that synthetic biology began in the early 1960s, even before genetic engineering.[8] Genetic engineering, if strictly defined, refers to genetic recombination—moving chunks of natural DNA from one location to another across species lines. This was achieved for the first time in the early 1970s and has been central to most biotechnology since that time. According to group 1 synthetic biologists, "synthetic biology is older than recombination technology."[9] When the technology of recombination arrived in the 1970s, many in the field saw it as more promising than synthetic biology because recombination offered the prospect of moving large segments of DNA that contained many genes whose functions were thought to be understood. Simply move them to the new context, it was thought, and the transplanted genes will work as before. Because it was generally believed that compared to DNA synthesis, genetic manipulation via DNA recombination would be "faster and more cost effective," biotechnology turned toward recombinant techniques.[10] Biologists from both groups agree that genetic engineering is an early and transitional strategy and that it has largely failed to deliver on what its proponents promised.

Even so, DNA synthesis technology has continued to advance, although out of the limelight. Researchers have learned to achieve faster synthesis of longer strands at lower cost. Not only that, but some truly novel and surprising advances have been made, for instance when Steven A. Benner's group learned in the 1980s not just to synthesize the analogue of natural DNA but to synthesize a wholly new type, using novel chemicals. In effect, they "created DNA containing two artificial genetic 'letters' in addition to the four that appear in life as we know it."[11] Natural DNA consists of four bases or letters in the genetic code, the familiar A, C, T, and G. Benner's group developed the ability to use two other bases never (to anyone's knowledge) used before by nature, to integrate these into DNA strands, and to develop systems by which these novel DNA codes are capable of drawing upon more than the standard (natural) repertoire of twenty amino acids to generate novel or unnatural proteins. More recently, researchers led by Peter G. Schultz "developed cells (containing normal DNA) that generate unnatural amino acids and string them together to make novel proteins."[12]

It is important to note the significance of not just DNA but RNA synthesis. A key function of RNA is to carry genetic information from the nucleus to the cytoplasm, where the "messenger RNA" (mRNA), translates the DNA code into the assembly instructions for proteins. Synthetic mRNA may have the potential to generate wholly new forms of proteins. In addition to mRNA, the cell depends upon nonmessenger or noncoding RNA (ncRNA) to perform many essential cellular functions. These include "splicing and editing RNA, modifying rRNA (ribosomal RNA), catalyzing biochemical reactions and regulating gene expression." Precisely because RNA molecules "play important and diverse regulatory roles in the cell by virtue of their interaction with other nucleic acids, proteins, and small molecules," RNA synthesis is attractive to researchers in synthetic biology. Compared to DNA, RNA is more "naturally versatile": "The causal relationship between sequence, structure and function significantly affects the interaction of RNA molecules with proteins, metabolites and other nucleic acids, making RNA a malleable and attractive molecule to drive programmable function."[13]

Group 2 synthetic biologists, coming more recently to the field of synthetic biology, are often informed by prior experience in other fields of engineering. They are like builders who have discovered new bricks, which some in this research community have dubbed "BioBricks." Biology, especially after the stunning successes of twentieth-century molecular biology, is a storehouse or parts store loaded with a completely unused set of engineering materials, the biological components of living systems. "This community seeks to extract from living systems interchangeable parts that might be tested, validated as construction units, and reassembled to create devices that might (or might not) have analogues in living systems."[14] The parts might be familiar (natural, in a way), but the organism into which they are put becomes, by their insertion, a novelty, an artifactual synthesis. Group 2 researchers give the word *synthesis* quite different meaning than do group 1 synthetic biologists. The component parts are not synthesized but extracted, purified, simplified, and rationalized with catalogue numbers and engineering specifications. "The parts come from natural living systems (that is, they are biological); their assembly is, however, unnatural" or *synthetic.*[15]

In this respect, group 2 synthetic biologists are indebted more to early efforts at recombinant DNA technology or genetic engineering than to the early attempts at DNA synthesis. Drew Endy quotes a 1978 comment by Waclaw Szybalski and A. M. Skalka: "The work on restriction nucleases not only permits us easily to construct recombinant DNA molecules and to analyze individual genes, but also has led us to the new era of 'synthetic biology.'" Nearly three decades later, Endy notes, despite all the successes, "the engineering of useful synthetic biological systems [is] still an expensive, unreliable and *ad hoc* research process," and certainly not yet *engineering* in the strict sense.[16]

Two papers, both published early in 2000, are often cited by group 2 researchers as the pioneering work in their field. In the first, Timothy Gardner and colleagues reported on their work with the bacterium *E. coli* to build a kind of on/off or toggle switch into the living cell. "The design is simple: two promoters and three genes. When the black gene is active, the gray gene and the reporter gene are silenced," and vice versa. Now:

> imagine if the reporter gene were exchanged with a biologically functional gene. Then a production facility could turn the secretion of a biomedical product on and off that otherwise would be toxic to the cells. Or, perhaps the cells could monitor waste sewage from a factory to detect violations of environmental laws.[17]

The other paper published in 2000, appearing in the same issue of *Nature* as Gardner's, is by Elowitz and Leibler.[18] It reports on what they call a "repressilator," modified cells that dampen down the production of one repressor protein when another is increased.

To the extent that group 2 synthetic biologists approach their work as engineers, they conceptualize by looking at the desired end of their work (a top-down approach) but they proceed in a multitiered bottom-up strategy. There are three levels of biological complexity, all of which are accessible to human intervention: "At the bottom of the hierarchy are DNA, RNA, proteins, and metabolites (including lipids and carbohydrates, amino acids, and nucleotides)." These complex organic chemicals, the fundamental components of living things, are represented as analogous to electronic components such as transistors and resistors. Just as electronic components are connected to create switches, logic gates, and other devices, so these biological components can be assembled to form the middle of the three levels: "The next layer, the device layer, comprises biochemical reactions that regulate the flow of information and manipulate physical process." The third and highest level, analogous to the integrated circuit, has been called the "module layer." Here, "the synthetic biologist uses a diverse library of biological devices to assemble complex pathways that function like integrated circuits." The highest level of engineering complexity, the module, might be thought of as an integrated set of biological functions or devices embedded within a host cell: "A module is a compartmentalized set of devices with interconnected functions that performs complex tasks. In the cell, modules are specific pathways, such as a meta-bolic pathway or a signal transduction pathway."[19]

The goal is control of the device based on an engineering understand-ing of each of the underlying levels: "We must ultimately understand how the function of a module or an entire biological system can be derived from the function of its component parts." To realize this full objective, however, the device-module-cell engineering process must include not just the cell in isolation (because its behavior as a single living cell remains unpredictable) but the cell in its population of similarly engineered cells:

> A biological device has no meaning isolated from a module; a module has no meaning isolated from a cell; a cell has no meaning isolated from a population of cells. This contextual dependence is an essential feature of living systems and is not an impasse, but rather a bridge to the successful engineering of living systems.

Just as the electronic or mechanical engineer may safely ignore quantum indeterminacy, so the future synthetic biologist can ignore the background noise of individual cells and their unpredictable behavior, concentrating instead on the largely predictable and therefore controllable behavior of the population of engineered cells. "As long as a significant number of the cell population performs our desired task, the unpredictability of events occurring at the molecular level should have minimal effect."[20]

Group 2 synthetic biologists describe their core strategies or engineer-ing methodologies as *standardization, decoupling,* and *abstraction.* By *stan-dardization,* they mean the creation of formal and widely agreed descriptions of biological functions and components. This is central to the mission of the Massachusetts Institute of Technology's (MIT's) "Standard Parts List for Synthetic Biology." According to Endy, one of the key de-velopers of the MIT parts list, its purpose is to "specify, organize, charac-terize, document, and freely provide a standard parts list of well-defined biological components that current and future synthetic biologists and en-gineers can use to compose ever more complex systems."[21]

The second strategy, *decoupling,* is based on:

> the idea that it is useful to separate a complicated problem into many sim-pler problems that can be worked on independently. . . . For example, one engineer might develop standard "power supply and chassis" cells that pro-vide known rates of nucleotides, amino acids and other resources to any engineered biological system placed with the cell, independent of the details of the system.[22]

This frees engineers to specialize and then to work together as teams with many specialties.

The third strategy, *abstraction*, is an attempt to cut through or bracket off some of the complexity of biological systems. The idea is to "allow individuals to work at any one level of complexity without regard for the details that define other levels." In the longer term, however, the suggestion is that "the parts and devices that comprise engineered biological systems should probably be redesigned and built anew so that they are simpler to model and easier to use in combination."[23] Elsewhere, group 2 synthetic biology strategies are described as "modularity, standardized structural and functional composition, hierarchical assembly, isolation from other components, characterized behavior, and standardized interfaces."[24]

An example of the work that can be done by the parts-list approach is the creation of a modified version of an existing bacteriophage (a virus that infects a bacterium). The report by Leon Chan and colleagues on work done by Drew Endy's team uses the term "refactoring," which they borrow from computer software engineering, to describe what is meant by modifying the organism. In its original context, refactoring refers to a process by which one software engineer examines the function of a piece of code and writes it in a simpler and more rational or minimal form. Chan and his colleagues examine the DNA code of the bacteriophage T7 and figure out a simpler, more rational substitute. "The goal of refactoring is to improve the internal structure of an existing system for future use, while simultaneously maintaining external system function."[25] As one software engineer improves upon another's work, so the synthetic biologist/ engineer improves upon nature, specifically on the processes of mutation and natural selection. The result is a "refactored" bacteriophage, T7.1, that is 30 percent "better" than nature. Commenting on this work, Knight points out that it "represents a redesign of over 30% of the T7 genome, removes complex gene overlaps, and rationalizes the sequence to ease future modifications."[26]

Not everything that counts as synthetic biology falls within these two groups. One of the more technically successful undertakings has been the attempt to engineer the simplest possible organism at the bacterial level. Where, in the context of these two approaches, do we put such attempts to engineer a minimal genome by removing genes? Researchers led by Craig Venter began not with synthesized DNA or with parts on a shelf but with an existing bacterium, *Mycoplasma genitalium*. This bacterium is among the simplest living things, having "the smallest genome of any organism that can be grown in pure culture. It has a minimal metabolism and little genomic redundancy. Consequently, its genome is expected to be a close approximation to the minimal set of genes needed to sustain bacterial life."[27] Of the 482 protein-coding genes that are found naturally in *M. genitalium*, researchers were able to deactivate one hundred, producing an organism that is in many ways novel and artificial.

Researchers in group 2 seem not to be impressed with DNA synthesis. Referring to work reported by Hamilton O. Smith and colleagues in 2003, in which researchers synthesized the entire DNA of bacteriophage phiX174 in fourteen days,[28] group 2 researchers find little value here in terms of new science because "the artificial sequences were only minor variants of the natural ones."[29] Comparing Venter's work with that of Endy and the refactoring of T7, W. Wayt Gibbs comments: "Re-creating a virus letter-for-letter does not reveal much about it, but what if the genome were dissected into its constituent genes and then methodically put back together in a way that makes sense to human engineers?"[30]

If the legacy of genetic engineering lives on among group 2 synthetic biologists, it does so in a new and systematic way:

> Synthetic biology extends the spirit of genetic engineering to focus on whole systems of genes and gene products. The focus on systems as opposed to individual genes or pathways is shared by the contemporaneous discipline of systems biology, which analyzes biological organisms in their entirety. Synthetic biologists design and construct complex artificial biological systems using many insights discovered by systems biologists and share their holistic perspective.[31]

Precisely because group 2 synthetic biologists wish to synthesize novel systems or organisms, they (far more than their genetic engineering forebears or their DNA-synthesizing rivals) must attend to the system.

It is perhaps ironic that while synthetic biology sounds reductionistic, researchers in the field (especially group 2 researchers) claim that they are *systems* biologists, perhaps of an applied sort. They reason that without knowledge of the system of the organism, any effort to modify the whole by manipulating the parts is a kind of prerational technology, a hit-or-miss experimentation. One researcher in synthetic biology speaks of the "core of systems biology" in terms that reflect at once an engineering spirit and a systems approach, as if "synthetic biology" and "systems biology" were interchangeable terms. Systems biology:

> aims at predicting the systemic properties in terms of the properties of the components and their interactions (cellular process in terms of molecular

interactions, organismal behavior in terms of populations of cells, and so on). If this program can be carried out at all levels of organization, building up successively on the previous one, it would be possible to design and control the functioning of living systems.[32]

Compared to the promises of the 1980s and nineties, detailed knowledge of genomes has provided less power than expected to predict the function of living systems. In biology generally, this has prompted a turn toward the system, from genes to genomes, from proteins to proteomics, indeed, to physiology. In medicine, the larger context of human physiological functions, not just the deterministic power of inherited DNA, must be taken into account in understanding health and disease. A recent study examined the interactive effects of genes in a systems approach to cancer: "The hypothesis that is beginning to revolutionize medicine is that disease may perturb the normal network structures of a system through genetic perturbations and/or by pathological environmental cues, such as infectious agents or chemical carcinogens." The complexity of interactive pathways suggests an end to simplistic thinking about control of diseases, as if a single-focus strategy will be effective. There is a second irony, nevertheless, in systems thinking. The complexity of living systems is taken more fully into account, but in the end, the promise of prediction and control reasserts itself: "Systems biology is a scientific discipline that endeavors to quantify all of the molecular elements of a biological system to assess their interactions and to integrate that information into graphical network models that serve as predictive hypotheses to explain emergent behaviors."[33]

Social, Ethical, and Theological Implications of Synthetic Biology

Should the claim that synthetic biology is nothing less than "Life 2.0" be dismissed as mere journalistic hyperbole? Researchers in the field are only slightly less audacious, for example, when they use software release nomenclature to refer to their previously mentioned work in refactoring the natural bacteriophage T7; Chan and his colleagues write, "we decided to attempt to engineer a surrogate genome, which we designated T7.1."[34]

Novelty and its exaggeration can be a two-edged sword for any technology. On the one hand, if the technology is nothing new, why fund it? Public research funding commitments and venture capital follow grand visions, backed up, of course, by convincing research but sold in the end to those who do not fully understand the research. The words used to describe the research are chosen not just to inform but to promote. Furthermore, sales pitches aside, venture capital demands patents, and patent law demands novelty. But claims of novelty can cut both ways, for instance when exaggerated claims of novelty that are intended to generate financial support result in heightened scrutiny and increased public anxiety.

The developers of synthetic biology have taken the initiative in addressing social and ethical questions. A 1999 publication on early work on a minimal genome was accompanied by an ethics article, the result of several conversations among researchers.[35] Annual meetings of synthetic biologists routinely include ethics sections, and some have called for a "SynBio Asilomar," hearkening back to the 1975 Asilomar conference that led to self-regulation among researchers in genetic engineering, pending the development of governmental structures. One appeal for a new Asilomar suggests, "That approach, which has since proven remarkably successful, bears emulating today."[36]

Whether self-regulation will be effective is a matter of debate. So far, however, few public voices have joined the debate, and there has been little or no public reaction to synthetic biology. This is surprising, considering the public response to genetic engineering and to specific areas of application such as genetically modified foods, especially in areas outside the United States. One exception is a recent statement, "Synthetic Biology— Global Societal Review Urgent!," also called an "Open Letter from Civil Society," which was released in 2006 on the Web and signed on behalf of thirty-five civil society organizations. This letter responds directly to ethics conversations that have been initiated by the researchers themselves calling upon each other to focus on the ethics issues and, at the least, to monitor themselves. According to the text, the document should be seen as "a joint letter calling on the synthetic biologists to withdraw from this self-governance approach." The letter rejects the idea that self-monitoring is adequate and argues instead that "Society—especially social movements and marginalized peoples—must be fully engaged in designing and directing societal dialogue on every aspect of synthetic biology research and products." The letter asserts, "Scientific self-governance doesn't work and is anti-democratic. It is not for scientists to have the determinant voice in regulating their research or their products."[37]

Skepticism about the sufficiency of self-governance may be widespread, but public scrutiny is no panacea. If scientists are thought incapable of acting in the public interest, will the addition of public advocacy groups necessarily improve the formula? More perspectives, of course, will join the debate, but more perspectives do not necessarily lead to more wisdom or justice.

What ethics concerns have been raised, either by the scientists or by others? The list at this point includes biosafety (the risk of accident or of some novel organism or DNA sequence escaping from the lab); biowarfare (the use of synthetic biology to create new weapons and the development of countermeasures); hacker culture (the creation of new DNA or RNA sequences just for fun or mischief); worrisome economic influences on research; and disruptive economic impacts as traditional resources and labor are replaced.[38] Critics and advocates of synthetic biology both agree that these are real concerns. Advocates offer some suggestions but few reassurances. Some suggest a monitoring system to see who is seeking information about the field, particularly biological components that might be used in weapons. Others argue for the necessity of a laboratory culture that not only maintains ethics standards but intentionally passes them to young researchers. One thing seems to be clear: "given the momentum and international character of research in synthetic biology, it is already too late to impose a moratorium, if indeed one was ever contemplated."[39]

When it comes to the basic issue of safety, the irony of novelty returns again, now in the form of a paradox, for it might very well turn out to be true that greater artificiality results in greater safety: "Making life is less worrying than modifying life."[40] The more novel, artificial, and nonnatural an organism is, the less chance it probably has of surviving in nature, where it might wreak havoc, mutate, and wreak still more havoc. "Life finds a way," according to the film *Jurassic Park*, but will synthetic life even survive, much less find a way to destroy its creators?

> The more different an artificial living system is from natural biological systems, the less likely it is that the artificial system will survive in the natural world . . . a completely synthetic life form that has eight nucleotides in its genetic alphabet would find survival very difficult if it were to escape from the laboratory. What would it eat?[41]

If novelty means safety, group 2 synthetic biologists are the most likely beneficiaries, as they themselves are quick to point out.

According to the summary section of a report on synthetic biology undertaken by the European Commission, the risks are sobering but probably manageable:

> In terms of risks, abuses and safety measures, it is not obvious that there is any aspect of synthetic biology that is qualitatively different from the way

such issues apply to biotechnology and genetic modifications, aside from the far greater capacity for manipulation and control that synthetic biology will afford (which has both positive and negative implications).[42]

The risks of synthetic biology, according to the report, are worth the potential benefits.

At the top of nearly every list of the short-term benefits of synthetic biology is the partnership between the Gates Foundation and the Berkeley laboratory of Jay Keasling. Gates Foundation money has been pledged to support research needed to bring to industrial scale the production of a naturally occurring remedy for malaria. The compound, artemisinin, is known to be effective in the treatment of the disease, which kills more than 1 million people each year, primarily in developing countries. Keasling's lab has already developed a synthetic biology process by which the complete synthesis of artemisinin can be achieved cheaply in the laboratory.[43] The current objective is to reduce costs still further, then to distribute the product. Needless to say, if this project is successful, synthetic biology as a field will bask in the warmth of global approval.

Other possible benefits of synthetic biology include organisms that will detect and destroy toxins, energy alternatives, new (and perhaps environmentally friendly) approaches to manufacturing, global climate remediation, perhaps by sequestering carbon, and numerous medical applications. Whether the potential benefits outweigh the risks remains to be seen. Accordingly, the European Commission report correctly notes that the public reaction might focus less on the ethics of risk/benefit analysis and more on cultural, philosophical, and even religious issues:

> it seems likely that the notion of creating entirely new life forms will also stimulate debates about the proper ethical boundaries of science: to some, this is sure to seem like "playing God." As was the case for reproductive technologies and stem-cell research, it seems likely that we do not as yet possess a conceptual ethical framework that can provide a common context for such debates: the science may have outstripped our ethical points of reference. We feel that such a debate should nonetheless be welcomed, but caution that it will be productive only if we can develop a more sophisticated appreciation of what is meant by "life" than is current in popular discourse.[44]

Concerns about violating the integrity of humanity, nature, or life, about abusing technology, about violating even the natural evolutionary process—sometimes construed pejoratively as "playing God"—are well represented in the theological literature that has developed in response to technology in general and genetic engineering and biotechnology in particular.[45] Whether synthetic biology will provoke new insight into these themes depends upon the responses of religious institutions and scholars. At the very least, the question of the human creature as creator (or "co-creator," as some have suggested) who contributes to the divine work of creation through new technology remains an open question, more urgent than ever. Some people of religious conviction see science as a new source of theology and technology as a new avenue of service in the grand work of creation. Others hold that theology's core ideas are firmly established by traditional insight and that technology is to be adopted with wariness if at all. As a discipline, synthetic biology is ill equipped to resolve its own relation to religious and moral traditions.

Will theology play a role in a public debate over science policy regarding synthetic biology? The ethicists who commented on the first efforts at developing a minimal organism show some cautious relief when they report:

> Although there is vigorous debate in some religious circles about the limits of human initiative in the new life sciences, the dominant view is that while there are reasons for caution, there is nothing in the research agenda for creating a minimal genome that is automatically prohibited by legitimate religious considerations. Moving forward with caution requires that the scientific communities be in continual conversation with the entire society, working together to address key ethical and religious concerns.[46]

Whether academic theology engages the discussion, whether more popular expressions of religion play a role, or even whether secular critics invoke religious themes to heighten the rhetorical force of their critique are all questions that remain for the future.

A recent survey of synthetic biology concluded that this field "clearly has the potential to bring about epochal changes in medicine, agriculture, industry, ethics, and polities, and a few decades from now it may have a profound influence on the definition of life, including what it means to be human."[47] If this is even remotely true, then synthetic biology will keep theology busy. Theology, which aims at critical reflection on all areas of life and culture and which asks how one might live with deep understanding and clarity of purpose, will need to take into account that all these areas expected to undergo change. Together with other areas of technology, such as nanotechnology, stem cell research, neuroscience, and related fields, synthetic biology will very likely play a key role in a future technological revolution that dwarfs the revolutions of the past. Whether fantasies of "transhumanism" will remain just that or whether their visions of radical life extension or cognitive enhancement will be realized to any degree, synthetic biology will probably play a role, both in their achievement and in our self-understanding as creatures for whom all things are possible. By what right, with what governance, guided by what vision, and to what end will we do these things?

The most interesting impact of synthetic biology, however, will be the way it changes basic ideas in biology. The century-old debate over Darwinian evolution, ranging from social Darwinism to "intelligent design," may not be directly affected, but our understanding of biological evolution surely will be. Already, synthetic biologists refer to their own work as truly "intelligent design." How will natural selection treat our handiwork, with its previously unused amino acids forming previously unassembled proteins? Is it possible to simulate evolution with computer programs, to move the venue of mutation and natural selection from *in vivo* to *in silico*, as some researchers now claim? Although still simple when compared to the complexity of life, the simulation of evolution via computer can be thought of as "a procedure aimed to reproduce *in silico* the feature that drives the design of genetic network architectures *in vivo*: evolution . . . [by means of] a computational algorithm that creates small gene networks.[48] As this research goes forward, what will we learn about the earliest stages of life on Earth, when the genetic code and the repertoire of amino acids were themselves evolving? What rules constrain the options that channeled the evolution of life down one path and not another, and what underlying chemistry and physics explain those rules. Will researchers learn to "create" life, and if so, what exactly will they have accomplished? What, after all, is life, and will efforts to create it force new clarity on how to define it?

One journalist's account of synthetic biology contains a wealth of suggestions as to how this field raises profound questions that may be explored critically by the theological community; for example, "this field may also help to answer some central questions about the evolution of life," a theme of great interest to some theologians. Furthermore, why is life built on only four nucleotides and only twenty amino acids? "Is there a particular reason why only 20 amino acids, and these particular 20, comprise the genetic code? Why hasn't the code evolved further?" Can synthetic biology, which has altered these fundamental rules of life, decipher how life wrote the rules in the first place? Can it create not just new proteins but new functions and new properties? "The move from creating new proteins to creating new life seems only a small step away."[49]

Special attention must be given here to the question of emergence within biology, according to which simple processes give rise to more complex functions and structures, a subject of some interest among scholars who have sought to integrate contemporary biology with philosophical and theological themes.[50] Synthetic biology, specifically the approach undertaken by group 2, is uniquely poised to offer new insight into this question. Researchers in the field often come to their work of biological engineering with a systems view and a multitiered approach, with level 1 complex chemicals being connected by engineers to create level 2 devices, which are then put together to create level 3 modules or "integrated circuits." One goal of this approach is to be able to swap out a specific element (a module, say) and then to be able to examine exactly the effect of the substitution on the behavior of the organism. Eventually, the hope is to be able to predict that effect based on knowledge of the modules in other organic systems. To the extent that the effort succeeds, it will reveal much about organic parts and wholes. The notion that certain features emerge with biological complexity will become far more precise and detailed. Perhaps human engineering will in the end show something about the ways in which physics and chemistry constrain how God might be thought to create. Principles of modularity and complexity that are discovered by synthetic biologists must first have been discovered by a patiently creating God.

It is widely asserted by researchers in synthetic biology that their work reveals new insight into biology. Recall the journalist's statement of the first goal of synthetic biology: "learn about life by building it."[51] Again, the success of synthetic biology cannot be predicted, and what it will teach us about living things and biological systems remains to be seen. To the extent that synthetic biology plays a major heuristic role for biology, it plays a similar role for theology, at least for any theology that is open to learning from science in general and wishes to reformulate its doctrines in light of new insight in fields such as biology. Acting on nature reveals the secrets of nature; by acting in new ways on organic structures, synthetic biology will reveal new secrets. How theology will interpret and incorporate these insights is a challenge to be faced by a new generation of theologians.

The heuristic potential of synthetic biology may shed dramatic new light on perennial questions such as: What is life? More likely, the new insight will come at a less grand level, with new understanding of the minimum material substrate for life. How do we comprehend more precisely the line that divides living and nonliving? Is it possible for life to function using different chemicals, or is life (wherever it exists) the same everywhere? How does this constrain evolution on Earth and on other planets? Questions such as these, which drive scientific curiosity and now also engineering audacity, are in the end questions of creation, of meaning, and of God.

Nature as Given, Nature as Guide, Nature as Natural Kinds: Return to Nature in the Ethics of Human Biotechnology

Gerald McKenny

A familiar passage in Descartes' *Discourse on the Method* is often cited as the paradigmatic expression of a new stance toward nature that emerged in the seventeenth century and, many believe, remains with us today. This stance is best characterized as a project to attain mastery over nature, but to treat this project simply as an assertion of the human will over nature, as is often done, is to fail to grasp the reason for its continuing appeal long after the initial mechanistic philosophy to which Descartes wedded it has been superseded. From the beginning this project was infused with a moral purpose. Indeed, it was this moral purpose that Descartes cited as the reason for publishing his *Discourse*, and it is in the context of his explanation of this reason that the familiar passage appears:

> But as soon as I had acquired some general notions in physics . . . I believed that I could not keep them secret without sinning gravely against *the law which obliges us to do all in our power to secure the general welfare of mankind.* For they opened my eyes to the possibility of gaining knowledge which would be very useful in life and of discovering a practical philosophy which might replace the speculative philosophy taught in the schools. Through this philosophy we could know the power and action of fire, water, air, the stars, the heavens and all the other bodies in our environment, as distinctly

as we know the various crafts of our artisans; and we could use this knowledge—as the artisans use theirs—for all the purposes for which it is appropriate, *and thus make ourselves, as it were, the lords and masters of nature.*

Descartes goes on to say that the mastery of nature is desirable not only
for facilitating enjoyment of the goods of the Earth but above all "for
the maintenance of health, which is undoubtedly the chief good and the
foundation of all the other goods in this life." The maintenance of health
is apparently not to be limited to the cure or elimination of disease. Because "the mind depends so much on the temperament and disposition of
the bodily organs," it is to medicine that we look in order "to make men
in general wiser and more skilful than they have been up till now"—an
indication of a broad program of human improvement that may also be
hinted at in Descartes' hope that medical knowledge "might free us from
innumerable diseases, both of the body and of the mind, and perhaps even
from the infirmity of old age."[1]

It would be a mistake to assume that Descartes' bold and visionary program typified the attitude of his time or that there is a direct line of
thought and practice linking this program to the biomedicine of our time.
If there is a Cartesian provenance here, it is by no means an unbroken
one. Yet the convictions that we (or society) are obligated to do all that is
reasonably in our power to promote human well-being, that this imperative is fulfilled in significant part through the control of nature for human
use, and that health, understood as freedom not only from infirmities but
also from limitations of body and mind, is fundamental to human well-
being are deeply ingrained in the moral life of late modern societies. These
convictions combine with commitments to autonomous choice, avoidance
of harm, and fairness that are enshrined in the most influential forms of
bioethics to constitute a contemporary version of the Cartesian program.
But if nature thus has significance in biomedicine only as that which is to
be brought under scientific and technological control in order to improve
somatic and mental functioning, then biomedicine may be said to be without nature in the sense that nature makes no normative claim on biomedical research and practice. The moral vision of the Cartesian program in
its current form would stand opposed to any moral vision for which nature
is the source of a normative claim.

In explicit contrast to this position, several prominent members of the
U.S. President's Council on Bioethics have called for biomedical science
and technology to respect the normative status of nature. Alert to the appeal of the moral vision deriving from Descartes, Michael Sandel, Leon

Kass, and Francis Fukuyama all gesture toward alternatives that would restrain that vision, if not eliminate it. These authors write mostly from explicitly secular perspectives, yet their pleas for the normativity of nature in biomedicine are eloquent articulations of claims that appear widely in responses to biotechnology from religious perspectives. For that reason they are well suited to raise the question of what stake theology has, if any, in the denial or affirmation of a normative status for nature in biomedicine.

It is important to distinguish this concern with the normativity of nature from other concerns that also prompt critiques of the Cartesian program. Criticism of the control of nature exercised by biomedical technology has been a persistent theme in bioethics and in histories and theories of medicine. A common line of inquiry charges that the objectification of the body in modern medical theory and practice abstracts the body from our ordinary experience of it, thus exacerbating the existential dimension of alienation from the body in the experience of illness while also rendering the body susceptible to social control, to professional or patriarchal power, and to commodification. Criticism in this vein seeks to expose the underside of modern biomedicine, to bring to attention the often disturbing effects and implications of biomedical knowledge and control of the body. However, with the partial exception of the concern over commodification, the normative commitments of this line of inquiry, to the extent that they are discernable, usually have to do with freedom in one form or another (authenticity, emancipation, resistance to power, self-formation) rather than with nature as such. This line of inquiry investigates the body as site of a struggle between these various forms of power and these various forms of freedom. By contrast, Sandel, Kass, and Fukuyama all argue that in one respect or another, nature makes a moral claim on us.

Nature as Normative: Three Conceptions

In what sense might nature make a moral claim on us? To answer this question it might help to broaden our focus to the biological sciences more generally, and especially to ecology and environmental studies, where questions about the moral status of nature have been widely discussed. In those discussions three distinct kinds of normative status have been ascribed to nature, and it is significant these are also the kinds of normative status that Sandel, Kass, and Fukuyama, respectively, ascribe to nature.

First, normative status may attach to nature as a realm whose objects and processes owe their existence and characteristics to forces operating independently of intentional human activity. This entails a particular idea of what nature is. In his essay in this volume, Stuart Newman captures this idea when he initially describes nature as "a world neither made nor influenced by human activity."[2] Newman writes in the context of biotechnology, but the same notion is expressed with relevance to ecology in the Wilderness Act of 1964, which famously defines wilderness as "an area where the earth and its community of life are untrammeled by man, where man himself is a visitor who does not remain."[3] In Bernard Williams's words, nature in this sense is that which "is not controlled, shaped or willed by us, a nature which, as against culture, can be thought of as just *there*."[4] In this first sense, then, we can say that nature is what is *given*. Opposition to biotechnology and to human encroachment on the Earth's ecosystems frequently appeals to nature in this sense, and it is usually the loss of nature in this sense that is meant by slogans such as the "end of nature." Because nature, according to this view, is what is independent of intentional human activity, to assign normative status to nature is to set moral limits on intervention as such. The issue is not so much that human interventions into nature may go awry or do more harm than good; rather, in Michael Sandel's terms, it is that human intervention into nature threatens to "leave us nothing to affirm or behold outside our own will."[5] Intervention into or alteration of nature is itself an object of moral concern apart from any moral evaluation of what is intended or effected by the intervention or alteration.

But normative status may be ascribed to nature in a second sense, finding in nature an immanent, prerational normative order that directs human activity. In ecology, a classic expression of this notion of nature as a guide to human activity is Aldo Leopold's dictum: "A thing is right when it tends to preserve the integrity, stability, and beauty of the biotic community. It is wrong when it tends otherwise."[6] In the field of human biotechnology, it is expressed in Leon Kass's call for "an ethical account of human flourishing based on a biological account of human life as lived, not just physically, but psychically, socially, and spiritually."[7] In their distinct ways, Leopold and Kass invoke nature as a guide to human activity. In contrast to the first position, their views of the normative status of nature allow for human interventions into natural processes, but they argue that nature is the ultimate source of the norms for such interventions. Nature in this view need not be represented as a fixed order, and the direction it gives to human activity need not consist in precise norms of conduct. But by this account nature does give direction to human activity, and human interventions are justified, on this view, to the extent that they conform to (or at least do not violate) a natural order, whether that order is represented as a state of equilibrium of forces, as with Leopold, or as a natural telos, as with Kass. To be without nature in this sense is to deny that nature contains or constitutes an immanent, prerational, normative order of this kind.

Finally, there is a third sense in which nature is said to possess normative status. When we inquire into the nature of a thing, we ask what kind of thing it is, and one way of answering this question is to refer to a natural kind of which it is an instance. Opponents of agricultural biotechnology who argue that transgenesis (the transfer of genes from one species to another) is unnatural often think of nature in this sense, while anxieties over whether genetic engineering or neuropharmacology will alter or eliminate an essential human trait also reflect this view of nature. To be without nature in this sense is to deny the reality of natural kinds, and this may also entail the denial that there are any natural boundaries between species or that there is any property or set of properties that identifies a species and sets it apart from other species. It is also to deny (in the case of human biotechnology) that there is any natural characteristic or set of natural characteristics that constitutes human beings as human. Those who take nature in this sense as normative often argue that biotechnology should not violate species boundaries or alter or eliminate certain human characteristics. Newman exhibits this view of the normativity of nature when he argues against transferring genes between species and generating chimeras.[8] Francis Fukuyama also has this view in mind when he identifies as the most pressing issue posed by biotechnology the

> fear that, in the end, biotechnology will cause us in some way to lose our humanity—that is, some essential quality that has always underpinned our sense of who we are and where we are going, despite all of the evident changes that have taken place in the human condition through the course of our history.[9]

There is no ideal term to express this sense of nature and its normativity, but it involves the notion that nature is ordered into kinds or species whose integrity must be respected.

These three senses of the normativity of nature often overlap in practice. For example, it is difficult to invoke human nature as a guide without indicating essential characteristics of human nature. When Kass argues that reproductive cloning violates the distinctively human meaning of sexual reproduction, he is arguing both that sexual reproduction is an essential feature of human nature and that we should look to it for direction in our thinking about which uses of reproductive technology are morally sound and which are not. However, it is still possible to distinguish a worry that biotechnology will eventually eliminate sexual reproduction (however that would be done) from a worry that certain forms or uses of reproductive technology violate the characteristically human meaning of sexual reproduction. The former is a worry that we will alter or destroy human nature; the latter is a worry that we will fail to take nature as our guide and will thereby degrade our nature, diminish its worth, or fail to fulfill it even if our interventions leave that nature intact.

In all three of these senses—as that which is given, as a guide to human activity, and as natural kinds or types—both the concept of nature itself and claims for its normative significance have been under constant attack in recent decades on scientific, philosophical, and moral grounds.[10] It is safe to say that claims for the normative status of nature have been out of fashion in bioethics. Yet arguments for the normative status of these three conceptions of nature by Sandel, Kass, and Fukuyama have recently brought these arguments to the forefront of bioethics, even if a major shift in the direction of taking such arguments seriously appears unlikely.

Nature as Given: Sandel

Could genetic knowledge and technology, regenerative medicine, neuropharmacology, and reconstructive surgery progress to a point where human capacities, performances, and appearances would all bear the marks of our intentional human activity to the extent that, in Sandel's words quoted above, there would be "nothing to affirm or behold outside our own will"? If so, we would be without nature in the first of our three senses. It is not clear exactly what would count as having arrived at such a state, but it is this prospect of a world in which we encounter only our own will that prompts Sandel, in two essays first published in 2004,[11] to argue that the increasing power of biotechnology to remake nature poses questions that go beyond the strictly ethical concerns with autonomy, rights, utility, and fairness that tend to dominate public debates over biotechnology, raising questions regarding the proper relation of human beings to God and to nature: Should human beings approach nature in an attitude of humility and awe or in an attitude of mastery, assertiveness, and control?

This question puts us in the realm of piety; ultimately at stake in the biotechnological alteration of nature is the proper attitude, stance, or disposition of human beings toward God. From this perspective, what is finally most troubling about the Cartesian program is its impiety; to strive for a world in which we affirm or behold only our own will is to express an improper religious sensibility, one that is inconsistent with our place in creation. Sandel, however, conflates what are actually rather different kinds of piety which have different theological meanings and practical implications. Before turning to Sandel, then, let us consider four stances of human beings toward God that are closely connected to the notion of nature as that which is given.

The first of these is reverence. Nature, we may say, sets a boundary or limit to human activity beyond which the latter exceeds the scope God has given to it. At some point, to alter or disturb the givenness of nature is to encroach on the divine. This thematic of boundary and transgression is deeply rooted in Western religious traditions (including, according to some scholars, the Yahwist strand in Gen. 1–11) and is probably the meaning most often suggested by the phrase "playing God" in debates over biotechnology.

Closely related to reverence is humility. Nature, as that which stands over against our intentional activity, confronts us with the limitations of our activity. Human power is finite, and so the aim of attaining complete mastery over what is given is dangerous and perhaps futile in the long run, however exhilarating our successes may be in the short run. To adopt such an aim is hubris, not only because it will eventually fail or go awry but also because it vastly overestimates human capacities and erodes or destroys a proper sense of the dependence of human beings on powers they do not control.

These first two stances of reverence and humility share a common theological preoccupation with the distinction between human beings and God. The remaining two stances also seem to belong together, but they are linked by a somewhat different theological sensibility. The third stance is gratitude. Nature, precisely as that which is not the product of human intentional activity, is a gift that should be received gratefully. Hannah Arendt had something like this in mind when, contemplating in 1958 the likelihood of a future marked by laboratory conception, genetically attained perfection, and an extended life span, she criticized the human being she saw emerging as being "possessed by a rebellion against human existence as it has been given, a free gift from nowhere (secularly speaking), which he wishes to exchange, as it were, for something he has made himself."[12]

Closely related to gratitude is a fourth stance, that of awe. Nature is a source of wonder at what exceeds us; standing over against our intentional activity, it reminds us that not everything in the world is to be made conformable to our will, use, or desire. The capacity for this kind of awe or wonder seems intimately connected with a capacity to be open to or to accept the value or worth of that which we do not control or design.

Sandel's two essays address two different audiences, one religious and one secular. The essay addressed to his religious audience reflects almost exclusively the stances of reverence and humility, while the one addressed to his secular audience reflects the stances of gratitude and awe. The former essay appears in a volume devoted to the work of the Jewish theologian David Hartman.[13] Commenting on Hartman's work, Sandel describes an ambivalence regarding human mastery of nature in Judaism. On the one hand, the sharp distinction between the creator and the creature has led to a permissive stance toward subjection of nature to human control and use. Judaism strongly denies that God is one with nature or is embodied in nature, and this has generally meant that there is relatively little restraint on human control and mastery of nature. On the other hand, humility before God sets limits on human power over nature. This means that in Judaism as Sandel understands it, it is God, not nature itself, who restrains human mastery of nature:

> The limits on the exercise of human powers over nature arise not from nature itself but from a proper understanding of the relation between human beings and God. If it is wrong to clone ourselves in a quest for immortality, or to genetically alter our children so that they will better fulfill our ambitions and desires, the sin is not the desecration of nature but the deification of ourselves.[14]

Extending some themes from Hartman's work, Sandel suggests three respects in which Judaism seems to curb the human tendency to self-deification: the acknowledgment of human finitude highlights the irreducible difference between humans and God; the Sabbath rest from domination of nature entails an attitude of humility toward God's creation; and the prohibition of idolatry might aptly apply to the remaking of human beings through biotechnology.

More significant than the content of these three suggestions, which he does not present as definitive, is Sandel's underlying conviction that what is theologically at stake in the human domination of nature is an illicit self-deification of humanity. For him, Judaism preserves the boundary between divine and human by restraining a human tendency to self-deification that threatens that boundary. The theological concern with human self-deification invokes the first two forms of impiety, namely, irreverence and hubris. Biotechnology potentially threatens the boundary between human beings and God, or at least fails to respect this boundary, and this is what is at stake for theology in the loss of nature as that which is simply given and not the product of our intentional activity. Sandel thus expresses in a distinctively Jewish voice what has also been uttered in different tones and with different accents on biotechnology by many Christian commentators, whose similar convictions about the distinction of creator and creature and the relation of human beings to God generate similar tensions between a permissible stance toward altering nature, exemplified best by those who support the technological alteration of nature by proposing that human beings are "co-creators" with God, and a restrictive stance, exemplified in popular form by the warning against "playing God."

Yet one of Sandel's major concerns in the essay is to overcome what he, following Hartman, thinks is a theologically and spiritually problematic oscillation in the thought of Hartman's distinguished teacher, Joseph Soloveitchik, between a thoroughgoing mastery of nature and a thoroughgoing submission before God. Like Hartman, Sandel seeks instead to show how permissibility and restraint are compatible with each other, comprising two aspects of a single moral and theological vision that restrains Promethean ambition within a general affirmation of human autonomy, initiative, and creativity in relation to nature. To combine the two stances, Sandel proposes that there be no restrictions on mastery of nature in order to restore human beings to wholeness in the face of disease but that the power to alter capacities and choose characteristics be reserved for God alone.[15]

From the perspective of Jewish bioethics, Sandel's position raises questions regarding what normative role theological considerations such as these should play in relation to Halakha (Jewish law), especially if the latter does not impose such restrictions on human mastery of nature. From the perspective of philosophical bioethics, Sandel assumes that the distinction between treating or curing diseases, on the one hand, and improving or enhancing human characteristics, on the other hand, can be consistently drawn and can be drawn in a way that makes it plausible to permit the former and proscribe the latter—assumptions that are widely questioned

in the bioethics literature. From within Sandel's own theological perspective, however, the most interesting question is whether the assumptions
he makes about the relation of human beings to God in respect of nature
perpetuate the very oscillation between mastery and submission that he
seeks to overcome. Nor is this simply a question for Sandel or for the kind
of Jewish theology he articulates. The scope of this question is broad
enough to include the oscillation between co-creation and playing God,
thus taking in a debate that extends to Christian theology as well.

The fear that human beings will become too much like God by striving
to improve human life by mastery and control of nature assumes that the
entire thematic of mastery and possession is the one best suited to characterize the complex relations between God, human activity, and nature. But
is nature best understood theologically, in Judaism or in Christianity, as
the scene of a divine-human struggle for mastery and possession, implicat-
ing biotechnology in an intrigue of boundary and transgression? Are not
the fear that human beings will become too like God by becoming masters
of nature and its opposite mood of exhilaration at the prospect of godlike
mastery in fact dialectically bound to each other? In short, do not Sandel
and Descartes simply occupy opposite sides of the same coin? For Sandel,
human beings are free to act as co-creators with God in the face of disease,
but the moment they confront the prospect of enhancing human traits,
they must resolutely refuse to play God. Besides placing enormous theological weight on a shaky distinction between therapy and enhancement,
this scheme seems to perpetuate the oscillation between mastery and submission that Hartman and Sandel find in Soloveitchik, rather than moving
beyond it.

Ironically, a theologically more satisfying alternative can be derived
from what Sandel writes about the relation of human beings to nature in
his secular essay. Here Sandel looks at emerging technologies directed at
increasing muscle capacity, memory, and height, and ponders what lies
ahead if these and other so-called enhancements become safe and effective. Yet in this essay, what is most troubling about the "Promethean aspiration to remake nature, including human nature, to serve our purposes
and satisfy our desires" is not its tendency toward self-deification but that
it "misses and may even destroy . . . an appreciation of the gifted character
of human powers and achievements."[16] What will happen, Sandel wonders, if genetic engineering leads us to regard our abilities and achievements as products of our deliberate design rather than as gifts of nature
that we cultivate? With this concern in mind, he contrasts an "ethic of
giftedness," which accepts that which is not the object of our design or

the product of our will, with an "ethic of willfulness," which subjects everything to our powers of striving.[17]

While the implicit contrast between Promethean theft and nature's gift places the conflict of these two ethical stances within a cosmic dimension, in this second essay the immediate objects of Sandel's worry are more mundane, having to do with the social effects of the mastery of nature. A brief summary of these social effects will help us elicit the theological relevance of the overall view of this essay. A sense of giftedness, Sandel proposes, conduces to openness to what is not designed, controlled, desired, or willed by us—an openness, that is, to the "other" or, in a deliberately quaint term he borrows from William F. May, to "the unbidden." The worry is that if our growing tendency to seek to determine the characteristics of our children through genetic and other technologies continues, we will be less willing to accept or value that which we do not control, that which does not conform to our desires or standards. Sandel next points to what he calls "hyper-agency," a condition that occurs with the expansion of technological control over what was once subject to fate. We are increasingly unable to limit our liability for the quality of our capacities and achievements by referring them to the inscrutability of providence or the fickleness of fortune, so that people are now held responsible—and hold themselves responsible—for every correctable "imperfection." Sandel's third concern strikes at the heart of liberal doctrines of justice. Like others who have explored the moral and political significance of luck, he believes that our solidarity with those whose abilities and achievements are more modest than our own depends on a sense that these abilities and achievements are contingent, so that if we begin to think of them as self-made rather than given, we will no longer think we owe anything to others.[18]

The distinctiveness of Sandel's position lies not in these arguments, which in one version or another appear widely in debates over the use of biomedical technology to improve or enhance human characteristics, but in the rhetorical force of the Promethean theme with its implicit theological drama, despite the insistence that the sense of giftedness in our relation to nature can be commended on secular grounds alone, made plausible by the threefold effect of the ethic of willfulness on our moral and social life. Yet if we pursue, as Sandel does not, the theological implications of the ethic of giftedness, we are more likely to arrive at the stances of gratitude and awe than at those of reverence and humility.

This becomes especially clear when we consider their relevance to Sandel's concerns with hyperagency and openness to what we do not control. To some extent, humility is the antidote to hyperagency; it introduces skepticism into our assumptions that by altering our natural capacities and characteristics, we can truly improve on nature, and that by improving them, we can make our lives and those of others better. But in these contexts, skepticism is usually invoked only as a warning to proceed with caution; it does not get at the roots of hyperagency. These roots are surely found in the seemingly infinite demand of a competitive society for high achievement and the rewards and punishments meted out accordingly, but these roots are nourished on a particular attitude toward nature. Nature, according to our first conception, refers to that which is given, that which is what it is apart from intentional human activity. But it matters how we understand givenness. If our capacities and characteristics are simply the product of chance, fortune, or accident, it is difficult to see on what grounds we should exempt them from our power to refashion them. Mere fate makes no normative claim. But to regard these capacities and characteristics as gifts from God is to ascribe worth to them just as they are.

It might follow from this that human responsibility is limited to cultivation of the gift and not for the gift itself. It would therefore be a mistake to hold ourselves and one another responsible for the quality of whatever we have the power to alter. If this line of thought is plausible, then gratitude, rather than humility, is the best defense against hyperagency. The related stance of awe implies that to encounter nature as a divine work that elicits wonder at what we did not design or what is not the expression of our will is to recognize in what we encounter a kind of value that does not fulfill an antecedent desire or conform to a plan or prior expectation. Recognition of this kind of value seems to be at some level a necessary condition of respect for human dignity.

If these are the theological implications of Sandel's position, how sound are they? On the positive side, emphasis on gratitude and awe as distinct from reverence and humility diminishes the role played by the Promethean myth in critiques of the Cartesian program. Use of that myth inevitably portrays biotechnology as a contest between a god jealous of divine prerogatives and an audacious yet beneficent champion of human well-being. In this contest, our sympathies quite understandably incline to Prometheus and by extension to the Cartesian program. Piety in this context appears grudging and petty, obstinately resisting humanitarian progress. But while the distinction between God and creation is central to both Jewish and Christian theology, the portrayal of the divine and human as locked in a contest of this sort is largely foreign to both traditions. By contrast, gratitude and awe point away from the economies of mastery and possession, of boundary and transgression, which underlie this use of the

Promethean myth. They pose a different kind of question to the Cartesian program: whether at some point its mastery of nature for human benefit obscures or threatens other, more fundamental kinds of worth. The issue here is less the usurpation of divine power than the rejection of divine good. The point is not that we should conclude that reverence and humility are unimportant for a theological evaluation of biotechnology. An adequate theological conception of the relation of human beings to God and nature will surely make room for all four stances. Yet there do seem to be sound theological reasons for granting priority to gratitude and awe.

There are problems with Sandel's second approach, too, and to a large extent they apply to his first approach as well. The major problem is that this first view of the normativity of nature seems to call for a sharp line between what is open to human intervention and what is to be exempted from it, yet it is difficult to determine at exactly what point the act of impiety occurs. Which interventions cross the line into irreverence and hubris or display ingratitude and disregard for what does not embody our will? One major attraction of Sandel's position is that it promises just the clarity we seem to want. In principle, at least, it is clear where we cease being legitimate co-creators with God and begin playing God: it is where we cross the line from restoring health to enhancing characteristics. In practice, though, neither that line nor its moral relevance is as clear as Sandel assumes. Nor is it clear what other line could be drawn in its place.

The underlying problem is that while the conception of nature as given draws a sharp line between what is and is not affected by human action, it is not clear that piety demands such a sharp line. As that which is what it is apart from human intervention, nature is lost the moment it is touched, so to speak. Yet we may wonder whether piety, at least in its latter two forms, is so easily violated. Are gratitude and awe incompatible with any human intervention whatsoever into that for which we are grateful or hold in wonder, or do they instead depend on factors such as the purpose of the intervention, the extent and degree of control we exercise, a recognition of the unconditional worth of the person that qualifies all of our efforts to alter her nature by a fundamental acceptance that does not depend on the success or failure of our alterations? If the latter, then piety cannot yield the moral clarity demanded by our first conception of the normativity of nature, and we may suspect that it will be hard pressed to counter the lure of the Cartesian program with its clarity of vision and tangibility of benefit.

However we arrange the relative priorities of these four stances, there appear to be inherent limitations to the relevance of this first approach to the normativity of nature. In light of these difficulties, it may be best not to expect attitudes or stances like these to do explicit normative work in bioethics. Nevertheless, the notion that something of incalculable worth would be lost if there were no longer anything that resists or eludes the human will seems to remain even if its normative implications for biotechnology are irreducibly vague, confronting us with goods that are imperiled by our determination to remake nature.[19]

Nature as Guide: Kass

Unlike Sandel, Leon Kass does not think of nature as what is independent of human fashioning, nor does he think its normative force lies in its sheer givenness. For him, nature is a robustly substantive notion, and he thinks we honor its normative status not by letting it be but by living in accordance with it.[20] Of the three senses in which nature is said to be normative, this is the one that enjoys the least favor in bioethics. Acutely sensitive to the ways nature has been invoked in similar ways to ground unjust social arrangements and morally abhorrent practices, aware of how nature and culture intertwine, and doubtful that nature in its contingency and variability can support morality, many contemporary moral thinkers recoil from the thought of nature as a moral guide. Meanwhile, from Christian or Jewish theological perspectives, nature may be thought to be fallen to such an extent that it offers no reliable guidance or broken in such a way that our moral task is to restore it rather than to take our bearings from it.

Against all of these views Kass affirms nature as the ground of judgments of what is good or right and the source of human flourishing. This brings him into proximity with those versions of the natural law tradition that hold that certain natural inclinations orient us, at least provisionally, to human flourishing. But while much natural law thought emphasizes the role of reason in directing these inclinations to the activities or forms of life that fulfill them or else, treating them as norms, is occupied with the question of whether it is ever permissible to violate them, Kass focuses more broadly on how features of our biological nature give rise to meanings, aspirations, and ways of being that give depth and grandeur to human life. Kass's position thus differs in some respects from traditions of natural law. For example, where his view of nature takes a physicalist turn, he finds normative significance in the forms of organisms or their parts and processes rather than in their functions, as is more common, and for him reflection does not consist in reason directing natural inclinations to the distinctively human good but rather in our conscious awareness of, struggle with, and partial transcendence of the finitude and mortality, neediness and dependence, and inherent limitations of embodied life that enable us to flourish.[21]

This emphasis makes Kass's position especially significant for a theological evaluation of biotechnology inasmuch as it places us directly before the question of how we should face human finitude and vulnerability: whether by finding the meaning and worth of human life in struggling with them and partially but never entirely rising above them or by gaining power over them through technology and mitigating or eliminating their resistance to our desires and ambitions. Yet we will see that this formulation of the question is problematic from certain theological perspectives.

We can summarize Kass's position in three claims. First, what gives human life its distinctive worth and meaning is rooted in our biological nature, so the use of technology to fulfill desires and aims that conflict with or disregard our biological nature is inherently dehumanizing. A particular conception of human dignity thus lies at the center of Kass's thought. It turns on the claim that the noblest human desires and longings and the deepest and most meaningful ideals and forms of attachment emerge out of our engagements with the needs and limitations of embodied life. For example, Kass argues that in our conscious awareness of our sexual nature and its incompleteness, sexual desire becomes "erotic longing for wholeness, completion, and immortality," a longing fulfilled only partially through a complementary other and more genuinely through the offspring of sexual union.[22]

Similarly, he argues against the champions of ageless bodies and an extended life span that awareness of mortality is a condition of much that counts as virtuous and worthy in human life.[23] In these and other contexts, Kass consistently draws attention to dignity as the elevation of embodied life through awareness of and struggle with its limitations, vulnerability, incompleteness, neediness, and dependence, opposing this to the common view that dignity consists in some feature distinct from our biological nature. He thus resists the tendency in bioethics to identify dignity with personhood or with the capacity for autonomous choice but, most important, he denies that dignity is compatible with the elimination of natural necessity or the overcoming of natural limitations. Of course, biotechnology promises to free us from such aspects of embodiment, and for Kass this is precisely the problem. The effort to eliminate or evade features of our biological nature, however well motivated, impoverishes and dehumanizes us by eliminating the conditions under which the deepest and richest desires, feelings, and ways of being are cultivated and expressed, disregarding these in favor of less noble (though in their own place legitimate) desires for health, comfort, peace of mind, and long life.[24]

It follows from all of this that the major task of bioethics is to discern, by reflecting on our embodied nature, which desires and aspirations contribute to the fulfillment of our embodied nature and which diminish it and degrade it. This brings us to Kass's second claim: our biological nature as he understands it is not what the life sciences, as currently practiced, take as their object. Modern biological science objectifies living beings, quantifying them, homogenizing them, reducing them to the functions of their parts, and so on.[25] Nature is reduced to an object of disengaged rational inquiry. By contrast, for Kass biological nature is "lived nature"; it has to do with everyday life in its concreteness, in all the dimensions in which we live it: physical, psychical, social, and spiritual. It is "life in its immediacy, vividness, and rootedness."[26] Despite this appeal to the ordinary, Kass also describes nature as "elusive" and in its higher forms "irreducibly mysterious."[27]

These two characteristics of biological nature—its everyday familiarity and its elusiveness—lead Kass to credit custom, taboo, and quasi-instinctual responses to new technologies while opposing the Promethean presumption to lay bare or explain away the mystery of nature. The ordinary and the mysterious seem to be epistemological opposites, one suggesting the transparency of the immediately familiar, the other, what is ultimately opaque, yet significantly, both are resistant to reason. Kass leaves little room for any form of reflection that falls between his own form of articulating intuition and the objectifying reason of modern rationalistic science and ethics.

This brings us to Kass's third claim, which is that neither biological science nor our public moral discourse in their current forms are capable of expressing and preserving the connection of our dignity to our biological nature, and in fact they pose the greatest threat to our ability to make this connection. While the same science that reduces nature to an object of disengaged rationality has undermined the ordinary experience of nature and thus also our confidence in the meanings and norms rooted in it, the expansion of notions of liberty and rights beyond the narrowly political confines of early liberalism into areas once governed by very different norms of private life has eroded social patterns and traditions of long standing that are the primary bearers of such meanings and norms.[28] The combination of urgency, even alarm, at the pace of biotechnological development in league with contemporary liberalism and modern science, and wistfulness, bordering on nostalgia, in the face of social and cultural change lends Kass's form of social conservatism its distinctive pathos.

For Kass the implications of the loss of nature as a guide are clear and disturbing. His argument runs something like this: the Cartesian program aims at knowledge of nature that will be useful in securing certain goods, chief among them somatic health and capability. But if we know nature only as instrumental to these goods, how can we be sure that the goods we aim at in subjecting nature to our rational control are genuine goods? If reason consists in rational mastery, then any good for which we make nature an instrument must ultimately be arbitrary, and the body will be treated as a mere instrument. According to Kass, then, there are only two alternatives: either we respect unmodified human nature as the source of what is worthy in human life and, as such, the standard for judging whether future developments in biotechnology contribute to human flourishing or detract from it, or we subject human nature to whatever technological mastery can achieve in accordance with our arbitrary desires.

Two consequences follow from the second alternative, with the loss of nature as a guide. We can sum them up under two headings, one having to do with the degradation of embodied life, that is, the reduction of biological nature to an instrument for desires that, lacking a genuine ground in our lived nature, are ultimately arbitrary, and the other having to do with dehumanization, that is, the reduction of human life to the pursuit of goods such as physical comfort, tranquility of mind, self-esteem, longevity, and so on—the shallow, pointless, and thoroughly diminished lives of Nietzsche's "last men" or of the inhabitants of Huxley's *Brave New World*.

We begin with degradation. Known only in objective and quantitative terms and possessing only instrumental value, the body can be reduced to its functional parts and treated as a mere means to any desirable end. Practices such as selling gametes, tissues, and organs will meet resistance only insofar as they violate norms of autonomy or justice. Yet rational mastery is not a pure exercise of the will for the sake of mastery; as Descartes proposed, it is carried out for the sake of certain kinds of good. This brings us to the theme of dehumanization. Rather than the elevation of biological nature through conscious awareness of and struggle with its neediness and limitations, rational mastery of nature aims to eliminate neediness and overcome limitations. It aims at a certain state of well-being characterized, as we have seen, by goods such as physical comfort, peace of mind, self-esteem, and longevity. It is thus to our humanitarian impulses that biotechnology appeals, but by seeking to eliminate neediness and overcome limitations, it threatens human dignity, effecting a "soft dehumanization."[29]

Thus while biomedicine remains the last refuge of the great modern myth of progress, Kass echoes Nietzsche by warning that what comes after nature may be empty of anything worth admiring. Yet there is an important difference between Kass and Nietzsche in this regard. Kass's celebration of the noble longings that emerge out of heroic struggle with limitation and necessity and disdain for the priority contemporary society gives to well-being, along with his interest in preserving dignity as a term of distinction against democratization of the concept, suggest an aristocratic ethos in opposition to a bourgeois one, a heroic ethic set against an ethic of ordinary life. Certain aspects of Kass's thought clearly confirm this impression.[30] At the same time, the nobility through struggle that Kass commends is found in exactly those areas of life an aristocratic ethic considers incapable of exhibiting excellence, namely, the domains of everyday life, especially that of the generation and rearing of children. It is ordinary life itself that Kass seeks to ennoble, or rather, to preserve from dehumanization.

We have suggested that one great advantage of Kass's position is its recognition that what is at stake in biotechnology is how we understand and face finitude and vulnerability. His vision is consciously tragic in a thoroughly classical sense: the effort to gain rational mastery over the conflicts, tensions, and limitations of life is enticing yet spells doom; the wise course is to look instead for meaning and purpose within the limitations of nature in accordance with reflection on time-honored custom. But the claim that biological nature is the origin and bearer of human meanings and aspirations is a naturalist claim, and it is worth considering this claim from a theological angle.

Both Jewish and Christian theologies offer grounds for suspicion that by making nature bear the entire weight of human meaning and aspiration, Kass demands of nature more than it can give.[31] There are grounds in both traditions for treating nature as a source and bearer of meaning, but the very aspects of nature that Kass emphasizes, namely, neediness and vulnerability, make it just as readily a challenge to meaning. To some extent, of course, there is wide agreement in these traditions with Kass's often rich descriptions of how the incompleteness of our biological nature leads us to seek completeness in others and makes us aware of our finitude. Yet the main currents of these traditions resist the notion that nature as we now experience it embodies these meanings adequately. If Jewish bio-ethicists are a reliable guide, this is especially the case in Judaism, which seems strongly suspicious of claims that neediness and vulnerability are ennobling.[32]

Christian theology has placed greater positive emphasis on biological nature as a reflection, albeit dimmed and refracted by the Fall, of a divinely created order, and this at least partially accounts for the affinity of Kass's position with some Christian theologies. But many Christian theologies hesitate to give biological nature the significance Kass gives it. Some of these theologies allot a greater role to reason in bringing biological nature to the fullness of the created good. Other theologies deny that nature in its fallen form, as we now know and experience it, adequately reflects the created order, which can be grasped only by revelation or some form of mystical knowledge rather than by reflection on biological nature. Still other theologies hold that any theological understanding of biological nature is incomplete until the effects of sin and the eschatological significance of the resurrected body are articulated.

In all of these cases the identification of our present knowledge and experience of biological nature, on the one hand, and the properly human meaning of biological nature, on the other hand, will diverge more than Kass seems to allow. This divergence may in turn open up moral space for efforts to eliminate or alleviate aspects of neediness and vulnerability and for at least some uses of biotechnology that enable people to enjoy a genuine though approximate participation in meanings rooted in nature when limitations of their biological nature would otherwise preclude it, though any such moral space would be bounded by moral injunctions which in practice might rule out some of the same interventions Kass rules out.

In sum, Kass's reflective biology asks too much of nature, while Cartesian mastery expects too little, and together they constitute a dialectical relation within naturalistic humanism. Nature by itself, even in the rich, generous way Kass understands it, as inclusive of psychic and spiritual striving, is unable to contain or fully to express the meaning and purpose of human life in whole or in part. It is neither a complete nor a completely reliable guide to the longings it manifests or to the partial fulfillments of these longings it affords, and to this extent, discontent with the limits nature sets to our longings and to their fulfillment is a theologically valid stance. The Cartesian program, by contrast, embodies the hope that neediness and vulnerability will be eliminated altogether. However, in spite of its quasi-utopian vision, this program despairs of the notion that nature in its neediness and vulnerability is capable of bearing any meaning at all.

Nature as Natural Kinds: Fukuyama

Could some development in biotechnology—in genetic engineering, perhaps, or in neurobiology—alter human nature itself, so that those who undergo the technique or inherit its effects are no longer instances of the same natural kind or members of the same species as those who remain unaltered? Any answer to this question must begin by gaining clarity on what would count as an alteration of nature in this sense and on what uses of biotechnology, if any, would have such an alteration as their effect.

Three considerations bring us closer to clarity on these matters. First, the alteration of human nature can refer to something that happens to the human species itself (or a significant part thereof) or to something that happens to individual members of the species. The first would involve a population effect, which may seem highly unlikely in light of the progress of biotechnology to date. Nevertheless, the alteration of the nature of an indeterminate number of individual human beings is still a matter of interest, given the questions that would arise regarding the moral and theological status of such individuals.

Second, a biotechnological intervention may have a profound effect on something that is essential to our nature without altering our nature. We can distinguish, for example, between a genetic intervention that permanently alters or eliminates the capacity to experience a certain range of emotions, on the one hand, from the ingestion of mood-altering drugs that temporarily suppresses those same emotional responses, on the other hand. It is at least plausible to argue that the former has an effect on our human nature (whether or not it constitutes the loss or transformation of our nature), while it is implausible to argue that the latter has such an effect.

Finally, we can, in principle at least, distinguish between the alteration of human nature and its loss or transformation into something else. We can imagine a research program that permanently alters cells so that the human lifespan expands to two hundred years. This would plausibly count as an alteration of human nature. However, it is less plausible to suppose that those whose cells were altered to bring about the increase would no longer be human beings but something else instead.

Fukuyama does not consistently take account of these distinctions, but he does present a distinctive concept of human nature. He rejects attempts to derive the concept of human nature from observation of behavioral constants along with attempts to identify human nature with some single characteristic or a set of characteristics taken to be essential. In the first case, it is not clear how the alteration or elimination of a contingently universal characteristic would affect human *nature*, while in the second case, assuming that the essential characteristics really do distinguish human beings from other beings in the natural world, it seems unlikely that human nature is under threat from biotechnology. Who, after all, can see the way from the present state of human gene transfer technology to the elimination or radical alteration of reason, consciousness, the capacities for language or morality, or whatever else may be proposed as a candidate for the essentially human characteristic(s)?

But what if human nature consists neither of contingent universals nor of essential characteristics but of the whole complex of evolved characteristics that are, in their sum, typical of the human species? If this is the case, then relatively modest alterations, such as the elimination of the genetic capacity for a certain range of aggressive behavior or emotional response, could be said to affect human nature itself. This is the view Fukuyama expounds in *Our Posthuman Future*. Biotechnology, he thinks, is on the verge of being capable of altering human nature itself, and this power, if used, will have ominous implications for many of the deepest moral commitments of modern liberal democracies.

Fukuyama's argument turns on the close relationship he sees between human nature and politics. His analysis is situated between two poles: Aristotle's insight that human nature is the ultimate ground of our notions of justice and the good and that it sets conditions, positive and negative, for political arrangements, on the one hand, and Nietzsche's insights into the instability of the notion of human dignity in modern liberal democracies and the political implications of its loss, on the other hand. Between these two poles runs the Hegelian narrative about modernity and liberal democracy familiar to readers of Fukuyama's *The End of History and the Last Man*, now corrected to meet the objection that history cannot end as long as science and technology continue to develop.

Against most modern theories, Fukuyama holds that rights are ultimately grounded in human nature: they reflect the wants, needs, and aspirations that a society recognizes and seeks to protect as most fundamental to our humanity. Political arrangements that respect what is most fundamental to human nature in this way will tend to thrive, while those that do not will ultimately prove unstable; liberal democratic orders, Fukuyama thinks, have fared better over time than totalitarian regimes because they reflect a more realistic view of human nature.[33] This is where biotechnology becomes significant. In the late twentieth century, Fukuyama suggests, technological advance (he is thinking primarily of information technologies) favored liberal democracy, while the social engineering projects that were so prevalent earlier in the century (he is thinking primarily of extreme efforts to modify behavior) ultimately failed because they went strongly against the grain of human nature, frustrating the social and political programs built around them. So goes the Aristotelian point. Now, however, with the possibility of altering human nature itself through biotechnology, social engineering will face fewer natural limits, setting the stage for new social experiments based, this time around, on sound science. Meanwhile the alteration of human nature will also mean that the ground of our moral sense will shift.[34] So goes the Nietzschean point.

It is this latter, Nietzschean point that gives Fukuyama's project its urgency. Liberal democracy rests on a conviction that "when we strip all of a person's contingent and accidental characteristics away, there remains some essential human quality underneath that is worthy of a certain minimal level of respect."[35] This is Fukuyama's concept of human dignity, and note that in this definition, dignity resides in "some essential human quality" that all human beings and only human beings share. This brings us to the point of the Nietzschean pole of the argument. Nietzsche, in Fukuyama's view, saw more clearly than do today's deniers of all notions of the essentially human that without the notion of a human essence that unites only and all human beings, belief in and commitment to human equality cannot survive: "If there is a continuum of gradations between human and nonhuman, there is a continuum within the human type as well." And as Nietzsche also saw, this meant liberation from all natural and social constraints for the strong and superficial happiness for the weak.[36]

However, while Nietzsche was convinced that notions of universal human dignity were inextricable from Christianity and would not survive the demise of the latter, Fukuyama ponders the persistence of such notions in liberal democratic societies even in the absence of any religious consensus. The reason for this persistence, he asserts (and here, of course, he departs from Nietzsche and returns to Aristotle), is that the notion of human dignity is not simply a cultural construction of Christianity but is grounded in human nature. However, the capacity of biotechnology to alter human nature threatens this fundamental tenet of liberal democracy by undermining the natural equality on which it is based.[37]

This is the context in which Fukuyama advances his particular conception of human dignity, his notion of what it is that confers moral status on all human beings. It is based, first, on the claim that human nature is the sum of species-typical characteristics and, second, on a biological theory of emergent complexity according to which the behavior of complex wholes is irreducible to the aggregate behavior of their parts. On these grounds Fukuyama proposes that human dignity consists in a complex whole, founded not on any single characteristic such as consciousness, language, and so on but on the whole in which all of these characteristics come together, a whole that itself is a species-typical (and thus a statistical rather than a metaphysical) universal that embraces all human beings and only human beings.[38] Because human nature consists in a complex, irreducible whole of this kind, alterations of parts have effects on the identity of the whole if they are significant enough. Thus biotechnology threatens human dignity by potentially disrupting "the unity or the continuity of human nature, and thereby the human rights that are based on it."[39] If that unity or continuity is disrupted, the natural equality of human beings, based on their common share in the complex whole that is their natural kind, is also disrupted, and it is difficult, Fukuyama thinks, to understand on what grounds moral and political equality could survive such a disruption.

The grounding of human rights in human nature, the relation of liberal democracy to human nature, the biostatistical conception of human nature, and the theory of emergent wholes all require more critical analysis than can be carried out here.[40] However, two points are especially relevant to the question of the normative status of nature. First, Fukuyama's worries about biotechnology are warranted only to the extent that biotechnology could indeed alter human characteristics in a way that changes the identity of the complex whole that is the ground of human dignity. But which interventions, real or imagined, have the potential to do this? Mindful of some of the uses for which mood-altering drugs are prescribed, Fukuyama offers as an example the potential restriction through neuropharmacology of the range of emotions that is typical of the human species. If a certain range of emotional responses is characteristic of the human species and part of the complex human whole, then it is reasonable to suppose that an alteration that had as its effect the loss of one end of this range would have an effect on human nature. But we have noted that unlike the genetic engineering of emotional capacities, which Fukuyama concedes is a long way off at best, mood-altering drugs do not affect human nature itself; they merely bring about temporary alterations (whether suppressions or expressions) of emotions and behaviors. The underlying biological capacities for emotional response remain. And as we also have noted, even if these drugs were capable of bringing about permanent alterations of the emotional or behavioral spectrum, it is unclear, on

Fukuyama's model, what kinds or degrees of alteration would affect the whole in such a way as to alter its identity. In other words, it is unclear what kinds or degree of alteration would involve the transformation of human nature into something else.

Second, it is unclear in the end whether the normative status of nature is secured by Fukuyama's account. According to him, the ultimate value to be protected from advances in biotechnology is the essential quality that makes human beings what we are in spite of all the contingency of our history.[41] Yet if we ask why it is so important to protect our nature, Fukuyama appeals to the moral values of equality and justice that are threatened by the biotechnological alteration of human nature.[42] What stands between us and the disastrous failures of totalitarian regimes, with their attempts at radical social engineering, is our nature, but now this barrier is about to be breached, imperiling the ground of our liberal democratic moral sense. But if the reason for resisting the alteration of human nature, on Fukuyama's account, is that such alteration would threaten our liberal democratic moral convictions, then in the last analysis it is not nature that is normative for Fukuyama but the moral vision of liberal democratic society. While politics for Fukuyama is ontologically dependent on human nature, in the wake of biotechnology the future of human nature as it now exists depends morally, for him, on our commitment to liberal democracy. Put differently, for Fukuyama it is important for the sake of the moral vision that sustains liberal democracy that we preserve the conditions that ground it, and it is for this reason that we must preserve human nature as it is. Ultimately, for Fukuyama, it is only in this instrumental sense that nature is normative.

What may we conclude about the normative status of nature in this third sense and the threat biotechnology poses to it?[43] The shortcomings of Fukuyama's position do not entail that the problem he addresses is not an important one. He rightly points out the link between human nature and human moral status, and this is what is at stake morally in this third conception of nature as normative. Whether or not human dignity and human rights derive from human nature, they are based on the notion that human beings possess a unique moral status that distinguishes them from the rest of the natural world, even when extrahuman nature is accorded some moral status. This claim seems in turn to presuppose that there is some set or range of characteristics that all human beings and only human beings share, on the basis of which they possess this unique moral status. If so, an alteration of human nature, if significant enough, could threaten the moral bond between those who have undergone it and those who have not.

It is important, in assessing this threat, to distinguish two senses in which natural kinds may be morally important. The first sense is ontological; the second is epistemological. With respect to the first sense we have questioned Fukuyama's assumption that biotechnological developments that are likely in the foreseeable future have the potential to make recipients of these technologies members of a different species or instances of a different natural kind.[44] If this ontological unity were broken, where would it leave us? Presumably, we would have to figure out how to treat members of the new species (and they us), just as we are now attempting to figure out how to treat nonhuman primates, given what we know about them, and in the past we had to figure out what status to assign beings such as angels, who resemble us in some ways but not in others.

Even if philosophical considerations and technological limitations lead us to conclude that no biotechnological alterations conceivable at present would compel us to judge that those who undergo them will be members of a different species or instances of a different natural kind, it is worth asking whether some alterations could result in differences that would make it difficult to perceive some human beings as members of the same species or instances of the same natural kind. In other words, a certain degree of similarity in perceivable biological properties seems to be a necessary condition for recognizing another entity as one of us, and alterations in ranges of intelligence, emotions, physical abilities, and other characteristics may become extensive enough to cross this epistemological threshold even without an ontological change. If so, Fukuyama's worries about the stability of our moral and political commitments in an age of biotechnology are warranted, even if we are skeptical about the likelihood that human nature itself will be transformed into something else.

Conclusion

Michael Sandel, Leon Kass, and Francis Fukuyama all set out in the hope that a conception of the normative significance of nature will set limits and give direction to recent and emerging uses of biotechnology where the moral and political order of liberal society, with its narrow focus on autonomy and justice (Sandel), its exaggerated humanitarianism (Kass), and its failure to secure its own grounds (Fukuyama), has failed. In each case we found that the appeal to nature identifies certain goods that are threatened by the contemporary version of the Cartesian program: kinds of worth that resist our will to mastery (Sandel), aspects of embodied life that are the source of human meaning (Kass), and commitments to equality of worth (Fukuyama). In each case, though, we found that the claim to establish nature as a norm was not sustainable, though for different reasons.

We are left in the uncomfortable position of recognizing that to be entirely without nature in any of these three senses would leave us morally impoverished while acknowledging that we are unable to draw clear lines that would indicate the point at which our moral impoverishment would occur. The lesson to be learned from all of this is that it is a mistake to expect nature to do the normative work these three thinkers assign it to do. The loss of nature brings with it the loss of certain goods that are dependent on nature or inextricable from it, and ultimately the defense of nature must take the form of an articulation and defense of those goods.

PART THREE

Geography and Nature

Nature's relationship to the disciplines of ecology and genetics is perhaps more immediately grasped than its relationship to geography. Geographer Edward Soja explains that the "spatial turn" driving new geographical studies has engaged nature from the beginning. Rather than from the study of rural "nature," the new geography emerged in the last decades from the study of urban space, that is, "second nature." Soja makes the provocative proposal that in terms of human history as well as social theory, the "second nature" of the built environment precedes the "first nature" of the biosphere: the space of the city precedes unmediated space as an interpretive framework and gives human order to it. After recounting the history and significance of the transdisciplinary "spatial turn," he sketches how spatial perspectives on nature can inform environmental and labor movements today. The first corollary of the primacy of urban spatiality is the universal "right to the city" and the pursuit of "spatial justice."

Soja's emphasis upon "second nature" is not uncontroversial. We might mistake Soja to be saying natural space is subordinate to urban space. In fact, he is saying that the development of urbanization begins both the absorption and degradation of nature. Nature is no longer isolatable and separate from urbanization, which is not to assign moral priority to either the city or nature. It is from the perspective of second nature that one begins to make sense of and identify value in first nature. Still, it is hard not to see in Soja's work the sort of anthropocentrism for which Christian theology has been criticized from environmental circles. How does "seeing nature spatially" impact the formation of theological and ethical judgments about nature, its decline, and its preservation? Timothy Gorringe and Sallie McFague both challenge the preeminence of urban spatiality, pointing out that cities are the centers of unsustainable consumption in the global North and West. Yet they also take up Soja's concerns about spatial justice and new theoretical perspectives and apply them to the Christian theological tradition.

If "first nature" is decisively altered by "second nature," how should that transformation alter Christian theological reflection in turn? Drawing upon Karl Barth's critique, Gorringe points out that natural theologies in the modern period often neglected their own inevitable social framing by "second nature." By denying their own local context, theologies of nature devolved into a "reactionary" romanticism of the natural world that in the twentieth century impaired their theological judgment. Moreover, God has God's own space, and so the space of (first) nature can never be the sole starting point for theological reflection. A true theology of creation must own up to the implication of first nature within second nature, such that nature is approached theologically only through careful attention to the "built environment," which includes urban spatiality.

While McFague hesitates to affirm Soja's emphasis on the city, she also proposes a major revision to Christian conceptions of nature. Rather than conceive the world as a machine, Christians should draw upon the tradition's resources to view the world as the "body of God." This metaphor emphasizes the sanctity and limits of nature's "body" and motivates response to the impending urban crisis. As scarce food and water remind us that like nature, we are perishable bodies before anything else, McFague questions the wisdom of giving "second nature" greater ethical attention than "first nature."

Does "seeing nature spatially" allow one to perceive injustices more clearly, as in Soja's concluding examples? How, acknowledging the urban space of our perspective and the spatiality of nature, can we still constructively critique urban growth, as both Gorringe and McFague recommend? How are ethical orientations influenced by divergent theological approaches to nature? And how are the spaces of "second nature"—especially the globalized megacities of the twenty-first century—transforming our access to and understanding of "first nature"?

Seeing Nature Spatially

Edward W. Soja

The last decade of the twentieth century has seen a remarkable change in the ways we look at the spatial aspects of human existence and how space affects society, behavior, politics, culture, and economic development. Twenty years ago, thinking critically about the spatiality of human life was largely confined to such fields as geography, architecture, and urban and regional studies. Today, spatial perspectives have entered a much wider variety of disciplines and discourses. In anthropology, economics, and art history, where spatial approaches had been developed to some degree in the past, there has been a significant renaissance. Spatial thinking has also spread widely into fields where explicitly spatial analysis has rarely been emphasized, such as literary criticism, rhetoric, poetry, ethnomusicology, film studies, media and communications, education and critical pedagogy, law, and accounting. To this list, reflecting the present context, must be added theology and religious studies.

Still, the diffusion of spatial perspectives has not entered the mainstream of most disciplinary discourses, and thinking spatially has all too often involved little more than adding to conventional writings a few flashy spatial metaphors and a reference or two to assertively spatial scholars. Increasingly, however, adopting a critical spatial perspective has begun to stimulate a deeper rethinking of core disciplinary issues and a vigorous questioning of long-established theoretical frameworks and foundational concepts. In these more profound and disruptive interventions, space is not just added *a posteriori* to existing modes of interpretation but is foregrounded as the primary or overarching interpretive perspective. This foregrounding—putting space first as a framework for critical analysis—is what I am doing in this essay with regard to the ways we conceive of and understand nature in its double sense of environmental context and essential quality.

Seeing nature from a spatial or geographical perspective is certainly not new. Geographers have always been involved in the study of nature and of human relations with the natural environment. My intent, however, is not to survey and draw insights from this traditional geographical literature but to approach the subject of nature from the more encompassing, richly explanatory and transdisciplinary, critical spatial perspective that has been developing over the past twenty years. Putting space first in looking at nature is, in this sense, an exploration of new ground and a search for new insights.

The core argument that I put forward is easily summarized but unusually difficult to accept, understand, and put into practice, for it clashes with long-standing and influential traditions of Western thought. Simply put, nature and society, and the relations between them, have been fundamentally urban for the past twelve millennia, since the formation of the first permanent urban settlements. Moreover, during this long duration, urbanization and urban spatial causality have been the primary forces behind the transformations of nature as well as all forms of societal development: economic, political, cultural, aesthetic. Even the best contemporary arguments that nature has been socialized, embedded in the dynamics of industrialization and reflexive modernization, and made into an essentially political project are not enough to explain why we may be "without nature." To understand nature today, we must put urban spatiality first.

The Chicago School and the Urbanization of Nature

There is no better place to begin to explore the urbanization of nature than in Chicago, famously described by William Cronon as "nature's metropolis." It is no coincidence that one of the best regional environmental histories of a city was written about Chicago and its multiscalar outreach, from the intensely local to the expansively global, and by a scholar who holds the telling position of the Frederick Jackson Turner Professor of

History, Geography, and Environmental Studies at the University of Wisconsin, Madison. This particular triple specialization, perhaps unique in American academia, provides an evocative platform from which to explore the geohistory of urbanized nature.[1]

In the 1920s and 1930s, what became known as the Chicago School of urban ecology deeply influenced the development of the social sciences in the United States and generated a way of thinking about cities that would create a specifically *urban* sociology. At the same time, it would also tempt the discipline of geography to consider redefining itself as the study of human ecology, fusing together its traditional physical and human duality. This distinctive spatial and ecological approach to studying cities drew heavily from German intellectual thought, ranging from Georg Simmel's conception of the fundamental nature or essence of urban life, to the philosophical debates about the theory and practice of historiography, to Hegelian and Marxian notions of "second" nature, that is, a socialized world created from a pristine "first" nature but increasingly separate and distinct, subject to its own laws of behavior and development.[2]

What most distinguished the Chicago School approach, however, was another German borrowing. The term *ecology* was first used in German natural science in the late nineteenth century and was to become the core concept for urban studies in Chicago. The root of the term is the Greek *oikos*, meaning "home," and is also the root term for economics, which preceded the word *ecology* and originally had to do with managing the affairs of the household. *Ecology* referred to a kind of natural management of the physical environment and its relations to the human organisms living within it. With very little social science theory to draw on, especially with regard to the city, the Chicago scholars adapted the natural science concept and applied it not to the physical or natural environment, which received very little specific attention, but to the socially and culturally constructed *urban environment*, creating the hybrid concept of "urban ecology."

Urban ecology represented the city as a social organism shaped by a mixture of physical and cultural processes. In particular, the urban ecologists drew on botanical science, with its developing notions of species invasion and succession, competition for space and location, and the movement toward an equilibrating "climax" or end-state vegetation. Following in the long tradition of social science imitating physical science, the Chicago School analogously extended and thereby socialized ecological concepts into the study of cities and urbanism generally.[3] For the Chicago

School, socialized or second nature was essentially urbanized and, for the most part, urban-generated.

The most representative and influential work of this collection of urban scholars is *The City: Suggestions for Investigation of Human Behavior in the Urban Environment* (1925), written by three of the leading Chicago sociologists, Robert Park, Ernest Burgess, and Roderick Mackenzie.[4] The City, capitalized here as in the original to signify an ambition to generalize about the essential qualities of all cities, was seen as an "ecological crucible" in which urbanism as a way of life was socially produced. Of particular interest in this urbanized approach to nature were so-called "natural areas," defined as territorial units whose distinctive physical, economic, and cultural characteristics are the product of the "unplanned operations of ecological and social forces."[5]

The ambitions of the Chicago School often extended still further to connect urban nature with human nature. In his introduction to a reissue of *The City* in 1967, Morris Janowitz states that the city is not simply an artifact or a background to social life. It "embodies the real nature of human nature. . . . It is an expression of mankind in general and specifically of the social relations generated by territoriality." Embedded in this glib urban humanism was an extraordinary assumption, one both rarely examined by the Chicago scholars and indeed virtually invisible—if not inconceivable—in most of Western social theory until very recently: that human beings as social animals and human culture more generally are *urban by nature*.[6]

Although the specific language of spatiality was rarely if ever used by them, the Chicago School was the first systematic effort by a collection of scholars to theorize and, more emphatically, to give significant explanatory power to what can be called the spatial specificity of urbanism, the ways in which cities are geographically organized and experienced. The foundational spatial model of urban life was Burgess's notion of "concentric zonation," a throwback in many ways to the land-use theories of the German political economist von Thünen as well as to Friedrich Engels' description of mid-nineteenth-century Manchester. From this perspective, human behavior in the urban environment is shaped and even *caused by* a particular geography consisting of a series of concentric rings extending outward from a generative nodal center and held together by a combination of powerful centrifugal and centripetal forces. Later theories supplemented the model with additional features—specialized axial wedges stemming from the preeminent center, racial and ethnic enclaves, and the possibility of multiple nuclei—but the foundational model of concentric zonation remained in the foreground.

A large proportion of the literature produced by the Chicago School consisted of empirical case studies of urban behavior investigating the formation of natural areas and subcultures that express this highly centralized concentricity. Whether the subject was the hobo, taxi-dance halls, land values, the chain store, the gang, the ghetto, or vice and prostitution, the aim was to show how these phenomena differed from zone to zone as products of the "unplanned operation" of ecological and social forces. Here, then, was another "invisible hand" shaping behavior, culture, social relations, and economic development, for the City was also seen as both the outcome and the medium of modernization. Chicago, with its center neatly defined by the Loop, was the primary laboratory for the theoretical and empirical study of urban ecology; yet the aim was not just to understand the particularities of Chicago nor even of the urbanized nature of cities as such, but to create a more general theory of human development in its fullest sense.

These larger ambitions and the accompanying focus on what many presumed to be extrasocial ecological processes led many sociologists (especially those who preferred the name *sociology* without an *urban* modifier) to abandon urban ecology, especially after World War II. Sociologists would not forget the Chicago School entirely but would selectively reconstruct its accomplishments to avoid any hint of environmental determinism and to endow it with merely historical significance in the development of other sociological methods treating race, ethnicity, and migration. It would be geographers, and later economists (as well as a few sociologists), who would carry forward many of the Chicago School traditions, mainly in the form of advanced statistical ecologies and urban economic model-building.[7]

There are a few specific points to remember about the Chicago School's understanding of the city's place in nature. For all its faults—and there were many—the Chicago School of urban ecology still stands out today, at a time when critical spatial perspectives have spread to almost every discipline, as the most concerted and successful attempt before the closing decades of the twentieth century to demonstrate the importance of *urban spatial causality*, namely, the ways in which the city as an urban agglomeration generates forces of creativity, innovation, economic development, and social change.[8] Attached to this notion of urban spatial causality was an even broader idea about the urbanization of nature, in its both physical and human forms. There are many studies of how humanity has transformed the physical environment for better and worse and likewise how the physical environment affects human behavior, and the powerful distinction between naïvely given first and creatively socialized second nature (the raw and the cooked, so to speak) has been with us for more than a century. What the Chicago School pioneered, however, was the notion that *physical and human nature are essentially urban* and that understanding the urbanization of (first and second) nature is best achieved by foregrounding a spatial perspective.

The Chicago School approach to urban spatiality was so exceptional and against the prevailing historical grain of Western social thought that it seemed incomprehensible, if not heretical, to most social scientists. After a brief period of widespread recognition and impact, urban ecology was either rejected as beyond the acceptable bounds of both liberal social science and radical scientific socialism or Marxism, or else it was simply ignored as a powerful force in social theory and practice. Part of the reason for these reactions has to do with the Chicago School approach itself. There were always, for example, certain ambiguous distinctions: between urban form and urban environment, between human and natural ecology, and between so-called first and second natures. That is, the Chicago School tended to dualize ecological and social forces without rigorously defining the mode of their relationship. This gave the unintentional appearance that physical or socialized nature was external to society, naïvely given and beyond the control of social forces, created through "unplanned" operations. That urban spatiality is precisely socially produced and therefore an integral and inherent part of human society itself may have been the intended argument, but it was never made sufficiently clear. Indeed it was this very notion that the space of nature is socially produced and therefore subject to substantive social change that would become the springboard for a radical reconceptualization of urban spatiality in the last decades of the twentieth century.

A few bold statements can help to summarize the contemporary legacy of the Chicago School with regard to the critical study of the urban spatiality of nature. First, socially constructed cityspace is not simply located in nature; it is the most powerful generative force socializing nature and stimulating societal development through this process. Second, the social space of nature in all its forms is urbanized and has been for at least twelve thousand years, ever since the first permanent human settlements arose in southwest Asia. In this sense, one can say that human societies have been "without nature," at least in its pristine, primordial, Edenic form, from their beginnings, despite various attempts to obscure and bury this loss.[9] In what follows, I try to explain these observations.

Ontological Struggles over Space and Time

The transdisciplinary spatial turn that has been occurring in recent years did not happen overnight. In its most significant sense, it is the product of complex ontological and epistemological debates about the nature of human existence and the way we accumulate knowledge about the world that have been going on for more than a century. Fundamentally, these debates revolve around the relations between space and time, or the spatiality and temporality of human existence. A strong argument can be made that from as far back as the middle of the nineteenth century, Western intellectual traditions have tended to prioritize time over space and, by extension, history over geography as modes of understanding the essential nature of being-in-the-world. This ontological priority has shaped prevailing epistemologies, affected theory-building and empirical science, and promoted a persistent precession of the historical over the geographical imagination, putting time and history first as an interpretive framework.

Among the most influential figures sustaining and rationalizing this ontological priority—putting time assertively ahead of space in understanding the nature of social being—was Martin Heidegger, whose classic work *Sein und Zeit* (1927) captured the foregrounding of time in the title. Heidegger began to question his own view of the relation between time, space, and social being in his later work, recognizing that being-in-the-world, *Dasein*, adds a certain thereness to human existence, a spatiality of being as he called it. Could it be that space, *Raum*, was as essential to being as time, *Zeit*? Should not the nature of being be thought of as existing in time and space simultaneously, with neither prioritized over the other? He explored the possibility seriously but eventually concluded, with some residual ambivalence, that the time of being-in-the-world, the history of being, continued to deserve a privileged position over life's inherent spatiality.[10]

Heidegger's ontological contemplations did not create the relative imbalance between time and space in Western social thought, nor did he intend to take away the causal or explanatory power of human spatiality. One might describe his conceptualization of time's relation to space as one of *primus inter pares*, a first among equals. But there were other forces that ruptured a more equitable view of the relative importance of time versus space, history versus geography, not just privileging time and history but also reducing space and geography to a mere background, container, or reflection of social life, with no autonomous force of its own. This subordination of space to time was particularly deeply embedded in the formation of the liberal social sciences and the emergence of a radical scientific socialism, also known as Marxist historical materialism. In the prevailing mainstreams of Western liberal and radical intellectual thought, the spatial dimension was persistently seen as external to society, an environmental background that was "naturally" given as a part of physical nature.[11]

One of the first influential scholars to identify and challenge this deep ontological bias was Michel Foucault. In an often-quoted observation from an interview by a group of radical French geographers in the 1970s, he began by asking, "Did it start with Bergson or before?" Here he was referring to the French philosopher Henri Bergson, who passionately wrote about the revelatory power of the historical imagination. Foucault then observed, thinking such folly was past, that in Western thought, "Space was treated as the dead, the fixed, the undialectical, the immobile. Time, on the contrary, was richness, fecundity, life, dialectic."[12] He suggested quite clearly that this contrast was both logically untenable and intellectually produced.

In some lecture notes from 1967, published as *Des espaces autres* (translated as "Of Other Spaces"), Foucault specifically located this ontological bias in the late-nineteenth-century "obsession" with history, "with its themes of development and of suspension, of crisis and cycle, themes of the ever-accumulating past, with its great preponderance of dead men and the menacing glaciation of the world."[13] The present, he optimistically predicted, will be the epoch of space, of simultaneity and juxtaposition, the near and far, the side-by-side and the dispersed. Reflecting this perceived imminence, Foucault would take the lead in a radical revisioning of the relations between space and time that would powerfully influence spatial thinking for decades to come.

Foucault would weave into nearly all his work a much more balanced spatiotemporality, especially with regard to the relations between space, knowledge, and power. History was not pushed into the background but was given co-priority in a critical *geohistorical* perspective. To create this rebalanced ontology, however, it was necessary to strengthen the powers of the spatial or geographical imagination. It can be argued that many of the most important insights in Foucault's work arose, in significant ways, from putting space first. For many reasons, including the persistent strength of a particular form of historicism in Western thought that peripheralized the importance of spatial thinking, Foucault's assertion of the primary importance of human spatiality and his call to develop a richer, stronger form of spatial thinking to match what had developed around time and history had relatively little effect until the 1990s, when it became a vital part of the transdisciplinary spatial turn.

Although not as directly and explicitly as Foucault, there were a few others in the 1960s and early 1970s raising similar questions about this ingrained philosophical tradition of invigorating time and history with dynamic, developmental, generative force while deadening and naturalizing space and geography into an extraneous condition or context. Significantly, this was a period of multiplying urban, anticolonial, and environmental crises, many of which were rooted in the uneven development, income disparities, and forms of territorial control evident in local, urban, regional, national, and international geographies. That these problems needed to be understood historically was obvious and unquestioned. The synchronic concatenation of crises on multiple scales, from the global to the local, however, seemed also to call for a more spatial or geographical understanding. In this sense, the spatial turn was as much part of the crisis-generated restructuring processes of the past three decades as were globalization, new information and communications technologies, and the shift from Fordism to post-Fordism.

The reassertion of a critical spatial perspective in Western social and political thought began during this period of crisis and instability. Summarizing broadly, three figures stand out as leading the way in significantly expanding the scope of the geographical imagination in ways that would justify and sustain the ontological and epistemological rebalancing of space and time, geographical and historical perspectives. As mentioned, Foucault played a key role not through explicit theorizations but by practicing his spatialized archaeology and genealogy of knowledge and power in his major writings. When he did attempt to conceptualize his approach, he described it as "heterotopology," the study of alternative or "other" spaces, a way of interpreting human spatiality that differed radically from all preexisting modes of spatial thinking.

Working in Paris at the same time as Foucault and developing a remarkably similar reconceptualization of space and spatiality was the Marxist metaphilosopher Henri Lefebvre. He, too, felt that existing spatial perspectives were useful but inadequate to the task of bringing spatial thinking to the same level achieved by thinking historically and socially, especially in the dialectical and historical materialism of Marx. Like Foucault, he criticized the bicameral nature of the geographical imagination, with its almost exclusive emphasis on materialist and idealist approaches, and worked to transcend this dichotomy with a radically new and different way of interpreting space and more specifically the effects of urban spatiality.[14]

Materialist approaches had concentrated on what Lefebvre called *perceived space*, measurable and mappable spatial practices that etched social relations into specific geographies. In contrast, idealist approaches had focused on *conceived space* and its cultural and ideological representations and semiotic imagery. The first involved "things in space" while the second dealt with "thoughts about space." Like Foucault, Lefebvre sought a more comprehensive and politically insightful way of looking at what he called *lived space*, the space that encompassed more than material spatial practices and ideational representations. Lived space occupies the scale and scope of lived time, of biography and history, and represents a way of thinking about space on an ontological and epistemological level similar to that of time.

The third key figure, David Harvey, began building his new version of spatialized Marxism in *Social Justice and the City*, published in 1973, one year before Lefebvre's major work *La production de l'espace* appeared in French (the English translation was published in 1991, the year of Lefebvre's death). Harvey begins his book with a creative and critical comparison of the historical and geographical imaginations and moves forward to develop an essentially new field of historical and geographical materialism, a Marxism that is simultaneously historical, geographical, and social. He would develop his reconceptualization of space and what he would call the "urban condition under capitalism" in many different ways over the next thirty years as the most influential figure in a new field of Marxist geography.

Some of the constraints of Marxist orthodoxy, especially the continued privileging of the historical and the social over the spatial, would blunt the specific impact of Harvey's work and that of other Marxist geographers on the ontological struggle to rebalance the triad of sociality, historicality, and spatiality. Putting space first as part of a rebalanced ontology of being and becoming was conceptually unacceptable to most Marxists, including those who considered themselves geographers and spatial analysts. Social relations, class struggle, and the forces behind capital accumulation were widely applied to explain geographical patterns and outcomes, but the possibility that these geographical outcomes could feed back to significantly affect class relations and capital accumulation was strongly resisted. Lefebvre's radical reconceptualization of specifically urban spatiality, for example, was seen as going too far, falling into an excessive spatialism that worked against revolutionary social consciousness and change.

Similar resistance existed in the liberal social sciences, where the historical and closely related sociological imaginations continued to deflect a causally empowered spatial epistemology. With a few exceptions, such as the Chicago School, spatial thinking and forms of geographical explanation, especially with regard to the generative forces arising from the spatial specificity of urbanism, played as little a role in the formation of Western social theory as they did in the development of Western Marxism. A similarly weak tradition of spatial explanation characterized all the specialized social science disciplines, from economics and political science to sociology and psychology. Spatial stirrings would occur on the fringes of the social sciences, but a more serious encounter would for the most part be delayed until the mid-1990s.

Over the period being discussed here—from the tumultuous and crisis-filled 1960s and early 1970s, when Lefebvre, Foucault, and Harvey called for a radically new mode of spatial thinking, to the mid-1990s and the transdisciplinary spatial turn—the field of geography was significantly transformed. Up to the last third of the twentieth century, geography remained an essentially descriptive discipline, markedly peripheral to the development of Western social theory and fundamentally acquiescent to the privileged place of history in the Western intellectual division of labor. Beginning in the 1960s, through what some called a quantitative and theoretical revolution, geography emerged as a positivist social science focused on increasingly sophisticated mathematical and statistical descriptions, theoretical formulations based on such spatial parameters as the frictional costs of distance, and other forms of analyzing the spatial organization of society.

Particularly pertinent to the discussion of nature, geography, unlike history, maintained its dual interest in both physical-environmental and human-social geographical studies, and geographers to this day consider themselves to be, if I can use the term loosely, the natural leaders in the study of human-environment (or culture-nature) relations. Physical and natural science had always informed the study of physical geography and, as mentioned above, influenced the geographical thinking of the Chicago School, but it would play only a minor supportive role in the making of human geography into a rigorous social science. Looked at somewhat differently, there was relatively little attention given to nature and the physical environment in the new scientific human geography. This also meant that the critical reconstruction of scientific human geography and its particular brand of spatial analysis that would occur after the early 1970s, under the influence of Marxist, feminist, and postcolonialist critiques, among others, would not be felt very strongly in physical geography. New approaches to nature would for the most part fall between the disciplinary cracks.

Over the last two decades of the twentieth century, however, a new field of critical human geography emerged and became the primary location for an eclectic range of spatial studies broadly exploring the manifold relations between "society and space," to cite the title of a key journal fostering these developments.[15] Although little explicit attention was given to the ontological struggles over space and time during this period, the community of scholars interested in spatial thinking was slowly expanding well beyond geography and the other traditionally spatial disciplines, such as urban and regional studies and architecture. While there continued to be antagonistic squabbles between competing critical perspectives, especially within geography, the accumulation of insightful studies about the spatiality of social life was sufficiently impressive to create the much wider, transdisciplinary diffusion of spatial thinking that has proceeded apace over the past decade.

Rethinking the Spatiality of Human Life

What, then, are the distinguishing features of the new spatial perspectives that have emerged from these ontological and epistemological struggles? Perhaps the most obvious starting point is the recognition that we are all inherently and unavoidably spatial beings. Our first act in coming into the world is to occupy space, and from the start we are participants in an interactive process in which we shape the spaces around us at the same time as they shape our being and becoming. This existential spatiality always combines with sociality and historicality, creating what Lefebvre described as a "triple dialectic" in which our lives develop through three encompassing, interactive, and mutually formative processes: the production of space, the making of history, and the constitution of society.[16] Even when putting the spatiality of being first as a means of breaking down tendencies to privilege sociality and/or historicality, the triple dialectic keeps us aware that our spatial lives are always simultaneously social and historical.

This radically revised "trialectical" ontology, as I have called it,[17] is only a starting point but a very significant one, for it signals the need for a concomitant revision of almost all established epistemologies, the ways in which we obtain accurate knowledge of the world. Just as everything in the physical world consists of three interactive qualities—space, time, and matter/energy—so, too, is the human world comprised of an ontological and epistemological triad: spatiality, historicality, sociality. We have long been comfortable with the notion that every individual, every social formation, every human society, exists in time and develops historically through time. What the rebalanced ontology makes us realize is that all history is always spatial, that history develops in and through space. Similarly, all social life is inherently, unavoidably, and saliently spatial. Just as there are no ahistorical societies, there are no aspatial societies or social relations.

This geohistorical understanding of the relations between society and space has not yet been widely recognized in all its implications, but accepting it entails that much of the knowledge about human life accumulated over the past two centuries may suffer from significant methodological flaws, namely a deficient explanatory emphasis given to spatiality. Likewise, foregrounding the spatial can generate radical new insights into traditional subject matter. To cite one particularly germane example, foregrounding the spatial generates a new perspective on the geohistory of nature itself and upends the conventional pastoral narrative of societal development over the last twelve thousand years.

To concretize further, every human, every spatial being, exists within a multilayered nesting of what can be described as nodal regions. The individual body (or the ego), with its surrounding bubbles of personal space reflecting and shaping behavior, is a model of the nodal region, a centralized space revolving around the (mobile) body and creating what the poet Adrienne Rich once called the "geography closest in." Beyond the body are much less mobile, socially produced nodal regions of varying scales and scopes. To describe these larger-scale nodal regions, however, requires a more specific geohistorical understanding, one that connects the spatiality of being directly to the urbanization process.

For most of the existence of *Homo sapiens*, the mobile nodal region of the human body was engaged in two levels of interaction, one in a set of social relations with a small number of other sapient beings, mainly hunters and gatherers, organized in bands that rarely contained more than forty individuals; and the other as a direct relation with nature and a relatively pristine natural environment and biosphere. Starting around twelve thousand years ago, however, another level of spatial interaction entered the picture, with a widened social scale and scope, bulging outward the reach of humanity. Human settlement, the movement of humans into materially constructed or built environments, created a new, more decidedly fixed geography. By its very nature, this new geography, with its temporal and social commitments to place, was also nodal and regional in its organization, in the sense of being an agglomeration of activities and built forms that extended social effects outward from the center to a periphery, an outer edge or boundary, the relation between center and periphery being both centrifugal and centripetal.[18]

This momentous step in the geohistory of societal development radically changed the relation between society and nature by creating an intervening and specifically urbanized nature, socially "cooked" and internalized rather than "raw" and detached. Prior to this urbanization process, social relations and human labor etched their effects directly on a natural environment, creating such forms as hunting territories, favored gathering areas, important sites for water and other resources, camping places, cave paintings, and so on. After the beginning of relatively permanent human settlement, a new socially produced geography was created and added to this, introducing an arena for a new level of dialectical interaction between society and space in which social processes and spatial forms shaped each other. Everyday life and societal development were no longer so directly shaped by relations with the natural environment alone. Urban agglomeration gave rise to a mediating, socially produced nature that altered the spatiality of social life up to the present day through the intrinsic generation of positive forces of innovation and creativity as well as negative processes associated with unequal power relations, increased social inequality, and growing environmental degradation.

The urban big bang that socialized nature may be the most important event in human geohistory, yet we know very little about it, its causes, and its consequences. It surely represents a crucial step in the early development of agrarian societies, since farming and animal husbandry emerged as urban-generated occupations, as Jane Jacobs argues in her 1969 classic, *The Economy of Cities*.[19] Incipient urbanization was also the trigger for a remarkable development of collective culture and religion that was associated with the construction of humanity's first truly "built" environments. The simple and moveable encampments that existed for more than 2 million years were replaced by more permanent stone buildings, pathways for mobility, painted walls, places for meeting and exchange. What followed the stimulus of urban agglomeration was the transformation of hunters, gatherers, and traders into farmers and herders, priests and shamans, kings and emperors, bureaucrats and warriors, and, later, industrialists and factory workers, scientists and technicians, professors and students, librarians and entertainers, software developers and political spin doctors, an urban-generated multiplication of human activities and occupations that continues to the present.

Recognizing the primary importance of urbanization in the geohistory of societal development over the past twelve thousand years is one of the most transformative, provocative, and, for many, difficult-to-accept insights to have arisen from the new spatial perspectives. On the one hand, it is stimulating new fields of inquiry centering on how contemporary urban agglomerations affect their resident populations and hinterland regions in both positive and negative ways. On the other hand, it is giving us new perspectives on the past, creating in many cases a radical revisioning of conventional wisdom.

Only with an appreciation for urban spatial causality can we make, after years of obfuscation, practical and theoretical sense of such prescient observations as that of Henri Lefebvre when he argued as far back as the 1960s that societal development is conceivable only in urban life, through the realization of urban society. Or the statement by Kathleen Kenyon, lead archaeologist in the excavation of ancient Jericho, one of the world's earliest urban settlements, that "Once man is settled in one spot, the rest follows."[20] Or the evocative claim made by Jane Jacobs that "without cities, we would all be poor," in essence recognizing that we would have remained hunters and gatherers without the intervention of permanent urban settlement.[21] If we can define a "space of creation" for human society, it would be decidedly urban in cause and effect.

Reflections on the Urban Spatiality of Nature

Seeing nature spatially starts with conceptualizing it as socially produced and inherently urbanized space. The urban spatiality of nature in essence "denaturalizes" nature and charges it with social meaning, connecting it to the dynamics of economic and cultural development and filling it with competitive politics and ideology. As an integral part of the spatiality of human life, nature is always mutable, subject to modification for good or bad. Raw physical nature may be naïvely or even divinely given to begin with, but once urban society comes into being, a new nature is created that blends into and absorbs what existed before. One might say that the

City *re-places* nature. There is no doubt that physical and biological processes continue to operate, but they become part of this urban replacement and are never beyond or entirely free from human modification.

Rather than a simple sequencing of first then second nature, the urbanization of nature is better described as a process of recursive hybridization, or what I have called a critical "thirding," that is, the creation of something new and different from the breakdown and reconstitution of binary distinctions.[22] First and second nature are conceptually as well as materially recombined in another nature that is significantly different from either of the originals yet includes them both in a more comprehensive frame. This socialized and spatialized "other" nature does not terminate reconceptualization at three levels, such as in a dialectic of thesis-antithesis-synthesis, but radically opens up the process to a continuous expansion, to the creation of new knowledges, requiring that we move beyond what we already know in an endless search for expanded ways of understanding being-in-the-world.

The City is thus seen as a crucible not so much of ecological processes, as in the Chicago School, but of sociospatial processes and the production of urbanity, hybridity, multiplicity, and difference. It is where not just the duality of first and second nature is reconstituted but where all totalizing dualisms and dichotomies are rethought and connected together: subject/object, natural/social, technological/biological, human/machine, city/countryside, center/periphery, sacred/profane, endogenous/exogenous, global/local, utopia/dystopia, order/chaos, capitalism/socialism. In this replacement, nature is absorbed into the complex and never completely knowable realm of what Lefebvre called "lived space" and Foucault termed "heterotopology."[23]

Our understanding of nature in its broadest sense must be contextualized at multiple regional scales, from the body to the planet. At each of these scales, original nature, physical as well as human, has been involved in a process of transformation from the very beginnings of urban society. Modern technological and scientific advances, from biogenetic manipulation to rainmaking, as well as punctured ozone layers, acid rain, and other forms of environmental degradation, do not signal some new trajectory for nature or a sudden estrangement from or destruction of the physical environment. In a significant sense, as noted above, we have been "without nature" in its purest, pristine, and naïvely given form for twelve thousand years.

The reconfiguration of nature does not mean that we can avoid any responsibility to address contemporary environmental problems by emphasizing their normality. On the contrary, it is new forms of spatial consciousness and environmental awareness that compel us to confront the radical degradation of physical and built environments. Seeing nature spatially helps us to demystify nature and thereby focuses our attention on specifically urban contexts, for it is here that the forces shaping, transforming, and destroying nature are collectively generated and where these processes can best be socially controlled and directed.

Although adopting a critical spatial perspective is not the only way to arrive at these realizations, seeing nature spatially compels one to revisit well-established ideas about the relations between environment and society. Viewing nature as urbanized, for example, makes it impossible to see natural and social worlds as separate and distinct. Such a dichotomous view of human-environment relations, with its oppositional and often combative logic, has to a significant degree been sustained and promulgated by the normal practices of the natural and social sciences, each charged with scientifically theorizing and analyzing the distinctive processes shaping these separate worlds and how one world affects and is affected by the other. The disciplines of history and geography (although certainly not all geographers and historians) have also tended to reinforce binary thinking by maintaining a strict dualism between physical and social worlds. While geographers have often sought to transcend its physical-human moieties (which disappeared from historiography long ago), the intellectual and interpretive dualism remains in force in most contemporary geographical research and writing.

This still prevailing view of society's dichotomized relation with nature has a language and what one might even call a mythology of its own. Society is seen as taming, conquering, destroying, exploiting, or else preserving, conserving, adapting to, revering, enjoying nature. Political divisions often revolve around utilitarian versus preservationist approaches to the physical environment, even when both sides see the possibilities for progress, development, recreation, and re-creation through cooperative action. In all these reactive behaviors, nature remains "out there," exogenous, separate, ruled by its own independent forces and dynamics. In its own way, nature also "reacts" by being alternatively magisterial and sacred, rich and bountiful, inert and passive, destructive and revengeful, showing off its natural beauty or striking back with awesome power.

Seeing nature spatially challenges this dichotomous mentality in at least two ways. The first arises from viewing nature as part of a sociospatial dialectic wherein there is a mutually formative relation between spatiality and sociality and hence between nature and society. Through this dialectic, sociality is spatially materialized and made concretely real and imagined; and in turn, spatiality (including the spaces of nature) is simultaneously socialized and politicized, filled with politics, culture, ideology, conflict, justice and injustice, and, most important, with the emphatic realization that it is subject to significant change through collective social action. Rather than being couched in a simple interactive duality, the nature-society relation is better seen as integral to this sociospatial dialectic, as incorporated into the social production of space and thereby inherently urbanized, always affected in some way by the spillover effects, negative and positive, of urban agglomeration. Spatializing and socializing nature as well as related concepts of ecology and environment in this way challenges our traditional understanding of what is natural and what is not. It makes us more effectively aware that everything we describe as natural is always already socialized, subject not just to natural laws but also to societal decisions and regulations.

Take the case of "natural" disasters or "natural" resources, for example. Seeing nature spatially suggests that there is no such thing as a natural disaster, if by this we mean an event that stands beyond political responsibility. An earthquake or hurricane becomes a disaster only in terms of its social context. Droughts without associated (and often preventable) famines may be described as natural but they are not disasters. Mother Nature never strikes back or gets even, nor is nature ever the cause of disaster in and of itself. Disasters are essentially socially created, the results of mutable economic and political decisions with respect to human settlement and productive activity as they are worked out on multiple scales from the local to the global. This does not mean that we should not study earthquakes, hurricanes, climate change, soil erosion, or global warming as physical processes but that we must never allow their physicality to obscure their significant connections to the social and political world, no matter what the spin doctors say.

The tragedy of New Orleans in the aftermath of Hurricane Katrina, for example, thus can be seen as arising from a failure of governance at the local, state, and especially federal levels to deal with specifically urban problems, from desperate poverty to crumbling infrastructure. That this failure is connected to the Office of Homeland Security, the Federal

Emergency Management Agency (FEMA), an obsession with antiterrorism, military spending, and everything associated with the war in Iraq opens up another story that has little to do with nature but a great deal to do with the need to denaturalize, politicize, and urbanize our way of thinking about nature. Especially pertinent here is the geohistory of the entire Lower Mississippi River Delta, the poorest and most racially stratified region in the United States. For the past century at least, in part because of the unusual power and influence of its often racially biased politicians in Congress and the presidency, the delta region, particularly New Orleans, has been marked by persistent neglect with regard to its extreme poverty and the needs of its large African-American population.[24]

The 2005 tragedy reinforces the need to denaturalize our understanding of nature. In much the same way as it can be argued that there are no natural disasters, it can be said that there is no such thing as natural limits to growth and societal development, especially when one sees them both arising from the stimulus of urban agglomeration. What is limiting growth and development and creating famine, poverty, and environmental degradation is not so much the absolute amount of food, shelter, clothing, and energy produced in the world but rather the overly concentrated geographical distribution of what we produce and consume. Most conventional approaches to nature and the natural environment obfuscate this fundamental distinction and detract from the need to focus attention on the geopolitics of redistribution.

Obscured in similar ways are the urban social origins and definition of natural resources and the related notion of natural endowments in terms of the wealth of nations. When nature is seen as detached from society and social spatialization, it distorts one's understanding of the causes and consequences of geographically uneven societal development. One country, area, or culture developing more rapidly and successfully than another, especially in the contemporary context, is often seen as either the result of a naïvely "given" distribution of natural resources (a roll of the dice, so to speak) or else as divinely given advantage (given to the "chosen people"). Japan, for example, is often praised as an anomaly for having reached high levels of economic development without abundant natural resources. For many, from secular economists to fundamentalist Christians, the United States is considered to have been unusually well endowed or uniquely blessed with natural resources.

Denaturalizing the uneven development process brings us back, in an admittedly roundabout way, to Chicago and William Cronon, as well as to the new economic geography or geographical economics mentioned above. Here we find abundant, persuasive arguments that so-called natural endowment plays a relatively unimportant role in economic development, whether one is speaking of cities, regions, or nation-states. As Cronon argues, what was most remarkable about Chicago's rise as the central city of the American heartland was the relative absence of any distinctive natural advantages of its site and immediate hinterland.[25] What mattered much more were the self-generating developmental effects of socially organized urban and regional geographies, according to which Chicago became the primary hub of an expanding and increasingly integrated system of varying urban agglomerations.

Cronon's work has been directly connected to the early development of the new geographical economics by perhaps its most prominent exponent and recipient of the 2008 Nobel Prize in Economics, Paul Krugman, also known for his insightful political commentary. Krugman's 1993 article "First Nature, Second Nature, and Metropolitan Location," was one of the earliest to recognize explicitly the relative importance of urbanized nature and the generative effects of urban agglomeration in economic development.[26] The paper begins with a reference to Cronon's "justly acclaimed" *Nature's Metropolis*, noting the remarkable "absence of any distinctive natural advantages of Chicago's site." Krugman goes on to say:

> As Cronon puts it, the advantages that "first nature" failed to provide the city were more than made up for by the self-reinforcing advantages of "second nature": the concentration of population and production in Chicago, and the city's role as a transportation hub, provided the incentive for still more concentration of production there, and caused all roads to lead to Chicago.

Arguments like Cronon's and Krugman's convey the need to see all aspects of the natural and human environment, from creativity and innovation to poverty and political oppression, in conjunction with the dynamics of urban agglomeration and by means of the explanatory power of urban spatial causality. Creativity, innovation, development, and change, as well as disasters, famines, and environmental degradation in all its forms are significantly, although not entirely, rooted in specifically urban processes and conditions.

Epilogue

An excellent contemporary example of the power of thinking spatially about nature is the development of the environmental justice movement

(EJM).[27] The struggle for environmental justice first emerged from the civil rights movement in the United States and with significant support from religious organizations. As an urban-based social movement, it built on a growing awareness that the negative effects of air and water pollution, hazardous waste production and disposal, fires and floods, as well as the implementation of federal environmental policies and regulations were disproportionately felt in African-American and other minority and poor communities and populations. Although it has become allied with some environmentalist groups, the EJM looks at nature in ways that differ significantly from mainstream environmentalism.

At the heart of these differences is the recognition that environmental problems and distributional injustices are socially produced and thus amenable to being resolved or ameliorated through social action. Just as important, environmental injustice is seen as related to industrial production and embedded in the specific geography of cities and regions. Both the public and the private sectors contributed to the creation and maintenance of these contextual injustices and have become the targets for seeking improvements. The search for environmental justice thus shifted attention away from the physical environment per se to the socialized, spatialized, and politicized urban environment.

Although the EJM revolved primarily around racial issues at first, it evolved in ways that connected it to a much wider range of discriminatory practices, and in particular to locational discrimination, which is the unequal treatment before the law of people based on their place of residence or place of work. In this sense, the EJM became a movement for what can be described as *spatial justice*. Seeing the problems of injustice and inequality spatially opened up new sources of solidarity and mobility and connected the EJM to the new spatial perspectives emerging over the last twenty years. The result has been an innovative strategic spatialization of the EJM.

Early examples of the struggle for environmental justice as spatial justice involved the siting of potentially hazardous facilities, from incinerators to prisons. New coalitions began to be mobilized linking community-based organizations and community-oriented labor unions to challenge these sites not simply as violating environmental regulations or zoning laws but for being intrinsically unjust in their geographical impact on local populations. These mobilizations built upon strong attachments to place-based community but also began to generate a new spatial awareness on a larger urban and regional scale.

Growing out of these mobilizations in some urban contexts has been the notion of residential "rights to the city," the argument that everyone living in the metropolitan region has an equal right to access the resources and advantages of the urban environment as well as to avoid its dangers and disadvantages.[28] Imbued with a new spatial consciousness, this expanded notion of civil rights argues that the organization of urban space is not "natural" or naïvely given; that this urban spatiality shapes our lives in ways that are both positive and negative, enabling as well as repressive; and that we can actively intervene to change current conditions and improve quality of life through an explicitly spatial politics.

One of the most stunning examples of this new spatial consciousness has been the Bus Riders Union (BRU) in Los Angeles.[29] In 1996, the BRU, a coalition of the working poor who depend on public transport, won a court case against the Metropolitan Transit Authority on the grounds that the costly plans for fixed-rail development discriminated both racially and *spatially* against the mainly bus-dependent population. By implication if not legal precedent, the BRU claimed that the transit plan for fixed-rail would bring much greater advantages to the predominantly white and relatively wealthy population of the suburbs and outer rings of the city than to the inner city and its massive concentration of immigrant working poor. In other words, the plan was racially and spatially unjust.

The end result of the BRU judgment has been the shift of potentially billions of dollars of public investment from a plan that would benefit the wealthy much more than the poor to a commitment to massive improvements in the bus network that would undoubtedly benefit the poor more than the wealthy. The BRU case has been continuously challenged in the courts both locally and at the federal level, blunting the possibility that the expanded (and spatialized) civil rights precedent could be extended to other forms of public planning and to other jurisdictions around the country, but the specific decision has significantly improved the transit needs of what is perhaps the largest agglomeration of the immigrant working poor in any U.S. city.

It is not a far stretch to say that such events as the success of the Bus Riders Union can be attributed at least in part to the putting into political practice of new ways of thinking spatially about nature, the environment, and the expansive effects of urban agglomeration. It is also within reason to envision the BRU and the rights to the city movement as just the beginning of more formidable and comprehensive coalitions of activist organizations seeking spatial justice at every geographical scale, democratizing our places of residence and work, our cities and regions, our national and global economies and cultures, all the spaces of nature we have created.

The Decline of Nature: Natural Theology, Theology of Nature, and the Built Environment

Timothy J. Gorringe

The Decline of Nature and the Rise of the City

As I write, a meeting called by the Brazilian government is considering the impact of persistent drought in the Amazon. Scientists attending the meeting predict that quite apart from the clearance of areas of forest the size of Belgium each year, the Amazon could be destroyed this century.[1] The polar ice caps are melting at a record rate. Both of these changes are due to global warming and have potentially devastating effects. Should the Gulf Stream go into reverse, the implications for world food security will be colossal. To those who argue that debates about ecoscarcity, natural limits, overpopulation, and sustainability are in fact debates about the preservation of a particular social order rather than the preservation of nature per se and that control over the resources of others is the real agenda, we have to respond that in the near rather than the distant future, the issue may be who has access to food supplies and who does not.[2]

Lifeboat ethics, the survival of the best armed, may be just around the corner. More than two thousand leading scientists issued a joint declaration in 1992 in which they warned that "many of our current practices put at risk the future that we wish for human society and the plant and the animal kingdoms, and may so alter the living world that it will be unable to sustain life in the manner that we know."[3] What they call "the living world" is what I take it is meant by "nature," and their grim warning speaks of "the decline of nature." As Robert Samuels puts it, God may not play dice with the universe, but humans do. In his view, "In geological time-frame, humanity could be in the last split second of its existence. Within the lifetime of the generation born today the planet could either be terminally ill, or on a path to sustainable recovery."[4]

The decline of nature in this sense is accompanied by the growth of the city. Of course cities are "second nature," in the sense that humans have created ecologies that include cities, which in turn have played an undeniably critical role in what we must still call, without a sneer, human progress. At the same time, cities have a troubled relation to "first nature," the living world which supports us. More than half the world's population now lives in cities, and the proportion of those who do so increases day by day. When it comes to global warming, the built environment has been described as "the principal villain" in the story.[5]

The ecological footprint is the amount of land required to feed a city or region, supply it with timber products, and absorb its carbon dioxide emissions. It has been calculated that the ecological footprint of London, with 11 million inhabitants, is 50 million acres, 125 times greater than its actual surface area.[6] The Organization for Economic Cooperation and Development (OECD) nations consume half the world's commercial energy, and 40 percent of this goes to heating, lighting, and providing air conditioning for homes and offices.[7] Some of this demand is generated by building that is insensitive to local conditions. Notoriously, Le Corbusier wanted "one single building for all nations and climates." Ignoring local climates means installing huge heating and air conditioning systems in offices, factories, homes, and hotels around the world.[8] The Sears Tower in Chicago uses more energy in twenty-four hours than an average American city of 150,000 or an Indian city of more than 1 million.[9] New York City uses as much electrical energy as the whole continent of Africa. The richest cities contribute most to worldwide environmental degradation because of their dependency on unsustainable levels of resource use.[10]

On these grounds it is argued that modern cities are inherently ecologically unsustainable because they need to import food, energy, and raw materials, produce more waste than they can cope with within their boundaries, and radically change the ecology of their sites. According to this view, the larger the concentration of population, the less sustainable is a given city, even if the city's hinterland is included in the equation.[11] For the architect Richard Rogers, "the world's environmental crisis is being driven by our cities. . . . The scale, and the rate of increase, of our consumption of resources, and the pollution it inflicts, is catastrophic."[12] In general terms, "the larger the city, the more dependent the city becomes on external ecosystems," both because consumption rises and because the internal capacity to produce food and energy is reduced.[13] Cities always had hinterlands, but these are now global. Given the amount of food ferried in by air, the footprint of any town with a large supermarket expands gigantically. I could go on, but the relation of the built environment and of cities in particular to the decline of nature is, I hope, fairly obvious.

Natural Theology as a Response to the Decline of Nature

If we wanted to respond theologically to the decline of nature, then terminologically, at least, "natural theology" suggests itself. In fact, in most of its forms, natural theology has nothing whatever to do with nature and appears on the stage long before significant urbanization, but it is interesting that forms of natural theology that concentrate especially on the beauty of nature appear at the dawn of modernity. Raymond of Sebonde's *Theologia naturalis, sive, Liber creaturarum* was written at the beginning of the fifteenth century and translated into French by Michel de Montaigne in the following century. It took up the idea of the book of nature, which went back at least to the fifth century, and was put on the *Index Librorum Prohibitorum* because, despite a conventional nod that grace is required to read the book of nature, Sebonde's text asserted that knowledge derived from creation was more certain than that derived from Scripture.[14] Raymond argues that knowledge of the book of creatures or of nature

> is necessary, natural, and fit for every man; by means of it he is enlightened, both as to himself and as to his Maker, and as to the whole duty of man as man; and moreover of the rule of nature, whereby everyone also is aware of all his natural obligations, whether to God or to his neighbour.

The knowledge derived from the book of nature

> is accessible alike to laymen and to clerks and to every condition of men and can be had in less than a month and without trouble. . . . It makes man cheerful, modest, kind and obedient, and causes him to hate all vices and sins and so love virtue. . . . Moreover it proves by means of what is most certain to every man by experience, that is by all the creatures and by the natural qualities of man himself and by man himself, and by what man

knows most assuredly of himself by experience, and above all by the inner experience which every man has of himself; and so this science seeks no other witness than a man's own self. At first this science appears very low and worthless, but in the end there cometh of it most noble fruit.[15]

Study of creatures leads us to the knowledge of God, but the love of God leads us back to love of the creatures:

> In the first place we loved the creatures because they were fair and good, and because they were serviceable to us, and so we loved them for our own sakes. But in the second place we loved them for their Creator's sake, because they are his and he made them; nay, we love also our own selves because we too are God's. And this love is perfect, good, enduring, excellent and constant, because it proceeds from the Creator who is the most excellent of all beings, the highest and supreme of all. And in this it is plain that love given to God is not wasted or diminished, nay it grows and is infinitely increased and expanded beyond all measure; since in the love of God are loved also all creatures and all things which belong to God.[16]

The optimistic view of human nature that Raymond implies is echoed in the rise of both landscape and still life painting in the sixteenth century. For both Counter-Reformation prelates and Calvinists, nature was one of the pleasures of the Christian mind. "Contemplation of nature was a means of becoming close to the Creator, because his Presence was to be found in all things."[17] There is a line between this affirmation of creation and the deism of the early eighteenth century, for which the created world was the manifestation of the divine perfection. "The Creation is a perpetual feast to the mind of a good man," wrote Addison. "Every thing that he sees cheers and delights him; Providence has imprinted so many Smiles on Nature, that it is impossible for a mind which is not sunk in more gross and sensual delights to take a survey of them without several secret sensations of pleasure."[18]

The landscape gardening of the eighteenth century was the correlate in the built environment of this view: a landscape apparently natural but wholly at the disposal of the landlord. Citing Jonas Hanway, who writes of Wilton House in 1757, David Solkin notes a deliciously ironic conflation of the landscape gardening of the aristocracy with the works of God:

> Since our time permits only a transient view of the noble Ornaments and costly collections at Wilton, let us hasten from the works of men, to the more glorious works of GOD! We may here contemplate the beautiful lawns on the south-east side of the house, and the bright streams which

water them. Over this river is a Palladian bridge of exquisite architecture, much admired by all connoisseurs. Above this, to the southward, you must not forget that noble rising ground, the summit of which is about a quarter of a mile. Here stands a very large equestrian statue of Marcus Aurelius, whose virtues are so much extolled by historians. From this eminence there is a view of the valley below, and of part of Salisbury, which looks very rural, the cathedral, as well as other parts of the city, being embowr'd with trees.

From the contemplation of beautiful nature, the mind is easily led to that of moral rectitude. True taste in the arrangement of material objects such as delight the senses, or exalt the heart, seems to have a great analogy with the harmony, or order, which the love of virtue inspires.[19]

As Solkin notes, when a Brownian park gives the appearance of being simply a continuation of nature, then the acquisitive tendencies that produced such grandiose place-making take on a semblance of equal naturalness.[20] This view of nature took class hierarchy for granted. A writer for the *Monthly Review* in 1760 argued:

If we read Nature in all her works, we may perceive, that she never intended an equality. She is various in all her productions; and this variety is no where more conspicuous than in the intelligent creation. As men are not formed with the same strength and proportion of body, neither are they endowed with the same vigour and capacity of mind. . . . From whatever cause it proceeds [this disparity] is the foundation of a natural superiority on the one hand, and of a natural inferiority on the other; from whence civil pre-eminence and subordination must necessarily result.[21]

Since the old justification of hierarchy as mirroring a heavenly order had been changed, a new justification of the class system had to be found, and "Nature" fitted the bill.

All this indicates how problematic this strand of natural theology is as a response to the decline of nature. As Alexander Pope and Edmund Burke famously illustrate in their poetry and writing, ruling worldviews can be read as nature's truth: providence becomes fate, the laws of the market become the laws of God, and whatever is, is right. This natural theology, in other words, is profoundly politically reactionary. In much eighteenth-century discourse, "Nature" is a site of mystification and is identified, in Edmund Thomas's words, with "the simple and primitive, as seen in children, peasants, savages, early men, and animals."[22] As such, it is, of course, opposed to the civilized, the urban. The contrast of town and country is ancient, but it is in the eighteenth century that William Cowper tells us that "God made the country, and man made the town":

> The love of Nature and the scenes she draws
> Is nature's dictate. . . .
> Lovely indeed the mimic works of art;
> But Nature's works far lovelier. . . .
> Beneath the open sky she spreads the feast;
> 'Tis free to all—'tis every day renewed;
> Who scorns it starves deservedly at home.

In cities, by contrast:

> Rank abundance breeds . . .
> . . . sloth and lust,
> And wantonness and gluttonous excess.
> In cities vice is hidden with most ease,
> Or seen with least reproach; and virtue, taught
> By frequent lapse, can hope no triumph there
> Beyond the achievement of successful flight.[23]

Flight from the city might not have been so successful, because as Keith Thomas notes, in early modern Britain, "agriculture was the most ruthlessly developed sector of the economy, small husbandmen were declining in number, wage labour was universal, and the vices of avarice, oppression and hypocrisy were at least as prominent in the countryside as in the town."[24] Still, the contrast was fed by the growth of Dickens' Coketown, which was the push factor behind Ebenezer Howard's dream of garden cities.[25] Today, at least in Britain, small market towns are the fastest-growing centers of population, and rural retreats are at a premium. At the same time, the green movement seems to encourage a sort of lightly paganized natural theology of a kind with which Raymond of Sebonde might have sympathized, and such a theology continues to have many more orthodox defenders. Its reactionary use in the past, however, ought to make us cautious and did in fact provoke a strongly critical response in the twentieth century.

Natural Theology and Ideology Critique

Karl Barth's attack on natural theology in the early 1930s has little connection with the kind of natural theology discussed above, although, had he been interested in Heidegger, he might have made the connection. However, he does highlight the ideological forces at work, in his view, in every form of natural theology.[26] Contemporary Barthians trace the attack to the inner logic of Barth's theological position: Barth's account of the hypostatic union in Christ, it is argued, simply leaves no room for belief in any kind of natural theology. In fact it rules it out.[27] But the argument that the rejection of natural theology is purely and simply a function of Barth's theological logic fails to account for the stridency of his argument. The ferocity of Barth's rhetoric has much to do with the situation, with the sense that natural theology has no defenses against the kind of idolatry implied in National Socialism. Barth writes:

> By "natural theology" I mean every (positive or negative) formulation of a system which claims to be theological, i.e., to interpret divine revelation, whose subject, however, differs fundamentally from the revelation in Jesus Christ and whose method therefore differs equally from the exposition of Holy Scripture. . . . [Such a system represents] an abstract speculation concerning a something that is not identical with the revelation of God in Jesus Christ.[28]

This definition has to be read in the light of the first thesis of the 1934 Barmen Declaration:

> "I am the Way and the Truth and the Life; no one comes to the Father but through me." . . . Jesus Christ, as he is witnessed to us in Holy Scripture, is the one Word of God whom we must trust and obey in life and in death. We reject the false doctrine that the Church can and must recognize as a source of its preaching, alongside the one Word of God, other events and powers, forms and truths than God's revelation.[29]

The question, for Barth, is how we discern where God is and who God is, and these questions are not merely academic but determine what we do with our lives. In the context of the struggle against fascism, opposition to natural theology took on a confessional significance; it became part of a life-and-death struggle. Only this, in my view, can explain the vehemence of Barth's arguments.[30]

Barth's arguments against natural theology are subjected to incisive and witty criticism by James Barr, who argues that Barth's position involves exegetical special pleading because it means that he had to discount the traditional source for natural theology, texts such as Psalm 19, Romans 1:19 and 20, and Acts 17, which had impressed even the dourest Reformers. Given this scriptural foundation, Barr seeks to impale Barth on the horns of a dilemma: either reject natural theology and give up the Scripture principle, or accept the Scripture principle and accept natural theology.[31] Barr argues that, as regards the political implications of natural theology, it is clear that adherence to it does not make one a fascist; natural theology might be developed in politically progressive ways, and certain appeals to natural law might be examples of that.[32]

There is no doubt that Barth's response to natural theology is disproportionate. At the same time, perhaps it might be understood more broadly in this way: the problem with natural theology is that like natural law, it is not natural at all, but socially constructed, as the eighteenth-century examples illustrate. Barth defines revelation as "what we cannot tell ourselves." In other words, rightly or wrongly, he believed that a theology of revelation made it possible to escape imprisonment by world-views. The huge discussion of Scripture in *Church Dogmatics* I/1 and I/2 is the attempt to establish that biblical interpretation is not imprisoned by context in quite the same way as natural theology. Barth argues that there is a dialectic of authority and freedom in Scripture, worked out in the ongoing discussion of the church, through which interpretation is constantly tested, thought through, and refined. This process makes possible a clearer idolatry critique—and, indeed, ideology critique—than natural theology is capable of. For Barth, any form of natural theology, whether it be the ontological argument or some version of the design argument, is fatally solipsistic; to use the terms of his 1916 lecture, "The Strange New World of the Bible," it only gives us human words about God. We do not hear the divine address to human beings which can overthrow the status quo and challenge the powers that be.

Developing a Theology of Creation

Once the onslaught on natural theology is out of the way, Barth moves, more interestingly, to the development of a theology of creation that essentially attempts to go back beyond deism and insist on God's living presence to the created world. It is this sense that was lost in the eighteenth century. Barth almost always uses the term *"die Schöpfung"* rather than *"die Natur"* partly because this is the term used in Scripture but also because it emphasizes intentionality, the divine engagement.[33] In Barth's picture, God ceaselessly and creatively engages with the created order, directing it to his own ends. Under God, creation has its own integrity. In the realm of nature, Barth writes, for all its distinctiveness, there is

> nothing which does not point to grace and therefore come from grace;
> nothing which can enjoy independent life or exercise independent

dominion. And conversely, for all the newness and particularity of the realm of grace, there is no place in it for anything unnatural, but from the creation everything is also nature.[34]

Barth agrees with Aquinas that grace does not destroy nature, but he cannot say it perfects it, because for him creation is "one vast symbol for grace."[35]

He is hostile to Schopenhauer because in him he finds a picture of nature without God, ending only in pessimism and despair.[36] What Barth takes from creation, by contrast, is a view of creation as *"die Wohltat,"* blessing, benefit, a gift of kindness. Creation as we know it in Christ is not yes and no but only yes—yes to Godself and yes to that which is willed and created by God. Creation is good because it is the product of the divine joy, honor, and affirmation. It is the goodness of God that takes shape in it, and God's good pleasure is both the foundation and the end of creation and is therefore its ontological ground.[37] The world whose reality is made known to us in revelation is good because it corresponds with the God who is good. Creation is good because God both actualizes it and justifies it. Its rightness, goodness, worth and perfection spring from its correspondence to the work of God's own Son as resolved from eternity and fulfilled in time.[38] We have to love and praise the created order because, as is clear in Christ, it is so pleasing to God. Creation therefore calls forth joy—a note sounded intensively throughout the account of creation. That we should seek joy is not merely a concession or permission but a command. Barth does not feel able to urge a "Christian optimism" but rather a "joy over the abyss," which he could also characterize as "Christian realism."

This account of creation produces its own ethic, which Barth calls, borrowing from Albert Schweitzer, "respect for life." He does not deal with the ecological crisis, but in the section on the killing of animals we get a clue to what his response would have looked like. He refuses to dismiss Schweitzer's contention that "ethics is infinitely extended responsibility to everything that lives" as "sentimental." "Those who can only smile at this point," writes Barth, "are themselves subjects for tears."[39] With regard to nonhuman life, human beings have to think and act responsibly. They are not lords over the Earth but on the Earth, and the exercise of freedom is one of care and stewardship. Barth allows the possibility of killing animals for food, but only as "a deeply reverential act of repentance, gratitude, and praise on the part of the forgiven sinner in face of the One who is the Creator and Lord of man and beast."[40] *Mutatis mutandis*, this could apply to much of the rest of the nonhuman creation.

Responding Theologically to the Decline of Nature: Critique

It follows from this brief account of Barth's approach to natural theology and his theology of creation that any theology learning from him will respond to the decline of nature in a twofold way: in terms of both critique and construction.

In response to the debt crisis and the inequities of the global economy, Ulrich Duchrow proposes that this is a confessional issue for the churches and that the Barmen Declaration should be our model. Conceiving the church as fundamentally being made up of discipleship groups, he urges a "prophetic resistance" that would tackle "the ideologies which the present system has been drumming into people's minds from childhood onwards and recognizing the idolatrous nature of these ideologies."[41] My first proposal, then, is that we can learn from Barth's opposition to natural theology that we need an ideology critique and that a theology of revelation can help discern and oppose the idolatrous presuppositions of the world in which we live. This critique will inform the praxis and reflection of discipleship groups acting first at local and then at regional, national, and international levels.

I maintain in the first place, then, that the ideology that lies behind the whole debate about the decline of nature is the doctrine of necessary and infinitely sustainable economic growth, which goes back to what Karl Polanyi calls the "great transformation" of the eighteenth century.[42] The acceleration of economic growth that began then is mirrored in the increase of population, which has doubled in the past forty years. This process is, in Fredric Jameson's words, both the best thing and the worst thing that has ever happened to us.[43] It is the best thing in terms of medicine, improvements in health and hygiene, improvements in housing, improvements in agriculture, and so forth, all of which have made the population explosion possible. It is the worst thing because precisely these changes may destroy us.

Writing in 1980, E. P. Thompson characterized the Western mind-set as "exterminism," referring not to the nuclear threat but to the threat posed by the sheer material success of our culture, arguing that the material volume of the modern economy is incompatible with ecological stability.[44] China and India now share this mind-set, and the rest of the world aspires to it. This ideology, I contend, is idolatrous in centering on consumption and in refusing limits. We have moved over the past century from a culture of conservation to a culture of consumerism. This was summed up by the American retail analyst Victor Lebow in 1956:

Our enormously productive economy . . . demands that we make consumption our way of life, that we convert the buying and use of goods into rituals, that we seek out spiritual satisfaction, our ego satisfaction, in consumption. . . . We need things consumed, burned up, worn out, replaced and discarded at an ever increasing rate.[45]

This process is idolatrous in that it puts a comforter god, like an infant's pacifier, in the place of the one who leads human beings from bondage to freedom and who does so through the "wilderness," the place of struggle.[46] The consumer economy essentially elects a life of well-fed slavery underwritten by the use of overwhelming force if the conditions for that slavery are challenged. This ideology has a theological correlate that is a form of natural theology, appealing as it does to "laws of nature" that guarantee the right to property and that teach us that capitalism follows from the attempt to "decipher the wealth hidden in creation by the Creator himself."[47]

Humans are, of course, part of the whole ecology of the planet. We differ from other aspects of the ecology in one crucial respect, however: we do not know when to stop. E. F. Schumacher argues that "Nature always . . . knows when to stop. Greater even than the mystery of natural growth is the mystery of the natural cessation of growth. . . . The system of nature, of which man is part, tends to be self-balancing, self-adjusting, self-cleansing."[48] We could respond that cancer is part of nature, and it stops only when it causes the death of its host organism. Death, including the death of whole species, may be part of this self-balancing. Some such self-balancing mechanism has to be accepted to explain the relative stability of the overall ecology. It is here that human beings produce imbalance. Aristotle defines human beings as "animals made for the polis" (*zōon politikon*). Perhaps we could gloss that by saying that we are part of nature as those creatures who have to decide when limits are reached. Accepting limits has always been part of human wisdom, and many teachers, including Aristotle, have defined maturity in terms of the acceptance of limits.[49] For Schumacher, "Any activity which fails to recognize a self limiting principle is of the devil."[50]

Today limits are vital because huge numbers mean huge impacts. Herman Daly and John Cobb, writing twenty years ago, note that "if 'needs' include an automobile for each of a billion Chinese, then sustainable development is impossible. The whole issue of sufficiency can no longer be avoided."[51] Today this situation is realized. Mathis Wackernagel and Williams Rees argue that "if everyone on Earth lived like the average Canadian or American, we would need at least three such planets to live sustainably."[52] To live in this way, it seems, is the human goal: per capita energy and material consumption have soared faster in the past forty years than human population has. In addition to being self-evidently ethical, the issue is political and spiritual: Who decides who can enjoy what, and at what cost?

Addressing inequalities in global consumption is essential if ecological damage is to be contained. We resist the notion that we should accept limits because we want to believe that we can have our cake and eat it and that it might be possible in time for everyone to share our lifestyle, because we ourselves are caught up in the whole process. "It is ultimately with the motor car and washing machine detergents that we do the damage," writes Rudolf Bahro, "rather than with bombs, nuclear power stations and dioxins. . . . A private dwelling full of comforts necessarily confirms the whole worldwide infrastructure—including the need for armaments, because in face of monstrous differences in standards it is a threatened luxury."[53] Hence there is no simple battle between good guys and bad guys, because the persuasive power of the global economy exists within each consuming self. The issue, again, is both political and spiritual: political in the sense that it can only be addressed by global political action, but spiritual in that it rests on addressing the illusion of infinite growth, the desire that Aristotle diagnoses as the key mark of human immaturity and injustice.

Responding Theologically to the Decline of Nature: Construction

Responding critically to Barth, Jürgen Moltmann sought to develop an ecological doctrine of creation in 1984, fifty years after the Barmen Declaration:

> Fifty years ago, discernment of the triune God revealed in Christ brought the church the assurance of faith; and today, in the same way, discernment of the God who is present in creation through his Holy Spirit can bring men and women to reconciliation and peace with nature. The salutary "christological concentration" in Protestant theology then, must be matched by an extension of theology's horizon to cosmic breadth, so that it takes in the whole of God's creation.[54]

Moltmann seeks to develop a Trinitarian theology of creation that understands human beings as part of the community of creation and that, because it is shaped by Jesus the Messiah, is directed toward the liberation of women and men and toward peace with nature. He evokes then, what he calls a "messianic theology of nature," an understanding of the human relation to the nonhuman world shaped by our understanding of Jesus the Messiah. Like Barth, Moltmann wants to insist that "the limited sphere of reality which we call 'nature' must be lifted into the totality of being which is termed 'God's creation.'"[55] This means that human beings are not, as Descartes declares, "masters and possessors of nature,"[56] but members of the one body, their special responsibility being to nurture and cherish the nonhuman world.

From Romans 8 we learn that the whole of creation is in bondage to transience and that there is a universal yearning for freedom. What we call "nature" is neither the pure primordial state nor perfection but, writes Moltmann, "a destiny to which creation is subjected: a continual process of annihilation, an all embracing fellowship of suffering, and a tense and anxious openness for a different future. To understand 'nature' as creation therefore means discerning 'nature' as the enslaved creation that hopes for liberty."[57] From this understanding of creation follows a particular spirituality, a spirituality of passion, care, and hope that addresses the domination of first nature and the spirituality behind that.

Moltmann also specifically raises the question of the homelike qualities of the world: "The embodiment of the messianic promises to the poor and the quintessence of the hopes of the alienated is that the world should be 'home.'"[58] A messianic theology of nature therefore explicitly raises the question of the built environment, or second nature, although Moltmann does not pursue this question.

Responding Theologically to "Second Nature"

"Second nature" is the world human beings have made for themselves, their home. The built environment, including great cities, is rightly described as a human ecology, but if ecology is, as Schumacher argues, self-balancing, might our headlong growth in every area ultimately mean our destruction? How do these considerations bear on our understanding of the built environment?

What geographers call the "spatial turn" was, curiously, already anticipated by Karl Barth in 1937. Drawing on the biblical language that talks of God's own place, Barth outlines a theology of divine spatiality that offers a theological grounding for all forms of created space and therefore for the built environment. In his discussion of time, Barth talks of God's "eminent temporality," that is, God's preceding, accompanying, and coming after time. It is this divine temporality, Barth says, that grounds our own temporality. In the same way, it is God's "eminent spatiality" that grounds our own created spatiality. Space, in other words, is not something contingent, something that will one day be annihilated, because it has its true and intrinsic ground in God. According to Barth, God is present to other things and is able to create and give them space because God in Godself possesses space apart from everything else.[59] What truth, Barth asks, could correspond to phrases like "in Christ," "in God" and "in the Spirit" if God were not genuinely and primordially spatial?

> If it is not an incidental or superfluous belief that we can obtain space from God and find space in him, but a truth which is decisive for the actuality of creation, reconciliation and redemption and the trustworthiness of the Word of God, we cannot evade the recognition that God himself is spatial.[60]

Barth also insisted that we take the language of "heaven" seriously, that it, too, is part of creation. Heaven is, according to Barth, the "whence, the starting point, the gate from which God sallies with all the demonstrations and revelations and words and works of His action on earth."[61] Barth considers that the existence of God's special "place" is essential for there to be genuine dialogue and intercourse between God and human beings. It is another created place that confronts our own but is otherwise unknown and inconceivable and therefore a mystery. It has its own inhabitants, the angels. For Barth, therefore, the created order, "nature," is not all of a piece but includes an element quite other, or, in the old terminology (which he rejects), a supernature. A Christian theology of the built environment can take its cue from these reflections.

The home of the utopian impulse in the twentieth century was architecture, and we all know the results. "It was one of the illusions of the 20s," writes Philip Johnson:

> We were thoroughly of the opinion that if you had good architecture the lives of people would be improved; that architecture would improve people, and people improve architecture until perfectibility would descend on us like the Holy Ghost, and we would be happy for ever after. This did not prove to be the case.[62]

Architecture and design have everything to do with the body, Robert Hughes reminds us, and the unredeemed body at that:

> Without complete respect for the body as it is, and for social memory as it stands, there is no such thing as workable or humane architecture. Hence,

most of the "classics" of Utopian planning have come to look inhuman or even absurd; they have ceased to work, and to a point where the social pretensions behind them no longer seem credible. Who believes in progress and perfectibility anymore? Who believes in masterbuilders or form-givers? . . . Memory is reality. It is better to recycle what exists, to avoid mortgaging a workable past to a nonexistent Future, and to think small. In the life of cities, only conservatism is sanity.[63]

Hughes's remarks make sense of Ernst Bloch's comment that "only the beginnings of another society will make genuine architecture possible again."[64] As with the global economy, the problems associated with the built environment are not primarily technical but spiritual, that is to say, they are fundamentally a question of values, of our understanding of the whole human project. The built environment, like the economy, is an expression of our spirituality. Human beings, says the Christian tradition, are body and soul in-formed by Spirit. Their whole constellation, what they are as body-soul unity, manifests their spirituality. As Walter Wink demonstrates, this goes beyond the individual to the collectivity.[65] The spirituality of a culture expresses itself in and therefore shapes ethics, but also art, literature, music, religion, cuisine, and building—the whole of everyday life. "The making of a society," says Raymond Williams, "is the finding of common meanings and directions, and its growth is an active debate and amendment under the pressures of experience, contact, and discovery, *writing themselves into the land.*"[66] The depth of a culture's spirituality undeniably waxes and wanes, and shallow periods produce poor, or at least unjust and unstable, environments. How are we to build dwellings and fashion settlements that are, to use the architect Christopher Day's words, life-renewing, soul-nurturing, and spirit-strengthening?[67] The interest in spirituality in our culture, I suggest, springs from an awareness of the need to renew the depths of our culture, without which we cannot make the world homelike.

Enthusiasts for cities are surely right in insisting that they are not just part of the problem but also part of the solution. Lewis Mumford believes the city played a key role in the emergence of a new society. "We must now conceive the city," he writes, "not primarily as a place of business or government, but as an essential organ for expressing and actualizing the new human personality—that of 'One World Man.'"[68] Mumford sees education as the main function of the city, enabling the change from a power economy to a life economy and thus global political and physical transformations.

Of course, to say that "the city" educates is shorthand for a whole range of social, political, and planning processes; perhaps the process would have to begin with educating the educators. Schumacher believes that a failure of education lies at the root of economic exterminism, the idea that growth will solve all our problems. We are suffering from a metaphysical disease, he suggests, by which he means a loss of clarity respecting fundamental convictions, and therefore the cure must be metaphysical: "Education which fails to clarify our central convictions is mere training or indulgence. For it is our central convictions that are in disorder, and, as long as the present anti-metaphysical temper persists, the disorder will grow worse."[69] Clarifying central convictions is what the church is about—is what brought people in fierce contest to Nicaea, Constantinople, and Chalcedon and later to Wittenberg and Barmen. In finding ways to house 8 billion or 12 billion people not just with dignity but with beauty, in finding ways to structure our settlements sustainably, a new, strong, and deep spirituality ranked alongside the marginalized and opposed to the powers of the big battalions is necessary. A theology of creation, rather than a natural theology, would be concerned with the nurturing of such a spirituality.

At the heart of that spirituality is a perception about justice. If all human beings are made in the image of God, then Christians cannot, as do neoliberal economists, dismiss the demands of egalitarianism as empty rhetoric.[70] Throughout the world there are "millions of homeless, incarcerated, prostituted, criminalized, brutalized, stigmatized, sick and illiterate persons," and the numbers are growing everywhere, as informational capitalism and the political breakdown of the welfare state intensify social exclusion.[71] The gap between rich and poor continues to grow, and this inevitably has repercussions in housing. A walk around any great city on Earth makes clear that this is one of the areas where injustice is most manifest. Globally the citizens of what Manuel Castells calls the Fourth World live in favelas, shantytowns, tent cities, without water or sewage, in tenements, sink estates, and neglected housing projects with rising damp, poor access to amenities, poor schools, and high crime rates. It is hardly surprising that foremost among the demands of Agenda 21 is the provision of adequate shelter for all.[72] An adequate theology of creation is also a liberation theology, a theology of justice that addresses itself to the issue of what constitutes adequate shelter.

A key aspect of the failure of justice in relation to both the built environment and the economy is deference to experts, the deskilling attacked by Ivan Illich.[73] A theology of creation that responds to the decline of nature seeks to take seriously the Pentecostal situation in which all God's people are prophets. In Britain, certainly, planning laws are quite consciously obstructive of people's creativity. At the same time the environmental crisis has underlined the fact that we cannot live without legislation. How is that contradiction to be resolved? The key point is that *ordinary people, the whole community, have to be part of the process.* This is implicit in the church's community charter, 1 Corinthians 12; where Jesus spoke of "kingdom," Paul speaks of a "body" "in-spired," breathed through, and empowered by Spirit. The whole body, Paul argues, has gifts to offer. The need for empowerment was recognized by the founding fathers of town planning, people like Ebenezer Howard, Patrick Geddes, and Peter Kropotkin, who thought of planning as a popular movement and regarded citizen participation to be the key. In Geddes's view, every citizen should have an understanding of the possibilities of his or her own city.[74]

Manuel Castells distinguishes between the "space of flows" and its actors, and the "space of place," in which most human experience and meaning is still based. The dominant global elites live in the space of flows and consist of "identity-less individuals," while on the other hand, "people resisting economic, cultural, and political disfranchisement tend to be attracted to communal identity."[75] The more power leaches into the "space of flows," the less genuine democracy there is and the less real debate there can be about the things that matter in the fabric of our lives. Environmental localism challenges the priorities of global capital; the latter is driven by an (anti)economic rationality that has no respect for place, destroying true *oikonomia*. Place, then, and planning in relation to place are at the heart of any theology of creation responding to "second nature." The church has a long experience in this area, as the discussion of enculturation in mission demonstrates. As Lamin Sanneh argues, it has been part of the genius of the Gospel to go into the vernacular in every place, thus stimulating local cultures, renewing them, and sowing seeds of revolution.[76] Following Jeremiah it is essential for Christians to settle down where they find themselves (Jer. 29:28), which is why churches have put up buildings everywhere, providing foci and facilities for the meeting and growth of local community.

Finally, at Pentecost the scattering that takes place at Babel is not reversed but confirmed as a blessing. All the different languages, the roots of culture, do not blend in some ethereal Esperanto. On the contrary, they become mutually intelligible. The "oneness" of the church is a unity in

diversity.[77] There is a promise of reconciliation precisely through the celebration of diversity. The same goes for the built environment: a homogenized environment is a poor environment. A world composed primarily of
suburbs, or edge cities, or megacities or a world that was merely "rurban"
would be the poorer. Human beings thrive on difference. Discussions of
"cities of difference" tend to focus on the need to guarantee respect for
different lifestyles, on finding space for the legitimacy of all groups. What
this respect for difference has actually generated, however, is that postmodern eclecticism in which all true difference disappears. In Castells's
terms, the coming of the space of flows leads to the generalization of ahistorical, acultural architecture.[78]

Castells warns that "irony becomes the preferred mode of
expression. . . . Because we do not belong any longer to any place, to any
culture, the extreme version of postmodernism imposes its codified code-
breaking logic anywhere something is built."[79] This architecture, writes
Jeffrey Cook, amounts to the "international trivialization of human life."[80]
Such trivialization is part of a good deal of contemporary culture and has
to be countered by a search for integrity and depth. A theology of creation
responding to "second nature" will look to the joyous celebration of difference in the fostering of the vernacular, which in turn can only be done
through real empowerment.

These thumbnail sketches of what it might mean for theology to respond to the decline of nature and to the place of "second nature" must
be weighed against the seriousness of the situation we face. "No one can
assure us that the worst will not happen," wrote Moltmann in 1995. "According to all the laws of experience: it will":

> We can only trust that even the end of the world hides a new beginning if
> we trust the God who calls into being the things that are not, and out of
> death creates new life. . . . Life out of this hope then means already acting
> here and today in accordance with that world of justice and righteousness
> and peace, contrary to appearances, and contrary to all historical chances
> of success. It obliges us solemnly to abjure the spirit, logic and practice of
> the nuclear system of deterrence and all other systems of mass annihilation.
> It means an unconditional Yes to life in the face of the inescapable death of
> all the living. That is the deeper meaning of the legendary Luther saying
> about "the apple tree" which he would plant today even if he knew that the
> world was going to end tomorrow.[81]

Ultimately it is this solemn and somewhat breathless theology of hope
that guides our response both to the decline of nature and to any account
of "second nature."

The Body of the World: Our Body, Ourselves

Sallie McFague

The title of these collected essays, *Without Nature?*, is an oxymoron. It is not possible to be "without nature." What *is* nature? Langdon Gilkey, theologian of nature, says nature has two meanings: "On the one hand, nature is represented in both archaic religion and modern science as the all-encompassing source or ground of all there is in concrete experience: the entities, inorganic and organic; the system of nature; ourselves; and even historical communities are products of nature."[1] In other words, there is nothing "outside" nature. But it is the second meaning Gilkey gives that raises the possibility of being "without nature": "nature as a word, a concept, a symbol, signals on the other hand our distinction from, even our distance from, this environment."[2] In this second meaning, nature is "in part the construction of mind, the object of an active, intelligent, and purposeful subject."[3] This second meaning allows us to reduce what is the source of our being (nature in the first meaning) "to a level below us; to a means, to a system of objects to be examined, manipulated, and used; to a warehouse for goods needed by us."[4]

This chapter explores issues and topics I have also explored in my volume *A New Climate for Theology* (Minneapolis: Fortress Press, 2008), chapter 7: "Where We Live: Urban Ecolotheology."

But as Edward Soja thoughtfully points out, the product of human interpretation and manipulation does not erase nature; rather, nature becomes a hybrid, as seen in urbanization. As Soja writes:

> The urban spatiality of nature in essence "denaturalizes" nature and charges it with social meaning. . . . Raw physical nature may be naïvely or even divinely given to begin with, but once urban society comes into being, a new nature is created that blends into and absorbs what existed before. One might say that the City *re-places* nature.[5]

Soja intends to undercut the conventional wisdom that views the natural and social worlds as separate, which he believes promotes dualism between nature and human beings. Rather, he suggests, we should focus on the hybrid—lived space—and especially on the city. By privileging space and place, everything changes, he asserts. We no longer indulge in the binary dualism of nature and culture but realize that since the beginning of agriculture and urbanization, nature has never been pristine. As he puts it, we have been "without nature" for twelve thousand years. There is no untouched nature, no wilderness; even Antarctica has become "urbanized," that is, socially and historically constructed.

Highlighting space is a necessary corrective to the Western and Christian emphasis on time and history. It has several advantages. First, it focuses our attention on the Earth (rather than heaven) by forcing us to attend to the humanized space of cities, where most of us human beings now live. It spotlights the need for habitat, for humanely built spaces, here and now, rather than eternal places in heaven. Second, it helps us to see that natural disasters are never only natural and forces us to accept some responsibility for the effects of global warming as well as poverty. Third, it raises issues of power and privilege in ways that a naïve focus on "first nature" fails to do. Who lives in the big house on the hill, and who lives in the shack beside the railway tracks? Fourth, it prohibits the romantic notion that all we need to do is to "get back to nature," as if nature were pure, good, and available as our guide in life.

Soja's argument for the priority of space and his assertion of the priority of cities as the hybrid place where we actually live is insightful. I intend to take it seriously and to suggest a theological contribution to just and sustainable city life, but first let me mention my critique. While I agree with his epistemological turn away from the Western focus on time and history to one of space and place, I fear that his hybrid spatial model of the city allows for and in fact encourages us to forget "first nature" as the source of our being.

Specifically, I wish to question Soja's statement that "the City *re-places* nature." He speaks of "a new nature" that "blends into and absorbs what existed before." Maintaining a distinction between nature and the city does not necessarily involve either binary logic or the erasure of one or the other. Antarctica is no longer separate from human interpretation and interference; nonetheless, there are in fact notable distinctions between spaces on Earth that are *relatively* untouched and the spaces of cities. Soja's position veers in the direction of eliminating differences, with priority given to human interpretation and control. While his position makes sense intellectually (all nature is now urbanized and/or interpreted to some degree), it is inadequate experientially, ethically, and factually. Soja's position fails to take sufficient account of the human experience of nature, the ethical demand of the "other" that it places on us, and the factual reality of human dependence on nature.

Human beings experience Antarctica and even a city park differently from the way they do a shopping mall or Disneyland. There is a sense of the "other" in a colossal iceberg or even a duck on a pond that is not found in a shopping mall or Disneyland. Prioritizing space and place need not mean eliminating the subjecthood of other life-forms, the intrinsic value of mountains, oceans, and forests as well as animal and plant populations, *even if* they are no longer totally pristine and untouched. There are relative states of nature-human interface that are not accurately described by "the City *re-placing* nature"; rather, the city and nature can be seen in a relationship of reciprocity. If we think of the city as absorbing or replacing nature, nature's intrinsic value and finite limits will be hidden from our view. What, then, will deter our appetite for unlimited, voracious overutilization of other life-forms and Earth processes? The Earth Charter lists as its first principle: "Respect Earth and life in all its diversity. Recognize that all beings are interdependent and every form of life has value regardless of its worth to human beings."[6] The hybrid model of city as nature tends to hide the "rights" of other life-forms as well as the necessity of our care for these others on whom we depend absolutely.

Nature Encompasses the City

For these reasons, it is not helpful to speak of the city as replacing nature, or as a new nature, or as absorbing nature. It is, I think, inadequate at experiential, ethical, and factual levels; but it is especially upon the fact of human dependence on nature that I would like to focus. While the city has in many ways replaced nature concretely as the habitat of most human beings, nevertheless we remain totally dependent on nature and its services. Nature in the first sense ("the all-encompassing source or ground of all there is")—and more specifically our own planet Earth, with its particular constitution of suitable elements—is the unique *sine qua non* of human life. No matter how much we transform "first nature," as epitomized by the city and by our myriad interpretations, it is not infinitely malleable.

Global warming is a powerful reminder of this truth. In the space of a few hundred years of excessive use of fossil fuels, human beings have managed to bring the planet to the brink of climate change so profound that many scientists fear we will soon reach a tipping point of uncontrollable, exponential rise in world temperatures. Our transformation of first nature, when we lived as hunter-gatherers, into second nature now confronts us with the deterioration and destruction of everything we hold dear. The human ability to distance ourselves from first nature, both by changing it and by objectifying it, is causing a deep forgetfulness to overtake us.

This forgetfulness is epitomized in the city dweller's relationship to food. Our ability to distance ourselves from first nature is nowhere more evident than in the ignorant denial of our dependence on nature for every mouthful we eat. As Michael Pollan puts it, in tracing "the natural history of four meals" back to their roots, "all flesh is grass." The scriptural text takes on new meaning when we consider that even a Twinkie or a Big Mac "begins with a particular plant growing in a specific patch of soil . . . somewhere on earth."[7] Our flesh (and the flesh that we eat) can be traced back to the grass that feeds us. Pollan writes: "At either end of any food chain you find a biological system—a patch of soil, a human body—and the health of one is converted—literally—to the health of the other."[8] And yet we city dwellers have forgotten this all-important piece of information: the inexorable, undeniable link between our health and the health of the planet. The physicality of the connection needs to be underscored, since, as Pollan points out, it is literally from body to body: "Daily, our eating turns nature into culture, transforming *the body of the world into our bodies and minds.*"[9] We need to relearn the importance of this most basic of all transformations: "For we would [then] no longer need any reminder that however we choose to feed ourselves, we eat by the grace of nature, not industry, and what we're eating is never anything more or less than *the body of the world.*"[10]

The city is therefore our greatest accomplishment and our greatest danger. Jerusalem, the city of desire and delight, is fast emerging as Babylon, the city of excessive luxury in the midst of extreme poverty. The city, which stands as the quintessential human habitation—civilized, diverse, cosmopolitan—is at the same time becoming the greatest threat to human well-being. An ecologist has warned that "of all the recognized ecological systems it is human urbanism which seems most destructive of its host."[11] Cities are energy hogs, sucking energy from near and far to allow some city dwellers to live at the highest level of comfort and convenience ever known, while many others exist in squalor. Cities of 12 million or more are divided, to be sure, by class, race, and gender, but also by the space they own and the energy they can command. A spacious condo overlooking the harbor, with all the electronic devices desired, is the sign of the successful city dweller. But having transformed first nature so thoroughly into the built, utilized environment, one too easily forgets that "first nature" remains the source of every mouthful we eat and every breath we take.

Peter Raven also questions whether we can do without nature. He summarizes our impact on the biosphere as follows: "Overall this condition can only be described as unsustainable; we are using its resources much more rapidly than they can be renewed and leaving for our children and grandchildren a planet that will be much less diverse, rich, healthy, and resilient than the one in which we live now."[12]

That we cannot do without "first nature" is the judgment not only of other contributors to the present volume but of other global experts as well. The recent United Nations Millennium Ecosystem Assessment represents the work of more than thirteen hundred experts worldwide, making it the first measurement of total human dependence on nature by the global scientific community.[13] The sobering conclusion of this massive study is that out of twenty-four essential services provided by nature to humanity, nearly two thirds are in decline. These services are numerous and all-encompassing, falling into three major categories: provisioning services (food, fiber, genetic resources, biochemicals and natural medicines, fresh water); regulating services (air, climate, water, erosion, disease, pest, pollination, natural hazard); and cultural services (spiritual and religious values, aesthetic values, recreation and ecotourism).[14] As the assessment states, "In effect, the benefits reaped from our engineering of the planet have been achieved by running down natural capital assets."[15] Yet nature's services are seldom appreciated; they are often hidden, particularly from city dwellers, for whom clean water simply comes from the faucet and food from the supermarket. Precisely because nature provides these services at no charge to the planet's inhabitants, technologically advanced societies can easily "gain the impression that we no longer depend on natural systems."[16] The first sentence of the assessment attempts to correct this misconception: "Everyone in the world depends on nature and ecosystem services to provide the conditions for a decent, healthy, and secure life."[17]

Needless to say, however, these necessary services are not shared equally. The difference between the rich and the poor on our planet can be measured by the availability or nonavailability of nature's services. Wealthy individuals benefit from an excess of food, clean water, freedom from disease, climate regulation, and so on, while poor people suffer from their lack. In societies where food, housing, and medical care are available to all regardless of the ability to pay, the gap between the rich and the poor is less pronounced and less painful. For this reason, the importance of the just distribution and the sustainability of nature's services cannot be overstated. The assessment concludes: "We must learn to recognize the true value of nature both in an economic sense and in the richness it provides to our lives in ways more difficult to put numbers on."[18] Such true value ranges from the taste of a cup of clean water to the sight of snow-capped mountains. Geographer David Harvey sums up the situation well with these sobering words:

> A strong case can be made that the humanly-induced environmental transformations now under way are larger scale, riskier, and more far reaching and complex in their implications (materially, spiritually, aesthetically) than ever before in human history. The quantitative shifts that have occurred in the last half of the twentieth century . . . imply a qualitative shift in environmental impacts and potential unintended consequences that requires a comparable qualitative shift in our responses and our thinking.[19]

Thinking Differently

The task before us—"a qualitative shift in our responses and our thinking"—is daunting. Yet such appears to be the overwhelming conclusion coming from all fields that study planetary health. As botanist Peter Raven says, this qualitative shift in thinking is also "a fundamentally spiritual task."[20] Until the eighteenth century, economics was considered a subdivision of ethics: the good life was understood to be based on such values as the common good, justice, and limits. Having lost this context for how to live on our planet, substituting the insatiable greed of market capitalism in its stead, we find ourselves without the means to make the shift in thinking now required. With the death of communism and the decline of socialism, Western society is left with an image of human life that is radically individualistic. The current major societal institutions in the West—government, economics, and religion—all support the assumption that the liberty, gratification, and salvation of the individual human person is the appropriate view of who we are in the scheme of things. This is diametrically opposed to how we should think of ourselves within an ecological worldview. It is impossible to imagine us acting differently—acting as "ecological citizens"—unless we internalize ecological values.[21]

One of the distinctive activities of religion is the formation of the imagination regarding human nature and our place in the scheme of things. As theologians widely agree, all theology is *also* anthropology. Religious traditions educate through stories, images, and metaphors, creating in their adherents deep and often unconscious assumptions about who human beings are and how they should act. It is at this point that the religions can make a significant contribution to the planetary crisis. For we live within the constructions of who we think we are; as these change, so might behavior. Thus, as many theologians and urbanists agree, utopian thinking—imagining what "might be" as well as prophetic witness against "what is"—should be recognized as an important step forward toward more just and sustainable living. As the slogan of nongovernmental organizations goes, "a different world is possible." But how do we get there? How can it become possible?

One small contribution toward this possibility is to change the metaphor by which we think of ourselves in the world. The metaphor that is conventional and widely accepted in twenty-first-century market capitalism is *the individual in the machine.* Human beings are seen as subjects in an objectified world that is there for our needs, desires, and recreation. The world is a "thing" to be utilized for human needs and pleasure. To see ourselves this way, however, is an anomaly in human history, for until the scientific revolution of the seventeenth century, as Carolyn Merchant and others have pointed out, the Earth was assumed to be alive, even as we are.[22] From the Stoics to the First Nations peoples, to medieval Christians, the organic quality of the Earth was unquestioned. But during the last few hundred years, it has become increasingly profitable to think of the world as more like a machine than a body. Since we always think in metaphors, especially at the deepest level of our worldviews, the nature of the metaphor becomes critical. If the machine model is dominant, then we will think of the world's parts as only externally related, able to be repaired, like cars, with new parts substituting for faulty ones, with few consequences for the Earth as a whole. With such a basic model in mind, it is hard for people to see the tragedy of clear-cutting forest practices or the implications of global warming.

Across many fields of study, however, the "body" is reemerging as a basic metaphor for interpretation and action. David Harvey mentions "the extraordinary efflorescence of interest in 'the body' as a grounding for all sorts of theoretical enquiries over the last two decades or so."[23] As we note above, this interest is hardly novel. From Protagoras's notion of the human body ("man") as the measure of all things, to the Stoic metaphor of the world as a living organism, to the First Nations' understanding of the Earth as the mother of us all, language of the body has historically been central to the interpretation of our place in the scheme of things. This is true of Christianity as well. As an incarnational religion, Christianity has focused on bodily metaphors: Jesus as the incarnate God, the Eucharist as the body and blood of Christ, the church as the body of Christ.[24]

To see bodily well-being as the measure of both human and planetary well-being is so obvious that it seems strange that it should need a revival. Gradually resurfacing is the realization that the appropriate metaphor for imagining our relation to the world is not *the individual in the machine* but *bodies living with the body of the Earth*. The food chain supports the centrality of this model: our eating transforms the body of the world into our bodies. However, behind twenty-first-century destruction of the planet as well as the impoverishment of the majority of its inhabitants lies a very different assumption about human beings: we are individuals with external relations to one another and to the planet itself.

Before proceeding further with the body model (or any other model), we must note that all metaphors are partial, none is adequate, and all need supplementation from other metaphors.[25] Metaphors are not descriptions; rather, they are the principal epistemological tool available to us on matters regarding our most basic assumptions about ourselves and our world. We judge metaphors not by descriptive agreement, but by a shock of recognition that follows initial disbelief. As Jacques Derrida points out, metaphor lies somewhere between nonsense and truth, and we entertain the nonsense for a while to see if it has any truth.[26] Thus to imagine the world as a machine or a body engenders an initial suspicion followed by an acknowledgment of possibility—and eventually, if the metaphor turns out to be an enduring model, acceptance and familiarity. In addition, however, to this criterion for a good metaphor, one other is crucial: What are the results of living within it? What does thinking within this model do to our acting within it?

We are now seeing the results of living within the machine model for several hundred years, and the verdict is overwhelmingly negative. Is it time to return to the model of the world and ourselves as body? The body as measure, as the lens through which we view the world and ourselves, changes everything. It means that human beings as bodies, dependent on other bodies and on the body of the Earth, are interrelated and interdependent in infinite, mind-boggling, wonderful, and risky ways. It means that *materialism*, in the sense of what makes for bodily well-being for all humans and for the Earth, becomes the measure of the good life. It combines the socialist and the ecological visions of human and planetary flourishing. It means that the good life cannot amount to the hoarding of basic resources by a few individuals for their own comfort and enjoyment. Rather, if we desire to take care of ourselves, we must also take care of the world, for we are, in this metaphor, internally related and mutually dependent on all other parts of the body. The metaphor of body—not just the human body but all bodies (all matter)—is a radically egalitarian measure of the good life; it claims that all deserve the basics of life: food, habitat, clean air and clean water.

This model turns our thinking upside down, for it makes two claims at odds with the mechanistic model. First, it claims that we human beings can no longer see ourselves as controlling all the other "parts"; rather, we must acknowledge that as the creature at the top of the food chain, we are totally dependent on all the others who are presumably "beneath us." Second, it compels us to acknowledge that the 20 percent of us who use 80 percent of the world's energy are responsible for the crushing poverty on our planet through our refusal to share resources equitably among all human beings and other creatures. In other words, this model helps us to see that sustainability and just distribution of resources are but two sides of the same coin: in order for the Earth to be healthy in the long term, the basic resources of life must be shared equitably among all creatures.[27] In other words, the individualistic, greedy assumptions of market capitalism are false; human beings cannot flourish apart from the flourishing of all the constituents that make up the Earth. The Earth is more like a body than like a machine, and we ought to return to the body model of our wiser forebears. This move, I believe, will help us in our central political task, as expressed by Harvey: "Suffice it to say that the integration of the urbanization question into the environmental-ecological question is a *sine qua non* for the twenty-first century."[28]

God Encompasses the World

Is the metaphor of the body also appropriate for thinking about the relationship of God and the world? If we were to imagine ourselves and the world in organic rather than mechanistic terms, what does this do to our concept of God? David Harvey gives us a clue when he states that basic geographical and environmental concepts must "also help to feed the hungry, clothe the naked, minister to the sick, and generally pursue the foundational aims of socialist/anti-capitalist politics."[29] It is fitting that Harvey should be quoting from Matthew 25, which identifies caring for the bodily needs of the poor with doing service to God. When the disciples ask Jesus how feeding a poor person can serve God, he replies, "Truly I tell you, just as you did it to one of the least of these who are members of my family, you did it to me" (Matt. 25:40). This key parable suggests that attention to the material needs of the oppressed is the mark of genuine Christian discipleship. Could it be then, that the model of the world as God's body might be an appropriate Christian way to imagine the relation of God and the world?[30]

As shocking as this question may seem, it is fully in keeping with the incarnationalism of Christianity. One of the most distinctive beliefs of this religion is that God became human, became flesh, in Jesus Christ. This incarnationalism is, however, also implicit in Hebrew religion, with its understanding of Emmanuel—God with us, here and now, on the Earth. This God is not a distant, unmoved Mover, as in Aristotelian thought, but the One who suffers with, delights in, punishes, and persuades the wayward tribe of Israel. Christianity claims that the Messiah has come and that God has appeared in human flesh in Jesus Christ. To see incarnationalism as the nature of God—that God is always with us on the Earth—and not simply in the onetime event of Jesus has been a deep strand in the history of Christian thought and is emerging once again in contemporary panentheism.

Panentheism says that God encompasses the world; God is internally related to every iota of creation as its source and sustaining power, but God is also more than the world.[31] The world is in God like a baby in the womb.[32] This understanding of the relation of God and the world differs from that of both theism and pantheism. Theism says that God is "above" the world and related to it only externally, as its creator and ruler, whereas pantheism identifies God with the world. Panentheism, broadly understood, is widespread among process theologians, feminist and ecological theologians, as well as Hindu and First Nations religions. This theological perspective understands the transcendence of God as radical immanence. The glory and power of God is manifest not in distance from the world but in intimacy with it as its source, sustenance, and renewal. For example, Augustine expresses this understanding of God in his *Confessions*:

> Since I do indeed exist and yet would not exist unless you were in me, why do I ask you to come to me? . . . Therefore, my God, I would not exist at all, unless you were in me; or rather, I would not exist unless I were in you "from whom and by whom and in whom all things exist." . . . To what place do I call to you to come, since I am in you? Or from what place are you to come to me? Where can I go beyond the bounds of heaven and earth, that my God may come to me, for he has said, "I fill heaven and earth"?[33]

When we speak of the relation of God and the world, we must always do so in metaphors and models. Thus we are not asking for a description of this relationship, for that is not available to us, any more than a poet can describe love, loss, death, or beauty. Poets and theologians work by way of metaphors, and in Christianity there have been several candidates to which the world as God's body can be compared. These include the deistic model (God as a clockmaker who sets the world in motion), the dialogical model (God in an I-Thou relationship with human beings), the monarchical model (God as king of the world with humans as subjects), and the agential model (God as human person who acts in the world).[34] Each of these models has its assets and its limitations, as all models do, but most of the popular Christian models have been anthropocentric, concerned mainly with the relation of God with human beings. None of these models support a God-world relationship that focuses on a just and sustainable planet as its goal. And yet a strong case can be made that the central Christian doctrines of creation and salvation are not just about eternal life for some human beings in another world but about the flourishing of all life on Earth.[35]

Therefore, in suggesting that we expand the model of body as a principle interpretive lens beyond our own bodies and the other bodies in the world to include "the body of God," we are not doing anything different from what theologians have always done when they attempt to speak of God. We are speaking metaphorically—heuristically, imaginatively, in an "as-if" fashion—and asking whether the model fulfils several criteria.[36] Does it fit with the Christian tradition? Yes, given the tradition's ancient and deep incarnationalism. Does it fit with contemporary understandings of reality? Yes, it is a major interpretive lens in many fields of study today and especially in political, feminist, and ecological circles. Would living within this model make things better for human beings and the planet? Yes, because it focuses on the just distribution of basic resources for humans and on the sustainability of the planet. Since we have only models, not descriptions, to work with, we must choose those that make sense in our time and result in human and planetary flourishing when lived out. Each theologian, like all other interpreters of human nature and destiny, can make only a small contribution to the current conversation of how to live better on our planet in our time. The challenge is universal and daunting, as summed up in the words of ecological economist Robert Costanza:

> Probably the most challenging task facing humanity today is the creation of a shared vision of a sustainable and desirable society, one that can provide permanent prosperity within the biophysical constraints of the real world in a way that is fair and equitable to all of humanity, to other species, and to future generations."[37]

I would like to suggest that the model of the world as God's body is one theological contribution that has standing within Christianity (as well as in other religions) and could be helpful in the planetary agenda that faces us. This contribution is made in a spirit similar to that of Timothy Gorringe in his book *A Theology of the Built Environment*, in which he attempts what he calls a liberation theology with a Trinitarian shape. Gorringe writes that "the relationships of the Triune God point us to community; the crucified God points us to the simultaneous presence of good and evil; the Spirit works in each place for human freedom."[38] Thus the grace of God meets us, as he puts it, in the ordinary, concrete places of human habitation and becomes the context—gift, not greed—that guides our actions. In a way not unlike the model of the world as God's body, Gorringe sees the land as gift: it is not ours but God's, and this acknowledgment allows for a change of consciousness and of action.

The Body of God

I would like now to investigate in more detail the contribution of the model of the world as God's body to twenty-first-century urban living. These contributions emerge from the two central streams in Christian thought: the sacramental and the prophetic, or the Catholic and the Reformed (or Protestant). The model of the world as God's body has both sacramental and prophetic dimensions.

THE SACRAMENTAL DIMENSION

If one lives within this model, one sees the world differently: not as an object or a machine or simply a resource, but as sacred, valuable, and needing our care. As mentioned above, the model of the world as God's body rests on an incarnational view of creation. Rather than seeing creation as separate from and external to God, something that God manipulates and controls (and hence that we can as well), an incarnational creation view sees nature as intimately related to God, as "within" God, as Augustine puts it. The world is God's body; hence creation, nature, bodies, and flesh are all "of God." The world, including nature, is not ours to do with as we wish. It all belongs to and tells us of God. The sacramental dimension claims that nature is an image of the divine; it is a reflection of God in all of God's diverse beauty.[39] Hence, while the sacramental dimension of the model connects us to God, it does so only through the millions of different bodies that make up God's "body." It suggests a celebration of bodies as well as concern for the care and feeding of bodies that underscores our respect for their intrinsic worth as part of God's creation. In other words, as sacrament of the divine, nature is other than and different from ourselves. The model of the world as God's body encourages an attitude of gratitude and humility toward the world, much as Gorringe's understanding of the land as gift.

The sacramental dimension of the model of the world as God's body prohibits us from folding first nature into second nature, since it suggests that nature, ours and everything else's, does not belong to us in the first place. It is "other." The interpretation of nature as sacrament of God demands a different stance, one suggested by Henry David Thoreau's belief that "wildness" was in the second-growth forest at Walden Pond in Concord. "Wildness" is in the mind as well as in reality; it is our recognition of otherness. In the words of philosopher Iris Murdoch: "Love is the extremely difficult realization that something other than oneself is real. Love . . . is the discovery of reality."[40] In other words, "love" is not a sentimental emotion or an act of charity; rather, it is the "objective" recognition that others exist and have intrinsic worth and rights to the basics of existence.

This sense of the "other" is evident also in the story of creation in Genesis. While Christianity has often been condemned as a chief contributor to environmental destruction through its mandate from Genesis to "subdue and dominate," one should also note a very different sensibility within that text. After each creation—of the light and darkness, the waters

and the land, the sun and the moon, all fish in the sea and birds in the air
and animals on the land, including human beings—God says, "It is good."
God then gives to every beast and bird and other living creature the green
plants to share among themselves. Having created all things and given
them food for flourishing, "God saw everything that he had made, and
indeed, it was very good" (Gen. 1:31). Two points stand out in this story:
God says of creation "it is good," not good for human beings (or even for
the divine self!), but simply "good." This is an aesthetic statement of intrinsic worth for each and every creature, echoing the first principle of the
Earth Charter. Second, the green plants are given to all living creatures to
share. In sum, God says of creation "it is good" seven times, but "subdue
and dominate" just once, and that within the context of the just distribution of plants to all creatures. This story supports both the intrinsic worth
of others and their right to the basics of existence.

An incarnational, Genesis-based creation story does not support replacing first nature by second nature. Rather, the organic model—the world
as the body of God—suggests a relationship more appropriately described
as "ecological unity." Bodies are related on a continuum by networks of
interrelationship and interdependence. The classical question from Plato
onward of the relationship of "the one and the many" is answered by
ecological unity, not with absorption or dualistic difference, but by way of
radical individuality within radical unity. Thus in an old-growth forest,
the health of the whole is dependent on the flourishing of all the parts,
each making its different contribution. Unlike the American image of the
melting pot, where all differences are assimilated, or the Canadian mosaic,
where differences sit side by side, ecological unity claims that the health
of the whole and of the parts is reciprocal. As stated earlier, sustainability
(the health of the whole) and distributive justice (the health of each of the
parts) are aspects of the same issue; one cannot occur without the other.
Likewise, second nature does not replace or absorb first nature nor stand
in a dualistic relationship to it. Rather, they are interrelated by complex
patterns of use and transformation, with the template being the fruitful
potential as well as inexorable limits of first nature.

Thus a sacramental understanding of the model of the world as God's
body suggests a sensibility that is appreciative of the world in its beauty
and value, sees the world as reflective of God, and is aware that as a body
made up of bodies, all parts must be fed and cared for. Such a sensibility
cannot imagine replacing the world—the body of God—by human interpretations and constructions. This would be neither appropriate nor realistic; rather, an attitude of gratitude for the wonder of the world and

recognition of our total dependence on it is the Christian response. Such an attitude toward the world acknowledges that human beings have indeed constructed the world in which we live and that there is no uninterpreted, pristine, or untouched nature left. Yet by living within the model of the world as God's body, one can nevertheless affirm that appreciation of and care for "others" is an imperative—and that it is the most realistic assessment as well.

THE PROPHETIC DIMENSION

While the sacramental dimension of the model encourages us to love others and realize their worth, the prophetic dimension focuses our attention on limits, namely the recognition that all bodies are finite, including the body of the world. All life-forms must have food, fresh water, clean air, and a habitat. The prophetic dimension stresses the finitude of the planet and the need for just and sustainable use of resources. More specifically, within the built environment resulting from twelve thousand years of gradual urbanization, the model of the world as God's body places severe limits on the excess, hoarding, greed, and injustice of some parts of the body: the well-off 20 percent of human beings who are contributing to the destruction of the planet and the impoverishment of fellow human beings.

The central issue at the third session of the World Urban Forum, which met in June 2006 in Vancouver, was the projection by the United Nations' latest evaluation on cities that slum living is now among the fastest-growing legacies of "civilization."[41] The conditions in many cities—those pushing 20 million—are already dire. By mid-century, city populations will double, from the present 2 billion to 4 billion, generating mind-boggling levels of need.[42] The forum met in Vancouver, widely praised as one of the most livable and well-built cities in the world. Vancouver epitomizes the "compact" city with its high-density population core of business and residential buildings, good public transit, numerous parks, and the greatest percentage of pedestrians and cyclists of any North American city. It is a dream city. But even Vancouver has "the lower East Side," an area of great poverty and drug addiction, an indication of things to come in the cities of the future, according to the forum. Vancouver is an example of the two sides of cities—the New Jerusalem and Babylon—with the latter projected as humanity's destiny.

Is the model of the world as God's body relevant to the upcoming urban crisis? The prophetic dimension of the model—the awareness of

the finitude, limits, and needs of bodies—suggests that it is. In fact, this
dimension must take center stage. The title of this volume (*Without Nature?*) proposes that being without nature may be possible. The prophetic
bodily sensibility, however, says: No! We do not now live "without nature," nor can we do so in the future. In fact, our very survival may well
rest on living within a different construction of nature, one closer to contemporary reality, in which second nature must be restrained. The model
of the world as God's body, which sees all bodies as needing the basics,
suggests a kenotic sensibility for today's well-off urban dwellers, so that
the projected slum dwellers may have space and place.

Kenosis means an emptying, a pulling back, a limiting. The term is traditional in Christian theology as a way to understand both God's creation
of the world and the incarnation in Jesus Christ. In creation, God allowed
"space" for others to exist by divine limitation, not as a self-denying act
but as affirmation of the other, in a way similar to the Genesis announcement, "It is good." In the incarnation, according to Pauline text, Christ,
"though he was in the form of God, did not regard equality with God as
something to be exploited, but emptied himself, taking the form of a slave,
being born in human likeness" (Phil. 2:6–7).[43] Kenosis is a unifying theme
in Christian thought, extending beyond God's actions in creation and the
incarnation to include the discipleship of followers. As Paul reminds his
flock: "Let each of you look not to your own interests, but to the interest
of others. Let the same mind be in you that was in Christ Jesus"; namely,
follow the self-emptying Christ. Kenosis—self-limitation that others
might have place and space to grow and flourish—is the way that God
acts toward the world and the way that Christians are to act toward one
another.

The notion of self-limitation for the well-being of others is widespread
among many religions, as evident in the emptying God in Buddhism and
Gandhi's notions of *ahimsa* and *satyagraha* (reverence for all living things;
soul or love force).[44] In spite of differences among the religions on many
issues, there appears to be no religion that supports "Blessed are the
greedy" (except, perhaps, the new "religion" of market capitalism). In
both Buddhism and Christianity, compassion toward others is based on
self-emptying, which, paradoxically, is also the way to true fullness; whoever would save their life must lose it.

At the heart of kenotic thinking is the assumption that bodies need
space. As benign as this might sound, it is one plausible description of
sainthood. Edith Wyschogrod, in her book *Saints and Postmodernism*, says

that "the term Other can be given a collective sense referring to the wretched of the earth." She goes on to say that "the saintly response to the Other entails putting his/her body and material goods at the disposal of the Other."[45] In other words, attention to others means attention to bodies, to the material needs of others, and this demands doing so with one's own body and the material goods one possesses. For well-off people, whose "ecological footprint" takes up most of the space on the planet, the prophetic and kenotic dimension of our model of the world as God's body is painful. It means pulling back, limiting oneself, learning to distinguish between "needs" and "desires," saying one has "enough," being willing to sacrifice for the common good. The new epistemological turn from time and history to space and place means for Christians, at least, the end of supposing that salvation is concerned with souls in heaven; now it is clearly acknowledged to refer to bodies on Earth. It means that the fortunate 20 percent must empty the self of its insatiable appetites so that others have the space for habitat, for food, and for life itself.

For city dwellers, the kenotic prophetic sensibility also means that second nature, or the built environment, must be minimized rather than maximized. It means small condos and apartments, not mansions; living spaces that go up, not out; small hybrid cars, not Hummers; food that is grown locally, not halfway around the world. It means saying "no" and saying "enough." Second nature is built upon first nature, and first nature is, increasingly, a vulnerable, deteriorating body unable to support the Western high-energy-use lifestyle. This realization should impact us at all levels: what we eat, our means of transportation, what we wear, the places we live, the parks where we play, the offices where we work. One of the greatest challenges of the twenty-first century is decent, livable conditions for the billions who will live in cities. We city dwellers need to take up less space, use less energy, lower our desires for more, attend to "needs" before "wants"—become small, in other words. The prophetic, kenotic sensibility demands that prosperous urban dwellers retreat from expansion and accept simplification at all levels of existence. Justice and sustainability demand that whatever we build upon first nature be shared with all other beings and be done within the limits of the planet's resources.

In sum, the second nature of the built environment should acknowledge that the base on which it is built and will continue to depend is first nature. Totalizing theories that eliminate first nature forget that we are *bodies* before all else. We cannot interpret or build unless we can eat. While we are also and at the same time interpreters and builders of our world, we are not its maker or master. There is something outside all our interpretations and constructions: the air we must breathe, the water we must drink, and the food we must eat. An understanding of second nature that underestimates the inescapable importance of first nature is not only unhelpful in our planetary crisis; it is also false. It does not help us to live as best we can, making decisions that are relatively better, even if Edenic first nature is no longer available. A model of the world as God's body reminds us of the sacredness, beauty, and importance of first nature at both the local and planetary levels. It reminds us that there is a difference between a small city lot zoned for a small park and such a lot tarred over for cars. It reminds us also that our planet is a limited physical entity able to support millions of different species as well as human beings, but only on a just and sustainable basis.

The kenotic God who opened up space for creation and who became empty in the incarnation is far removed from the image of an absolute, unmoved ruler who controls others by demanding total obedience. The power of the kenotic God lies in giving space that others might live, dying to the self that others might live. This strange reversal—losing one's life to save it—is also the sensibility that is needed if our planet is to survive and prosper. Giving space is a basic Christian doctrine, but it is also deep in the center of most religions and it is felt in the hearts of all people, religious or not, who know that "love is the discovery of reality," the realization that something beside oneself is real. Other bodies exist and must be fed and cared for. Once that acknowledgment is internalized, there is no going back to the assumption that individuals can pursue their own good apart from the good of others.

The model of the world as God's body is a possible contribution from an incarnational religion to twenty-first-century urban life. It suggests a context, a way of thinking, a construction within which to live that underscores the beauty and intrinsic value of what is left of first nature as well as our inexorable dependence on it. It helps to situate human beings in an appropriate stance toward the world, a stance of gratitude and care: gratitude for the wonder of living on this beautiful planet (as the poet Rilke puts it, "Being here is magnificent"), and care for its fragile, deteriorating creatures and systems, for "just as you did it to one of the least of these who are members of my family, you did it to me." We do not own the Earth, we do not even pay rent for it; it is given to us "free" for our lifetimes, with the proviso that we treat it with the honor it deserves, appreciate it as a reflection of the divine, and love it as our mother and our neighbor.

PART FOUR

Anthropology and Nature

Media reports in 2008 spoke frequently of the "human catastrophe" of flooding in the Midwestern states. Presumably this designated the tragic impacts of exceptional ecological events for families and communities in the affected areas. The banal phrase, however, conceals a provocative juxtaposition reminiscent of suggestions by Edward Soja and Michael Fischer: a "natural catastrophe" is made catastrophic by its social appropriation, that is, precisely by its human origins and effects. In this more radical sense, every natural catastrophe is a human catastrophe, not only in terms of its painful consequences for individuals but as a social product. Where does the autonomously "natural" end and the social agency of human natures begin? This section on anthropology addresses how human institutions and technologies intersect with experiences of "the natural."

Michael Fischer delves into the political and social spaces emerging from and conditioning human experiences of the natural and of the self. Our institutions come to manifest particular understandings of life and of being, but they never do so univocally, since all institutions develop from multiple interests, communities, and legal negotiations. Fischer explores four different notions of nature in terms of such complicated discourses: the nature manifested in the distribution of natural resources or more dramatically in natural catastrophes; the nature that proceeds from technical and cultural productions; the natures rebuilt "inside out" by genetic research; and the nature that confronts us in the alterity of other sentient beings. Each of these instances allows Fischer to investigate interrelated narratives by which we attempt to gain some purchase on our place in the world despite our incomplete knowledge of it. The plural identities of human nature, whether individual or social, emerge from this interplay of narratives.

Lisa Sowle Cahill posits that nature is "polyvalent," particularly as it simultaneously delineates that which is and that which ought to be. Nature designates not only physical structures but also social and psychological structures. Rather than depend on the fixity of human nature, Cahill insists on the possible sanctification of nature, an ethical hope that human natures can grow collectively more just. In light of Fischer's essay, Cahill's perspective offers directions for mediating the diverse narratives that inform human nature. Theology's new condition is not being without nature but appropriating our moral nature in interdependence with a global community. Situating ourselves in relation to the world community and understanding the self in that social and political context suggests that the proper—even "natural"—human function is an ethic of care for those who are disadvantaged.

Thomas Carlson addresses the relationship between human nature and the technological possibility of personal re-creation. Carlson identifies a stream of philosophical and theological anthropology that defines the human, paradoxically, as that which can never be finally defined. If this is true, it would be a threat to human nature if technology eliminated all chance and ignorance or if reactions to genetic technology insisted on a single human definition. If, as Heidegger suggested, the distinctive characteristic of remaining open, unpredictable, and capable of wonder is fundamentally linked to being created or being "given," does technology foreclose possibility or facilitate it? In response, Carlson proposes, by reference to Michel Serres, that the human possibility might be understood in terms of love, that is, a natural openness that precludes definition.

Emergent Forms of Un/Natural Life

Michael M. J. Fischer

Nature is an ambivalent term meaning both what is other to us and what is essentially ourselves. Even as our selves (our characters, our bodies, our selfhoods), nature is often "other," that from which we attempt to separate ourselves and upon which we are dependent, which we attempt to control but which always escapes our reach.

Four kinds of nature defining self and other seem to have risen to the top of political, philosophical, and moral agendas in the past quarter century: (1) so-called "natural" catastrophes and the problems traditionally associated with the "control of nature" (ecological nature); (2) "industrial" accidents and the unintended negative consequences of new technologies associated with first-order industrial processes and the military-industrial complex as well as with renewed calls for deliberative democracy, social accountability, and environmental justice related to older environmental interests in remediation, preservation, and conservation (environmental nature); (3) contestations over agricultural and medical biotechnologies (and the life sciences more generally), and their potential for reorganizing conceptual categories of life, the viability of human beings and their habitats, as well as more targeted concerns about genetic and pharmacological enhancements and inequalities (nature in the life sciences); (4) shifting relations with companion species, both domesticated (including modified organisms for medical research) and wild (particularly viruses, such as avian flu strains that map the changing relations among species and habitats) (coevolutionary nature).

We live (again) in an era in which new ethical and political spaces are thrown up that require action and have serious consequences but for which the possibilities of giving adequate reasons quickly run out.[1] Traditional ethical and moral guides seem not always helpful, particularly when some of the very categories of discussion (such as "nature") have morphed, disaggregated, and become distributed. We are often left to negotiate multiplicities of interests and trade-offs in serial legal battles or other tournaments of decision-making over time. As an anthropologist, I am interested in the ways emergent forms of life embed institutional and ethical orientations, inventions, and productivities and how these vary or contrast in different places and times. Are there pressures toward new "reflexive" or "second-order modernization" institutions, or do we fail to learn from one crisis to the next, allowing involution of institutions, hierarchies, and sanctioned behaviors? What social, literary, and material technologies are used to frame and negotiate trade-offs, crises, and dilemmas? I take it as given that "one cannot change only one thing"; interconnections are interesting, puzzling, surprising, and they spur us to reframings and new institutions. This might be called the "ecological rule."

Narrating First Nature: Catastrophe, Deep Play, Repetition, and Social-Ecological Learning

As the devastation of Hurricane Katrina unfolded in 2005, I mused over whether it was surreally following a radio script of 1931 by Walter Benjamin, *"Die Mississippi Überschwemmung 1927"* ("The Flooding of the Mississippi 1927").[2] Benjamin did a series of radio "children's stories" on catastrophes, the Lisbon earthquake of 1753 being another celebrated one.[3] Both tales continue to have resonances for today. In the Lisbon quake tale, Benjamin asked if new predictive technologies (seismology for earthquakes, satellite monitoring for hurricanes) would successfully enable the avoidance of future crises. In the Mississippi River tale, Benjamin directly addressed social failures.

The 1927 flood, caused by heavy rains from August 1926 through the spring of 1927 displaced over 1 million people from the Lower Mississippi River region (from Cairo, Illinois, to the Gulf Coast). Some 23,000 square miles flooded from Virginia to Oklahoma. People took refuge on the tops of levees. Some 660,000 were fed by the Red Cross.[4]

The impact of the heavy rains was exacerbated by poor engineering decisions to improve the flow of the Mississippi River. At issue was not only the struggle against the meandering of the great river to make it stay in its banks and flow "efficiently" from north to south; more to the point for Benjamin was the dynamiting of the dikes that protected rural regions, making vulnerable the land and the homes of the rural poor for the interests of New Orleans. Troops were called out to suppress threat of civil war. As in 2005, St. Bernard Parish was flooded, but in 1927 the breaking of the dikes was neither a natural nor a necessary event but a political decision to send a message to the New York and Chicago financial institutions that measures would be taken to protect the city of capital, the *Hauptstadt*. New Orleans was not only the great port for agriculture but also the banking center for the sugar and cotton interests of the Mississippi Valley. Despite these measures, the New Orleans banks were nonetheless wiped out, and agriculture already in depression in the Mississippi Valley was further devastated.

Poor African-American sharecroppers in Greenville, Mississippi, and elsewhere were prevented from evacuating (lest they leave for good) and were pressed into rebuilding the levees at gunpoint (albeit paid a dollar a day). Echoes might be heard in the 2005 Bush administration's lifting of the rules on paying workers the going rate. Instead of either employing local labor at the legal rate or giving work to the many local illegal Mexican immigrants hiding from the authorities in the devastated city and surrounding areas, the Bush administration brought in fresh Mexican labor from Texas.

Benjamin commented on the destruction of the electronic communications system that ran along the levees. In 2005, again, one of the system failures was our much-vaunted communications networks, hampering first responders and rescue workers.

As a coda, Benjamin added the story of three brothers stranded on a roof. Despairing that any rescue boats would stop for them, one jumped to his death just before the other two were rescued. This figures as a miniature to the larger story and is part of Benjamin's polemic against techno-optimism. Catastrophes, Benjamin says, blast us out of the continuum of history and provide illuminations of different orderings of nature, history, limits to strategic planning, cost-benefit accounts, and other claims of rational prudence. They function analogously to traditional theological parables of human beings' best-laid plans gone awry due to inevitably partial knowledge.

The 1927 flood was a transformative event in a number of regards. First, it dramatically changed the way Americans thought about the federal government's responsibility for its citizens.[5] Previously the federal government had felt little obligation to provide food or shelter to disaster victims. President Coolidge refused to visit the disaster areas but did send Herbert Hoover, empowered him as a cabinet-level officer, and put him into the military chain of command. Hoover coordinated relief efforts of the Red Cross and other agencies. The newsreel imagery of the disaster and Hoover's coordination of relief propelled him into the presidency. Some of this footage can be seen in the documentary *Fatal Flood* produced by Chana Gazit and released in 2001.[6]

Second, the 1927 floods changed race relations in the Delta and across the United States. Three times as many African Americans migrated to Chicago, Detroit, Houston, and Los Angeles in the wake of the flood as would do so during the Depression of the 1930s, which is usually counted as the cause of the Great Migration. Previously, because of labor shortage, the laborers and sharecroppers had been treated relatively well, but after the prevention of evacuation and forced labor in the immediate aftermath of the flood, patrimonial relations with plantation owners were broken.[7]

Third, the 1927 flood changed the way in which the Army Corps of Engineers attempted to control the river.[8] Rather than work against the river's momentum, containing the river within narrow banks to increase the speed of water flow, and self-dredging for navigation (the so-called "levees only" strategy), the Corps moved to a strategy of working with and leveraging the flow of the river, directing it via "outlets" and Eads' jetties, named after the engineer James Eads. In 2005 a design flaw eerily similar to the "levees only" strategy operated: canals built in the 1960s to speed shipping funneled Katrina storm surges from the Gulf of Mexico into Lakes Pontchartrain and Borgne and on into the city.[9]

The 1928 Flood Control Act initiated the United States' largest civil engineering project (Project Flood) and shifted relations between the federal government and the states, constructing safety valves, controlled spillways, and fuse-plug levees. In the 1940s the Mississippi Basin Model, a forty-acre physical model of the river, was built by German prisoners of war. It was used as an experimental system for testing large floods and control systems until 1973.[10]

Whether Hurricane Katrina in 2005 will have some similar transformative effects remains to be seen, but a number of features articulate even broader concerns than those of 1927. There are suggestions of connections with anthropogenic climate warming, not just with civilian addiction to fossil fuels but possibly with Cold War military experiments disrupting the chemical and electromagnetic circuits of the planet.[11]

I want to pose three kinds of analytic frames here: deep play, the balance between decentralized and centralized control systems, and reflexive social institutions and dialogic narrative capacities.

DEEP PLAY

Catastrophic events and their associated political contestations often become deep play: sites where dynamically a number of meaning structures "implode" or intersect and where society dramatizes to itself the meaning of its own representations about the moral order. It is said from various "rational" and "cultural" (e.g., Cajun backcountry) points of view that controlling the Mississippi River in whole or in some of its parts (e.g., destroying wetlands along its banks) is hubristic and self-defeating. Yet, as with many death-defying sports (and some dangerous and death-challenging technologies), the struggle with the Mississippi has also been seen as the grandest of human agons: the Corps of Engineers against nature.

The struggle with the Mississippi is a deep play in the Geertzian sense,[12] giving meaning to endeavors to define human nature against its others. Overinvestments of money, passion, and political resources constitute a nexus in which multiple registers of meanings are densely knotted. New Orleans, after all, is the great port of Midwestern agriculture, a great transshipment port of oil and petroleum, and the cultural entrepôt of French, Cajun, African-American, and Southern cultural distinction. But in a Benjaminian flash of catastrophic illumination, it also reveals the irrationalities of class and racial inequality, of the ethical (or social justice) unconcern on the part of political and financial elites, of bureaucratic fiefdoms, and of technological decay and miscalculation.

The cost-benefit calculations of 1965, for instance, remain unchanged forty years later. Cost-benefit analysis itself might be challenged as a questionable methodology when lives are at stake. A measure of unconcern might be the only token funding for the 1998 plan to save wetlands and rebuild the Louisiana coast (the Louisiana Coastal Area Project, or Coast 2050). This play of plan and underfunding is a deep-play demonstration of meaning and values, dramatized, televised, and for a time put out for public discussion. One might narrate these meanings, as is usually done in the press, as a play of "indictments" and "defenses," in a mock-litigious, American-style shadow play of skeptical "civic epistemology," where "truth," "fact-finding," and "meaning" are said to be established through adversarial contestation, but where testimony under oath cannot be sub-poenaed or compelled. The existential and ethical deep-play agons are refracted as well in plays, in music, and in debates about how much aid and succor should be provided by the government and how much by civil society and "faith-based" organizations.[13]

BALANCE BETWEEN DECENTRALIZED AND CENTRALIZED CONTROL OR GOVERNANCE SYSTEMS

This second set of questions about alternative social organizations has be-come "mission critical": What sorts of centralized or decentralized gover-nance might be most effective in dealing with future hurricanes or similar events, including the building and maintaining of seawalls, levees, and wetland defenses, but also the prepositioning of emergency supplies, the bolstering of local responders, shelters, and evacuation facilities. Walter Benjamin's question resonates: What use are our predictive abilities if the social institutions exacerbate the damage?

The comparative case of the seawall in the Netherlands, built after the devastations of the 1953 floods, has been primarily discussed in technolog-ical terms, but an anthropological science and technology approach should also turn attention to the political and organizational robustness required. The 1953 floods killed almost two thousand people and forced the evacua-tion of seventy thousand. It could have been much worse. Half the coun-try, including Amsterdam and Rotterdam, is below sea level. Dramatically, a Dutch sea captain sank his boat in a widening breach to protect Rotter-dam. The project to improve the sea defenses with a new design that allows water through to maintain the wetlands in at least a portion of the coast caused a huge domestic debate. The new design and the debate also shifted the relations between the central state and local water councils.

Decentralized water councils have long been connected to Dutch dem-ocratic and self-reliance organizations. Over the course of the twentieth century, the state water-control authorities created a symbiotic system of state planning and the outsourcing of construction and maintenance to private sector companies. The new effort required new organizational forms, both in negotiating the new plans and in construction and mainte-nance.[14] In the end, a compromise in the new design was dictated by the politics of budgets, as described in Wiebe Bijker's 2002 article. One leaves Bijker's account worried with the Dutch about how secure the system is, even though it currently seems to be functioning well.

The Dutch debate continues as to whether one can hold the sea back as the land sinks. Perhaps, it is debated, one ought to invest in floating cities; indeed, in parts of the Netherlands new construction is required to be on pontoons. Other experiments for comparative attention are the floodgates on the Thames, those on the Adriatic to protect Venice, the superlevees being built in Japan, the concrete shelters on stilts in Bangladesh built in the aftermath of the 1991 hurricane and storm surge, and California's "smart" levees using "time-domain reflectometry" sensors to monitor whether the dikes are weakening.[15]

The loss of life and livelihood in these comparative cases of the Netherlands and Bangladesh should refocus attention on deep play structures of meaning embedded in modalities of social organization. An estimated eight hundred to a thousand lives were lost immediately in the Hurricane Katrina flooding (not considering excess mortality figures in the ensuing years), and almost immediately questions were raised about how many of these were from the poor, disabled, and minority communities and what would happen to these communities and people as the city rebuilt and perhaps in the process gentrified. Kerry Emanuel, one of the scientists studying the connections of hurricanes with climate warming, pointed out in an interview that "tropical depression Jean the previous year—it was just a depression—killed almost 2,000 people in Haiti. Hurricane Mitch in 1999 killed 11,000 people in Central America. And a decade before that, a hurricane in Bangladesh killed 100,000 people."[16] Emanuel suggests that the United States is relatively lucky in having been able to prevent loss of life, that people should be encouraged to stop building along vulnerable coastlines, and that the differences between the vulnerability of the poor and rich are replicated in international comparative terms as in class terms within New Orleans. Charles Perrow, a sociologist of vulnerabilities in high-risk technologies, argues that New Orleans should be maintained at about one third its pre-Katrina size—large enough to sustain the vital port functions, but small enough to be defended with Dutch-style technologies against future storms and sinking coasts.[17] New Orleans is already at two thirds its pre-Katrina size.

Even more went wrong in the New Orleans case with the breakdown of evacuation and relief preparedness. A previous evacuation effort in 2004 had resulted in gridlock on the highways. The repeat highway problems in 2005 indicate a certain failure in social learning. As Katrina approached, newsmen prepared reports on the 1965 Hurricane Betsy disaster, when eighty-one people died, 250,000 were evacuated, the ninth ward was flooded, people had to be rescued from their rooftops, and rumors flew that water was pumped out of the mayor's Lake Vista subdivision into the Ninth Ward and even that the Industrial Canal was deliberately breached to flood out black people. Worst-case scenarios, with computer-generated Sea, Lake and Overland Surges from Hurricanes (SLOSH) models (run by the National Hurricane Center) had long been in circulation.[18] One wonders if any of the modelers or first-responder agencies had thought much about Charles Perrow's models of "normal accidents" (as he titles his book on managing risk in high-tech industries). It was reported that a $1 million hurricane simulation exercise in New Orleans in 2004 exposed many communication and logistical problems that remained unfixed.[19] Speculation began about what the long-term effects of the trauma would be on those who would remain separated from their social networks in the Ninth Ward and elsewhere—whether we would see, for instance, a spate of suicides (two suicides were reported among the police during the storm). In sum, governance questions regarding the balance and integration of regional plans (such as Coast 2050) with decentralized local initiatives and knowledge, ecological planning for cities such as New Orleans, and federal level coordination remain deeply problematic. "Learning from catastrophe" is a social institutional issue par excellence. It is also a cultural arena of "deep play" in which multiple interests, strategies, passions and investments interact, often in unacknowledged ways, in planning documents and bureaucratic politics.

REFLEXIVE SOCIAL INSTITUTIONS AND DIALOGIC
NARRATIVE CAPACITIES

The third set of questions, therefore, has to do with the creation of flexible and reflexive social institutions of second-order modernity that can make use of a rich interchange of communications and dialogue between decentralized capillary powers of decision-making and central nodes of macro-coordinated support. Despite the multidimensionality of the deep play surrounding a catastrophe and the following reconstruction, restitution, and rehabilitation, planning tends to elicit from government and major relief agencies a monological rather than dialogical form of mapping complexity within a semiclosed world of expertise that assumes everything can be viewed from a commanding height: the Mississippi Basin Model that was used from the 1940s to 1973; a FEMA office in Washington; a simulation model in a university. One of the interests of comparison with the Dutch case is to probe the possibilities of on-the-ground community involvement and investment in complex sociotechnical systems, particularly under long-term anticipated changes such as climate warming and rising sea levels.

From a hydrological point of view, both the 1927 floods and the 2005 hurricane flooding, despite their quite different causes and directionality, are part of a long series of Mississippi floods (1858, 1862, 1867, 1882, 1884, 1888, 1890, 1927, 1965, 1993, 1995, 1997, 1998, 2001). In 1965 Hurricane Betsy flooded New Orleans as Katrina did in 2005, and it was in 1965 that standards were last set for the strength of the levees on a dubious basis of cost-benefit analysis. The most significant of these floods in recent memory were the 1993 floods (both the fourth "hundred-year flood" in eight years, and a "five-hundred-year" event, causing some $12 billion in damage). The causes of the 1993 flooding included an unusual shift in the jet stream that blocked a cold front and kept heavy rains over the Mississippi for six weeks. By August, 1,083 levees had failed.

This 1993 flooding stimulated some changes in floodplain management, reinforced by the Upper Mississippi floods in 2001. Instead of rebuilding in the floodplain, houses and even whole towns (e.g., Valmeyer, Illinois, in 1993; parts of Davenport, Illinois, in 2001) were moved away from the floodplain. Federal incentive programs for restoring wetlands began; an estimated half of all wetlands of the Mississippi Basin are said to be gone, and in the Delta some of the farmland, now used for catfish farming, gets its water by pumping from the aquifers below. One study found that 40 percent of flood insurance payments go to repeat victims, who represent 2 percent of policyholders; one house worth $114,000 received payments worth $806,000 for sixteen floods over eighteen years.[20]

Apart from these ecological, technical, and social management problems, there has been speculation about the role of climate change (as well as murky questions about the impact of military experiments on the atmosphere).[21] While no direct correlation between individual events and climate change can be established, it is statistically the case that we are in a warming phase and that there is a correlation between warming waters and the energy that goes into more intense hurricanes. The 1940s and 1950s were a period of intense and strong hurricanes, followed by a lull in the 1970s and 1980s, and we appear to be in another upswing. From the statistics of the Atlantic storms (11 percent of total storms) there is no way to associate the increasing intensity of hurricanes with anything but a natural cycle. On the other hand, Kerry Emanuel also says that globally it appears that "the intensity of hurricanes is going up owing to global warming, and their duration is increasing, as well."[22] He does not think that we will see any direct evidence in the immediate future; it will take time for the connections to become evident. In half a century the connections will be more evident—insurance companies: take note. In the meantime, particularly during the 1970s and 1980s (when there was a lull in the

intensity of tropical storms), there have been significant construction and
population growth along vulnerable coastlines.[23]

For New Orleans, climate change is experienced most directly by rising
sea levels, which will put the city lower and lower below sea level over
time. As shown by Amsterdam, Galveston, and other places around the
world, this is not necessarily an insurmountable engineering or social
problem, but it is one that requires local knowledge and investment. For
the greater New Orleans region, rising sea levels are but one factor contributing to the collapse of the coastal area, together with the loss of allu-
vium which is washed out to sea by the channeled Mississippi but would
otherwise be deposited along the riverbank, shoring up the coast and nurturing the wetland's protective zones. Deposits of nitrogen and other
chemicals from fertilizer runoff (and perhaps other sources) in the allu-
vium cause hypoxia, creating dead zones in the Gulf, and land slumping
due to depressurization from offshore oil drilling further contributes to
loss of wetlands.[24]

We thus come full circle in these first narratives of nature. "Catastrophe" and "deep play" provide windows into our responses, passions, and
meaning structures. They help us see ourselves as not particularly puny
microorganisms in the larger scales of the universe and our multiple
worlds or frames of reference. Even very small organisms, we learn from
ecological studies, have cascading effects that can change larger-scale
systems.[25]

Second Natures: German Modes of Production, French Parliaments of Things, and American Regulatory Sciences

The contamination events at Minimata, Japan (mercury poisoning from
Chisso Corporation's chemical factory's wastewater over the 1932–1968
period affecting some 2,265 people in official counts by 2001), Love Canal
(21,000 tons of toxic waste found buried in Niagara Falls township in New
York State, causing declaration of a public health emergency), Bhopal,
India (42 tons of toxic methyl isocyanate released from a Union Carbide
plant in 1984, killing thousands within two weeks and many more since),
Chernobyl (1986 nuclear reactor release of radioactivity which badly contaminated the immediate area in the Ukraine and also drifted over large
parts of Eastern and Northern Europe and beyond), and Woburn, Massachusetts (dumping of carcinogenic toxic waste from tanneries and three
industrial plants and ill-advised drilling of two water wells by the city,

causing a cluster of leukemia cases and an important book and film that helped transform public awareness) form a series of engagements with the complexity of our environment and nature different from earthquakes, hurricanes, and tsunamis. They have to do with our chemical industries, our bodies, and our engagements with high-hazard, high-consequence missions, including medicine and public health, aeronautics and space flight, and nuclear industries. It was Friedrich Hegel and the generations that would conceptualize the transitions between the first and second industrial revolutions who elaborated the notion that men and women create around themselves a reworked nature, a second nature, a technological and cultural nature that is increasingly difficult to separate from nostalgias for a lost, primal, and mythic first nature. In literature and rhetoric, this lost pastoral was used to criticize and critique industrial, urban society.[26]

But it is within the politically "green" lineage of concern (from Rachel Carson and Barry Commoner onward in the 1960s United States, and from the election in 1983 of the Greens in Germany) that a different register of work has emerged, probing for voluntaristic, politically organized ways in which society could be reorganized to protect itself from the dark sides of its own production.[27] While there are striking parallels across countries in the processual or dramaturgical responses to industrial disasters that affect the environment and public health across national boundaries,[28] there are also dramatic differences in cultural politics, in the presuppositions of how political decisions should be legitimately resolved (Sheila Jasanoff's "civic epistemologies"), and in the unstable coalitions of actors "called forth" by particular conjunctures of crises, social pressures, and double-bind commitments (Kim Fortun's "enunciatory communities").[29]

The concept of "enunciatory communities" constituted in the vortex of contradictory demands helps make clear the importance of dialogical accounts (multiple play of arguments across interests, values, perspectives) that are often pushed into the background of monological expert summaries. In the Bhopal case, to take the double binds of three of the key enunciatory communities: the State of India, the women's association of affected families, and the lawyers for the victims. The Indian state attempted to represent the victims and at the same time publicly assert the hospitality of India to foreign capital. The women's association of methyl isocyanate gas–injured families asserted women's agency and yet had to recruit a male leader, who unfortunately fell into a typical male patriarchal mode of leadership antithetical to the women's organization. The lawyers for the gas-injured needed to appeal the dismissal of their suit in New

York against Union Carbide on jurisdictional grounds (because their clients would get less compensation in Indian courts than would American victims of similar accidents on U.S. soil, an invidious double standard of justice) without thereby asserting the incompetence of Indian courts to provide fair trials. The Indian government was a party to charges of not enforcing safety regulations as well as having conflicting interests in the legal outcome. The lawyers wanted to force Indian courts to hold the Indian state accountable.[30]

Enunciatory communities and dialogical narrative formats are among the conceptual tools that can register and incorporate the multiple points of view that are required in *real time*, lest complex social systems under crisis conditions break down. The best-known of these formulations is, perhaps, Ulrich Beck's notion that we are entering a second-order modernization, coordinated and governed through new reflexive social institutions.[31] We increasingly live, he argues, in risk societies, producing risks and dangers that are not calculable in the way the insurance industry constructed actuarial tables for factory accidents in the nineteenth century. Beck's narrative begins as a delightful, almost parodic, reprise of the language of Karl Marx on the transformation of feudal modes of production into industrial capitalist ones. It has the same doubleness of rhetoric, being simultaneously hortatory for a politics without which the transformation cannot occur and descriptive of the internal institutional pressures to save old capitalist and bureaucratic forms from their brittleness and simplistic rationalities. Marx's notion of new modes of production arising from the accumulated pressures and contradictions of older modes of production is adapted by Beck to frame a structural account of shifts and changes.[32]

Beck's elegant argument is that our chemical and nuclear industrial processes, among others, are producing risks that we cannot see without scientific instruments, that respect no political or class boundaries, and whose causality and thus liability are hard to trace. In preindustrial society, risks were largely not man-made. In industrial society, insurance systems were based on understandings of systematic causation and statistical probabilities, so that rules of liability and compensation could be devised. But in risk society, risks accumulate slowly, are not limited in time and space, affect future generations, and are often testable only after the fact. The globe thus becomes used as a laboratory for toxic waste, the spread of illness vectors, and cascades of nonlinear causalities that make accountability diffuse and rules that the polluter pays hard to enforce.

In such circumstances corporate behavior becomes a shell game of defensive and competitive actions, as when one industry publicizes risks of another industry (for instance, the nuclear industry publicizing the ozone hole[33]). The ad campaigns so generated contribute to wild swings in public mood between hysteria and cynicism. Politicians are urged to make dramatic policies based on such mood swings. "Parapublic" expert bodies are created by political leaders to contain public anxiety and often to narrow and contain public debate. The logic of social divisions is reorganized sometimes along sectoral lines rather than class lines, with, for instance, tourist industries opposed to chemical industries. (The Po Valley is one of Beck's exemplars since it is both a crucial tourist landscape and the heart of industrial production in Italy. The tourist industry wants green environments free of the pollution by-products of the chemical industries. The political stakes and social divisions, Beck argues, thus fall out differently in risk society than in industrial society).

Some of these differences between industrial and risk society contribute to the decay and brittleness of legacy industrial-society institutions.[34] For instance, demands for ever-higher standards of scientific accuracy and causal linkage can be used to minimize risk and the need to take counteraction.[35] But other features militate toward reparative and potentially transformative institutional forces such as pressures toward green production and the use of consumerism to drive ecological consciousness (rights of consumers to clean air and water; increasing market segments for organic food; citizen pressure toward mobilization of socially administered security). One of the key features of these new institutional forms is "reflexive" social organizations that are able to integrate and use input from many different positions in society rather than relying on isolated top-down expertise of policy planners, factory designers, or laboratory scientists.

Minimata, Love Canal, Woburn, and Bhopal all provide case examples of the agonistic battles to evolve "reflexive" social organizations. The "dramatological" pattern of citizens having to struggle against older corporate and bureaucratic structures is one of citizens noticing cancer clusters or seemingly patterned illnesses, demanding from the state epidemiological surveys, being denied by the state and corporate authorities on the ground that the alleged causality is impossible, that the industrial processes in question were carefully constructed in the lab.[36] That shop-floor practices are frequently different from lab practices is often overlooked and denied, and in the case of the Union Carbide plant in Bhopal, safety features were being dismantled because the entire plant was scheduled to be closed and moved. Citizens thus are forced to find scientists and epidemiologists who can collect sufficiently rigorous data to stand up in court, and once this barrier is passed, a long and arduous community organizing process must be launched to get remediation, restitution, compensation, and medical and other help. In the Minimata case, the effort was still ongoing after thirty years, in the Bhopal case new charges were filed on the twentieth anniversary, and in Woburn, community activists are still fighting after twenty years.

Love Canal spawned a toxic-chemical clearinghouse alliance for communities across the country. Superfund legislation in the United States mandated citizen action panels, providing the citizens some funding to hire technical experts in their battles with corporations, military installations, and government facilities. Tactics of both citizen organizing and corporate defense have evolved over time. In the Louisiana chemical corridor, older civil rights organizing traditions helped with environmental organizing, only to be countered by petroleum companies organizing their own "grassroots" organizations, a tactic which is the subject of at least one corporate "how to" guide.[37] The Bhopal case involved litigation in the United States as well as India, and the parallels with struggles over Union Carbide's plant in Institute, West Virginia, illustrate that the Bhopal struggles were not merely due to "Third World backwardness." In West Virginia, capital was less mobile but labor was made mobile, with Mexican labor brought in to stop local union organizing. The post-9/11 concerns about terrorism reversed the drive toward right-to-know postings on the Internet of emission releases and worst-case scenarios for local residents.[38]

Still the argument for second-order modernization or "reflexive" social institutions remains vital and more general than these particular cases of breakdown. Silvio Funtowicz and Jerome Ravetz note that "policy-relevant science," or what Jasanoff more felicitously calls "regulatory science," operates differently from normal science (in Thomas Kuhn's sense) or even consultancy science (where there is thought to be an application of available knowledge to well-characterized problems); instead, highly uncertain, contested knowledge is generated in support of health, safety, and environmental decisions, and this requires a quite different sort of peer review, one that is extended to multiple stakeholders.[39]

One of the most intractable (and hence interesting) renegotiations of governance of environmentally damaged and hazardous areas is described in Joe Masco's 2006 study of the lands surrounding the Los Alamos National Laboratory, with quite different legal resources, perspectives, traditions, and data collection among the Los Alamos scientists (whose past hiding of facts has lost them credibility as objective stewards), Pueblos and Nuevomexicanos (both of whom are dependent upon Los Alamos for

jobs), Anglos (often with romantic New Age environmentalism discon-
nected from local political economies), and Washington bureaucrats.[40] No
longer is Los Alamos or Washington (or the University of California, as
operator of Los Alamos) in control of all information or legal standing.
This example should provide a comparative probe for other such sites
around the world and connects the institutional reflections of this section
with the shifts in environmental management and the climate warming
debates in which the Inuit are engaged (see note 23).

The degree to which local knowledge, tacit skills, and intuition build
up over long periods of practice and experience is critical to the flexibility
and robustness of complex systems, whether they are "traditional" knowledge (as with the Pueblo and Inuit) or "situated" on the "shop floor" of
nuclear power and chemical plants or large engineering projects such as
the space shuttle, or in medical operating theaters and emergency disaster
relief organizations.[41] These are arenas that will repay detailed ethnographic attention in the coming years as the sites for some of the most
consequential of ethical decision-making. Philosophically (epistemologi-
cally, methodologically), if not practically, the French tradition of political
ecology and what Bruno Latour calls the "parliament of things" can perhaps help keep thinking in this arena from falling into overly simple formulations.[42] Luc Ferry begins his 1992 book in this French political-
ecology tradition by reminding readers about older "natural contracts"
that drew together social and human-insect-animal relations in ways different from our own natural contracts. In sixteenth-century France, wee-
vils and beetles were put on trial, accused by villagers of destroying their
crops. Trials were held for insects, reptiles, rats, mice, leeches. Even dolphins were excommunicated for blocking navigation in a port.[43]

The idea of natural contracts in the French tradition has been picked
up by Michel Serres not so much as a matter of rights and standing in
court, as in the famous 1972 law review article by Christopher Stone,
"Should Trees Have Standing?"[44] Rather, Serres points out that social-
contract theory in political philosophy was implicitly local, taking nature
as given and as available for appropriation. As technological extensions
make human reach global, this implicit relation to the environment encounters new forms of feedback and resistance. Human societies need to
move from positions of parasitism to ones of symbiosis with natural cycles.
Serres's notion of a natural contract, Kerry Whiteside explains, is not an
ethical act in which people come to an agreement, nor is it grounded in a
view of a preexisting nature that is given judicial recognition (as in the
sixteenth-century examples), but it is rather a literal *con-trahere* (gathering

together), as in the image of tightening the ropes of the rigging of a sail-
boat, "a complex set of constraints and freedoms in which each element
receives information through every adjustment."[45]

Bruno Latour's "political ecology" focuses this French tradition of
thought as one of shifting competences among "mélanges of things that
transcend human control and of actions imputable to mankind."[46]
Whereas premoderns sacralized nature and feared nature's wrath, mod-
erns attempted to create purified worlds they could control in science and
politics. Today, however, Latour suggests, hybrids have broken through
these efforts at purification; global warming, nuclear waste, and genetically
engineered plants are among some of these unruly mélanges. In his provocative formulation, he suggests that what is needed is to give such hybrids or mélanges seats in our parliaments and representative assemblies,
a parliament of things. The point seems to be that already all such
"things" are matters of controversy and disputation among scientists but
also among human rights activists, ecologists, government agencies, and
others. These negotiations and backstage wars of position (to adopt a
Gramscian formula) need to be made visible, explicit, and part of our open
representative assemblies. Latour insists that there is no nature independent of human interests and practices that might be used as a standard for
preservation or restoration, that life is always in an experimental mode,
and that what we need to pay attention to are the mediating instruments,
inscriptions, and practices that form what we call "objects."

There is an institutional move here, which perhaps can be seen if read
together with Foucault's trajectories and assemblages of biopower. The
modern creation of disciplines (labor/economics, language/linguistics,
life/biology) for Foucault begins with the collection of social statistics,
which can then be used by the state to discipline both bodies and populations.[47] Other material devices, such as the arrangements of prisons,
schools, and clinics, contribute to the construction of such disciplining.
Latour pays attention to the material assemblages of things and people,
the "mélanges of things that transcend human control and of actions imputable to mankind" in his studies of the rise of bacteriology (Pasteur's
carefully staged public demonstrations; the creation of the laboratory as
an obligatory point of passage; the reversal of ratios of power between
farmers and scientists),[48] of intelligent transportation systems (the shifting
coalitions enrolled to make a futuristic technological system come into
being or fail to come into being),[49] and of the constitutional court that
adjudicates new laws in quite a different fashion from the way science
would.[50]

Latour suggests that the parliament of things would allow the contours of hybridization or mélange composition to be observed and that the "moral effect" comes not from applying a priori ethical schemas but from a slowing down and modernization of the production of hybrids. This is not unlike the idea of "slow motion" ethnography that Wen-Hua Kuo uses in his recent dissertation on the International Conference on Harmonisation (ICH) of clinical trials among the United States, European Union, and Japan.[51] At issue for Japan is the claim that because Japanese bodies are different in nature from European ones (drug dosages, for instance, are often adjusted), clinical trials must use Japanese bodies. In part this is an obvious political-economy ploy to create a space for a Japanese clinical-trial industry and to block American and European–based pharmaceutical companies from dominating the market. But by patiently and carefully examining the exchanges at ICH meetings, the arguments about the state of the pharmaceutical market in Japan, and how clinical trials are done there, Kuo tries to show that more is at stake, that a hybridization of medical culture is at issue. Japan is also positioning itself to become an obligatory point of passage for larger regional and global markets, with the idea of building a genomics database (which other Asian countries can ill afford).

In all these cases (chemical industry accidents, nuclear accidents, and biological safety and efficacy), unitary expertise narratives seem increasingly less robust than dialogic (not two person, but *dia*-logic, cross argument) ones, involving persons differentially located, with different "stakeholder" interests, or, in Kim Fortun's terminology, enmeshed in different "enunciatory communities."[52]

Nature inside Out: The Double Career of Bioethics in Cultures of Trust, Procedure, and Skepticism

Beyond second natures, we are now, via genomics and proteomics, polymer engineering, material sciences, and other new molecular and nanotechnologies, entering into the promises of regenerative medicine, of rebuilding our natures inside out. The story of the remaking of our natures—from cellular, genetic, or tissue level up, using technological manipulations too small to be seen by the naked eye, revealed thus only through the mediation of scientific instruments and graphical interfaces, and also heavily mediated and interpreted by advertising technologies on the part of companies, on the one hand, and religious groups, on the other—contains at least four moments. First there is the evolution of institutions of regulation in their different public-sphere settings. England, Jasanoff argues, relies heavily on trust in experts, while Germany relies more on procedural correctness, and the United States on litigation to test and establish regulatory rules.[53] These presuppositions about how decisions must be made are embedded in historically contrasting institutional developments.

Second, there are contrasting policy outcomes, as in the application of the precautionary principle for genetically modified organisms in Europe versus "good science" calculations of probabilities and risk in the United States. The former is more cautious and more embedded in German procedural and bureaucratic traditions. American entrepreneurial traditions view the precautionary principle as inhibiting investment and market support for innovation and development of new technologies. In the case of stem cells, in England the House of Lords voted to permit cloning of human stem cells at the same time that President George W. Bush, on the advice of Senator Bill Frist, blocked federal spending on stem cell research except for the use of already existing stem cell lines (which proved to contain fewer and fewer viable stem cells as time went on, most of which were unsuitable for research on human diseases because they had been immortalized in mouse cells). In England a "pre-embryo" category (blastocysts to the development of the primitive streak at fourteen days) was accepted by the House of Lords,[54] whereas in the United States the term "embryo" (or even "unborn child") was dominant. President Bush's Council on Bioethics translated "reproductive cloning" into "cloning to produce children," shifting the connotations away from reproductive rights, and "therapeutic cloning" into "cloning for biomedical research," shifting connotations away from therapy toward experimental uncertainty and lack of control.[55]

Third, the histories and evolution of deliberative democratic forms are not only different in different countries but also now include considerable transnational histories of treaties, conventions, arbitrations, and adaptation of rules from one another. After the Asilomar conference on safety issues surrounding recombinant DNA technologies in 1975, for instance, U.S. National Institutes of Health (NIH) rules on the handling of recombinant DNA were widely adopted outside the United States, and today clinical trial facilities in India and elsewhere tend to follow NIH protocols closely so as to be able to provide services for companies dependent on the American market. On the other hand, good manufacturing practice (GMP) rules for therapeutic cell technologies (stem cells for bone marrow transplant) differ somewhat between the U.S. Food and Drug Administration (FDA) specifications and those of the European Union.

Fourth, the battles of marketing campaigns to control the semiotics of new drugs and other biotechnologies—as in the above example of "pre-embryos" versus "unborn children"—can sharply affect the understandings and political room for maneuver of physicians, patients, politicians, and others. Indeed, all four moments involve the boundary work of what is natural or unnatural, of the relation between what can and what should be done, and between what is socially possible (not just ideally possible) and what is socially preventable (and does not return by another route).

Molecular biology techniques have undergone rapid development, beginning in the mid-1970s with the breakthrough in recombinant DNA and proceeding to the biotechnology revolution of the 1980s that brought assisted reproduction technologies, genetic engineering, genomics, the promises of individualized therapies, and now the nuclear transfer technologies of therapeutic (and potentially somatic) stem cell cloning. In the popular press and public discourse into the 1990s, concerns surrounding these techniques often focused on potential category confusions and blurrings: What is your kinship if your genetic material is cloned from a parent? Should organ transplant donors and recipients have any moral ties? What would be the status of living with xenotransplant organs, that is, organs from another species (for example, would one have to live with lifelong monitoring in the beginning, and could that be ethically enforced)? Will human-assisted gene transfer among plants and potentially among mammals change the course of evolution?

Anthropologically (and sociologically) more interesting, however, are the coproductions of social venues for decision-making as these technologies are shaped, because it is in these slow-motion, recursive, repetitive, and contested settings that new ethical stakes become visible, moral systems are developed, fears are distinguished from real danger, and utopian hopes are separated from real possibilities. In contrast to accounts of the evolution of regulatory institutions for dealing with social, ethical, and legal concerns that are simply chronological—by implication, self-correcting, gradual social learning toward flexible, adaptable, second-order modernization or reflexive institutions—the work of Jasanoff and Herbert Gottweiss reminds us that civic epistemologies, moral traditions, and cultural politics look different in different countries.[56] Moreover, the work of João Biehl, Paul Farmer, Fortun, Kuo, Adriana Petryna, Kaushik Sunder-Rajan, and others reminds us that global politics (variously called "the new world order," "neoliberalism," "empire," and "globalization") also have effects that reach far down into the fates of localities and individuals.[57]

"Ethical, social, and legal issues" (ELSI) is the formula from the Human Genome Project of the 1990s that set aside a small percentage of money for discussions about these issues,[58] but these concerns go back to efforts to regulate and provide oversight for the use of human subjects in experimentation (the Nuremberg Code of Medical Ethics of 1945; the Helsinki Declaration of the World Medical Association of 1964; the Beecher Report of the Harvard Medical School of 1966; and the belated exposure by the *New York Times* in 1972 of the Tuskegee syphilis experiments, which withheld treatment long after a penicillin treatments were available[59]), which produced institutional review board (IRB) oversight for federally funded research in the United States. More broadly, these concerns led to the introduction of "bioethics," a term coined in 1970 by Van Rensselaer Potter and promoted by the Hastings Center (founded 1969), the Kennedy Institute of Ethics at Georgetown University (1971), the issuing of the 1978 Belmont Report (which established the three ethical standards of respect for persons, beneficence, and social justice), and the 1980-to-1983 Presidential Commission for the Study of Ethical Problems in Medicine and Biomedical and Behavioral Research.

Potter intended "bioethics" to refer to biology and values, encompassing medicine, environment, public health, and spirituality.[60] But the term was instead rapidly professionalized into a focus on informed consent and the rights of individual patients. This was a period when the frontiers of medical knowledge were shifting from how to cure or prevent infectious diseases to chronic diseases as the key problem of First World medicine. In medical ethics, it was the time of a shift to an emphasis on patient autonomy.[61]

Professionalized bioethics has been severely criticized for being captured by medical schools and more recently by pharmaceutical and biotech companies to provide the ethical veneer on practices they wish to pursue, and criticized, too, by social medicine proponents for its individualist ethics rather than concern with access, inequality, and social justice. Yet, as Jasanoff suggests, a funny thing happened on the way to the forum. As biotechnology in the 1980s moved from laboratory research to the marketplace, civil society also appropriated bioethics as a vehicle for gaining a voice in policy and ethical oversight. Hence the "double career" of bioethics: a formal professionalized form and a more open one in the public sphere. Jasanoff suggests, moreover, that these public-sphere forms work through different civic epistemologies in England, Germany, and the

United States, which she tags with the shorthand labels of, respectively, trust, procedure, and skepticism.[62]

In the 1970s, public concerns over potential escape of genetically engineered organisms from the laboratory and ecological and evolutionary implications of transferring DNA from one species to another were handled by calling for a self-imposed moratorium. Then, at the 1975 Asilomar conference on DNA, regulatory controls were proposed that were made into NIH guidelines. By 1979 the debate over the safety of recombinant DNA research had been contained (to resurface later, however, in Germany and Switzerland regarding bovine growth hormone). As experience accumulated, the NIH guidelines were gradually relaxed. Jasanoff suggests that the experts at the time were not able to conceive that in the future this technology might destabilize kinship or farmers' rights to replant seeds.[63] An important feature of such parapolitical modes of control (presidential commissions, National Academy of Sciences studies, etc.) is the way in which they narrow what is to be considered and thereby contain public discord. As technologies move into the marketplace, Jasanoff suggests, these techniques of containment become subject to public scrutiny and contestation, and at the same time broad ideological positions become more nuanced.[64]

In the United States, 1980 saw dramatically changing institutional and patronage environments for the biosciences and for the creation of a new power-knowledge nexus emerging around the new biotechnology institutions. Four arenas were changing: modes of funding, parapolitical modes of expert regulation (and containment of disputes), market forces and the relation of scientists to the market, and legal rulings and guidelines. This was the year of the Bayh-Dole Act, which fostered rapid development of new biotechnologies by encouraging NIH-funded research at universities to be patented and licensed to the private sector. The 1980 Chakrabarty Supreme Court case opened the floodgates to patenting of life forms as manufactured products, processes, and new composition of matter.[65] Another case, *Foundation on Economic Trends v. Heckler*,[66] found that the public interest was not satisfied by expert review, but required more open deliberative processes. The 1980 Superfund legislation (the Comprehensive Environmental Response, Compensation, and Liability Act) provided for citizen action panels or remediation review boards with some funding to empower citizens to hire their own experts independent of government agencies.

This was a period in which advertising became more and more sophisticated as well. Copyright, patent, trademark, and brand names, Donna

Haraway suggests, are the "genders" (generic marks, "directional signals on maps of power and knowledge") of "asymmetrical, congealed processes which must be constantly revivified in law and commerce," especially in our new world of creating transuranic elements and transgenetic organisms.[67] The FDA in 1991 streamlined approvals for biotech food by introducing the criterion of "substantial equivalence." Review would only be triggered if there was an indication that toxic or allegeric reactions were caused by substitutes or changes in nutritional content. What is important, the FDA reasoned, is the product, not how it is made.

This rationale required revision in the later 1990s struggles over "organic food" labeling. As Jasanoff points out, in 1993 recombinant bovine growth hormone (rBGH), also known as recombinant bovine somatotropin (rBST), was approved despite its questionable need in a dairy industry that already produced surpluses, its likelihood to aid only large producers (and drive out small ones), and its possible effects of mastitis in the animals.[68] Monsanto opposed labeling of rBST. Labeling is a powerful tactic in building a market. Lack of labeling means it is harder for consumers to opt out. Labeling, Monsanto argued, could negatively affect markets by suggesting that something was wrong. The civic epistemological form that opposition in the United States was forced to take was of developing counterscientific arguments such as that rBST is not obviously "substantially equivalent" because it has additional amino acid subunits (linker proteins).

Similar struggles over the labeling of organic foods in the 1990s eventually conceded to the organic growers and their lobbies that foods treated with irradiation or produced with the use of sewage sludge as fertilizer, also genetically modified (GM) foods, could not be labeled "organic." Not only the product was important, but also how it was made. By the time this point was conceded by the U.S. Department of Agriculture, organic farming had become a $6 billion industry producing 2 percent of the nation's food and was growing at a rate of 20 percent a year.[69]

Opposition to genetically modified foods, Jasanoff points out, was always part of wider issues (agricultural practices, nature preservation, integrity of food) and national styles of civic epistemology or cultural politics. In England, the crisis over bovine spongiform encephalopathy (BSE; mad cow disease) in 1996 created a breakdown in confidence in the Ministry of Agriculture, Fisheries and Food and contributed to the defeat of the Conservative government. New deliberative democratic forums were created to rebuild confidence under the new Labour Party government. A public debate, "GM Nation?" was organized through a Web site, and more than six hundred public meetings were publicized via the Genewatch Web site. A citizens' jury was organized by Greenpeace with the University of Newcastle and the Consumer's Association and with sponsorship by Unilever and the Co-op Group. The Prime Minister's Strategy Unit did a cost-benefit analysis, presenting models and precautionary methods in public seminars to prepare people for potential "Shocks and Surprises." The government chief science advisor organized an expert advisory process with open meetings and expanded panel membership. Jasanoff notes that in view of displays of scientific and social unknowns through these attempts at public education, the government announcement of March 2004 to go ahead with commercial growing of GM crops came as a surprise and was felt to be a betrayal.

At issue in England in civic epistemological terms was the culture of trust in experts, whereas in the United States, as illustrated in the cases of the first commercially grown genetically engineered food granted a license (in 1994) for human consumption, the FlavrSavr tomato, as well as the rBST and organic foods examples mentioned above, the market (and litigation) became the arbiter, as it did again later in the 2000 case of genetically modified StarLink corn (produced by Aventis), which was found to have entered the human food chain for which it was not licensed, causing a recall of three hundred food products.

In Germany, public hearings introduced after the Green Party gained seats in Parliament were gradually withdrawn as the political tactics of environmentalists became obstructionary (e.g., demanding that all documents be translated into German, and other delaying tactics). Not only was it argued that public hearings make sense only if they actually function as a Habermasian public sphere, requiring an informed public; but questions of "whose rationality" were increasingly foreclosed (e.g., in the rBST debate, whether this technology would hurt small businesses was not discussed, only whether it was a safe and could help production of large farms).[70]

Issues of process in Germany are tied, Jasanoff argues, to constitutional requirements that the state protect human dignity. In Germany's stem cell debates, the Christian Democratic Union (CDU) and Christian Social Union (CSU) invoked this doctrine to forbid even the import of embryonic stem cells created abroad. The Social Democratic Party (SPD) voted to allow importing stem cells for research on the grounds that these are not embryos proper and so do not require the same level of protection. The reprehensible act, if such it was, of creating stem cells had already taken place outside Germany and the cells in any case were not capable of becoming fully human. The Free Democratic Party (FDP) voted to allow imports because they could benefit humanity and would not harm human beings or potential human beings. The law that passed in 2002 allowed import under supervision by an expert committee established by the Robert Koch Institute. This moved the discussion back into a contained deliberative environment, away from public debate.

Jasanoff summarizes part of her three-nation comparative study by saying that the rise of bioethics illustrates Foucault's account of how the growth of biopower ropes ethical debates into larger national narratives. In the United States the narrative is one of medical and agricultural innovation, in Germany it is one of building a principled *Rechtsstaat*, and in the United Kingdom it one of maintaining a well-ordered space for research.[71] The European Union becomes not so much a source for higher-level rulings as a political resource in federal and *Länder* (local state) negotiations. Wen-Hua Kuo's 2005 analysis of the International Conference on Harmonisation of Technical Requirements for Registration of Pharmaceuticals for Human Use (ICH) reveals a similar pattern. Taiwan is not an official member (analogous to the European Union not being a sovereign nation or a superstate with overriding authority), but provides a mediating role facilitated by its cadre of returned diasporic biostaticians.[72]

I conclude this "double helix" account of new challenges to our sense of the [un]natural coming from the new biotechnologies as well as the institutions through which we recursively and repeatedly revisit and renegotiate our cognitive understandings and visceral feelings by thinking about xenotransplantation as deep play. It is a deep play of the fantasies of abolishing disease and immortalizing life, sometimes at the expense of human rights, informed consent, equity, and access.[73] The American physicists went ahead with the bomb for Nagasaki, as Oppenheimer memorably put it, because it was "technically sweet." So, too, today physicians and patients often go ahead with heroic experimental trials because they are caught up in what Mary-Jo Good calls the "biotechnical embrace," doing what technically can be done, under the Hippocratic formulation of preserving and extending life, because it can be done, sometimes at the expense of the good death.[74] The Austrian cartoonist Manfred Deix captures some of the fantasies and nightmares surrounding biotechnologies in the picture of a genetically engineered pig altered to be already a huge sausage, or in his mutant monsters (think post-Chernobyl) who have voting rights.[75]

Xenotransplantation is one site among the biotechnologies where, because the science is so hard, there is some time to experiment with some creative thinking toward new institutions and new ways of bringing into being an informed citizenry on a global scale that can provide civil society oversight, accountability, and decision-making. Prominent immunologist and xenotransplantation researcher Dr. Fritz Bach's call for a moratorium on clinical trials provides an overview of some of the changing venues for ethical and policy deliberation.[76] Old institutions of medical ethics seem insufficient. The promise of a supply of organs from pigs, primates, or other mammals for increasing numbers of patients on waiting lists for organs is the public justification for xenotransplantation research. (The other promise is that such research expands basic immunological knowledge that will be helpful whether or not xenotransplantation emerges as better therapy than, say, regenerative medicine.) On the other hand, the threat of zoonosis (and specifically of known and possibly unknown retroviruses from pig populations) that could unleash a pandemic like HIV/ AIDS, however small the risk, is not something that can be dealt with through medical ethics models of doctor-patient relations, or by hospital ethics committees (which negotiate patient demands for heroic care versus doctors' judgments that such care is fruitless and will cause needless suffering), or even by national-level regulatory institutions.

Older methods of self-regulation by scientists in the Asilomar style of dealing with the fears about recombinant DNA in the 1970s seem no longer possible or adequate, and the recent experience of Monsanto with the "terminator seed"[77] in the controversies over genetically engineered crops shows that the refusal to engage in public consultation can lead at minimum to public relations fiascoes. Dr. Bach has been experimenting not only with education modules at the high school, church, and grassroots levels and with national committee structures at the political level in several countries in both the First and Third Worlds but also with new modes of global Web-based public consultation seeded with a network of opinion leaders in various countries.[78] It will be interesting to watch this and other experiments in new institution and public critical knowledge building, especially in an environment in which calls for even limited moratoriums draw the ire of those who find it harder under such circumstances to raise research money and venture capital to push the science further.

Bach's interventions have come a long way from the model of Asilomar in 1975 and the handling of concerns over recombinant DNA research in the 1970s. That trajectory is one of the changing possibilities for parapolitical modes of expert self-regulation and containment of disruptive disputes and public politics. At issue in many of the debates over biotechnologies are questions of public safety. But equally at issue are the "gut feelings" and highly emotional stances that people adopt in regard to what they feel is "natural." The anthropologist is interested in how fast or slowly feelings about what can count as "natural" can change and in what facilitates or blocks such change. This is what Durkheim would have called the *conscience collective* or moral sensibility, what Jasanoff more recently calls civic epistemologies, and what is often called by moral conservatives the "slippery slope" leading to ethical confusion, to which many scientists often reply that in scientific work and new knowledge production we are always already on slippery slopes. To deal with the slipperiness, we need to characterize it and understand it better, not try to black-box it.

Companion Species: Animal Models, Sentinels, Alterities, Phenomenologies

J. M. Coetzee's published version of his 1997–1998 Tanner Lectures, *The Lives of Animals*, foregrounds the debates over "animal rights," but evokes in the wings four series of questions about just what the natures of animals are in relation to: (a) human genetics, evolutionary development, and transitional medical artifacts such as the OncoMouse that promise regenerative medicine to replace the slash, burn, and poison of today's brute medicine; (b) "the morality of the table," or human ecologies of food and illnesses such as obesity and diabetes; (c) sentinels of climate warming and habitat change; and (d) coevolving species that repeatedly mirror our sense of being in the world in uncanny and refractory ways.[79] Coetzee's character Elizabeth Costello, mother, English professor, and animal rights moralizer, stands in for Wendell Berry, Troy Duster, Jim Hightower, Winona LaDuke, Michael Pollan, Peter Singer, Vandava Shiva (all of whom contributed to *The Nation*'s special issue on food), and many others who both rightly and irritatingly remind us of the sins of the social systems in which we participate and are complicit.[80] Costello argues that in tasting the flesh of living things, we violate animal rights and may be tasting sin, a trope that interprets the biblical story of the tree of knowledge in a particularly masochistic way.

Sin and *rights* may not be the most appropriate terms for thinking about our animal relations. Animal models, animal sentinels, companion species, and phenomenologies of emotion may be much more appropriate. Literature and philosophy all too often use animals as symbolic tokens but betray a disabling lack of interest in actual animals, their socialities, their sensoria, or how to interact with them. Thinking of lab animals and work animals,

Donna Haraway asks what would happen to our conceptual and ethical stances if we thought of responsibility in terms of the category of labor rather than rights. She complains about Deleuze and Guattari's appropriations of wolf packs and particularly their dismissal of pet and other animal training relations as merely regressive narcissism rather than as critical epistemological and ethical sites.[81]

Similarly, Jacques Derrida points out that while philosophers attribute muteness and therefore often also melancholy to animals, it is the human philosophers whose language, calculus of responsibility, and *responsiveness* fail.[82] At best, Derrida demonstrates, invoking his cat, it is the return gaze of the animal that provides philosophers with an optical space in which to contemplate key zero points of phenomenology—nausea, shame, suffering—for recovering bodily nonoptical modes of being.

Haraway gently criticizes her younger self, the author of *Primate Visions*, for not having gone into the field with the primatologists as an anthropologist would have and thus for having perhaps slighted the noncognitive but critical ways in which people (primatologists, in this case) have learned to interact with, respond to, and become included in the communication styles of animals. And so we turn to animal models, animal sentinels, companion species, and phenomenologies of affective communication.

ANIMAL MODELS, EXPERIMENTAL SYSTEMS, AND (UN)NATURAL KINDS

In arguing quite rightly against genetic determinism, the molecular biologist Stuart Newman argues quite dubiously in favor of a classical notion of "natural kinds."[83] The notion of "natural kinds" seems hard to reconcile with contemporary ecological understandings or with unfolding of knowledge within molecular biology itself. At issue are at least two troubling dilemmas: the use of animal models in medical research; and the use of life-forms as technological instruments. I deal with the first dilemma together with Haraway's interventions on companion species (both lab animals and work animals). I deal with the second dilemma together with animal sentinels (including viruses as cross-species delivery systems).

Newman makes two crucial claims: that "species are 'natural kinds' . . . because they exhibit causal homeostatic mechanisms that enforce their type-specificity"; and that an epigenic or "plasticity-based 'phenotype first, genetic programs later' scenario, rather than the gradualist, gene-driven processes of neo-Darwinism, makes the whole enterprise of improving phenotypes of plants and animals by genetic tinkering . . . all but irrational."[84] The claims for evolutionary developmental biology against genetic fundamentalism are an important corrective to much hype in contemporary science and biotechnology. Still, this is only one area of transformative ideas about nature that are being both discovered and "rewritten" (in the sense of creating objects, materials, and biologicals that have not previously existed). Newman's caution about experiments that seem to jump across the slow testing of natural selection seems well taken. On the other hand, his formulation seems insufficiently open to the slow, incremental nature of the experimental discovery procedures that he seems to argue against. The sciences involved are not easy, and the time they take should allow us to understand the self-organizing properties and constraints (including homeostatic ones).

Newman is correct that in arenas such as agriculture and ecology we desperately need to find alternatives to the self-destructive industrial organizations and financial drivers that destroy us. To begin to do this, it may be helpful to turn to animal sentinels and animal companions.

ANIMAL SENTINELS: ECOLOGIES OF FOOD, ILLNESS, BIODIVERSITY, AND CLIMATE CHANGE

The likelihood of an H5N1 avian flu pandemic has emerged in recent years as one of the most feared (or perhaps most hyped) of threats to human populations. It is a more dangerous virus than SARS, experience with which has already put public health authorities on alert about the critical need to report outbreaks and the self-defeating dangers of denial or hiding of cases.[85] The H5N1 avian flu threat is belatedly recalling from repressed "memory" the 1918 influenza that killed millions around the globe. And it is one of a series of recent viruses and retroviruses, including HIV/AIDS, Ebola virus, and dengue virus, that can cross species and reinscribe into our consciousness our symbiotic repertoires.

Viruses operate as double figures in both the popular and scientific imaginaries of nature: (1) as a figure of thought for a variety of biological processes that disturb the understanding of "natural kinds," species, and evolutionary trees; (b) as means of drug delivery and new materials fabrication that reconfigure the sense of the boundaries of natural kinds into more permeable and new ecologies of interaction. As figures that disturb the understanding of natural kinds, viruses are one of a series, including infectious agents (bacteria, viruses), symbiogenetic forms and parasites (e.g., the wasp-polydnavirus-caterpillar association), jumping genes and lateral transfer.[86] Understanding the molecular mechanisms of host-parasite interactions could lead to a variety of new, hopefully more biologically gentle therapies.

As biological tools, viruses are used as drug delivery vehicles and are part of the experimental and still dangerous technology of genetic engineering, but they are also now being used in nanofabrication technologies. Viruses subvert their hosts to reproduce themselves, but we are now learning to repay the favor and turn them into new optics and electronic material assemblers. For example, Angela Belcher's MIT lab has produced the first virus-assembled nanoelectrode and virus-assembled battery and is working on a virus-based transistor.

Belcher bombards a semiconductor wafer with nontoxic viruses to see which react, looking for ones with the chemical functionality matching the target material. Once found, the virus's genes are manipulated so that they make protein coats that collect molecules of cobalt oxide and gold. Once altered, the viruses are inserted in a bacterial host, which replicates or clones millions of copies. They align on a polymer surface to form ultrathin wires (circa 6 nanometers or six billionths of a meter). Because viruses are negatively charged, they can be layered between oppositely charged polymers to form thin, flexible sheets that serve as an anode. (Batteries are anodes and cathodes separated by electrolytes.) Nanowire structures are used to assemble thin lithium ion batteries (from the size of a grain of rice to that of a hearing aid battery). The necessary reactions can all be done at room temperature and pressure. The energy density of these batteries is two to three times that of other batteries. By harnessing the electrostatic nature of the self-assembly process with the functional properties of the virus, highly ordered composite thin films combine the function of the virus and polymer systems.

Viruses, bacteria, parasites, and the like provide experimental systems for exploring the permeability and symbiotic repertoires of natural kinds. Comparative genomics tracks some of the commonalities across living forms. But it is really ecological studies that provide some of the most worrisome questions about our futures by both tracking cross-species transfers that simultaneously map ecologies of human practices and transfer of organisms, and cataloguing, regulating, and redirecting the destruction of biodiversity and climate change.

Mobilization around the term "biodiversity" dates from the 1986 National Forum on Biodiversity, sponsored by the National Academy of Sciences and the Smithsonian Institution, led by Walter Rosen, and including such key figures as Paul Ehrlich, Ernst Meyer, Peter Raven, and E. O.

Wilson.[87] The organizers announced: "The species extinction crisis is a threat to civilization second only to the threat of nuclear war."[88] These already senior figures could afford to join the newly growing field of conservation biology, which understood itself to be scholarly advocacy and was viewed for that reason with some apprehension by the National Academy.

At issue are a series of wonderful (for the anthropologist and science studies scholar) ambiguities about not only how to guesstimate the decline of biodiversity but what such concepts as "ecological system," "keystone species," or even "species" and "habitat" should mean. On the one hand, it is crucial to the enterprise to emphasize how little we know about and how much research needs to be done on the functional role of species in ecosystems. David Takacs quotes Peter Raven: "We know so little about biodiversity, the interchangeability of biodiversity in communities and all the rest that we don't know what the limits are."[89] At the extreme is E. O. Wilson's observation that "the little things that run the world" (bacteria and insects) are hardly evident on the endangered species lists, which primarily include either large animals that humans relate to or small creatures that are useful to block development that should be opposed on other grounds but the Endangered Species Act of 1973 is the available tool to hand.

Still, on the other hand, the notion of biodiversity gets around both the charges that proponents wildly inflate the estimated rates of extinction and the endless task of making a species-by-species case for ecological integrity when we do not really know what makes for such integrity (whether one should be protecting maximum genetic diversity, genetically distinct populations, communities of tightly integrated organisms, or larger ecosystems). Protection for larger animals requiring larger home ranges can serve as umbrellas for other organisms.

Even so, there are ambiguities in managing populations using tools such as those that measure minimal viable populations (MVP), the smallest populations that could survive genetic drift or catastrophic events. Debates about culling and about defining ecosystems, are inevitably political and draw in economic interests. Among the most interesting efforts to leverage political and economic interests and make the market incentives work in a green direction is the Costa Rican experiment of commodifying biodiversity around pharmaceutical, ecotourist, and scholarly renewable industries.[90] Especially interesting is the idea of retraining rural local people to treat their environments as intellectual resources, thereby enchanting the environment in new ways and capturing traditional knowledges, as well as building computerized databases with their help.

Conceptually, this expansive view of biodiversity and ecology leads to what Takacs calls metaphysical holism. Again he quotes Peter Raven: "Peace, social justice, human order, the protection of biodiversity, the production of or promotion of a stable biosphere are all inextricably inter-woven."[91] Warwick Fox says that the knowledge-producing process of try-ing to protect biodiversity is a "this-worldly realization of as expansive a sense of self as possible."[92] This view is on the surface unexceptionable but, as the case of E. O. Wilson increasingly makes clear, can be a kind of priestly calling on the part of sociobiologists convinced that encoded in our genes is a biophilia evolved in hunter-gatherer pasts that has under-gone remarkably little evolution, culturally, institutionally, or otherwise. As Takacs nicely argues in his final chapter, the self-contradictory mix of apocalyptic crisis, urgency, and need for expertise that only people like Wilson can supply is indeed a kind of charismatic and priestly call to faith, with many metaphysical, unsubstantiable, claims, such as biophilia, made vociferously.[93]

While the trope of the "disappearance of nature," often attributed to Bill McKibben,[94] turns out to be a nostalgic one (nature doesn't disappear, it changes, impoverishes, etc.), somewhat like the pastoral image used in the nineteenth century to critique industrialization and its destruction of the wild, perhaps the most trenchant structural argument for the loss of biodiversity and thus the loss of sustainable, complex, "wild" ecosystems is that of Steven Meyer.[95] Meyer argues that while the Earth will continue to teem with life, it will be an increasingly homogenized assemblage se-lected for compatibility with human beings. He claims that the extinction rate is now over three thousand species a year, while less than one new species appears over the same period; hence within the next one hundred years half the Earth's species and a quarter of the genetic stock will disappear.

The argument is a structural one: there is a hierarchy of three kinds of species. *Weedy species* are adaptive, flourish in variety of ecological settings, switch easily between food types, breed prolifically, and often have their needs met more efficiently by humans. For example, raccoon populations are five times denser in suburbs than in the wild; aquatic plants such as hydrilla thrive in waterways enriched with runoff from farms, suburbs, and sewage treatment facilities; rats and white-tailed deer reach pest propor-tions around human habitation. *Relic species* do not thrive in human-domi-nated environments and survive either in isolated areas or as managed "boutique populations," as do African elephants, giant pandas, Sumatran rhinoceroses, and most of Hawaii's indigenous plants. *Ghost species* continue to exist but are past the tipping point of population collapse. These include African lions, gray wolves, and prairie dogs. Meyer claims that 90 percent of the stocks of tuna and swordfish are gone (sturgeon, which used to populate the East coast of the United States, have been gone for many years), and that more lions live as pets and in zoos in the United States (10,000) than worldwide in the wild (7,000).[96]

Meyer argues that while various factors in this "dumbing down" seem manageable, once one understands their cumulative interactions, they become unmanageable. While some ameliorative efforts seem to work (whooping crane numbers are increasing; tiger numbers in India's Sunderban forest region seem stable), most prohibitory (protection) regimes are focused on relics and ghosts; most refuges and reserves are too small and thus illusory; and the slogan of "sustainable communities" is usually an anthropomorphic use policy based on calculations of how much can be harvested, not on ecological models, with the result that much is driven by global markets. "The race," Meyer says, "to save the composition, structure and origin of biodiversity is over: we've lost." What we can and should do, he argues, is "to purge ourselves of the humanistic love affair with the wild, landscape, and aesthetics," and do research on the functions of what is here and how it lives.

However apocalyptic one might judge the ecological and species extinction crisis to be, the sentinel feedback that is given to us by our animal and plant environment is not to be disregarded. Obesity and diabetes (via the foods we eat) are signals. So too are endocrine hormone disruptions (of the chemicals we ingest and inhale) and multiple chemical sensitivity syndromes (caused by incremental, interactive, cumulative encounters with toxic elements). Cross-species infectious diseases, the succession of invasive species, the devastation of tropical forests and possible disruption of the Earth's carbon cycle, the softening of the tundra and the disturbance of whale and caribou migration in the Arctic are all sentinel feedback signals. The use of freshwater dolphin censuses are signals that help measure the water quality of the Orinoco River.[97]

ALTERITIES AND COMPANION SPECIES: RESEARCH,
DOMESTICATED, AND WILD ANIMALS

I return to Haraway's and Derrida's complaints that most of the literary and philosophical literatures that use animals to think with do not actually deal much with the actual lives of these animals.[98] These literary and philosophical meditations do not consider the anthropological literature on how cultures categorize, name, and use different classes of animals, how animals carry mythic armatures of ecological knowledge, or how affect gets attached to animal figures through structural positioning in classifications from the domestic to the wild.[99] Deleuze and Guattari create new philosophemes with animal categories—wolf pack as a figure for multiplicity; orchid-wasp as a figure for symbiosis—but at the expense of the "points of view" of animals, and most grievously, as Haraway complains, they dismiss pet and other training relations as merely regressive narcissism rather than as overlapping arenas of differential phenomenologies.[100]

In this context, Haraway is perhaps one of the most useful of thinkers at the moment, coming from the broad world of the history of biology and science studies, both in the trajectory of her career from *Primate Visions* to *When Species Meet*, and in thinking about the unresolved struggles that particularly research animals pose, struggles that will grow in public awareness as biotechnologies continue to expand. With Haraway, perhaps we can prepare the ground for how to think intelligently about the dilemmas of the real world of illness and death, killing and making live, and *responsiveness* to companion species of all sorts, a responsiveness that parallels but is not exactly the same as earlier ecological notions of feedback in systems that will collapse or deteriorate if the component flora and fauna are misused or destroyed.[101]

In her 1989 *Primate Visions*, Haraway took on the newly developing profession of primatology as it began to use anthropological-style fieldwork to study baboons, chimpanzees, lemurs, and then other animals in their natural habitats and societies rather than in laboratories or artificial colonies. *Primate Visions* turned the tables on the researchers, exploring their intellectual genealogies, hierarchies, and, above all, the ways in which they projected human cultural concerns onto their nonhuman subjects of study. This was elegantly done by charting decade by decade how changing theories of primate sociality correlated with changing popular human cultural anxieties. Second, it focuses attention on female primatologists, helping raise their profile in a male-dominated field but criticizing them, in a friendly, puzzled way, for buying into the then-faddish sociobiology. Third, it contributes to the wider anthropological critique of sociobiology's importation of American folk theories of reproduction, competition, aggression, sexuality, and status and of sociobiology's crude genetic reductionism (long before one could even map the genome or begin to unravel the mediations of protein, cellular, and other functionalities). Fourth, it was a tour de force and exemplary exercise in using (and keeping carefully distinguished) popular culture materials about animals (hunting and photo shooting in the wild), interview and archival materials on a science in formation, and the gradually growing positive knowledge gained about animals and their socialities.

As noted above, it is quite in character that Haraway should in her most recent work reflect back on *Primate Visions* and gently criticize her younger self for not having gone into the field with the primatologists as an anthropologist would have and thus for perhaps having slighted the noncognitive but critical ways in which people (primatologists, in this case) have learned to interact with, respond to, and become included in the communication styles of animals. The trajectory of Haraway's work builds a new perspective. In her 1985 "Cyborg Manifesto," an essay in *Simians, Cyborgs, and Women,* Haraway began to speculate on mixed technical and biological systems that would lead to the creation of animals with human genes and illnesses for medical research such as the OncoMouse.[102]

In her 1997 *Modest_Witness@Second_Millennium.FemaleMan@_Meets_ OncoMouse™: Feminism and Technoscience,* her concerns with the relations between technologies, animals, and humans have evolved into a set of reflections on the grammar of these relations in material reality as well as conceptually.[103] These grammatical relations are signaled in the focus on cyborg creatures such as the OncoMouse, a humanly modified genetic organism (unlike the original NASA mouse fitted with an osmotic pump) designed to aid in research on human diseases. The grammatical relations are signaled in the title of the book and in section titles, adapting the usages of the computerized information environment in which biology has become infiltrated, embedded, and facilitated.[104] And they are conceptually signaled by Haraway's neologism "material semiotic objects"—that is, real-world objects whose coming into being configures the way our semiotic and symbolic worlds work. OncoMouse is not only a biological organism but a legal one that generated court cases and new understandings of the intellectual property rights regime that in the 1980s transformed the doing of biology and biotechnologies.

At issue throughout *Modest_Witness@Second_Millennium* is the challenge that biology is civics, that biology is inseparable from political relationships and that rearranging biological relations simultaneously has civic implications. The several strands of grammatical relations alluded to above are also markers of our civic politics. Copyright, trademark, and brand have become, she wrote in a brilliant *bon mot,* our genders, generic marks on maps of power and influence. One of the essays in the volume is on the material and biological crossings (and material-semiotic changes they help produce) of the DuPont Corporation in polymer chemistry (nylon, rayon, synthetics), transuranics (nuclear power), and the new world of transgenics—a cross section of our changing first and second natures.

But it is with *The Companion Species Manifesto* and *When Species Meet* that Haraway begins to signal three important themes: that to mistake pets as children is to endanger both the human and the animal (alterity is real and needs to be worked with in any useful animal-human ethics); that species contain rich histories of coevolution with humans in their biology, labor regimes, and pedigree (consumption-branded) regimes; and that living with and loving animals can be a way of learning to live and work with diversity.[105] I am particularly struck in a chapter on laboratory animals in *When Species Meet* by the honesty of struggle with commitments that resist simultaneous and seamless closure. These commitments are to medicine, to science, and to protecting animals from suffering as much as possible. Haraway commits herself to thinking about how the humans in the lab might work, think, and interact with their animals otherwise.

Animal models for medical research attract the ire of animal rights activists but are still thought by most biomedical researchers to be necessary and not yet replaceable by computer models, regenerative tissue engineering, or other techniques. Of particular interest for the discussions of the nature of animals is that many, if not most, laboratory animals are genetically modified artifacts. This is particularly true of research mice and rats, which make up 95 percent of research animals, although the range of animals as experimental systems extends from nematodes (roundworms) and drosophila (fruit flies) to mice, dogs, cats, and nonhuman primates (mainly monkeys imported from abroad).

Of particular interest in the current context of arguments about the (un)natural is Haraway's observation that "rights" language seems philosophically inappropriate, even if legal initiatives on such grounds may occasionally have tactical value.[106] Some utilitarian "rights" arguments invoke pain and suffering as phenomenological grounds on which rights might be attributed.[107] But while Haraway also invokes animal suffering and affect, she recognizes the alterity of animals and does not assimilate them to the same, a point that she makes through a series of anecdotes about dog training and collaboration in agility competitions as well as through contrasts between dog breeds.[108]

"Intersubjectivity," Haraway points out, "does not mean 'equality.' . . . It does mean paying attention to the conjoined dance of face-to-face significant otherness." Again: "To regard a dog as a furry child" demeans both, setting up children to be bitten and dogs to be killed.[109] Moreover, dogs have been bred for different subjectivities: meta-retrievers, bred for herding, are not interested in chasing balls on the beach but can be totally obsessed with chasing retrievers as they chase balls, attempting to block and herd them away from the balls. Border collies, bred through generations of competitive sheep herding trials, became popular pets when shown on British television, but then were frequently abandoned when owners could not satisfy the dogs' needs. Living ethically in such heterogeneous relationships, Haraway suggests, is a training ground in alterity.

Acknowledging the emotional dynamics or responsiveness of animals, she asks how the humans in the lab might work, think, and interact with their animals otherwise. One thinks here of Karin Knorr-Cetina's *Epistemic Cultures*, showing how laboratories modify the organisms they form into experimental systems, but also how the human investigators are remade into socialities whose dynamics are quite different in a high-energy physics lab and in a molecular biology lab. At issue is that for the time being, until methods can be developed that will not require the making ill and sacrificing of animals in the service of medical research, in the laboratory as in nature, killing and illness are required.[110] As a first step toward a less brutal relationship with our companion species in the lab, Haraway wonders about involving more hemophiliacs in laboratory work with hemophiliac dogs used to study hemophilia.

ANIMALS AND PHENOMENOLOGIES OF AFFECTIVE COMMUNICATION

The philosophemes of Wittgenstein's lion; Levinas's dog, Bobby; and Derrida's cat all indicate something similar about our relations to our companion species, but they do not go as far as Haraway. The philosopher Stanley Cavell interprets the encounter with Wittgenstein's "mute lion" ("If a lion could talk, we would not understand him") as generating self-reflexivity: "sooner or later it makes us wonder what we conceive knowledge to be." But dog and horse trainer Vicki Hearne objects: the lion is reticent, not mute, and it has presence; indeed, "if the chimpanzee Washoe learns human language and still remains dangerous," Cavell's epistemological mirror becomes confusing. For Hearne and Haraway, "the shared language of animal training makes possible a common world between beings with vastly different phenomenologies."[111]

Levinas's dog, Bobby, the "last Kantian in Germany," recognized and restored the humanity of the prisoners in Nazi camp 1492 (uncannily the date of Columbus's discovery of North America and of the expulsion of Muslims and Jews from Granada) through a responsiveness that the Nazis denied in their stripping of the prisoners down to their presumptive species biology, their animality (a zero point undone by Goebbels' "I decide who is Jewish"). As Haraway also echoes in relatively more civilized circumstances, Levinas does not fail to acknowledge that humans also eat meat. But against Heidegger's 1949 callous leveling of the difference between genocide and industrial agriculture, Levinas uses the juxtaposition of genocide and industrial agriculture to raise questions about the various and different claims upon consciousness. As Derrida would more explicitly thematize, Heidegger's obtuseness is an object lesson in the ideology of difference. Levinas uses the fact of our consuming flesh as a zero point that exposes how the "I" is dependent on others, prior to distinctions between ego and nonego. Derrida radicalizes this: "There is no such thing as animality, but only a regime of differences without opposition."[112]

Nausea and shame rivet us to our bodies and have served from Kierkegaard to Derrida as phenomenological touchstones for thinking about how the physiological body provides a substrate for consciousness. What philosophers fail to do is to expand this insight toward comparative ethology or even historical change. Derrida at least elaborates on Levinas, using the story of his cat, whose gaze, when Derrida is naked, brings on a kind of shame of revealed intimacy. As with Wittgenstein's lion, this could be taken merely to mean that there is a bestiary at the origins of philosophy, that the cat's gaze instills self-consciousness. But Derrida speaks of the animal's point of view, something occluded by Cavell's reading and by philosophical discourse generally. As Steve Baker explains: "Believing that human conceptions of the animal are stuck in a language which generally does animals few favors, Derrida puns *animaux* into '*animots*,' presenting these language-laden composite creatures as something close to . . . botched taxidermy."[113] "*Animots*" puns on *mot*, French for "word." Haraway's more material-semiotic version is to speak of dogs as *metaplasms* (from the Greek *metaplasmos*, remodeling or remolding), having separated from wolves, according to mitochondrial studies, some 50,000 to 150,000 years ago ("at the dawn of *Homo sapiens*"), feeding off human-discarded food and thus coevolving with us.

Derrida's cat and his "shame" also index something like Wittgenstein's forms of life, language games, and metalinguistic meanings carried by the kinesthetics and pragmatics of communication. As Gregory Bateson says, "If you want to know what the bark of a dog 'means' you look at his lips, the hair on the back of his neck, his tail and so on;" and "if you say to a girl, 'I love you,' she is likely to pay more attention to the accompanying kinesics and paralinguistics than to the words themselves."[114] For the anthropologist, this indexing between the physiological and phenomenological also carries historically differentiated and socially formed anxieties.

Using a century and a half of clinical reports on agoraphobia as both an index of changing pressures on the collective technobody (empty squares at the hearts of rebuilt European cities; urban freeways; and shopping malls) and the closely associated descriptions of nausea and shame in the phenomenological existentialisms of the late nineteenth and early twentieth centuries (Kierkegaard's objectless anxiety, Edvard Munch's agoraphobic painting *The Scream*, Dostoyevsky's agoraphobic *Underground Man*, Heidegger's abyss of death as the ground of authenticity, Levinas's analysis of nausea and shame, Sartre's nausea and nothingness), Kathryn Milun points out that these function as zero signs. Zero signs refer only to themselves. They occlude an organizing dimension, like the vanishing point in one-point linear perspective drawings, an invisible point that establishes the grid around which all other signs in its field are organized. Such zero points and their occluded organizing functions, as Levinas and Derrida delight in exposing, open up a space for dissension and recover social contexts occluded by the zero sign.[115]

Such is the function of companionate species, who, through comparative ethology, comparative genomics, animal experimental models, and sentinels of ecological deterioration and health, open up for us frozen categories, relationships, knowledges, and bases for ethical reconsideration.

Conclusions: The Four Trials of Anthropologies to Come

At the end of *The Elementary Forms of Religious Life*, Durkheim argues that religion and science do not stand in a relationship of replacement; rather, at the boundaries of what each society takes to be empirically knowable (science) are questions that demand answers supplied by "religion," itself seen as a product of deeply socially structured relationships.[116] E. E. Evans-Pritchard called this the two-spear theory of causality.[117] Both science and religion are thus always changing with respect to one another. Return to religion, Jacques Derrida points out in his commentary on Kant's similar notion of religion at the limits of reason, is never a return to the same but more like respiration, a return after taking a break, a renewal of inquiry.[118] As with Derrida's *animots*, Levinas worries that anthropomorphism, allegory, and other figural aspects of language can collapse crucial differences.[119] And yet, of course, some of the art of differences and *différances* in Levinas and Derrida comes from the multiplying of meaningful figurations. I am intrigued by the seeping-through of religious traces in the ambiguous denials/acknowledgments of E. O. Wilson's Baptist fundamentalisms (genetic, biophilial), Haraway's Catholicism (material-semiotic incarnational symbols, the "Christian realism" which she claims to decipher in much American science), Levinas's and Derrida's Judaism (expulsion, errancy of signification), and, indeed, the title of this anthology, which I take to be worrying the notions of natural law.

My inquiry into the empirical places where ethical, political, and policy-making decisions are (re)formulated, adjudicated, and negotiated are an anthropologist's experimental effort to locate where contemporary theology could come into play with our emerging technosciences. This essay groups these into four "trials" or places of moral testing: from nature as a place of *context or environment*; to nature as *contingency, accident, and risk*; nature as *nano- and molecular culturing, cultivation, Bildung, from the inside out and bottom up*; and nature as *dealing with and accepting alterity*.

Old metaphysical words such as "soul" or "presence" have meaning in today's world only by taking on a (weak) metaphorical or translational cast. They gesture toward helping people work through (and clarify) the conflicts in their lives and among the social forces in which they participate. Parables and stories have always been part of this tradition. They help point us to interconnections in society, to the ecological complexity of changing things rather than allowing the market, competition, or accumulation to define the "nature" of things. In this sense the old stories of Moses and Khizr, the Muslim version of Elijah, who travels back and forth between this world and the next and who in the Qur'an has encounters with Moses, still apply: we humans are always in possession of only partial knowledge (that is what we have to work with), with which we fashion our moral robustness (a social thing) as well as our ethics (a personal thing). We are tested with these tools in repetitive, recursive, ever slightly changing tournaments and ways.

So, too, the internal debates of religious traditions more generally provide narrative forms for ethnographic analysis of the social interests at stake. Like "justice" as an aspiration in contrast to actual decisions of the "law," the terms *values, ethics,* and *morals* operate as aspirations, as regulatory ideas, as odd-job terms, generally left unspecified or specified only in the context of particular cases. When dogmatized and claimed to be instantiated or perfectly embodied, they often undermine their own credibility. Just as minority opinions in legal decisions sometimes become majority ones in the future, so too with the formulations of religious thought.

In the scholastic traditions of the three monotheistic traditions, in the logical debate traditions of Buddhism, Hinduism, and Jainism, and in the parable-telling of Native American traditions, there is always dialectical room for alternative interpretation, particularly at the limits of reason and tradition. The old Aristotelian modes—visceral emotion, cognitive reason, and character—are institutionalized today as advertising, science and technology, and civic epistemologies.

To explore and define these positions, this essay deploys the notions of (1) narratives (Benjamin's catastrophes, Geertz's "deep play"); (2) second natures (modes of production, parliaments of things, litigations, and contestatory, emergent "enunciatory communities"); (3) nature inside out (new biologies and biotechnologies, new forums for social definition of what is un/natural); and (4) expansion of symbiotic repertoires with our animal familiars, analogues, and coevolutionary species. I use the dialogues (cross-arguments) between comparative ethology, animal training, comparative genomics, and other emerging scientific fields, on the one hand, and phenomenological, philosophical, and psychiatric notions of agoraphobia, nausea-shame, and pleasure, on the other, to come back to the question of the collective technobody with which I begin the first section.

My interest is in the changing "coevolution" of sites of dilemmas and ethical-political decision-making, from reflexive social institutions of second-order modernities to regulatory forums differently handled by different civic epistemologies; to tournaments of ethics rounds in medical settings including changing definitions of mental and social health as agoraphobia (once defined in relation to space, now defined by pharmaceutical medicine as panic attacks without reference to space); to sites of interspecies and intercultural negotiation of radically different phenomenologies and social consciousnesses.

What might all this mean for an *anthropos* and an anthropology to come? Let me sum up with five hypotheses or queries:

1. Historically speaking, "nature" is an odd-job word, unlike "culture," which has an analytic history in anthropology as a quasi-technical frame of analysis. "Nature" no doubt has a history from classical times through the natural-law tradition but in more recent times has increasingly lost its foundational referents and instead is a covering label for the paradoxical ambiguity with which I began (nature is that which is both our other and our "essential" self); and as our knowledge expands and reconfigures itself, this ambiguity also expands.[120]

2. Cross-culturally speaking, only in a heavily Christianized or "globalatinized" world can one speak of the "death of God" or the dissolution

of a foundational "natural law."[121] One need not be a holy fool, Sufi saint, Hindu guru, Jain monk, Zen or dialectical Buddhist, Talmudist, or Spinozan to recognize that "God" diffuses into nature, leaving traces of divinity everywhere, and that the decisions of the world are in the hands of the creatures and forces of the world. Thus to speak of its death or absence seems not to make any sense, nor does the nineteenth-century fear (intensified by World War I) that without rules (metaphorized in traditional moral language as God), nihilism and chaos would ensue. "The death of God" and "without nature" are pre-mid-twentieth-century European philosophemes.

3. In the *anthropos* and anthropology to come, nature can be no more than the output of humble, partial, experimental systems, meaning this less as a Darwinian idea than a contemporary interoperable, kludgy, workaround, molecular, nano, and genetic, algorithmic, but also tissue and polymer conglomerate view, in which our epistemology is always already entwined, mediated, mutated, or transduced into (dis)harmonic registers of Lévi-Strauss–like symphonies of meaning.

4. At issue here is a structure of feeling that as the world changes, as scientific and pragmatic knowledges expand, our very vocabulary also shifts, increasingly inflected by the sciences and technologies of our time and the epistemologies and instrumentations through which they are elaborated. We need to embrace these languages and interrogate them for their "zero points" and other naturalizing and occluding features in order to keep them, as well as our ethical stances in the world, lively and informative.[122]

5. An anthropology to come will need to be collaborative and intercultural, not only across traditional cultures but across cultures of specialization, and will need not only to incorporate the lively languages of the new technosciences but also to reread, redecipher, and redeploy the palimpsests of traditional knowledges. Such collaboration is not easy: as with animal training, it involves coordination, translation, exchange, and responsiveness to different phenomenologies, epistemologies, ways of doing, and ways of knowing.

Nature, Change, and Justice

Lisa Sowle Cahill

> Of things that exist, some exist by nature. . . . Each of them has within
> itself a principle of motion and of stationariness [and an] innate
> impulse to change.
>
> ARISTOTLE, *Physics*[1]

Preliminaries

The title of this collection is "Without Nature? A New Condition for
Theology." This theme captures a premise: that theology up until now
has assumed a concept and reality of nature that has vanished. More specifically, a formerly clear and certain concept of nature has been dislodged
by a few decades'-worth of technological innovation, for example and especially in human and agricultural genetics, and by the ability to replace
or supplant human parts and functions with artifacts of technology. The
boundaries of the species are in doubt, as are the lines drawn between
nature and artifice and between natural beings and their environments. To
this, some react with alarm and denounce the new powers; others see these
powers as providing an evolutionary opportunity, perhaps even an opportunity to escape the strictures of human mortality.

My thesis is that nature can serve as a condition for theology, in much
the same way that it usually has, if we grant that nature—at least human
nature—is a historical and social reality to which change is integral. This
idea is not at all new and should evoke neither horror nor new ambition.
For instance, Aristotle recognized that "man" is by nature a social and

political animal, one of whose most characteristic activities is the exercise of practical reason. Reason, society, and politics do not always work for good ends. Unfortunately, some of the most enduring traits of "human nature" are self-promotion, violence, and greed. To take nature as a condition for theology (or for any sort of ethics) requires us to acknowledge not only that nature is historical but that it is polyvalent.

Since the word "nature" is equivocal, different concepts of nature must be distinguished. "Nature" can refer either to beings, states, activities and relationships that exist actually and de facto (the "descriptive" sense of nature) or to those that should exist because they constitute more authentic or fulfilling forms than those that prevail (the "normative" sense of nature). While modern science uses the term "nature" in the former, descriptive sense, philosophers and theologians who use "nature" as a norm or talk about a "natural law" mean the latter, normative sense. Ethical *norms* can be based on, though not directly derived from, *facts* of nature that can be described empirically. The concept of nature in the normative sense also contains an implicit reference to change, since it is equated not with what simply is but with that which present existence can and ought to become. But defining normative nature requires a good deal of interpretation and judgment concerning states and behaviors that we actually see. Which of these are good, just, and contribute to human flourishing? Nature-related norms, as expressing a normative concept of nature, are known socially, relationally, inductively, and historically and exhibit both continuity and change—just like nature itself. Indeed, the historical argument about how to define justice and social justice is precisely what constitutes philosophical and theological ethics.

In much of the literature about nature, norms, and biotechnology, the difference between descriptive and normative accounts is neglected. Moreover, three problematic assumptions are pervasive:

1. *"Nature," in the sense of human nature, concerns primarily the human body and derivative psychosomatic traits.* Debates about nature tend to envision discrete members of the species, especially as potential objects of technological intervention. For example, the prospect that genomics and biotech will alter human beings radically is a (or the) key problem entertained.

2. *In the past, theology and ethics worked with a "clear and distinct" idea of nature to guide action and reflection.* Nature was accepted as a "given," reflected God's unchanging design, and defined humanity's proper place, sphere, and destiny.

3. *Science (biotechnology) is changing nature to such an extent that we no longer know what it is.* This suggests infinite malleability—even metamorphosis into the posthuman. Transhumanists are perhaps the most attention-grabbing proponents of this trajectory. According to the "Transhumanist Declaration," it is feasible to redesign "the human condition, including such parameters as the inevitability of aging, limitations on human and artificial intellects, unchosen psychology, suffering, and our confinement to the planet earth."[2] We should be able to get rid of illness, aging, and death—"we" being elites with money, of course. Transhumanists will have no truck with "customary injunctions against playing God, messing with nature, tampering with our human essence, or displaying punishable hubris."[3] The theological counterpart, or "counter-reformation," is the view of humans as God's "cocreators" who are charged to improve what we are given, using measures like genetics, though with respect for the deity and with greater concern about social exclusion and access.

My responses to these assumptions are as follows:

1. Reducing the meaning of nature to physical nature—that is, the human body, and even more narrowly, the human genes—makes it seem easier to pin down a clear concept of nature. But nature is more than the human body. It is also human psychology (intelligence, freedom, emotions, imagination, and spiritual capacity). Nor is nature only *individual* bodiliness and psychology; it is also *social* identity and behavior.

2. Theological and religious ethics do not assume that nature cannot change, for the transformation of human nature is key to theological ethics. Theological ethics does assume that there is continuity in human characteristics, but its main concern is with the social relationships that humans create, which are also part of "nature." And certainly, while social relationships exhibit some continuity across times and cultures, they also can, do, and should change. Theological ethics urges humans to embody patterns of social existence that reflect human community under God and assumes that natural forms of society can be transformed by divine power, gift, or participation. Examples from Christian tradition are the commands to "Love the Lord your God with your whole heart, mind, and soul; and your neighbor as yourself"; the parable of the Good Samaritan from the Gospel of Luke; and the proclamation of St. Paul that there is neither Jew nor Greek, slave nor free, male nor female, for you "are all one in Christ Jesus." The nature of human *social* behavior, especially the transformation of destructive patterns of behavior, is the ultimate focus of Christian ethics.

3. Nature does change, then, but this undermines neither the possibility of moral judgment nor the normative contribution of theological ethics. Nature is and has always been a complex constellation of traits and capabilities oriented around purposes and goals. Nature has always been changing. Still, it is possible to discern lasting continuities in good and bad human habits and conduct, especially social conduct. From the standpoint of Christian theology, "we" should change human nature, if we can, toward more inclusive concern for the common good and a preferential option for the poor.[4]

Finally, even if theology does not have a new condition of naturelessness, it does have a new condition of global interdependence and needs a global ethical consciousness to match it. "Mainstream" North Atlantic "First World" ethics and bioethics worry considerably about "ourselves"—our powers, our actions, our impact on us and our cultures and futures. Interestingly, human genetic enhancement and transhumanism, pro or con, are not big topics in global bioethics from the developing world. Those speaking on behalf of the poor give much more airtime to the "natural" tendency of those who control technologies to use them selfishly and exploitatively. Yet the 2.8 billion people in the world living on less than $2 a day are not given much attention on the Transhumanist Web site, nor on that of the Biotechnology Industry Organization.[5] This skewing of the issue of the future of human nature deters us as philosophers, theologians, cultural critics, activists, and policy-makers from fully engaging the most important quandary posed by the topic: how to change the rapid, global institutionalization of new technological prowess in ways that do not exponentially undermine participatory democracy and access to benefits for the least well-off.

In this article I develop the connections among nature, change, and justice by addressing the coexistence in human nature of change and continuity; the "goods" and "bads" of human nature; and the possibility of human nature's positive transformation, supported by religion and theology.

Continuity and Change in Human Nature and Its Goods

Theologian Peter Scott makes the case that all creatures participate with God in a dynamic reality characterized by unity, sociality, and openness, all of which reflect the character of reality as "becoming" rather than static "being." "Ruled out is the claim that God validates a *specific* order." Scott defines humanity as "the temporal emergence of embodied selves-in-relation." He notes that "nature can thus refer to human embodiment, the natural conditions which allow the emergence of the social life of humanity and the totality of processes and structures of the universe." I would only add that beyond the human body, "nature" also includes human intelligence, will, emotions, and capacity for intersubjective recognition, all obviously part of what Scott names as "the natural conditions which allow the emergence of the social life of humanity." In any event, as Scott maintains, "humanity can be understood as other than nature, in continuity with nature and part of the totality of nature," depending on the aspects or activities of humanity one intends to indicate. An evident implication is that humans are always a part of nature, so they never have an "objective" standpoint "outside" nature from which to analyze it.[6]

Peter Scott backs up his claims with theologies of the Trinity and of Christ. For example, just as the Logos is differentiated from God yet one with God, so creatures are differentiated from God yet in unity with God, differentiated from one another yet in relationship to all. God relates to humanity in a temporal and spatial way in the incarnation and is "in nature"; humans are also in nature and, in a temporal, spatial, historical way, relate to other creatures and to God.[7]

Ecological identities must therefore be understood as given yet not static: human identities are to be interpreted relationally with reference to God and nature; natural identities are to be interpreted relationally with reference to God and humanity; the divine identity is to be interpreted relationally (that is, as triune) by reference to the act of God in incarnation as fleshly: social and natural.[8]

Scott is not unique among theologians in making claims for the relationality and sociality of nature, including human nature, as well as for the unity of humanity, God, and nature through creation, incarnation, and the activity of God as Spirit. Sallie McFague's *Models of God* and *The Body of God* are landmark contributions in a similar vein.[9] Ecofeminist theology in general is an important and increasingly global resource, also credited by Scott.[10] According to Jürgen Moltmann, "the communities found in nature" enjoy with "human persons and communities" the "fellowship of the Holy Spirit." "That is why it is appropriate to talk about *the community of creation*, and to recognize the operation of the life-giving Spirit of God in the trend to relationship in created things."[11]

These authors do not buy the prevalent modern preconception that "nature" can and should be defined in terms of clear and distinct ideas empirically verified (reflecting Newton, Locke, Hume, and Descartes).[12]

They reject the idea that the edges of what is "natural" can be conclusively established as well as the idea that such boundaries are necessary to ethical analysis and to a cogent politics of nature. The social and relational view of nature they endorse is also a view of nature as historical and changing.

These insights are not exclusive to theology and certainly not to contemporary theology. (In contrast, concerns about the well-being of the natural environment, about the dangers to it attendant upon human action, and about the agency of the natural universe in its own right are relatively recent.) For instance, Aristotle sees "nature" as designating not unchanging aspects of a being that are available to observation as clear and distinct traits but rather its mysterious propensity to change while retaining identity (its form). Every natural being has both an impulse to change in certain typical ways ("for instance the property of fire to be carried upwards") and a recognizable and continuous identity as the "subject" or "substance" in which the propensity inheres. Each kind of being has its own proper function and activity, derived from the appropriate natural ends or goals to which it tends.[13]

A constitutive goal for humans, Aristotle says, is the happiness derived from association with others in friendship and politics.[14] Since "man is a social and political being," practical reason and practical activity go into what human nature is and means.[15] This entails *change*, because human beings and societies are constituted in time, place, and history. The characteristics that define human nature are not absolutely invariant but have a relatively fluid quality. Yet human identity is constituted by core goals and aspirations, capabilities and activities, and virtues and satisfactions that remain recognizably similar among humans and in one's own identity. There is also similarity of basic material and social conditions necessary to friendship, politics, and happiness. It is fair to say that for Aristotle, change occurs within certain limits, or at least on a certain defined trajectory, constituted by the "form" of a being that gives it its specific identity.

Aristotle's thirteenth-century theological interpreter, Thomas Aquinas, adopts a similar approach to defining human nature as social and teleological. For Aquinas too, nature provides an essential continuity and stability to ethics and politics—yet nature is not unchanging. To what degree it can change for Aquinas has been a matter of extensive interpretive debate, especially among Catholic theologians. It suffices to say at least that for Aquinas, practical morality and politics require negotiation of the requirements of human nature in relation to concrete particularities of circumstance and that "practical rectitude" according to nature is not the same always and everywhere in every matter.[16] Today we might ask whether the fact that freedom is a distinctive characteristic of human beings means that human nature and its goods are more deeply disposed to change and be changed than Aristotle and other premodern authors envisioned.

Indeed, as Elaine Graham points out, it is "impossible to speak of a pristine, unadulterated 'human nature' without considering the ways in which humans have always, as it were, co-evolved with their tools and technologies," as well as conditions in their environments, both material and social. In the creation of material cultures, "humanity cannot but refashion itself as integral elements of that world."[17] "'Human nature' ceases to be a fixed category and re-emerges as a constantly changing set of possibilities and configurations."[18] The complex, variable, and evolving realities of human life include but exceed what can be discovered by the natural and human sciences. Some realities, such as love, hatred, grief, wonder, friendship, faith, and hope, are better captured in media such as art, literature, music, and religious symbols and ritual. The classics of human cultures reveal commonalities of emotion, imagination, and even moral value across time and place.

Theological ethicist Stephen Pope commends the fact that evolutionary psychologists "think of human nature as the collection of species-typical goal-directed mechanisms designed by natural selection."[19] Nature is comprised by "species-wide orientations to certain important classes of goods," such as food, security, mating and nurturing of offspring, and social alliances that serve these and other ends.[20] According to Pope, it is better to think of nature not as unchanging or clearly demarcated but as constituted by "species-wide regularities," a better term than "universals."[21] These regularities are linked to physiological processes and functions that have a genetic component, guaranteeing their consistent appearance, and with it, a shared "natural" substratum of human experience and society.[22] Yet even the stability characteristic of human nature is derived from humanity's characteristic purposes and activities and is interdependent with motion and change.[23] It also does not exclude but presupposes freedom—understood contextually and historically. According to one commentator on Aristotle, "a natural being becomes and reveals its nature as it grows, changes, and moves through time. Nature, understood as an end and a beginning all at once, is an ongoing process."[24] Intellectual, moral, and political activities progressively constitute the nature of a human being, a being that is historical, creative, and adaptive.

The "Goods" of Human Nature

What exactly is fulfilling for human beings and relationships, what contributes to the human good or flourishing, calls for interpretation and judgment. Even if the human good or goods is or are recognized similarly across cultures, we are still rightly impressed by the diversity of interpretations to which cultures have given rise and to the conflicts these differences apparently spawn. Can human nature and its goods be more or less precisely defined? And can normative interpretations be proposed in any generally persuasive way?

Aristotle defines the human good as happiness, attained through a life of virtue and of certain material and social benefits conducive to friendship, politics, and philosophical contemplation. Just as on the definition of nature, Aristotle defines the good and happiness via an experiential and inductive approach to knowledge, using as the standard of truth not modern science but consensus and the authority of those whose virtue and example are proof of their wisdom. Generally speaking, happiness is a life of activity guided by practical reason, a life in society with others and enjoying a certain level of security and respite from subsistence labor. Aristotle suggests that the sort of life most closely approximating the divine would be a life of contemplation, and contemplation of the truth for its own sake is part of the complete good for human beings. We may debate whether contemplation is better than human society or merely a necessary component of a full human life, but what no one seriously debates is Aristotle's apprehension of basic human goods: material and social security, fulfillment of basic needs, relations of love and friendship, and political participation. These core aspects of human nature, and the evaluation of them as "good," are not really all that debatable, though diverse cultures have diverse ways of securing, celebrating, and institutionalizing them.[25]

"Justice" for Aristotle refers to the quality of relations that accord with reason and practical wisdom; those things that are just "produce and preserve happiness for the social and political community." Just as he says, "There are some things which, though naturally just, are nevertheless changeable, as are all things human. Yet in spite of that, there are some things that are just by nature and others not by nature."[26]

This is where "cultural difference" enters in contentiously. Justice refers to the systems or processes of allocation defining access to human goods. Aristotle spells out the varieties of justice in terms of fair and proportionate social relations, including distribution of goods, and rectification of imbalances and inequalities. Yet Aristotle had no problem with slavery and assumed the subordinate position of women.[27] The uncertainty of *normative* judgments about nature and "the natural," especially what are naturally just relations to human goods, is precisely why it is so appealing for those considering biotechnology to seek a simple and specific biological standard by which to encourage or prohibit certain interventions. This does not solve the problem, however, if the ethical criterion is too simple and too biologically focused to deal with the human reality, good and bad. Just as there is continuity in human embodiment, providing recognizable similarity within change, so there are recognizable human goods and valued relationships that help us sort out the productive from the destructive expressions of human nature—to sort out fundamental justice from injustice.

For Aquinas, human nature also follows the good as structuring nature teleologically. Aquinas begins by asking not about the boundaries and biological markers of human nature but about the inclinations to the good that guide human activity to happiness. He essentially appeals to experience-backed consensus on this matter, supporting his proposals with various authorities, including Aristotle, Augustine, and Scripture. Aquinas frames his inquiry into the "natural" around the premise that it is natural to human beings to do good and avoid evil: "The good is that which all things seek."[28]

Most important, "man" has "an inclination to good, according to the nature of his reason, which nature is proper to him." The ultimate human good is God, but the human inclination to seek both the highest good and finite goods is expressed through practical social and political activity. Common to humans in all societies are dispositions "to know the truth about God, and to live in society," to "shun ignorance," and to "avoid offending those among whom one has to live."[29] Humans also have inclinations to happiness-producing activities that they share with other living things, such as self-preservation, sexual intercourse, and the education of offspring. All these inclinations, ruled by reason and expressed practically, belong to "human nature."[30] They refer simultaneously to biological traits and functions and to social relationships that express, institutionalize, and protect them in ways that serve individual and social well-being. Such relationships are just, rendering to everyone that which he or she deserves.[31]

Note that Aquinas selects out of his rendering of "natural inclinations" other human propensities that are socially destructive though quite pervasive, for example, violent competition and abandonment of offspring. For both Aristotle and Aquinas, "nature" is both a descriptive and a normative concept. It indicates common human activities and the goals to which they lead, but it does so after having designated some human goals, activities, and relationships, and not others, as contributing to human flourishing and happiness and hence as serving "justice" in human relationships. The contrary goals, activities, and relationships are designated by Aristotle as "vice" and by Aquinas as "sin," even though they are naturally occurring. These are of course historical, social, and hence somewhat contingent judgments, which vary in their certainty depending on their specificity, on their dependence on local conditions, on the degree of good or harm in which they result, and on how broad a consensus a particular judgment can evoke. Like Aristotle, Aquinas accepts slavery and women's naturally inferior status, though Aquinas defends slavery not on its primary "naturalness" but on its "utility."[32]

The lesson here is that although it is right to speak of certain basic human goods that are generally known, the inductive and historical process of coming to knowledge is never free from error and bias. This is even more true of good and just relations, especially relations of access to goods. Knowledge, including the prudential knowledge of ethics and politics, reflects cultural circumstances and concerns and often cultural priorities and blind spots. Thus the process of discerning human goods and normative human relationships must be dynamic, dialogical, and constantly self-correcting.

A recent neo-Aristotelian framework for understanding human nature is the "capabilities" approach of Martha Nussbaum, an approach that in its basic dimensions I find compatible with Aquinas as well.[33] Though Nussbaum herself does not call this a "theory of human nature," I think it could be considered one, assuming that "nature" is relational, social, historical, and known inductively to exhibit "species-wide regularities" with regard to certain features. It is these features that she names "capabilities." The revisable list of capabilities Nussbaum offers includes life; bodily health; bodily integrity; senses, imagination, thought; emotions; practical reason; affiliation (relationship to others, including the social bases of one's own self-respect and dignity); relationship to other species; play; and political and material control over one's environment.[34] The defining human capabilities are enabled by the regularities of human physiology, including the human genotype, and might be undermined or enhanced by genetic redesign or by the introduction into human beings of "artificial" components. Yet the ethically relevant question for Nussbaum would be not the specific origin of these or other deliberately enabled traits but how well they serve human dignity and freedom within societies and institutions that support similar basic capabilities for all, including women and members of all social and economic classes. She does not try to draw absolute lines but grants a certain contingency to judgment.

Martha Nussbaum recognizes that the importance she assigns to freedom and self-determination characterizes her as a modern liberal democrat.[35] Here she essentially makes a normative statement about patterns of access to goods—as ideally governed by equality. She maintains, rightly in my view, that individual freedom requires the same basic capabilities that are valued across cultures by people with varying priorities. Basic needs and capabilities are known, appreciated, and recognized globally, despite the fact that forms of fulfillment will vary, as will allocation patterns. On basic issues of hunger, poverty, AIDS, or rape, social frameworks will provide different values and solutions having to do both with goods and with social status. Nevertheless, as Nussbaum says, there are essential dimensions of human experience as embodied and social that enable people from different cultures "to proceed as if we are all talking about the same human problem."[36]

Now, beyond Aristotle, a question that could be posed today is whether even "basic" human capacities, activities, and aspirations might change *drastically*, producing discontinuity with what the "human" has so far been. If so, would the resulting beings still be "human"? It seems to me that recognizable similarity is part of the definition of a nature or human nature; but it also seems that not even the transhumanists are proposing evolutions that bear no recognizable similarity to the human as we know it. After all, their aim is to survive, not be replaced. Fascination with futuristic scenarios can distract us from bigger and more urgent "human" problems that humans face right now. Such distractions may even be instrumental in producing a deliberately false consciousness about the problems that most deserve our efforts.

Indeed, if we could solve some of the globally urgent problems of social justice and democratic participation, then possible radical changes in human nature would not seem so dangerous. The main thing people fear is not change itself but the arrival of change under the aegis of greater control over the majority by a minority wielding the new technologies. This is the underlying message of *1984*, *Animal Farm*, *Gattaca*, and Kazuo Ishiguro's award-winning novel *Never Let Me Go* (though I think Ishiguro's dominant theme is the avoidance of our own mortality—another phenomenon operative in posthumanist fantasies).

Moreover, we already have the problem of possibly fuzzy species boundaries with signing gorillas, dolphins, and the recent *Homo floriensis* controversy. There is no reason the trend could not go in several directions, with humans at the midpoint of a spectrum, or the hub of a wheel, or an intersection of a web, rather than at the zenith of a single evolutionary trajectory. Richness, diversity, and lush proliferation are part of the beauty of nature, which we ordinarily encourage and protect. The real problem for "human nature" is not expanding nature but abusive and unjust nature.

The essential ethical question is the question of justice, not the question of change. Justice must be defined. It is not autonomy alone, nor only the right to produce and purchase goods (like biotech "advances") on the market. Justice includes equal access to the basic goods of life and participation in the common good. Defining the line between justice and injustice is obviously a challenge; decreasing the latter in favor of the former is an even more massive one. To do that, we must confront the totality of human nature—and confront it honestly.

The "Bads" of Human Nature

Nature is both beneficent and destructive, sometimes harmonious, sometimes competitive and violent. Likewise, speaking in purely factual terms, there is a *natural* human disposition to evil as well as to good.

Competition, violence, and destruction are part of human nature. War, genocide, torture, illegal incarceration and execution, human trafficking, domestic abuse of women and children, and commercial exploitation of the natural environment all come readily to mind. Let me begin with a few ostensibly more benign examples closer to applications in humans of genetics and biotechnology. According to a recent article in *Foreign Policy*, a mere 1 percent of the 1,556 drugs developed between 1975 and 2004 were for tuberculosis (TB) or the so-called "neglected diseases" that cannot command research dollars because they affect millions of poor people.[37] A report from an independent international initiative, the Commission on Health Research for Development, defined the root cause as the "10/90" gap: 10 percent of health research money is spent globally on problems that affect 90 percent of the world's population.[38] Diseases including AIDS, TB, malaria, hookworm, Guinea worm, river blindness, and polio cause permanent disability and death to millions in the developing world, exacerbating a cycle of illness and poverty.

Some of these diseases could perhaps be attacked using pharmacogenomics, or by discovering and controlling genes that either provide immunity from or susceptibility to given diseases. Research is in fact under way to target and genetically disable malaria-carrying mosquitoes. In a world no more futuristic than that of transhumanists, nanotechnology might discover and eradicate infesting worms or allay the effects of blindness. Stem cell research might lead to other ways to restore function for people devastated by polio. But these enterprises are not big priorities for "Big Pharma" or its investors and stockholders, no doubt including many of us and the institutions for which we work. Even the benefits of current genetic research on illnesses that afflict both rich and poor, like alcoholism and muscular dystrophy, will be sold on the market by private enterprise following the profit motive.

The contemporary human sciences, especially sociobiology and evolutionary psychology, help shed light on these dismal facts of human life. Despite a tendency to explain human nature in reductionist terms, evolutionary sciences can offer the ethicist greater understanding of the fact that humans display a great and complex variety of traits and behaviors. A significant proportion of human traits evolved because they were supportive of the goals of reproduction and survival. Yet they are still evolving in interaction with our environment, including the social networks and institutions that humans have designed. The given and the chosen are inextricable and mutually interdependent parts of human nature. Together they explain human existence as we know it and indicate opportunities for change.

To generalize, evolutionary psychology explains certain basic tendencies in human behavior in terms of the natural selection of biologically and genetically grounded (not necessarily determined) traits that enabled humans to solve adaptive problems faced by our hunter-gatherer ancestors.[39] For the great majority of our history, humans existed in small nomadic bands, foraging for food. Forming protective alliances, hoarding resources, and showing aggression toward outsiders provided evolutionary advantages. Humanity's evolutionary past provides us with certain species-typical bodily components, needs, and capacities; cognitive capabilities; emotional and psychological ranges and responses; and capacities and desires for social interaction and connection.

The moral agency characteristic of and unique to humans takes shape on the basis of a great variety of complex cognitive and emotional capacities and on the basis of goals and inclinations that may conflict with one another. Moral agency is grounded on an inclination of humans to seek out social membership and to depend on networks of reciprocal cooperation and commitment, but reciprocity is selective. Meanwhile, the institutions through which individual agency is organized and coordinated can diminish the sense of individual responsibility while magnifying the effects of many concerted individual choices. Humans "naturally" reconcile evolved inclinations to engage in prosocial behavior with other human inclinations to behave selfishly and aggressively, by forming groups that promote self-interest via intragroup cohesion and dominance of outsiders. This is not the only type of moral behavior that is natural to humans and societies, but it is a very familiar one.[40]

The North American theologian and social ethicist Reinhold Niebuhr identified a tendency of group behavior that he termed "collective egotism."[41] By dedicating oneself to the ideology and agenda of a group, one can align one's fragile and finite self with a transcendent cause and, in the name of that cause, seek power and prerogatives, in effect overcoming anxiety about one's own finitude. Groups and their elites play on this tendency to conscript the loyalty of individuals to serve the aims of the larger group and to protect the authority and interests of elite control. In Niebuhr's view, this whole process is a symptom of sin in the world and is the cause of injustice and violence. To call a social pattern sinful, of course, is also to admonish us to moral responsibility. Despite the determinism of some sociobiology, humans are not fated to act always for reasons that are primarily selfish. Nature may provide parameters and conditions of our freedom, but freedom is part of nature nonetheless.

In a magisterial book on the social factors that help marshal human behavior around evil and genocide, James Waller also lights some paths to change.[42] Waller's first contribution is the use of social and evolutionary psychology to clarify the origin of the social dynamic that leads to evil as destructive social violence, and clarify, too, its frequency and the difficulty of countering it. His second contribution is to understand the steps necessary to do so.

According to Waller, we are burdened with three evolved tendencies of human nature that help create a human "capacity for extraordinary evil—ethnocentrism, xenophobia, and the desire for social dominance."[43] These are inclinations that our nature has handed us, not determinants of moral outcomes. However—and here it is salutary to keep in mind Niebuhr's "collective egotism"—there is a powerful impetus for groups to rationalize such behavior as good, necessary, and fair, and for individuals to seek to belong to groups that help aggrandize their own claims to goods. This works especially well when individuals or groups feel under threat, real or perceived. Of course, it is in the interests of both individuals and groups to exaggerate threat in order to justify aggression and the expropriation of more goods.

Waller argues that motivation to extraordinary violence is much more likely when personal self-interest or advancement is involved, when cultural belief systems encourage obedience to authority and a high degree of ideological commitment, and when a "culture of cruelty" is created in the immediate social context. A culture of cruelty requires and builds on socialization to engage in violence against others, often via professional roles. This socialization is accomplished by means of escalating commitments to participate in violence, ritual conduct legitimizing violence or the roles entailing it, and the repression of individual conscience. Cruelty is bolstered by group bonds that diffuse responsibility, deindividuate agency, and enforce conformity to peer pressure and by the merger of role and person in such a way that an individual agent comes to believe that acting morally consists in fidelity to one's role, often one's professional role. Finally, extraordinary violence depends on us-them thinking, that is, seeing adversaries as guilty and deserving of persecution, as nonhuman, or as both.[44]

Waller exposes his readers to several horrifying first-person accounts of real instances of genocide and murder from Nazi death camps, Vietnam, Cambodia, East Timor, Kosovo, Srebrenica, Rwanda, and Guatemala. He shows that these crimes were not committed by psychopaths or monsters but by ordinary people for whom evolutionary, personal, and social factors came together in a perfect storm to create a capacity, indeed an eagerness, to do extraordinary evil. This kind of evil is not even rare. Though most societies do not in fact commit genocide, Waller reminds us that "buried in the midst of all our progress in the twentieth century are well over a 100 million persons who met a violent death at the hands of their fellow human beings. That is more than five times the number from the nineteenth century and more than ten times the number from the eighteenth century."[45] It is not hard to imagine that hundreds of millions more have met their deaths from the institutionalized violence of poverty and lack of access to food, clean water, sanitary living conditions, and minimal health care.

"Destructive social violence" may seem like an extreme characterization of the negative social potentials of genetic engineering and biotechnology. Yet a similar dynamic in the social acceptance, implementation, and institutionalization of these sciences accounts for by far the greater part of their moral objectionability. These innovations may not lead to outright violence but they are already participating in patterns of social oppression and exclusion—resulting in suffering, illness, and death—that rapid scientific manipulation of the human body can exacerbate at great speed and with global scope.

For extraordinary evil, socialization maneuvers need to be strong and well structured. Yet ordinary social evil is enabled in a similar if less coercive way. The "professions" and "discourses" of science, business, and even academia involve participants in strategies that rationalize, ritualize, and disguise self-interested behavior that is detrimental to other persons, other groups, and the common good. All these sectors of modern culture become complicit in the use of biotechnology as an instrument of structural violence when, with promises of "relief of human suffering," they seek prestige or profit by rationalizing technologies that will benefit only a few; when they socialize practitioners into professional roles and peer organizations that take current trends for granted; when they demonize every critic as a "reactionary" or a member of the "religious right"; and when they escalate commitment to the "progress" of biotechnology by incrementally crossing barriers against risk to human subjects, payment of so-called "donors," creation of research embryos, market-driven patenting and pricing, and so on.

Religion can also be part of the problem of extraordinary violence—sadly obvious in Waller's cases of genocide. In the case of biotechnology and genetics, some complicity of religion in unethical developments may be due to the desire of religious bioethicists to have a voice in the halls of power, where government policy is made and corporate ethics committees are convened. However, I believe that by far the greater cause is the tendency of religious groups and theologians to identify the wrong problems as key. The most significant ethical issues of economic justice and the use and abuse of health care resources have been grievously neglected by many, if not most, of the official religious representatives in the United States, and too often by theological bioethicists. This makes us "guilty bystanders," in the phrase of social psychologist Ervin Staub, a child Holocaust survivor. A "bystander" to social evil is an individual or a collection or organization of individuals who witness what is happening but remain passive. "This passivity encourages perpetrators."[46]

Yet, according to Waller, it is not necessarily true that groups always behave less morally than individuals. Sometimes groups are catalysts for social justice and social change and may even oppose destructive collective behavior. Waller takes issue with part of Niebuhr's analysis.[47] True, Niebuhr identifies a common dynamic of group identification that is often found when groups adopt oppressive or violent policies and actions. Groups can bind people together around shared grievances and lead them to undertake more extreme behavior than they would as individuals, magnifying the evil any one individual could accomplish alone. Yet the same sort of bonding and concerted strength occur when groups form identity around cooperative or humanitarian aims.[48]

Transforming Nature: Roles of Religion and Theology

The analyses of James Waller, Stephen Pope, and Ervin Staub show that as humans, we are equipped "naturally"—by genes and by many other dimensions of our history—for social behavior that can be either inclusive and cooperative or aggressive and discriminatory. Despite the apparent odds in favor of the latter, Waller urges us not to despair. By understanding the conditions that make humans more likely to exhibit fear, aggression, and dominance, we will learn how to inspire compassion, cooperation, and altruism. We are already equipped naturally (by evolution) with dispositions toward love of kin, kin altruism, reciprocal altruism, and enduring reciprocal alliances in the form of friendships and civic and political membership. Our capacities for empathy and our contextual freedom permit us to encourage and enhance such alliances.

The evolved human ability to respond with empathic identification to the feelings and needs of those to whom our own self-interest is bound (kin and allies) is the basis of our ability to recognize the needs and feelings of everyone as part of a moral program of universal dignity and equality. The trick is to get humans to extend their naturally self-serving emotions and preferences to nonkin, nonmembers, "strangers," and even "enemies," even when it does not serve their immediate success strategy or that of their group. This is precisely a key role of religious narratives, stories, and practices oriented around maxims such as "All are made in the image of God," "Love your neighbor as yourself," and "Do unto others as you would have others do unto you." Individuals, organizations, and communities, including religious communities, are capable of "active bystandership." I concur with Staub that ideologies and worldviews can be constructive as well as destructive, enabling followers to assume risk for those outside the group and to work together "for a shared cause."[49]

Theologians also work with concepts of human goods, but the role of religion and theology is not to define the basics of human nature in an original way. Theologians define natural goods and capabilities through a process of reflection similar to that of philosophers and in fact rely largely on philosophy and other sources of information about the human condition, such as history, literature, the natural and human sciences—as well as on sources of occasional "disinformation," including scientific inaccuracy and cultural bias. Aquinas's use of Aristotle, his assumptions about gender and slavery, and his inaccurate picture of reproductive biology are good examples of this fact. Religion and theology offer *orientations of relationship* with regard to the realities and goods of human existence. Religion and theological ethics shape worldviews around an experience of God that influences believers' perceptions of "who should get what." They do this by mediating human realities through symbolic matrices such as "creation," "sin," "sacrifice," and "redemption," that connect the human with the divine in specific ways.

For example, Kathryn Tanner offers a characterization of basic human goods and rights that is not all that different from Nussbaum's but stresses the point that all human beings are due these equally as creatures of God.[50] As far as ethics and politics are concerned, religious symbol systems communicate and prioritize certain kinds of *relationships* and *responsibilities* among created beings. Theological ethics concerns relationships that define access to goods, status, or well-being among creatures and the responsibilities of humans to respect and support the access of other human beings or of nonhuman beings.

Though we often speak of religion's world-envisioning symbol systems as "narratives," they are practical, not just forms of discourse. Members of religious communities are formed by liturgical practices and moral practices to interact with their world in general, and with human "nature" in particular, in ways that embody the relation to ultimate reality—for Christians, God as revealed in Jesus Christ—mediated by their defining beliefs and symbols. Theology reflects on, systematizes, and draws out the practical implications of these narratives, symbols, and practices. Philosophy, literature, and art take up parallel tasks in different ways and on the basis of distinctive worldviews. We can even say that "descriptive" disciplines, including history and the sciences, are guided to some extent (sometimes a large extent) by a normative agenda that shapes questions asked and "realities" presented. But the task of a theological ethics is to define and prioritize relationships and responsibilities on the basis of an experience of God or "sense of the divine" that requires a certain ordering or orientation of human life against an ultimate horizon of meaning and destiny.[51]

For example, William Schweiker states the imperative of Christian responsibility thus: "in all actions and relations we are to respect and enhance the integrity of life before God."[52] God's identity "constitutes the identity of the community through commitment to justice and mercy," and "the core moral insight of Christian faith is specified in terms of knowledge and love of others."[53] Similarly, for Peter Scott, "the blessing of God's presence in creation" reveals and commends "the basic human solidarity to be with and for one another."[54] Further, for Scott, the Christian experience of "the fellowship of the Holy Spirit" (1 Cor. 12:13) reveals and commends reordered relationships with the whole of nature, including a politics of "the fellowship in sociality of humanity and nature as the gift of the Spirit."[55]

In a statement that is highly typical of contemporary Christian social ethics, the African-American theologian Dwight Hopkins maintains that "from the Christian perspective, Jesus announces his sole purpose on earth to privilege the poor—the homeless, the hungry, the thirsty, the prisoner, people enslaved by labor, the abused women, humans lorded over by the powerful, the brokenhearted, the oppressed, the stranger, those without clothing, and the lowly."[56] His book is aptly named *Being Human*. In a book with the equally pertinent title *An Economy of Grace*, Kathryn Tanner remarks that:

> what is notable about Christianity . . . is its attempt to institute a circulation of goods to be possessed by all in the same fullness of degree without diminution or loss, a distribution that in its prodigal promiscuity calls forth neither the pride of superior position nor rivalrous envy among its recipients.[57]

We are to distribute goods in imitation of God, overcoming "the differences in worthiness and status that rule the arrangements of a sinful world."[58] Note that the value of basic human goods such as home, food, drink, clothing, freedom, physical and sexual safety, respect, happiness, welcome, and social equality is not in question and is not the point being made by Jesus's example and by Christian moral teaching. The point is that classes of persons excluded from these goods should be actively included by Christian communal and political practices: the poor, the homeless, prisoners, slaves, women, and the oppressed in general. Exclusion is not denied as a fact but it is judged and rejected as "sin."

The Christian worldview and symbols, as reflecting and mediating an experience of God, do not only *commend* radical and revolutionary inclusion of all, especially "the poor," in social relationships of sharing and solidarity. They also *announce* renewed social relationships as already proleptically available and effective in the life of the faith community and in the activities of Christians in their social worlds. Narratives and practices forming Christian identity around the presence of God in all creation, Jesus's resurrection, the sending of the Spirit, and an eschatology of God's inbreaking and final redemptive action in history communicate radical transformation as a present possibility. In the words of Peter Scott, the resurrection of Jesus Christ "points forward to the completion of nature, human and non-human, in eschatological glory." Creation not only has "an orientation to the future," it is "living 'out of' that future."[59] Dwight Hopkins is surely speaking eschatologically when he says, "By removing the systemic structures of human evil while transforming the internal demon of individualism, all of humanity can eventually live together on the same horizontal level. Consequently, the wealthy ultimately cease to exist in culture."[60] Ted Peters suggests that the genetic enhancement of human nature could represent "transformation on behalf of improved human flourishing . . . attuned to God's eschatological promise."[61]

The eschatological expectation of Christianity and the moral and political transformations implied necessarily lead the theologian on to two further considerations: the intransigent reality of evil (going back to "human nature" and even genetics); and the theological validation or devising of practical strategies to combat it. Such strategies may be viewed as part of human nature's potential as social and historical, and will take into account the new global situation of human communication, agency, and collective action. Social technologies, and not only genetic, nanotechnological, or transhuman ones, are also part of the changing picture of human nature.

Theologians and all those who are members of faith traditions have much work to do to give sufficient practical traction to Waller's observation that "the teachings of most religious belief systems are replete with affirmations of the dignity of human life and the responsibilities of human beings to respect and preserve that dignity."[62] In my view, we must begin by coming to terms with the practical effects (or lack thereof) of our teachings. We must then invest in practical efforts to socialize, educate, and enlighten human nature so that prosocial behavior conforming to our highest moral aspirations will be more widely realized. As Peter Scott maintains, it is not enough to have a theology of nature: a politics is necessary too. What are some actual strategies that can lead us closer to the "fellowship in the Spirit" that the New Testament proclaims?[63] Space does not allow a lengthy response here.[64] I would like to stress one particular aspect of any adequate answer: globalization.

The institutions—scientific, medical, commercial, political, and regulatory—that are mediating applied genetics into the worldwide marketplace and cultures are just at the point of emergence. This makes intervention all the more urgent and affords ethicists and activists a window of opportunity for change. Michael Fischer's essay in this volume is helpful in this regard. Fischer is immediately aware that bioengineering is a social as well as biological phenomenon and that power and interests are very active in defining what their social institutionalization and impact will be. Fischer states specifically that public regulation will be required, and he begins to indicate the necessarily global (if piecemeal) nature of such regulation by comparing differences in regulatory initiatives in the United States and the United Kingdom. His most important point, however, is that new forms of deliberative democracy and "open deliberative processes," guided by interest in the economic ramifications of biotech, have "forced governments to expand their regulatory forums."[65]

Although religion is not a major part of Fischer's analysis, some people with religious affiliations, and religiously sponsored organizations themselves, have been part of the pressure for a more global and participatory approach to biotechnology. Fischer does mention venues that in the early days of interest in genes and ethics were hospitable to theological contributions: the Hastings Center, the Kennedy Institute of Ethics at Georgetown, the Belmont Report, and the 1980-to-1983 Presidential Commission for the Study of Ethical Problems in Medicine and Biomedical and Behavioral Research.[66] He also mentions that bioethics has penetrated the realm of civil society, and civil society is the dwelling place of most religious institutions.

Civil society, deliberative democracy, and open deliberative processes are taking increasingly global forms. These are aided by the World Wide Web, the Internet, and other communications technologies, as well as transportation opportunities that permit events such as the international AIDS conferences, the world congresses sponsored by the International Association of Bioethics, and protests at global trade talks. Though elites are more likely to attend than "grassroots" representatives, the latter are not lacking, and activists of every stripe and class are on wide display.

These transformations are part of human nature as social, as political, and of course as changing. Our religious and moral charge is to maximize their potential for participation and democracy, including heretofore excluded persons, groups, and interests. Our mandate is also to encourage, if not ensure, global participation that results in more egalitarian access to basic human goods, rather than in violent responses to disadvantages that groups have experienced or fear that they may experience, or in more effective means to conscript disproportionate goods for proprietary use. Which of these conversions of human nature is any specific technology likely to embody? I will leave that question as the guide to assess it morally, with the theological proviso that the Christian moral standard is—or at least should be—the preferential option for the poor.

Technological Worlds and the Birth of Nature: On Human Creation and Its Theological Resonance in Heidegger and Serres

Thomas A. Carlson

If the category of nature seems to grow questionable today, it does so largely in relation to a late-modern or postmodern humanity that devises and exercises technological and scientific powers that appear threatening, both existentially and conceptually, not only to "nature" but also to the "human," and perhaps above all to the human in whatever we might count as *its* distinctive nature. Appeals, then, to "save" our human nature grow more energetic in the measure that emerging technoscience promises to reshape categories long held to define securely or locate clearly the human in its nature. In this direction, nearly everything can seem up for grabs, from the place, scope, and character of human intelligence and agency—on which the human may have less exclusive claim than once thought, in contrast both with the animal and with the machine—to the borders of so-called natural human life.

Thus it is that a figure such as Leon Kass can warn—in reference to emerging biotechnical powers associated with genetic and reproductive technologies, neuroscience and psychopharmacology, artificial organs, and the like—that "human nature itself lies on the operating table, ready for alteration," and that "for anyone who cares about preserving our human-ity, the time has come to pay attention" so that we might resist the evange-lists of a "posthuman future."[1] So likewise can a writer such as Bill

McKibben worry, with equal energy if from another end of the political and cultural spectrum, that "staying human in an engineered age" will require that we address and close off the possibility raised by genetics today "that we will engineer ourselves out of existence."[2]

In order to clarify what may be at stake in such anxieties surrounding the human, its nature, and their potential loss, we should inquire, of course, into the assumptions being made about human nature that would allow our increasingly technological worlds even to suggest such a threat. Along those lines, I would note straightaway that warnings about the need to protect and preserve the human in its nature can tend in two different, if not contradictory, directions (often taken by a single individual).

For many, especially those working from the presuppositions of a modern liberal humanism and its individualistic conception of the human, the ostensible threat of technological and scientific development—from genetics and biotechnology to cybernetics and artificial intelligence—concerns the intellectual and agentive self-possession or self-determination, and hence also the responsibility, that is or should be distinctive to any human being. On this take, the human being is understood first and foremost as an individual endowed "by nature," recall, with certain rights and properties, beginning with the right and property of individual property itself. Given such an understanding, human nature, as well as nature more broadly, can understandably seem threatened by scientifically driven technology that escapes the control of human individuals—often, indeed, turning back to act upon human existence to reshape its conditions in unexpected, uncontrolled, and hence dispossessing or even inhuman ways.

In her 1999 book *How We Became Posthuman: Virtual Bodies in Cybernetics, Literature, and Informatics*, N. Katherine Hayles demonstrates well, I think, that a good deal of anxiety over perceived technoscientific threat to the human is premised on such liberal humanist suppositions that the human is rightly and best understood in terms of such individual self-possession and self-determination, so that a technological world exercising intelligence and agency beyond the intentions of any human individual and, indeed, acting back upon us in a manner beyond our control could appear as a danger to the human itself. As Hayles points out, the father of "cybernetics" himself, Norbert Wiener, worries along just these liberal humanist lines that "the science of control might rob its progenitor of the very control that was no doubt for him one of its most attractive features."[3]

This first direction of concern, stemming largely from liberal humanist premises, can be contrasted with an opposite worry, perhaps the more interesting and the one on which I will focus here: a worry not about ostensible threats to the definition or location and hence to the autonomy and control of the human, but more about the threat of too much certainty or too much security concerning just who and where the human is or should be—a certainty and security often seen to go hand in hand with a will to mastery thought to be operative within technoscientific attempts to mold or indeed to control all of nature, human and otherwise. Along this latter path, one no longer assumes that the human should be in control, or autonomous, in order then to debate whether and how technology and its science either increase or undermine such control or autonomy; rather, one suspects that something essential about human nature is threatened—or already lost—within those forms of thinking and living that assume as highest good and as primary goal the very project of such control. One suspects that the drive to eliminate all chance and unknowing from human experience through rational calculation and technological self-assertion fundamentally undermines or misunderstands our distinctively human freedom and finitude—which might themselves speak against any secure definition or comprehension of the human.

It can be illuminating, I think, to frame these two different directions of concern over the implications of technology for the nature of human existence in light of two different tendencies within the history of theological anthropology. Within that history, the idea that the human is created in the image of God can be taken in two divergent senses, one more positive, or *kataphatic*, and the other more negative, or *apophatic*. The first posits some definition or knowledge of what or who, in its basic nature, the human is or should be; it lets the human know its place as image of God. The second insists, rather, that as an image of God, the human is, like that God, ultimately beyond any final definition or secure comprehension, which means beyond the kind of location that alone allows for definition. This latter tendency in the history of theological anthropology—one emphasizing that the human itself is a mystery or incomprehensible, and one thus claiming that the distinction or definition of the human may well be its lack of distinction or definition—has significant analogues in modern and contemporary philosophies that understand the human and its nature not as defined and knowable given but as an irreducibly open question and always ongoing project, the function of an inexhaustible possibility that might demand an indeterminate figure of the human as work of an "indiscrete image."[4]

If versions of such negative anthropology can be traced through modern and contemporary philosophy just as well as through the deeper histories of theological speculation on the human, in both directions the definition of the human as lacking definition is often meant to highlight the inescapably creative or poetic—and, indeed, technological—character of the human as open question and ongoing project. To forget the human's definitive lack of definition, from this perspective, to provide an answer on the human as defined or definable actuality, would be to efface the human as creature—and creator—of always open possibility.

A key question, then, with respect to the human and our emerging technological worlds is whether and how the technological threatens to efface the human as open question by turning the human into a managed actuality; or whether and how our technological being rather intensifies even as it depends on the questionable character of the human—and on the always open possibility of human nature as ongoing creation or, indeed, birth. Attending to its theological resonance, I engage this question here through a comparative reading of Martin Heidegger, rightly influential exemplar of this first claim, and Michel Serres, a recent proponent of the second, and I aim through that reading to advance an understanding both of human nature as a form of ongoing birth and of technologically structured worlds—which in fact all worlds are—as a condition of such birth.

An extreme of the human's removal from the openness of questioning or of its reduction to the logic of manageable actuality can be glimpsed in the "total lack of questioning" that Heidegger associates with modern metaphysics and with the machination of modernity's technoscientific culture. These in concert, Heidegger insists, would subject all of nature—human and otherwise—to the project of a rational comprehension and calculation whose relentless concern with organization and manipulation, planning and production, aspires ultimately to a thoroughgoing control of existence.

In his much discussed 1953 lecture "The Question Concerning Technology," Heidegger argues that the essence of technology in modernity is to be seen not so much in our tools themselves as in modernity's distinctive way of staging—of "enframing" or "constructing"—the real, its distinctive way of setting those conditions according to which and thus the manner in which beings are ever allowed to appear at all.[5] Reducing all being, including human being itself, first to objectivity and eventually to what he calls "standing-reserve" (*das Bestand*), the "enframing" (*das Gestell*) of being in the essence of modern technology brings beings to appearance in a manner that might be contrasted with that of *poiesis*. While *poiesis* "brings forth" beings in a way that the human for whom those beings appear remains open to a call that the human does not produce or control, enframing "sets upon" being or "challenges forth" being in and through processes of regulating and making, in such a way that the real must show itself as that which is stored up and kept constantly accessible for human comprehension, manipulation, and exploitation.

This difference between technological enframing and poetic revealing can be glimpsed, Heidegger suggests, in the difference between a Rhine River dammed up and kept on store, at our command, as a reliable source of energy for the machinations of an industrialized and capitalistic humanity, and a Rhine River that appears in the poetry of Friedrich Hölderlin, where we encounter the Rhine not as hydroelectric power plant under the control of technologically calculating man but as something more like an artwork whose self-revealing, comparable to that of a "nature" that modernity would have eclipsed and forgotten, calls to man on its own terms rather than answering conditions set by man.[6]

These two figures of the Rhine, stemming from two different modes of revealing, suggest, indeed, two quite different faces of nature. Whereas the Rhine that appears in or as poetic artwork would recall an understanding of *physis* as the coming forth of something into appearance out of itself (the core of Heidegger's definition of the phenomenon), the Rhine that appears as power plant—or, for that matter, as an occasion for prepackaged vacation experience—answers to a more modern sense of nature as a calculable coherence of forces open to the rational representation or comprehension and hence the technological manipulation, exploitation, or even mastery of man.[7] While the former face of nature requires the openness of man to that for whose appearance he does not set the conditions, to that which he does not produce conceptually or technically, the latter form of nature would be the function of a human thought and practice that closes the human to any appearance or any call that the human does not first condition by such rational-technical means.

The real threat to humanity signaled by modern technology, from this perspective, is not to be found in the lethal devices with which we might irreparably damage or destroy actually existing humans or the natural world they currently inhabit; the threat rests more in "the possibility that it could be denied to [man] to enter into a more original revealing [than that of technological enframing] and hence to experience the call of a more primal truth."[8] Man is closed to such a call insofar as "the illusion comes to prevail that everything man encounters exists only as his construct" such that "it seems as though man everywhere and always encounters only himself."[9] In such "subservience to the challenging forth of enframing," modernity's technological human "fails to see himself as the one spoken to, and hence also fails . . . to hear in what respect he ek-sists, in terms of his essence, in a realm where he is addressed, so that he can never encounter only himself."[10]

In these terms of enframing and standing-reserve, "The Question Concerning Technology" extends the definition and critique of modern metaphysics that Heidegger develops at some length in earlier writings such as *Introduction to Metaphysics* (1935), "Age of the World Picture" (1938), and the posthumously published *Contributions to Philosophy (From Enowning)* (1936–1938).[11] If every metaphysics involves an understanding of being and a definition of truth, he posits, the metaphysics that grounds technological modernity, coming to expression in a founding figure such as René Descartes, understands being as objectivity and truth as the certainty achieved by a rational, thinking human subject who represents to itself all being as thus objectified.[12] Conceptually, this rational subject becomes the ground and measure or, indeed, the producer of all that is (or of all that is allowed to appear as a being), and the logic of such conceptual production carries over into the technological forms of making that come to shape modern culture so deeply.

While perhaps seeming to stand at odds with traditional Christian theology, where created man would be humbly subjected to his Creator God and hence stand more in the passive position of reception than in the self-assertive position of active production, the reign of human technicity in modernity, on Heidegger's account, actually repeats and extends the theologic of a Christian metaphysics in which every being (save God) is a created being, conceived and brought forth by the Creator, who is himself taken as the highest being and first cause of all other beings. Just as for Christian metaphysics every being appears only as conceived and produced by this highest being, God, to whose causal control all is subjected, so for modern metaphysics and its technicity, beings appear first and mainly as the rationally conceivable and producible and hence technologically manageable (and even that which may initially appear beyond rational comprehension and calculation is taken as *eventually* comprehensible and calculable; this is the attitude that Max Weber well defines at the heart of a disenchanted world[13]). "It is in this connection," Heidegger writes in *Contributions to Philosophy*:

> that what belongs to machination now [in the transition from Greek *physis* to the medieval Christian *actus*] presses forward more clearly and that *ens* becomes *ens creatum* in the Judaeo-Christian notion of creation, when the corresponding idea of God enters into the picture. Even if one refuses

crudely to interpret the idea of creator, what is still essential is beings' being-caused. The cause-effect connection becomes all-dominating (god as *causa sui*). That is an essential distancing from *physis* and at the same time the crossing toward the emergence of machination as what is ownmost to beingness in modern thinking.[14]

Such a metaphysical conception of God as highest being and cause of all other beings finds an exemplary modern instance, for Heidegger and his heirs, in the interpretation of God according to Leibniz's principle of sufficient reason, which holds that "nothing is without reason, or no effect is without a cause."[15] In his close reading of Leibniz in the 1957 work *The Principle of Reason*, Heidegger emphasizes that the ideal of completeness or perfection operative in the principle of sufficient reason, as tied especially to the security of calculation concerning objectified being, is key to understanding modernity as a technological age. "Without really understanding it," Heidegger writes:

> we know today that modern technology intractably presses toward bringing its contrivances and products to an all-embracing, greatest-possible perfection. This perfection consists in the completeness of the calculably secure establishing of objects, in the completeness of reckoning with them and with the securing of the calculability of possibilities for reckoning. . . . Modern technology pushes toward the greatest possible perfection. Perfection is based on the thoroughgoing calculability of objects. The calculability of objects presupposes the unqualified validity of the *principium rationis*. It is in this way that the authority of the principle of reason determines the essence of the modern, technological age.[16]

If in this way the principle of sufficient reason entails the will to a rational completeness and objective calculability that are echoed in the will to mastery of a technological modernity, the conception of God as first cause according to the principle of sufficient reason effectively subjects that God to the human project of conceptual and practical mastery of "the world."

Within this frame, God serves as that one being who allows us to account for all other beings in their totality, and thus he supports our effort to represent or conceive the world as a whole—to reduce the world to a "world-picture" or a "worldview," which means to an object of representation that we, the rational subject, form or define and thus, on the basis of such definition, comprehend and seek to manage.[17] Thus conceived as a highest causal being who, by rendering reason, allows us to represent or comprehend the world, to make some rational sense of it, this God of reason—sometimes called the God of the philosophers—really makes the rational *human subject* the measure and condition for the appearance of all beings—including, to begin with, God, and then, by extension, all of nature.

Both nature and its God, then, no longer give themselves on their own terms, to which we would have to answer; rather, they are made to answer and appear in accordance with the conditions of *our* rational capacities and the needs of our technological self-assertion. The conception of God as highest cause, in short, goes hand in hand with the conception—which means the objectification—of nature in terms of a rationality that enables calculation and its technological forms of control: "In the light of causality, God can sink to the level of a cause, a *causa efficiens*. He then becomes even in theology the God of the philosophers, namely of those who define the unconcealed and the concealed in terms of the causality of making, without ever considering the essential provenance of this causality."[18]

Of course, all of this, for Heidegger, entails a way of thinking that misunderstands human existence and worldhood alike by attempting to make present as a defined object what in fact cannot be so represented, and for two interrelated reasons: first, because we find ourselves always already within a world and so cannot stand outside or apart from it as a representing subject in relation to a represented object; and second, because in any case, "world" means an irreducibly open network of reference relations, which are relations of practice and possibility, and not a bounded thing whose outlines could be located so as to constitute a definite, objective, and discretely present actuality. If, within the thinking that reduces world to picture and God to cause, nature presents itself "as a calculable complex of forces," and if such a presentation "can indeed permit correct determinations," it remains the case, Heidegger warns, "that in the midst of all that is correct the true will withdraw."[19]

This distinction between the correct and the true can be understood productively, I think, in relation to the difference Heidegger makes between the "ontic" and the "ontological," insofar as these signal two different ways of understanding possibility. If "the correct" concerns a thinking that represents and calculates with regard to actual or eventually actual beings (thus amounting to an ontic thinking), "the true" would concern that opening or unconcealment in which alone any such beings might ever appear as beings—but which itself could never be made exhaustively present in any given being nor in the sum total of all eventually actual beings (thus amounting to an ontological thinking). By tracing all beings, as such and in their totality, back to yet another being (albeit a "highest being"), the metaphysical conception of God, as exemplified in the principle of sufficient reason, forgets the difference between possibility taken in an ontic sense and possibility taken in an ontological sense.

We can sense what is at stake in this difference between ontic possibility, which concerns an eventually actual this or that, and ontological possibility, which concerns the structural and temporal openness of the "to be," in light of the analysis in *Being and Time* (1927) of finite human existence as being-in-the-world: in that finite, worldly existence, I am, as *Dasein*, always still yet "to be" (or always still "not yet" all that I "can be"), according to a potentiality for being that is never converted into or exhausted by any present actuality (any ontic being) that I might represent or comprehend so as to relate to it as an object of rational calculation and technological control.

Heidegger's critique of Christian metaphysics, of its extension in the principle of sufficient reason, and of the technoscientific culture defined by that principal can thus be read to concern, at bottom, this reduction of ontological possibility, which remains finally incalculable and unmanageable, to the logic of ontic actuality, which sustains the project of mastery that Heidegger sees at the heart of modernity's calculative thought and technological being. Both the God of the philosophers and the rational subject of modern metaphysics would exercise such a reduction of the ontological to the ontic, of world to picture, and of nature to the calculable coherence of forces, in and through the dominating logic of the cause-effect relation.[20] Through the foreclosure of possibility effected by this domination of the cause-effect relation or through the "preponderance of the makeable and self-making," Heidegger worries, technological modernity threatens to eclipse the self-giving of nature and the finite human's constitutive openness to the foreign.[21]

The question arises here, however, whether more recent theorizations of our technological worlds might not offer a slightly different perspective and whether that perspective might not open or recall alternative understandings of human creation and its theological resonance.

Among contemporary philosophers in the European context, Michel Serres stands out for his deeply affirmative stance on the creative potential of our emerging technoscientific worlds—a stance highlighting *within* the technoscientific sphere forms of possibility that Heidegger mainly believes that sphere to close off. Through the technological realm itself, Serres suggests, we are perhaps unsettling more than we are extending the logic of modern and Christian metaphysics as Heidegger understands them, and we are doing so by engaging in forms of creation that are not amenable to the logic of rational representation and calculation, technical production and control—which means also not constrained by the priority of actuality over possibility or by the reduction of all possibility to the eventually actual.

Serres evokes such interplay between creation and possibility through an explicit rewriting of the scene with which Leibniz concludes his *Theodicy*. There, the character Theodorus is led by the goddess Pallas to the summit of a bottomless pyramid, which represents the actual, the only, and the best world, below which stands the infinity of possible worlds that God, in his role as reason of creation, considered ahead of time but finally did not choose and thus abandoned. In our technological worlds today, Serres suggests, we are in effect turning from the notion of that one and actual world, as preformed in its necessity and intelligibility according to the principle of sufficient reason, and we are exposing ourselves to the infinitely possible or the virtual—as the irreducibly open future of a human self-creation that transpires by means of technological and scientific networks that always exceed us and recurrently re-create us.

Such self-creation is notable here for two related reasons. First, it unsettles the understanding of God that many, with Heidegger, consider *the* metaphysical concept par excellence, that is, God as some version of the principle of sufficient reason, a highest being and first cause that guarantees the necessity and the intelligibility of the natural order; and second, it understands the human, correspondingly, as defined by its lack of settled definition or, which amounts to the same, as finding its nature in processes of ongoing birth made and kept possible by just such lack. Along these two lines, creation is best understood not as preformation of the eventually actual but as the sustained opening and cultivation of the possible in its possibility.

If metaphysics, as Heidegger understands it, conceives God according to a logic of causality and intelligibility that is taken up and extended by modernity's calculative thought and technological culture, and if Heidegger and his heirs take Leibniz's principle of sufficient reason as metaphysical name par excellence for such a God, Serres finds in our technological worlds an occasion to rethink causality and the principle of reason in a manner that departs from the modernity of Heidegger's analysis. "The causality of the producer," Serres insists in his 2004 book *Rameaux*, is weaker than Heidegger's modernity would have us believe, and creation, notably in the technological sphere, does not amount to "preformation."[22] In other words, the logic of finality that dominates the cause-effect relation as conceived in modernity's calculative thought is, as often as not, resisted and unsettled by the technological itself: "You would have never to have held one in your hand in order to believe that a tool is always made for one and only one use, clearly conceived and fully mastered [*asservi*]," Serres insists, going on to note that "the story of technologies participates in the same contingency as that of evolution."[23] This proves to be so in the measure that the worlds we create technologically also re-create us in unexpected ways, such that we actually participate in the open and ongoing creation, or birth, of nature "itself."

Indeed, in the natural realm as in the technological—and the two prove, for the human who emerges in Serres, inextricable—we are not subjected to the already given and fixed laws of a stable actuality so much as we are ever newborn, constantly opened and opening ourselves to unforeseeable slippages and shiftings between actuality and possibility. "We live not so much immersed in a fatal series of foreseeable causes, in an irrecusably necessary reality," Serres elaborates:

> as in an extraordinary game where the actual or the probable lose their weight in relation to the inactual, to the symbolic, to the unforeseen. . . . What appears here and now dramatic and pressing soon dissipates, and that whose importance no one sees becomes, in a patient or sudden way, the essential. What is necessary today veers quickly toward the impossible, and the contingent, suddenly, changes into necessity, the reasonable into the imbecilic and the alien into the rational.[24]

From this perspective, which recognizes the instability and the incalculable character of evolving cause-effect relations where the rational is ever exposed to the alien, the principle of sufficient reason and understandings of creation bound to it would need to be reimagined.

The conception of creation as preformation, which supposes "that there could exist a reason that integrates the totality of causes in such a way that the course of subsequent time would deploy that reason and refer back to it alone,"[25] must give way to the contingency and unknowing that give creation its freedom. If the vocal opponents of evolution today, and indeed of scientific thinking more broadly, speak often in the name of a God whose "creation" would amount to just this kind of preformation, the understanding of creation opened here would resonate with a God who himself remains open to or participant in the kind of contingency and unknowing we might see in our own biological—and technological—evolution:

> Contingent, we fabricate the contingent; evolution produces us as producers of evolution. . . . [T]he more our knowledge advances, the more we notice our contingency, that of the world and of our actions. Except in

cases of extreme simplicity, we have made and we will make the unforeseen. The more we approximate the Creator, the less we imitate providence. We do not pre-form anything or anyone: teachers do not form parrots. . . . Children disobey: *felix culpa*, that happy fault sometimes allows them to avoid the obstacles accumulated by our formats. . . . Let me highlight the definition of our new era: contingent evolution produces a producer of contingent evolution.[26]

Integral to this understanding of a human creation conditioned by unknowing is a determination of the human as inescapably indeterminate. Tensed dynamically between the necessity of reliable formats or codes and the contingency of unforeseeable branching of format and rewriting of code, a creation distinct from preformation requires the human unknowing and indetermination that would allow for something other than the programmatic repetition that can be figured as much by divine providence as by notions of genetic determinism or technological automatism. The image of creative humanity that emerges here is one in which the human proves creative—and technological—thanks to its indetermination and unknowing as well as the reverse: the more programmed the creature, the more set in its place, the less creative and adaptable; the less programmed the creature and the less set in its place, the freer for technological and other forms of creativity.

Such a take on the human as creative and technological thanks to its indetermination or lack of definition has a deep and varied history, from relatively recent biological and evolutionary understandings of the human as neotenic or pedomorphic back into the long traditions of mystical theology, where the human is with striking recurrence understood to be creative insofar as it remains, like the Creator God in whose image the human is made, beyond comprehension or definition, which means beyond discrete location.[27] Very notably in the nascent modernity of figures such as Nicholas of Cusa, Giordano Bruno, and Giovanni Pico della Mirandola, these traditions suggest that the creative human imitates the Creator God not through the mimetic repetition of fixed or pregiven archetypes so much as in the free and dynamic creation of new forms that have no prior models, or ways of being that are without precedent.[28]

In this way, the human can be understood to imitate the divine act of creation ex nihilo, and creation without pregiven archetypes would entail also, in the absence of any one given end, an infinite multiplication of ends by and for the human.[29] From this perspective, the principle of sufficient reason could be understood to derive from an anxious refusal of the world's being "without reason," its absence of any one foundation or end—and hence from a refusal of the world's resistance to the comprehensive representation of any "world-picture." It is this absence of finality and this impossibility of comprehensive representation, I contend, that keep open the space and time of free human creation, just as it is such an absence of finality, far more than any objective threat, that may best account for the anxieties engendered by our emerging technologies.[30]

Reading the technological along these lines can open for us an important alternative to the Heideggerian take on technological modernity—so as even to suggest an ethical affirmation of the cybernetic, which would itself prove intimate to the natural. By contrast with Heidegger, for whom the cybernetic becomes perhaps *the* figure of modernity's drive to total control through the "coercive steering" of relentless calculation, organization, planning, production, and so on, Serres understands the cybernetic in terms related to its maritime origins, that is, in terms of creative adaptation to those incessant variations—of our worlds and of ourselves, of the natural and the sociocultural in their interplay—that we never fully foresee, no less control, but in which we inevitably and essentially participate:[31] "Let us govern productions whose behavior we never—once and for all and before the fact—decide. Following the lessons obtained in the course of their evolution, let us inflect our decisions in real time, in practicing the prudence of the pilot."[32]

Against the kinds of acosmism and gnosticism that do often shape the discourse and thinking of many cyberenthusiasts today, the cybernetic ethic suggested by Serres would highlight and attend to the complex and inextricable ties, and hence the fundamental con-tract, between man and world or between the human and nature and hence between the ethico-political and the natural-scientific—both sides now construed in broader and more relational terms than is the norm for a modernity that tends to think the social world without the natural, and vice versa. As our discussion should by now suggest, such a "natural" contract must also be understood as an essentially "virtual" contract, for it concerns not only the actuality that is now or will eventually be but also the open possibility of what could be and hence the future of possibility itself; it concerns, that is, nature in the sense of ongoing and unmasterable birth. "Let us agree on the natural contract with daughters and sons, *naturae* and *naturi*, those women and men [*celles et ceux*] of the future generations. As a complementary audaciousness, the same status as subject of right is extended to possible things, *natura*, to the things to come."[33] If we think the natural and the virtual in these terms, together, then the future of birth comes to form the "transcendental condition of knowledge and action."[34] How to think and act in relation to these things and persons to come, such that we might keep open for them the possibility of birth, and hence of nature? The response to such a question will need, among other things, to reflect on the nature of worldly care with respect to futurity.

Heidegger himself already offers important clues pointing in this direction in *Being and Time*, where he distinguishes between two extremes of the positive care, or solicitude (*Fürsorge*), that an individual might exercise toward others. This distinction seems to me especially suggestive in light of the contrast evoked above—through the examples of parent and teacher—between creation and preformation. In one extreme of positive solicitude, Heidegger notes, I can "jump in" for the other or take the place of the other (*sich an seine Stelle setzen, für ihn einspringen*) in such a way that I take over his concern, actualizing for him his projected possibilities so as even to deprive the other of his own potentiality-for-being, thus placing him in a dependence, or in-authenticity, through which I dominate or dispossess him. "This kind of solicitude," Heidegger writes:

> takes over for the Other that with which he is to concern himself. The Other is thus thrown out of his own position; he steps back so that afterwards, when the matter has been attended to, he can either take it over as something finished and at his disposal, or disburden himself of it completely. In such solicitude the Other can become one who is dominated and dependent, even if this domination is a tacit one and remains hidden from him. This kind of solicitude, which leaps in and takes away "care," is to a large extent determinative for Being with one another.[35]

At the other extreme of my solicitude for the other, by contrast, I do not jump in for the other so as to make things actual for him, but I leap ahead of him in order to make possible for him his own distinctive possibility or potentiality for being, or care. I "*leap ahead* of him [*ihm voraussp-ringt*] in his existential potentiality-for-Being," as Heidegger puts it:

> not in order to take away his 'care' but rather to give it back to him authentically as such for the first time. This kind of solicitude pertains essentially to authentic care—that is, to the existence of the Other, not to a '*what*' with which he is concerned; it helps the Other to become transparent to himself *in* his care and to become *free for* it.[36]

As I note above, in "The Question Concerning Technology" Heidegger worries that technology, by reducing the logic of all possibility to the logic of eventual actuality, aims to place all being, natural and human, "on call" for man, so that man is himself closed to any call whose conditions he has not already established as familiar. Recalling that worry here, we can say that the essence of modern technology for Heidegger threatens to do to man what this first form of solicitude in *Being and Time* does to the other: take away from him the freedom—which means also the burden and the danger—of genuine care by reducing the other's existential projection of possibility to the calculative forecast or providence of some actuality, all of which effectively deprives the other of a genuine world. Both the solicitude that "jumps in" and the technology that would reduce all being to calculated and managed actuality deprive the other of what is most his own—which is precisely not an actuality, nor a given nature in the sense of defined property, but an open potentiality for being in the world, or a nature in the sense of ongoing birth.

When Heidegger worries that the essence of technology may close human being to the foreignness of any genuine call, the worry is, in other terms, that the incalculable openness of our ontological possibility, the never yet determined or exhausted "to be" in which alone the worldly human being exists, will be reduced to or confused with the mere calculation, organization, and management of ontic possibilities—possibilities, that is, that are or can eventually be converted into some present, objectively defined actuality.[37] In all of its strangeness, the call to which Heidegger and his heirs want to keep the human open is that which calls us not simply away from ourselves but also, thereby, back to ourselves and to what is most "our own." But what is most our own is emphatically not a possession or property, not a nature in the sense of traits held secure, but instead the possibility or potentiality of that nature which entails birth.

It is such a nature, as capacity for birth, that more recent thinking like Serres's can see operative, as Heidegger mainly does not, within our technological worlds today. Indeed, one might today glimpse as operative in and through the technological something akin more to a solicitude that leaps ahead in order to open possibility than to one that jumps in to predetermine actuality. This is where an evocation of the parent and teacher, in the distinction between creation and preformation, can be instructive. What the technological may give, on this take, would be much like that which caring parents and teachers aim to give: not finished actuality but the open possibility of another existence that would itself have the capacity for care.

As any thoughtful parent or teacher well realizes, however, we can never actually see clearly or determine with unshakable certainty when it is that we are leaping ahead so as to give the other her genuine possibility and thus her care, and when it is that we are more jumping in to make everything actual for her—already managed or programmed—in such a way that she loses her care. How we decide on such a distinction in any given moment and thus how we work to make care and its possibility possible for others is in fact a deep mystery—and one that has everything to do, I suspect, with love. On this point and perhaps even on technology's capacity to conspire with such love, we might finally posit a suggestive if unexpected proximity between the differing tendencies of thought that I am sketching out with Heidegger and Serres.

If Heidegger takes the openness of possibility to be what is most threatened by the essence of technology in modernity, he also suggests at points that our technological existence may yet expose us to something like that foreign call that calls us back to ourselves by calling us beyond ourselves, or even something like that indetermination in which Serres sees the freedom of our nature as a freedom of birth: "Human beings are caught [*gestellt*], claimed, and challenged," Heidegger states in his 1966 interview with *Der Spiegel*:

> by a power that is revealed in the essence of technology. The experience that humans are structured [*gestellt*] by some-thing that they are not themselves and that they cannot control themselves is precisely the experience that may show them the possibility of the insight that humans are needed by Being. The possibility of experience, of being needed, and of being prepared for these new possibilities is concealed in what makes up what is most modern technology's own. Thinking can do nothing more than to help humans to this insight, and philosophy is at an end.[38]

If the essence of technology can well close man to possibility and its call through a reduction of all being to actuality or even to the standing-reserve that swallows world and care alike, it may also reveal to the human, as this passage suggests, that the human, as *Dasein*, is always already conditioned and called by something that the human does not and cannot control. If such a condition and call "make possible," if they keep open the possibility of birth or the birth of possibility, and in such a way that humans are "needed by Being," then they may also, in a fundamental way, entail the work of love.

As Heidegger suggests in his 1947 "Letter on Humanism," it may well be that to "make possible" or to "let be" another person or thing means in the end to love or to favor that person or thing (*sie lieben, sie mögen*). Such love enables, I would emphasize, not by giving this or that actuality but by granting the possibility of possibility itself:

Such favoring is the proper essence of enabling [*des Vermögens*], which not only can achieve this or that but also can let something essentially unfold in its provenance, that is, let it be. It is on the "strength" of such enabling by favoring that something is properly able to be.[39]

If this take on love in Heidegger, like the distinction just noted between two extremes of solicitude, can be read to extend, implicitly, conceptions of love and care operative in the St. Augustine to whom the young Heidegger attends explicitly, the recent work of Serres also evokes more straightforwardly a Christian-Pauline sense of love when he suggests the need to glimpse or to place love at the heart of the natural and hence virtual contracts that we form throughout our technological worlds today.[40] If the nature of the human, as natal, is to remain "without nature," if it is ever to exceed, by altering recurrently, the givenness of code and the fixedness of definition, then it might well be love and its generosity that sustain a humankind conditioned by the strangeness of relations it cannot calculate or comprehend:

> Charity, finally, saturates with love our relations with others. Inverting the contractual relationships, political or juridical, of our old forms of belonging, this total tie [*lien total*] to others is bound up with a complete doubt about reciprocity. No matter what response meets it . . . it still loves, it "excuses all, *believes* all, *hopes* all, bears all" (I Cor. 13:7). Its omnitude integrates faith and hope and plunges, with even less assurance, into the fluctuating and dangerous contingency that is characteristic of relations. Adventurous and generous—from the same family as humankind [*genre humain*] the word generosity repeats the word gentile, used in the expression that defines Saint Paul as the Apostle to the gentiles, that is, to the strangers—this integration allows the new *I* to be in relation with the universality of people [*des hommes*], no matter what origin their form of belonging might claim. . . . Faith, hope and love describe the non-ontology of this subject: its non-installation, its non-assurance.[41]

Might such nonbelonging, such openness to our own strangeness, suggest one way to understand the unconditional condition of our ongoing and always technological birth, one way to glimpse the sense in which we are, in our nature, without nature? And if so, how might we enact a love that answers to such a condition?

PART FIVE

Theology without Nature?

The title of this volume is posed with a question mark as a provocation to encourage reflection. Ultimately, many of the contributions from different disciplinary fields resist the suggestion that contemporary ethics is "without nature." Since nature is the indispensable substrate of human life, and since the relationship to nature is always mediated by "second nature," one cannot become divested of nature, as nature was never unambiguously owned. Each of the three papers in this section suggests that we are not "without nature" because the relationship to nature has always been more hermeneutically complex than mere possession or dispossession would allow. Each also proposes a new framework for reapproaching old questions about nature: a general ethics of "life," the "ecosociality" of nature's political representation, and a reconstruction of "grace."

William Schweiker proposes that contemporary bioethics and ecological ethics share a common concern for the status of life, whatever the status of nature may be. But it is a theological mistake for ethics to promote reverence for life itself rather than for life's integrity. Indeed, the "integrity of life" functions well as a more practical substitute for older concepts of "nature." Since the term "life" indicates the human, the animal, and the broader ecosphere unequivocally, it helps curb Western religious tendencies toward anthropocentrism. At the same time it gestures toward human value that persists despite its increasingly dramatic determination by genetic and other technologies. Ethical action, then, amounts to relieving the agon inherent to life, that is, to restoring harmony to the living whole, whose unity is God. Where the concept of "nature" separates God and the world and permits the human being to withdraw herself from the biosphere, the concept of "life" roots human dignity precisely within its natural home and links all forms of life more intimately with the "Life" that is divine.

Peter Scott points out the political shortcomings of the rhetoric of "postnaturality." Scott helpfully notes how the political use of a given concept of nature has always worked hand in hand with its ecological or biological use. From this perspective, the function of nature in theology and ethics has been to establish legitimacy, and one can parse the political modes through which nature is grasped. Although nature is always represented in some way or another within every polity, its function is often to segregate human pursuits from nonhuman interests. Not only can humanity never be without nature; they belong together in a more original and never escapable relationship. Neglecting nature's political role within human communities can blind one to the occasions when the relationship breaks down, entering into tragic or apocalyptic modes.

Kathryn Tanner demonstrates how recent biological accounts of human plasticity in fact accord with the most ancient Christian theological understandings of human nature. That human nature is indefinite is a consequence of its being an image of the undefinable God. Just as God cannot be confined to a single definition or name, so, too, human being is intrinsically open to multiple possibilities and unconstrained by a single essence. Theological distinctions of nature and grace are therefore not imperiled by changing understandings of the natural in the contemporary physical and social science. Human nature is constantly reconstituted by virtue of its desire for and participation in the infinitely indeterminate God, of which it is an image.

Should We Reverence Life? Reflections at the Intersection of Ecology, Religion, and Ethics

William Schweiker

On many accounts we live in an age in which human and nonhuman life is endangered through environmental crisis, genetic manipulation, genocide, disease, and on and on. In this time, how ought one to think about the *worth* of life? This question is in many ways at the heart of the most heated debates in the United States and around the world. For many people it is obvious that morally and religiously sensitive individuals will endorse the belief that life is "sacred" and thus worthy of reverence, especially human life. For these people, we ought not to alter human life irrevocably nor lessen the distinctive value of the person from conception to death. Conversely, there is a host of thinkers and also popular movements that insist we must "unsanctify human life" in order to acknowledge the moral standing of animals and other forms of nonhuman life, including ecosystems. Still others look forward to a posthuman future through the genetic manipulation of the species. From debates about terrorism to stem cell research, from problems of global warming and biological diversity to euthanasia and abortion, the question of the value or moral standing of life in its various forms specifies a discursive space of religious, moral, and political contestation.

The task of this essay is to explore and assess just one of the terms of the current debate, namely, the idea of reverence for life. I want to do so in order to isolate problems in that idea and also to set forth in somewhat programmatic terms an ethics aimed at the *integrity of life*. The decisive move is to grasp that the will-to-live, and thus life qua life, is not an adequate focus for a contemporary ethics nor even the proper grounds of moral considerability. One needs to distinguish between the vitality of living beings and that at which vitality or power aims, or what it seeks or imposes upon itself, that is, integrity. The integrity of life is related but not reducible to the specific traits, capacities, and goods of a living being. At least this is what I am arguing. However, I imagine that immediate interest in this topic is really about how to answer the question that forms the title of the essay: Should we reverence life?

First of all, who is the "we" addressed in this question? I am using it in an inclusive sense to denote anyone who might ask about the moral status of life and living things. In this respect, my concern is with a subset of the orienting questions about "nature" posed by this book, since the scope of nature exceeds the realm of the living, at least conceptually speaking. The relevant "we" of this essay, then, is those persons and communities concerned about "living nature." Further, the title question does not presuppose specific religious convictions; moreover, a valid answer to it cannot, in my judgment, be specified just for members of some community, religious or not. In what follows, I draw on religious resources for the purposes of understanding our shared moral situation and the demands of responsibility. Those resources are not self-validating, however.

About my answer to the question: it is, in a nutshell, yes and no. The answer is yes, we ought to view life reverently because, despite its ambiguity, the discourse of "reverence for life" intends to signal the depth and seriousness of moral being, a depth and seriousness that is too easily eroded or ignored in a situation when all forms of life can be enfolded within the reach of technological power. Responsibility is about how people organize and are accountable for the exercise of power in response to others. The idea of "reverence for life" denotes, then, the way in which the moral quality of human existence depends on how we respond to what has worth outside of human determination and power. The conditions of responsibility, that is, the reality and worth of others as well as accountability for power at one's disposal, are things we reject or lose at grave peril to our existence as well as to the sustainability of life on this planet. This is why I hope to show that a religious claim encoded in the language of reverence continues to echo in social and personal life. However, it is also part of my argument that an adequate answer to the framing question of this essay must be no. The discourse of "reverence for life" is theologically confused and does a very poor job of clarifying and answering the moral issues we need to address, including that to which we are responsible. So my argument is not going to fall into the usual ideological options playing themselves out in current social life.

This essay moves in some broad steps. First, we need some clarity about what the idea of "reverence for life" means and how it might relate to "respect for life" or "dignity of life" or "sanctity of life." The second step is to chart the range of questions that swirl around debates over reverence for life. If we can attain some purchase on such ideas and questions, we might gain insight into the deeper currents working in the contemporary social world. These two initial steps of the essay form a moral interpretation of the social situation found in technologically advanced nations like our own. The third step is to turn to the history of modern thought and briefly to engage the thinker who launched the idea of "reverence for life" into ethics. As is well known, Albert Schweitzer was a theologian, biblical scholar, medical doctor, musician, Nobel Prize winner, and a man interested in various religions. He famously developed an ethics of reverence for life that continues to influence thought. While there are other positions one needs to address on this topic, why I have chosen to explore Schweitzer's ethics will become clearer in the pages that follow.[1]

The journey of reflection now outlined leads, finally, to some critical and constructive reflections on my part about the integrity of life, rather than reverence for life, as the core of a viable ethics of responsibility for our age. This ethics must speak to the widespread and pervasive sensibilities now permeating global social life, but in a way that will mark a cognitive gain over the evocative but problematic discourse of reverence for life. The cognitive gain, surprisingly enough, will entail theological insights necessary to decode currents in social existence and to reassess how to think about the moral status of life. This is not to suggest that one must be explicitly religious in order to be moral. That claim is patently false, in my judgment. I do contend that religious and theological reflection, the kinds of judgments and forms of understanding they entail, can and must help us to diagnose and also respond to what is happening in our global social situation.

Let me turn now to the confusion surrounding the idea of the reverence for life.

Conceptual Confusions

At first blush, the question "Should we reverence life?" seems like a big question and, indeed, a big problem. There can be little doubt about its social, political, and religious resonance. Answers to it pit conservatives against progressives. It is often used to cast religious people as antiscientific and woodenly dogmatic or conversely to paint advocates of genetic manipulation, abortion, or voluntary euthanasia as somehow against life. The rhetoric reached a shrill pitch in the supposed clash between a culture of life and a culture of death, to note terms used by both John Paul II and President George W. Bush. Yet it is also true that some deep ecologists and ecological theologians speak of the Earth as sacred and thereby encourage reverence for the whole ecosystem and with it all forms of life. Whether one followed with horror and pity the spectacle of Terri Schiavo's death, puzzled through debates surrounding stem cell research, or worried over deforestation and climate change, it is hard to miss this question or the fact that the idea of "reverence for life" denotes both a widespread sensibility and also a big problem.

The phrases "reverence for life," "sanctity of life," "dignity of life," and "respect for life" are ubiquitous in American and worldwide social discourse. Given all of this confusion, we need some sense of the meaning of these concepts, or at the very least some indication of how I intend to use them. Reverence and respect, I submit, are about moral attitudes or dispositions we ought to adopt toward human and nonhuman life; they relate to other concepts such as sympathy or compassion, which I cannot explore here. The idea of "reverence" more precisely designates the attitude or posture of deep affection and even religious awe and deference. Traditionally, it meant the proper response to the holy or sacred. "Respect" is a concept that specifies the attitude toward or acknowledgment of the moral standing of some being that focuses on recognition and nonintervention rather than awe or deference. While "respect" has often been limited to human life, given the Kantian legacy of modern Western ethics, it has recently been extended to nature by Paul Taylor and others.[2] Presumably, respect is evoked by the moral worth of the other, whether human or nonhuman, but the focus is on one's disposition or willingness to treat that other as an end in itself, not merely as a means.

While respect and reverence are about attitudes or dispositions to act and to respond to others, "dignity" and "sanctity," conversely, seem to articulate the moral worth in question; they encapsulate the conditions of moral considerability, that is, why something or someone matters morally. "Dignity," arising out of the ancient Hellenistic thought world, denotes height, excellence, and honor, whereas "sanctity," with an array of religious or sacral resonances, specifies something as holy or sacred, what is set apart, inviolable. Nowadays thinkers specify different qualities of a being that warrant the use of dignity or sanctity or some other idea to indicate the grounds of moral standing. Some look to sentience; others focus on rationality or capabilities. This is one point of dispute between my argument and Schweitzer's, since, as we see below, he focuses on the "will-to-live" as the ground of moral considerability, whereas I am trying to articulate the "integrity" of life.

In this way two concepts (reverence/respect) with different meanings specify the posture or attitude one can and should take morally toward others, human or nonhuman. The other two concepts (sanctity/dignity) aim to articulate the standing or claim to considerability of self and other, human or nonhuman, which is meant to evoke the correlate attitude and response. Reverence is to sanctity what respect is to dignity, we might say. Each couplet encompasses an attitude or disposition and a claim about the standing or importance of some human, nonhuman, or divine reality. In fact, each side of a couplet infuses the other: recognition of and response to dignity is respect; a sense of reverence reveals the sacred. What bedevils too much current ethics is that the couplets have been pulled apart. Subjectivist theories in ethics look just to peoples' moral intuitions, attitudes, or feelings; objectivist theories, fearing relativism, try to specify moral standing without reference to subjective responses. The trick, in terms of moral and theological reflection, is to keep both sides of the dynamic in play, namely, concepts for what we are responding to that are not reducible to our reactions, and also the complex social and psychological dynamics at play in moral attitudes and feelings.

In this essay I can examine only the reverence/sanctity couplet and must leave the consideration of other big ideas (e.g., respect/dignity) to another inquiry. The reason for this focus is twofold. First, the idea of the reverence for life has served as an intersection between environmental ethics and bioethics that is important for this book. It helpfully links what is too often torn asunder (human and nonhuman life) and thereby lets us think about the intersections among these concerns. Second, within the welter of moral concepts that structure current social life, "reverence," it would seem, traffics between recognition of and care for the preciousness of finite life and the awe and obeisance usually due the sacred, the divine. In this light, part of the confusion in the present situation is that discourse properly predicated of the human relation to the divine has migrated to name an attitude toward nondivine, finite life. The way "reverence" has come to be predicated of human and nonhuman finite life is part of the story I want to tell throughout this inquiry into our posttheistic condition.

Things become conceptually more confusing if we turn to the idea of "life." At issue are two related but distinct questions: What is life? And what is it about life that evokes reverence or respect, that is, how can one rightly predicate sanctity or dignity of a living thing? The question of how to define life is no doubt one of the longest-standing in Western thought, ranging from ancient and medieval discussions about kinds of souls, or the power of animation, to current debates about artificial life. Importantly, the religions, and certainly Christianity, make distinctions between physical, social, spiritual, eternal, and divine life. One can thereby specify the condition in which a person might be physically living and yet spiritually dead. Christians also claim, with Saint Paul, that new life is being in another, in Christ. Logical problems arise, then, about the predication of "life" to different beings or states ranging from the sentient to the divine. This is one point at which theological analysis becomes essential in social and moral thought, since we need clarity about the diversity of meanings the idea "life" bears. For the purpose of this essay, by "life" I simply mean processes on whatever scale marked by interaction within an environment, reproduction, the consumption and processing of energy, the ability to produce waste, some measure of purposiveness, and the threat of disintegration or death. Different living things carry on these processes differently, but those differences are not too salient for the purpose of this discussion.

Other problems dog us if we try to make sense of what it is about "life" that warrants terms like "sanctity" or "dignity." Is there a hierarchy in life, so that animate life has worth because it is created by the living God but human beings have even greater value because they are created in the *image* of this God? Is the dignity or sanctity of life taken to be a nonderivable attribute of life that undistorted moral perception grasps? Do we say that what matters is sentience and hence the capacity to feel pain and to have some kinds of interests? Can we examine our own will-to-live, as Schweitzer does, and logically extend this to other living things, however life is defined? Is the worth of life intrinsic to a being, just inhering in it, or is the worth of life always instrumental, in relation to some purposes?[3]

A complete response to the question that frames this essay would have to address all of these matters about how to define life and how to specify the conditions of its value. That is obviously not possible here. I want to keep matters open in order to grasp the range of debates that fall within the semantic field of reverence for life. So I work with a rather capacious and intuitive sense of the concept of life and then spend most of the time asking about whether such life rightly evokes reverence or respect, or some other attitude. That is Schweitzer's gambit as well. Before engaging his thought, it is important next to grasp the kinds of debate provoked by the discourse of reverence for life.

The Range of Questions

Aside from clashes found in popular discourse and the media around abortion or euthanasia, there are debates about life that touch more technical matters in ethics. Let me note three that structure the remainder of this inquiry.

First, there is the question of the domain or scope of value. Some thinkers, such as Peter Singer, insist that we have to "unsanctify" human life so that we can attend to the moral standing and rights of other forms of life.[4] His contention is that the discourse of the "sanctity of human life" and its correlate attitude of "reverence" relies on untenable religious claims that in fact warrant the immoral treatment of nonhuman forms of life. As Friedrich Nietzsche puts it, "When will we have completely de-deified nature?"[5] The concern, as Singer puts it, ought to be with sentience and preference utility. Other thinkers, religious and nonreligious ones, also challenge what they see as the anthropocentrism of Western religion and ethics. Theologians such as Sallie McFague, Gordon Kaufman, and James Gustafson argue that too often Western thought has constricted the domain of value to what furthers human purposes. Without denying the unique responsibility of human beings, the domain of value, seen theologically or metaphysically, extends beyond the well-being of our species. Whether one uses the religiously fraught rhetoric of "reverence" or theocentrism, we are living through a global clash about whether to expand our perception of moral worth to include nonhuman life, to retain traditional anthropocentric boundaries, or to expunge appeals to the "value" of life from public discourse as philosophically and scientifically untenable. I submit that the rhetoric of "reverence for life" is precisely the way in which the question of God or God's death is being posed in our time after the end of traditional theism.

The second basic question in dispute about the rhetoric of the reverence for life concerns the status of human self-understanding. A host of thinkers, ranging from the German philosopher Jürgen Habermas to social critics such as Francis Fukuyama and the Protestant theologian Paul Ramsey, worry that we are transforming the born into the made, as they put it.[6] Genetic engineering, ideas about cloning, and rhetorically charged

discourse about cyborgs among some postmodern thinkers seem to undercut the biological conditions of human self-understanding and replace
them with a celebration of (technological) power. The confusion of the
born and the made threatens our normative self-understandings as creatures who know themselves in and through biological lineage. Withdraw
the facts of birth and death, and human consciousness is altered.

The force of this point should not be missed. For much of this civilization's history, to be a moral creature, to have the form of awareness
marked by the sense of responsibility, meant precisely that our ability to
act was bounded by perceptions of worth recalcitrant to that power. That
moral limit was defined by the gods, fate, Nature, or the Living God and
also the awareness of birth and death, which discloses the tenuous worth
and preciousness of life. Mortality and divinity, we might say, provided a
moral space of reasons within which to understand the meaning, purpose,
and limits on human power. Maybe angels are creatures with normative
self-understandings uncoupled from the fact of mortality, and certainly a
"monster" is a being chained to mortality but not morality, but, at least in
the traditions that have shaped this civilization, to be human is to live
with some sense of responsibility and aspiration always made possible and
limited by mortal life and an order of being, the Deity or Nature, that
exceeds humankind. The debate about the moral status of finitude, as this
book shows, articulates anew long-standing assumptions about what
makes human beings moral creatures, neither angels nor monsters. What
if the very conditions of our finitude now fall within the scope of our
power? In the terms of this volume's title, what would establish the moral
status of a humanity "without Nature"?

Beyond questions about the scope of value or the conditions of our
normative self-understanding as finite and yet moral beings, we can now
uncover a third arena of debate. Albert Camus, in typically spirited language, writes that the only serious philosophical question is why one
should not commit suicide. "Judging whether life is or is not worth living," he writes, "amounts to answering the fundamental question of philosophy."[7] Of course Camus' claim entails a specific conception of
philosophy, but the point is not hard to grasp. Given the threats of death,
sorrow, loss, and unhappiness as well as moral outrage over innocent suffering, the tyranny of ignorance, and all manner of oppression, is human
life worth living, both in a moral and a nonmoral sense? Is it good to be
alive, and are we justified in living when our lives are necessarily sustained
at the expense of other forms of life? The big question is not, with apolo-
gies to Shakespeare, whether to be or not to be. The pressing question,

humanly and ethically speaking, is whether it is *good* to be. It is not surprising that some ancient authors cursed the day they were born.

However, in an age when many forms of life are endangered on this planet through the radical expansion of human power, concentration on the question of suicide seems a rather narrow preoccupation of the individual. We are now forced to pose the question in a wider, more capacious way. One needs to ask if and why life itself, and not just human life, can and should evoke reverence, and if so, what that means for a sense of responsibility. If life does evoke some sense of worth that cannot be wantonly trammeled, then finite existence as such places limits on human power and wants. If that is so, should one endorse, as the Roman Catholic magisterium does, an ethics of life that insists on the sanctity of human life from conception to death?[8] Conversely, if life makes no claim to recognition, if it bears no moral standing, then all forms of life, including human life, are made instrumental to other purposes. And if that is true, ought we then to engineer species, exploit the natural environment at will, forsake the claim of future generations upon us as nothing but misguided moralizing about life and its worth? Deciding if life has worth that places limits on the exercise of human power while also being a condition of normative self-understanding amounts to answering what might in fact be the only serious question of our age.

Once the question "Should We Reverence Life?" is asked in this particular way, then ethical responsibility is deepened. The idea of "reverence for life" seems to pick out and articulate a longing for some sense of what is inviolable, what ought not to be demeaned or destroyed, a sense even of what is holy and so can require actions and policies for its enhancement. And this poses a profound challenge. As the theologian Jürgen Moltmann puts it: "Whether humanity *ought* to live, or ought to become extinct, is a question which cannot be answered through the dictates of rational expediency, but only out of a love for life."[9] There is a sense among many people that the moral rightness and validity of the human project is bound up with how one responds to the claim of the inviolable. This sense bespeaks the religious tenor of our current moral and social situation.

At this level of reflection, one is tempted to say that "reverence for life" brings the Good down to earth. What was once reserved for a good that transcended the world of finite life, the *summum bonum* or God, has within the flow of Western and global history been progressively incarnated in humanity and now in finite life itself. This development is not the career of modern nihilism. What is happening is not just an idolatry of the finite, although that, too, might be the case. "Reverence for life" articulates a

longing for what is inviolable within an age scarred by the constant violation of human and nonhuman life and thereby in search of a moral justification of the human adventure in the face of ongoing evil. The language
of "reverence" seems to have migrated from God to finite life even while
the echo of the divine-human relation remains faintly heard in this discourse. In this context, I can turn to the ethics of Albert Schweitzer. This
foray into his thought will enable us to probe further the concerns just
identified and also to chart the limits of the discourse of the reverence for
life for answering vexing moral and religious matters.

Absolute Reverence for Life

Albert Schweitzer argued that an ethics of the reverence for life is absolute. It presents a moral demand and possibility that can never be fully
realized in human history. The struggle to fulfill this responsibility deep-
ens human life. Schweitzer was accordingly critical of an ethics of compromise, as he called it, which sought to provide the means to relieve absolute
responsibility by providing answers to moral conflicts. He resolutely insisted that "the good conscience is an invention of the devil."[10] The moral
life is the justification of the human project in a universe wherein life
thwarts, destroys, and competes with life.

Schweitzer held that an adequate theory of civilization must be ethical
and be affirmative of the world and of life. The idea of an ethics of reverence for life is meant to meet this twofold demand.[11] In continuity with
eighteenth-century rationalism and especially the reflexive philosophy of
René Descartes, Schweitzer sought to examine immediate self-consciousness.[12] When we do so, he argued, we come to realize that the core of
consciousness is not the *cogito*, the "I think" (Descartes), nor time consciousness (Bergson), nor, as Kant believed, the transcendental unity of
apperception and the law of pure practical reason. Schweitzer's point was
that the "I think" is empty; to think at all is to think about something.
The first datum of consciousness is actually the will-to-live: " 'What is the
immediate fact of my consciousness?' . . . 'To what do I always return?'
We find the simple fact of consciousness is this, *I will to live*."[13] And as he
notes, "When my will-to-to live begins to think, it sees life as a mystery
in which I remain by thought. I cling to life because of my reverence for
life."[14]

Below, we see that an ethics of the integrity of life also begins reflexively, but it is "integrity," and not the brute will-to-live, that is most basic.

At this juncture one must grasp that, for Schweitzer, if one follows the will-to-live to its conclusion consistently, it is obvious that all beings are moved by the will-to-live. In fact, the will-to-live would seem to be the primary feature of the universe, a reality that I affirm in myself and must acknowledge in every living thing. At the origin of consciousness is the will-to-live and as such also a primary affirmation of that life. The will-to-live is self-evidently good.[15] The will-to-live, rather than sentience or being created by God or rationality, is the ground of moral considerability, as I call it above. Insofar as nonhuman and human life is driven by the will-to-live, then life itself has moral standing and ought to evoke reverence.

While the affirmation of life is the first spiritual act of experience, as Schweitzer calls it, this experience brings with it an immediate consequence, one that moves in the direction of ethics and the ultimate purpose of human action:

> What happens is that one realizes that he is but a speck of dust, a plaything of events outside his reach. Nevertheless, he may at the same time discover that he has a certain liberty, as long as he lives. . . . Hence our dependence upon events is not absolute; it is qualified by spiritual freedom. Therefore, when we speak of resignation it is not sadness to which we refer, but the triumph of our will-to-live over whatever happens to us.[16]

The affirmation of life in oneself leads via thinking to *resignation*, a kind of sincerity of self rooted in vulnerability to events beyond one's power but also the freedom to transcend that fact in the capacity to choose to exist or to leave existence, to endure or to end one's life. Knowledge provides the insight that the will-to-live is everywhere and thereby reveals the extent of our dependence. However, it is not obvious that an affirmation of my life entails the demand to reverence another's life. It would be possible, as Schweitzer knew, to reverence the will-to-live as the will-to-power, the domination of the weak by the strong.[17] How does he make the move from the will-to-live to the ethics of the reverence for life?

Schweitzer insisted that the attitude one can and ought to take toward other forms of life must be consistent with self-appraisal. "If I am a thinking being," he writes, "I must regard other life than my own *with equal reverence*." For all his vitalism, Schweitzer was a moral rationalist.[18] Endorsing Kant's principle of universalizability as the true form of morality, an ethics of the reverence for life means that every life is given equal reverence. This led Schweitzer to insist on the moral standing of nonhuman life. "Ethics are responsibility without limit towards all that lives," he writes.[19] Evil is what annihilates or hinders or hampers life; good is helping or saving or enabling life to its highest development. Moral responsibility is thereby expanded to the point that every moral agent is responsible for all living things. We might call this "absolute reverence for life" in order to capture Schweitzer's insistence on an absolute ethics, an ethics without compromise. "A man is truly ethical," Schweitzer notes, "when he obeys the compulsion to help all life which he is able to assist, and shrinks from injuring anything that lives."[20]

Matters are more complex, however. Schweitzer is keenly aware that life competes with life:

> The world is a ghastly drama of will-to-live divided against itself. One existence makes its way at the cost of another; one destroys the other. One will-to-live merely exerts its will against the other, and has no knowledge of it. But in me the will-to-live has come to know about other wills-to-live. There is in it a yearning to arrive at unity with itself, to become universal.[21]

What does ethics mean in that case? Is it absolute, rational, and active, but also tragically futile? As he notes, it is "a painful enigma for me that I must live with reverence for life in a world which is dominated by creative will which is also destructive will, and destructive will which is also creative."[22] The enigma of creative and destructive will is not resolved. In the face of this division within the will-to-life, the ethical person brings to a momentary end the "ghastly drama" of reality in acts of goodness *to any form of life*.[23] The destiny of ethical existence, he writes, is to "choose for my activity the removal of this division in the will-to-live against itself, so far as the influence of my existence can reach."[24] When one so acts, Schweitzer insists, one experiences a union, a mystical participation, in the infinite Will in which all of life is one. That is the mystical significance of ethics and the moral justification of the human adventure. It is a kind of redemption or moral salvation from the horrors of existence.

The theological dimension of Schweitzer's ethics is the form in which to grasp the meaning of the division in the will-to-live. Arising from the plight of our moral experience, his position moves conceptually between theism and pantheism. Ethical theism, as Schweitzer calls it, "presupposes a God who is an ethical Personality, and who is, therefore, so to speak, outside the world . . . [and] it must hold fast the belief that God is the sum total of the forces working in the world—that all that is, is in God."[25] Ethical theism, in a word, tries to preserve the difference between God and the sum total of states of affairs and thereby escape the charge of crude pantheism. Yet if the ethics is to warrant the predication of "reverence" to life, it must also assert that "all that is, is in God."

Schweitzer's ethics is mystical in at least two senses. First, it seeks to enunciate the divine being beyond the categorical distinctions that haunt the human mind and traditional theism (transcendence and immanence). Second, it specifies an immediate unity of self and God in the ethical act: "Neither knowledge nor hope for the future can be the pivot of our life or determine its direction. It is intended to be solely determined by allowing ourselves to be gripped by the ethical God who reveals Himself in us, and by our yielding our will to His."[26]

From Reverence to Integrity

Schweitzer's ethics is a grand thing. It addresses precisely the range of questions isolated at the outset of this essay. First, the ethics for the reverence of life expands the realm of moral value beyond narrow anthropocentrism. Second, insofar as human beings are rational agents, the full depth of moral responsibility is also acknowledged. It is hard to imagine that Schweitzer would endorse technical intervention aimed at changing the biological conditions necessary for our normative self-understanding as moral beings, that is, an alteration of the will-to-live that is the grounds for the absolute ethical mandate. Finally, by insisting on the will-to-live and then an ethics aimed at stopping the ghastly drama of existence, Schweitzer indicates that in which the goodness of life consists. He has an answer for Camus' question, but one that is wider than anxiety about individual existence. Through his ethical mysticism, a religious vision that mixes theism and pantheism clarifies why it is right to reverence life. All that is, is in God and thereby is rightly due reverence. Theological language migrates from the transcendent personal God to the drama of life while providing a form in which to understand the turmoil of existence.

This ethics is also not without grave problems. One must take care lest the idea of reverence for life too easily backs actions and policies that violate moral intuitions and sensibilities. Do I encounter deadly cancer cells destroying a dear friend reverently when I hope for the success of chemotherapy that will kill living cells? Do we encounter life reverently when we seek to protect the subtle ecology of a hardwood forest by restricting all human access to it, knowing that jobs will be lost, families will be endangered, children will go hungry? In order to support his family, does the poor man who sells the retina in one of his eyes pay due reverence to life? The idea of reverence for life is so inflated and so vague that it poorly articulates the sensibility it hopes to express.

Furthermore, despite Schweitzer's insistence on an "absolute ethics" and his own self-sacrifice to carry out medical work in Africa, it seems that his kind of ethical mysticism can provide too easy a salvation from the ghastly drama of existence. In the tooth-and-claw struggle of existence, I am justified, I participate rightly in the being of God, if in some small way I stop the division within the will-to-live. Schweitzer expresses this by noting that if one rescues an insect from a pool of water, that ethical act on behalf of life can be experienced as mystical participation in the unity of life. What does that really mean? In my judgment, the ethics is gravely underdetermined. There is no principle for distinguishing morally between forms of life in situations of conflict where hard choices have to be made. In the end, it seems that Schweitzer's position is grand but also grandly vague. The same problem dogs every ethics that latches onto the discourse of the reverence for life. What, then, ought we to do? I am bold enough to sketch some constructive claims along the lines of the questions that structure this essay.

Methodologically, the ethics of the integrity of life begins, as Schweitzer's does, with the primitive data of our experience of self-awareness as embodied, social, reflective, living beings. Insofar as human beings are living, then we instantiate what is present in various degrees in every living being.[27] But unlike in Schweitzer's ethics, what is basic is not life qua life, whether conceived as vitality or will. What is crucial in an ethics of integrity is that a living being seeks or imposes on itself the integration of several capacities and their goods into a fleeting and perhaps never completely attainable complex coherence, that is, integrity. It is not just vitality or power or the will-to-live that defines worth, but rather, power that is organized, integrated, in our being with and for others. Integrity, or its lack, is not just a predicate of human beings. Living beings also struggle for integrity in different ways precisely due to the diversity of their forms and interactions with their environments through which power or vitality is organized.

Human beings, for instance, must aim at but also create the integration of basic, social, and reflexive capacities and goods in a way different from, say, nonhuman animals or ecosystems. This is the distinctly moral and cultural task of human life: we strive to organize vitality as subjectivity and power as community. The moral question is the integrity of self and the integrity of a community. Indeed, we might say that a human being's integrity is both more complex and more fragile than other forms of life because it is not predetermined by the powers it self-organizes. The violation of our reflexive capacities, say in deception or forced ignorance, can violate our basic and social goods as well. Conversely, it is possible to alter, deny, or enhance some human capacities, say through genetic manipulation or medical intervention, without thereby threatening the integrity of human life. The limit on intervention, manipulation, or the enhancement of a form of life is respect for its integrity amid interactions with its world. Respect and enhancement, rather than reverence, are the attitudes and dispositions correlating to "integrity" as the reality that encapsulates moral considerability.

Thus, contrary to Schweitzer's ethics for the reverence for life, the first point is that "life" is not a brute datum but manifests purposiveness aimed at integrity, not just brute will but organized power, defined by the kind or form of life that is in question. Granting continuities between human and nonhuman life, the vitalities of existence rise in human life to the act of self-formation and cultivation and therefore freedom.[28] Given this, that which grants moral considerability is not life qua life but the integrity of life in diverse forms. The integrity of life is thereby related but not reducible to raw vitality, the will-to-live, or the various goods and capacities a living being struggles to integrate. The distinction of levels of powers and goods enables us to insist on an absolute moral demand to respect and enhance the integrity of life without loss of the means to make moral distinctions and judgments. Some capacities and power can be justifiably sacrificed, but if and only if that does not demean or destroy the integrity of a form of life, human or nonhuman.

What, then, about the second question that circulates in contemporary social life, namely, the conditions for our normative self-understanding as moral beings and what this implies for an ethics? Schweitzer, as we see above, was a moral rationalist, in that human beings, while bound to all others through the will-to-live, can and must rationally universalize maxims of their actions. He rightly notes the biological conditions of normative self-understanding and also rejects anthropocentrism as a standard of value without thereby denying the distinctive moral responsibility of human beings. Yet his argument, as we also see above, inflates the scope of human responsibility while leaving the criteria for judgment underdetermined. The idea of integrity likewise expands the scope of moral value insofar as it concerns the integrity of all life, not just human life, and, further, the struggle for integrity by any living being is interdependent with others. In a quite literal sense, we are implicated in other forms of life, aiding or thwarting the will-to-integration.

This implication of life within life is the condition for the inescapable tragic fact of finite existence that comes to expression in our most pressing questions about whether life is indeed good. The very fact that human beings ask that question, in Camus' restricted form or in a more expansive ecological way, discloses that the integrity of human life is bound to our reflective capacity to wonder about, assess, and value the purposiveness of life and thereby to act upon oneself in response to others, to give shape to life with and for others. From this act of conscience, the creative assessment and shaping of personal and social life, arises moral responsibility as well as a distinct form of goodness. That is to say, by acting on an imperative to respect and enhance the integrity of life, human beings either bring into being a form of moral goodness or violate that demand and thereby destroy a distinctly moral good. So, beyond basic, social, and reflexive goods and capacities, human beings can aim at the *moral integrity* of their lives, wherein a distinctive good is enacted which is related but not reducible to basic, social, and reflexive goods. That is the shape of normative self-understanding and its various conditions.

The demand of responsibility is thereby hardly underdetermined. Quite the contrary is the case. Once these distinctions are made, an absolute ethics can also meet the more proximate demands for making valid moral judgments. One can specify the capacities and goods involved in situations of conflict and the extent to which, under the absolute demand both to respect and to enhance the integrity of life, actions that deny or thwart some goods and capacities are warranted. It is possible, again, to sacrifice certain goods within some domain of life if and only if that does not violate its integrity. For instance, one might judge, as some land ethics do, that in order to respect and enhance the integrity of a specific ecosystem, it is warranted to reduce a certain population of nonhuman animals. However, there are necessary limits on the means to the management of that ecosystem precisely because the integrity of the system is interdependent with the forms of life that constitute its own life. Likewise, there are situations, say in war or medical treatment, in which it is valid to intervene, deny, and even sacrifice human goods if and only if in doing so the individual's integrity is neither demeaned nor coercively diminished. Distinguishing the good of integrity as an absolute demand from the proximate goods and capacities of life enables us to retain the gravity of ethics without loss of the means to make and validate specific judgments.[29]

At this juncture we seem to have returned to what Schweitzer calls the ghastly drama of existence, that is, to the contemporary longing for the inviolable and the search for what might morally justify the human adventure in a world that is radically finite and tragic. One might well utter, with Saint Paul: "Who will rescue me from this body of death?" (Rom.

7:24, NRSV). As noted at the outset of these reflections, it is my sense that the discourse of reverence and sanctity poses the question of God in our social situation, insofar as religious discourse has migrated to the realm of finite life, and yet there is also a longing to give sense to the horrors of existence, a longing for redemption or justification. In this respect, my exercise in moral and social thought throughout this essay is also and has always been a labor of theological reflection.

Schweitzer's ethical mysticism, we saw, was fashioned as a response to the involvement of human life in the division of life against itself. His ethics for the reverence of life is nothing else, at bottom, than an account of moral salvation. It is a way of understanding the meaning of existence when life's drama is apprehended as being in God. The same religious impulse, whether recognized or not, seems at work in other forms of ecological and bioethics, even among thinkers, like Singer, who work endlessly to deny any religious significance to the moral life. There seems to be a longing for justification or an escape from any need for one. A theological ethics for the integrity of life hardly wants to dodge this social fact. Again, I have no interest in claiming that one must be explicitly religious in order to be moral. Yet given that religious questions arise within and circulate through the range of moral challenges that confront us in our age, a theologian is warranted in offering a religious response.

Nowadays it is usual for Christian theologians to answer these problems by turning to the discourse and faith of their church tradition or by trying to reimagine the divine in ways that speak to contemporary ecological consciousness.[30] Consistent with the method of an ethics of the integrity of life, theological discourse cannot be drawn from traditional resources and imposed willy-nilly on social realities, nor is it sufficient simply to reimagine God in an ecologically friendly way. Theological ethics, on my account, is a way of analyzing and articulating the lived structure of reality in order to provide meaning, orientation, and guidance for life.[31] It draws on many resources, including those of a specific religious tradition.

In bringing this essay to a close, what, then, am I really saying theologically? In fact, I am engaging the religious question all along, even if not by means of explicitly theological discourse. The ethics of the integrity of life is rooted in the struggle of living beings to draw together, to integrate, their existence against powers that thwart it, the forces of disintegration. Insofar as the struggle to organize power is never settled and in human beings touches the rectitude of our lives, the aim for the "integrity" of life names what religiously is called the desire for God. The scope of value is inclusive of living beings but even exceeds this insofar as human life reaches beyond itself toward an integrity related but not reducible to finite capacities and goods. This is what Saint Augustine means when he notes in the *Confessions* that "God" is the life of one's life.

Further, "God" designates not only the ultimate good of life but also a source of our moral restlessness, the demand of responsibility. The reflective demand to respect and enhance the integrity of life that arises within our interdependence with other forms of life on this planet is, theologically taken, nothing other than the testimony of a divine claim on life grasped in the depths of moral interactions. This is why, I believe, the discourse of "reverence" and "sanctity" continues to resonate even outside explicit religious communities. How we relate to other forms of life forces the question of what is holy, what is inviolable; this question is found among many of the world's religious traditions. The moral life is a prism for religious sensibilities. Finally, interdependence with other realms of life coupled with the moral depths and seriousness of human existence comes to its most heated expression in the disquietude about life's worth and the longing for some peace amid the tragic facts of existence. For some people, ethical mysticism will answer this longing for salvation. For others, the longing for the inviolable and the gnawing awareness that our lives are in the moral balance remains mute. There are other religious responses as well, say, the experience of redemption in Christ or Buddhist Enlightenment.

Most fundamentally, an ethics for the integrity of life holds that we cannot and will not answer our deepest moral and spiritual longings merely through the continual extension of power to alter life. The quest for salvation from the conflict of life within life will hardly be answered by denuding life of worth and celebrating power as the root of goodness. That kind of response to the challenges of the drama of life is self-refuting and in fact is a harsh servitude. There is a decisive limit on the drive to extend human power in order to alter and thereby escape the tragic facts of life. Even altered, enhanced, or cyborg life will be tragic life. The integrity of one's existence is found in how one responds to that which limits power, namely, the vulnerability of others, human and nonhuman. It is not just the limit that mortality places on our striving. Theologically construed, that limit is found in the whole community of life, including divine life.[32] What is important morally in this theological vision is that we who live in an age of endangerment to every form of life must cultivate a sense of the insufficiency of power to answer our plight. Paradoxically enough, once we are freed from the dream of attaining the integrity of our lives through the limitless extension of power, we are then freed to respect and enhance the integrity of finite life with its limitations.

Put in more classical Protestant Christian terms, and so to use my own religious tradition, there is no active works-righteousness; human power and effort alone will not save us or bring about the Reign of God. The longing for God ought to remain a longing for God. That is the spiritual demand of this age. Life is not a second god. Finite life has its own good of integrity, but this life is not rightly the object of reverence. Our task, morally and religiously, is to respect and enhance the integrity of life, to answer the call of responsibility, and in that to find rectitude of conscience, if not ultimate salvation.

Conclusion

These reflections are a rather complex journey through the dense moral spaces of high-modern societies. I am trying to bring some clarity to conceptual confusions as well as to isolate an interlocking set of questions that swirl around the public debate over the worth of life in an age of global endangerment. I am also bold enough to show that theological reflection can and must be carried on within moral and social thought precisely because the big problems we now face are not without their religious resonance. And, finally, I am beginning to sketch an ethics centering on responsibility for the integrity of life that can, at least in principle, speak to some of the confusions, questions, and longings of our situation.

In the face of big problems we need to think big thoughts. This is not to suggest that thought alone will change the course of events; it is to insist that future life now lies vulnerable before human powers. Without a sensibility for the good of finite existence and the intelligence to labor responsibly for what is right, our power will triumph in nothing but ignorance and loss. Against that grim possibility, the challenge, possibility, and even joy before us are to lay hold of the claim of responsibility and to act on behalf of the integrity of life. In that labor is to be found the inner dynamics of our moral being and also an answer to why humanity *ought* to live.

The End of Nature and the Last Human?
Thinking Theologically about "Nature"
in a Postnatural Condition

Peter Manley Scott

Part I

THE ARGUMENT

In this essay I propose that we find ourselves in a postnatural condition. Stressing the *post* in postnatural indicates that in following after nature, the human is mixed up with nature; the separation of humanity and nature cannot be maintained. Emphasizing the *natural* in postnatural indicates that nature has not disappeared; nature still exceeds and encompasses the human. We are not "without" nature but we are "after." Furthermore, we must speak of what I call the "haveability" of nature, yet not in ways that separate the human from nature or in ways that suggest that the human can master the nonhuman. Nature is haveable and yet elusive. Although there is no pure nature for us to have—nature is always a constituted nature—yet nature cannot be contained and mastered by us. This nature is haveable yet beyond our control.

This postnatural circumstance is a theological condition *and* a political circumstance. Theology and politics cannot here be separated. How we think about nature has political determinants and consequences. Let me give you a small example to illustrate this claim. On August 7, 2006, the Environmental Audit Committee of the British House of Commons issued a report calling for urgent political action to reduce U.K. carbon dioxide emissions. As is well known, there is a majority scientific view that such emissions are the major contributor to anthropogenic climate change. The committee singled out the transport industry, especially air travel, as the only sector in the U.K. economy where carbon dioxide emissions are rising, as they have been doing since 1990.[1] As the committee's report was released, the British Broadcasting Corporation (BBC) was already posting a summary of a radio interview with Prime Minister Tony Blair, broadcast the same day, in which the prime minister advised individual citizens to undertake "carbon audits" on their domestic energy consumption, thereby in turn urging people to take individual responsibility. In his own words, "let's try and enable the individual to make their contribution too [to the reduction of CO_2 emissions]."[2]

On that same day, Friends of the Earth and Greenpeace responded by dubbing the prime minister's response as too individualistic and calling for legislation. The Friends of the Earth press release concluded by "calling for new legislation to force all government departments to make tackling climate change an aim of their policies."[3] The "low-cost" airlines also responded to the committee's report, making their usual populist argument that increasing air passenger duty (tax) would have a punitive effect on the financial ability of the poorest to fly away on vacation, a view later partially endorsed by a government minister. Preferred solutions seem to involve purchasing newer, more fuel-efficient planes and further negotiations on the availability of "cheap" flights at the level of the European Union.

In this one news cycle we have many representations of nature and of British participation in that nature. We have nature presented as a sink that is rapidly filling to capacity, the presentation of technical fixes as a solution, and an abiding sense of the short-term priority of the human interest. The problem of transport and CO_2 emissions is also internationalized by reference to negotiations with the European Union, individualized by reference to households, and deferred by reference to targets to be met in five years' time. In this *West Wing*–style operation of politics, the representations of nature are multiple and easily contained.[4]

This essay is concerned to oppose such strategies of containment. In line with my affirmation of a postnatural condition, I wish to ask how nature could be understood in our politics as haveable and less containable? Or, as British political philosopher John Keane presents the matter, how shall we think about "the growing need of the human species to give

institutional recognition to our fundamental dependence on nature itself"?[5] Put differently, nature needs to be haveable in our politics in the
manner of grit. For Friends of the Earth and Greenpeace, the British
prime minister's response lacks grit. Yet nature is never unmediated and
so is never directly present in our political actions. Nature as a social phenomenon is always already constituted in and through social relations; we
cannot in any straightforward fashion appeal to the grittiness of nature.

For European modernity, the relationship between nature and society
is an old issue, reconsideration of which may help in opposing strategies
of containment. Modernity is the passage from one order to another, in
which newness is privileged. "Modernity," writes David Ingram, "is defined by a consciousness of novelty."[6] In this new order, how is nature to
be understood, and what is its relation to the human? This has been a
central concern of Enlightenment and post-Enlightenment philosophers.
For example, Terry Pinkard records that in his lectures on the philosophy
of nature, Hegel was concerned to refuse, on the one hand, a mystical
conception of nature and, on the other, a mechanistic conception of nature. For Hegel, the first was irrational, dogmatic, and therefore reactionary; the mechanism of the second seemed to be opposed to our sense of
ourselves as free. Given Hegel's commitment to reform, neither version
of natural order seemed inviting.[7]

In promoting my concept of the postnatural, I am noting this European
concern over the concept of nature as part of a progressive politics. In this
perspective, declaring ourselves without nature makes little political sense.
You may banish the issue of natural ordering, but, like Banquo's ghost,
it will return to spoil the feast. Instead, the theological condition of the
postnatural affirms part of what is meant by being without nature but attempts to develop this critically. That is, I seek to affirm that nature is
always mediated and yet that we may also speak of the haveability of nature
to our politics. And in turn, what must be refused are the common ways
in which the haveable in-betweenness of nature is occluded: temporal deferral; spatial redistribution (injustice); amelioration through technology
(that is, private enterprise and the market). The condition of becoming
postnatural—which is a theological condition—must resist the standard
strategies that deny nature's political representation.

To summarize, I argue that we should characterize our present situation
as postnatural and affirm both the haveability and unruliness of nature. Yet
I wish to make this case as part of a larger theological argument: that
modernity has wrestled with how to understand nonhuman nature and

how that nonhuman nature relates to the human. In refusing the description "without nature," I am accepting a double obligation: (1) to offer an
elaboration of this postnatural condition, and (2) to work out what is morally normative in our postnaturality. This is an old struggle but also—and
this is new—a matter of our present survival.[8]

PROBLEMS WITH DISCOURSES OF "THE END"

The postnatural is, I say above, an aid to thinking about both the haveability and the uncontainability of nature. In contrast, it is difficult to see how
the phrase "without nature" assists in explicating the haveability of nature
in our politics. If we are indeed without nature, then nature *cannot* be
haveable in our politics. Thereby a fundamental question goes unasked: in
the condition of being without nature, do we have a defeat of our politics
because the effort no longer needs to be made to try to represent nature
in political actions?

In order to rethink being without nature and its unhappy political consequences, I offer the postnatural as a critical term: it seeks to indicate the
limits of our knowledge and action. By it, I join with Louis Dupré in his
historical interpretation that nature is a premodern and modern—indeed,
antitheological—invention; nature emerges as graceless, as somehow dis-
associated from the purposes of God.[9] And I join Bruno Latour in his
affirmation of amodernity. For Latour, modernity separates nature and
society and seeks to maintain the boundary between them in a work of
ontological policing.[10] The modern effort is remarkable yet unpersuasive,
for we have always been hybrid beings.[11]

Thus we are postnatural; that is to say, neither may we escape from
nature nor are we obliged to conform to it. We are mixed entities participating in a wider environment by way of our machines. This postnatural
order is neither given, nor can it be overcome.[12] Some sense of the diversity of our postnatural, participatory life can be discerned if we note the
variety of ways in which we consider nature. For example, in his brief
introduction to the phenomenon of climate change, Mark Maslin suggests
that there are four "myths" of nature: nature as benign; as ephemeral; as
perverse or tolerant; and as capricious.[13] It takes only a moment's thought
to see that such myths invite very different practical responses.

We can further develop this critique by noting that discourse on "without nature" is an endist discourse; that is, it is concerned with the end of
a state of affairs. Of this discourse I want now to ask two questions: (1)

What is involved in working with endist discourses? (2) Is the environmental understanding of nature—so common in endist discourse on nature—the only option in the construal of nature in a postnatural
condition?

   1. What is involved in working with endist discourses? When considering endist discourse, it is important to note two points—we might call
them ontological points—about such discourse.[14] First, if we are in a new
condition or state of "without nature," what is the cause of this new condition? What are the forces or tendencies that cause this new condition? If
we are without nature, is this the result of the willing of individuals or
communities, or are we referring here to undirected systemic change? And
if this state of the end of nature is not intended, is it still possible to speak
of a telos for the process?

   Second, and intimately related to the first point, the matter of human
action, its basis and scope, is immediately raised. What possibilities for
change are now open? To be without nature—is that a fixed state or not?
If yes, are we at the state of the last human in the sense that the scope for
political action is radically circumscribed? If no, in what ways thereby
must the description of "without nature" be amended, and through this
amendment how shall we come to understand the scope for action in and
through our dependencies with nature?

   In case this is unfamiliar, I want to rehearse these two points a little
further. Is the state of being "without nature" satisfying for the human?
Is it in some fashion ontologically, morally, and politically appropriate?
Does it, to borrow a phrase from political philosopher C. B. Macpherson,
correspond to "the needs, aspirations and capacities of modern man"?[15]
This, according to Francis Fukuyama, raises an old question about universal history.[16] To put the matter in the manner of Fukuyama, does history
provide us with evidence of a pattern that might be understood as culmi-
nating in a condition of being "without nature"? Or is the condition of
being "without nature" an alien and deeply troubling state that must be
subverted or resisted? And this point—about subversion and resistance—
connects to my worries about human agency: if the condition of being
"without nature" is somehow natural to us, then what we will *not* wish to
do is to refuse or subvert this condition. If, however, we conclude that
being without nature is an *inappropriate* condition—in some fashion not
natural—then what follows?

   Many of our current discussions about nature can be contextualized in
this fashion. In other words, we are troubled as to whether the condition
of being without nature is appropriate or not. In a recent intervention,

German philosopher Jürgen Habermas argues that the development of medical therapies that change human genes should be resisted.[17] His argument is that the exercise of human freedom is constitutive of human identity. He considers that a person growing up with the knowledge that their genetic code has been altered according to the desires of their parents experiences a significant incursion into what we mean by freedom. Freedom is natural, not artificial; freedom, the ground of our autonomy, is somehow given. If the conditions of that freedom are altered genetically, then our autonomy is abridged; we have been treated as a means (to someone else's view of a good life) rather than as an end.[18] Our sense of self, our freedom, and our agency are thereby denatured, designed for us rather than acquired by us. If being without nature means permission to engage in far-reaching genetically based medical therapies, then Habermas is calling that condition into question. Habermas's argument provides us with an example of my point that endist discourse on nature raises the issue as to whether being without nature is a natural condition and whether that condition, in turn, denies the possibility of free human action.

2. Is the environmental understanding of nature—so common in endist discourse on nature—the only option in the construal of nature in a post-natural condition? As is well known, end-of-nature discourse typically understands nature environmentally. Bill McKibben's *The End of Nature* is exemplary here; in this popular book, we are offered a lament for a lost innocence. Once, McKibben contends, reference to nature meant reference to that which is different from the human; now, in the globalization of human action, all is artificial and nature's transcendence is lost.[19] This argument is ontological and moral, as can easily be seen when comparing McKibben's position against certain emphases in Romanticism. For example, in his *Notebooks*, in an entry dated 1802, Samuel Taylor Coleridge writes: "In Natural Objects we feel ourselves, or think of ourselves, *only by Likenesses*—among men too often by *Differences*. Hence the soothing love-kindling effect of rural Nature/the bad passions of human societies."[20] If McKibben is right in our being at the end of nature, then only differences remain, and what Coleridge calls the "love-kindling effect of rural Nature" is abridged or curtailed. Indeed, Coleridge immediately proceeds to ask, in alarmingly postmodern fashion, "And why is Difference linked with Hatred?" In the colonization of Nature by Society, we are confronted by bad passions and the construction of differences. Here nature is educative: we proceed by way of the pedagogic identification of likenesses.

Nonetheless, Romanticism's nature is already a reaction. That is, nature as educative in a Romantic idiom arose within and toward the *end* of

European Enlightenment. For Northern Europe and Western modernity, nature had earlier been deployed in a yet different way—that is, not environmentally nor Romantically—and had suggested a form of politics. A case can certainly be made that the European Enlightenment promoted a specific concept of nature and in a fashion that had important consequences for human society. Hungarian Marxist György Lukács makes this argument: in developing its concept of nature, albeit along mechanistic lines, the Enlightenment hoped that rational science would purge teleologies and anthropomorphisms from nature.[21]

Part of this Enlightenment hope, Lukács claims, is that on the basis of a rational nature a rational society may be formed. What, however, is the relationship between a purged nature and society? If the hope is for a unified ontology of nature and society—that is, of a rational society—then in what ways is society to be derived from nature? For, as Raymond Williams remarks, "in the idea of nature is the idea of man . . . the idea of man in society, indeed the ideas of kinds of societies."[22] Put otherwise, conceptions of nature imply and support certain conceptions of society.

In Anglo-Saxon modernity, the political use of nature has focused on the theme and concept of the "state of nature," a staple in the contractarian construals of the basis of human society, especially in the work of Thomas Hobbes and John Locke. From a European perspective, then, to declare our situation to be without nature calls into question the "state of nature." In the state of nature, we are presented with the essence or nature of the human prior to society, so to speak.[23] Whether it is the Hobbesian emphasis on self-preservation or the Lockean emphasis on securing basic needs, we are being offered an account of natural right.

Such state of nature arguments have traditionally been employed to provide transhistorical justification for the contractualist foundations of the early modern polity and, crucially, for a defense of private property. (The natural human of the state of nature precedes all societies.) To assert the givenness of "life, liberty and the pursuit of happiness" is in its essentials a Lockean argument. Being without nature thereby interrupts one use of the concept of nature: the provision of a transhistorical standard. If there is no transhistorical standard, it becomes hard to know *how* to judge whether "without nature" is a good position to be in. In this deployment, the concept of nature operates in support of a particular conception of reason. Additionally, therefore, to be "without nature" raises questions about the capacities of reason.

So far, I am arguing that "without nature" is a troubling phrase. First, the phrase invites us into a world of endist discourse where the issue of the appropriateness or habitableness of our present circumstance as well as the matter of the possibility and scope of political action is raised. Second, if we think about nature in terms of a state of nature, we are invited to think of the loss of nature as a transhistorical standard.[24] To declare ourselves to be without nature is both to invoke the perils of endist discourse and to focus on only one meaning of nature—namely, nature as environmental. In our modern polity, nature has functioned in other ways, most especially in state of nature arguments. We live by a *concept* of nature, and that concept is—as I hope to show in the next section—bound up with the power of political legitimacy.

THE NATURE OF LEGITIMACY

Which concept of nature do we live by? Answering this question is made more complicated if we note that contemporary arguments over nature are at the same time arguments over legitimacy. To repeat Raymond Williams: "[I]n the idea of nature is the idea of man . . . the idea of man in society, indeed the ideas of kinds of societies."[25] Traditionally, state of nature arguments have contributed to the legitimacy of governance in the kind of society that is the modern liberal polity. That is, in the modern polity the state of nature contributes to establishing how political actions are morally founded and exploring the source of their authority. I offer some examples of nature's relation to legitimacy before discussing the concept of legitimacy more fully.

Debates over the genetic engineering of crops, the mapping of the human genome, and the development of genetics-based medical therapies raise this matter of legitimacy. Are these manipulations of nature permissible? What scope is there for restricting manipulation, if any? These considerations are handled in different ways. In the mapping of the human genome, for example, legitimacy was granted by separating the technical issues concerned with gene sequencing from various ethical, legal, and social issues. Moral and other questions were thereby distinguished from technical issues and set apart for separate consideration. The wish of some U.S. scientists to secure federal funding and move ahead rapidly was met by permitting the scientific work of mapping to proceed without reference to ethical and other concerns.[26] Engagement with the ethical, legal, and social issues was accepted as the way questions about the legitimacy of the mapping project were to be addressed. We are invited to accept the view that we should regard as legitimate or illegitimate the *applications* of such mapping. However, the mapping work itself is unproblematic. Scientific research into nature somehow sits outside our moral compass as if nature should be understood as *preceding* society and thereby as somehow benign and neutral—just *is*.

Legitimacy in reference to nature functions in other ways as well. In a previous article, I address the matter of political legitimacy in the context of the British government's 2004 decision to permit the commercial farming of genetically modified (GM) maize. While I accept that the British government has the power to make this decision, I question whether it has the authority.[27] What I did not appreciate at the time is the way that nature is cited as a source of legitimacy in democratic discourse. And this citation leads to a conundrum: Western democracies both manipulate nature and appeal to nature as a source of legitimacy. That is, how can the manipulation of the transhistorical not undercut nature as a source of legitimacy? Neither did I see clearly that consideration of whether we are with or without nature also affects the other sources of legitimacy—will, history—in Western democracies.

I mention the other sources of legitimacy above, so let us proceed to a more detailed consideration of these. Legitimacy is concerned with the moral quality of governance or the practice of governing on the basis of a moral principle. In *Democracy and Dictatorship*, Italian political philosopher Norberto Bobbio presents three sources of political legitimacy: will, nature, and history.[28] For modern Western democracies, will is explicated by reference to the people; nature by reference to the state of nature; and history by reference to the future. People, state of nature, future: these are the three sources of legitimacy, however imperfect their outworking may be in practice.

The issue of political legitimacy in an endist circumstance is, of course, the central concern of Francis Fukuyama's *The End of History and the Last Man*.[29] For Fukuyama, the great ideological struggle of history—the competition between economic systems—is over. And "without nature" might be read analogously: the competition between different accounts of nature is over. Formally, the questions that Fukuyama raises regarding history are identical to mine regarding nature. What is important about Fukuyama's work is that although he claims that there is only one source of legitimacy today—the sovereign will of the people—in his actual writing he appeals to the other sources referred to by Bobbio. That is, he appeals to nature and to history also. For nature, he appeals to transhistorical standards; and for history, he appeals to its ending.[30]

Fukuyama's appeal to a transhistorical standard, which he calls a concept of nature, presents an interesting question to any "without nature" discussion. The sharpness of his challenge is in the conundrum he poses: some transhistorical standard is required, but if we are "without nature," that standard cannot be discerned in nature. If that standard cannot be discerned, which means that there is no human nature, what guides toward appropriate *human* action do we have? Fukuyama's response is, of course, to argue that the transhistorical standard does still exist, and that standard brings history to a close.[31] But what if we do not wish to bring history to a close, must we then refuse the transhistorical standard? Excellent, we all cry, let us give up on transhistorical standards—for are we not already without nature? But then, all reference to the natural is ruled out, and a sort of ecological relativism sets in. We end up wishing to affirm the dangers of an ecological crisis but without reference to the natural. We are close to McKibben here; we desire the otherness of nature as a way of transcending human activity, yet it is through human activity that the natural has been rendered artificial and so no longer transcends us. The condition that provokes the need for the natural standard is the same condition that denies the actuality of the standard.

Fukuyama's response to this conundrum is traditional and elegant. We need a concept of nature, that is, we need a concept of human nature that in turn relates us to a wider nature. Traditionally in Anglo-Saxon discourse, such a concept of nature has been provided by the state of nature, as proposed by Thomas Hobbes and John Locke. This much we have already noted. As is well known, Fukuyama prefers Hegel and the dialectic of the master and slave. He sets aside the natural desire for preservation and goods, as he finds them in Hobbes and Locke, and opts for what he regards as Hegel's compelling psychological insight that it is human nature to transcend natural or physical need. In Fukuyama's own words: "Hegel . . . understands man as a moral agent whose specific dignity is related to his inner freedom from physical or natural determination. It is this moral dimension, and the struggle to have it recognized, that is the motor driving the dialectical process of history."[32]

What is interesting about Fukuyama's position is not the appeal to liberal democracy. His specific position here is unpersuasive. He seems to think that liberal democracy is the only meaning of democracy, thereby overlooking *social* democracy; he fails to see that his position undermines agency; and then he decides that he needs to revise this undermining by identifying the thymotic elements of democracy in order to defend a certain sort of aristocratic action. Nonetheless, what is interesting is that Fukuyama tries to develop a transhistorical standard. In the appeal to a moral basis of universal history, he argues that where we have arrived at with liberal democracy and liberal capitalism is rational; given human nature, it is appropriate or fitting. This condition is universal and without contradiction. Thus one should not be concerned about the narrow scope of political action that the end of history bestows on us. For there is no other circumstance where the last human should wish to be.

In our discussion of "without nature" the same issue is raised: Are we at the condition of "without nature" as a matter of arbitrariness or because this is a suitable and satisfactory position for humanity? It seems to me that we keep getting the second answer. We should be here: history, progress, the future, providence have brought us to the point where we should genetically manipulate and map. There is a rightness to our actions; a liberal polity is saying that we should be here, and seeks legitimacy and thereby authority from this declaration. In my view, Fukuyama at least tries directly to face—and answer—the question: Why should we think like this? Of course, Fukuyama's question is different; he inquires whether liberal democracy is proportionate to being human. Formally, however, his question and mine are identical: Given that we are here, should we be here? Is being without nature (my concern) or history (Fukuyama's issue) somehow proportionate to being human?

And yet. If Fukuyama's transhistorical standard brings nature to a close, must I refuse all reference to nature as transhistorical standard? To jettison nature in order to keep history open seems a high price to pay. If I declare that our condition is without nature, I keep history open and I hold open the possibility of meaningful political action; that is, I hold open the possibility of revolution. Yet is revolution opposed to natural standards? Must I choose between people and the future, on the one hand, and nature, on the other, as sources of political legitimacy? Put otherwise, is it possible to maintain both the importance of nature as a transhistorical standard and the openness of history—that a concept of nature may be deployed in support of governing on the basis of a moral principle that does not deny nature nor bring history to a close? Here emerges the value of the concept of the postnatural: nature is haveable, is grit in the technological machine, and yet, in the constituting of that machine, opens out into human action. Revolution is a postnatural event and draws legitimacy from the concept of the postnatural.[33]

Part II

In the second part of the essay, I want to concentrate on the theme of legitimacy in a postnatural context. I am suggesting that legitimacy might be developed in a postnatural direction by reference to the representative, the tragic, and the apocalyptic. Indicating the limits of knowledge and action, the themes of representation, the tragic, and the apocalyptic suggest ontic clues as to salient features of the world. Here I am drawing on Charles Taylor, who suggests that we need some account of a "moral order" that informs "an identification of features of the world, or divine action, or human life which make certain norms both right and (up to the point indicated) realizable."[34]

From a theological perspective, such a postnatural moral order needs to make consistent and constitutive reference to the ways of God with the world: a postnatural—always theological—anthropology. Nor is this an imposition upon political modernity by theological interests. Even modernity, as Taylor argues, may also be considered a moral order, even if of an attenuated kind; even modern individualism may be appreciated as a new form of sociality. Moreover, such reference to moral order is at the center of Fukuyama's concerns, as it was for Hegel. Although Fukuyama employs such terms as "rational" and "noncontradictory," central to his argument is that the end of history is a moral order.[35] Here I try to develop a theological account of a moral ordering that is sensitive to ecological distresses and is articulated by reference to God's action in atoning work, creative activity, and eschatological consummation. I thereby offer a theological outline of the postnatural human as an essay in moral order, and, as such, as a contribution to political legitimacy for a postnatural condition, and thereby as transhistorical.

THE POSTNATURAL: REPRESENTATIVE POLITICS, TRAGIC RELATIONS, AND APOCALYPTIC HISTORY

In this section, I seek to humanize nature as a source of political legitimacy and I seek to naturalize the will of the people and history as sources of political legitimacy. For a postnatural context, I am suggesting that each of these sources of legitimacy needs to be made more complex toward the articulation of a moral order: (1) the will of the people by reference to the political representation of nature; (2) the state of nature by reference to the tragic quality of our relations with nature, not least in relation to technology/machines; (3) the future by reference to the closing-in of the apocalyptic.[36] These indicate a postnatural condition in which the separation of humanity from nature is comprehensively called into question and yet some attempt is made to indicate the differences between the human and the nonhuman. Moreover, this condition is neither brute fact nor revisable contract. Instead, it identifies the common realm in which the human is always already placed, in which the mutual involvement of the human and nonhuman both structures the field of human action and also secures the openness of such action. Let me now try to indicate how this is so.

The Representative   How should humans represent the nonhuman in their political practices?

In one of his working notes for *Ethics*, Bonhoeffer writes: "civil servant, soldier, minister, scholar. *Principle of vicarious representative action*: one for the other—fights, works, administers, studies."[37] This, so to speak, is the creaturely aspect of the reconciling dynamic of Christ's work; representatives are exemplars of Christ's objective sacrifice. If Christ's sacrifice rescues the actuality of creatures from prideful forgetfulness of the ecological conditions of the human habitat into what Colin Gunton calls "the living out of creaturely being," representative actions enable others to overcome such forgetfulness.[38] Such forgetfulness may take many forms, including, paradoxically, the attempted mastery of nature, in which human creatures struggle to forget or set aside their creatureliness. (In that such forgetfulness is often called stewardship, efforts to repristinate the notion of stewardship must also be rejected.)

Is this representation revocable or not? And if this representative role has been given to humanity irrevocably, *how* is it given? To be a representative requires acting for the other. A representative is not a substitute and should not obscure the one for which she acts. Instead, a representative seeks vicariously to relate or present the interests of another. (We are familiar enough with this role when a doctor represents the interest in life of a patient who, for a medical reason, cannot speak for herself or when elected officials in an indirect democracy represent their electors in democratic deliberations.) The task of the postnatural representative is to remind postnatural humanity of its situatedness in nature, of humanity's productive embedding in natural conditions.

Nonetheless, an important principle of representation presents a difficulty for my argument. In the representative state, we have the representation of people, not of interests. Nature is not a person and so must be an interest; yet as an interest, nature cannot be represented. A democratic conundrum! Nor is this matter adequately addressed by drawing the human and the nonhuman closer together (by suggesting that the higher mammals enjoy, for example, a capacity for language or by granting rights to nature). Neither strategy renders nature into a person. Thus it seems to me that the issue needing elaboration is the democratic representation of nature.

In a previous work, when I tried to address this issue of the democratic representation of nature, I sought to avoid claiming that nature is a person. Furthermore, I denied that, given the complexity of modern societies, a direct democracy is possible in which nature is somehow present in the democratic realm.[39] In other words, of the two options—nature is designated a person; the interests of nature are represented in direct democracy—neither is easily available to us. It is not easy to grasp how nature is a person nor to discern how complex modern societies could be governed in practice by direct democratic arrangements. Next, I sought to claim that nature should be represented *in*directly in democratic negotiation. In this regard I privileged the knowledge of those groups that are identified with or claim to represent nature: specific groups must enact indirect representation.

Nonetheless, there are difficulties with this proposal. How are these groups identified? Is the matter of *knowledge* of nature overstressed here? In what senses does the human creature share a nature with other creatures so as to be able to assume the role of the representative?

The last question is the most fundamental, and an answer logically precedes answers to the first two questions. In what ways, then, may we speak of representation? What are the logic and mode of representation? And what is its ontology? There are differing logics and modes of representation, as follows:

> Representation by a solicitor or a doctor: the solicitor represents my case at law, not me *totaliter*; the issue here is expert knowledge on the part of my representative. This is not a total representation and it is revocable (I can dismiss my solicitor).
>
> Political representation: this is undiluted; my Member of Parliament represents my national political interests comprehensively as a matter of vocation. Within the fixed term of the period of election, this representation—save corruption, death, and so on—is not revocable.
>
> The representation of nature combines these; it is not total (nature exceeds us as *extra nos*) but it is irrevocable (although humans may deny that irrevocability).

To understand how this is so, we need to inquire after the ontology of representation. What are the ontological conditions of representation such that the human participates in the nonhuman, and the nonhuman in the human, yet not only by way of knowledge? I offer the following suggestion: the human is the perfect summary of the natural but not its full substitute; the human cannot substitute entirely for the natural. If the human cannot fully substitute for nature, nor can it perfectly represent the nonhuman; and yet the human is the summary or concentration of nature. Political representation of nature builds upon these commitments: not full substitution—although the human does what nature cannot do for itself, namely, speak for the nonhuman in political negotiation—and yet also not full representation, but irrevocable representation, for the human is the recapitulation of nature. To say "human" is to say "nature," but nonidentically. The substitution of nature by humanity does not cancel nature; the representation of nature by the human is never perfect but neither can it be avoided.[40]

If the above is right, what needs to be grasped in political representation is the precise combination of representation and substitution. Nature is not personal and so cannot be fully substituted by the human. So we have partial substitution and irrevocable representation—the former qualifies the latter. This indicates a direct democracy of the human-natural; a postnatural democracy tends toward direct democracy. (In that I am drawing on a conceptuality associated with atonement theory here, is it significant that Hobbes is a methodological atheist and Locke a Socinian—therefore neither is interested in atonement theory? Thus their accounts of natural right cannot grasp the ways in which we participate in nature and nature in us. Whereas Hobbes and Locke invest in mechanism, contract, and property, I invest in social relations, analogical participation, and the common realm of nature, humanity, and God.) Thus the postnatural will of the people is always a representative, substitutionary will: nature must be represented but can never be fully represented. The grittiness of democracy is increased by the demand that nature is always represented, but also a sense of its unruliness is maintained by accepting that the substitution of nature by the human is never complete. When matters of ecological sustainability are raised, we should therefore encourage experiments in direct democracy as a way of acknowledging that the human represents nature properly, but not fully.[41]

However, since direct democracy does not always function well in the complexity of modern societies, indirect democracy must also be practiced. Given that the representative role of the human is irrevocable and yet that the representative's knowledge is incomplete, caution and patience will here be important considerations. What will be crucial here is to what extent decisions taken are reversible. Decisions must be taken, yet in ways that respect the insecurity of the representative's knowledge. It would be interesting to explore this combination of action and caution in such pressing issues as nuclear power, land management, and oil exploration. Those persons or groups who will be strongly affected by the irreversibility of such decisions or who have close knowledge of the likely impacts of such decisions would be important representatives in this democratic process of negotiation. Offering situated ecological forms of knowledge or testimony as to the consequences of such decisions would be a vital part of their representative role. It is likely that fresh experiments in direct democracy would intersect with the holders of such knowledge and testimony.

Put differently, political representation of nature must resist the standard strategies that deny nature's representation. As we see in the first section of this chapter, these strategies are: (1) temporal deferral, in which the failure to take action now means that certain ecological states or trends will become irreversible; (2) spatial redistribution, in which irreversible injustice is visited upon poorer and/or nonwhite communities; (3) amelioration through technology (that is, private enterprise, market), in which the irreversibility of decisions is sidelined by reference to technological development that, it is hoped, will either reverse the irreversibility or attend to the unwelcome consequences of irreversibility (thereby magically rendering irreversibility as being without consequence).

The Tragic If these strategies must be resisted, what may be affirmed theologically? That the way in which the human opens out onto the nonhuman involves the tragic. Why is this so? The human acts as a representative of the nonhuman to present the common relations between the human and nonhuman based in participation in social life. This, we might say, is the default position in the doctrine of creation: postnatural humanity is always after nature in the senses of both exceeding yet also following nature. The human represents such common creatureliness in any circumstance. Humanity and nature may thereby be understood as *citizens* in a common realm.[42]

Is this too easy, however? To argue for the ecosociality of nature and humanity to explicate the postnaturalness of humanity may indicate something of the quantity and quality—the dialectic, if you will—in which humanity-nature relations are founded. Yet in this consideration of the political representation of nature, if politics is founded on the Schmittian distinction "between friend and enemy" and so is concerned with the exercise of force or violence, how violence is to be understood in relation to nature remains unclear.[43] We do on occasion talk of violence against nature; an oil spill at sea might be an example. Yet this is clearly a highly analogical use, as are the occasions when we speak of natural violence against the human; a tsunami might be a good example here. Indeed, we certainly do not wish to accept Schmitt's friend/enemy distinction and then apply that to nature—as if to say that nature is our enemy.

Nonetheless, if politics is founded on the acknowledgment of the employment of violence, perhaps we should say that through our political actions pressure is placed upon our natural conditions—the interweaving hybridity that we may call humanity-nature. My earlier example from British politics in August 2006 may illustrate the point: if there is change to our climate, and if some of that change may be sourced to human economic action, then the in-betweenness of nature is being subjected to stress. How should we respond to that? If we are to act responsibly, to what precisely are we responding, given the numbers of ways in which nature is presented in our political actions and discourses?[44] To affirm an ethics of responsibility in our postnatural political world, we need to address the matter of postnatural *standards*.

Moreover, these political actions governed by an ethics of response to postnatural standards will often be tragic. For in our postnatural circumstance, nature is not available to provide us with the requisite natural standards. Yet it is in this very failure to provide that nature supports us; the unsatisfactory incompleteness of nature's directedness toward the human is the manner of nature's support and—however difficult to interpret—the provision of natural standards.[45] That is why our relationship with nature is tragic: this relationship bears the weight of what we need to expel from our society, either as fearful or pitiable. The task of theological anthropology is to remind us of the pitiable. Of course, what must be sacrificed in this noncultic, nonmythological reading is *ourselves*. We require, then, a new subject, a sacrificial agent, to be the "last human."

What we are doing at present, of course, is inventing a new *pharmakos* in order to defend and sustain our own security. The latest *pharmakos* is the terrorist, whom we fear but cannot pity. Such a fearful subject must either be degraded (as in the pens at Guantánamo Bay) or expelled (recall the shock in Britain that it was *British* Muslims who were responsible for the explosions in London on July 7, 2005, and the attempts to blame their trips to Pakistan for their "indoctrination"). Yet our longer-term survival, let alone security, turns upon a resistance to scapegoating and the renewal of *sacrificial* actions: the nurturing of pity rather than fear. In our relationships with nature, that means understanding the difference between humanity and nature as tragic. This tragic difference is not the difference that requires the domination of the other in a necessarily unsuccessful effort to complete it, nor the exclusion of the other in the desperate desire to control it. Instead, what is required is a sense of the incompleteness of nature, of its varied engagement with us; in its fractured state, nature acts in our support.[46]

The tragic question is therefore: How are we to act morally if such action jeopardizes us, the agents? Additionally, if our actions have consequences that we do not and cannot foresee, how should we act? With regard to nature, we must be judge in our own cause—and yet we cannot act only "humanly" now, but also "naturally." To be a just act, such acts of judging will be sacrificial acts in which we are placed at risk.[47] To be the "last human" calls into question what it means to judge in our own cause. Yet we must do so in the hybrid mediations of an impure nature. The postnatural invokes the tragic.

The Apocalyptic   The apocalyptic is the practice and style of thinking of the powerless, those with the least stake in the system. Apocalypse is usually catastrophic; it is a style of discourse that expects—and looks forward to—historical discontinuities, a revolution. In this rupture there is an unveiling, a disclosing of the true meaning of history. And this unveiling is disruptive. Indeed, it is often associated in its Christian form with the theme of death and judgment. On account of this emphasis on disruption, it is those without much investment in the system who thereby maintain a political interest in apocalypse. If eschatology refers to the problem of access to God's own goodness, then, as Jürgen Moltmann writes, the apocalyptic is what stops Christian eschatology from being overoptimistic.[48] How might the condition of the postnatural be cured of any tendencies toward overoptimism?

Certainly, we should note that the rule of God has the quality of finality. "Many modern "apocalypses" are not truly apocalyptic," writes Colin Gunton, "because they do not envisage some form of divine action that is ontologically final."[49] That is, the rule of God is concerned with judgment. Because it is concerned with judgment, the rule of God is thereby fundamentally normative. To say that creation has a place in God's purposes is not a descriptive but rather a normative statement. We are referred to how the world will finally be with God. In the consummation of God's ruling, attention is directed not only to transformation by divine agency but also to the normative quality of God's goodness. In eschatology we are not concerned with a description of future states but instead with the final moral ordering of this world and what the final consummation means for the life of God.[50]

One way of construing the apocalyptic in terms of judgment and crisis would be to build into our theory of human-nature interaction some account of impartiality. That is, our inquiry needs to stress how political representation between the human and the nonhuman must be operated *impartially*. "Do the rights of individual human beings," asks Seán McDonagh, "always and forever take precedence over the rights of other species to survive?"[51] Thus, in theological perspective, both humanity and nature must be treated impartially. The notion of impartiality is a way of thickening our account of the relations between nature and humanity and suggests a broadening of what we mean by the common good. That is, the common good can be served only by means of the testing required by the switching of perspectives that the notion of impartiality invites.[52] Such a way indicates self-judgment and the requirement of conversion. Such impartiality would be very hard to practice. For, habitually, we side with ourselves against nonhuman nature. Impartiality here means the criticism of dominant narratives that we tell about ourselves in relation to nature; this, then, is a militant impartiality. Moreover, such militant impartiality is part of the postnatural condition.

Apocalyptic thinking, I say above, is a style of thought practiced by the powerless, by those without a stake in the present system. Christian eschatology recommends a God who does not close down but rather *closes in*.[53] If God is closing down, then we must hurry. However, if God is closing in, then we must review, change, and convert. As Seán McDonagh puts it, "Christians in local churches are being called to imitate the Master and give their lives 'for the life of the world.'"[54] We should be impatient for change, but only if this is the change of conversion, of self-assessment, of sometimes calling ourselves into question by judging naturally as well as humanly.

THE LAST HUMAN?

So far, I am arguing that the endist discourse of "without nature" raises the issues of human action and the matter of transhistorical standards. Yet one matter remains unattended to: In my steady defense of a postnatural moral order, what do I mean by the "last human"?[55]

The last human indicates that the natural has given way to the postnatural. We are the last human because we cannot understand ourselves as we have done in the past as interacting with some separate zone called nature, usually in some attempt to get beyond nature. Neither can we understand ourselves as not human, for if we do that, we have only two options: to

consider ourselves as either gods or animals. Both options thrust us outside the God-founded and -oriented sociality of humanity and nature.
Claims to divinity and animality are, in any case, disastrous political options as they fund idolatries and persecutions. The last human is therefore
not a state but a *task*: to interpret ourselves as human not in distinction
from the nonhuman but by reference to a common sociality of representation, the tragic, and the apocalyptic. The last human is in process of
becoming.

To be the last human is to identify a realm of political action in which
the human acts naturally as well as humanly, knowing that nature must be
represented, that such representative acts will be tragic, and as such will
need to respond to the approach of God through the criticism of narratives
in which humans are always given the primacy. I am recommending an
ecclesial epistemology in which trust may yet be reestablished by the effort
of representation, impartially and yet tragically.

A final question: How is the postnatural transhistorical? The postnatural may be understood as transhistorical in that: (1) it refers to the finality
of God's action in such fashion to require militant yet impartial action in
which the narrative of primacy of the rich human is not granted the default
position; (2) it refers also to the condition or quality of our interactions
with nature, the tragic—suggesting a certain concept of nature as *pro nobis*
but also *extra nos* in which, again, we are the ones whose primacy may have
to be called into question and in which nature is to be pitied rather than
feared; (3) finally, it refers to that which needs direct and indirect democratic representation: the transcendence of nature requires political constitution in the manner of the human representation of it. Nature exceeds
the human by way of action, divine and human, which also identifies humanity and nature as coactors. The postnatural transhistorical is given by
and in praxis, which both preserves and destroys. Put differently, nature is
presence toward negotiation, that is, both constituting and dispossessing.

What is resecured in this fashion is the possibility and actuality of
agency. In that our relationships are tragic, we cannot identify clearly the
dividing line between the human and the natural so as to stop history dead.
Since God closes in on the nonhuman as well as the human, humanity is
required to act impartially and therefore perhaps not always to defend this
generation's primacy. Moreover, as represented politically in a postnatural
condition, nature participates in political processes and thereby is reconstituted and reidentified in terms of political agency.[56] As such, ecclesial
epistemology recruits a civic epistemology: trust in a morally chastened,
active democracy that seeks metanoia.

To be in this postnatural condition is to be not in some end state but rather in a realm in which human action is characterized by reference to representing nature politically in ways that acknowledge the tragic quality of human activity and work militantly and impartially for the postnatural good. The postnatural condition is one in which nature and mediations are never absent. What is never absent, also, is grit in the operations of the common realm. Such grit specifies human action as vicarious, tragic, and militantly impartial; the last human acts vicariously, tragically, and impartially. The postnatural is, then, a theological condition. And who would wish to be without it?

Grace without Nature

Kathryn Tanner

Must Christian theology have an interest in a stable, fixed, and clearly demarcated human nature, the sort of nature that biogenetics calls into question? If Christian theology can follow the lead of biogenetics in this regard, how would grace—the idea of a free gift of God beyond our natural created endowments—need to be reconceptualized, absent any reference to such a nature? By exploring a commonly overlooked and underdeveloped understanding of the way humans are created in the image of God, I try to show that Christian theology need not assume a human nature of the sort called in question by biogenetics. I then develop an account of grace without nature in conversation with modern controversies, particularly in Catholicism, over the relationship between nature and grace.

Human "Nature"

Theological discussion of human beings, prompted by the Genesis verses about their creation in the image of God, often amounts to the effort to specify some set of clearly bounded, self-enclosed properties, a given human nature, which both reflects the divine nature and sets humans off from all other creatures. Humans are created in the image of God because, unlike other creatures, they have reason or free will or the ability to rule over others as God does. Or so the story commonly goes.

A radical deflection, however, of this concern to specify a sharply defined, clearly delimited human nature comes about in Christian theology when the Word of God, a divine person or principle, rather than human nature, is taken to be the primary image of God. The image in the Genesis verse, "Let us make humankind in our image" (Gen. 1:26), is understood Christologically to refer to the second person of the Trinity. The image of God is primarily, then, a divine image and not a human one. Human beings do not image God in and of themselves. They come to image God only when they take on that divine image and are deified, formed according to the divine Word as Christ's humanity was.

With this loss of a primary preoccupation with human nature per se as the image of God comes an odd refocusing of what is of interest about human beings. Since human beings do not image God in and of themselves but only when radically reworked into the divine image through Christ, it is the plasticity of human nature that becomes important. Plasticity is the capacity that allows humans to image God.

Because of this interest in plasticity or radical transformability, theologians of this ilk often exhibit a concern for natural processes of growth through nourishment.[1] All living creatures become themselves by taking in things from outside themselves; seeds, for example, require food from without in order to germinate. Humans, because they are made to be in the image of God, require God for their nourishment. In heaven, indeed, God will be our only food and drink:

> While our present life is active amongst a variety of multiform conditions, and the things which we have relations with are numerous, for instance, time, air, locality, food and drink, clothing, sunlight, lamplight, and other necessities of life, none of which, many though they be, are God—that blessed state which we hope for is in need of none of these things, but the Divine Being will become all [1 Cor. 15:28], and instead of all, to us, distributing Himself proportionately to every need of that existence. . . . God [will] become . . . locality, and home, and clothing, and food, and drink, and light, and riches, and dominion, and everything thinkable and nameable that goes to make our life happy.[2]

In the case of all other livings things, whatever they take in is formed according to the limits of their preestablished natures. For example, the natural resources assimilated by a plant for its nourishment—light, water, nutrients from the soil, and so on—are transformed to conform to the plant's nature. The plant remains itself, becoming merely a bigger and better version of itself, when there is genuine nourishment for the plant's good. When human beings take in God as their proper nourishment, they come out, to the contrary, as God. They are turned thereby into the matter, so to speak, for a new divine organization of what they are. They become God's image, rather than God's image becoming theirs; humans are reworked according to God's pattern of living, rather than God being reworked according to a human one. Like what happens to light, water, and soil—but now with a peculiar reversal of consequences from the usual scenario—men, women, children, Greek and Jew, free and slave all go into the process of reformation and come out with a divine identity, as Gregory Nazianzen says:

> This is the great mystery planned for us by God . . . to . . . recover his image and refashion the human, that we might all become one in Christ . . . that we might no longer be male and female, barbarian, Scythian, slave or free (which are identifying marks of the flesh), but might bear in ourselves only the form of God, by whom and for whom we came to be, and be shaped and imprinted by him to such an extent that we are recognized by this alone.[3]

In keeping with this general interest in plasticity, human beings in these theologies are often compared to soft wax, which a vast variety of seals might indent to their image, or called mirrors of that which they gaze upon. Like vessels that gain their character from their contents, humans take on new identities according to the uses to which they put themselves.

Expressed less metaphorically (and in a more contemporary idiom), one could say that human life takes a variety of forms depending on what it is that people care about.[4] As Augustine puts it, "Such is the strength of love, that the mind draws in with itself those things which it has long thought of with love, and has grown into them by the close adherence."[5] Human beings exercise self-reflective powers; they are able to make an object of themselves in projects of self-fashioning and refashioning, following changeable judgments about what is most important to them: fancy cars, the respect of their peers, wisdom, and so on. They attach themselves to these objects of desire and draw them into themselves, so to speak, as variable organizing principles of their lives. Gregory of Nyssa says, "Human nature adapts itself to the direction of thought and it changes according to whatever form it is inclined to by the impulse of free choice."[6] This means—to return to a previous metaphor—that:

Human nature is in fact like a mirror, and it takes on different appearances according to the impressions of free will. If gold is held up to the mirror, the mirror assumes the appearance of gold and reflects the splendor of gold's substance. If anything abominable is held up, its ugliness is impressed in the mirror.[7]

Reflective capacities of self-judgment mean humans can try to reshape in a self-critical fashion even those desires they cannot help having. One may have the natural desire in this sense to eat, but one need not shape one's life around the importance of food—asceticism is a case in point. Humans have the capacity to use the passions of their animal natures (as Nyssa would term them)—for example, their natural attraction to what benefits them—as instruments of either virtue or vice.[8] Natural attraction may propel them toward, say, profligacy—or God. Humans have the power to cultivate or discourage natural drives and tendencies, making efforts, for example, to alter their intensities through stimulation or neglect or to rework the way they figure in one's life as a whole. Indeed, these self-reflective powers account for why human lives can become so horrible, much more horrible than those of other animals; the anger, for example, that an animal might fleetingly feel when faced with an opponent can be husbanded by the human mind—dwelt upon—so as to pervade all one's dealings with others in a host of variable forms—envy, malice, conspiracy, deceit—with the result that one's whole nature is traced anew after that design.[9]

Human beings have plastic powers, self-formative capacities, and it is the fact that those capacities are not determined to one thing as natural desires are—the fact that those capacities need not incline in a predetermined direction according to the givens of one's nature or essential definition (following here a Thomistic understanding of natural desire)—that accounts for the heightened variability of their effects in operation. People turn out in wildly different ways for better or for worse. Or one might say that the self-formative capacities of humans do have a nature but the particular nature of rational volition is just to have no definite nature to which it must be true in the way that animals must be true to their natures when acting properly for their own good. Humans can think of a variety of things that it would be good to do in certain respects or for certain purposes, and what they decide about what is most important to them in the course of such deliberations determines in great part the character of their lives, the identity they come to exhibit in their acts; *that* is their nature.

The Eastern Church's stress on free will as the image—or often secondarily, rule in the sense of self-rule—can now be taken in a new light, not as the promotion of some vaunted power in a positive sense, an imitation of divine omnipotence, but as an interest in the unusual plasticity of human lives absent any predetermined direction by nature. Free will is an indication of variability. Their unusual powers of self-determination mean humans can become anything along the continuum of ontological ranks, from the bottom to the top.

Humans, it is true, are determined to God: being formed in the image of God is their good by nature. But that is just *not* to be determined in any particular direction, as other things are, since God is the absolute good and not a limited one. Humans might have a nature that imitates God only by not having a clearly delimited nature. Every other creature imitates God by expressing the goodness that God is in a limited form; they are good by being a definite something—a pig or a rock, indeed the best pig or rock they can be. While humans are a definite sort of creature distinct from others and in that sense of course still have a particular nature (they are not God who alone is different from others by not being a kind of thing), humans still stand out by their failure to be clearly limited by a particular nature as other creatures are.

Failure of definition by remaining ill defined is not so much the point; what is primarily at issue here is a failure of definition through excessive love. Humans seem to have an underlying concern for what is absolutely good per se—for God—for what is not merely good in certain respects but fully good in a perfectly unlimited way. They want in some sense to *be* that absolute good rather than a particular sort of thing by being formed in and through a relationship with it, for example, by knowing the absolute truth that is God, the absolute good for human cognition that comes by way of God's very presence to the mind. Their strangely unlimited character would then be the fundamental reason for traditional theological preoccupation with human intelligence and will when discussing the way humans are the image of God. These faculties are of interest because of their excessive openness, because, one might say, of their attraction to formation through what exceeds their own or any limited nature.

All the qualities of humans typically highlighted by Gregory of Nyssa, Athanasius, Irenaeus, and Cyril of Alexandria (the theologians I am interested in here) have something to do with human rational capacities. And there is probably a good reason for this, even from a more modern point of view less enamored of a mind-matter dualism, if indefinite plasticity, the nature that is no nature, is what these theologians are trying to get at.

It is important to see, however, that plastic or nonnatured *bodies* are the ultimate issue even for these early church theologians. At the end of the day, it is human bodies that are to be remade into Christ's body.

Human beings form themselves with reference to a whole host of outside influences—people, places, animate and inanimate influences, what have you—both spiritual and material things. What is formed is their whole lives, irrespective of any division between the material and the spiritual. When our minds are therefore formed according to the divine image, so are our bodies. When the mind is "adorned by the likeness of the archetypal beauty . . . the nature which is governed by it [i.e., the body] . . . is adorned by the beauty that the mind gives, being, so to say, a mirror of the mirror."[10]

Human materiality is essential to the image of God so as to take the whole of existence to God. This is why angels or disembodied pure intelligences are not traditionally said to be the image. Only in virtue of the fact that they have bodies can the whole world hope in humans. Humans demonstrate that, appearances to the contrary (especially in the cultural and philosophical milieu of the early church), the material world itself is plastic—by extension just as plastic to divine influence, one might hope, as human lives. God formed humans out of the dust of the earth so that when formed in the image of God, humans might show that the earth, too, can be made over in God's image; both matter and mind are made for a single grace.[11]

The new genetic technologies that blur species boundaries serve only to confirm such a theological hope in the plasticity of bodies generally. It is not merely the bodies of human beings that are radically transformable through the exercise of their rational capacities for choice. Expanded by technological know-how, these same human capacities prove the alterability of the entire world. Animal bodies, for example, are now just as clearly alterable as human ones and in a far more literal way than previously conceived. These new technologies, like all exercise of human free will, can be used for good or ill, with the stakes raised enormously now that humans can make monsters of more than themselves. The good, which Christians ultimately identify with God, remains the hoped for end of radical transformability.

Grace

Interest in a self-contained, clearly bounded human nature dissolves when human life is understood to be created in the image of the Word of God or Christ. But what becomes of grace without such a nature? If it is just human nature not to have a nature, have we not lost along with it a clear sense of the difference between nature and grace? That grace is not nature, something more than our natural created endowments, is quite easy to see when human nature is considered self-sufficient and complete in its own terms, but how might such a difference be sustained now?

The problem may not be as difficult as first appears. Henri de Lubac convincingly demonstrated some time ago that a self-contained, sharply bounded human character has not always been the prerequisite for Christian understanding of the graciousness of God's gift in Christ.[12] For most of Christian history, indeed, articulation of the fact that what human beings are to become in Christ is a gracious gift from God did not require reference to a concept of a pure human nature, that is, a simply self-contained human character with its own humanly achievable ends apart from any special divine help.

The idea of pure nature, as de Lubac shows, is implicated in a distinctively modern naturalism without any obvious compatibility with Christian faith. In a naturalistic vein, the idea of pure nature suggests, in other words, the self-sufficiency of the natural apart from the God who creates and saves it. It suggests that human nature is most properly itself without God's grace. And it has the effect of making God's grace an extrinsic addition to human life, something we could very well do without. Grace becomes an optional, even superfluous addition to human life, which is lived quite well on its own terms.

As an alternative to the idea of pure nature, de Lubac suggests in his *Surnaturel* the return to an Augustinian-inflected Thomism in which humans have a natural desire for a supernatural end unattainable by their own powers. The grace of Christ obviously cannot be an external addendum if human nature is ordered of itself to God.

The problem for de Lubac's position, and a host of theologies like his, is showing the gratuity or unowed character of grace and, secondarily, the integrity of the human apart from grace without lapsing once again into an appeal to pure nature. A Thomistic account of natural desire (because of its Aristotelian appeal to essential nature-based finalities) suggests, first of all, that humans are moving on their own accord toward God on the basis of their natural capacities. This is a kind of incipient naturalism even if the final end of such natural drives requires the outside help of God and is beyond those drives' created capacities. Whether or not humans achieve the end that only God's grace can provide, they have the dignity of a life devoted to such an end with all the preliminary goods achievable simply by their own powers. Life without God's grace is still worthwhile, and in this way the idea of a nature sufficient of itself is broached. Even if what they can achieve on their own is subordinated to that final end and placed on a single historical trajectory with it rather than being self-contained, humans still seem capable of achieving quite a lot independently of the grace God gives in Christ. The actual gift of grace therefore retains the impression of being an appendage. Naturalism, some kind of purely natural state apart from grace, again seems here the prerequisite for gratuity of the very sort that de Lubac is trying to avoid.

A self-generated dynamism on the way to God makes it hard, in the second place, to avoid the suggestion that the essential nature of humanity demands the gifts that only God can give, that is, the beatific vision of God face-to-face. God has created them with the sort of constitution that makes seeing God face-to-face their natural end, what they are naturally attracted to; and unless God is willing to frustrate God's own intentions, it would seem that the actual gift of grace follows necessarily from God's gift to humans of such a nature.

A major problem, one might say, with a natural desire for God, understood in Thomistic terms, is its focus on our final destiny as a human state. God is the absolute truth and the absolute good that drives us forward in constant dissatisfaction with any form of knowledge or goodness short of God; that is what the natural desire for God amounts to as a kind of ongoing human dynamism or movement toward God. One pictures, then, an unrolling sequence of human states—for example, an ideally progressively better understanding of God with a final human state at the end, as perfect a knowledge of God as is possible by way of divinely elevated human capacities. It becomes hard to see the radical character of the gap, so speak, between what we are and what we are given in Christ, since the human consequences of the latter are in this way pressed to the fore.

The natural desire for God in a Thomistic sense carries us along a trajectory of varying human states, those without or with the help that only God can give, if this natural desire for God is to reach its term. The gratuity of grace therefore also tends to be argued for in terms of this axis of varying human states, its gratuity demonstrated, that is, by some sort of discontinuity between the human character with which we were created and the human state we will enjoy by means of God's grace. The natural desire or orientation to that final human state always exists itself, however, to bridge the gap and lessen the discontinuity; the gap can never be wide enough to avoid the suggestion of some sort of continuity between the two, thereby lessening the gratuity of grace.

On the theological account I offer, alternatively, we image God in the strongest way when we have the divine image for our own through unity with it. We image God only secondarily, in a weaker sense, in our own humanity when the divine image we possess through unity with it reworks our humanity into a human version of itself. It is not just plasticity, then, that is at issue when considering humans as the image of God, but plasticity of a certain sort: openness to, essential dependence upon, the influence of the alien or foreign—God, who is other than creatures, what they are not.

On this view of grace, the focus is therefore on the gift of God's very self, with human states being that primary gift's secondary consequences. And this means that the gratuity of grace can now be assured by the very difference between God and creatures, between the gift of God and any and all human states.[13] The difference between creator and creature does the work now of showing how grace is gratuitous, and therefore this grace is gratuitous even if it is always enjoyed by us without the prior existence of any merely natural human state of nonenjoyment:

> The soul itself, even though it may be always wise—as it will be, when set free from all eternity—will be wise through participation in the changeless Wisdom, which is other than itself. For even if the atmosphere was never bereft of the light which is shed on it, there would still be the difference between its being and the light by which it is illuminated.[14]

As the gift of God's very self, the gift of salvation in Christ is as gratuitous, unowed, and freely given as anything can be, because of the gap between God and creatures. There can be some mediating continuum between human states, no matter how low the one and how elevated the other, but not between God and creatures. The gift of God's very self is never anything less than unexacted.

On this account of creation and salvation in the image of God, humans do not have a natural desire for God apart from the actual gift of God's own self to them. Desire for God is not strictly speaking a self-generated desire stemming from the character of human nature per se, since human nature has not been made to exist on its own. Instead, it is by participating in God, sharing in God's own life, that we come to desire God. The only natural desire for God we have is the one that participation in God gives rise to; and there is no effort to imagine human nature and its desires in some original state apart from that gift. The effect of this is not, then, to play down our natural desire for God in the way Thomistic appeals to a desire for God that is only elicited by grace typically do;[15] the gift of God that produces the desire is always given, and the desire itself is still natural, as we see below.

We naturally desire the source of the good that has been good to us;
we naturally desire what we are not in virtue of the fact that what we are
not is superior to ourselves, better than what we would be without it, as
Nyssa points out: "As long as a nature is in defect as regards the good, the
superior existence exerts upon this inferior one a ceaseless attraction
towards itself."[16] We therefore do not move toward God on our own apart
from some prior gift of God's own goodness spurring us on:

> For to the Godhead it properly belongs to lack no conceivable thing which
> is regarded as good, while the creation attains excellence by partaking in
> something better than itself; and further, [it] not only had a beginning of
> its being, but also is found to be constantly in a state of beginning to be in
> excellence, by its continual advance in improvement, since . . . all that it
> has acquired becomes by participation a beginning of its ascent to some-
> thing still greater.[17]

The gift of God's own self is not pictured here as a secondary temporal
addition to a human nature that exists at the start without it. Instead, it is
given to humans from the very first. The difference between nature and
grace is therefore not demonstrated by spacing the two gifts out temporally in a way that implies that human nature, without the actual gifts of
grace and with only a desire or orientation for them, is a real human state
at a particular historical time, a kind of pure nature in that sense, even if
ordered to grace.

Because humans are not pictured as properly existing at first on their
own, there indeed is not the same impetus to show how human nature
without the gift of God is still somehow ordered to it. It is the temporal
spacing between two historical states—humans existing first without and
then with the actual gift of God—that opens up the possibility of an extrinsic relation between them; if humans at some point exist on their own
without the gift of God, why do they need it at all? The temporal spacing,
then, produces the need to show how the one is ordered to the other. And
with this intrinsic ordering of human nature to God's grace comes the
problem of suggesting that grace is owed to humans: created with a nature
essentially ordered to it, human beings seem due the grace of God that is
to be theirs later. The imaginative prerequisite and impetus for the idea
of an intrinsic ordering of human nature to God's grace is gone now that
human nature is never properly considered to exist without the grace of
God. There is no way for the gift of God's self to appear a superfluous
addition to human nature if one cannot even imagine human nature existing without it.

It is true that sin brings the loss of the gift of grace as a sort of historical stage to which grace must then be added. Such a loss might be thought to prompt once again, particularly in Catholic circles worried about an extrinsic grace, a consideration of how humans without the gift of God are still ordered to it, in virtue of whatever purely natural desires remain under conditions of sin. But on the account I am offering, retention of a desire for God in a state of sin might be better understood as the product of the continuing influence of the very same gift with which we started. That gift is still being offered even as we turn away from it in sin. When we shut our eyes to the light of God, it is we who produce the barrier to the light, without the light of God itself retiring or withdrawing from us.[18] God is still present to us, in other words, through the gift of the Holy Spirit making the second person of the Trinity available to us as the organizational principal of our lives, and it is only because of that fact—its ongoing influence despite our refusal—that we retain any desire for God at all, an attraction to God as our good, even as we lead lives of sin.

In contrast to a Thomistic account of a natural desire for God, I propose that the gift of God's self is not natural to us if one considers the character of human nature on its own terms. God is just not the sort of thing that can accord with a creature's nature; grace is alien or foreign to us just because we have a created nature and are not ourselves divine. Even when we enjoy the gift of God's own life, it never becomes natural to us in the sense of becoming our own property; it remains alien to us in its very divinity. We are elevated beyond our human natures when we are saved; and the powers we enjoy—eternal life, for example—are properly divine powers that no creature ever enjoys in and of itself. Human nature and the benefits of the divine life it now enjoys remain quite distinct.

If not ours by nature, then, the gift of God is still, one might say, naturally ours or natural to us.[19] It is naturally ours because having this gift is to be our ordinary or proper state as God's creatures. The gift of God is natural to us in that it is from the first and constantly proffered to us (apart from sin, and, as we saw above, maybe even then, too). As de Lubac says, "Adam found [the help of God] naturally, as something normally at his disposal, and always as it were within his reach, without having to ask for it first. He did not have to seek God, because God was already near him."[20] As our ordinary and proper condition, the enjoyment of such an exterior or alien gift of God's self is simply what it means to be human. The quite hypothetical question of whether human beings might have been created without this gift of grace is then tantamount to asking whether humans might not have been created human at all but as some other sort of creature with a more self-contained existence, its operations content with the finite goods that accord with the limitations of its own nature as an animal's operations are.

The desire for God is naturally ours in the same sense. It is what we would ordinarily and properly display in virtue of a participation in God that is always to be granted to us as our normal state. We would not, then, acquire such a desire from without by, say, being taught it by another; Saint Basil the Great explains, "instruction in yearning for the divine does not come from outside; but simultaneously with the fashioning of the living creature."[21] Though requiring cultivation and capable of falling into neglect, such a desire is not learned but natural to us in the same sense that love of one's benefactors—love, for example, of children for their parents—is natural to us.[22]

Therefore the loss of the gift of God's self does us harm; its loss creates an unnatural state in us, manifest by the suffering that ensues. Life with the gift of God's very self must be natural to us in the sense that we live excellently with it—this gift is for our good—and in that its loss brings about our misery and destruction. Alienated from God, we die in both body and soul; we suffer a literal death, that is, and the character of our lives is corrupted. As Nyssa puts it:

> Seeing that ignorance of the true good is like a mist . . . and when that mist grows denser a cloud is formed so thick that Truth's rays cannot pierce through these depths of ignorance, it follows further that with the total deprivation of the light the soul's life ceases altogether; for we have said that the real life of the soul is acted out in participation of the Good; but when ignorance hinders this apprehension of God, the soul which thus ceases to partake of God, ceases also to live.[23]

Absent a Thomistic account of the natural desire for God, not just the gratuity of grace but the integrity of human nature can be better secured, too. As I suggest above, the Thomistic account always brings with it some suggestion of a hypothetical or subordinate natural completion of human desire in the effort to secure both the gratuity of grace and the integrity of our natures.[24] For example, it might be said that human nature is capable of knowing the God of the philosophers, even if the Trinity exceeds its grasp. One can know something about God by one's natural powers, no matter how provisional. Philosophy appears here as a kind of natural completion of the human desire to know.

On the account I am offering, to the contrary, one can say without any hedging that human nature is complete only with the gift of God's own self, in that human capacities have no excellence of operation without that gift; naturalism is therefore more thoroughly repudiated. Cyril of Alexandria, for example, and Augustine, too, famously distinguish between our existence and our well-being and claim that the latter is a function of God's own entrance within us. We are rational creatures, and that is a sort of image of God—a weak sort—but when we know well, then we are the image of God in a strong sense in virtue of the fact that the truth itself, God, has entered within us to give us the truth. The excellent functioning of our native capacities is not a self-sufficient operation, then, in the sense of simply unrolling from our own capabilities, but requires a strong dependence on the very powers of God that have become ours for the taking in some extraordinary gift of God to us of what is not ours by nature.

Rather than making the problem of human integrity more acute, the integrity of human nature follows here, as the gratuity of grace does, from the idea of participation in, the gift to us of, what we are not that is part and parcel of this view of God-given human excellence. It is simply part of the definition of receiving something foreign or alien, something from outside oneself, that its being given and taken away do not affect one's essential character.[25] This is just to say, for example, that, although we do not know well without the gift of the truth which is God (and in that sense we require God for the completion of our rational natures), we are rational with or without it.[26]

NOTES

WITHOUT NATURE?
David Albertson

1. Friedrich Nietzsche, *Werke*, ed. Karl Schlechta (Munich, Germany: Carl Hanser, 1958), 1:231–232. See Joachim Ritter and Karlfried Gründer, eds., *Historisches Wörterbuch der Philosophie [HWPh]* (Basel, Switzerland: Schwabe, 1984), 6:491. Translations are the author's unless otherwise noted. I thank Cabell King for his several contributions to this introduction. Many of the points made here express conclusions we reached together in conversations leading up to the present volume.

2. Bill McKibben, *The End of Nature* (New York: Anchor Books, 1989).

3. Jeff Goodell, *Big Coal: The Dirty Secret Behind America's Energy Future* (Boston: Houghton Mifflin, 2006), 16.

4. Goodell recounts one example:

According to one EPA study, the runoff from [strip mines] is sometimes three to five times higher than in undisturbed areas, which means that five inches of rain—about the amount that fell in southern West Virginia from June 13 to June 19, 2003—has the same effect as would fifteen to twenty-five inches. . . . What bothered [one landowner living in the shade of a West Virginia strip mine] most was not losing her front yard to the floodwaters. It was the attitude of the engineer from the coal company who showed up the morning after. [She] noticed him standing out in her yard and waded through the muck to see what he wanted. "The first thing out of his mouth was, 'We are not responsible for this. It was an act of God.'"

Ibid., 38.

5. Clark L. Erickson, "Prehistoric Landscape Management in the Andean Highlands: Raised Field Agriculture and Its Environmental Impact," *Population and Environment* 13.4 (Summer 1992):286; Clark L. Erickson, "Agricultural Landscapes as World Heritage: Raised Field Agriculture in Bolivia and Peru," in *Managing Change: Sustainable Approaches to the Conservation of the Built Environment* (Los Angeles: Getty Conservation Institute, 2003), 187.

6. Quoted in James Trefil, *Human Nature: A Blueprint for Managing the Earth—By People for People* (New York: Times Books, 2004), 87.

7. Charles Moore, "Trashed: Across the Pacific Ocean, Plastics, Plastics Everywhere," *Natural History* 112.9 (November 2003), available at http://www.naturalhistorymag.com/1103/1103_feature.html.

8. Darshak M. Sanghavi, "Preschool Puberty, and a Search for the Causes," *New York Times*, October 15, 2006.

9. See Plato, *Laws* 889e–890d, in *Platonis Opera*, ed. John Burnet (Oxford: Clarendon, 1907), 5:334–335.

10. Aristotle, *Metaphysics* 5:1015a.1–3, in *The Metaphysics*, trans. Hugh Tredennick (Cambridge, Mass.: Harvard University Press, 1933), 1:220.

11. Ibid., 5:1015a.14–19, 1:222.

12. Boethius, *Contra Eutychen*, I.52–53, in *The Theological Tractates*, trans. H. F. Stewart, E. K. Rand, and S. J. Tester (Cambridge, Mass.: Harvard University Press, 1973), 80.

13. HWPh, 6:484, citing Cicero, *De finibus* V:25, 74: *consuetudine quasi alteram quondam naturam effici*. Cicero alludes to Aristotle's notion of the friend as "another I" (ho philos allos autos; verus amicus . . . tamquam alter idem).

14. *HWPh*, 6: 485, citing Augustine, *Contra Julianum* 1.69.14–5, 1.69.42 (CSEL 85.1, 76–77).

15. *HWPh*, 6:485, citing Augustine, *De diversis quaestionibus ad Simplicianum* 1.11 (CCSL 44, 16).

16. Boethius, *De fide catholica*, 239–240, in *The Theological Tractates*, trans. H. F. Stewart, E. K. Rand, and S. J. Tester (Cambridge, Mass.: Harvard University Press, 1973), 68.

17. See Henri de Lubac, *The Mystery of the Supernatural*, trans. Rosemary Sheed (New York: Crossroad, 1998); Henri de Lubac, *A Brief Catechesis on Nature and Grace*, trans. Richard Arnandez (San Francisco: Ignatius, 1984).

18. Louis Dupré, "The Dissolution of the Union of Nature and Grace at the Dawn of the Modern Age," in *The Theology of Wolfhart Pannenberg*, ed. Carl E. Braaten and Philip Clayton (Minneapolis, Minn.: Augsburg, 1988), 96. This article was later expanded into Dupré's seminal book, *Passage to Modernity. An Essay in the Hermeneutics of Nature and Culture* (New Haven, Conn.: Yale University Press, 1993).

19. Hans Urs von Balthasar, "Der Begriff der Natur in der Theologie," *Zeitschrift für Katholische Theologie* 75 (1953):452–461.

20. Although intended in a somewhat different sense, the prescient judgment of Gordon Kaufman holds true:

> If we are to make theological use of the modern notion of nature . . . we shall have to engage in theological reconstruction going down to the deepest roots of the Western religious sensibility and vocabulary. . . . What the outcome, or even the

main direction, of such far-reaching reconstruction might be, I cannot say, but there is little question in my mind that it would transform Christian faith (as we now know it) in far more profound ways than seem to be imagined by many who now blithely call for a theology of nature or for ecological theology.

Gordon Kaufman, "A Problem for Theology: The Concept of Nature," *Harvard Theological Review* 65 (1972):355.

21. See the important study by Andreas Speer, *Die Entdeckte Natur: Untersuchungen zu Begründungsversuchen einer "scientia naturalis" im 12. Jahrhundert* (Leiden, Netherlands: Brill, 1995).

22. See M.-D. Chenu, *Nature, Man and Society in the Twelfth Century*, ed. Lester Little and Jerome Taylor (Toronto: University of Toronto Press, 1997).

23. See Willemien Otten, "Nature and Scripture: Demise of a Medieval Analogy," *Harvard Theological Review* 88.2 (1995):257–284.

24. Andreas Speer, "The Discovery of Nature: The Contribution of the Chartrians to Twelfth-Century Attempts to Found a *Scientia Naturalis*," *Traditio* 52 (1997):138.

25. Nikolaus M. Häring, *Commentaries on Boethius by Thierry of Chartres and His School* (Toronto: PIMS, 1971), 555, 1.2. Otten notes that "Thierry appears to break with the tradition of Augustine-based Genesis interpretations by explaining the creation and formation of the world as dependent not so much on a single divine act, but rather as a gradual development from secondary causes." Otten, "Nature and Scripture," 274.

26. See William of Conches, *Dragmaticon philosophiae*, I.7.3, in *Guillelmi de Conchis Opera omnia*, vol. 1, ed. Italo Ronca, Corpus Christianorum Continuatio Medievalis CLII (Turnhout, Belgium: Brepols, 1997); see also Ronca's English translation with commentary in William of Conches, *A Dialogue on Natural Philosophy: Dragmaticon philosophiae*, trans. with intro. and explanatory notes by Italo Ronca and Matthew Curr (Notre Dame, Ind.: University of Notre Dame, 1997).

27. William, *Dragmaticon philosophiae*, VI.7.3.

28. See George D. Economou, *The Goddess Natura in Medieval Literature* (Cambridge, Mass.: Harvard University Press, 1972).

29. Carlos Steel, "Nature as an Object of Science: On the Medieval Contribution to a Science of Nature," in *Nature in Medieval Thought: Some Approaches East and West*, ed. Chumaru Koyama (Leiden, Netherlands: Brill, 2000), 128.

30. *Adelard of Bath, Conversations with His Nephew: On the Same and the Different, Questions on Natural Science, and On Birds*, ed. and trans. Charles Burnett (Cambridge, U.K.: Cambridge University Press, 1998), 97–99.

31. Steel, "Nature as an Object of Science," 132.

32. Ibid., 133.

THE WORLD IN ORDER
Lorraine Daston

1. Wislawa Szymborska, "View with a Grain of Sand," in *View with a Grain of Sand: Selected Poems*, trans. Stanislaw Baranczak and Clare Cavanagh (San Diego, Calif.: Harcourt Brace, 1995), 135–136.

2. Aristotle, *Nicomachean Ethics*, 1152a27–35, in *The Complete Works of Aristotle*, 2 vols., ed. Jonathan Barnes (Princeton, N.J.: Princeton University Press, 1995), 2:1820.

3. "Rache der Natur," *Berliner Kurier*, June 10, 2003, 2.

4. Arnold I. Davidson, "The Horror of Monsters," in *The Boundaries of Humanity: Humans, Animals, Machines*, ed. James J. Sheehan and Morton Sosna (Berkeley: University of California Press, 1991), 36–67.

5. Elisabeth Blair MacDougall, "A Paradise of Plants: Exotica, Rarities, and Botanical Fantasies," in *The Age of the Marvelous*, ed. Joy Kenseth (Hanover, N.H.: Hood Museum of Art, Dartmouth College, 1991), 145–157.

6. William Shakespeare, *The Winter's Tale*, 4.4.86–87.

7. Lorraine Daston and Katharine Park, *Wonders and the Order of Nature, 1150–1750* (New York: Zone, 1998), 303–328.

8. Augustine of Hippo, *Confessions*, III.8; trans. R. S. Pine-Coffin (London: Penguin, 1961), 64–66.

9. For a first attempt, see the essays and bibliography in Lorraine Daston and Fernando Vidal, *The Moral Authority of Nature* (Chicago: University of Chicago Press, 2004).

10. Aristotle, *Physics*, II.8, 199b26–30; trans. Philip H. Wicksteed and Francis M. Cornford, Loeb edition, 2 vols. (London: William Heinemann, 1929), 1:178–179.

11. Aristotle, *Politics*, I.ii, 1252a24.–1252b9; trans. H. Rackham, Loeb edition (Cambridge, Mass.: Harvard University Press, 1990 [1932]), 4–7.

12. Plato, *Republic. Books I–V*, trans. Paul Shorey (Cambridge, Mass.: Harvard University Press, 2003 [1930]), 434a–b, 371.

13. Ibid., 395d, 235.

14. J. Krynen, "Naturel. Essai sur l'argument de la nature dans la pensée politique française à la fin du moyen age," *Journal des Savants* (April–June 1982):169–190, at 179.

15. Aristotle, *Physics*, II.i, 193b8–13; 1:114–115. In one the very few passages in which Aristotle applies the term *para physin*, "contrary to nature," as a moral epithet to condemn usury, it is because this practice makes something

artificial grow and reproduce like a natural kind; Aristotle, *Politics*, I.iii.23, 1258b6–8; 51.

16. See, e.g., Guillaume de Lorris and Jean de Meun, *Roman de la rose*, trans. André Landry, 2 vols. (Paris: H. Champion, 1971–1982); see also Mechthild Modersohn, *Natura als Göttin im Mittelalter* (Berlin: Akademie Verlag, 1997), for associated imagery.

17. Plato, *Republic*, 415a–b, 305.

18. Current values concerning the desirability of human diversity in society march hand in hand with analogous claims about the desirability of biodiversity in nature, and both appeal to intuitions about the multiplicity and harmony among natural kinds, each perfect of its type.

19. In her study of evil in Hindu mythology, Wendy Doniger gives a striking example of this ethos in relation to the Sanskrit *dharma*, the semantic field of which overlaps with that of "nature" in its original sense: even those with evil *dharma* (e.g., thieves or demons) are enjoined to follow it lest the order of things, absolute *dharma*, be overturned. Wendy Doniger O'Flaherty, *The Origins of Evil in Hindu Mythology* (Berkeley: University of California Press, 1980 [1976]), 46, 94–95.

20. Augustine, *Confessions*, III.8; trans. William Watts, Loeb edition, 2 vols. (Cambridge, Mass.: Harvard University Press, 1995 [1912]), 2:127–129.

21. Yan Thomas, "Imago naturae: Note sur l'institutionnalité de la nature à Rome," *Théologie et droit dans la science politique de l'état moderne* (Rome: École française de Rome, 1991), 201–227, esp. 206–208.

22. Giuliana Lanata, *Legislazione e natura nelle novelle giustinianee* (Naples: Edizioni scientifiche italiane, 1984), 189–204.

23. Jacques Chiffoleau, "Contra naturam: Pour une approche casuistique et procédurale de la nature médiévale," *Micrologus* 4 (1996):265–312, esp. 267–278. Hence the regularity with which heretics (and infidels like Jews and Muslims) were accused of sodomy and incest by Christian theologians after the eleventh century.

24. Thomas Aquinas, *Summa theologica*, IIa–IIae, 154.12.

25. See, e.g., James Davidson, *Courtesans and Fishcakes: The Consuming Passions of Classical Athens* (London: Fontana, 1997), 179–180.

26. Euripides, *Medea*, in *Cyclops-Alcestis-Medea*, ed. and trans. David Kovacs, Loeb edition (Cambridge, Mass.: Harvard University Press, 1994), ll. 103–104 at 304–305; ll. 1339–1343 at 418–419. Euripides in his *Bacchae* employs similar bestial imagery for another case in which a mother murders her son, that of the crazed Agave, who is deceived by Dionysus into tearing her son Pentheus limb for limb. She is described as a "lioness," and she mistakes Pentheus for "the whelp of a desert lion." Euripides, *Bacchae*, trans.

Arthur S. Way, Loeb edition (Cambridge, Mass.: Harvard University Press, 1988), 898–899 at 1174.

27. Euripides, *Medea*, 333. Compare Sophocles, *Oedipus Tyrannus*, in which a blight upon crops, cattle, and women in childbirth and a plague in Thebes signal some undetected act of pollution: "A blight is on the buds that close the fruit, a blight is on the flocks of grazing cattle and on the women giving birth, killing their offspring; the fire-bearing god, hateful Pestilence, has swooped upon the city and harried it." Sophocles, *Oedipus Tyrannus*, in *Ajax-Electra-Oedipus Tyrannus*, trans. Hugh Lloyd-Jones, Loeb edition (Cambridge, Mass.: Harvard University Press, 1994), 329. Seneca, *Medea*, in *Tragedies*, trans. Frank Justus Miller, Loeb edition (Cambridge, Mass.: Harvard University Press, 1979 [1917]), 282.

28. For Aristotle on slavery, see Aristotle, *Politics*, I.3–6, 1253b1–1255a2, at 12–25.

29. John Stuart Mill, "Nature" (comp. 1850–1858), *Three Essays of Religion* (1874), in *Essays on Ethics, Religion and Society*, ed. J. M. Robson, with an intro. by F. E. L. Priestley (London: Routledge, 1996), 373–402, at 373.

30. Quoted in Thomas Mallon, "The Red Sheep," *New Yorker* (October 16, 2006), 176–182, at 182.

31. Christine M. Korsgaard, *The Sources of Normativity*, ed. Onora O'Neill (Cambridge, U.K.: Cambridge University Press, 1996).

32. Robert Boyle, *A Free Inquiry into the Vulgarly Received Notion of Nature*, ed. Edward B. Davis and Michael Hunter (Cambridge, U.K.: Cambridge University Press, 1996 [1686]), 15.

33. On Darwin, see Lorraine Daston, "How Nature Became the Other: Anthropomorphism and Anthropocentrism in Early Modern Science," in *Biology as Society, Society as Biology*, ed. Sabine Maassen, Everett Mendelsohn, and Peter Weingart (Dordrecht, Netherlands: Kluwer, 1995), 37–56.

34. Immanuel Kant, *Kritik der praktischen Vernunft*, ed. Karl Vorländer (Hamburg: Felix Meiner, 1993 [1788]), [289], 186.

35. George Eliot, *Essays of George Eliot*, ed. Thomas Pinney (New York: Columbia University Press, 1963), 413; quoted in George Levine, *Dying to Know: Scientific Epistemology and Narrative in Victorian England* (Chicago: University of Chicago Press, 2002), 109.

36. On the connection between seasonability and justice in Hesiod, see Laura Slatkin, "Measuring Authority, Authoritative Measures: Hesiod's *Works and Days*," in *The Moral Authority of Nature*, ed. Daston and Vidal, 25–49.

37. The Pindar poem from which this fragment (169) comes has been lost. Translation (slightly modified) from Herodotus, *The Histories*, III.38, trans. A. D. Godley, 2 vols., Loeb edition (Cambridge, Mass.: Harvard University Press, 1995 [1921]), 2:51.

OUR COMMON RESPONSIBILITY TO NATURE
Peter H. Raven

1. Bill McKibben, *The End of Nature* (New York: Random House, 1989).

2. Some of the data in the following paragraphs are adapted from Peter H. Raven, "Science, Sustainability and the Human Project," *Science* 297 (2002):954–958.

3. Richard H. Grove, *Green Imperialism: Colonial Expansion, Tropical Island Edens and the Origins of Environmentalism, 1600–1860* (Cambridge, U.K.: Cambridge University Press, 1995).

4. On terrestrial consumption, see Peter Vitousek, Paul R. Ehrlich, Anne H. Ehrlich, and Pamela A. Matson, "Human Appropriation of the Products of Photosynthesis," *BioScience* 36 (1986):368–373. I have extrapolated the data to the present. On water consumption, see Sandra L. Postel, Gretchen Daily, and Paul R. Ehrlich, "Human Appropriation of Renewable Fresh Water," *Science* 271 (1996):785–787.

5. In terms first expounded clearly in a pathbreaking article by Ehrlich and Holdren, our impact (I) equals the product of population, affluence (consumption), and technology: I = PAT. Each of these factors has increased rapidly over the recent past, thus greatly increasing our impact on the Earth's sustainability. Paul R. Ehrlich and John P. Holdren, "Impact of Population Growth," *Science* 171 (1971):1212–1217.

6. See http://www.globalfootprint.org/ and William E. Rees, Mathis Wackernagel, and Phil Testemale, *Our Ecological Footprint: Reducing Human Impact on the Earth* (Gabriola Island, British Columbia: New Society Publishers, 1995).

7. A further inequity that the world confronts is the disparity in scientific capacity between rich and poor countries. About 90 percent of the world's scientific output takes place in countries that account for about 18 percent of the world's population. The remaining 10 percent of the world's scientific output is contributed by Brazil, China, Mexico, and India. These four countries have approximately 40 percent of the world's population, which means that the remaining countries, with another 40 percent of the world's population, have, in general, little or no scientific or technical capacity. This means, very simply, that their ability to make decisions about the best management and use of their own resources on the basis of their own knowledge is very limited, and they also have difficulty in making the best use of technologies and scientific advances developed elsewhere. In an age when science and technology drive most of the increased industrial output, they are increasingly deprived and isolated. It is clearly important to attempt to redress this balance as rapidly as possible, since a sustainable world is one in which all partners can cooperate on a more or less even footing in the management of our own resources.

8. See Rodolfo Dirzo and Peter H. Raven, "Global State of Biodiversity and Loss," *Annual Reviews of Ecology and Systematics* 28 (2003):137–167; Raven, "Science, Sustainability and the Human Project."

9. For example, see Lesley Hughes, "Climate Change and Australia: Trends, Projections and Impacts," *Australian Ecology* 28 (2003):423–443.

10. Chris D. Thomas et al., "Extinction Risk from Climate Change," *Nature* 427 (2004):145–148.

11. Aldo Leopold, *Sand County Almanac* (New York: Oxford University Press, 1949), 216.

12. Donella H. Meadows, Jorgen Randers, and Dennis L. Meadows, *The Limits to Growth* (New York: Universe Books, 1972).

13. World Commission on Environment and Development (Brundtland Commission), *Our Common Future* (Oxford: Oxford University Press, 1987). The Earth Summit also brought into sharp focus the huge difference between the concerns of the governments of industrialized countries, a fifth of the world's population with a per capita income of more than $20,000 and a life expectancy of seventy-five years, with those of the developing countries, four fifths of the world's people, with a per capita income of about $1,200 and a life expectancy of sixty-three years. Some 1.3 billion people live in acute poverty with incomes of less than $1 per day; an estimated 890 million of them receive less than 80 percent of the U.N.-recommended minimum caloric intake and thus are literally starving.

14. Norman Myers and Jennifer V. Kent, *The New Consumers. The Influence of Affluence on the Environment* (Washington, D.C.: Island Press, 2004).

15. Donella H. Meadows, Dennis L. Meadows, and Jorgen Randers, *Beyond the Limits* (Post Mills, Vt.: Chelsea Green, 1992).

16. Norman Myers, *Ultimate Security. The Environmental Basis of Political Stability* (New York and London: W. W. Norton, 1995).

17. Kai N. Lee, *Compass and Gyroscope, Integrating Science and Politics for the Environment* (Washington, D.C.: Island Press, 1993).

18. Peter H. Raven, "Sustainability: Prospects for a New Millennium," in *Science and the Future of Mankind: Science for Man and Man for Science* (Vatican City: Pontifical Academy of Sciences, 2001), 132–154.

19. Norman Myers with Jennifer V. Kent, *Perverse Subsidies: Tax $s Under-cutting Our Economies and Environments Alike* (Winnipeg, Manitoba: International Institute for Sustainable Development, 1998).

20. Willy Brandt, *North-South: A Program for Survival* (Cambridge, Mass.: MIT Press, 1980).

21. Allen L. Hammond, *Which World? Scenarios for the 21st Century—Global Destinies, Regional Choices* (Washington, D.C.: Island Press, 1998).

22. Kai N. Lee, *Compass and Gyroscope: Integrating Science and Politics for the Environment* (Washington, D.C.: Island Press, 1993).

23. See Yvonne Baskin, *The Work of Nature: How the Diversity of Life Sustains Us* (Washington, D.C.: Island Press, 1997); Gretchen C. Daily, ed., *Nature's Services: Societal Dependence on Natural Ecosystems* (Washington, D.C.: Island Press, 1997).

24. See Juliet B. Schor, *The Overspent American: Why We Want What We Don't Need* (New York: HarperCollins, 1998).

25. Paul Hawken, *The Ecology of Commerce* (New York: HarperCollins, 1993).

26. Paul Hawken, Amory Lovins, and Hunter Lovins, *Natural Capitalism. Creating the Next Industrial Revolution* (New York: Little, Brown, 1999); Gordon Conway, *The Doubly Green Revolution: Food for All in the Twenty-First Century* (London: Penguin, 1997).

27. William Cronon, "The Trouble with Wilderness; or, Getting Back to the Wrong Nature," in *Uncommon Ground: Toward Reinventing Nature*, ed. William Cronon (New York: W. W. Norton, 1995), p. 90.

28. Edward O. Wilson, "Is Humanity Suicidal?" *New York Times Magazine*, May 30, 1993, 24–28.

WITH RADICAL AMAZEMENT: ECOLOGY AND THE RECOVERY OF CREATION
William French

1. Edward O. Wilson, "Is Humanity Suicidal?" *New York Times Magazine*, May 30, 1993, 24. This is reprinted in Edward O. Wilson, *In Search of Nature* (Washington, D.C.: Island Press, 1996), 183–199. See also Peter Raven, "Biodiversity and Sustainability: Our Common Responsibility to Nature," in this volume.

2. See John Robert McNeill, *Something New under the Sun: An Environmental History of the Twentieth-Century World* (New York: W. W. Norton, 2000), where he takes the words from Ecclesiastes to suggest how new certain environmental challenges are. See also Richard Leakey and Roger Lewin, *The Sixth Extinction: Patterns of Life and the Future of Humankind* (New York: Doubleday, 1995).

3. Bill McKibben, *The End of Nature* (New York: Random House, 1989).

4. Hans Jonas, *The Imperative of Responsibility: In Search of an Ethics for the Technological Age*, trans. Hans Jonas and David Herr (Chicago and London: University of Chicago Press, 1984), 2–8.

5. Julien Offray de La Mettrie, *Machine Man and Other Writings*, ed. Ann Thomson (Cambridge, U.K.: Cambridge University Press, 1996). See also Leonora Cohen Rosenfield, *From Beast-Machine to Man-Machine: Animal Soul in French Letters from Descartes to La Mettrie* (New York: Octagon Books, 1968), 54; Julien Offray de La Mettrie, *L'Homme Machine: A Study in the Origins of an Idea*, critical ed. with intro. and notes by Aram Vartanian (Princeton, N.J.: Princeton University Press, 1960), 13–39, 95–113.

6. Immanuel Kant, *Foundations of the Metaphysic of Morals*, trans. Lewis White Beck (Indianapolis and New York: Bobbs-Merrill, 1959), 46. See also Carolyn Merchant, *The Death of Nature: Women, Ecology and the Scientific Revolution* (San Francisco: HarperSanFrancisco, 1989).

7. Gordon D. Kaufman, "A Problem for Theology: The Concept of Nature," *Harvard Theological Review* 65 (July 1972):337–366.

8. See Jonas, *Imperative of Responsibility*, 2–8.

9. Lester R. Brown and Christopher Flavin, "A New Economy for A New Century," in Lester R. Brown et al., *State of the World 1999* (New York and London: W. W. Norton, 1999), 5–9.

10. Albert Borgman, *Technology and the Character of Contemporary Life: A Philosophical Inquiry* (Chicago and London: University of Chicago Press, 1984).

11. See Wendell Berry, *The Unsettling of America: Culture & Agriculture*, 2nd ed. (Sierra Club Books, 2004); Wendell Berry, *A Gift of Good Land: Further Essays Cultural and Agricultural* (New York: North Point, 1982). Also see Peter Singer, *Animal Liberation* (New York: Harper Collins, 2002).

12. See Anna L. Peterson, *Being Human: Ethics, Environment, and Our Place in the World* (Berkeley: University of California Press, 2001), 1–50.

13. William James, "The Moral Equivalent of War," in *War and Morality*, ed. Richard A. Wasserstrom (Belmont, Calif.: Wadsworth, 1970), 12–13.

14. See Barry Commoner, *Making Peace with the Planet* (New York: Pantheon, 1990).

15. John Rawls, *A Theory of Justice* (Cambridge, Mass.: Harvard University Press, 1970).

16. Ibid., 512.

17. See Mary Midgley, *Animals and Why They Matter: A Journey around the Species Barrier* (New York: Penguin, 1983), 49–51.

18. But there remains a minority tradition in modern Protestant thinking that affirms a distinct Protestant natural-law view. See Stephen J. Grabill, *Rediscovering the Natural Law in Reformed Theological Ethics* (Grand Rapids, Mich.: Eerdmans, 2006); Michael Cromartie, ed., *A Preserving Grace: Protestants, Catholics, and Natural Law* (Grand Rapids, Mich.: Eerdmans, 1997).

19. Karl Barth, *Church Dogmatics*, vol. III, bk. 2, *The Doctrine of Creation*, trans. Harold Knight et al. (Edinburgh: T. & T. Clark, 1960), 43.

20. Joseph Sittler, *Essays in Nature and Grace* (Philadelphia: Fortress, 1972), 67.

21. Gustaf Wingren, *The Flight from Creation* (Minneapolis: Augsburg, 1971), 24.

22. For one of the founding classics of twentieth-century Catholic "personalism," see Emmanuel Mounier, *Personalism*, trans. Philip Mairet (Notre

Dame and London: University of Notre Dame Press, 1952). See likewise Karl Rahner, *Foundations of Christian Faith: An Introduction to the Idea of Christianity*, trans. William V. Dych (New York: Seabury, 1978); Bernard J. F. Lonergan, *Insight: A Study of Human Understanding* (New York: Harper & Row, 1958); Bernard Häring, *Morality Is for Persons: The Ethics of Christian Personalism* (New York: Farrar, Straus and Giroux, 1971).

23. See William C. French, "Subject-Centered and Creation-Centered Paradigms in Recent Catholic Thought," *Journal of Religion* 70.1 (January 1990):48–72.

24. Gustavo Gutiérrez, *A Theology of Liberation: History, Politics and Salvation*, trans. Caridad Inda and John Eagleson (Maryknoll, N.Y.: Orbis, 1973), 174.

25. See Pope John Paul II, *Solicitudo rei socialis* (On Social Concern) (Washington, D.C.: United States Catholic Conference, 1987), 45, 64–66, secs. 26, 34. John Paul II's fullest treatment was his World Day of Peace address on January 1, 1990, "The Ecological Crisis: A Common Responsibility," in *"And God Saw That It Was Good": Catholic Theology and the Environment*, ed. Drew Christiansen and Walter Grazer (Washington, D.C.: United States Catholic Conference, 1996), 215–222. This book includes a number of statements on ecological issues from Catholic bishops' conferences around the globe.

26. Cardinal Karol Wojtyła (Pope John Paul II), *The Acting Person*, trans. Andrzej Potocki (Dordrecht, Netherlands: D. Reidel, 1979). See George Weigel, *Witness to Hope: The Biography of Pope John Paul II* (New York: Cliff Street Books, 1999), 125–130.

27. Pope John Paul II, *Laborem exercens* (On Human Work) (Washington, D.C.: United States Catholic Conference, 1981), 9–14, 26, 53–55, paras. 4–6, 12, and 25.

28. For a helpful treatment of the historical sweep of the natural-law tradition, see Alexander Passerin d'Entrèves, *Natural Law: An Introduction to Legal Philosophy*, 2nd ed. (London: Hutchinson, 1970). See also Jean Porter, *Nature as Reason: A Thomistic Theory of the Natural Law* (Grand Rapids, Mich.: Eerdmans, 2005); and Anthony J. Lisska, *Aquinas's Theory of Natural Law: An Analytic Reconstruction* (Oxford: Clarendon, 1996).

29. See Mounier, *Personalism*; Häring, *Morality Is for Persons*; Wojtyła, *Acting Person*; and Charles E. Curran, *The Catholic Moral Tradition Today: A Synthesis* (Washington, D.C.: Georgetown University Press, 1999).

30. See Germain Grisez, *Beyond the New Theism* (Notre Dame, Ind., and London: University of Notre Dame Press, 1975); and John Finnis, *Natural Law and Natural Rights* (Oxford: Clarendon, 1980).

31. Thomas Aquinas, *Summa Theologiae*, 5 vols., trans. Fathers of the English Dominican Province (Westminster, Md.: Christian Classics, 1948).

32. See Aquinas, "Treatise on the Creation" and "Treatise on Work of the Six Days," in *Summa Theologiae*, 1:229–254, 324–359 (1a, qq. 44–49, 65–74). Finnis and Grisez privilege the "Treatise on Law," with its stress on the principle of practical reason. See Germain G. Grisez, "The First Principle of Practical Reason: A Commentary on the *Summa Theologiae*, 1–2, Question 94, Article 2," *Natural Law Forum* 10 (1965):168–201; Germain Grisez, Joseph Boyle, and John Finnis, "Practical Principles, Moral Truth, and Ultimate Ends," *American Journal of Jurisprudence* 32 (1987):99–151.

33. Lloyd L. Weinreb, *Natural Law and Justice* (Cambridge, Mass.: Harvard University Press, 1990), 97–126.

34. Richard M. Gula, *Reason Informed by Faith: Foundations of Catholic Morality* (New York: Paulist, 1989), 231–249.

35. Martin Heidegger, *The Question Concerning Technology and Other Essays*, trans. William Lovitt (New York: Harper Torchbooks, 1977), 12–21.

36. See Max Oelschlaeger, *Caring for Creation: An Ecumenical Approach to the Environmental Crisis* (New Haven, Conn., and London: Yale University Press, 1994).

37. See David R. Loy, "The Religion of the Market," in *Visions of a New Earth: Religious Perspectives on Population, Consumption, and Ecology*, ed. Harold Coward and Daniel C. Maguire (Albany: State University of New York Press, 2000), 15–28. See Alan Durning, *How Much Is Enough: The Consumer Society and the Future of the Earth* (New York: W. W. Norton, 1992); John De Graaf et al., *Affluenza: The All-Consuming Epidemic* (San Francisco: Berrett-Koehler, 2002).

38. See Herman E. Daly, *Beyond Growth: The Economics of Sustainable Development* (Boston: Beacon, 1996), 5–12, 31–44.

39. Al Gore, *Earth in the Balance: Ecology and the Human Spirit* (Boston: Houghton Mifflin, 1992), 170.

40. Ibid., 182–196; Barry Commoner, *The Closing Circle: Nature, Man and Technology* (New York: Bantam Books, 1974), 249–291; more recently, Lester R. Brown, *Eco-Economy: Building an Economy for the Earth* (New York: W. W. Norton, 2001), 7–8, 21–23, 77–95.

41. See Norman Myers, *Ultimate Security: The Environmental Basis of Political Stability* (New York and London: W. W. Norton, 1993); Commoner, *Making Peace with the Planet*; and William French, "Contesting Energies: The Biosphere, Economic Surge, and the Ethics of Restraint," in *The Challenge of Global Stewardship: Roman Catholic Responses*, ed. Maura A. Ryan and Todd David Whitmore (Notre Dame, Ind.: University of Notre Dame Press, 1997), 119–134.

42. See Thom Shanker, "Proposed Military Spending Is Highest since WWII," *New York Times*, February 4, 2008.

43. For a recent treatment of Vice President Dick Cheney's post-9/11 thinking about the need to mitigate any terrorist threat at all costs, see Ron Suskind, *The One Percent Doctrine: Deep Inside America's Pursuit of Its Enemies Since 9/11* (New York: Simon & Schuster, 2006).

44. See Gore, *Earth in the Balance*, 196; Winston Churchill, "The Locust Years," in *Blood, Toil, Tears and Sweat: The Speeches of Winston Churchill*, ed. David Cannadine (Boston: Houghton Mifflin, 1989), 114–128.

45. See Peter L. Berger and Thomas Luckman, *The Social Construction of Reality: A Treatise on the Sociology of Knowledge* (Garden City, N.Y.: Anchor Books, 1967). On the rise of sociology and the ascendancy of the category of "culture" over "nature" to explain human action and behavior, see Carl N. Degler, *In Search of Human Nature* (Oxford: Oxford University Press, 1990), 187–211.

46. See Berger and Luckman, *Social Construction of Reality*.

47. See John R. Searle, *The Construction of Social Reality* (New York: Free Press, 1997).

48. See French, "Subject-Centered and Creation-Centered Paradigms."

49. See David Tracy, *Plurality and Ambiguity: Hermeneutics, Religion and Hope* (San Francisco: Harper & Row, 1987).

50. Charlene Spretnak, *The Resurgence of the Real: Body, Nature and Place in a Hypermodern World* (Reading, Mass.: Addison-Wesley, 1997), 64–79. See also David Ray Griffin, ed., *Spirituality and Society: Postmodern Visions* (Albany: State University of New York Press, 1988); Michael E. Soulé and Gary Lease, eds., *Reinventing Nature? Responses to Postmodern Deconstruction* (Washington, D.C.: Island Press, 1995).

51. Borgman, *Technology and the Character of Contemporary Life*, 41–43.

52. See, e.g., James A. Nash, "Seeking Moral Norms in Nature: Natural Law and Ecological Responsibility," in *Christianity and Ecology: Seeking the Well-Being of Earth and Humans*, eds. Rosemary Radford Ruether and Dieter T. Hessel (Cambridge, Mass.: Harvard University Press, 2000), 227–250.

53. Thomas Berry, *The Dream of the Earth* (San Francisco: Sierra Club Books, 1988), 123–137; Thomas Berry, *The Great Work: Our Way into the Future* (New York: Bell Tower, 1999), 21–32.

54. Berry, *Great Work*, 13–14. See also Saint Augustine, *The Literal Meaning of Genesis*, trans. John Hammond Taylor, Ancient Christian Writers Series, vol. 1 (New York: Newman, 1982), 117, 162–163, 172–176.

55. See James M. Gustafson, *Ethics from a Theocentric Perspective*, vol. 1, *Theology and Ethics* (Chicago and London: University of Chicago Press, 1981), 195–279. See also James M. Gustafson, *A Sense of the Divine: The Natural Environment from a Theocentric Perspective* (Cleveland, Ohio: Pilgrim, 1994).

56. Berry, *Dream of the Earth*, 123–137.

57. Reinhold Niebuhr, *The Interpretation of Christian Ethics* (New York: Seabury, 1979), 13–18.

58. See Theodore Hiebert, "The Human Vocation: Origins and Transformations in Christian Traditions," in *Christianity and Ecology: Seeking the Well-Being of Earth and Humans*, eds. Rosemary Radford Ruether and Dieter T. Hessel (Cambridge, Mass.: Harvard University Press, 2000), 135–154; William C. French, "Soil and Salvation: Theological Anthropology Ecologically Informed," in *The Whole and the Divided Self*, eds. David E. Aune and John McCarthy (New York: Crossroad Herder, 1997), 158–181.

59. Iris Murdoch, *The Sovereignty of Good* (London and New York: Ark Paperbacks, 1970, repr. 1986), 56.

60. Abraham Joshua Heschel, *God in Search of Man: A Philosophy of Judaism* (New York: Farrar, Straus and Giroux, 1955), 45, 43, 47.

IN THE WORLD: HENRI LEFEBVRE AND
THE LITURGICAL PRODUCTION OF NATURAL SPACE
Cabell King

1. H. Paul Santmire, *The Travail of Nature: The Ambiguous Ecological Promise of Christian Theology* (Philadelphia: Fortress, 1985).

2. Rachel Carson, *Silent Spring* (Boston: Houghton Mifflin, 1962), 277.

3. Bill McKibben, *The End of Nature* (New York: Doubleday, 1989), 47–48.

4. Ellen Meloy, *Eating Stone: Imagination and the Loss of the Wild* (New York: Vintage, 2005), 327.

5. See Peter H. Raven, "Biodiversity and Sustainability: Our Common Responsibility to Nature," in this volume.

6. On natural order, see Lorraine Daston, "The World in Order," in this volume.

7. Michael Scanlon, "Language and Praxis: Recent Theological Trends," *Proceedings of the Catholic Theological Society of America* 43 (1988):83; cited in Mary Catherine Hilkert, *Naming Grace: Preaching and the Sacramental Imagination* (New York: Continuum, 1997), 178.

8. "It happens that we use the same word to designate nature in man (human nature: instinct, need, desire) and nature without man, before man, outside of man." Henri Lefebvre, "Nature and Nature Conquered," in *Introduction to Modernity*, trans. John Moore (London: Verso, 1995), 134. First published as *Introduction á la modernité*, 1962.

9. "[Matter] is both the condition for production and the product of action itself, the place for mankind and the object of its pleasure: the earth." Ibid., 133.

10. The following text is an example where the division of inside and outside is infused with language of resource and product:

Nature designates . . . two "beings" in a confused way. On the one hand it points to the "human being," the "human nature," which will emerge and is already emerging from history, which will never be able to separate itself completely from nature as a given. The human being is forced to dwell with antinature (abstraction) painfully and long, and is already trying to return to nature, to put down roots, to find meaning in it, and peace of mind. On the other hand, nature designates the origin, what history has emerged from, something which both transforms and reveals itself in the succession of forms taken by action, by abstraction, by the signs which underpin and facilitate action, and by human power.

Ibid., 134.

11. Ellen Meloy's language beautifully proposes nature's potential to confront us: "*Homo sapiens* have left themselves few places and scant ways to witness other species in their own world, an estrangement that leaves us hungry and lonely. In this famished state, it is no wonder that when we do finally encounter wild animals, we are quite surprised by the sheer *truth* of them." Like McKibben, Meloy explicitly asserts nature as independent of humans and seems almost unaware that the problem she articulates is not about nature's own integrity. Animals occupy a different world than humans. They are somehow independently true. The failure she laments regards opportunities for interaction and communication, that is, our already socialized apprehension of that which is natural. Meloy, *Eating Stone*, 3.

12. Lefebvre, "Nature and Nature Conquered," 133.

13. Ibid., 132.

14. Ibid., 137.

15. Henri Lefebvre, *The Production of Space*, trans. Donald Nicholson-Smith (Malden, Mass.: Blackwell, 1991), 71.

16. Ibid., 49.

17. This example is taken from Paul Hawken, Amory Lovins, and L. Hunter Lovins, *Natural Capitalism: Creating the Next Industrial Revolution* (Boston: Little, Brown, 1999), 155–156.

18. See Gretchen C. Daily, ed., *Nature's Services: Societal Dependence on Natural Ecosystems* (Washington, D.C.: Island Press, 1997); Robert Costanza et al., "The Value of the World's Ecosystem Services and Natural Capital," *Nature* 387 (May 15, 1997):253–260.

19. R. Bruce Hull, *Infinite Nature* (Chicago: University of Chicago Press, 2006), 17.

20. Physicist James Trefil is actually quite optimistic about human industry and maintains a strong mechanistic view of nature, so he has minimal anxiety about environmental degradation. With little remorse he prophesies the death of nature:

If nature is defined to be that which is independent of human beings, then nature will cease to exist (if it has not done so already). From now on, the distinction between "human" and "nature" will become less and less meaningful, less and less useful in thinking about the world. "Nature" will become human.

James Trefil, *Human Nature: A Blueprint for Managing the Earth—by People for People* (New York: Henry Holt, 2004), xiv.

21. Jean-Joseph Goux, *Symbolic Economies: After Marx and Freud*, trans. Jennifer Curtiss Gage (Ithaca, N.Y.: Cornell University Press, 1990), 158.

22. John Reader, *Cities* (New York: Grove, 2004), 297, citing a report from the U.K. Forestry Commission in the *Independent*, March 31, 2002.

23. Lefebvre, "Nature and Nature Conquered," 138.

24. Alexander Schmemann, *World as Sacrament* (London: Dartman, Longman and Todd, 1965), 14.

25. Ibid., 17.

26. Ibid., 18.

27. Michel de Certeau, *The Practice of Everyday Life*, trans. Steven Rendall (Berkeley: University of California Press, 1984), xi.

28. Schmemann, *World as Sacrament*, 15.

29. Ibid., 140–141.

RENATURED BIOLOGY: GETTING PAST
POSTMODERNISM IN THE LIFE SCIENCES
Stuart A. Newman

1. William Bateson, *William Bateson, F. R. S., Naturalist: His Essays and Addresses* (Cambridge, U.K.: Cambridge University Press, 1928).

2. Mark Greene, Kathryn Schill, Shoji Takahashi, et al., "Ethics: Moral Issues of Human-Nonhuman Primate Neural Grafting," *Science* 309 (2005):385–386.

3. Paul Gross, Norman Levitt, and Martin Lewis, *The Flight from Science and Reason* (New York: New York Academy of Sciences, 1996); Noretta Koertge, *A House Built on Sand: Exposing Postmodernist Myths about Science* (New York: Oxford University Press, 1998).

4. Nuffield Council on Bioethics, *Genetically Modified Crops: The Ethical and Social Issues* (London: Nuffield Council on Bioethics, 1999), 15, available at: http://www.nuffieldbioethics.org/fileLibrary/pdf/gmcrop.pdf.

5. Any conception of "nature" apart from human activity must also include the material and social cultures of nonhuman animals. For differing views on the value of untransformed nature, see Bill McKibben, *The End of Nature* (New York: Random House, 1989); McKibben, *Enough: Staying Human in an Engineered Age* (New York: Henry Holt, 2003); Virginia I. Postrel, *The Future and Its Enemies: The Growing Conflict over Creativity, Enterprise, and Progress* (New York: Free Press, 1998); Ray Kurzweil, *The Singularity Is Near: When*

Humans Transcend Biology (New York: Viking, 2005); Jeremy Rifkin, *The Biotech Century: Harnessing the Gene and Remaking the World* (New York: Jeremy P. Tarcher/Putnam, 1998).

6. Keekok Lee, *The Natural and the Artefactual: The Implications of Deep Science and Deep Technology for Environmental Philosophy* (Lanham, Md.: Lexington Books, 1999).

7. See Nuffield Council on Bioethics, *Genetically Modified Crops.*

8. An agricultural scientist: Nina V. Fedoroff, "Agriculture: Prehistoric GM Corn," *Science* 302 (2003):1158–1159. Policy analysts: Henry Miller and Gregory Conko, *The Frankenfood Myth: How Protest and Politics Threaten the Biotech Revolution* (Westport, Conn.: Praeger, 2004).

9. See Allen Buchanan, Dan W. Brock, Norman Daniels, and Daniel Wikler, *From Chance to Choice: Genetics and Justice* (Cambridge, U.K.: Cambridge University Press, 2000).

10. It can be argued that neo-Darwinism, the reigning paradigm in evolutionary theory for more than half a century, is an important progenitor or "boundary condition" of the postmodernism of cultural theory. I return to this in a later section. See Gerd Müller and Stuart A. Newman, "The Innovation Triad: An EvoDevo Agenda," *Journal of Experimental Zoology. Part B. Molecular and Developmental Evolution* 304 (2005):487–503; Stuart A. Newman and Gerd Müller, "Genes and Form: Inherency in the Evolution of Developmental Mechanisms," in *Genes in Development: Re-Reading the Molecular Paradigm*, ed. Eva M. Neumann-Held and Christoph Rehmann-Sutter (Durham, N, C.: Duke University Press, 2005), 38–73.

11. Miller and Conko, *Frankenfood Myth.* See also Lee Silver, *Challenging Nature: Science in a Spiritual World* (New York: Ecco, 2006).

12. David Noble, *The Religion of Technology: The Divinity of Man and the Spirit of Invention* (New York: Knopf, 1997); Mary Midgley, *Science as Salvation: A Modern Myth and Its Meaning* (London and New York: Routledge, 1992).

13. Terry Eagleton, *After Theory* (New York: Basic Books, 2003) 58.

14. On the resistance of scientists, see Josh Schollmeyer, "Minority Report," *Bulletin of the Atomic Scientists* 61 (January/February 2005):38–39.

15. The reality was different. Eugenics, the attempt to improve human heredity by social policy, was a prestigious research agenda in the United States and Great Britain in the first half of the twentieth century, and forced sterilizations motivated by these ideas were performed throughout North America and Scandinavia at least through the 1970s. The exclusive association of eugenics and eugenicist policies with the Nazis, though the received view throughout the post–World War II period, is a vast oversimplification. See Daniel J. Kevles, *In the Name of Eugenics: Genetics and the Uses of Human*

Heredity (New York: Knopf, 1985); Elof Axel Carlson, *The Unfit: The History of a Bad Idea* (Cold Spring Harbor, N.Y.: Cold Spring Harbor Laboratory, 2001).

16. The Green Revolution was a program initiated by the Rockefeller Foundation in Mexico in 1944 that subsequently spread into South and Southeast Asia, involving improved crop seeds and extensive use of chemical fertilizers, herbicides, and pesticides. It is credited with saving hundreds of millions of people from starvation.

17. Lysenkoism was the Soviet doctrine, common from the 1930s through the mid-1960s but ultimately considered to have little scientific basis, that biological traits can be altered by physiological means in a fashion that can be passed on to subsequent generations. It declared genetics a "bourgeois pseudoscience" and promoted nongenetic techniques, such as exposure of seeds to cold and fertilizers, to increase agricultural yields.

18. For technology's impacts among the poor, see Vandana Shiva, *Stolen Harvest: The Hijacking of the Global Food Supply* (Cambridge, Mass.: South End Press, 1999). The Green Revolution, for example, increased the number of dispossessed people and reduced biodiversity.

19. Ian Hacking, *The Social Construction of What?* (Cambridge, U.K.: Cambridge University Press, 1999); Eagleton, *After Theory.*

20. David J. Hess, *Science Studies: An Advanced Introduction* (New York: New York University Press, 1997); Alan H. Goodman, Deborah Heath, and M. Susan Lindee, eds., *Genetic Nature/Culture: Anthropology and Science beyond the Two-Culture Divide* (Berkeley: University of California Press, 2003).

21. Jean Baudrillard, *Simulacra and Simulation*, trans. Sheila Faria Glaser (Ann Arbor: University of Michigan Press, 1994); Richard Rorty, *Truth and Progress* (Cambridge, U.K., and New York: Cambridge University Press, 1998). There are many definitions and characterizations of postmodernism. While my presentation here draws heavily on the critical views of this phenomenon in Jameson and Eagleton, I am not unsympathetic to the useful ironical and other rhetorical aspects of the querying of received social realities by some postmodernist theorists and artists. See Fredric Jameson, *Postmodernism, or, the Cultural Logic of Late Capitalism* (Durham, N.C.: Duke University Press, 1991); Eagleton, *After Theory.*

22. Bruno Latour, *Politics of Nature: How to Bring the Sciences into Democracy* (Cambridge, Mass.: Harvard University Press, 2004).

23. For resistance from the political right, see Paul Gross and Norman Levitt, *Higher Superstition: The Academic Left and Its Quarrels with Science* (Baltimore, Md.: Johns Hopkins University Press, 1994). For resistance from scientists, see Alan D. Sokal and Jean Bricmont, *Fashionable Nonsense: Postmodern Intellectuals' Abuse of Science* (New York: Picador USA, 1998). For resistance from cultural critics, see Jameson, *Postmodernism*; Eagleton *After Theory.*

24. Eagleton *After Theory*, 67–68.

25. Reviewed in Stuart A. Newman, "The Fall and Rise of Systems Biology," *Genewatch* 16 (2003):8–12.

26. Francis Bacon, *The Advancement of Learning and New Atlantis* (Oxford: Oxford University Press, 1979).

27. Stuart A. Kauffman, *The Origins of Order* (New York: Oxford University Press, 1993); Ricard V. Solé and Brian C. Goodwin, *Signs of Life: How Complexity Pervades Biology* (New York: Basic Books, 2000); Gerd B. Müller and Stuart A. Newman, eds., *Origination of Organismal Form: Beyond the Gene in Developmental and Evolutionary Biology* (Cambridge, Mass.: MIT Press, 2003).

28. For example, see Steven Pinker, *The Blank Slate: The Modern Denial of Human Nature* (New York: Viking, 2002); Jon Entine, *Taboo: Why Black Athletes Dominate Sports and Why We Are Afraid to Talk about It* (New York: Public Affairs, 2000).

29. For example, see John Dupré, "Making Hay with Straw Men: Review of Steven Pinker, *The Blank Slate: The Modern Denial of Human Nature*," *American Scientist* 91 (2003):69–72.

30. Jeff Sessions, September 12, 2005, Testimony of U.S. Senator Jeff Sessions (R-AL) on Day 1 of hearings on the nomination of John Roberts to be Chief Justice of the U.S. Supreme Court, available at http://www.washingtonpost.com/wp-dyn/content/article/2005/09/13/AR2005091300693_pf.html.

31. Sheldon Krimsky and Roger P. Wrubel, *Agricultural Biotechnology and the Environment: Science, Policy, and Social Issues* (Urbana: University of Illinois Press, 1996); Stanlew W. Ewen and Arpad Pusztai, "Effect of Diets Containing Genetically Modified Potatoes Expressing *Galanthus nivalis* Lectin on Rat Small Intestine," *Lancet* 354 (1999):1353–1354; Anita Bakshi, "Potential Adverse Health Effects of Genetically Modified Crops," *Journal of Toxicology and Environmental Health, Part B* 6 (2003):211–225; Miguel A. Altieri, *Genetic Engineering in Agriculture: The Myths, Environmental Risks, and Alternatives* (Oakland, Calif.: Food First Books/Institute for Food and Development Policy, 2004); Alexandra Hüsken and Antje Dietz-Pfeilstetter, "Pollen-mediated intraspecific gene flow from herbicide resistant oilseed rape (Brassica napus L.)," *Transgenic Research* 16 (2007): 557–569; Howard V. Davies, "GM Organisms and the EU Regulatory Environment: Allergenicity as a Risk Component," *Proceedings of the Nutrition Society* 64 (2005): 481–486; Eric J. Baack, "Engineered Crops: Transgenes Go Wild," *Current Biology* 16 (2006):R583–584.

32. ERS/USDA, Annual Report (2005), Economic Research Service, U.S. Department of Agriculture, available at http://www.ers.usda.gov/Data/BiotechCrops.

33. Miller and Conko, *Frankenfood Myth*; Nina V. Fedoroff and Nancy Marie Brown, *Mendel in the Kitchen: A Scientist's View of Genetically Modified Foods* (Washington, D.C.: Joseph Henry, 2004).

34. I am not suggesting that agribusiness has refrained from attempting to make modifications that would make produce more appealing to the end user and thus more competitive. Rather, the determinants of quality have proved elusive and difficult to manipulate by genetic engineering.

35. On the stubborn concerns about GM crop production, see Davies, "GM Organisms"; David Schubert, "Regulatory Regimes for Transgenic Crops," *Nature Biotechnology* 23 (2005):785–787, author reply 787–789.

36. On institutional and anthropological conflicts, see Chaia Heller and Arturo Escobar, "From Pure Genes to GMOs: Transnationalized Gene Land-scapes in the Biodiversity and Transgenic Food Networks," in Alan H. Goodman, Deborah Heath, and M. Susan Lindee, eds., *Genetic Nature/Cul-ture: Anthropology and Science beyond the Two-Culture Divide* (Berkeley: University of California Press, 2003), 155–175; Sheila Jasanoff, *Designs on Nature: Science and Democracy in Europe and the United States* (Princeton, N.J.: Princeton University Press, 2005).

37. Leslie Clarence Dunn, *A Short History of Genetics* (New York: McGraw-Hill, 1965).

38. Stuart A. Newman, "The Human Chimera Patent Initiative," *Medical Ethics Newsletter* (Lahey Clinic) 9:4 (2002):7; Jason Scott Robert, *Embryology, Epigenesis, and Evolution: Taking Development Seriously* (Cambridge, U.K., and New York: Cambridge University Press, 2004).

39. Reviewed in Schubert, "Regulatory Regimes."

40. J. O. Andersson, "Lateral Gene Transfer in Eukaryotes," *Cellular and Molecular Life Sciences* 62 (2005):1182–1197.

41. Rafael Zardoya, Xiaodong Ding, Yoshichika Kitagawa, and Maarten J. Chrispeels, "Origin of Plant Glycerol Transporters by Horizontal Gene Transfer and Functional Recruitment," *Proceedings of the National Academy of Sciences U.S.A.* 99 (2002):14893–14896.

42. Kent J. Bradford, Allen Van Deynze, Neal Gutterson, Wayne Parrott, and Steven H. Strauss, "Lessons from Plant Breeding, Biotechnology and Genomics," *Nature Biotechnology* 23 (2005):439–444.

43. Günter P. Wagner, Ginger Booth, and Homayoun Bagheri-Chaichian, "A Population Genetic Theory of Canalization," *Evolution* 51 (1997):329–347; Mark L. Siegal and Aviv Bergman, "Waddington's Canalization Revisited: Developmental Stability and Evolution," *Proceedings of the National Academy of Sciences U.S.A.* 99 (2002):10528–10532.

44. Miller and Conko, *Frankenfood Myth*; Fedoroff and Brown, *Mendel in the Kitchen*.

45. National Academy of Sciences, *Research with Recombinant DNA* (Washington, D.C.: National Academy of Sciences, 1977); Susan Wright, *Molecular Politics: Developing American and British Regulatory Policy for Genetic Engineering, 1972–1982* (Chicago: University of Chicago Press, 1994); National Research Council Board on Biology, Committee on Scientific Evaluation of the Introduction of Genetically Modified Microorganisms and Plants into the Environment, *Field Testing Genetically Modified Organisms: Framework for Decisions* (Washington, D.C.: National Academy, 1989) 14.

46. National Research Council, *Field Testing GM Organisms*, 15.

47. Organisation for Economic Co-operation and Development, *Safety Evaluation of Foods Derived by Modern Biotechnology: Concepts and Principles* (Paris: OECD , 1993).

48. Erik Millstone, Eric Brunner, and Sue Mayer, "Beyond 'Substantial Equivalence,'" *Nature* 401 (1999):525–526; Les Levidow and Joseph Murphy, "Reframing Regulatory Science: Trans-Atlantic Conflicts over GM Crops," *Cahiers d'économie et sociologie rurales* 68/69 (2004):47–74; Richard Caplan and Skip Spitzer, "Regulation of Genetically Engineered Crops and Foods in the United States," Genetically Engineered Food Alert briefing paper (2001), available at http://www.gefoodalert.org/library/admin/uploadedfiles/Regulation_of_Genetically_Engineered_Crops_and.htm; Bradford et al., "Lessons from Plant Breeding."

49. I. R. Rowland, "Genetically Modified Foods, Science, Consumers and the Media," *Proceedings of the Nutrition Society* 61 (2002):25–29; Jan Peter Nap, Peter L. J. Metz, Marga Escaler, and Anthony J. Conner, "The Release of Genetically Modified Crops into the Environment. Part I. Overview of Current Status and Regulations," *Plant Journal* 33 (2003):1–18; Davies, "GM Organisms"; Schubert "Regulatory Regimes."

50. Statement adopted by the U.S. Department of Agriculture's National Organic Standards Board's April 1995 meeting. See lines 920–931 of the minutes of that meeting, available at http://www.ams.usda.gov/AMSv1.0/getfile?dDocName = STELPRDC5057442. See also the Organic Trade Association, "Organic Foods Production Act Backgrounder," available at http://www.ota.com/pp/legislation/backgrounder.html.

51. Martin Teitel and Kimberly A. Wilson, *Genetically Engineered Food: Changing the Nature of Nature* (Rochester, Vt.: Park Street Press, 2001). For evidence that organic foods may not provide all the benefits claimed by their supporters, see Anthony Trewavas, "A Critical Assessment of Organic Farming-and-Food Assertions with Particular Respect to the UK and the Potential Environmental Benefits of No-Till Agriculture," *Crop Protection* 23 (2004):757–781; Jasanoff, *Designs on Nature*.

52. Miller and Conko, *Frankenfood Myth*; Bradford et al., "Lessons from Plant Breeding."

53. Fedoroff, "Prehistoric GM Corn."

54. T. Ramsay, "The Difficulties of Defining the Term 'GM,'" *Science* 303 (2004):1765; P. Grun, "The Difficulties of Defining the Term 'GM,'" *Science* 303 (2004):1765; Nina V. Fedoroff, "The Difficulties of Defining the Term 'GM'; Response," *Science* 303 (2004):1765–1767.

55. Mary Warnock, *A Question of Life: The Warnock Report on Human Fertilisation and Embryology* (Oxford and New York: Blackwell, 1985).

56. For an example of caution, see Rudolf Jaenisch and Ian Wilmut, "Developmental Biology: Don't Clone Humans!" *Science* 291 (2001):2552. For more affirmative views, see Arthur L. Caplan, "What If Anything Is Wrong with Cloning a Human Being?" *Case Western Reserve Journal of International Law* 35 (2003):369–384; Russell Blackford, "Human Cloning and 'Posthuman' Society," *Monash Bioethics Review* 24 (2005):10–26.

57. Louis M. Guenin, "The Set of Embryo Subjects," *Nature Biotechnology* 21 (2003):482–483.

58. For example, in response to petitions by the biotechnology companies ViaGen and Cyagra for permission to introduce the meat and milk of cloned animals into the food supply, the U.S. Food and Drug Administration has provided assurances of the equivalence of cloned livestock to their noncloned counterparts. See Larissa Rudenko, John C. Matheson, and Stephen F. Sundlof, "Animal Cloning and the FDA—The Risk Assessment Paradigm under Public Scrutiny," *Nature Biotechnology* 25 (2007):39–43.

59. The original report is I. Wilmut, A. E. Schnieke, J. McWhir, A. J. Kind, and K. H. Campbell, "Viable Offspring Derived from Fetal and Adult Mammalian Cells," *Nature* 385 (1997):810–813. For enthusiastic responses, see Nathan Myhrvold, "Human Clones: Why Not?" *Slate.com*, March 14, 1997, available at http://www.slate.com/default.aspx?id=1903; Senator Tom Harkin, Comments at Hearings of the Subcommittee on Public Health and Safety of the Senate Committee on Labor and Human Resources, March 12, 1997, available at. http://www.cnn.com/HEALTH/9703/12/nfm/cloning/index.html.

60. Ronald Bailey, "Send in the Clones," *Reason* (June 1998), available from *ReasonOnline* at http://reason.com/9806/bk.bailey.shtml.

61. Chimpanzee Sequence and Analysis Consortium, "Initial Sequence of the Chimpanzee Genome and Comparison with the Human Genome," *Nature* 437 (2005):69–87.

62. Richard Lewontin, "The Confusion over Cloning," *New York Review of Books* 44 (1997):20–23; Stephen Jay Gould, "Individuality: Cloning and the Discomfiting Cases of Siamese Twins," *The Sciences* 37 (1997):14–16.

63. Eva Jablonka and Marion J. Lamb, *Epigenetic Inheritance and Evolution* (Oxford: Oxford University Press, 1995).

64. Giuseppe Testa and John Harris, "Genetics: Ethical Aspects of ES Cell-Derived Gametes," *Science* 305 (2004):1719.

65. David Cameron, "Stop the Cloning," *Technology Review* May 23, 2002, available at http://www.mit-technology-review.com/articles/02/05/wo_cameron052302.asp; Jaenisch and Wilmut, "Don't Clone Humans!"

66. Rudolf Jaenisch and Stuart A. Newman, "Debating Therapeutic Cloning," *Medical Crossfire* 4 (2002):48–52.

67. Sue Chan, "Stanford to Develop Stem Cells: First Institution to Embrace Process Considered to Be Cloning," Associated Press, December 11, 2002, available at http://www.cbsnews.com/stories/2002/12/10/tech/main532566.shtml.

68. See the Web site of the International Society for Stem Cell Research (ISSCR) at http://www.isscr.org/about/index.htm.

69. Kristen Philipkoski, "Clone Newcomer Bends U.N.'s Ear," *Wired News* June 1, 2004, available at http://www.wired.com/medtech/health/news/2004/06/63636. This organization, formerly the Human Cloning Policy Institute, as of 2006 had an approximately 50 percent overlap in its board of directors with Weissman's ISSCR.

70. Carole B. Fehilly, S. M. Willadsen, and Elizabeth M. Tucker, "Interspecific Chimaerism between Sheep and Goat," *Nature* 307 (1984):634–636; Sabine Meinecke-Tillman and B. Meinecke, "Experimental Chimaeras—Removal of Reproductive Barrier between Sheep and Goat," *Nature* 307 (1984):637–638.

71. David Dickson, "Legal Fight Looms over Patent Bid on Human/Animal Chimaeras," *Nature* 392 (1998):423; Rick Weiss, "What Is Patently Offensive? Policy on 'Immoral' Inventions Troubles Legal, Medical Professionals," *Washington Post* May 11, 1998, A21.

72. Newman, "Human Chimera Patent Initiative"; Stuart A. Newman, "My Attempt to Patent a Human-Animal Chimera," *L'observatoire de la génétique* 27 (April–May 2006), available at http://www.ircm.qc.ca/bioethique/obsgenetique/zoom/zoom_06/z_no27_06/za ...no27_06_01.html.

73. National Public Radio, *All Things Considered* April 15, 1998.

74. Natalie DeWitt, "Biologists Divided over Proposal to Create Human-Mouse Embryos," *Nature* 420 (2002):255; Daylon James, Scott A. Noggle, Tomasz Swigut, and Ali H. Brivanlou, "Contribution of Human Embryonic Stem Cells to Mouse Blastocysts," *Developmental Biology* 295 (2006):90–102.

75. Tom Bearden, "Extended Interview: Irving Weissman," *Online Newshour* July 2005, available at http://www.pbs.org/newshour/bb/science/july-deco5/chimeras_weissman-ext.html .

76. Midgley, *Science as Salvation*; Donna Haraway, *Modest_Witness@Second_Millennium.FemaleMan©_Meets_OncoMouse™: Feminism and Technoscience* (New York: Routledge, 1996); Nancy K. Hayles, *How We Became Posthuman: Virtual Bodies in Cybernetics, Literature, and Informatics* (Chicago:

University of Chicago Press, 1999); Jürgen Habermas, *The Future of Human Nature* (Cambridge, U.K.: Polity, 2003).

77. Lee M. Silver, *Remaking Eden: How Genetic Engineering and Cloning Will Transform the American Family* (New York: Avon, 1998); Gregory Stock, *Redesigning Humans: Our Inevitable Genetic Future* (Boston: Houghton Mifflin, 2002); Francis Fukuyama, *Our Posthuman Future: Consequences of the Biotechnology Revolution* (New York: Profile Books; Farrar Straus & Giroux, 2002); Buchanan et al., *From Chance to Choice.*

78. Greene et al., "Ethics: Moral Issues."

79. Nato Thompson, *Becoming Animal: Contemporary Art in the Animal Kingdom* (North Adams, Mass. and Cambridge, Mass.: Massachusetts Museum of Contemporary Art, distributed by MIT Press, 2005).

80. David L. Hull, "The Effect of Essentialism on Taxonomy: Two Thousand Years of Stasis," *British Journal for the Philosophy of Science* 15 (1965):314–326, 16:311–318; Ernst W. Mayr, *The Growth of Biological Thought: Diversity, Evolution, and Inheritance* (Cambridge, Mass.: Belknap, 1982).

81. Robert A. Wilson, ed., *Species: New Interdisciplinary Essays* (Cambridge, Mass.: MIT Press, 1999); specifically in that volume, Richard Boyd, "Homeostasis, Species, and Higher Taxa," 141–186; Paul Griffiths, "Squaring the Circle: Natural Kinds with Historical Essences," 209–228; Robert A. Wilson, "Realism, Essence, and Kind: Resuscitating Species Essentialism?" 187–207. See also Stuart A. Newman and Gerd B. Müller, "Epigenetic Mechanisms of Character Origination," *Journal of Experimental Zoology. Part B. Molecular and Developmental Evolution* 288 (2000):304–317.

82. Reviewed in Eugenie C. Scott, *Evolution vs. Creationism: An Introduction* (Westport, Conn.; London: Greenwood, 2004).

83. Michael J. Behe, *The Edge of Evolution: The Search for the Limits of Darwinism* (New York: Free Press, 2007).

84. Michael Ruse, *The Evolution Wars: A Guide to the Debates* (Santa Barbara, Calif.: ABC-CLIO, 2000); Robert Wright, "Meaning of Life TV," series of interviews, *Slate.com*, 2006, available at: http://meaningoflife.tv; Freeman Dyson, "Religion from the Outside," *New York Review of Books* 54 (2006):4–8; Francis S. Collins, *The Language of God: A Scientist Presents Evidence for Belief* (New York: Free Press, 2006).

85. The title of the unpublished essay sent by Alfred Russel Wallace to Charles Darwin in 1858, spurring the latter's publication of his own similar theory of evolution, was "On the Tendency of Varieties to Depart Indefinitely from the Original Type." The malleability of organismal type, despite experience to the contrary, remains a tenet of the neo-Darwinian synthesis. See Alfred Russel Wallace, "On the Tendency of Varieties to Depart Indefinitely from the Original Type," *Proceedings of the Linnean Society of London* 3 (1858):53–62.

86. George Monbiot, "A Life with No Purpose," *The Guardian* (London), August 16, 2005.

87. Richard Dawkins, *The God Delusion* (Boston: Houghton Mifflin, 2006).

88. I am not suggesting here that conclusions about ultimate meaning are within the purview of natural science. Rather, my point is that the assertion that people must relinquish their sense of life's meaning because (1) this is what Darwinism implies, and (2) Darwinism provides a satisfactory account of evolution will not be a persuasive recruiting technique for evolution skeptics if neither of these two things is the case.

89. Jonathan Weiner, *The Beak of the Finch: A Story of Evolution in Our Time* (New York: Knopf, 1994).

90. Reviewed in Müller and Newman, "Innovation Triad."

91. Niles Eldredge and Stephen J. Gould, "Punctuated Equilibria: An Alternative to Phyletic Gradualism," in *Models in Paleobiology*, ed. T. J. M. Schopf (San Francisco: Freeman Cooper, 1972), 82–115.

92. Stephen Jay Gould, "Darwinian Fundamentalism," *New York Review of Books* 44 (1997):34–37.

93. Olivier Pourquié, "The Segmentation Clock: Converting Embryonic Time into Spatial Pattern," *Science* 301 (2003):328–330.

94. Small gene-associated variations are, of course, what neo-Darwinism appeals to as well. But in this newer view, the inherent (often "nonlinear") dynamical properties of the system the genes or gene products are part of can convert small molecular changes into global reorganization of activity or structure. See examples in Müller and Newman, *Origination of Organismal Form*.

95. Gabor Forgacs and Stuart A. Newman, *Biological Physics of the Developing Embryo* (Cambridge, U.K.: Cambridge University Press, 2005).

96. Newman and Müller, "Epigenetic Mechanisms"; Mary Jane West-Eberhard, *Developmental Plasticity and Evolution* (Oxford and New York: Oxford University Press, 2003).

97. C. H. Waddington, "Canalization of Development and the Inheritance of Acquired Characters," *Nature* 150 (1942):563–565.

98. "Self-organization" is a term used to describe the capacity of certain materials, nonliving as well as living, to assume preferred forms by virtue of their inherent physical properties. For applications of this concept to developing embryos, see Forgacs and Newman, *Biological Physics*. On the Cambrian explosion, see Stephen Jay Gould, *Wonderful Life: The Burgess Shale and the Nature of History* (New York: W.W. Norton, 1989).

99. Jean M. Carlson and John Doyle, "Complexity and Robustness," *Proceedings of the National Academy of Sciences U.S.A.* 99 Suppl. 1 (2002):2538–2545.

100. Massimo Pigliucci, *Phenotypic Plasticity: Beyond Nature and Nurture* (Baltimore, Md.: Johns Hopkins University Press, 2001); West-Eberhard, *Developmental Plasticity*.

101. I owe this insight to Prof. Marion Blute. See Charles Darwin, *On the Origin of Species by Means of Natural Selection, or, The Preservation of Favoured Races in the Struggle for Life* (London: J. Murray, 1872 [1859]).

102. For a review, see Stuart A. Newman, "The Pre-Mendelian, Pre-Darwinian World: Shifting Relations Between Genetic and Epigenetic Mechanisms in Early Multicellular Evolution," *Journal of Bioscience* 30 (2005):75–85.

103. Daniel C. Dennett, *Darwin's Dangerous Idea: Evolution and the Meanings of Life* (New York: Simon & Schuster, 1995).

104. Far from denying the efficacy of natural selection, these biologists typically presented an expanded picture in which the role of selection in preserving and reinforcing successful, marginally distinctive phenotypes was complemented by the dynamics of developmental processes in generating novelties.

105. See note 17 on Lysenkoism.

106. B. Zavadovsky, "The 'Physical' and the 'Biological' in the Process of Organic Evolution," in *Science at the Crossroads*, ed. Nikolai Bukharin (London: Frank Cass, 1931) 69–80; Richard Levins and Richard C. Lewontin, *The Dialectical Biologist* (Cambridge, Mass.: Harvard University Press, 1985).

107. Christiane Nüsslein-Volhard, *Coming to Life: How Genes Drive Development* (New Haven, Conn.: Yale University Press, 2006).

108. For example, see Geerat J. Vermeij, *Evolution and Escalation: An Ecological History of Life* (Princeton, N.J.: Princeton University Press, 1987); Weiner, *Beak of the Finch*; Michael Pollan, *The Botany of Desire: A Plant's Eye View of the World* (New York: Random House, 2001); Carl Zimmer, *Evolution: The Triumph of an Idea* (New York: HarperCollins, 2001). As they are contemporary works, "gene-language" pervades these writings, but this is not their main subject.

109. Mary Midgley, *Evolution as a Religion: Strange Hopes and Stranger Fears* (London and New York: Methuen, 1985); Michael Ruse, *The Evolution-Creation Struggle* (Cambridge, Mass.: Harvard University Press, 2005).

110. Brian Charlesworth, "Evolution: On the Origins of Novelty and Variation" (review of Marc W. Kirschner and John C. Gerhart, *The Plausibility of Life: Resolving Darwin's Dilemma*), *Science* 310 (2005):1619–1620.

111. Orthogenesis, the idea that evolving systems have an innate tendency to change in certain preferred directions, is generally condemned by neo-Darwinists. But the EvoDevo conclusion that there are preferred forms for living tissues dictated by their inherent material properties (see the segmentation example, above) provides a rationale for a concept of orthogenesis that is entirely consistent with modern biology.

112. Edward O. Wilson, *The Diversity of Life* (Cambridge, Mass.: Belknap Press, 1992).

113. Kerri Smith, "Homing in on the Genes for Humanity," *Nature* 442 (2006):725.

114. Francis Crick, *Life Itself: Its Origin and Nature* (New York: Simon and Schuster, 1981).

115. The phrase "context of no context" was coined by the late cultural critic George W. S. Trow, who used it in reference to popular culture. See George W. S. Trow, *Within the Context of No Context* (Boston: Little, Brown, 1981).

116. Freeman Dyson, "The Darwinian Interlude," *Technology Review* March 2005, available at http://www.technologyreview.com/read_article .aspx?id = 14236&ch = biotech. An expanded version of this piece subsequently appeared in Freeman Dyson, "Our Biotech Future," *New York Review of Books* 54 (2007):4–8.

117. See Silver, *Challenging Nature.*

118. Miller and Conko, *Frankenfood Myth.*

119. Lee, *Natural and the Artefactual;* Joel Kovel, *The Enemy of Nature: The End of Capitalism or the End of the World?* (London: Zed Books, 2002).

120. Acknowledgments: I would like to thank the following individuals for comments and suggestions on earlier drafts of this chapter: David Albertson, Laurent Arnoult, Philip Bereano, Ramray Bhat, Marion Blute, Charles Brummer, Alex Dajkovic, Richard Grossman, Cabell King, Vidyanand Nanjundiah, Sarah Newman, Edward Soja, Tina Stevens. Discussions with Ronald Brady before his untimely death stimulated my interest in concepts of "the natural."

SYNTHETIC BIOLOGY: THEOLOGICAL QUESTIONS
ABOUT BIOLOGICAL ENGINEERING
Ronald Cole-Turner

1. Ernesto Andrianantoandro, Subhayu Basu, David K. Karig, and Ron Weiss, "Synthetic Biology: New Engineering Rules for an Emerging Discipline," *Molecular Systems Biology* 2 (2006):1744.

2. Farren J. Isaacs, Daniel J. Dwyer, and James J. Collins, "RNA Synthetic Biology," *Nature Biotechnology* 24/5 (2006):545.

3. William J. Blake and Farren J. Isaacs, "Synthetic Biology Evolves," *Trends in Biotechnology* 22.7 (2004):321.

4. W. Wayt Gibbs, "Synthetic Life," *Scientific American* 290.5 (2004):75.

5. Ibid.

6. Steven A. Benner and A. Michael Sismour, "Synthetic Biology," *Nature Reviews Genetics* 6.7 (2005):533–543.

7. Ibid., 533.

8. Historical summaries of DNA synthesis often point to H. G. Khorana, "Polynucleotide Synthesis and the Genetic Code," *Federation Proceedings* 24 (1965):1473–1487.

9. Peer Stähler, Markus Beier, Xiaolian Gao, and Jörg D. Hoheisel, "Another Side of Genomics: Synthetic Biology as a Means for the Exploitation of Whole-Genome Sequence Information," *Journal of Biotechnology* 124.1 (2006):206–212.

10. Ibid., 207.

11. Gibbs, "Synthetic Life."

12. Joseph A. Piccirilli, Steven A. Benner, Tilman Krauch, Simon E. Moroney, and Steven A. Benner, "Enzymatic Incorporation of a New Base Pair into DNA and RNA Extends the Genetic Alphabet," *Nature* 343 (1990):33–37; Gibbs, "Synthetic Life."

13. Isaacs et al., "RNA Synthetic Biology."

14. Benner and Sismour, "Synthetic Biology," 533.

15. Ibid.

16. Drew Endy, "Foundations for Engineering Biology," *Nature* 438 (2005):449–453.

17. A. Malcolm Campbell, "Meeting Report: Synthetic Biology Jamboree for Undergraduates," *Cell Biology Education* 4 (2005):19–23, citing Timothy S. Gardner, Charles R. Cantor, and James J. Collins, "Construction of a Genetic Toggle Switch in *Escherichia Coli*," *Nature* 403 (2000):339–342.

18. Michael B. Elowitz and Stanislas Leibler, "A Synthetic Oscillatory Network of Transcriptional Regulators," *Nature* 403 (2000):335–338.

19. Andrianantoandro et al., "Synthetic Biology," 1744, 1747.

20. Ibid.

21. Drew Endy, "MIT: Department of Biological Engineering," faculty Web page, available at http://www.cdpcenter.org/research_scientists/scientists/drew_endy.

22. Endy, "Foundations," 451.

23. Ibid., 451–452.

24. Thomas F. Knight, "Engineering Novel Life," *Molecular Systems Biology* 1 (2005):1, in a discussion of Leon Y. Chan, Sriram Kosuri, and Drew Endy, "Refactoring Bacteriophage T7," *Molecular Systems Biology* (Sept. 2005).

25. Chan et al., "Refactoring."

26. Knight, "Engineering Novel Life," 1.

27. John I. Glass, Nacyra Assad-Garcia, Nina Alperovich, et al., "Essential Genes of a Minimal Bacterium," *Proceedings of the National Academy of Sciences* 103.2 (2006):424–430.

28. Hamilton O. Smith, Clyde A. Hutchinson III, Cynthia Pfannkoch, and J. Craig Venter, "Generating a Synthetic Genome by Whole Genome

Assembly: PhiX174 Bacteriophage from Synthetic Oligonucleotides," *Proceedings of the National Academy Of Sciences* 100.26 (2004):15440–15445.

29. Knight, "Engineering Novel Life," 1.

30. Gibbs, "Synthetic Life."

31. Andrianantoandro et al., "Synthetic Biology," 1744.

32. Jose M. G. Vilar, "Modularizing Gene Regulation," *Molecular Systems Biology* (March 2006).

33. Leroy Hood, James R. Heath, Michael E. Phelps, and Biaoyang Lin, "Systems Biology and New Technologies Enable Predictive and Preventative Medicine," *Science* 306.5696 (2004):640–643.

34. Chan et al., "Refactoring."

35. Mildred K. Cho, David Magnus, Arthur L. Caplan, Daniel McGee, and the Ethics of Genomics Group, "Genetics: Ethical Considerations in Synthesizing a Minimal Genome," *Science* 286.5447 (1999):2087–2090.

36. Jonathan B. Tucker and Raymond A. Zilinskas, "The Promise and Perils of Synthetic Biology," *New Atlantis* 12 (Spring 2006):25–45.

37. ETC Group, "Open Letter on Synthetic Biology: Synthetic Biology—Global Societal Review Urgent!," May 17, 2006, available at http://www.etcgroup.org/en/materials/publications.html?pub_id = 11.

38. See ETC Group, "Open Letter"; Tucker and Zilinskas, "Promise and Perils."

39. Tucker and Zilinskas, "Promise and Perils," 44.

40. "Synthetic Biology: Playing Demigods," *The Economist* 380.8493 (2006).

41. Benner and Sismour, "Synthetic Biology," 541.

42. Directorate-General for Research, European Commission, *Synthetic Biology: Applying Engineering to Biology* (Luxembourg: Office for Official Publications of the European Communities, 2005), 18–19, available at ftp://ftp.cordis.europa.eu/pub/nest/docs/syntheticbiology_b5_eur21796_en.pdf.

43. Dae-Kyun Ro, Eric M. Paradise, Mario Ouellet, et al., "Production of the Antimalarial Drug Precursor Artemisinic Acid in Engineered Yeast," *Nature* 440.7086 (2006):940–943.

44. Directorate-General for Research, European Commission, *Synthetic Biology*, 19

45. Ronald Cole-Turner, "Biotechnology and the Religion-Science Discussion," in *The Oxford Handbook of Religion and Science*, ed. Philip Clayton and Zachary Simpson (Oxford: Oxford University Press, 2006), 1646–1673.

46. Cho et al., "Genetics: Ethical Considerations," 29.

47. Tucker and Zilinskas, "Promise and Perils," 44.

48. Blake and Isaacs, "Synthetic Biology Evolves," 322.

49. Andrea Rinaldi, "A New Code for Life," *EMBO Reports* 5 (2004):336–339.

50. Niels Henrik Gregersen, ed., *From Complexity to Life: On the Emergence of Life and Meaning* (Oxford: Oxford University Press, 2003).

51. Gibbs, "Synthetic Life," 75.

NATURE AS GIVEN, NATURE AS GUIDE, NATURE AS NATURAL KINDS:
RETURN TO NATURE IN THE ETHICS OF HUMAN BIOTECHNOLOGY
Gerald McKenny

1. René Descartes, "Discourse on the Method," in *Descartes: Selected Philosophical Writings*, trans. John Cottingham, Robert Stoothoff, and Dugald Murdoch (Cambridge, U.K.: Cambridge University Press, 1988), 47 (emphasis added).

2. Stuart A. Newman, "Renatured Biology: Getting Past Postmodernism in the Life Sciences," in this volume.

3. Wilderness Act, P.L. 88–577, 78 Stat. 890; 16 U.S.C. 1121 [note], 1131–1136, available at laws.fws.gov/lawsdigest/wildrns.html.

4. Bernard Williams, "Must a Concern for the Environment be Centred on Human Beings?" in *Making Sense of Humanity and Other Philosophical Papers* (Cambridge, U.K.: Cambridge University Press, 1995), 240.

5. Michael J. Sandel, "The Case against Perfection: What's Wrong with Designer Children, Bionic Athletes, and Genetic Engineering," *Atlantic Monthly*, April 2004, 62.

6. Aldo Leopold, "The Land Ethic," in *A Sand County Almanac* (Oxford: Oxford University Press, 1949), 224–225.

7. Leon Kass, *Life, Liberty, and the Defense of Dignity: The Challenge for Bioethics* (San Francisco: Encounter Books, 2002), 21.

8. Newman, "Renatured Biology."

9. Francis Fukuyama, *Our Posthuman Future: Consequences of the Biotechnology Revolution* (New York: Farrar, Straus and Giroux, 2002), 101.

10. For example, from within ecology alone, the ubiquity of anthropogenic influence on the Earth's ecosystems is said to obviate the notion of nature as given, while the "ecology of flux," which denies that there is a natural state of equilibrium to which ecosystems tend, is said to render Leopold's dictum inapplicable. Meanwhile, it is a staple of neo-Darwinian theory that species do not have fixed essences.

11. Michael Sandel, "Mastery and Hubris in Judaism," in Sandel, *Public Philosophy: Essays on Morality in Politics* (Cambridge, Mass.: Harvard University Press, 2005), 196–210. Originally published in *Judaism and Modernity: The Religious Philosophy of David Hartman*, ed. Jonathan W. Malino (Aldershot, U.K., and Burlington, Vt.: Ashgate, 2004), 121–132. Sandel, "The Case against Perfection,"

12. Hannah Arendt, *The Human Condition* (Chicago: University of Chicago Press, 1958), 2–3. Arendt's concern is entirely intrahuman: it involves

what she sees as the modern alienation of human beings from the Earth. It is not a religious concern; it is significant that she does not speak of gratitude and that her "free gift" is without a giver, "from nowhere." Still, her picture of nature as a gift rejected by its recipients in favor of their own artifice quite readily evokes the thought of ingratitude toward the giver.

13. Sandel, "Mastery and Hubris in Judaism."

14. Ibid., 201.

15. Ibid., 202–203, 210. See also Sandel, "Case against Perfection," 57.

16. Sandel, "Case against Perfection," 54.

17. An interesting point of Sandel's is that societies that aspire to be egalitarian valorize the striver who succeeds by hard work and dedication in spite of limited talent over the naturally gifted person, whose inherent advantages may invite suspicion rather than admiration. Such societies, he suggests, may be inclined to value biomedical enhancements as a triumph of striving (albeit a technological form) over giftedness. The opposite argument has been made by other opponents of biomedical enhancement technologies, who distinguish technological means from genuine human effort.

18. Ibid., 60, 62.

19. Outside of ethics, this sensibility perhaps indicates an important theological point: that nature may have a status or worth before God that is not mediated through human beings. The "writings" or "wisdom literature" of the Jewish and Christian scriptural canons give expression to this point, especially Psalm 104 and Job 38–41.

20. For example, while Sandel rejects efforts to alter human capacities on the grounds that they violate an ethic of givenness, as we have seen, Kass rejects such efforts because they violate the fully natural human meaning of cultivation of talents and abilities. Enhancement technologies treat the organism as a mere object of technological manipulation rather than working through the characteristically human forms of activity that are involved in practices such as education and training.

21. Regarding physicalism, see Kass's remark that the meaning of lineage to human identity is marked in our navel, which connects us with our ancestors, and our genitalia, which link us with our descendents; Leon Kass, *Life, Liberty, and the Defense of Dignity: The Challenge for Bioethics* (San Francisco: Encounter, 2002), 101. Here form does the work that teleological function once did in Catholic manuals of moral theology.

22. Ibid., 156.

23. Ibid., 265–68. See also President's Council on Bioethics, *Beyond Therapy: Biotechnology and the Pursuit of Happiness* (Washington, D.C.: The President's Council on Bioethics, 2003), 183–192.

24. Kass, *Life, Liberty, and the Defense of Dignity*, 17–18.

25. Ibid., 281–293.

26. Ibid., 134; see also 18.

27. Ibid., 93n., 296.

28. Ibid., 12–15, 44–45, 50–52, 135.

29. Ibid., 7.

30. See Ibid., 4–8, 15–16, 244–256; and President's Council, *Beyond Therapy*, 17–20, 252–266.

31. In the Christian tradition, many of these suspicions are based on the notion that human nature participates in a good that transcends it and from which all of human nature, including biological nature, derives its ultimate meaning. From this perspective, it is expected that some indication of this good will be reflected in all of human nature, including biological nature, but that its meaning cannot be derived from consideration of biological nature even when the latter is understood as broadly and nonreductively as Kass understands it.

32. See Ronald M. Green, "Jewish and Christian Ethics: What Can We Learn from One Another?" *Annual of the Society of Christian Ethics* 19 (1999):3–21, esp. 14–16.

33. Fukuyama, *Our Posthuman Future*, 106, 117, 127–128.

34. Ibid., 13–16, 82–83, 101–102.

35. Ibid., 149.

36. Ibid., 155.

37. Ibid., 156.

38. Ibid., 130–131, 140–143, 162–172.

39. Ibid., 172.

40. One of these points, the relation of liberal democracy to human nature, has always depended on Fukuyama's Hegelian narrative in order to explain the late arrival of liberal democracy. Meanwhile, the Iraq War has dealt a blow (though for Fukuyama, not a fatal one) to the claim of the historical inevitability of liberal democracy.

41. Ibid., 101.

42. Ibid., 9–10.

43. It is worth noting that the prospect of being without nature in this third sense arises not only in the context of biotechnology but also in the challenges to notions of human nature from neo-Darwinian and philosophical attacks on the applicability of concepts of species and natural kinds to biological entities generally; from studies in ethology and other sciences, on the one side, and "cyborg" reflections, on the other side, which have raised doubts about the reality of the boundaries between human beings and other entities; and, of course, from the field of genomics. Whether any of these developments render the notion of human nature obsolete may be just as doubtful as

we have found it to be in the case of biotechnology, at least in its currently foreseeable forms.

44. It is notable that the hypothetical scenario concocted by Lee Silver, in his provocative *Remaking Eden* (New York: Avon, 1997), envisions thousands of years for the incremental inheritance of genetic changes through prenatal selection to result in two distinct species.

SEEING NATURE SPATIALLY
Edward W. Soja

1. William Cronon, *Nature's Metropolis: Chicago and the Great West* (New York: W. W. Norton, 1991). Chicago also has another, more personal attraction as a starting point. I began my professional life as a geographer and spatial theorist just across the northern boundary of Chicago, in Evanston, where I taught in the now-disbanded Department of Geography at Northwestern University from 1965 to 1972. Although my practical and theoretical interests have since shifted from the older Second City to the new one, centered in Los Angeles, Chicago and its environs continue to hold a special place in the development of my critical geographical imagination as well as that of many other spatial thinkers. Although the once prestigious Department of Geography at the University of Chicago, like that at Northwestern, no longer exists as such, Chicago stands out as the iconic birthplace of critical spatial thinking about cities and the interplay between urbanization and ecological processes, themes that will thread their way through all the discussion that follows.

2. The Marxian or historical materialist tradition had little to say specifically about cities, lumping them together with the physical environment as the contingent background to the "making of history," but its emphasis on historical and social processes and the power of individual and collective consciousness influenced the scholars of the Chicago School as well as the liberal social sciences as a whole. The distinction between first and second nature would later be developed much more explicitly, and in reference to Chicago, by Cronon in *Nature's Metropolis*. For Simmel, see Georg Simmel, "The Metropolis and Mental Life" in *The Sociology of Georg Simmel*, trans. Karl Wolff (New York: Free Press, 1950), 409–424.

3. The natural science perspective also brought with it a strong inclination toward Darwinian evolutionary theories and related notions of competition, mutation, and "survival of the fittest," to the point that many characterized the Chicago School approach to urban life as a form of social Darwinism.

4. Robert Park, Ernest Burgess, and Roderick Mackenzie, *The City: Suggestions for Investigation of Human Behavior in the Urban Environment* (Chicago: University of Chicago Press, 1925). Park was the primary intellectual funnel

of German influences on the Chicago School, and his essay, "The City: Suggestions for the Investigation of Human Behavior in the Urban Environment," published in 1915 (*American Journal of Sociology* 20.4: 577–612), was a powerful precursor of what was to come. Burgess was the original theorist of the concentric-ring model that became so closely associated with the Chicago School and its inheritors in such fields as geography and economics.

5. These terms are discussed further in Edward Soja, *Postmetropolis: Critical Studies of Cities and Regions* (Oxford and Malden, Mass.: Blackwell, 2000), 84–94.

6. Henri Lefebvre was one of the first to make this existential urbanism explicit when he stated in *Le droit à la ville; Espace et politique* (Paris: Anthropos, 1968) that the development of society is conceivable only in urban life, through what he called "the realization of urban society." Very few scholars, even close followers of Lefebvre's work, would understand this powerful notion of urban causality: that the city is not just a reflection of social relations but one of its essential driving forces.

7. For many years, the focus of geographers and economists was on the form or morphology of cities, rarely venturing into the realms of urban spatial causality directly. See, e.g., Brian J. L. Berry and John D. Kasarda, *Contemporary Urban Ecology* (New York and London: Macmillan, 1977). Significantly, however, it would be from the combination of the new economic geography and a revived geographical economics that the most exciting new work would be done on how cities endogenously generate creative, innovative, and developmental forces.

8. In recent years, a new field has emerged in the borderlands between geography and economics, focusing on the generative, developmental, and other "spillover" effects of urban agglomeration and what are called urbanization economies. I return to these arguments about urban causality later in the paper.

9. This does not mean that natural or ecological processes do not operate in the city or that they do not have significant effects on urban life. What we have been without for so long is an all-encompassing, unitary, and preordained nature as our extrasocial environment.

10. Some background to these arguments can be found in Maria Villa-Petit, "Heidegger's Conception of Space," in *Critical Heidegger*, ed. C. Macann (London: Routledge, 1996), 134–157.

11. These and earlier arguments regarding Heidegger's concept of spatiality are drawn primarily from Edward Soja, *Postmodern Geographies: The Reassertion of Space in Critical Social Theory* (London: Verso, 1989).

12. Michel Foucault, *Power/Knowledge: Selected Interviews and Other Writings 1972–77*, ed. Colin Gordon (New York: Pantheon, 1980), 70.

13. Michel Foucault, "Of Other Spaces," *Diacritics* 16 (Spring 1986):22.

14. Henri Lefebvre, *The Production of Space*, trans. D. Nicholson-Smith (Oxford and Malden, Mass.: Blackwell, 1991). For an extended discussion of Foucault's and Lefebvre's concepts of space, see Edward Soja, *Thirdspace: Journeys to Los Angeles and Other Real-and-Imagined Places* (Oxford and Malden, Mass.: Blackwell, 1996).

15. Two interesting facts about the journal *Society and Space* merit noting. First, it was named in part to link up with an older French journal, *Espace et Societé*, which in its origins and early development was closely associated with Henri Lefebvre. Second, the journal has always been part of a series of journals under the general title *Environment and Planning*, reflecting the much wider connections of the new critical human geography.

16. Lefebvre, *Production of Space*. Anthony Giddens would capture this triple dialectic in his concept of the time-space structuration of social relations. See Giddens, *A Contemporary Critique of Historical Materialism* (Berkeley and Los Angeles: University of California Press, 1987).

17. Soja, *Thirdspace*.

18. See Soja, *Postmetropolis*, 19–26.

19. Jane Jacobs, *The Economy of Cities* (New York: Random House, 1969).

20. Kathleen Kenyon, *Archaeology in the Holy Land* (London: Ernest Benn, 1960), 20, cited in Soja, *Postmetropolis*, 27.

21. The full quote from Jacobs is:

Cities are the mothers of economic development, not because people are smarter in cities, but because of the conditions of density. There is a concentration of need in cities, and a greater incentive to address problems in ways that haven't been addressed before. This is the essence of economic development. Without it, we would all be poor.

Steve Proffitt, "Jane Jacobs: Still Challenging the Way We Think about Cities," *Los Angeles Times* October 12, 1997.

22. See Soja, *Thirdspace*.

23. Lefebvre, *Production of Space*; Foucault, "Of Other Spaces."

24. For an excellent discussion of the Lower Mississippi Delta region and its history of racism and governmental neglect, see Clyde Woods, *Development Arrested* (London: Verso, 1998).

25. See Cronon, *Nature's Metropolis*.

26. Paul Krugman, "First Nature, Second Nature, and Metropolitan Location," *Journal of Regional Science* 33/2 (1993):129–144. See also Paul Krugman, Masahisa Fujita, and Anthony J. Venables, *The Spatial Economy* (Cambridge, Mass.: MIT Press, 1999).

27. Robert D. Bullard, ed., *Confronting Environmental Racism* (Cambridge, Mass.: South End Press, 1993). See also Ronald D. Sandler and Phaedra C.

Pezzullo, *Environmental Justice and Environmentalism* (Cambridge, Mass.: MIT Press, 2007).

28. The original concept of the right to the city is associated with Henri Lefebvre. See "Right to the City" in *Writings on Cities/Henri Lefebvre*, trans. Eleonore Kofman and Elizabeth Lebas (Oxford and Malden, Mass.: Blackwell, 1996), 61–181. In recent years, a growing local, national, and international movement has been developing based on Lefebvre's ideas. For example, a *World Charter for the Right to the City* was declared at the World Social Forum (2002) and published by UNESCO (2005); and in 2007 a Right to the City Alliance was formed in Los Angeles linking regional organizations across the United States. For more on the Right to the City Alliance, see www.rightto thecity.org and www.tides.org/fileadmin/tf_pdfs/TheRightToTheCity.

29. Edward Soja, *Seeking Spatial Justice* (Minneapolis: University of Minnesota Press, forthcoming).

THE DECLINE OF NATURE: NATURAL THEOLOGY, THEOLOGY OF NATURE, AND THE BUILT ENVIRONMENT
Timothy J. Gorringe

1. Paul Brown, "Drought Threatens Amazon Basin," *The Guardian*, July 17, 2006.

2. David Harvey, *Justice, Nature and the Geography of Difference* (Oxford: Blackwell, 1996), 148.

3. Union of Concerned Scientists, "1992 World Scientists' Warning to Humanity," http://www.ucsusa.org/about/1992-world-scientists.html.

4. Robert Samuels, "Environmental accountability, users, buildings and energy," in *Global Warming and the Built Environment*, ed. Robert Samuels and Deo K. Prasad (London: Taylor and Francis, 1996), 19.

5. Allan Rodger, "Sustainable Development, Energy Policy Issues and Greenhouse," in *Global Warming and the Built Environment*, ed. Robert Samuels and Deo K. Prasad (London: Taylor and Francis, 1996), 96. In Britain the use of buildings accounts for 46 percent of carbon dioxide emissions, and when construction is added, it is more than 50 percent. Energy is consumed in vast quantities at every stage of the process—in the production of bricks, cement, steel, aluminum, glass, plaster; in their transport and assembly; and then heating, cooling, and lighting buildings once they are built. The construction industry uses an estimated 3 billion tons of raw materials per year—40 percent of the total flow into the global economy. Really to understand the part played by the built environment in the environmental crisis, however, we have to ask what the implications are of the fact that half of humankind now live in cities. "As primary consumers cities use up fossil fuels hundreds of thousands of times faster than they can accumulate in the earth." Herbert Girardet, *The Gaia Atlas of Cities*, rev. ed. (London: Gaia, 1996), 106.

6. International Institute for Environment and Development, *Citizen Action to Lighten Britain's Ecological Footprints*, 1995, http://www.gdrc.org/uem/footprints/IIED-UK_footprints.pdf.

7. Maf Smith, John Whitelegg, and Nick Williams, *Greening the Built Environment* (London: Earthscan, 1998), 6.

8. Ibid., 42.

9. Graham Haughton and Colin Hunter, *Sustainable Cities* (London: Regional Studies Association, 1994), 14.

10. Mike Jenks, Elizabeth Burton, and Katie Williams, *The Compact City: A Sustainable Urban Form?* (London: Routledge, 1998), 4.

11. Patrick N. Troy, "Environmental Stress and Urban Policy," in *The Compact City: A Sustainable Urban Form?* ed. Mike Jenks, Elizabeth Burton, and Katie Williams (London: Routledge, 1998), 200.

12. Richard Rogers, "Learning to Live with the City," *The Independent* February 13, 1995.

13. Haughton and Hunter, *Sustainable Cities*, 70.

14. *Theologia naturalis* was put on the Index of banned books in 1595, but in 1564, the prohibition was reduced to encompass only the Prologue, which remained on the index until 1896. The idea of the "book of nature," it has been argued, was implicit in the very idea of creation by the Word. Giuseppe Tanzella-Nitti, "The Two Books Prior to the Scientific Revolution," *Annales Theologici* 18 (2004):51–83. It is also implied by the metaphor of creation as a roll or scroll (e.g., Isa. 34:4). Philo had already spoken of "Nature" as behaving like Wisdom in teaching human beings, and this view was reiterated in Christian teaching. G. Harder and Colin Brown, eds., *Dictionary of New Testament Theology* (Exeter, U.K.: Paternoster Press, 1980), 2:658. In Sermon 68, Augustine urges his congregation to consider the "great book, the very appearance of created things. . . . Look above you; look below you! Note it; read it! God, whom you wish to find, never wrote that book with ink. Instead, He set before your eyes the things he had made." *The Essential Augustine*, ed. Vernon J. Bourke (Indianapolis: Hackett, 1974), 123. By the twelfth century, reference to this book had become commonplace. Hugh of Saint Victor spoke of the book of nature, running parallel to the book of grace in Scripture, in which "each particular creature is somewhat like a figure, not invented by human decision but instituted by the divine will to manifest the invisible things of God's wisdom." Hugh of Saint Victor, *Didascalia* 7.4.

15. Cited in Clement C. J. Webb, *Studies in the History of Natural Theology* (Oxford: Clarendon, 1915), 296.

16. Ibid., 306.

17. Pamela Jones, "Federico Borromeo as a Patron of Landscapes and Still Lifes: Christian Optimism in Italy ca. 1600," *Art Bulletin* 70.2 (June 1988):265.

18. Cited in Basil Willey, *The Eighteenth Century Background* (Harmondsworth, U.K.: Penguin, 1962), 67.

19. Jonas Hanway, quoted in David Solkin, *Richard Wilson* (London: Tate Gallery, 1983), 116.

20. Solkin, *Richard Wilson*, 123. Lancelot "Capability" Brown was an influential landscape architect in eighteenth-century England. London's Hyde Park, though not designed by Brown, is perhaps the most famous example of the style he introduced.

21. Quoted in Ibid., 69.

22. Cited in Raymond Williams, *The Country and the City* (London: Hogarth Press, 1985), 259.

23. William Cowper, *The Task*, 1.412–435, 1.686–692.

24. Keith Thomas, *Man and the Natural World* (Harmondsworth, U.K.: Penguin, 1984), 246.

25. See Ebenezer Howard, *Garden Cities of To-morrow*, ed. F. J. Osborn, with and introductory essay by Lewis Mumford (London: Faber and Faber, 1946).

26. On Barth's theology as ideology critique, see Timothy Gorringe, *Karl Barth: Against Hegemony* (Oxford: Oxford University Press, 1999).

27. See Bruce McCormack, "Review of T. J. Gorringe, *Karl Barth: Against Hegemony*," *Scottish Journal of Theology* 55.2 (2002):238.

28. Karl Barth and Emil Brunner, *Natural Theology* (London: Bles, 1936), 74–75.

29. See Gorringe, *Karl Barth*, 131. The Barmen Declaration, drafted in large part by Barth, was the response of the "Confessing Church" Christian resistance movement in Nazi Germany to the Nazi-supported "German-Christian" movement.

30. So Friedrich-Wilhelm Marquardt: "Barth's total negation of natural theology was a polemical action from a not yet fully developed theological position and a means of political encounter with Nazism. In politically quieter times both before and afterwards Barth could not only affirm this theology but take it up. The *extra Calvinisticum* made this possible." Friedrich-Wilhelm Marquardt, *Theologie und Sozialismus: Das Beispiel Karl Barths* (Munich: Kaiser, 1985), 263. On rather different grounds, so also Stephen Webb: "Barth confronts the unlimited power of fascism with the jealous power of God, playing one exclusive rhetoric against another; this explains, in part . . . his condemnation of natural theology." Stephen Webb, *Re-Figuring Theology: The Rhetoric of Karl Barth* (Albany: State University of New York Press, 1991), 168. Hermann Diem disagrees, arguing that Barth never totally rejected natural theology and did not deny it on political grounds. See Hermann Diem, "Karl Barth as Socialist," in *Karl Barth and Radical Politics*, ed. George Hunsinger (Philadelphia: Westminster, 1976), 135.

31. James Barr, *Biblical Faith and Natural Theology* (Oxford: Clarendon, 1993),103–105.

32. Ibid., 111–113.

33. It is significant that the Hebrew Bible has no word for "nature" that denotes the natural world exclusively in the context of creation. The Greek term *physis* occurs only in late biblical writings influenced by Greek philosophy, and then rarely. In Wisdom of Solomon and in Maccabees, *physis* refers to an essential quality, similar to Ionian thought (e.g., 4 Macc. 13:27, Wisd. of Sol. 13:1) or the whole world of creation (3 Macc. 3:29). The statement that "It is wrong to reject Nature's favours" (4 Macc. 5:8) recalls Marcus Aurelius: "To Nature, whence all things come and whither all return, the cry of the humble and well instructed heart is, 'Give as thou wilt, take back as thou wilt.'" Marcus Aurelius, *Meditations*, trans. Maxwell Staniforth (Baltimore, Md.: Penguin, 1964) 10.14, p. 157. In the New Testament it is Paul (who at university in Tarsus had obviously studied Stoic philosophy) who uses the term most frequently to speak of human behavior that conforms or fails to conform with what seems to be natural. The fact that this includes men wearing their hair short whilst women wear it long illustrates the extent to which his view of nature is socially constructed (1 Cor. 11:14). Some people, he tells the Christians in Rome, have rejected natural (*physiken*) sexual intercourse for unnatural (*para physin*) (Rom. 1:26); at the same time some Gentiles who live just lives do so *physei*, by nature (Rom. 2:14). This recalls Chrysippus's comment that one should live "by following nature" (quoted in A. H. Armstrong, *An Introduction to Ancient Philosophy* [London: Methuen, 1947], 126). In 1 Corinthians, Paul contrasts the *psychikos* and the *pneumatikos* man (1 Cor. 2:14). Although Jerome translated *psychikos* as *animalis*, it quickly was translated as *naturalis* by Augustine: the "natural man does not receive the things of the Spirit of God," a translation that, as one commentator puts it, has nothing to recommend it except familiarity. As Paul used it, *psychikos* was not deprecatory: it meant "the body, animated by soul," but in the context of the dispute with Pelagius about nature and grace, it came to have a negative sense.

34. Karl Barth, *Church Dogmatics* III/1 (Edinburgh: T&T Clark, 1958), 62.

35. Hans Urs Von Balthasar, *The Theology of Karl Barth* (San Francisco: Ignatius, 1992), 124. Creation is not grace, but there is an analogous relation between the two. Creation is, says Barth, "a unique sign of the Covenant, a true sacrament; not Jesus Christ as the goal, but Jesus Christ as the beginning (the beginning just because He is the goal) of creation." Barth, *Church Dogmatics* III/1, 232.

36. Barth, *Church Dogmatics* III/1, 334–340.

37. Ibid., 330–331.

38. Ibid., 370.

39. Karl Barth, *Church Dogmatics* III/4 (Edinburgh: T&T Clark, 1961), 349.

40. Ibid., 355.

41. Ulrich Duchrow, *Global Economy: A Confessional Issue for the Churches?* (Geneva: WCC, 1986), 66.

42. Karl Polanyi, *The Great Transformation* (Boston: Beacon 1957, orig 1944). The necessity of growth lies in the fact that efficiencies gained by the division of labor demand larger markets to meet expanded production. Machines increase production but have to turn out more and sell more in order to pay for themselves. Innovations drive old products from the field and call forth yet more innovations. Money has to be borrowed to pay for new machinery, and the system of interest is self-perpetuating: my business has to grow to pay back the interest on the money I have borrowed, which requires new loans, and so on. Lynn White's suggestion that the Genesis dominion text, Genesis 1:28, lies behind the ecological crisis is impossibly idealist.

43. Fredric Jameson, *Postmodernism, or, the Cultural Logic of Late Capitalism*, 47.

44. E. P. Thompson, *Writing by Candlelight* (London: Verso, 1980).

45. Cited in Alan T. Durning, *How Much Is Enough?* (London: Earthscan, 1992), 21.

46. Speaking of the new urban developments in the United States, which he calls "Edge City," Joel Garreau notes that the shopping mall is the new spiritual center and that "there is apparently no reason for any 'ceremonial centres' dedicated to a 'life more abundant' to be at the core of Edge City." Garreau, *Edge City* (New York: Anchor Doubleday, 1991), 65.

47. So *Toward the Future: Catholic Social Thought and the U.S. Economy; A Lay Letter* (Notre Dame, Ind.: Quodlibetal Publications, 1984), analyzed in Duchrow, *Global Economy*, 169.

48. E. F. Schumacher, *Small Is Beautiful* (London: Sphere, 1974), 122.

49. Aristotle, *Nicomachean Ethics* 3.10.

50. Schumacher, *Small Is Beautiful*, 129.

51. Herman E. Daly and John B. Cobb, *For the Common Good: Redirecting the Economy toward Community, the Environment, and a Sustainable Future* (Boston: Beacon Press, 1989), 76.

52. Mathis Wackernagel and Williams E. Rees, *Our Ecological Footprint* (Gabriola Island, British Columbia: New Society, 1996), 13.

53. Rudolph Bahro, *Avoiding Social and Ecological Disaster: The Politics of World Transformation* (Bath, U.K.: Gateway, 1994), 92.

54. Jürgen Moltmann, *God in Creation* (London: SCM, 1985), xii.

55. Ibid., 21.

56. René Descartes, *Discourse on Method and Other Writings*, trans. F.E. Sutcliffe (Harmondsworth, U.K.: Penguin, 1968), 78.

57. Ibid., 39.

58. Ibid., 5.

59. Karl Barth, *Church Dogmatics*, vol. II, bk. 1 (Edinburgh: T&T Clark, 1957), 474.

60. Ibid., 475.

61. Karl Barth, *Church Dogmatics*, vol. III, bk. 3 (Edinburgh: T&T Clark, 1960), 433.

62. Cited in Robert Hughes, *The Shock of the New*, 2nd ed. (London: Thames and Hudson, 1991), 164.

63. Ibid., 207, 211.

64. Ernst Bloch, *The Principle of Hope*, trans. Neville Plaice, Stephen Plaice, and Paul Knight (Oxford: Blackwell, 1986), 737.

65. See Walter Wink, *Unmasking the Powers: The Invisible Forces that Determine Human Existence* (Minneapolis: Fortress, 1986), 24ff.

66. Raymond Williams, "Culture Is Ordinary," in *Resources of Hope* (London: Verso, 1989), 4; emphasis added.

67. Christopher Day, *Places of the Soul: Architecture and Environmental Design as a Healing Art* (London: Thorsons, 1993), 7.

68. Lewis Mumford, *The City in History* (Harmondsworth, U.K.: Penguin, 1991 [1961]), 653.

69. Schumacher, *Small Is Beautiful*, 83.

70. See, e.g., John Gray, *Beyond the New Right* (London: Routledge, 1994).

71. Manuel Castells, *End of Millennium* (Oxford: Blackwell, 1998), 164–165.

72. Agenda 21 is an ecological agenda for the twenty-first century initiated by the European Union and intended to guide planners to build according to sustainable norms.

73. Ivan Illich, *Deschooling Society* (Harmondsworth, U.K.: Penguin, 1973) 24.

74. Patrick Geddes, *Cities in Evolution* (London: Williams and Norgate, 1915), ch. 13.

75. Manuel Castells, *The Power of Identity* (Oxford: Blackwell, 1997), 356.

76. Lamin O. Sanneh, *Encountering the West* (London: Marshall Pickering, 1993).

77. Jürgen Moltmann, *The Church in the Power of the Spirit* (London: SCM, 1977), 342.

78. Manuel Castells, *The Rise of the Network Society* (Oxford: Blackwell, 1996), 418.

79. Ibid., 376.

80. Jeffrey Cook, "Environmentally Benign Architecture," in *Global Warming and the Built Environment*, ed. Robert Samuels and Deo K. Prasad (London: Taylor and Francis, 1996), 132.

81. Jürgen Moltmann, *The Coming of God* (London: SCM, 1996 [1995]), 234.

THE BODY OF THE WORLD: OUR BODY, OURSELVES
Sallie McFague

1. Langdon Gilkey, *Nature, Reality, and the Sacred: The Nexus of Science and Religion* (Minneapolis, Minn.: Fortress, 1993), 178.

2. Ibid., 179.

3. Ibid., 179.

4. Ibid., 179.

5. Edward W. Soja, "Seeing Nature Spatially," in this volume.

6. See "The Earth Charter" at the Web site of the Earth Charter Initiative, http://www.earthcharter.org.

7. Michael Pollan, *The Omnivore's Dilemma: A Natural History of Four Meals* (New York: Penguin, 2006), 17.

8. Ibid., 9.

9. Ibid., 10; emphasis added.

10. Ibid., 411; emphasis added.

11. Jeffrey Cook, "Environmentally Benign Architecture," in *Global Warming and the Built Environment*, ed. Robert Samuels and Deo K. Prasad (London: Spon, 1994), 143.

12. Peter H. Raven, "Biodiversity and Sustainability: Our Common Responsibility to Nature," in this volume.

13. UNEP Millennium Ecosystem Assessment, Statement from the Board, "Living Beyond Our Means: Natural Assets and Human Well-being," http://www.millenniumassessment.org/documents/document.429.aspx.pdf, 16.

14. Ibid., 17.

15. Ibid., 5.

16. Ibid., 6.

17. Ibid., 3.

18. Ibid., 5.

19. David Harvey, *Spaces of Hope* (Berkeley: University of California Press, 2000), 220.

20. Raven, "Biodiversity and Sustainability."

21. See Seppo Kjellberg, *Urban Eco Theology* (Utrecht, Netherlands: International Books, 2000), 46.

22. Carolyn Merchant, *The Death of Nature: Women, Ecology and the Scientific Revolution* (San Francisco: Harper and Row, 1983).

23. Harvey, *Spaces of Hope*, 97.

24. For further elaboration, see Sallie McFague, *The Body of God: An Ecological Theology* (Minneapolis, Minn.: Fortress, 1993).

25. For discussion of the epistemological and theological role of metaphor and model, see Sallie McFague, *Metaphorical Theology: Models of God in Religious Language* (Minneapolis, Minn.: Fortress, 1982); and McFague, *Models of God: Theology for an Ecological, Nuclear Age* (Minneapolis, Minn.: Fortress, 1987).

26. Jacques Derrida, "White Mythology: Metaphor in the Text of Philosophy," *New Literary History* 6 (1974):41–42.

27. For further elaboration of this and related issues, see Sallie McFague, *Life Abundant: Rethinking Theology and Economy for a Planet in Peril* (Minneapolis, Minn.: Fortress, 2000).

28. David Harvey, *Justice, Nature and the Geography of Difference* (Oxford: Blackwell, 1996), 429.

29. Ibid., 5.

30. See McFague, *Body of God.*

31. For an overview, see John B. Cobb, Jr., and David Ray Griffin, *Process Theology: An Introductory Exposition* (Philadelphia: Westminster, 1976).

32. See, e.g., Arthur R. Peacocke:

> Mammalian females . . . create within themselves, and the growing embryo resides within the female body and this is a proper corrective to the masculine picture—it is an analogy of God creating the world within herself. . . . God creates a world that is, in principle and in origin, other than him/herself but creates it, the world, within him/herself.

Arthur R. Peacocke, *Creation and the World of Science* (Oxford: Clarendon, 1979), 142.

33. Augustine, *The Confessions of St. Augustine*, Books 1–10, trans. F. J. Sheed (New York: Sheed and Ward, 1942), I.2, pp. 3–4.

34. McFague, *Life Abundant*, ch. 3.

35. See Sallie McFague, "Is God in Charge? Creation and Providence," in *Essentials of Christian Theology*, ed. William C. Placher (Louisville, Ky.: Westminster John Knox, 2003), 93–116.

36. For a fuller discussion of criteria in the use of theological models, see McFague, *Life Abundant*, ch. 3.

37. Robert Costanza et al., *An Introduction to Ecological Economics* (Boca Raton, Fla.: St. Lucie Press, 1997), 179.

38. T. J. Gorringe, *A Theology of the Built Environment: Justice, Empowerment, Redemption* (Cambridge, U.K.: Cambridge University Press, 2002), 17.

39. The natural theology tradition of Roman Catholicism, epitomized by Thomas Aquinas, sees creation as a reflection of God. It is not just human beings who are made in the image of God; rather, all creatures are. As Thomas expresses it:

> But creatures cannot attain to any perfect likeness of God so long as they are confined to one species of creatures; because, since the cause exceeds the effect in a

composite and manifold way. . . . Multiplicity, therefore, and variety, was needful in the creation, to the end that the perfect likeness of God might be found in things according to their measure.

Quoted in Arthur O. Lovejoy, *The Great Chain of Being: A Study in the History of an Idea* (Cambridge, Mass.: Harvard University Press, 1933), 76.

40. Iris Murdoch, "The Sublime and the Good," *Chicago Review* 13 (Autumn 1950):51.

41. Stephen Hume, "We Are Seeing the Urban Future and It Is Slums— Slums on a Frightening Scale," *Vancouver Sun* June 21, 2006, A17. See further the UN report, *State of the World Cities 2004/2005: Globalization and Urban Culture* (London: Earthscan, 2004).

42. "Report of the Third Session of the World Urban Forum," June 19–23, 2006, Vancouver, British Columbia, http://www.unhabitat.org/down loads/docs/3406_98924_WUF3-Report.pdf, 3.

43. See, e.g., George F. R. Ellis, "Kenosis as a Unifying Theme for Life and Cosmology"; Keith Ward, "Cosmos and Kenosis"; and Jürgen Molt- mann, "God's Kenosis in the Creation and the Consummation of the World," in *The Work of Love: Creation and Kenosis*, ed. John Polkinghorne (Grand Rapids, Mich.: Eerdmans, 2001).

44. See John B. Cobb, Jr., and Christopher Ives, eds., *The Emptying God: A Buddhist-Jewish-Christian Conversation* (New York: Orbis, 1998).

45. Edith Wyschogrod, *Saints and Postmodernism: Revisioning Moral Philos- ophy* (Chicago: University of Chicago Press, 1990), xxii.

EMERGENT FORMS OF UN/NATURAL LIFE
Michael M. J. Fischer

1. For example, see the classical moral philosophy and social theory formu- lations in Ludwig Wittgenstein, *On Certainty*, ed. G. E. M. Anscombe and George Henrik von Wright (New York: Harper and Row, 1969); Ulrich Beck, *Risk Society: Towards a New Modernity* (London: Sage, 1986/1992); Michael Gibbons, Camille Limoges, Helga Nowotny, Simon Schwartzman, Peter Scott, and Martin Trow, *The New Production of Knowledge: The Dynamics of Science and Research in Contemporary Societies* (London: Sage, 1994); also com- mentary in Michael M. J. Fischer, *Emergent Forms of Life and the Anthropolog- ical Voice* (Durham, N.C.: Duke University Press, 2003).

2. Walter Benjamin, "Die Mississippi Überschwemmung 1927," in Ben- jamin, *Gesammelte Schriften*, ed. Rolf Tiedemann and Hermann Schweppen- häuser. (Frankfurt: Suhrkamp, 1989), 7:237–43. See also Jeffrey Mehlman, *Walter Benjamin for Children: An Essay on His Radio Years* (Chicago: University of Chicago Press, 1993).

3. Walter Benjamin, "The Lisbon Earthquake," in *Selected Writings, Volume 2, 1927–1934*, ed. Michael W. Jennings, Howard Eiland, and Gary

Smith (Cambridge, Mass.: Harvard University Press, 1931), 536–540. For more on the dates of Benjamin's participation in the programs "Jugend-stunde" and "Stude der Jugend" of the Sudwestdeutschen Rundfunk of Frank-furt, see Sabine Schiller-Lerg, *Walter Benjamin under der Rundfuk: Programmarabeit zwischen Tehorie und Praxis* (Munich: K.G. Saur, 1984).

4. I follow here the account of historian John M. Barry in *The Rising Tide: The Great Mississippi Flood of 1927 and How It Changed America* (New York: Simon and Schuster, 1997).

5. Ibid.

6. Chana Gazit, prod., *Fatal Flood* (PBS Video, 2001).

7. Barry, *The Rising Tide*.

8. Ibid.; Anuradha Mathur and Dilip da Cunha, *Mississippi Floods* (New Haven, Conn.: Yale University Press, 2001).

9. See John Bohannan and Martin Enserink, "Scientists Weigh Options for Rebuilding New Orleans," *Science* 309 (2005):1808–1809.

10. See J. E. Foster, *History and Description of the Mississippi Basin Model* (Vicksburg, Miss.: Army Engineer Waterways Experiment Station, 1971) and Mathur and da Cunha, *Mississippi Floods.*

11. Rosalie Bertell, *Planet Earth: The Latest Weapon of War* (London: The Women's Press, 2001).

12. See Clifford Geertz, "Deep Play: The Balinese Cockfight" in *The Interpretation of Culture* (New York: Basic Books, 1973), 412–53.

13. Cornell West sardonically uses New Orleans blues and jazz to under-score the meaning structures of the long-term deep play:

> New Orleans has always been a city that lived on the edge. The white blues man himself, Tennessee Williams, had it down in *A Streetcar Named Desire*—with Elysian Fields and cemeteries and the quest for paradise. When you live so close to death, behind the levees, you live more intensely, sexually, gastronomically, psychologi-cally. Louis Armstrong came out of that unbelievable cultural breakthrough unprec-edented in the history of American civilisation. The rural blues, the urban jazz. It is the tragi-comic lyricism that gives you the courage to get through the darkest storm. . . . This kind of dignity in your struggle cuts both ways, though, because it does not mobilise a collective uprising against the elites.

Cornell West, "Exiles from a City and from a Nation," *The Observer* (U.K.) September 11, 2005.

It is a repetitive deep play. In 2001 the play *An Evening with* [Hurricane] *Betsy*" dramatized the bitter conspiracy rumors during the floods in New Orleans in 1965; such rumors circulated again during and after Katrina, rumors about sacrificing the poor neighborhoods and, indeed, trying to rid the city of them, rumors that while literally untrue nonetheless express a cer-tain kind of truth and reality. David Remnick, "High Water: How Presidents and Citizens React to Disaster," *New Yorker* October 3, 2005, 48, 53.

14. Wiebe Bijker, "The Oosterschelde Storm Surge Barrier: A Test Case for Dutch Water Technology, Management, and Politics," *Technology and Culture* 43 (2002):569–584.

15. William Broad, "High Tech Flood Control, with Nature's Help," *New York Times* September 6, 2005, D1, 4.

16. Kerry Emanuel, television interview, "Hurricanes and Climate Change," *Living on Earth*, aired September 2, 2005, available at www.loe.org/shows/shows.htm?programID = 05-P13–00035.

17. Charles Perrow, Arthur Miller Lecture in Science and Ethics, Massachusetts Institute of Technology, October 22, 2007. See also Charles Perrow, *Normal Accidents: Living with High-Risk Technologies* (Princeton, N.J.: Princeton University Press, 1999); Charles Perrow, *The Next Catastrophe: Reducing Our Vulnerabilities to Natural, Industrial, and Terrorist Disasters* (Princeton, N.J.: Princeton University Press, 2007).

18. Remnick, "High Water," 48, 52, 53.

19. Rick Klein, "Ex-FEMA Chief Spreads the Blame," *Boston Globe* September 28, 2005.

20. Michael Grunwald, "Disasters All, But Not as Natural as You Think," *Washington Post* May 6, 2001, B1

21. There has been speculation about whether the Ground Wave Emergency Network (GWEN) might have had something to do with the unusual weather pattern involved in the 1993 floods. GWEN is said to be an emergency communications military network using extremely low frequency (ELF) radiation of 72–80 hertz. Both the Soviet Union and the United States experimented with geophysical warfare techniques that leverage instabilities in the environment. The speculation is that "an 'electronic dam' can be set up using ELF generators—a magnetic field is created which stalls or blocks a weather front, therefore causing a torrential rain over an area" (Rosalie Bertell, *Planet Earth: the Latest Weapon of War* [London: The Women's Press, 2001]). The Benjaminian World War I image that "new constellations rose in the sky," (Benjamin, *One-Way Street, and Other Writings*, trans. Edmund Jephcott and Kingsley Shorter [London: New Left Books, 1979, orig. 1928]) is here echoed in the airglow reported over the Midwest on September 23, 1993, during the flooding. An unusual lightning flash rising from the clouds upward instead of downward was reported, possibly part of a larger series of such events, such as the airglow before the 1976 Tangshan earthquake in China (in which 650,000 died) and mysterious ELF pulsed waves before the 1986 and 1987 quakes in California, the 1988 quake in Armenia, the 1989 quakes in Japan and Northern California, and the 1994 quake in Los Angeles. Such speculations are hard to evaluate, given military secrecy. All the more reason for determined monitoring and sleuthing by civilian groups and investigative journalists as part of civil society "checks and balances" and as a way of exploring the

theoretical possibilities of ecological interconnections. See Rosalie Bertell, *Planet Earth: The Latest Weapon of War* (London: Women's Press, 2000), 131–132, 136.

22. Emanuel, "Hurricanes and Climate Change."

23. The climate change debate, when seen in relation to local or regional patterns, becomes sociologically even more interesting. In addition to concerns about the effect on coastal areas of rising ocean levels, the Amazon and the Arctic are touchstones of research and debate about climate warming. Even more than the politically tinged debate in the United States, with the so-called "contrarians," funded by the oil and gas industry, who argue against the existence of a climate crisis and against the validity of the scientific consensus of the Intergovernmental Panel on Climate Change (IPCC), the debate in the Amazon has high political stakes for Brazil in terms of economic growth versus more conservative ecological sustainability policies, but also in terms of sovereignty and freedom from global pressures on national policies and in terms of the development of a scientific establishment independent of European or U.S. interests. The Large-Scale Biosphere Atmosphere Experiment (LBA) has been internationally funded to determine the role of the Amazon in the global carbon cycle: Is it a carbon sink, that is, able to remove greenhouse gases from the atmosphere? What is the Amazon's role in regulating the global environment and its sustainability? Most U.S. scientists assume the Amazon is a large *source* of carbon, while European Union scientists try to prove that it is a small *sink*. U.S. scientists think that the new growth forests in the Northern hemisphere are carbon sinks and argue that countries with sinks would be allowed to emit more greenhouse gases under international treaties such as the Kyoto Protocol to the United Nations Framework Convention on Climate Change (UNFCCC or FCCC). If the Amazon is a sink, deforestation would be more of a problem and Brazil could seek funds from more developed countries to preserve the forest from being cut down for agricultural and other development schemes. Tower experiments to determine if the Amazon forests are sink or source, performed in the city of Manaus, Brazil (by the University of Edinburgh), and performed in the state of Pará, Brazil (by Harvard), provide contending results and disagreements over method and interpretation. The Manaus experiment seems to show the Amazon is a sink; the Harvard experimenters claim it is closer to a steady state (as one might expect from traditional theory about old-growth forests). Satellite data provided by NASA are viewed with suspicion by Brazil as being tainted by American interest in using international controls on environmental policy as a way to control Brazil's growth. Brazil's ability to provide its own scientific analyses is hampered, it is felt by some government policy-makers, by the training and ongoing networks of influence that Brazilians get in the

United States and Europe. See Myanna Lahsen, "Transnational Locals: Brazilian Experiences of the Climate Regime," in *Earthly Politics: Local and Global in Environmental Governance*, ed. Sheila Jasanoff and Marybeth Long (Cambridge, Mass.: MIT Press, 2004), 151–172.

In the Arctic, the Inupiaq near Barrows Point, Alaska, and the Inuit of Canada are on the front lines. It is quite evident that the climate is warming, the tundra is softening, the whale and caribou migrations are changing, and sea levels are rising. Barrows Point has been a major climate research station for over a hundred years, along with other research stations around the Arctic. But correlating Inupiaq observations and ecological knowledge with scientific runs of data and complex climate models (i.e., general circulation models) is not seamless. Indeed, while general physics laws have convinced many scientists of the IPCC claims about anthropogenic causes of climate warming, the general circulation models are far too complex, too abstract, and too general to make the argument on their own. It appears "that massive [climate] changes could come from inputs much smaller than the models' margins for error" (Charles Wohlforth, *The Whale and the Supercomputer: On the Northern Front of Climate Change* [New York: North Point, 2004], 167). Some policy analysts now understand that responses to climate change will proceed from local decisions, in the slow, adaptive way that complex systems adjust. Local governments and states have adopted carbon reduction standards and some corporations are cutting carbon emissions. Ron Brunner, a policy analyst at the University of Colorado, writes that some climate modelers think of their work as writing an "operator's manual . . . for Spaceship Earth" (cited in ibid, 278) But as Charles Wohlforth puts it:

> The whole enterprise rests on a logical fallacy: events in an infinitely complex world, full of constantly adapting people and natural systems, cannot be predicted reliably by a mathematical code. Understanding climate change, as well as responding, must happen inside individual human beings, in their minds and in their bones, through judgment and trial and error, in the way the Inupiaq, and all people, learn the truth by living it. We need modern science, Ron wrote, but we also needed a ten-thousand year old science based on the human experience of concrete places and events. (Ibid.)

A recent new turn in the Inuit story is the preparation of legal grounds for filing suit in international courts against the United States or in federal court against U.S. corporations on human rights grounds—not so much individual human rights as the rights of a culture to survive. The Inuit seek a ruling by the Inter-American Commission on Human Rights (an investigative organ of the Organization of American States), which has a history of treating environmental degradation as a human rights issue. The acknowledgment by the United States of anthropogenic sources of climate warming in official reports and the signing of the Rio and Kyoto treaties provide legal grounds. Whatever the legal consequences, it is an sophisticated publicity ploy enrolling both the media and established nongovernmental organizations with legal expertise, such as the Center for International Environmental Law in Washington, D.C., and EarthJustice in San Francisco. See Andrew Revkin, "Eskimos Seek to Recast Global Warming as a Rights Issue," *New York Times* December 15, 2004.

24. Joel K. Bourne, "Gone with the Water: The Louisiana Bayou, Hardest Working Marsh in America, Is in Big Trouble with Dire Consequences for Residents, the Nearby City of New Orleans, and Seafood Lovers Everywhere," *National Geographic* October 2004.

25. Wohlforth, *Whale and the Supercomputer*, 149, citing MIT meteorologist Edward Lorenz, a pioneer of chaos theory and the butterfly effect calculations.

26. Leo Marx, *The Machine in the Garden* (New York: Oxford University Press, 1964). One could elaborate a "deep play" account of each of these chemical and toxic disasters. Perhaps Richard Power's novel *Gain* (New York: Picador, 1999) is precisely that. It deals with the growth of a chemical corporation that provides employment and valued commodities and perhaps also causes breast cancer. Investigative journalist Colin Crawford's *Uproar at Dancing Rabbit Creek: Battle over Race, Class, and the Environment* (Reading, Mass.: Addison-Wesley, 1996) deals with the political competitions that allow or block the siting of toxic waste facilities. Much more is at stake culturally than just waste disposal. On Woburn, see Jonathan Harr, *A Civil Action* (New York: Vintage, 1995).

27. See Rachel Carson, *Silent Spring* (New York: Houghton-Mifflin, 1962); Barry Commoner, *Science and Survival* (New York: Viking Press, 1966); Barry Commoner, *The Closing Circle: Nature, Man, and Technology* (New York: Knopf, 1971); Eva Kolinsky, ed., *The Greens in West Germany* (New York: St. Martin's Press, 1989); and E. Gene Frankland, Paul Lucaridie, and Benoit Rihoux, eds., *Green Parties in Transition: The End of Grass Roots Democracy?* (Burlington, Vt: Ashgate, 2008).

28. Michael Reich, *Toxic Politics: Responding to Chemical Disasters* (Ithaca, N.Y.: Cornell University Press, 1991).

29. Sheila Jasanoff, *Designs on Nature* (Princeton, N.J.: Princeton University Press, 2005); Kim Fortun, *Advocacy after Bhopal: Environmentalism, Disaster, New Global Orders* (Chicago: University of Chicago Press, 2001).

30. Fortun, *Advocacy after Bhopal*.

31. Ulrich Beck, *Risk Society: Towards a New Modernity*, trans. Mark Ritter (New York: Sage Publications, 1992, orig. 1986).

32. Similar accounts arise out of green politics and regulatory sciences more generally in so-called "Mode Two" knowledge (Gibbons et al., *New*

Production of Knowledge) or "postnormal" science (Silvio O. Funtowicz and Jerome R. Ravetz, "Three Types of Risk Assessment and the Emergence of Post-Normal Science," in *Social Theories of Risk*, ed. Sheldon Krimsky and Dominic Golding [Westport, Conn.: Praeger, 1992], 251–274), in the cosmopolitics of global harmonization conventions (Wen-Hua Kuo, *Japan and Taiwan in the Wake of Bioglobalization: Drugs, Race and Standards*, PhD dissertation, Massachusetts Institute of Technology, 2005), and perhaps in the more philosophically eccentric tradition of French "political ecology": Bruno Latour, *Politics in Nature* (Cambridge, Mass.: Harvard University Press, 2004); Michel Serres, *The Natural Contract*, trans. Elizabeth MacArthur and William Paulson (Ann Arbor: Michigan University Press, 1995, orig. 1990); Kerry H. Whiteside, *Divided Natures: French Contributions to Political Ecology* (Cambridge, Mass.: MIT Press, 2002).

33. See, for instance, the ads for nuclear power as "clean" or "green" sources of energy, detailed at http://www.greenpeace.org/international/about/deep-green/nov-08-atomic-renaissance-interrupted.

34. The preceding and many other systematic features of difference between industrial and risk society are elaborated by Beck for the 1980s (in Ulrich Beck, *Risk Society: Towards a New Modernity*, trans. Mark Ritter [Thousand Oaks, Calif.: Sage, 1992, orig. 1986.]), in an updated transnational set of observations for the 1990s (in Ulrich Beck, *What Is Globalization?* trans. Patrick Camiller [London: Blackwell, 2000, orig. 1997]), and in three volumes for the early twenty-first century: Ulrich Beck, *Power in the Global Age: A New Global Political Economy*, trans. Kathleen Cross (Cambridge, U.K., and Malden, Mass.: Polity, 2005); Ulrich Beck, *The Cosmopolitan Vision*, trans. Ciaran Cronin (Cambridge, U.K., and Malden, Mass.: Polity, 2006); Ulrich Beck and Edgar Grande, *Cosmopolitan Europe* (Cambridge, U.K.: Polity, 2007).

35. For an example, see Aaron B. Wildavsky, *But Is It True? A Citizen's Guide to Environmental Health and Safety Issues* (Cambridge, Mass.: Harvard University Press, 1995).

36. For Italy, Japan, and the United States, see Reich, *Toxic Politics*.

37. Barbara Allen, *Uneasy Alchemy: Citizens and Experts in Louisiana's Chemical Corridor Disputes* (Cambridge, Mass.: MIT Press, 2003); Edward Griefe and Martin Linsky, *New Corporate Activism* (New York: McGraw Hill, 1995). See also Sheldon Rampton and John C. Stauber, *Trust Us, We're Experts* (New York: Penguin, 2001).

38. Fortun, *Advocacy after Bhopal*; Perrow, *The Next Catastrophe*.

39. Thomas Kuhn, *The Structure of Scientific Revolutions* (Chicago: University of Chicago Press, 1962); Funtowicz and Ravetz, "Three Types of Risk Assessment"; Jasanoff, *Designs on Nature*.

40. Joseph Masco, *The Nuclear Borderlands* (Princeton, N.J.: Princeton University Press, 2006).

41. For nuclear and chemical knowledge, see Constance Perin, *Shouldering Risks: The Culture of Control in the Nuclear Power Industry* (Princeton, N.J.: Princeton University Press, 2004); Fortun, *Advocacy after Bhopal*. For engineering knowledge, see Diane Vaughan, *The "Challenger" Launch Decision: Risky Technology, Culture, and Deviance at NASA* (Chicago: University of Chicago Press, 1997).

42. Bruno Latour, *The Politics of Nature* (Cambridge, Mass.: Harvard University Press, 2004); Latour, "From Realpolitik to Dingpolitik—or How to Make Things Public," in Latour, ed., *Making Things Public: Atmospheres of Democracy* (Cambridge, Mass: MIT Press, 2005).

43. Luc Ferry, *The New Ecological Order* (Chicago: University of Chicago Press, 1995).

44. Serres, *Natural Contract*; Christopher Stone, "Should Trees Have Standing? Towards Legal Rights for Natural Objects," *Southern California Law Review* 45 (1972):450–501. Stone is cited in Ferry, *New Ecological Order*.

45. Whiteside, *Divided Natures*, ch. 4.

46. Latour, *Politics in Nature*.

47. Michel Foucault, *The Order of Things: An Archaeology of the Human Sciences* (New York: Pantheon, 1971, orig. 1966). See also Morris Janowitz, *Social Control of the Welfare State* (New York: Elsevier, 1976).

48. Bruno Latour, *The Pasteurization of France* (Cambridge, Mass: Harvard University Press, 1988); Latour, *The Politics of Nature*; Latour, "From Realpolitik to Dingpolitik."

49. Bruno Latour, *Aramis, or, The Love of Technology* (Cambridge, Mass.: Harvard University Press, 1993).

50. Bruno Latour, "Regeln für die neuen wissenschftlichen und sozialen Experimente," plenary, Darmstadt Colloquium, March 30, 2001.

51. Kuo, *Japan and Taiwan*.

52. Fortun, *Advocacy after Bhopal*.

53. Jasanoff, *Designs on Nature*.

54. On the debate in the House of Lords, see ibid., 152–55. She points out that "the term 'pre-embryo' was ready to hand from the field of animal development," but that the term was also grounded in the physical mark of the "primitive streak" as well as drawing upon religious and secular authorities. The primitive streak is a furrow like structure of epiblast cells that will form endoderm and mesoderms, and around which the bilaterally symmetric embryonic structures will align. Errors at this stage can cause cancers. Several of the religious authorities, such as earlier statements by the Archbishop of York, used in the debate argue that matter that exists before these structures form cannot reasonably be ascribed characteristics of personhood.

55. Ibid., 195.

56. Ibid.; Herbert Gottweiss, *Governing Molecules: The Discursive Politics of Genetic Engineering in the United States and Europe* (Cambridge, Mass.: MIT Press, 1998).

57. João Biehl, *The Will to Live: AIDS Therapies and the Politics of Survival* (Princeton, N.J.: Princeton, University Press, 2008); Paul Farmer, *AIDS and Accusation: Haiti and the Geography of Blame* (Berkeley: University of California Press, 1990); Paul Farmer, *Infections and Inequalities: The Modern Plagues* (Berkeley: University of California Press, 1999); Paul Farmer, *Pathologies of Power: Health, Human Rights, and the New War on the Poor* (Berkeley: University of California Press, 2003); Fortun, *Advocacy after Bhopal*; Kuo, *Japan and Taiwan*; Adriana Petryna, *Life Exposed: Biological Citizens after Chernobyl* (Princeton, N.J.: Princeton University Press, 2001); Kaushik Sunder-Rajan, *Biocapital: The Constitution of Postgenomic Life* (Durham, N.C.: Duke University Press, 2006).

58. See http://www.genome.gov/10001618.

59. Jean Heller, "Syphilis Victims in U.S. Study Went Untreated for 40 Years," *New York Times*, July 26, 1972, 1.

60. Van Rensselaer Potter, *Bioethics: Bridge to the Future* (Englewood Cliffs, N.J.: Prentice-Hall, 1971). See also James E. Trosko, and Henry C. Pitot, "In Memoriam: Professor Emeritus Van Rensselaer Potter II (1911–2001)," *Cancer Research* 63 (April 1, 2003):1724.

61. Jonathan D. Moreno, "In the Wake of Katrina: Has Bioethics Failed?" *American Journal of Bioethics* 5.5 (2005):W18.

62. Jasanoff, *Designs on Nature*.

63. Ibid., 101 and passim.

64. Ibid., 101, ch. 7.

65. *Diamond v. Chakrabarty*, 447 U.S. 303 (1980).

66. *Foundation on Economic Trends (Jeremy Rifkin) et al. v. Margaret M. Heckler, Secretary of the Department of Health and Human Services, et al., Regents of the University of California, a Corporation*, 756 F.2d 143 D.C. Cir. (1985).

67. Donna Haraway, *The Companion Species Manifesto: Dogs, Humans and Significant Otherness* (Chicago: Prickly Pear Press, 2003).

68. See Jasanoff, *Designs on Nature*, ch. 5.

69. Jasanoff, *Designs on Nature*.

70. See ibid. for an account of these maneuvers and arguments.

71. Ibid., ch. 7.

72. Wen-Hua Kuo, "Japan and Taiwan in the Wake of Bio-globalization: Drugs, Race and Standards" (PhD diss., Massachusetts Institute of Technology, 2005).

73. The following few paragraphs draw from the section "Deep Play in the Life Sciences™: Markets versus Deliberative Democracy" in chap. 1 and sections of chaps. 2 and 9 of Fischer, *Emergent Forms of Life*.

74. Mary-Jo DelVecchio Good, "L'Abbraccio biotechnico: Un invito al trattemento sperimentale," in *Il spaere della quarigole*, ed. Pino Donghi (Spoleto, Italy: Laterza, 1996); Mary-Jo DelVecchio Good, "Metaphors for Life and Society in Health and Illness and the Biotechnical Embrace," paper presented at the International Symposium on Health and Illness, Bologna, Italy, 1998; Mary-Jo DelVecchio Good, "The Biotechnical Embrace," *Culture, Medicine, and Psychiatry* 25.4 (2001):395–410.

75. Manfred Deix, *Good Vibrations, Eine Retrospective* (Vienna, Austria: Museums Betriebsgesellschaft, 2000).

76. See Fischer, *Emergent Forms of Life*, ch. 1.

77. The technology is nicknamed "terminator" because it produces plants that do not produce a second generation, requiring farmers to purchase new seeds for each new planting season. These terminator seeds were widely opposed on the grounds that they are purely a means of consolidating control over farmers (as had already been done, if less completely, with earlier hybrid seeds which also required repurchase each year in order to maintain even quality; hence there was less protest from American farmers already used to annual purchase of hybrid seeds than from third-world farmers used to saving seeds for the following year's replanting). The technical name for terminator technology is genetic use restriction technology (GURT). There are two types: so-called "variety level," or V-GURT, which produces sterile seeds, and "trait," or T-GURT, which produces fertile plants with seeds that farmers can save for the next season, but has genetically enhanced properties that are turned on or off by the application of chemicals sold by the seed company. The technology was developed by the U.S. Department of Agriculture together with the Pine Land Company, and was taken up by Monsanto. Initially V-GURT was field-tested and generated global opposition on the grounds that its efforts to protect the company's intellectual property rights through production of sterile seeds was especially onerous for third-world farmers. In the faces of global protests, Monsanto agreed not to commercialize this technology. More recently T-GURT is back on the table. Monsanto claims that this is a way to control unwanted genetic features from hybridizing with other plants. But Monsanto also attempted to enforce intellectual property rights in cases where farmers claimed that they had not planted Monsanto seeds but their crops had apparently been contaminated by pollen or genetic drift from Monsanto licensed fields. The negotiations over this technology continue, as they do more generally regarding genetically modified crops. Allegations of trade war tactics are rife, particularly against the European Union, for forcing trade partners in Africa to forego planting genetically-modified crops on pain of being denied access to sell in European markets. See Robert Paarlberg, *Starved for Science: How Biotechnology is Being Kept out of Africa* (Cambridge, Mass.: Harvard University Press, 2008).

78. See Fischer, *Emergent Forms of Life*, ch. 1.

79. J. M. Coetzee, *The Lives of Animals* (Princeton, N.J.: Princeton University Press, 1999). On the relation of animal natures and food ethics in Coetzee, see Jennifer Schuessler, "The Novelist and the Animals: J. M. Coetzee's Unsettling Literature of Animal Rights," *Boston Globe* October 12, 2003.

80. See *The Nation*, special issue on food, 283 (2006): 7.

81. Haraway, *Companion Species Manifesto*. Haraway is referring to Giles Deleuze and Felix Guattari, *A Thousand Plateaus: Capitalism and Schizophrenia*, trans. Brian Massumi (Minneapolis: University of Minnesota Press, 1983, orig. 1980), ch. 2.

82. Jacques Derrida, "And Say the Animal Responded?" in *Zoontologies: The Question of the Animal*, ed. Cary Wolfe (Minneapolis: University of Minnesota Press, 2003). See also Alice A. Kuzniar, *Melancholia's Dog: Reflections on Our Animal Kinship* (Chicago: University of Chicago Press, 2006).

83. See Stuart Newman, "Renatured Biology: Getting Past Postmodernism in the Life Sciences," in this volume.

84. Ibid.

85. On SARS, see, for instance, Arthur Kleinman and James L. Watson, eds., *SARS in China: Prelude to Pandemic?* (Stanford, Calif.: Stanford University Press, 2005), and Tommy Koh, Aileen Plant, and Eng Hin Lee, eds., *The New Global Threat: Severe Accute Respiratory Syndrome and Its Impacts* (Singapore: World Scientific Pulbishing Company, 2003).

86. The Cortesia congregate wasp, like many Hymenoptera, lays eggs in the host, in this case the tobacco sphinx caterpillar, which dies when the larvae burst out to develop first into pupas and then flying wasps. Along with the eggs come virus particles that manipulate the physiology of the caterpillar so that the wasp larvae can develop. See Eric Espagne, Catherine Dupuy, Elisabeth Huguet, et al., "Genome Sequence of a Polydnavirus: Insights into Symbiotic Virus Evolution," *Science* 306 (October 2004):286–289. More generally, see the work of Lynn Margulis on symbiosis, Michel Serres on parasites, Gilles Deleuze and Felix Guattari on rhizomes, and Stefan Helmreich on the breakdown of genealogical or arboreal models in marine biology: Margulis, *The Symbiotic Planet: A New Look at Evolution* (New York: Basic Books, 1998); Lynn Margulis and Dorion Sagan, *Microcosmos: Four Billion Years of Microbial Evolution* (Berkeley: University of California Press, 1997); Margulis and Sagan *What Is Life?* (Berkeley: University of California Press, 2000); Margulis and Sagan, *Acquiring Genomes: The Theory of the Origin of Species* (New York: Basic Books, 2003); Serres, *Natural Contract*; Deleuze and Guattari, *A Thousand Plateaus*; Helmreich, "Trees and Seas of Information: Alien Kinship and the Biopolitics of Gene Transfer In Marine Biology and Biotechnology," *American Ethnologist* 30.3 (2003): 241–259; Helmreich, *Alien Ocean: Anthropological Voyages in Microbial Seas* (Berkeley: University of California Press, 2009).

87. See the collection of papers presented there, Edward O. Wilson and Frances M. Peter, eds., *Biodiversity* (Washington, D.C.: National Academy Press, 1988).

88. David Takacs, *The Idea of Biodiversity: Philosophies of Paradise* (Baltimore, Md.: Johns Hopkins University Press, 1996), 38.

89. Cited in ibid., 88.

90. See William Allen, *Green Phoenix: Restoring the Tropical Forests of Guanacaste, Costa Rica* (New York: Oxford University Press, 2001); Nalini Nadkarni and Nat Wheelwright, eds., *Monteverde: Ecology and Conservation of a Tropical Cloud Forest* (New York: Oxford University Press, 2000); and Luis A. Vivanco, *Green Encounters: Shaping and Contesting Environmentalism in Rural Costa Rica* (New York: Berghahn Books, 2006).

91. Ibid., 96.

92. Warwick Fox, *A Theory of General Ethics: Human Relationships, Nature, and the Built Environment* (Cambridge, Mass.: MIT Press, 2006).

93. Takacs, *The Idea of Biodiversity*.

94. Bill McKibben, *The End of Nature* (New York: Random House 1989).

95. Stephen M. Meyer, *The End of the Wild* (Cambridge, Mass.: MIT Press, 2006).

96. Ibid.

97. On endocrine hormone disrupters, see Sheldon Krimsky, *Hormonal Chaos: The Scientific and Social Origins of the Environmental Endocrine Hypothesis* (Baltimore, Md.: Johns Hopkins University Press, 2000); Sara Wylie, "Living the Landscape: Natural Gas Development and the Cultivation of Contested Disease" (paper presented at the annual meeting of the Society for the Social Study of Science, Vancouver, 2006); David O. Norris and James A Carr, *Endocrine Disruption: Biological Basis for Health Effects in Wildlife and Humans* (New York: Oxford University Press, 2006). On cross-species diseases, see Mike Davis, *The Monster at Our Door: The Global Threat of Avian Flu* (New York: New Press, 2005). On conditions in the Arctic, see Wohlforth, *Whale and the Supercomputer*. On dolphins in the Orinoco, see Indira A. R. Lakshmanan, "In Colombia, a Race to Count the Dolphins," *Boston Globe* October 21, 2006, A1, 6.

98. Haraway, *Companion Species Manifesto*; Derrida, "And Say the Animal Responded?" The rich literature on animals as tropes is extensive. On uses of animals in recent art, see Steve Baker, *The Postmodern Animal* (London: Reaktion Books, 2000). On animals as figures of transference, see Akira Mizuta Lippit, *Electric Animal: Toward a Rhetoric of Wildlife* (Minneapolis: University of Minnesota Press, 2000); Cary Wolfe, *Animal Rites: American Culture, the Discourse of Species, and Posthumanist Theory* (Chicago: University of Chicago Press, 2003). On anthropomorphism, see Lorraine Daston and Greg Mittman,

eds., *Thinking with Animals: New Perspectives on Anthropomorphism* (New York: Columbia University Press, 2005). On melancholia, see Kuzniar, *Melancholia's Dog*. Daston and Mittman *Thinking with Animals*, does acknowledge some historical changes, such as the sentimentalization of pets in urbanizing England and contemporary insistence on anthropomorphizing animals. For instance, *National Geographic*, in a documentary about rehabilitating abandoned pet orangutans, insisted the filmmakers anthropomorphize the animals as a way of capturing sentimental interest. Similarly, biodiversity and ecological protection campaigns claim to need to use celebrity animals both for protecting the animals and to enhance ethologists' own celebrity and participation in such campaigns. Lippit, *Electric Animal*, engagingly suggests that in the late nineteenth and early twentieth centuries, the figure of the animal shifts from ritual sacrifice and communication with the next world to circuits of spectral communication in anticipation of and response to a parallel function of psychoanalysis and the cinema both operating as supplements of the subject. "Everywhere animals disappear," Lippit quotes John Berger as saying, leading to a sense of panic. "Animals never entirely vanish," says Lippit. "Rather they exist in a state of perpetual vanishing. Animals enter a new economy of being," the spectral, the undead, the mourned, in which the zoo is one melancholy site. Pierre Hadot, *The Veil of Isis: An Essay on the History of the Idea of Nature*, trans. Michael Chase (Cambridge, Mass.: Belknap Press of Harvard University Press, 2006, orig. 2004) surveys Western tropes of nature from ancient Egypt to modern France and notes how repetitive they are.

99. See Lévi-Strauss's comparative epistemological investigation of how names of birds, dogs, cattle, and race horses form contrastive sets, and Leach's essay on animal categories and verbal abuse: Claude Lévi-Strauss, *The Savage Mind* (Chicago: University of Chicago Press, 1966), 203–208; Edmund Leach, "Animal Aspects of Language: Animal Categories and Verbal Abuse," in *New Directions in the Study of Language*, ed. E. H. Lenneberg (Cambridge, Mass.: MIT Press, 1964). Lévi-Strauss's *Mythologies* is a compendium of mythically restructured ecological knowledges. Claude Lévi-Strauss, *Introduction to a Science of Mythology*, 4 vols. (London: Jonathan Cape, 1969–1981, orig. 1964–1971).

100. Deleuze and Guattari, *A Thousand Plateaus*.

101. Donna Haraway, *Primate Visions: Gender, Race and Nature in Modern Science* (New York: Routledge, 1989); Donna Haraway, *When Species Meet* (Minneapolis: University of Minnesota Press, 2008).

102. Donna Haraway, *Simians, Cyborgs, and Women: The Reinvention of Nature* (New York: Routledge, 1991). See also Donna Haraway, "Manifesto for Cyborgs: Science, Technology and Socialist Feminism in the 1980s," *Socialist Review* 80 (1985):65–108.

103. Donna Haraway, *Modest_Witness@Second_Millennium.FemaleMan©_ Meets_OncoMouse™: Feminism and Technoscience* (New York: Routledge, 1997).

104. Take, e.g., the antimicrobial "grammar" of peptides being used to explore ways of combating drug-resistant pathogenic bacteria. The "grammar" was recognized by a pattern recognition algorithm from language research. Patterns in amino acid sequences include wordlike sequences that can be swapped without changing the functioning of the peptide. New peptides can thus be constructed that differ from all known peptides. These can attach to membranes of bacteria that are otherwise resistant to drugs. Whether this is merely a fancy metaphor for a variant of standard computational methods or not, the point here is that algorithms and information technologies are the tools of discovery and manipulation. See Christopher Loose, Kyle Jensen, Isidore Rigoutsos, and Gregory Stephanopoulos, "A Linguistic Model for the Rational Design of Antimicrobial Peptides," *Nature* 443 (2006):867–869.

105. Haraway, *Companion Species Manifesto*; Haraway, *When Species Meet.*

106. Two examples already mentioned are the suggestion that trees might be given standing in environmental conservation law suits; and the Inuit and other indigenous people's lawsuits under human rights law on grounds of destruction of traditional habitats and cultural ways of living.

107. For example, see Peter Singer, *Animal Liberation* (New York: Ecco, 2002).

108. In discussing the different dog-training traditions of Vicki Hearne, Susan Garrett, and others, Haraway provides a lovely anecdote about her six-year-old godson's first puppy training lesson. The boy was taking karate lessons at the time and had learned the ritual of facing an opponent eye to eye and bowing before a match. "Marco," Haraway writes, at first treated [Cayenne] like a microchip implanted truck for which he held the controls." Cayenne learned the cues and sat for him:

> Marco, I said, Cayenne is not a cyborg truck: she is your partner in a martial art called obedience. You are the older partner and the master here, you have learned how to perform with your body and eyes. Your job is to teach the form to Cayenne. Until you can find a way to teach her how to collect her galloping puppy self calmly and hold still and look you in the eye, you cannot let her perform the "sit" command.

Haraway, *Companion Species Manifesto*, 41.

109. Ibid.

110. Karin Knorr-Cetina, *Epistemic Cultures: How the Sciences Make Knowledge* (Cambridge, Mass.: Harvard University Press, 1999). Haraway, unlike Ray C. Greek and Jean Swingle Greek (*Sacred Cows and Golden Geese: the Human Cost of Experiments on Animals* [New York: Continuum, 2000]), does

not accept the argument that animal experimental systems are no longer scientifically necessary or are all too often misleading.

111. Cavell and Hearne are quoted in Wolfe, *Animal Rites*, 3–5. Washoe died October 30, 2007, aged forty-two. Born in West Africa, and adopted at ten months by cognitive scientists R. Allen and Beatrix T. Gardiner, by age five she had learned some American Sign Language, and became a celebrity. In 1980 she was adopted by Deborah and Roger Fouts and moved to Central Washington University. The degree of chimpanzee language-learning capacities remains controversial. Washoe's obituary appeared, among other places, in the *New York Times* on November 1, 2007.

112. David Clark, "On Being 'The Last Kantian in Nazi Germany': Dwelling with Animals after Levinas," in *Animal Acts: Configuring the Human in Western History*, ed. Jennifer Ham and Matthew Senior (New York: Routledge, 1997), 174–175. Calling his dog "the last Kantian in Germany" recalls for Levinas momentarily both Odysseus' dog in Ithaca, "the last true Greek in Ithaca," and the dogs in Exodus who participated in the miracle through the holding of their barking while the Egyptians mourned their firstborn: "not a dog shall growl." See also Emmanuel Levinas, *On Escape* (Stanford, Calif.: Stanford University Press, 2003). The phrase from Derrida (quoted by Clark) is from "On Reading Heidegger: An Outline of Remarks to the Essex Colloquium," *Research in Phenomenology* 17 (1987): 171–188. See also Derrida, *The Animal That Therefore I Am*, trans. David Wills (New York: Fordham University Press, 2008, orig. 2006).

113. Baker, *Postmodern Animal*, 74.

114. Gregory Bateson, *Steps to an Ecology of Mind* (New York: Random House, 1972), 370, 374; cited in Wolfe, *Animal Rites*, 40.

115. Kathryn Milun, *Pathologies of Modern Space* (New York: Routledge, 2007), 37.

116. Emile Durkheim, *The Elementary Forms of the Religious Life*, trans. J. W. Swain (New York: Free Press, 1915, orig. 1912).

117. E. E. Evans-Pritchard, *Witchcraft, Oracles and Magic among the Azande* (Oxford: Clarendon Press, 1937).

118. Jacques Derrida, "Faith and Knowledge: The Two Sources of 'Religion' at the Limits of Reason Alone," in *Religion*, ed. Jacques Derrida and Gianni Vattimo, (Stanford, Calif.: Stanford University Press, 1998, orig. 1996), 1–78. *Re-ligere*, to tie back, is one etymology of religion, a reknotting, perhaps, in the Lacanian sense.

119. "But enough of allegories! We have read too many fables and we are still taking the name of a dog in the figurative sense . . . Bobby and I are not like [Odysseus's] dog and his master"; quoted in Clark, "On Being the Last Kantian," 152, 168.

120. Michael M. J. Fischer, "Cultural Analysis as Experimental Systems," *Cultural Anthropology* 22.1 (January 2007):1–65.

121. "Globalatinized" is Derrida's term for a global world dominated by Western European Christianized forms of public discourse.

122. Scott Gilbert suggestively linked the four bodies of four scientific research domains with different metaphorical transductions to the social world in a 1993 lecture delivered at the Massachusetts Institute of Technology, "Reconstructing the Body in the Intercultural University." The *neural body*, deriving from nineteenth-century divisions between brain and body, has adapted to computer-friendly visions of science as acultural. (As suggested by the work of Simmel, Durkheim, Freud, Benjamin, Taussig, Ronell, and Milun, the history of the social and physical nervous system is much more complex and less acultural than suggested by Gilbert here.) Before the 1960s the *immune body* and the lymph system were a popular metaphor for defense of the body, albeit technically already misleading, as Fleck argued in 1935, and for distinguishing self from nonself; after the 1960s, obsessions with cancer transformed the immune body into a metaphor of the body out of control; Ludwik Fleck, *Genesis and Development of a Scientific Fact* (Chicago: University of Chicago Press, 1935). The *genetic body*, Gilbert suggests, parallels the medieval view of the soul, which survives the death of the body and is the body of potentials, of repertoires of phenotypes. The genetic body is a separate culture in which most ordinary people are illiterate. While this formulation yields too much to the often misleading and quite old trope of the book of life, critiqued by Lily Kay, it is the case that we are learning to write new biologies; Lily Kay, *Who Wrote the Book of Life? A History of the Genetic Code* (Palo Alto, Calif.: Stanford University Press, 2000); Hans-Jorg Rheinberger, *Toward a History of Epistemic Things: Synthesizing Proteins in the Test Tube* (Palo Alto, Calif.: Stanford University Press, 1997). The *phenotypic body* is increasingly seen as epiphenomenal to the other three bodies. Gilbert's point is not really to insist on the legacy correlations between ethnicity and the metaphors of the genetic body, defense and the metaphors of the immune body, or cultural "memes" and the neural body. Rather, he is reacting against intercultural studies existing apart from the contemporary sciences and is symmetrically suggesting that there is waiting time in biology labs that could be used to read the accounts of Fleck or Emily Martin, or in molecular biology labs to write grant proposals for non-Western cultures or to take regular field trips to see and experience real animals. Emily Martin, *Flexible Bodies: Tracking Immunity in American Culture from the Days of Polio to the Age of AIDS* (Boston: Beacon, 1994). See also Scott F. Gilbert, "Resurrecting the Body: Has Postmodernism Had Any Effect on Biology?" *Science in Context* 8 (1995):563–577; Gilbert, "The Genome in Its Ecological Context: Philosophical Perspectives on Interspecies Epigenesis," *Annals of the New York Academy of Science* 981 (2003):202–218.

NATURE, CHANGE, AND JUSTICE
Lisa Sowle Cahill

1. Aristotle, *Physics*, trans. R. P. Hardie and R. K. Gaye, bk. 2, pt. 1, available at The Internet Classics Archive, http://classics.mit.edu/Aristotle/physics.2.ii.html.

2. Citations from the World Transhumanist Association Web site at www.transhumanism.org/index.php/WTA/index/.

3. Nick Bostrom, "Transhumanist Values," World Transhumanist Association, available at www.transhumanism.org/index.php/WTA/more/transhumanist-values/.

4. The ethical norm of a preferential option for the poor emerged in liberation theology, refers back to the biblical prophets and Jesus's ministry of the inclusive kingdom or reign of God, and has been incorporated into Catholic social teaching. See, for example, John Paul II's 1987 encyclical, *Sollicitudo rei socialis*, no. 42.

5. See the Web site of the Biotechnology Industry Organization (BIO) at www.bio.org. BIO, however, does provide links to other organizations that do address issues of bioethics and global poverty, such as the Kennedy Institute for Ethics, Georgetown University, and the Center for Bioethics at the University of Minnesota.

6. Peter Scott, *A Political Theology of Nature* (Cambridge, U.K., and New York: Cambridge University Press, 2003), 44, 55, 192, 193.

7. Ibid., 173–174, 54–55, 181.

8. Ibid., 199.

9. Sallie McFague, *Models of God: Theology for an Ecological, Nuclear Age* (London: SCM, 1987); Sallie McFague, *The Body of God: An Ecological Theology* (London: SCM, 1993).

10. See Heather Eaton, *Introducing Feminist Theologies* (New York and London: Continuum, 2005).

11. Jürgen Moltmann, *The Spirit of Life: A Universal Affirmation*, trans. Margaret Kohl (Minneapolis, Minn.: Fortress, 2001), 225.

12. Forebears of this model of the knowledge of human nature are the eighteenth-century intellectuals Isaac Newton, John Locke, David Hume, and René Descartes. Hume's *Treatise of Human Nature* aimed to identify, on the basis of empirical observation, certain universal traits of the human mind and emotions and the laws that govern these traits. Hume was influenced by Newton's distinction between conjecture and empirical investigation as well as his interest in mathematical quantification. Hume also adopted the Lockean premise that a valid definition of human nature could rely only on experience. Descartes distrusted sense experience and turned instead to the elemental experience of thought as the most secure basis of knowledge. Yet he similarly

aspired to "clear and distinct" intellectual perceptions of truths (*Meditation IV*).

13. Aristotle, *Metaphysics*, trans. Richard Hope (Ann Arbor: University of Michigan Press, 1952) V; Aristotle, *Nichomachean Ethics*, trans. Martin Ostwald (Upper Saddle River, N.J.: Prentice Hall, 1999), I.7.4–5.

14. Ibid., X.6.12–13.

15. Ibid., IX.9; Jill Frank, "Citizens, Slaves, and Foreigners: Aristotle on Human Nature," *American Political Science Review* 98/1 (2004): 92.

16. Thomas Aquinas, *Summa Theologica*, trans. Fathers of the English Dominican Province (New York: Benziger, 1957) I–II. Q 94.a 4.

17. Elaine Graham, "In Whose Image? Representations of Technology and the 'Ends' of Humanity," in *Future Perfect? God, Medicine and Human Identity*, ed. Celia Deane-Drummond and Peter Manley Scott (London; New York: T&T Clark, 2006), 62–63.

18. Ibid., 64.

19. Stephen J. Pope, *Evolution and Christian Ethics* (Cambridge, U.K., and New York: Cambridge University Press, 2007), 129.

20. Ibid., 131.

21. Ibid., 130.

22. See Gordon Graham, "Human Nature and the Human Condition," in *Future Perfect? God, Medicine and Human Identity*, ed. Celia Deane-Drummond and Peter Manley Scott (London; New York: T&T Clark, 2006), 36.

23. Frank, "Citizens, Slaves, and Foreigners," 99.

24. Ibid., 101.

25. See Aristotle, *Nichomachean Ethics*, I.1–5, X.6–8.

26. Ibid., V.1, 7.

27. For an argument that Aristotle did not see slavery as an unchanging natural condition, see Frank, "Citizens, Slaves, and Foreigners," 94–97. For Aristotle on the subordination of women, see Aristotle, *Politics*, in *Aristotle's Politics and Poetics*, trans. Benjamin Jowett and Thomas Twining (New York: Viking, 1957), I.12–13, III.6.

28. Aquinas, *Summa Theologica*, I-II. Q 94.

29. Ibid., I–II. Q 94. a 2.

30. Ibid., I–II. Q 94. a 2. reply obj. 2.

31. Ibid., II–II. Q 58. a 1.

32. For Aquinas on the status of women, see Aquinas, *Summa Theologica*, I. Q 92. For Aquinas's defense of slavery, see Aquinas, *Summa Theologica*, II–II. Q 57. a 3. reply obj. 2.

33. Martha Nussbaum, "Human Functioning and Social Justice: In Defense of Aristotelian Essentialism," *Political Theory* 20 (1992): 202–246.

34. Nussbaum offers multiple versions of this list. A fairly recent one can be found in Martha Nussbaum, *Women and Human Development* (New York; Cambridge, U.K.: Cambridge University Press, 2000), 78–80.

35. Martha Nussbaum, *Sex and Social Justice* (New York; Oxford: Oxford University Press, 1999), 9, 73–75.

36. Martha C. Nussbaum, *Love's Knowledge: Essays on Philosophy and Literature* (New York; Oxford: Oxford University Press, 1990), 46–47; see also 26, 28, 95–96.

37. Erika Cheek, "Quest for the Cure," *Foreign Policy* (July–August 2006):28–36.

38. Ibid., 29.

39. James Waller, *Becoming Evil: How Ordinary People Commit Genocide and Mass Killing* (Oxford: Oxford University Press, 2002), 145–149. Waller cites as his key sources on evolutionary psychology two "pioneers" in the field, psychologist Leda Cosmides and anthropologist John Tooby, both at the University of California at Santa Barbara (ibid., 145). For present purposes, I am presenting this field of research very schematically. For an extensive treatment in relation to religion and ethics, see Pope, *Evolution*.

40. Pope, *Evolution* 143–153, 250–267.

41. Reinhold Niebuhr, *Moral Man and Immoral Society* (New York: Charles Scribner's Sons, 1932); Reinhold Niebuhr, *Nature and Destiny of Man*, vol. I, *Human Nature* (New York: Charles Scribner's Sons, 1941), 218–219.

42. Waller, *Becoming Evil*.

43. Ibid., 153.

44. Ibid., 20.

45. Ibid., x.

46. Ervin Staub, *The Psychology of Good and Evil: Why Children, Adults, and Groups Help and Harm Others* (Cambridge, U.K., and New York: Cambridge University Press, 2003), 4.

47. Waller, *Becoming Evil*, 33–35.

48. Ibid., 35.

49. Staub, *Psychology of Good and Evil*, 547.

50. Kathryn Tanner, *The Politics of God: Christian Theologies and Social Justice* (Minneapolis, Minn.: Fortress, 1992), 176–187.

51. James M. Gustafson, *A Sense of the Divine: The Natural Environment from a Theocentric Perspective* (Cleveland: Pilgrim, 1994).

52. William Schweiker, *Responsibility and Christian Ethics* (Cambridge, U.K., and New York: Cambridge University Press, 1995), 3.

53. Ibid., 177, 217.

54. Scott, *Political Theology*, 192.

55. Ibid., 202.

56. Dwight N. Hopkins, *Being Human: Race, Culture and Religion* (Minneapolis: Fortress, 2005), 80.

57. Kathryn A. Tanner, *An Economy of Grace* (Minneapolis: Fortress, 2005), 25.

58. Ibid.

59. Scott, *Political Theology*, 176.

60. Hopkins, *Being Human*, 80.

61. Ted Peters, "Perfect Humans or Trans-Humans?" in *Future Perfect? God, Medicine and Human Identity*, ed. Celia Deane-Drummond and Peter Manley Scott (London; New York: T&T Clark, 2006), 16.

62. Waller, *Becoming Evil*, 179.

63. Scott, *Political Theology*, 4–6, 201–202.

64. I attempt a more complete analysis in *Theological Bioethics: Participation, Justice and Change* (Washington, D.C.: Georgetown University Press, 2005), which includes chapters on "National and International Health Access Reform" and "Biotechnology, Genes, and Justice."

65. Michael M. J. Fischer, "Emergent Forms of Un/Natural Life," in this volume.

66. Ibid.

TECHNOLOGICAL WORLDS AND THE BIRTH OF NATURE: ON HUMAN
CREATION AND ITS THEOLOGICAL RESONANCE IN HEIDEGGER AND SERRES
Thomas A. Carlson

1. Leon Kass, *Life, Liberty and the Defense of Dignity: The Challenge for Bioethics* (San Francisco: Encounter Books, 2002), 4.

2. Bill McKibben, *Enough: Staying Human in an Engineered Age* (New York: Henry Holt, 2003).

3. N. Katherine Hayles, *How We Became Posthuman: Virtual Bodies in Cybernetics, Literature, and Informatics* (Chicago: University of Chicago Press, 1999), 111.

4. I elaborate this sense of the human as indiscrete image, along with these connections between apophatic forms of theological anthropology and contemporary philosophical approaches to the human as open question, in Thomas A. Carlson, *The Indiscrete Image: Infinitude and Creation of the Human* (Chicago: University of Chicago Press, 2008).

5. Martin Heidegger, "The Question Concerning Technology," in *Basic Writings: Revised and Expanded Edition*, ed. David Farrell Krell (San Francisco: Harper Collins, 1993); originally published as Martin Heidegger, "Die Frage nach der Technik," in *Vorträge und Aufsätze* (Stuttgart: Verlag Günther Neske, 1964).

6. Ibid., 321.

7. For Heidegger's definition of the phenomenon, see, e.g., *Being and Time*, where it is defined as "that which shows itself in itself" (*das Sich-an-ihm-selbst-zeigende*); Martin Heidegger, *Being and Time*, trans. John Macquarrie and Edward Robinson (Oxford: Basil Blackwell, 1962), 54; Martin Heidegger, *Sein und Zeit* (Tübingen: Max Niemeyer Verlag, 1986), 31.

8. Heidegger, "Question Concerning Technology," 332. It is not surprising that this concern to keep the human open to a call for which the human does not set or control the conditions becomes one of the central issues of twentieth-century thought among post-Heideggerians such as Emmanuel Levinas, Jacques Derrida, and Jean-Luc Marion, all of whom attend not only to the relative threat of technology to such a call but also to the potential religious import of the call—thus linking in essential ways, I think, the question of technology and the question of religion in modern and contemporary thought.

9. Ibid.

10. Ibid.

11. Martin Heidegger, "The Age of the World Picture," in *The Question Concerning Technology and Other Essays*, trans. William Lovitt (New York: Harper and Row, 1977); originally published as Martin Heidegger, "Die Zeit des Weltbildes," in *Holzwege* (Frankfurt am Main, Germany: Vittorio Klostermann, 1950). Martin Heidegger, *Contributions to Philosophy (From Enowning)*, trans. Parvis Emad and Kenneth Maly (Bloomington: Indiana University Press, 1999); originally published (posthumously) as Martin Heidegger, *Beiträge zur Philosophie (Vom Ereignis)* (Frankfurt am Main, Germany: Vittorio Klostermann, 1989).

12. That every metaphysics involves an understanding of being and a definition of truth is the fairly clear and accessible definition of "metaphysics" that Heidegger offers and develops in the first pages of "Age of the World Picture."

13. See, for example, "Science as a Vocation," in *From Max Weber: Essays in Sociology*, ed. H. H. Gerth and C. Wright Mills (New York: Oxford University Press, 1946), 139.

14. Heidegger, *Contributions to Philosophy*, 88.

15. Leibniz, cited and discussed at length both in Martin Heidegger, *The Principle of Reason*, trans. Reginald Lilly (Bloomington: Indiana University Press, 1991), 21; originally published as Martin Heidegger, *Der Satz vom Grund*, vol. 10 of *Gesamtausgabe* (Frankfurt am Main, Germany: Vottorio Klostermann, 1997); and in the earlier 1929 engagement with Leibniz in Martin Heidegger, *The Essence of Reasons: A Bilingual Edition Incorporating the German Text of* Vom Wesen des Grundes, trans. Terrence Malick (Evanston, Ill.: Northwestern University Press, 1969), 15.

16. Heidegger, *Principle of Reason*, 121. As Jean-Luc Marion emphasizes, the Leibnizian principle of sufficient reason, within whose bounds Leibniz conceives God, marks an extension into modern thought of what begins in Descartes as an "onto-theo-logy" of the *causa*:

> Leibniz's principle of sufficient reason seeks out God in the figure of the ultimate cause: "This is why the ultimate reason of things must lie in a necessary substance.

... This is what we call God" [Leibniz, *Monadologie* § 38]. Here, to be sure, reason is substituted for *causa* when it is time to designate the ultimate term; but besides the fact that Descartes had already posited the equivalence of *causa* and (*sive*) *ratio*, reason merely achieves for Leibniz a sufficiency that is still limited by cause. The onto-theo-logy of *causa* thus points toward Leibniz, through Spinoza, and beyond him.

Jean-Luc Marion, *On Descartes' Metaphysical Prism: The Constitution and Limits of Onto-theo-logy in Cartesian Thought*, trans. Jeffrey L. Kosky (Chicago: University of Chicago Press, 1999), 126.

17. While modern metaphysics would capture the world as picture, a more genuine philosophy, for Heidegger, inhabits an open questioning that answers to the irreducible possibility of worldhood in its essential tie to our Being-in-the-world, a possibility that itself cannot be represented "as such" in any given actuality, whether already achieved or yet to come.

18. Heidegger, "Question Concerning Technology," 331.

19. Ibid.

20. See also Heidegger, *Contributions to Philosophy*, 77.

21. Ibid., 88.

22. Michel Serres, *Rameaux* (Paris: Le Pommier, 2004), 198 and 199, respectively. This work should be read in the context of three others that with it form what Serres calls "Le Grand Récit," a text that seems to me one of the more far-reaching among recent attempts to interpret technological humanity in affirmative and creative terms: Serres, *Hominescence* (Paris, Le Pommier, 2001); Serres, *L'Incandescent* (Paris: Le Pommier, 2003); and Serres, *Récits d'humanisme* (Paris: Le Pommier, 2006).

23. Serres, *Rameaux*, 199.

24. Ibid., 131.

25. Ibid., 161.

26. Ibid., 201.

27. I elaborate these biological and mystical approaches to the human in chaps. 1 and 3, respectively, of Carlson, *Indiscrete Image*.

28. On this, see, in addition to chap. 3 of Carlson, *Indiscrete Image*, the major studies by Hans Blumenberg, *The Legitimacy of the Modern Age* (Cambridge, Mass.: MIT Press, 1985); and Louis Dupré, *Passage to Modernity: An Essay in the Hermeneutics of Nature and Culture* (New Haven, Conn.: Yale University Press, 1993).

29. In this direction, and with explicit reference to Heidegger's reading of Leibniz, see also Jean-Luc Nancy, *La création du monde ou la mondialisation* (Paris: Galilée, 2002).

30. "We assume today, then, what we assume since the beginning, a mastery of our productions that is unequal, weak, and sometimes nil, varying like

the principle of sufficient reason. Granting a slight shift in scale, nothing new under the sun. If our terrors, ordinary today, have less to do with those risks whose idea supposes an insufficient mastery than with this non-finality of our new artifacts, we can relativize these anxieties with the idea that past cultures did not master any better the pseudo-finalities of the Ancients." Serres, *Rameaux*, 200.

31. In his Heraclitus seminar with Eugen Fink, Heidegger does raise the possibility of a "non-coercive steering" that might be distinguished from the cybernetics that define our age of modern science and technology; his energies are given mainly, however, to concern over this latter, especially as it relates to the "cybernetic biology" that emerges from "the information-theoretical interpretation of the biological" and its "attempt . . . to actively steer." In Martin Heidegger and Eugen Fink, *Heraclitus Seminar*, trans. Charles H. Seibert (Evanston, Ill.: Northwestern University Press, 1993), 12–13.

32. Serres, *Rameaux*, 202.

33. Ibid., 227. See also the works dedicated specifically to the natural contract, Michel Serres, *Le contrat naturel* (Paris: Éditions François Bourin, 1990); translated by Elizabeth MacArthur and William Paulsen as *The Natural Contract* (Ann Arbor: University of Michigan Press, 1995); and Serres, *Retour au Contrat naturel* (Paris: Bibliothèque nationale de France, 2000).

34. Serres, *Rameaux*, 227.

35. Heidegger, *Being and Time*, 158; *Sein und Zeit*, 122.

36. Ibid., 158–159; 122.

37. It is worth noting another recent and influential version of this distinction in Jacques Derrida's differentiation between, on the one hand, messianicity as an open structure of futurity or anticipation never realizable as such in any present, and on the other hand, the various messianisms that would aim or claim to fill such anticipation and thus effectively close any genuine futurity.

38. Martin Heidegger, "*Der Spiegel* Interview with Martin Heidegger," in *Martin Heidegger and National Socialism: Questions and Answers*, ed. Günther Neske and Emil Kettering, trans. Lisa Harries (New York: Paragon House, 1990), 57; originally published as "Noch nur ein Gott kann uns retten," *Der Spiegel*, May 31, 1976, publication of the interview with Rudolf Augstein and Georg Wolff that took place on September 23, 1966. A similar point is made already in the early 1938 lecture published as "Age of the World Picture":

> But as soon as the gigantic in planning and calculating and adjusting and making secure shifts over out of the quantitative and becomes a special quality, then what is gigantic, and what can seemingly always be calculated completely becomes, precisely through this, incalculable. This becoming incalculable remains an invisible shadow that is cast around all things everywhere when man has been transformed into *subjectum* and the world into picture.

Heidegger, "Age of the World Picture," 135.

39. Martin Heidegger, "Letter on Humanism," in *Basic Writings: Revised and Expanded Edition*, ed. David Farrel Krell (San Francisco: Harper Collins, 1993), 220; Heidegger, "Brief über den 'Humanismus,'" in *Wegmarken* (Frankfurt am Main, Germany: Vittorio Klostermann, 1967), 316. Along these lines, see also the rest of the passage quoted here from "Letter on Humanism":

> As the element, Being is the "quiet power" of the favoring-enabling, that is, of the possible. Of course, our words *möglich* [possible] and *Möglichkeit* [possibility], under the dominance of "logic" and "metaphysics," are thought on the basis of the definite—the metaphysical—interpretation of Being as *actus* and *potentia*, a distinction identified with the one between *existentia* and *essentia*. When I speak of "the quiet power of the possible" I do not mean the *possibile* of a merely represented *possibilitas*, nor *potentia* as the *essentia* of an *actus* of *existentia*; rather, I mean Being itself, which in its favoring presides over thinking and hence over the essence of humanity.

Heidegger, "Letter on Humanism," 220.

40. On this resonance of Augustine in Heidegger, see Thomas A. Carlson, "With the World at Heart: Reading Cormac McCarthy's *The Road* with Augustine and Heidegger," *Religion and Literature* 39.3 (2007): 47–71.

41. Serres, *Rameaux*, 90–91.

SHOULD WE REVERENCE LIFE? REFLECTIONS AT THE INTERSECTION OF
ECOLOGY, RELIGION, AND ETHICS
William Schweiker

1. In my discussion of Schweitzer's thought I will be drawing on some of my previous writings. See esp. William Schweiker, "The Spirit of Life and the Reverence for Life," in *God's Life in Trinity*, ed. Miroslav Wolf and Michael Welker (Minneapolis, Minn.: Fortress, 2006), 22–31.

2. See Paul W. Taylor, *Respect for Nature: A Theory of Environmental Ethics* (Princeton, N.J.: Princeton University Press, 1986). It is interesting in this light that Immanuel Kant, in his deduction of freedom and formulation of the categorical imperative, notes that what commands one's "respect" is something that is found "holy" in oneself, namely, rational freedom. In this respect, a religious claim, only fully developed in his philosophical theology, is at the core of Kant's ethics.

3. The Czech philosopher Erazim Kohák, in his account of the moral sense of nature, speaks about the ingression of value, while others get at the same point by saying that moral value supervenes on the natural, nonmoral conditions and traits of something. See Erazim Kohák, *The Embers and the Stars: An Inquiry into the Moral Sense of Nature* (Chicago: University of Chicago Press, 1984).

4. See Peter Singer, *Unsanctifying Human Life* (Oxford: Blackwell, 2002).

5. Friedrich Nietzsche, *The Gay Science: With a Prelude in German Rhymes and an Appendix of Songs*, ed. Bernard A. Williams, trans. Josefine Nauckhoff and Adrian Del Caro (Cambridge, U.K.: Cambridge University Press, 2002), 109.

6. See Francis Fukuyama, *Our Posthuman Future* (New York: Farrar, Straus and Giroux, 2002); and Paul Ramsey, *Fabricated Man* (New Haven, Conn.: Yale University Press, 1970). Also see Jürgen Habermas, *The Future of Human Nature* (Cambridge, U.K.: Polity, 2003); Donna Haraway, *Simians, Cyborgs, and Women: The Reinvention of Nature* (New York: Routledge, 1991); and Leon Kass, *Life, Liberty and the Defense of Dignity* (San Francisco: Encounter, 2002).

7. Albert Camus, *The Myth of Sisyphus and Other Essays*, trans. Justin O'Brien (New York: Vintage International, 1991), 3.

8. See Joseph Cardinal Bernardin, *Consistent Ethic of Life* (New York: Sheen and Ward, 1988); and John Paul II, *Veritatis Splendor* (Dublin: Veritas Publications, 1998).

9. Jürgen Moltmann, *The Spirit of Life: A Universal Affirmation*, trans. Margaret Kohl (Minneapolis: Fortress, 2001), xii.

10. Albert Schweitzer, *The Philosophy of Civilization*, trans. C. T. Campion (Buffalo, N.Y.: Prometheus, 1987), 318.

11. Of course, the question of the relation, if any, between ethics and metaphysics or a theory of the universe or a mythopoetic conception of reality has been hotly debated among moral philosophers and theologians. Generally speaking, modern ethics has rejected any connection, whereas all forms of religious ethics and now most forms of "postmodern ethics" seek to explore the moral significance of some vision of reality, some construal of the moral space of reality. On this, see Iris Murdoch, *Metaphysics as a Guide to Morals* (London: Penguin, Allen Lane, 1992); William Schweiker, *Power, Value and Conviction: Theological Ethics in the Postmodern Age* (Cleveland: Pilgrim, 1998), and Franklin I. Gamwell, *The Divine Good: Modern Moral Theory and the Necessity of God* (San Francisco: HarperCollins, 1990).

12. Schweitzer's thought worked at the interface of religion, ethics, and what we now call ecological concern. That is one reason for me to engage his work. But there is another reason. Most twentieth-century ethics took the famous "turn to language" and so explored the meaning of moral concepts, forms of moral discourse, the character of public actions, especially through ideas about justice. What often got lost was a concern for human moral consciousness. Indeed, the philosopher Seyla Benhabib notes that "the paradigm of language has replaced the [modern] paradigm of consciousness." Interestingly enough, questions in ecological ethics about perceptions of the value of nonhuman life as well as recent discussions surrounding genetic manipulation

and research have, thankfully, pushed the question of moral consciousness again into the forefront of ethical inquiry, a welcome development in my judgment. Insofar as Schweitzer fastens on consciousness and the will-to-live as basic to his ethics, he might have something to contribute to the current discussion, at least by way of problems to avoid. See Seyla Benhabib, *Situating the Self: Gender, Community and Postmodernism in Contemporary Ethics* (New York: Routledge, 1992), 208.

13. Albert Schweitzer, "The Ethics of Reverence for Life," *Christendom* 1 (1936):225–239; repr. in Henry Clark, *The Ethical Mysticism of Albert Schweitzer: A Study of the Sources and Significance of Schweitzer's "Philosophy of Civilization"* (Boston: Beacon, 1962), 180–194; and reproduced with permission of the World Council of Churches at http://www1.chapman.edu/schweitzer/sch.reading4.html. This and subsequent quotations are from the online version.

14. Ibid.

15. For a related argument, if cast in different terms, see Hans Jonas, *The Imperative of Responsibility: In Search of an Ethics for the Technological Age* (Chicago: University of Chicago Press, 1984).

16. Schweitzer, "Ethics of Reverence for Life."

17. In fact, the various philosophies of life divided at precisely this point. Friedrich Nietzsche, for instance, traced out the implications of the will-to-life as sheer vitalism. Arthur Schopenhauer saw life as essentially suffering and believed that the wisdom of life consisted in pessimism as well as the liberation of intellect from its servitude to will.

18. Schweitzer once noted to the theologian Karl Barth that whereas in the face of the confusion of nineteenth- and twentieth-century thought Barth returned to the Reformation, Schweitzer himself sought the insight of the eighteenth-century Enlightenment thinkers.

19. Schweitzer, *Philosophy of Civilization*, 311.

20. Ibid., 310.

21. Ibid., 312.

22. Ibid. One should remember that Schweitzer studied Schopenhauer and also Asian traditions, including Jainism. The claim that ultimate reality (creative will) is creative and destructive is consistent with these forms of thought, and therefore a full treatment of this ethics requires a foray into comparative religions. That work is, of course, not possible in this essay. See Arthur Schopenhauer, *The Basis of Morality*, trans. A. B. Bullock, 2nd ed. (Mineola, N.Y.: Dover, 2005).

23. It is for this reason that Schweitzer, somewhat like Kant, draws a sharp distinction between theoretical and practical reason. Theoretical reason, what Schweitzer calls knowledge, can aid in ethical reflection, but the domain of moral existence is really the place of practical reason.

24. Schweitzer, *Philosophy of Civilization*, 313.

25. Albert Schweitzer, *Christianity and the Religions of the World*, trans. Johanna Powers. (New York: Henry Holt, 1939), 81. Also see Lois K. Daly, "Ecofeminism, Reverence for Life, and Feminist Theological Ethics," in *Liberating Life: Contemporary Approaches in Ecological Theology*, ed. Charles Birch, William Eaken, and Jay B. McDaniel (Maryknoll, N.Y.: Orbis, 1990), 86–110.

26. Schweitzer, *Christianity and the Religions of the World*, 78.

27. This is a reflexive or broadly existential or experimental method. See William Schweiker, *Responsibility and Christian Ethics* (Cambridge, U.K.: Cambridge University Press, 1995).

28. For a related argument, see Mary Midgley, *The Ethical Primate: Humans, Freedom and Morality* (London: Routledge, 1998).

29. The issues in moral theory at stake in the claims are analogous to debates in Roman Catholic ethics about "proportionalism." Germain Grisez, for instance, argues that "In voluntarily acting for human goods and avoiding what is opposed to them, one ought to choose and otherwise will those and only those possibilities whose willing is compatible with a will towards integral human fulfillment." Because of this, Grisez and others insist that one cannot draw distinctions between premoral and moral goods in order to legitimate some actions against premoral goods. The position I am advancing requires these distinctions, and others, since integrity is not reducible to its conditions. See Germain Grisez and Russell Shaw, *Fulfillment in Christ* (Notre Dame, Ind.: University of Notre Dame Press, 1991), 70. On this, see Schweiker, *Responsibility and Christian Ethics*, chap. 5.

30. One hears about the Earth as the Body of God or the divine as the principle of creativity or the connection of Gaia and God or the need to adopt "biophilia" or a sense of the divine and a theocentric perspective on the natural world. For important options, see Sallie McFague, *The Body of God: An Ecological Theology* (Minneapolis: Augsburg, 1993); and James M. Gustafson, *Ethics from a Theocentric Perspective*, 2 vols. (Chicago: University of Chicago Press, 1981, 1984).

31. See William Schweiker, *Theological Ethics and Global Dynamics: In the Time of Many Worlds* (Oxford: Blackwell, 2004).

32. If space allowed, I could enter the complex array of theological concepts and symbols ranging from "creation" to the *imago dei* and even into ideas about salvation in order to provide the forms with which to articulate and grasp the religious meanings uncovered about the scope of value, normative self-understanding, and also the longing for the inviolable. That would provide additional means to think otherwise than the kind of ethical theism found in Schweitzer's thought. That work is not possible in the present inquiry.

THE END OF NATURE AND THE LAST HUMAN? THINKING THEOLOGICALLY
ABOUT "NATURE" IN A POSTNATURAL CONDITION
Peter Manley Scott

1. "Air Tax Hike Would 'Hit the Poorest,'" *BBC News* August 7, 2006, available at http://news.bbc.co.uk/1/hi/uk_politics/5253444.stm.

2. "Blair Urges Home Pollution Checks," *BBC News* 7 August 7, 2006, available at http://news.bbc.co.uk/1/hi/uk_politics/5251312.stm.

3. Friends of the Earth, "Call for Greener Transport Policies in Damning Report," press release, August 7, 2006, available at http://www.foe.co.uk/resource/press_releases/call_for_greener_transport_07082006.html.

4. At the end of this media game, we learn furthermore that governments will respond to climate change by seeking to adapt to its effects rather than to mitigate its causes. In taking this adaptation approach, the wealthier countries will be at an advantage over their poorer counterparts, thereby sustaining their existing economic advantage.

5. John Keane, "Introduction," in Norberto Bobbio, *Democracy and Dictatorship* (Cambridge, U.K.: Polity, 1989, 1997), xxiii.

6. David Ingram, *Habermas and the Dialectic of Reason* (New Haven, Conn.: Yale University Press, 1989), 79.

7. Terry Pinkard, *Hegel: A Biography* (Cambridge, U.K.: Cambridge University Press, 2000), 563.

8. For a comprehensive demonstration of this, see Peter Raven, "Biodiversity and Sustainability: Our Common Responsibility to Nature," in this volume.

9. Louis Dupré, *Passage to Modernity: An Essay in the Hermeneutics of Nature and Culture* (New Haven: Yale University Press, 1993), 174–181.

10. Bruno Latour, *We Have Never Been Modern* (London: Harvester Wheatsheaf, 1993).

11. See Peter Manley Scott, "We Have Never Been Gods: Transcendence, Contingency and the Affirmation of Hybridity," *Ecotheology* 9.2 (August 2004):199–220, at 200. Although written from different sources and for a different purpose, there is some overlap in my position here and Soja's recommendation of a "trialectical ontology" of spatiality, historicality, and temporality; see Edward W. Soja, "Seeing Nature Spatially," in this volume. There is further overlap with the Christological framing of a common realm of God, nature, and humanity in terms of sociality, temporality, and spatiality that I propose. Peter Manley Scott, *A Political Theology of Nature* (Cambridge, U.K.: Cambridge University Press, 2003), chap. 7. My position, however, also contains the theological claim that nature may be understood as an active subject.

12. See Scott, "We Have Never Been Gods," 213–216.

13. Mark Maslin, *Global Warming: A Very Short Introduction* (Oxford: Oxford University Press, 2004), 37.

14. See György Lukács, *The Ontology of Social Being*, vol. 1, *Hegel* (London: Merlin, 1978), 11–13.

15. C. B. Macpherson, *The Political Theory of Possessive Individualism: Hobbes to Locke* (Oxford: Oxford University Press, 1962, 1964), 2.

16. Francis Fukuyama, *The End of History and the Last Man* (Harmondsworth, U.K.: Penguin, 1992), 51.

17. Jürgen Habermas, *The Future of Human Nature* (Cambridge, U.K.: Polity, 2003), 16–74.

18. See Robert Song, "Knowing There Is No God, Still We Should Not Play God? Habermas on the Future of Human Nature," *Ecotheology* 11.2 (June 2006):191–211, at 192–195.

19. Bill McKibben, *The End of Nature* (New York: Anchor Books, 1990), 48.

20. Samuel Taylor Coleridge, *Notebooks: A Selection*, ed. Seamus Perry (Oxford: Oxford University Press, 2002), 29.

21. Lukács, *Ontology of Social Being*, 5–6. There are some splendid examples of this tendency to be found in Keith Thomas's *Man and the Natural World*, whose summary is as follows:

> In place of a natural world redolent with human analogy and symbolic meaning, and sensitive to man's behaviour, they [the naturalists] constructed a detached natural scene to be viewed and studied by the observer from the outside, as if by peering through a window, in the secure knowledge that the objects of contemplation inhabited a separate realm, offering no omens or signs, without human meaning and significance.

Keith Thomas, *Man and the Natural World* (Harmondsworth, U.K.: Penguin, 1984), 89.

22. Raymond Williams, *Problems in Materialism and Culture* (London: Verso, 1980), 71.

23. Cf. Macpherson, *Political Theory of Possessive Individualism*, who argues against this, and thus assists my argument by indicating that there is no unmediated nature.

24. It is into this vacuum that arguments such as Fukuyama's are sucked.

25. Williams, *Problems in Materialism and Culture*, 71.

26. See Peter Manley Scott, "Is the Goodness of God Good Enough? The Human Genome in Theological and Political Perspective," in *Brave New World: Theology, Ethics and the Human Genome*, ed. Celia Deane-Drummond (London: T & T Clark, 2003), 294–318, at 299–300.

27. Peter Manley Scott, "Anarchy in the UK? GM Crops, Political Authority and the Rioting of God," *Ecotheology* 11.1 (March 2006):32–56.

28. Bobbio, *Democracy and Dictatorship*, 83.

29. Francis Fukuyama, *The End of History and the Last Man* (Harmondsworth, U.K.: Penguin, 1992), 161.

30. Ibid., 138–139.

31. Ibid., 207.

32. Fukuyama, *End of History*, 45.

33. Cf. Raven, "Biodiversity and Sustainability": "Nothing less than a new industrial revolution and a new agriculture are required to make possible the sustainable world of the future."

34. Charles Taylor, "The Moral Order: The Transition to Political Modernity," in *Religion & Political Thought*, ed. Michael Hoelzl and Graham Ward (London: Continuum, 2006), 259–267, at 260.

35. Fukuyama, *End of History*, 337–338.

36. Perhaps these three points correspond to Fischer's presentation of political institutions, "deep play," and narrative as ways of interpreting ecological issues: see Michael M. J. Fischer, "Emergent Forms of Un/Natural Life," in this volume.

37. Dietrich Bonhoeffer, *Ethics* (Minneapolis, Minn.: Fortress, 2005), 388–389 n. 2.

38. Colin E. Gunton, *The One, the Three and the Many* (Cambridge, U.K.: Cambridge University Press, 1993), 226.

39. See Scott, *Political Theology of Nature*, 201–232.

40. This suggests that Bruno Latour's position, as Fischer reports it— "there is no nature independent of human interests and practices"—is too strong. See Fischer, "Emergent Forms of Un/Natural Life."

41. Colin Crouch, *Post-Democracy* (Cambridge, U.K.: Polity, 2004), 113, recommends temporary citizens' assemblies as a way of renewing substantive democracy. This proposal might be explored ecologically; such assemblies might be tasked with drawing up legislation toward the protection of the environment or scrutinizing ordinary legislation for its ecological deficit.

42. This paragraph is from Peter Manley Scott, "Postnatural Humanity? Bonhoeffer, Creaturely Freedom and the Mystery of Reconciliation in Creation," in *Mysteries in the Theology of Dietrich Bonhoeffer*, ed. K. B. Nielsen, Ulrik Nissen, and Christiane Tietz (Göttingen, Germany: Vandenhoeck & Ruprecht, 2007), 112–134.

43. Carl Schmitt, *The Concept of the Political* (Chicago: University of Chicago Press, 1996), 26.

44. Theology offers some responses here: natural (moral) law, orders of creation, mandates, stewardship. It seems to me that only the first and last survive, and yet neither is helpful in the discussion of *postnatural* standards.

45. Terry Eagleton, *Sweet Violence: The Idea of the Tragic* (Oxford: Blackwell, 2003).

46. What is also to be refused is nature as abyssal or focal that requires the difference of fear but then renders that fear as benign.

47. Cf. Donald MacKinnon, *Explorations in Theology*, (London: SCM, 1979), 5:182–195.

48. Jürgen Moltmann, *The Coming of God* (London: SCM, 1996), 234.

49. Colin E. Gunton, *The Triune Creator: Historical and Systematic Considerations* (Edinburgh: Edinburgh University Press, 1998), 219.

50. Daniel W. Hardy, "Eschatology as a Challenge for Theology," in *The Future as God's Gift*, ed. David Fergusson and Marcel Sarot (Edinburgh: T & T Clark, 2000), 151–158.

51. Seán McDonagh, *To Care for the Earth* (London: Geoffrey Chapman, 1986), 190.

52. Cf. Raven, "Biodiversity and Sustainability": "Food security, health, social justice—all are dependent on rising above our parochial and perhaps ingrained views of how to live and learning together how to manage our planetary home for our common benefit."

53. Walter Lowe, "Prospects for a Postmodern Christian Theology: Apocalyptic without Reserve," *Modern Theology* 15.1 (1999):17–24, esp. 20.

54. Seán McDonagh, *The Greening of the Church* (London: Geoffrey Chapman, 1990), 198.

55. For Fukuyama, the last man is the thymotic human. This is a response to Nietzsche's critique of the slavery, the unfreedom of democracy.

56. Again, this is not far from Soja, "Seeing Nature Spatially": "spatiality (including the spaces of nature) is simultaneously socialized and politicized, filled with politics, culture, ideology, conflict, justice and injustice, and, most important, with the emphatic realization that it is subject to significant change through collective social action." My reservation over this formulation is that it suggests that the spaces of nature are colonized by other—historical?— forces, leading to a denaturing. For a wider critique of socialist ecology and a fuller elaboration of the criticism that nature in the thought of some socialist ecologists is somewhat inert, see Scott, *A Political Theology of Nature*, chap. 6.

GRACE WITHOUT NATURE
Kathryn Tanner

1. The general trajectory I am tracing runs through theologians such as Irenaeus, Athanasius, Gregory of Nyssa, and Cyril of Alexandria in the early church. For this concern for natural processes of growth through nourishment in particular, see, e.g., Irenaeus, "Against Heresies," in *Ante-Nicene Fathers*, vol. 1 (Grand Rapids, Mich.: Eerdmans, 1989), bk. 4; and Gregory of Nyssa, esp. Nyssa, "On Infants' Early Deaths," in *Nicene and Post-Nicene Fathers*, vol. 5 (Peabody, Mass.: Hendrickson, 1994), where he is no doubt trying to fathom

the deeper meaning of the Genesis call to "grow and multiply" and the Genesis prohibition on certain forms of eating.

2. Gregory of Nyssa, "On the Soul and the Resurrection," in *Nicene and Post-Nicene Fathers*, vol. 5 (Peabody, Mass.: Hendrickson, 1994), 452.

3. Gregory Nazianzen, Oration 7.23, *Nicene and Post-Nicene Fathers*, vol. 7 (Grand Rapids, Mich.: Eerdmans, 1983), 237.

4. See Harry G. Frankfurt, *The Reasons of Love* (Princeton, N.J.: Princeton University Press, 2006).

5. Saint Augustine, "On the Holy Trinity," *Nicene and Post-Nicene Fathers*, vol. 3 (Grand Rapids, Mich.: Eerdmans, 1956), Book 10, ch 5, 138.

6. Saint Gregory of Nyssa, "Fourth Homily," *Commentary on the Song of Songs* (Brookline, Mass.: Hellenic College, 1987), 92. See also Nyssa, "On the Soul and Resurrection," 457: "Human nature is such that whatever it may wish to be," it "becomes that very thing."

7. Nyssa, "Fourth Homily," 92.

8. Nyssa, "On the Soul and Resurrection," 442.

9. Gregory of Nyssa, "On the Making of Man," *Nicene and Post-Nicene Fathers*, vol. 5, ch. 18.3–4, 408.

10. Nyssa, "On the Making of Man," ch. 12.9; the discussion continues into secs. 10–11, 399.

11. Gregory of Nyssa, "An Address on Religious Instruction," in *Christology of the Later Fathers*, ed. Edward Hardy (Philadelphia: Westminster, 1953), sec. 6, 279.

12. See Henri de Lubac, *Surnaturel* (Paris: Aubier, 1946).

13. See Henri de Lubac, *Augustinianism and Modern Theology*, trans. Lancelot Sheppard (New York: Crossroad, 2000), 233–234.

14. Augustine, *City of God*, trans. Henry Bettenson (New York: Penguin, 1972), bk. 11, ch. 10, 441–442.

15. For example, Cajetan thinks that apart from grace, we do not positively desire God at all.

16. Gregory of Nyssa, "Against Eunomius," *Nicene and Post-Nicene Fathers*, vol. 5, bk. 1.22, 62.

17. Nyssa, "Against Eunomius," bk. 8.5, 210.

18. Gregory of Nyssa, "On Virginity," *Nicene and Post-Nicene Fathers*, vol. 5, ch. 12, 357.

19. David L. Balás, *Metousia Theou: Man's Participation in God's Perfections According to Saint Gregory of Nyssa* (Rome: Herder, 1966), 149.

20. De Lubac, *Augustinianism*, 90, recounting Augustine's position.

21. Saint Basil the Great, "Long Rules," in *On the Human Condition*, trans. Nonna Verna Harrison (Crestwood, N.Y.: St. Vladimir's Seminary, 2005), question 2, answer 1, 112.

22. Basil, 'Long Rules," 112–115.

23. Nyssa, "On Infants' Early Deaths," 376.

24. See de Lubac, *Augustinianism*, 154–157.

25. See Cyril of Alexandria, *Commentary on John*, trans. E. B. Pusey (London: Walter Smith, 1885), bk. 11, ch. 7.6, 503, discussing kingly power as a human attribute.

26. This essay is the mere outline of a theological position. Much more could be said, but I hope I have said enough to give my reader the general idea why one might want to maintain, if one is a Christian theologian, that it is human nature not to have a nature, and some understanding of what grace might mean in that case if God is the very image that we are to become. In this way, Christian theology might follow the lead of the contemporary biological sciences while being all the more true to itself.

David Albertson is Assistant Professor of Religion at the University of Southern California. He is the author of several articles on Nicholas of Cusa.

Lisa Sowle Cahill is J. Donald Monan, S.J., Professor at Boston College, where she has taught Theology since 1976. She is a past president of the Catholic Theological Society of America (1992–1993), a past president of the Society of Christian Ethics (1997–1998), and a fellow of the American Academy of Arts and Sciences. Her recent publications include *Bioethics and the Common Good* (2004); *Theological Bioethics: Participation, Justice and Change* (2005); and an edited collection, *Genetics, Theology, Ethics: An Interdisciplinary Conversation* (2005).

Thomas A. Carlson is Professor in the Department of Religious Studies at the University of California, Santa Barbara. He is the author of *Indiscretion: Finitude and the Naming of God* (1999) and *The Indiscrete Image: Infinitude and Creation of the Human* (2008). Editor of the Religion and Postmodernism series at the University of Chicago Press, he is also translator of several works by the French philosopher Jean-Luc Marion, including *God without Being* (1991); *Reduction and Givenness: Investigations of Husserl, Heidegger, and Phenomenology* (1998); and *The Idol and Distance* (2001).

Ronald Cole-Turner holds the H. Parker Sharp Chair of Theology and Ethics at Pittsburgh Theological Seminary. He was instrumental in organizing the International Society for Science and Religion in 2002. He is the author of *The New Genesis: Theology and the Genetic Revolution* (1993), and coauthor of *Pastoral Genetics: Theology and Care at the Beginning of Life* (1996). He is the editor of *Human Cloning: Religious Responses* (1997), *Beyond Cloning: Religion and the Remaking of Humanity* (2001) and *Design and Destiny: Jewish and Christian Perspectives on Human Germline Modification*

(2008) and coeditor of *God and the Embryo: Religious Voices on Stem Cells and Cloning* (2003).

Lorraine Daston is Director at the Max Planck Institute for the History of Science and Visiting Professor in the Committee on Social Thought at the University of Chicago. She is the author of *Classical Probability in the Enlightenment* (1988) and coauthor (with Katharine Park) of *Wonders and the Order of Nature, 1150–1750* (2001), both winners of the History of Science Society's Pfizer Prize. She is editor of *Biographies of Scientific Objects* (2000) and *Things that Talk: Object Lessons from Art and Science* (2004). Her most recent book, coauthored with Peter Galison, is *Objectivity* (2007).

Michael M. J. Fischer is Andrew W. Mellon Professor in the Humanities and Professor of Anthropology and Science and Technology Studies at the Massachusetts Institute of Technology. He was previously the Director of the Center for Cultural Studies at Rice University, and from 1996 to 2000 he was the Director of the Program in Science, Technology and Society at MIT. He is the author of *Iran: From Religious Dispute to Revolution* (1980); *Anthropology as Cultural Critique: An Experimental Moment in the Human Sciences* (with George Marcus, 1986); *Debating Muslims: Cultural Dialogues in Postmodernity and Tradition* (with Mehdi Abedi, 1990); *Emergent Forms of Life and the Anthropological Voice* (2003); *Mute Dreams, Blind Owls and Dispersed Knowledges: Persian Poesis in the Transnational Circuitry* (2004); and *Anthropological Futures* (2009).

William French is Associate Professor of Theology and Director of the Center for Ethics at Loyola University Chicago. He serves on the board of the National Catholic Center for Holocaust. His research focuses on ecological issues and war and peace concerns. He is the recipient of a Louisville Institute Grant for research on his current book, *Natural Law and Ecological Concern*.

Timothy J. Gorringe is St. Lukes Professor of Theological Studies at the University of Exeter. His recent works include *Karl Barth: Against Hegemony* (1999); *A Theology of the Built Environment* (2002); and *Furthering Humanity: A Theology of Culture* (2004).

Cabell King is completing a PhD in Theology in the Divinity School at the University of Chicago. His research concerns conceptions of space and time in the work of Henri Lefebvre and their significance to Theological Anthropology and Ecological Ethics.

Sallie McFague is Distinguished Theologian in Residence at the Vancouver School of Theology in British Columbia. Her books include *Models of God* (1987); *The Body of God* (1993); *Super, Natural Christians* (1997); and *Life Abundant: Rethinking Theology and Economy for a Planet in Peril* (2000).

Gerald McKenny is Associate Professor of Christian Ethics and Director of the John C. Reilly Center for Science, Technology, and Values at the University of Notre Dame. He is joint principal investigator of "Altering Nature: How Religions Evaluate Biotechnology," a four-year project sponsored by the Ford Foundation, and author of *To Relieve the Human Condition: Bioethics, Technology, and the Body* (1997), a Choice Award winner.

Stuart A. Newman is Professor of Cell Biology and Anatomy at New York Medical College in Valhalla, New York. He is a founding member of the Council for Responsible Genetics and is currently a Fellow of the Institute on Biotechnology and the Human Future. He is coeditor of *Origination and Organismal Form: Beyond the Gene in Developmental and Evolutionary Biology* (2003) and coauthor of *Biological Physics of the Developing Embryo* (2005).

Peter H. Raven is President of the Missouri Botanical Garden and George Engelmann Professor of Botany at Washington University in St. Louis. He is a member of the Board of Trustees of the National Geographic Society and chairs its Committee for Research and Exploration; he has been the recipient of Guggenheim and MacArthur Foundation fellowships. In 1999 *Time Magazine* named him one of its "Heroes of the Planet." He is author of more than four hundred articles and sixteen books.

William Schweiker is Edward L. Ryerson Distinguished Service Professor of Theological Ethics at the University of Chicago Divinity School. His books include *Mimetic Reflections: A Study in Hermeneutics, Theology and Ethics* (1990); *Responsibility and Christian Ethics* (1995); *Power, Value and Conviction: Theological Ethics in the Postmodern Age* (1998); *Theological Ethics and Global Dynamics: In the Time of Many Worlds* (2004); and, with David Klemm, *Religion and the Human Future: An Essay on Theological Humanism* (2008).

Peter Manley Scott is Senior Lecturer in Christian Social Thought and Director of the Lincoln Theological Institute at the University of Manchester. He is author of *Theology, Ideology, and Liberation* (1994), *A Political Theology of Nature* (2003), and *Anti-Human Theology* (2010) and coeditor of the *Blackwell Companion to Political Theology* (2004); *Future Perfect?* (2006); *Remoralizing Britain?* (2009); and *Nature, Space, and the Sacred* (2009).

Edward W. Soja is Distinguished Professor of Urban Planning at the University of California at Los Angeles, where he teaches in the Regional and International Development area. His publications include *Postmodern Geographies: The Reassertion of Space in Critical Social Theory* (1989); *Thirdspace: Journeys to Los Angeles and Other Real-and-Imagined Places* (1996); and *Postmetropolis: Critical Studies of Cities and Regions* (2000).

Kathryn Tanner is the Dorothy Grant Maclear Professor of Theology at the University of Chicago Divinity School. She is author of *God and Creation in Christian Theology* (1988); *The Politics of God* (1992); *Theories of Culture* (1997); *Jesus, Humanity, and the Trinity* (2001); and *Economy of Grace* (2005).

Hastings Center, 260, 302
Harvey, David, 190–91, 226–30 *passim*
Hawken, Paul, 52
Hayles, N. Katherine, 305
Hearne, Vicki, 276
Hegel, Georg Wilhelm Friedrich/Hegelian, 62, 93, 172, 183, 251, 344, 351, 353
Heidegger, Martin, 66, 187, 208, 240, 277–78, 304, 307–20
Heisenberg, Werner, 132
Heraclitus, 28
Herodotus, 28–29
Heschel, Abraham, 79
Hightower, Jim, 266
Hitler, Adolf, 71
HIV/AIDS, 265, 268, 292–93, 302
Hobbes, Thomas, 348, 351, 356
Hölderlin, Friedrich, 308
Holy Spirit, 214, 286, 300, 373
homosexuality, 18, 23–25, 64
Hoover, Herbert, 244
hope, 96, 215, 220, 240, 288, 320, 335, 364, 368
Hopkins, Dwight, 300–1
horror, 17–18, 24–25, 27, 132
Howard, Ebenezer, 208, 219
Hughes, Robert, 216–17
Hull, R. Bruce, 91
Human Genome Project, 260
human rights, 18, 31, 174–75, 256, 264
humanism, 13, 170, 184, 305
Hume, David, 26, 286
humility, 77, 158–59, 162–64, 233
Hurricane Katrina, 30, 198–99, 242–49 *passim*
Huxley, Aldous, 168
hybrids/hybridity, 196, 222–23, 256–57, 358–59
   animals, 121
   cars, 237
   plants, 17

idolatry/idol, 27, 82, 92, 209–13 *passim*, 331, 361
Illich, Ivan, 218
imagination, 32, 187–91, 227, 288, 291
impiety. *See* piety/impiety
in vitro fertilization (IVF), 116–17
incarnation/incarnationalism, 228–38 *passim*, 279, 286. *See also* Jesus Christ
Ingram, David, 344

Institute for Cancer/Stem Cell Biology and Medicine, 119–20
intellectual property
   animals and, 108, 111, 121–22, 130, 145, 297
   gender and, 261–62, 274–75
   U.S. Patent and Trademark Office, 121–22
International Association of Bioethics, 302
International Conference on Harmonisaton (ICH), 257, 264
International Society for Stem Cell Research (ISSCR), 120
Irenaeus of Lyons, 367
irrigation, 2, 40, 59
Ishiguro, Kazuo, 292

Jacobs, Jane, 194–95
Jaenisch, Rudolf, 119
James, William, 59–60
Jameson, Fredric, 212
Janowitz, Morris, 184
Jasanoff, Sheila, 114, 251, 254, 258–64, 266
Jeremiah, Book of, 219
Jesus Christ
   anthropomorphism and, 36
   Christology, 62, 214, 364
   Creation and, 211
   human life and, 328, 369
   hypostatic union in, 209, 214
   image of God and, 368–69
   incarnation and, 228, 230, 236, 299, 368
   kenosis and, 236–38
   nature and, 81, 214–15
   poverty and, 300
   redemption in, 95–96, 340, 370–71
   revelation in, 209, 214, 299
   sacrifice and, 301, 354
   spatiality and, 216
   unity in, 219, 284, 365, 368
   as Word of God, 209
Joel, Book of, 71
John, Gospel according to, 85
John Paul II, 63–64, 326
Johnson, Philip, 216
Joyce, James, 105
Judaism, 76–79, 159–61, 163, 165, 169–70, 272, 284, 365
Just, E. E., 129